Get the eBook FREE!

(PDF, ePub, Kindle, and liveBook all included)

We believe that once you buy a book from us, you should be able to read it in any format we have available. To get electronic versions of this book at no additional cost to you, purchase and then register this book at the Manning website.

Go to https://www.manning.com/freebook and follow the instructions to complete your pBook registration.

That's it!
Thanks from Manning!

Programmer's Guide
to Apache Thrift

RANDY ABERNETHY

MANNING

Shelter Island

For online information and ordering of this and other Manning books, please visit
www.manning.com. The publisher offers discounts on this book when ordered in quantity.
For more information, please contact

    Special Sales Department
    Manning Publications Co.
    20 Baldwin Road
    PO Box 761
    Shelter Island, NY 11964
    Email: orders@manning.com

Manning Publications Co.
20 Baldwin Road
PO Box 761
Shelter Island, NY 11964

Development editors:	Cynthia Kane, Jennifer Stout
Technical development editor:	Pim van Oerle
Review editor:	Ozren Harlović
Project editor:	Lori Weidert
Copyeditor:	Katie Petito
Proofreader:	Alyson Brener
Technical proofreader:	Akon Dey
Typesetter:	Gordan Salinovic
Illustrator:	Chuck Larson
Cover designer:	Marija Tudor

ISBN 9781617296161
Printed in the United States of America
1 2 3 4 5 6 7 8 9 10 – SP – 24 23 22 21 20 19

Dedicated to my mom, Kay.
You are an inspiration to me in everything I do.

brief contents

contents

foreword

I first met Randy on the Apache Thrift mailing lists, where we both grew from contributing enthusiasts to committers and finally to PMC members of the Apache Thrift project. Later on I met him a few times in person, and we formed a bond—the kind many programmers are familiar with—while working on a piece of open source software across two continents.

Isn't it funny how that works? At the same time there are heavy conflicts in certain areas of the world, countless open source projects are bringing people together, to communicate freely and build bridges—across oceans, across continents, and across cultures. And if there is any Apache project that best fits this picture of communication and connections, it's probably Apache Thrift.

When I became aware of Apache Thrift for the first time, I quickly realized its potential. This RPC and serialization framework is a powerful and enabling technology. It's easy to use and extremely flexible, and it supports a wide range of target languages and dialects—more than 20 at the time of this writing. Besides establishing connections across languages, Thrift also supports the application developer by crossing platform boundaries.

The consequences of this new freedom for developers are overwhelming. For the first time, we're in a position where we can literally choose the right tool for the job, on the platform we find most suitable, without having to think too much about how we can integrate it all. This fact alone lets Thrift fit very well in today's microservice, cloud-native world.

There's a good chance that you bought this book to find out how you can unleash the nearly unparalleled capabilities of the Apache Thrift framework for your projects. You want to know about the possibilities, use cases, and applications, or how the serialization part could help you with your message-queue–based system. You want to see examples and code and have them explained.

This book gives you all the answers. Randy did a great job creating it, preparing and fine-tuning countless examples to keep pace with the latest developments of the Apache Thrift project. What you hold in your hand is the single most comprehensive publication about Apache Thrift available today.

JENS GEYER
SENIOR SOFTWARE ENGINEER,
VSX VOGEL SOFTWARE GMBH

preface

I've been in technology, often in coding roles, for about 30 years. During the dot-com era, I created an institutional equities trading platform that turned into a broker-dealer transacting somewhere around a billion US dollars a day. Needless to say, making sure the technology ran smoothly was a constant concern.

At that company we created technology bits in the line of trading with C++. Building the web-based frontend bits required some JavaScript. When we turned our hands to creating the internal monitoring and support systems, Active Server Pages, and, later, C# were the easiest tools to use. As much as possible, we wanted the language-based systems to interact, rather than have to reinvent bits from one language to the other ourselves.

The platform was based on Windows NT (later Windows 2000), and the RPC elements of the platform were COM+ and described in MS IDL, Microsoft's interface definition language. While I had used IDL on Unix systems in the past, this was the first big thing I had done in IDL. As the project developed, I became more and more enamored with the engineering processes the IDL abstraction enforced on our organization.

Everything central to the system was represented in IDL, including messages used to place orders and report executions. Interfaces that described the ways in which you could interact with the market data system or the order entry system were concisely defined in a beautifully abstract way. When we hired new engineers, the first thing we asked them to do was dig into the IDL. It was the best way to understand this vast platform without ever clouding or fixing our ideas with implementation code.

Our architecture meetings also focused on the IDL, because the interfaces and structure of the overall platform were critical but the implementation really wasn't. If you got the implementation wrong, you could rewrite it without impacting anyone else. If you got the interface wrong, the problem would propagate and often becoming debilitating.

There were challenges as well. My wish list included, as time rolled on, the ability to interoperate with Linux systems. Given that these were the "Linux is a cancer" days at Microsoft, that wasn't happening. I also wanted to be able to evolve our IDL without having to rebuild the world each time. A critical flaw in many distributed system technologies is that they don't allow one element to be updated without also updating all of those interacting with it.

Fast-forward to 2009: I was preparing to architect and develop another trading platform, and I reflected on my IDL wish list. Was it possible that somewhere out there in the cybersphere someone had open-sourced my dream technology for distributed computing? It wasn't long before I discovered Apache Thrift. I was stunned. Here was a system that worked with every commercially viable programming language and platform, included a compact but elegant IDL, and, most importantly, supported a critical set of features enabling interface evolution. I've been an Apache Thrift fan ever since.

In today's world of microservices and cloud-native systems, where new services are deployed multiple times a day, not having interfaces that support evolution and backward compatibility is a nonstarter. Apache Thrift delivers elegance, evolution, and the performance necessary to support the real-time needs of multiple microservices collaborating where a single monolith once prevailed.

The only thing missing was a book.

acknowledgments

While documenting a comprehensive serialization and RPC framework that operates across more than 20 programming languages was no small task, imagine what it took to create such a thing! My most profound thanks must first and foremost go to the Apache Thrift developers.

I must also thank my family for putting up with me writing chapters and committing patches in the middle of family gatherings and holidays over the course of several years. Thanksgiving and Christmas holidays turned into chapter-production activities, and no one yelled at me for staring at my laptop for hours while the family played Risk, Settlers of Catan, or what have you.

I owe a special thanks to the folks at Manning. I have to be the biggest laggard they have ever dealt with. No matter how late I was, they were as professional and supportive as a firm could be. In particular I'd like to thank Jenny Stout, who is not only a wonderful person but a great editor; Akon Dey, for his fantastic technical insights; and Kevin Sullivan, for driving the book to completion and helping me with all the final issues necessary to button up the book.

I'd also like to give a huge thank you to the reviewers who took the time to read the chapters and provide invaluable feedback, including Barry Alexander, Carlos Saltos, Chris Snow, Daniel Bryant, Ezra Simeloff, Georges Clerc, Jerry Goodnough, Palak Mathur, Raphaël P. Barazzutti, Ray Morehead, Robin Coe, Rock Lee, and Thomas Lockney. Jens Geyer was without doubt my most stalwart sounding board, providing detailed and thoughtful commentary and guidance from beginning to end. Roger Meier made sure I didn't miss important topics along the way and shared some of his compelling Apache Thrift IoT projects. Ben Craig kept me honest; when I couldn't get a good example done, Ben would push me to patch Thrift so that I could. He also saved me from falling into the pit between C++98 and C++11 or committing concurrency crimes. Jake Farrell, the PMC chair, provided encouragement and bore the burden of pushing new Apache Thrift versions out the door while the book developed, managing the complex set of package releases that grows with every new language.

about this book

Programmer's Guide to Apache Thrift was written to make learning how to use Apache Thrift drastically easier. Open source projects are famous for substandard documentation, and Apache Thrift has traditionally been a poster child for this stereotype. In retrospect, I can see why this is the case! This book and the accompanying source code repository should help newbies get started quickly and enable old hands to design better interfaces.

Who should read this book

Programmer's Guide to Apache Thrift is for anyone serious about mastering Apache Thrift. Both beginners and experienced Apache Thrift developers will find valuable bits of insight and useful reference material, making it easier to develop quality, extensible interfaces in Apache Thrift.

How this book is organized

The book has 17 chapters divided into three parts:

- Part 1 imparts introductory concepts, basic architecture knowledge and Apache Thrift set up, and basic debugging insights. Developers new to Apache Thrift should probably read this part thoroughly, while current Apache Thrift users may want to simply skim it.
- Part 2 covers the Apache Thrift system layer by layer, working from the lowest layer, transports, through to the highest layer, servers. Programmers seeking an in-depth understanding of Apache Thrift should read this part end to end.

Those interested in a higher-level understanding of Apache Thrift can skim the chapters here, with perhaps a deeper dive into chapter 6, which covers the Apache Thrift IDL in detail.

- Part 3 provides language-based walk-throughs that not only demonstrate the use of Apache Thrift in some of the most popular programming languages, but also continue the journey through use cases and features. Part 3 ends with chapter 17, which looks at Apache Thrift serialization in messaging systems, contrasts Apache Thrift IDL with other popular interfaces, such as REST/HTTP, and finally digs into Apache Thrift RPC performance. I would recommend everyone read the chapters on the languages they're interested in, as well as Chapter 17, which provides important summary information and Apache Thrift best practices.

About the code

This book contains many examples of source code, both in numbered listings and in line with normal text. In both cases, source code is formatted in a `fixed-width font like this` to separate it from ordinary text. Sometimes code is also **in bold** to highlight changes from previous steps in the chapter, such as when a new feature adds to an existing line of code.

In many cases, the original source code has been reformatted; we've added line breaks and reworked indentation to accommodate the available page space in the book. In rare cases, even this was not enough, and listings include line-continuation markers (➡). Additionally, comments in the source code have often been removed from the listings when the code is described in the text. Numbered markers ❶ accompany many of the listings, and mark particular lines and elements discussed in the text.

Source code for the examples in this book is available for download from the publisher's website at https://www.manning.com/books/programmers-guide-to-apache-thrift or on GitHub at http://github.com/randyabernethy/thriftbook.

liveBook discussion forum

Purchase of *Programmer's Guide to Apache* includes free access to a private web forum run by Manning Publications where you can make comments about the book, ask technical questions, and receive help from the author and from other users. To access the forum, go to https://livebook.manning.com/#!/book/programmers-guide-to-apache-thrift/discussion.

You can also learn more about Manning's forums and the rules of conduct at https://livebook.manning.com/#!/discussion. Manning's commitment to our readers is to provide a venue where a meaningful dialogue between individual readers and between readers and the author can take place. It is not a commitment to any specific amount of participation on the part of the author, whose contribution to the forum remains voluntary (and unpaid). We suggest you try asking the author some challenging questions lest his interest stray! The forum and the archives of previous discussions will be accessible from the publisher's website as long as the book is in print.

Online resources

Need additional help?

- The Apache Thrift mailing lists and IRC chat are both useful resources (https://thrift.apache.org/mailing).
- The Thrift tag at StackOverflow (stackoverflow.com/questions/tagged/thrift) is a great place both to ask questions and to help others. Helping someone else is a great way to learn!

about the author

RANDY ABERNETHY is a partner at RX-M LLC, a leading cloud-native systems consultancy. He has been an Apache Thrift user for almost a decade and is currently an Apache Thrift committer and PMC member. He has a passion for distributed systems technology and markets, frequently working with clients in the capital markets and financial services spaces.

about the cover illustration

The figure on the cover of *Programmer's Guide to Apache Thrift* is captioned "L'agent d'affaires." The illustration is taken from a collection of works by many artists, edited by Louis Curmer and published in Paris in 1841. The title of the collection is *Les Français peints par eux-mêmes*, which translates as *The French People Painted by Themselves.* Each illustration is finely drawn and colored by hand, and the rich variety of drawings in the collection reminds us vividly of how culturally apart the world's regions, towns, villages, and neighborhoods were just 200 years ago. Isolated from each other, people spoke different dialects and languages. In the streets or in the countryside, it was easy to identify where they lived and what their trade or station in life was just by their dress.

Dress codes have changed since then and the diversity by region, so rich at the time, has faded away. It is now hard to tell apart the inhabitants of different continents, let alone different towns or regions. Perhaps we have traded cultural diversity for a more varied personal life—certainly for a more varied and fast-paced technological life.

At a time when it is hard to tell one computer book from another, Manning celebrates the inventiveness and initiative of the computer business with book covers based on the rich diversity of regional life of two centuries ago, brought back to life by pictures from collections such as this one.

Part 1

Apache Thrift overview

Apache Thrift is an open source, cross-language serialization and remote procedure call (RPC) framework. With support for more than 20 programming languages, Apache Thrift can play an important role in many distributed application solutions. As a serialization platform, it enables efficient cross-language storage and retrieval of a wide range of data structures. As an RPC framework, Apache Thrift enables rapid development of complete cross-language services with little more than a few lines of code.

Part 1 of this book will help you understand how Apache Thrift fits into modern distributed application models, while imparting a high-level understanding of the Apache Thrift architecture. Part 1 will also get you started with basic Apache Thrift setup and debugging and includes a look at building a simple cross-language "hello world" service.

Introduction to Apache Thrift

This chapter covers
- Using Apache Thrift to unify polyglot systems
- Simplifying the creation of high-performance networked services
- Introducing the Apache Thrift modular serialization system
- Creating a simple Apache Thrift cross-language microservice
- Comparing Apache Thrift with other cross-language communications frameworks

Modern software systems live in a networked world. Network communications are critical to the tiniest embedded systems in the Internet of Things through to the weightiest of relational databases anchoring traditional multitier applications. As new software systems increasingly embrace dynamically scheduled, containerized microservices, lightweight, high-performance, language-agnostic network communications are ever more important.

But how to wire all these things together, the old and the new, the big and the small? How do we package a message from a service written in one language in such a way that a program written in any other language can read it? How do we design services that are fast enough for high-performance, backend cloud systems but accessible by frontend scripting technologies? How do we keep things lightweight to support efficient containers and embedded systems? How do we create interfaces that can evolve over time without breaking existing components? How do we do all of this in an open, vendor-neutral way, and, perhaps most important, how can we do it all precisely once, reusing the same communications primitives across a broad platform? For companies such as Facebook, Evernote, and Twitter, the answer is Apache Thrift.

This chapter introduces the Apache Thrift framework and its role in modern distributed applications. We'll look at why Apache Thrift was created and how it helps programmers build high-performance, cross-language services. To begin, we'll consider the growing need for multi-language integration and examine the role Apache Thrift plays in polyglot application development. Next, we'll look at the two key functions of Apache Thrift, serialization and RPC, and walk through the construction of a simple Apache Thrift service. At the end of the chapter we'll compare Apache Thrift to several other tools offering similar features to help you determine when Apache Thrift might be a good fit.

1.1   *Polyglotism, the pleasure and the pain*

The number of programming languages in common commercial use has grown considerably in recent years. In 2003, 80% of the Tiobe Index (http://www.tiobe.com/index.php/tiobe_index) was attributed to six programming languages: Java, C, C++, Perl, Visual Basic, and PHP. In 2013, it took nearly twice as many languages to capture the same 80%, adding Objective-C, C#, Python, JavaScript, and Ruby to the list (see figure 1.1). In early 2016 the entire Tiobe top 20 didn't add up to 80% of the mind share. In Q4 2015, Github reported 19 languages all having more than 10,000 active repositories (http://githut.info/), adding Swift, Go, Scala, and others to the list.

2003 Tiobe Index top four quintiles

Language	Rating	Cumulative
Java	23.08%	23.08%
C	18.47%	41.55%
C++	15.56%	57.12%
Perl	9.42%	66.54%
(Visual) Basic	7.81%	74.35%
PHP	4.76%	79.11%

2013 Tiobe Index top four quintiles

Language	Rating	Cumulative
C	17.81%	17.81%
Java	16.66%	34.47%
Objective-C	10.36%	44.82%
C++	8.82%	53.64%
PHP	5.99%	59.63%
C#	5.78%	65.41%
(Visual) Basic	4.35%	69.76%
Python	4.18%	73.94%
Perl	2.27%	76.21%
JavaScript	1.65%	77.87%
Ruby	1.48%	79.35%

Figure 1.1   **The Tiobe Index uses web search results to track programming language popularity (http://www.tiobe.com).**

Increasingly, developers and architects choose the programming language most suitable for the task at hand. A developer working on a Big Data project might decide Clojure is the best language to use; meanwhile, folks down the hall may be doing front-end work in TypeScript, while programmers in the basement might be using C with embedded systems (no aversion to sunlight implied). Years ago, this type of diversity would be rare at a single company; now it can be found within a single team.

Choosing a programming language uniquely suited to solving a particular problem can lead to productivity gains and better quality software. When the language fits the problem, friction is reduced, programming becomes more direct, and code becomes simpler and easier to maintain. For example, in large-scale data analysis, horizontal scaling is instrumental to achieving acceptable performance. Functional programming languages such as Haskell, Scala, and Clojure tend to fit naturally here, allowing analytic systems to scale out without complex concurrency concerns.

Platforms drive language adoption as well. Objective-C exploded in popularity when Apple released the iPhone, and Swift is following suit. Go is the language of the booming container ecosystem, responsible for Docker, Kubernetes, etcd, and other essentials. Those programming for the browser will have teams competent with JavaScript or TypeScript, while the game and GUI world still often codes in C++ for top-performing graphics. These choices are driven by history as well as compelling technology underpinnings. Even when such groups are internally monoglots, languages mix and mingle as they collaborate across business boundaries.

Many organizations who claim monoglotism make use of a range of support languages for testing and prototyping. Dynamic programming languages such as Groovy and Ruby are often used for testing, while Lua, Perl, and Python are popular for prototyping, and PHP has a long history with the web. Build systems such as the Groovy-based Gradle and the Ruby-based Rake also provide innovative capabilities.

The polyglot story isn't all wine and song, however. Mastering a programming language is no small feat, not to mention the tools and libraries that come with it. As this burden is multiplied with each new language, firms may experience diminishing returns. Introducing multiple languages into a product initiative can have numerous costs associated with cross-language integration, developer training, and complexity when building and testing. If managed improperly, these costs can quickly overshadow the benefits of a multi-language strategy.

One of the key strengths of Apache Thrift is its ability to simplify, centralize, and encapsulate the cross-language aspects of a system. Apache Thrift offers broad support, in tree, for polyglot application development. Every language mentioned previously is supported by the Apache Thrift project, more than 20 languages in all, and growing (see table 1.1). This unrivaled direct support for existing languages and the Apache Thrift community's rapid addition of support for new languages can help organizations maximize the potential of polyglotism while minimizing the downsides. The more our programs mirror the dialog on the floor of the United Nations General Assembly, the more we'll need professional translators such as Apache Thrift to streamline communications.

Table 1.1   Languages supported by Apache Thrift

AS3	C	C++	C#
D	Dart	Delphi	Erlang
Go	Haskell	Haxe	Java
JavaScript	Lua	Node.js	Objective-C
OCaml	Perl	PHP	Python
Ruby	Rust	Smalltalk	TypeScript

1.2   *Application integration with Apache Thrift*

Whether your application uses multiple platforms and languages or not, it's likely that its operations span multiple processes over networks and time. At times these processes will need to communicate, either through a file on disk, through a buffer in memory, or across networks. Two central concerns are associated with inter-process communications:

- Type serialization
- Service implementation

Let's consider each in turn.

1.2.1   *Type serialization*

Serialization is a basic function in any cross-platform/language exchange. For example, imagine an application for the music industry that uses NATS as a messaging system to move song data between processes (see figure 1.2). Using NATS, the team can send/receive messages rapidly between their remote processes written in Java and Python. The question is, can the programs read the musical messages when sent by another language? Python objects are represented differently in memory than Java objects. If a Python program sent the raw memory bits for its music track data to a Java program, fireworks would ensue.

To solve this problem, we need a data serialization layer on top of the messaging platform. Why not send everything back and forth in JSON, one might ask? Using a standard format such as JSON is part of a solution; however, we must still answer questions such as: how are data fields ordered when sending multi-field messages, what happens when fields are missing, and what does a language that doesn't directly support a data type do when receiving that data type? These and many other questions

Figure 1.2   Apache Thrift can be used to serialize data in cross-platform messaging scenarios.

cannot be answered by a data layout specification such as JSON, YAML, or XML. Different languages frequently produce different, though legally formatted, documents for the same dataset.

IDL AND TYPES

Apache Thrift provides a modular serialization framework that addresses these issues. With Apache Thrift, developers define abstract data types in an Interface Definition Language (IDL). This IDL can then be compiled into source code for any supported language. The generated code provides complete serialization and deserialization logic for all of the user's defined types. Apache Thrift ensures that types written by any language can be read by any other language. The following listing shows Apache Thrift IDL type definitions for a hypothetical music application.

Listing 1.1 Apache Thrift IDL type definitions

```
namespace * music

enum PerfRightsOrg {
    ASCAP = 1
    BMI = 2
    SESAC = 3
    Other = 4
}

typedef double Minutes

struct MusicTrack {
    1: string title
    2: string artist
    3: string publisher
    4: string composer
    5: Minutes duration
    6: PerfRightsOrg pro
}
```

Some people complain that creating IDL is an extra step, slowing the development process. I've found that it's the opposite. IDL forces you to carefully consider your interfaces in isolation, free of noisy implementation code. This may be the most important time you spend on a system design. IDL is also lightweight, easy to modify and experiment with, and often useful as a communications tool on the business side.

Users may say schemaless systems are more flexible and that IDL is brittle. The truth is, whether you document your schema or not, you still have a schema if you're reading and interpreting data. Implied (undocumented) schemas can be the source of fairly treacherous application errors and create a burden on developers who need to interact with the data or extend the system. If you have no definition for the data layout you read and write except the code that reads and writes it, it will be slow going when you want to extend the system. How many bits of code throughout the system depend on this implied schema? How do you change such a thing?

The popularity of NoSQL systems, many of which are schemaless, creates another role for IDL. You can now document your types in a single place and use those types in service calls, with messaging systems and in storage systems such as Redis, MongoDB, and others.

Several systems reverse the process and generate their schema from a given coded solution. Annotation-driven systems, such as Java's JAX-RS, can work this way. This approach makes it easy to allow implementation details to bias the interface definition, straining portability and clarity. It's generally much more work to modify implementation code than it is to modify IDL. Also, you have no guarantee that another vendor's code generator will create compatible code from a foreign schema. This is a problem any time multiple vendors are involved in a communications solution.

Apache Thrift sidesteps many of these problems by providing a single source of truth, the IDL. Apache Thrift supplies vendor-independent support for a single IDL across a wide array of programming languages, and the Apache Thrift cross-language test suit is constantly at work verifying interoperability as the framework grows.

INTERFACE EVOLUTION

IDL creates a contract that all parties can rely upon and that code generators can use to create working serialization operations, ensuring the contract is adhered to. Yet IDL schemas need not be brittle. Apache Thrift IDL supports a range of interface evolution features which, when used properly, allow fields to be added and removed, types to be changed, and more.

Support for interface evolution greatly simplifies the task of ongoing software maintenance and extension. Modern engineering sensibilities such as microservices, Continuous Integration (CI), and Continuous Delivery (CD) require systems to support incremental improvements without impacting the rest of the platform. Tools that supply no form of interface evolution tend to "break the world" when changed. In such systems, changing an interface means all the clients and servers using that interface must be rewritten and/or recompiled, then redeployed in a big bang.

Apache Thrift interface evolution features allow multiple interface versions to coexist seamlessly in a single operating environment. This makes incremental updates viable, enabling CI/CD pipelines and empowering individual Agile teams to deliver business value at their own cadence.

Continuous Integration (CI) and Continuous Delivery (CD)

Continuous integration is an approach to software development wherein changes to a system are merged into the central code base frequently. These changes are continuously built and tested, usually by automated systems, providing developers with rapid feedback when patches create conflicts or fail tests. Continuous Delivery takes CI one step further, migrating successfully merged code to evaluation/staging systems and ultimately into production, many times per day. The goal of continuous systems is to take many small risks and provide immediate feedback rather than taking large risks and delaying feedback over long release cycles. The longer integration is delayed, the more patches are involved, making it more difficult to identify and repair conflicts and bugs.

MODULAR SERIALIZATION

Apache Thrift provides pluggable serializers, known as protocols, allowing you to use any one of several serialization formats for data exchange, including binary for speed, compact for size, and JSON for readability. The same contract (IDL) can remain in place even as you change serialization protocols. This modular approach allows custom serialization protocols to be added as well. Because Apache Thrift is community managed and open source, you can easily change or enhance functionality and push it upstream when needed (patches are always welcome at the Apache Thrift project).

1.2.2 Service implementation

Services are modular application components that provide interfaces accessible over a network. Apache Thrift IDL allows you to define services in addition to types (see listing 1.2). Like types, IDL services can be compiled to generate stub code. Service stubs are used to connect clients and servers in a wide range of languages.

Listing 1.2   /ThriftBook/part1/hello/sail_stats.thrift

```
service SailStats {
    double get_sailor_rating(1: string sailor_name)
    double get_team_rating(1: string team_name)
    double get_boat_rating(1: i64 boat_serial_number)
    list<string> get_sailors_on_team(1: string team_name)
    list<string> get_sailors_rated_between(1: double min_rating,
                                           2: double max_rating)
    string get_team_captain(1: string team_name)
}
```

Imagine you have a module that tracks and computes sailing team statistics and that this module is built into a Windows C++ GUI application designed to visualize wind flow dynamics. As it happens, your company's web dev team wants to use the sail stats module to enhance a client-facing, Node.js-based web application on Linux. Faced with multiple languages and platforms and the "laziness" axiom (wanting to write as little code as possible), Apache Thrift could be a good solution (see figure 1.3).

With Apache Thrift we could repackage the sail stats functions as a microservice and provide the Node.js programmers with access to the service through an easy-to-use Node.js client stub. To create the sail stats microservice we need only define the service interface in IDL, compile the IDL to create client and server stubs for the service, select one of the prebuilt Apache Thrift servers to host the service, and then assemble the parts.

PREBUILT SERVER SHELLS

It's important to note that, unlike standalone serialization solutions, Apache Thrift comes with a complete set of server shells, ready to use, in almost all the supported languages. This sidesteps the difficult and repetitive process of building custom network servers. The prebuilt Apache Thrift servers are also small and focused, providing

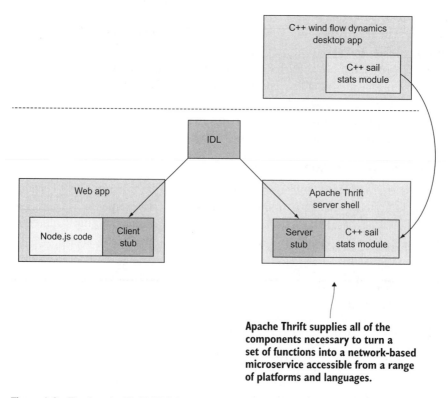

Apache Thrift supplies all of the components necessary to turn a set of functions into a network-based microservice accessible from a range of platforms and languages.

Figure 1.3   The Apache Thrift RPC framework enables cross-platform services.

only the functionality necessary to host Apache Thrift services. A typical Apache Thrift server will consume an order of magnitude less memory than an equivalent Tomcat deployment. This makes Apache Thrift servers a good choice for containerized micro-services and embedded systems that don't have the resources necessary to run full-blown web or application servers.

Microservices and Service Oriented Architecture (SOA)

The microservice and SOA approaches to distributed application design break applications down into services, which are remotely accessible, autonomous modules composed of a set of closely related functions. Such systems provide their features over language-agnostic interfaces, allowing clients to be constructed in the most appropriate language and on the most appropriate platform, independent of the service implementation. These services are typically (and in the best case) stateless and loosely coupled, communicating with clients through a formal interface contract. Services may be internal to an organization or support clients across business boundaries. The distinction between SOA services and microservices is subtle, but most agree that microservices are a subset of SOA services in which the services are more atomic and independently deployable.

MODULAR TRANSPORTS

Apache Thrift also offers a pluggable transport system. Apache Thrift clients and servers communicate over transports that adapt Apache Thrift data flows to the outside world. For example, the TSocket transport allows Apache Thrift applications to communicate over TCP/IP sockets. You can use prebuilt transports for other communications schemes, such as named pipes and UNIX domain sockets. Custom transports are easy to craft as well. Apache Thrift also supports offline transports that allow data to be serialized to disk, memory, and other devices.

A particularly elegant aspect of the Apache Thrift transport model is support for layered transports. Protocols serialize application data into a bit stream. Transports read and write the bytes, making any type of manipulation possible. For example, the TZLibTransport is available in many Apache Thrift language libraries and can be layered on top of any other transport to achieve high-ratio data compression. You can branch data to loggers, fork requests to parallel servers, encrypt, and perform any other manner of manipulation with custom-layered transports.

1.3 Building a simple service

To get a better understanding of the practical aspects of Apache Thrift, we'll build a simple "hello world" microservice. The service will be designed to supply various parts of our enterprise with a daily greeting, exposing a single "hello_func" function that takes no parameters and returns a greeting string. To see how Apache Thrift works across languages, we'll build clients in C++, Python, and Java.

1.3.1 The Hello IDL

Most projects involving Apache Thrift begin with careful consideration of the interface components involved. Apache Thrift IDL is similar to C in its notation and makes it easy to define types and services shared across systems. Apache Thrift IDL is plain text saved in files with a ".thrift" extension (see the following listing).

> **Listing 1.3   /ThriftBook/part1/hello/hello.thrift**

```
service HelloSvc {            ❶
    string hello_func()       ❷
}
```

Our hello.thrift IDL file declares a single service interface called HelloSvc ❶ with a single function, hello_func() ❷. The function accepts no parameters and returns a string. To use this interface we can compile it with the Apache Thrift IDL compiler. The IDL compiler binary is named "thrift" on UNIX-like systems and "thrift.exe" on Windows. The compiler expects two command line arguments, an IDL file to compile and one (or more) target languages to generate code for. Here's an example session that generates Python stubs for HelloSvc:

```
/ThriftBook/part1/hello$ ls -1
-rw-r--r-- 1 root root     88 Feb 16 17:01 hello.thrift
/ThriftBook/part1/hello$ thrift --gen py hello.thrift        ❶
/ThriftBook/part1/hello$ ls -1
drwxr-xr-x 4 root root   4096 Feb 17 00:16 gen-py            ❷
-rw-r--r-- 1 root root     88 Feb 16 17:01 hello.thrift
```

In the previous session the IDL compiler is invoked with the –gen py switch ❶, which causes the compiler to create a gen-py directory ❷ to house the emitted Python code for your hello.thrift IDL. The directory contains client/server stubs for all the services and serialization code for all the user-defined types in the IDL file.

1.3.2   *The Hello server*

Now that we have our support code generated, we can implement our service and use a prebuilt Apache Thrift server to house it. The following listing provides a sample server coded in Python.

Listing 1.4   /ThriftBook/part1/hello/hello_server.py

```
import sys
sys.path.append("gen-py")                                   ❶
from hello import HelloSvc

from thrift.transport import TSocket
from thrift.transport import TTransport                      ❷
from thrift.protocol import TBinaryProtocol
from thrift.server import TServer

class HelloHandler:                      ❸
    def hello_func(self):
        print("[Server] Handling client request")
        return "Hello from the python server"

handler = HelloHandler()                          ❹
proc = HelloSvc.Processor(handler)

trans_svr = TSocket.TServerSocket(port=9090)              ❺
trans_fac = TTransport.TBufferedTransportFactory()            ❻
proto_fac = TBinaryProtocol.TBinaryProtocolFactory()            ❼
server = TServer.TSimpleServer(proc, trans_svr, trans_fac, proto_fac)  ❽
server.serve()       ←┐
                      ❾
```

At the top of our server listing we use the built-in Python sys module to add the gen-py directory to the Python Path. This allows us to import the generated service stubs for our HelloSvc service ❶.

Our next step is to import several Apache Thrift library packages. TSocket provides an endpoint for our clients to connect to, TTransport provides a buffering layer, TBinaryProtocol will handle data serialization, and TServer will give us access to the prebuilt Python server classes ❷.

The next block of code implements the HelloSvc service itself through the Hello-Handler class. This class is called a handler in Apache Thrift because is handles all of the calls made to the service. All the service methods must be represented in the Handler class; in our case this is the `hello_func()` method ❸. In real projects, almost all of your time and effort is spent here, implementing services. Apache Thrift takes care of the wiring and boilerplate code.

Next we create an instance of our handler and use it to initialize a processor for our service. The processor is the server-side stub generated by the IDL compiler that turns network service requests into calls to the appropriate handler function ❹.

The Apache Thrift library offers endpoint transports for use with files, memory, and various network types: the example here creates a TCP server socket endpoint to accept client connections on TCP port 9090 ❺. The buffering layer ensures that we make efficient use of the underlying network, transmitting bits only when an entire message has been serialized ❻. The binary serialization protocol transmits our data in a fast binary format with little overhead ❼.

Apache Thrift provides a range of servers to choose from, each with unique features. The server used here is an instance of the TSimpleServer class, which, as its name implies, provides the most basic server functionality ❽. Once constructed, we run the server by calling the `serve()` method ❾.

The following example session runs our Python server:

```
/ThriftBook/part1/hello$ ls -l
drwxr-xr-x 4 randy randy 4096 Jan 27 02:34 gen-py
-rw-r--r-- 1 randy randy  732 Jan 27 03:44 hello_server.py
-rw-r--r-- 1 randy randy   99 Jan 27 02:24 hello.thrift
/ThriftBook/part1/hello$ python hello_server.py
```

The Python server took approximately seven lines of code, excluding imports and the service implementation. The story is similar in C++, Java, and most other languages. This is a basic server, but the example should help you see how much leverage Apache Thrift gives you when it comes to quickly creating cross-language microservices.

1.3.3   A Python client

Now that we have our server running, let's create a simple Python client to test it, as shown in the following listing.

Listing 1.5   /ThriftBook/part1/hello/hello_client.py

```
import sys
sys.path.append("gen-py")
from hello import HelloSvc        ❶

from thrift.transport import TSocket          ❷
from thrift.transport import TTransport        ❸
from thrift.protocol import TBinaryProtocol         ❹
```

```
trans = TSocket.TSocket("localhost", 9090)       5
trans = TTransport.TBufferedTransport(trans)       6
proto = TBinaryProtocol.TBinaryProtocol(trans)      7
client = HelloSvc.Client(proto)              8

trans.open()              9
msg = client.hello_func()         10
print("[Client] received: %s" % msg)      11
trans.close()        ◁┐
                  12
```

The Python client begins by importing the same HelloSvc module used by the server, but the client will use the client-side stubs for the hello service ❶. We'll also import three modules from the Apache Thrift Python library. The first is TSocket, which is used on the client side to make a TCP connection to the server socket ❷; as you may guess, the client must use a client-side transport compatible with the server transport. The next import pulls in TTransport, which will provide a network buffer ❸, and the TBinaryProtocol import allows us to serialize messages to the server ❹. Again, this must match the server implementation.

Our next block of code initializes the TSocket with the host and port to connect to ❺. We'll wrap the socket transport in a buffer ❻ and finally wrap the entire transport stack in the TBinaryProtocol ❼, creating an I/O stack that can serialize data to and from the server.

The I/O stack is used by the client stub, which acts as a proxy for the remote service ❽. Opening the transport causes the client to connect to the server ❾. Invoking the `hello_func()` method on the Client object serializes our call request with the binary protocol and transmits it over the socket to the server, then deserializes the returned result ❿. The program prints out the result ⓫ and then closes the connection using the transport `close()` method ⓬.

Here's a sample session running the above client (the Python server must be running in another shell to respond):

```
/ThriftBook/part1/hello$ ls -l
drwxr-xr-x 3 randy randy 4096 Mar 26 21:45 gen-py
-rw-r--r-- 1 randy randy  386 Mar 26 21:59 hello_client.py
-rw-r--r-- 1 randy randy  535 Mar 26 16:50 hello_server.py
-rw-r--r-- 1 randy randy   95 Mar 26 16:28 hello.thrift
/ThriftBook/part1/hello$ python hello_client.py
[Client] received: Hello from the python server
```

While it takes more work than your run of the mill "hello world" program, a few lines of IDL and a few lines of Python code have allowed us to create a language-agnostic, OS-agnostic, and platform-agnostic service API with a working client and server. Not bad.

1.3.4 A C++ client

To broaden your perspective and demonstrate the cross-language aspects of Apache Thrift, let's build two more clients for the hello server, one in C++ and one in Java. We'll start with the C++ client.

First we need to compile the service definition again, this time generating C++ stubs:

```
/ThriftBook/part1/hello$ thrift --gen cpp hello.thrift       ❶
/ThriftBook/part1/hello$ ls -l
drwxr-xr-x 2 randy randy 4096 Mar 26 22:25 gen-cpp
drwxr-xr-x 3 randy randy 4096 Mar 26 21:45 gen-py
-rw-r--r-- 1 randy randy  386 Mar 26 21:59 hello_client.py
-rw-r--r-- 1 randy randy  535 Mar 26 16:50 hello_server.py
-rw-r--r-- 1 randy randy   95 Mar 26 16:28 hello.thrift
```

Running the IDL compiler with the --gen cpp switch ❶ causes it to emit C++ files in the gen-cpp directory, roughly equivalent to those generated for Python, producing C++ headers (.h) and source files (.cpp). The gen-cpp/HelloSvc.h header ❶ contains the declarations for our service, and the gen-cpp/HelloSvc.cpp source file contains the implementation of the service stub components.

The code for a HelloSvc C++ client with the same functionality as the Python client appears in the following listing.

> **Listing 1.6   /ThriftBook/part1/hello/hello_client.cpp**

```cpp
#include "gen-cpp/HelloSvc.h"
#include <thrift/transport/TSocket.h>
#include <thrift/transport/TBufferTransports.h>
#include <thrift/protocol/TBinaryProtocol.h>
#include <boost/make_shared.hpp>
#include <iostream>
#include <string>

using namespace apache::thrift::transport;      ❶
using namespace apache::thrift::protocol;
using boost::make_shared;                        ❷

int main() {
    auto trans_ep = make_shared<TSocket>("localhost", 9090);
    auto trans_buf = make_shared<TBufferedTransport>(trans_ep);
    auto proto = make_shared<TBinaryProtocol>(trans_buf);
    HelloSvcClient client(proto);

    trans_ep->open();
    std::string msg;                             ❸
    client.hello_func(msg);
    std::cout << "[Client] received: " << msg << std::endl;
    trans_ep->close();
}
```

Our C++ client code is structurally identical to the Python client code. With few exceptions, the Apache Thrift meta-model is consistent from language to language, making it easy for developers to work across languages.

The C++ `main()` function corresponds line for line with the Python code with one exception; `hello_func()` doesn't return a string conventionally, rather it returns the string through an out parameter reference ❸.

The Apache Thrift language libraries are generally wrapped in namespaces to avoid conflicts in the global namespace. In C++ all of the Apache Thrift library code is located within the "apache::thrift" namespace. The `using` statements here provide implicit access to the necessary Apache Thrift library code ❶.

Apache Thrift strives to maintain as few dependencies as possible to keep the development environment simple and portable; however, exceptions do exist. For example, the Apache Thrift C++ library relies on the open source Boost library. In this example, several objects are wrapped in boost::shared_ptr ❷. Apache Thrift uses shared_ptr to manage the lifetimes of almost all of the key objects involved in C++ service operations.

Those familiar with C++ will know that shared_ptr has been part of the standard library since C++11. While the sample code is written in C++11, Apache Thrift supports C++98 as well, requiring the use of the Boost version of shared_ptr (C++98 support will likely be dropped in the future, moving all Boost namespace elements to the std namespace).

The following listing shows a Bash session that builds and runs the C++ client.

Listing 1.7 Bash session running C++ client

```
$ ls -l
drwxr-xr-x 2 randy randy 4096 Mar 26 22:25 gen-cpp
drwxr-xr-x 3 randy randy 4096 Mar 26 21:45 gen-py
-rw-r--r-- 1 randy randy  641 Mar 26 22:36 hello_client.cpp
-rw-r--r-- 1 randy randy  386 Mar 26 21:59 hello_client.py
-rw-r--r-- 1 randy randy  535 Mar 26 16:50 hello_server.py
-rw-r--r-- 1 randy randy   95 Mar 26 16:28 hello.thrift
$ g++ --std=c++11 hello_client.cpp gen-cpp/HelloSvc.cpp -lthrift      ❶
$ ls -l
-rwxr-xr-x 1 randy randy 136508 Mar 26 22:38 a.out
drwxr-xr-x 2 randy randy   4096 Mar 26 22:25 gen-cpp
drwxr-xr-x 3 randy randy   4096 Mar 26 21:45 gen-py
-rw-r--r-- 1 randy randy    641 Mar 26 22:36 hello_client.cpp
-rw-r--r-- 1 randy randy    386 Mar 26 21:59 hello_client.py
-rw-r--r-- 1 randy randy    535 Mar 26 16:50 hello_server.py
-rw-r--r-- 1 randy randy     95 Mar 26 16:28 hello.thrift
$ ./a.out                                                             ❷
[Client] received: Hello thrift, from the python server
```

Here we use the Gnu C++ compiler to build the hello_client.cpp file into an executable program ❶. Clang, Visual C++, and other compilers are also commonly used to build Apache Thrift C++ applications.

For the C++ build we must compile the generated client stubs found in the HelloSvc.cpp source file. During the link phase the "–lthrift" switch tells the linker to scan the standard Apache Thrift C++ library to resolve the TSocket and TBinaryProtocol library dependencies (this switch must follow the list of .cpp files when using g++ or it will be ignored, causing link errors).

Assuming the Python Hello server is still up, we can run our executable C++ client and make a cross-language RPC call. The C++ compiler builds our source into an a.out file that produces the same result as the Python client when executed ❷.

1.3.5 A Java client

As a final example let's put together a Java client for the service. Our first step is to generate Java stubs for the service, as shown in the following listing.

Listing 1.8   Generating Java stubs

```
/ThriftBook/part1/hello$ thrift --gen java hello.thrift          ❶
/ThriftBook/part1/hello$ ls -l
-rwxr-xr-x 1 randy randy 136508 Mar 26 23:07 a.out
drwxr-xr-x 2 randy randy   4096 Mar 26 22:25 gen-cpp
drwxr-xr-x 2 randy randy   4096 Mar 26 23:23 gen-java
drwxr-xr-x 3 randy randy   4096 Mar 26 21:45 gen-py
-rw-r--r-- 1 randy randy    641 Mar 26 22:36 hello_client.cpp
-rw-r--r-- 1 randy randy    386 Mar 26 21:59 hello_client.py
-rw-r--r-- 1 randy randy    535 Mar 26 16:50 hello_server.py
-rw-r--r-- 1 randy randy     95 Mar 26 16:28 hello.thrift
```

The --gen java switch causes the IDL compiler to emit Java code for our interface in the gen-java directory ❶, creating a HelloSvc class with nested client and server stub classes. The following listing provides the source for a Java client that parallels the prior Python and C++ clients.

Listing 1.9   /ThriftBook/part1/hello/HelloClient.java

```
import org.apache.thrift.protocol.TBinaryProtocol;
import org.apache.thrift.transport.TSocket;
import org.apache.thrift.TException;

public class HelloClient {
    public static void main(String[] args) throws TException {
        TSocket trans = new TSocket("localhost", 9090);
        TBinaryProtocol protocol = new TBinaryProtocol(trans);
        HelloSvc.Client client = new HelloSvc.Client(protocol);

        trans.open();
        String str = client.hello_func();
        System.out.println("[Client] received: " + str);
        trans.close();
    }
}
```

In typical Java form, the `main()` method lives inside a class with the same name as the containing file and the rest of the code is a rehash of the previous clients. The one noticeable difference is that the Java client has no buffering layer above the endpoint transport because the socket implementation in Java is based on a stream class that buffers internally, so no additional buffering is required.

The following listing shows a build and run session for the Java client.

Listing 1.10   Build and run session for the Java client

```
/ThriftBook/part1/hello$ javac -cp /usr/local/lib/libthrift-1.0.0.jar:\    ❶
                              /usr/share/java/slf4j-api.jar:\               ❷
                              /usr/share/java/slf4j-nop.jar \    ◀
        HelloClient.java gen-java/HelloSvc.java         ◀                   ❸
/ThriftBook/part1/hello$ ls -l                             ❹
-rwxr-xr-x 1 randy randy 136508 Mar 26 23:07 a.out
drwxr-xr-x 2 randy randy   4096 Mar 26 22:25 gen-cpp
drwxr-xr-x 2 randy randy   4096 Mar 26 23:34 gen-java
drwxr-xr-x 3 randy randy   4096 Mar 26 21:45 gen-py
-rw-r--r-- 1 randy randy   1080 Mar 30 00:04 HelloClient.class
-rw-r--r-- 1 randy randy    607 Mar 29 23:48 hello_client.cpp
-rw-r--r-- 1 randy randy    657 Mar 30 00:04 HelloClient.java
-rw-r--r-- 1 randy randy    384 Mar 29 23:48 hello_client.py
-rw-r--r-- 1 randy randy    535 Mar 26 16:50 hello_server.py
-rw-r--r-- 1 randy randy     95 Mar 26 16:28 hello.thrift
/ThriftBook/part1/hello$ java -cp /usr/local/lib/libthrift-1.0.0.jar:\
                              /usr/share/java/slf4j-api.jar:\
                              /usr/share/java/slf4j-nop.jar:\
                    ❺      ./gen-java:\
                              . \
                    HelloClient
[Client] received: Hello thrift, from the python server
```

The Java compile includes three dependencies; the first is the Apache Thrift Java library jar ❶. The IDL-generated code for our service also depends on SLF4J, a popular Java logging façade. The slf4j-api jar ❷ is the façade and the slf4j-nop jar ❸ is the nonoperational logger that discards logging output. The Java files generate byte code in .class files for our HelloClient class as well as the HelloSvc class ❹.

To run our Java HelloClient class under the JVM we must modify the Java class path as we did in the compilation step, adding the current directory and the gen-java directory, where the HelloClient class and HelloSvr class files will be found ❺. Running the client produces the same result we saw with Python and C++.

Beyond running standard build tools in our respective languages, it didn't take much effort to produce our Apache Thrift server and the three clients. In short order, we've built a microservice that can handle requests from clients created in a wide range of languages. Now that we've seen how basic Apache Thrift programs are created, let's look at how Apache Thrift fits into the overall application integration landscape.

The Apache Thrift tutorial

In addition to the code examples included with this text, the Apache Thrift source tree provides a tutorial. The tutorial is based on a central tutorial IDL file defining a calculator service from which client and server samples in each language are built. This tutorial is simple but demonstrates many of the capabilities of Apache Thrift in every supported language. The tutorials can be found under the tutorial directory below the root of the Apache Thrift source tree. Each language-specific tutorial is found in a subdirectory named for the language. A Makefile is provided to build the tutorial examples in languages that require compilation. The source tree also provides many tests throughout the tree, all of which provide useful examples.

```
/thrift/tutorial$ ls

as3            c_glib     cpp      csharp      d
dart           delphi     erl      gen-html    go
haxe           hs         java     js          netcore
nodejs         ocaml      perl     php         py.tornado
py.twisted     py         rb       rs          shared.thrift
tutorial.thrift
```

1.4 The communications toolkit landscape

SOAP, REST, Protocol Buffers, and Apache Avro are perhaps the technologies most often considered as alternatives to Apache Thrift, though many others exist. Each technology is unique and each has its place. The following sections provide a brief overview of the key players in the software communications landscape, followed by a summary of the features fielded by Apache Thrift and a discussion of where Apache Thrift fits in the milieu.

1.4.1 SOAP

Simple Object Access Protocol (SOAP) is a W3C recommendation (https://www.w3 .org/TR/2007/REC-soap12-part1-20070427/) specifying a Service Oriented Architecture (SOA)-style remote procedure call (RPC) system over HTTP. SOAP relies on XML for carrying its payload between the client and server and is typically deployed over HTTP, though other transports can also be used. Optimizations are available that attempt to reduce the burden of transmitting XML, and SOAP has versions that use JSON, among other offshoots. Related technologies, such as XML-RPC, operate on similar principles. Unlike RESTful services, which directly use HTTP headers, verbs, and status codes, SOAP and XML-RPC systems tunnel function calls through HTTP POST operations, missing out on most of the caching and system layering benefits found in RESTful services.

The key benefit of HTTP-friendly technologies is their broad interoperability. By transmitting standards-based text documents (XML, JSON, and others) over the ubiquitous HTTP protocol, almost any application or language can be engaged. Human-readable XML/JSON payloads also greatly simplify prototyping, testing, and debugging. On the downside, each language, vendor, and, often, each company provide their own scheme for generating stubs. You have no guarantees that code generated by different SOAP WSDL (Web Service Description Language) tools will collaborate.

SOAP was one of the principle technologies used during the evolution of Service Orientation and is still widely used in older systems. SOAP offers a number of WS-* standards established by the Oasis standards body, addressing authentication, transactions, and other concerns (https://www.oasis-open.org/standards). Few new SOAP services appear to be coming online, and most considering SOAP today find REST simpler, faster at scale, and more compelling as a public API solution.

1.4.2   *REST*

REST is an acronym for REpresentational State Transfer, a term coined by Dr. Roy Fielding in his 2000 dissertation (https://www.ics.uci.edu/~fielding/pubs/dissertation/rest_arch_style.htm). REST is the typical means for web browsers to retrieve content from web servers. RESTful web services use the REST architectural style to leverage the infrastructure of the web. The well-understood and widely supported HTTP protocol gives REST-based services broad reach. REST-based services typically use the JSON format for payload transmission, making client/server requests human-readable and easy to work with.

RESTful services are unique in that their interfaces are based on resources accessed through URIs and manipulated through HTTP verbs, such as GET, PUT, POST, and DELETE. When done well, this is referred to as a Resource Oriented Architecture (ROA). ROAs produce significant benefits when scaling over the web. For example, standard web-based caching systems can cache resources acquired using the GET verb, firewalls can make more intelligent decisions about HTTP delivered traffic, and applications can leverage the wealth of technology associated with existing web server infrastructure. HTTP headers can negotiate payload formats, cache expirations, security features, and more. In-browser clients can leverage the native features of the browser, and the list goes on.

One concern with ROA is that monolithic applications are composed of modules that expose functions or methods internally. Module operations don't typically map naturally to resource-based interfaces. This can make decomposing a monolith into RESTful microservices more work than decomposing the same code into RPC-based microservices.

When developers refer to APIs or services today, they're usually talking about REST APIs/services. The RESTful approach has become nearly ubiquitous when it comes to implementing public interfaces. The ecosystem is vast and the developer skills are widespread. REST, however, does have its drawbacks.

It's important to keep in mind that REST is an architectural style, not a standard or a technology framework. Two different teams might build the same REST service in different and incompatible ways. While this might be said of any solution, it's particularly true of REST due to the broad set of perspectives on how REST should be done and the several toolkits, schema mechanisms, and documentation systems in use. For example, the RESTful world offers at least three competing platforms for service definition and code generation: RAML, Swagger, and API Blueprint, though the more recent Swagger-based Open API Initiative (OAI) appears like it may unify the space.

Several communications models are not addressed by REST. REST is, by definition, a client/server architecture and, in practice, it's implemented over HTTP, a request/response-based protocol. REST doesn't address serialization concerns or support messaging or data streaming.

One of the most important issues with RESTful interfaces is their overhead in backend systems. The advent of HTTP/2 (https://http2.github.io/) does much to address the overhead associated with HTTP header and JSON text transmission; however, no amount of external optimization is likely to allow a REST service to perform at the level of a purpose-built binary solution such as Apache Thrift. In fact, Protocol Buffers and Thrift were created by Google and Facebook respectively to alleviate the performance issues associated with RESTful services in high-load server systems.

1.4.3   *Protocol Buffers*

Google Protocol Buffers (PB) (https://developers.google.com/protocol-buffers/) and Apache Thrift are similar in function, performance, and from a serialization and IDL standpoint. They were built by different companies (but by several of the same people) to do the same thing. Official Google Protocol Buffer language support is limited to Java, Python, Objective-C, C++, Go, Ruby, and C#. This is a moving target and support for new languages is added over time. Protocol Buffers are used by a large community of developers.

Google Protocol Buffers focuses on providing a monolithic integrated message serialization system through the main project. Several RPC-style systems for Protocol Buffers are available in other projects, in particular, the HTTP/2-based gRPC (grpc.io). The gRPC system trades web platform integration through HTTP/2 for speed; Apache Thrift and Protocol Buffer TCP-based services typically run 4-6 times faster. Many developers feel the modular serialization and transport features of the Apache Thrift framework and the in-tree language and server support provide an advantage. Others prefer the simple integrated serialization scheme offered by PB.

Another difference between the platforms is support for transmission of collections. Apache Thrift supports transmission of three common container types: lists, sets, and maps. Protocol Buffers supplies a repeating field feature rather than support for containers, producing similar capabilities through a lower-level construct. Newer versions of PB add map simulation with several restrictions. Protocol Buffers supports signed and unsigned integers, while Apache Thrift supports only signed integers.

Apache Thrift, however, supports unions and other minor IDL features not found in Protocol Buffers.

Protocol Buffers are robust, well-documented, and backed by a large corporation, which contrasts with the community-driven nature of Apache Thrift. This is evident most clearly in the quality of the documentation for the two projects, Google's being noticeably superior (and I'm being kind).

1.4.4   Apache Avro

Apache Avro (https://avro.apache.org/) is a serialization framework designed to package the serialization schema with the data serialized. This contrasts with Apache Thrift and Protocol Buffers, both of which describe the schema (data types and service interfaces) in IDL. Apache Avro interprets the schema on the fly while most other systems generate code to interpret the schema at compile time. In general, combining the schema with the data works well for long-lived objects serialized to disk. However, such a model can add complexity and overhead to real-time RPC style communications. Arguments and optimizations can be made to turn these observations on their head, but most practical use of Apache Avro has been focused on serializing objects to disk; Avro isn't used for RPC in the wild.

Apache Thrift versions

The Thrift framework was open sourced by Facebook in 2007 and became an Apache Software Foundation incubator project in 2008:

0.2.0	released 2009-12-12
0.3.0	released 2010-08-05
0.4.0	released 2010-08-23
0.5.0	released 2010-10-07

Project moved to top-level status in 2010:

0.6.0	released 2011-02-08
0.6.1	released 2011-04-25
0.7.0	released 2011-08-13
0.8.0	released 2011-11-29
0.9.0	released 2012-10-15
0.9.1	released 2013-07-16
0.9.2	released 2014-11-16
0.9.3	released 2015-10-11
0.10.0	released 2017-01-06
0.11.0	released 2017-12-03
0.12.0	released 2019-01-04

1.4.5   *Strengths of Apache Thrift*

The strength of the Apache Thrift platform lies in the completeness of its package, its performance and flexibility, as well as the expressiveness of its IDL. Apache Thrift was created to provide cross-language capabilities comparable to REST but with dramatically improved performance and a significantly smaller footprint.

PERFORMANCE

To get a sense for the relative performance of several of the communications approaches described here, look at the test results in figure 1.4 (these tests are created and covered in detail in chapter 17). The chart displays the time required to make one million API calls to a single service implemented with several communications technologies. All of the servers were coded in Java and the same client, also coded in Java, was used in all cases, though the necessary bindings are used to call the service backend under test. Each bar shows the number of seconds the requests took to complete against a different implementation running on the same machine. The tests were performed in isolation over the local loopback on a system with no other activity. Multiple runs of each test were completed and no outliers were discovered. The sole service function accepts a string and returns a small struct. The service implementation is identical in all cases, performs no logic, and returns a static struct to highlight the service and serialization overhead.

The first bar shows the elapsed time for the service when implemented with SOAP. A standard Java SOAP service coded in JAX-WS, deployed on Tomcat 7, was used for the test. The serialization overhead associated with XML and the load incurred by Tomcat and HTTP make this the worst performer in the group, at more than 350 seconds.

The second bar shows the results of the same test but against a REST service created with Java and JAX-RS. Though the comparison normalizes as many variables as possible, REST-based services are defined with HTTP verbs and IRIs, not functions. The

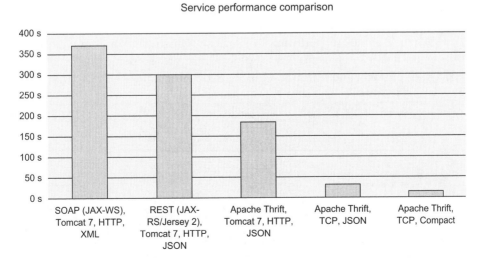

Figure 1.4   Time to complete 1 million service requests for various Java servers

implementation here is a simple GET request (no caching), passing the input string as a query parameter and receiving the resultant struct in a JSON payload. This is noticeably faster than the SOAP example at about 300 seconds, largely due to the lack of a caller payload, improved serialization performance of JSON over XML, and the significantly smaller JSON reply payload.

The last three bars are Apache Thrift server cases. The first is as close to an apples-to-apples comparison with the REST example as can be had with Apache Thrift. An Apache Thrift server was created with the same one method service, packaged as a servlet, deployed on Tomcat, and configured to use the JSON protocol over an HTTP transport. The result is a significant improvement in performance. This is attributable to the serialization benefits produced by the purpose-built Apache Thrift client/server stubs, among other efficiencies.

The real performance gains arrive when Tomcat and HTTP are left behind. The final two bars show the performance of compiled Apache Thrift servers running over TCP with JSON and Compact protocols respectively. Both are an order of magnitude faster and an order of magnitude smaller in memory.

While your mileage will vary with different languages, different levels of concurrency, different server shells, different services, and different frameworks, the previous example case provides a frame of reference and explains why many firms have moved large-scale backend services away from REST/SOAP and/or JSON serialization when under pressure for performance. Migrating to Apache Thrift from REST or SOAP could enable the same hardware to support 10 times the traffic. Backend systems using a microservice approach often require multiple backend services to collaborate to complete a client request, prioritizing backend service repressiveness.

Certain developers contemplate REST with payloads serialized using Protocol Buffers or Apache Thrift; however, this doubles the toolkit burden and complexity, misses out on the significant benefits to be had by eliminating HTTP, and gives up the endearing "human-readable payload" property typically associated with REST. It's an altogether unsatisfying combination.

When it comes to performance, Apache Thrift offers a complete package with near REST-class interoperability, significantly improved performance, and the widest range of protocol and transport choices. See figure 1.5.

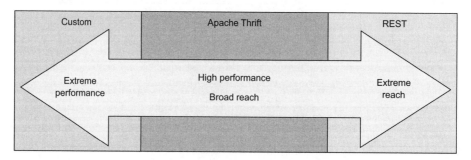

Figure 1.5   Apache Thrift balances performance with reach and flexibility.

REACH

Apache Thrift offers support in tree for a comprehensive set of programming languages but also an impressive range of platforms. Apache Thrift can be a good fit for embedded systems, offering support for Java's Compact Profile and small footprint servers for C++ and other languages.

Apache Thrift is a natural fit for typical enterprise development environments, with support for Java/JVM and C#/CLR/.Net Core on Windows, Linux, and OSX. Apache Thrift is also a perfect fit for cloud-native systems, offering small footprint servers in many languages perfect for container packaging. See figure 1.6.

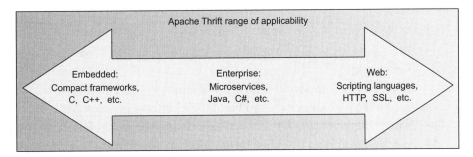

Figure 1.6   Apache Thrift is an effective solution in embedded, enterprise, and web technology environments.

Apache Thrift integrates well with the world of the web also, including native support for languages such as JavaScript and TypeScript. Apache Thrift offers HTTP, TLS, WebSocket, and JSON support. Mobile solutions on IOS and Android are also easy to build with support for Objective-C and Java.

1.4.6 *Take away*

You have many viable communications schemes to choose from today and they all have their place. As a default API option and particularly if you want broad accessibility over the public internet, REST may be your best choice. If speed is your priority, you can write your own native binary protocol or use something edgy like Cap'n Proto (https://capnproto.org). If you are principally serializing to disk, look at Apache Avro. If you want a solid, name-brand, high-speed serialization system, consider FlatBuffers (https://google.github.io/flatbuffers), or if you need RPC services as well, perhaps Protocol Buffers and GRPC will fit the bill.

However, if you want...

- *Servers and Serialization*—A complete serialization and service solution in tree
- *Modularity*—Pluggable serialization protocols and transports with a range of provided implementations
- *Performance*—Lightweight, scalable servers with fast and efficient serialization
- *Reach*—Support for an impressive range of languages, protocols, and platforms

- *Rich IDL*—Language-independent support for expressive type and service abstractions
- *Flexibility*—Integrated type and service evolution features
- *Community Driven Open Source*—Apache Software Foundation hosted and community managed

. . . in one package, then Apache Thrift belongs at the top of your consideration list. In the next chapter we'll look at the architecture of Apache Thrift and examine transports, protocols, and servers in more detail.

Summary

Here are the most important points to take away from this chapter:

- Apache Thrift is a cross-language serialization and service implementation framework.
- Apache Thrift supports a wide array of languages and platforms.
- Apache Thrift makes it easy to build high performance services.
- Apache Thrift is a good fit for service-oriented and microservice architectures.
- Apache Thrift is an Interface Definition Language (IDL)–based framework.
- IDLs allow you to describe interfaces and generate code to support the interfaces automatically.
- IDLs allow you to describe types used in messaging, long-term storage, and service calls.
- Apache Thrift includes a modular serialization system, providing several built-in serialization protocols and support for custom serialization solutions.
- Apache Thrift includes a modular transport system, providing built-in memory disk and network transports, yet makes it easy to add additional transports.
- Apache Thrift supports interface evolution, empowering CI/CD environments and Agile teams.

Apache Thrift architecture

In the first chapter, we discussed Apache Thrift's place in the distributed application development landscape and created a set of programs demonstrating a simple cross-language service. In this chapter, we take a sweeping look at the overall Apache Thrift framework. We'll break down the framework into layers, examining each layer in turn. Understanding how the facets of Apache Thrift function and fit together at a high level will allow us to dig into the topics in part II of this book with a solid conceptual understanding of Apache Thrift overall.

The Apache Thrift Framework can be organized into five layers (see figure 2.1):

- The RPC Server library
- RPC Service Stubs
- User-Defined Type Serialization
- The Serialization Protocol library
- The Transport library

Applications requiring a common way to serialize data structures for storage or messaging may need nothing more than the bottom three layers of this model.

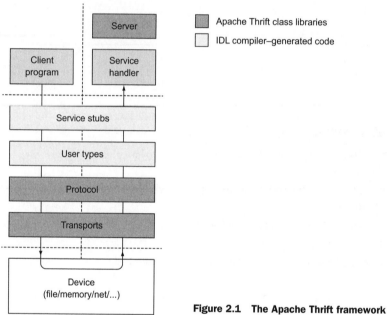

Figure 2.1   The Apache Thrift framework

The top two layers include the Apache Thrift library of RPC servers and the IDL compiler-generated service stubs, adding RPC support to the stack.

Apache Thrift is conceptually an object-oriented framework, though it supports object-oriented and non-object-oriented languages. The Transport, Protocol, and Server libraries are often referred to as class libraries, though they may be implemented in other ways in non-object oriented languages. The classes within the Apache Thrift libraries are typically named with a leading capital T, for example, TTransport, TProtocol, and TServer.

2.1   *Transports*

At the bottom of the stack we have transports (see figure 2.2). The Apache Thrift transport library insulates the upper layers of Apache Thrift from device-specific details. In particular, transports enable protocols to read and write byte streams without

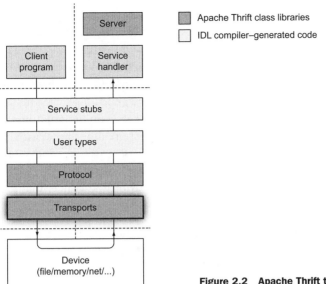

Figure 2.2   Apache Thrift transports

knowledge of the underlying device. This allows support for new devices and middleware systems to be added to the platform without impacting the upper layers of software.

For example, imagine you developed a set of programs to move stock price quotations over the Sockets networking API. After the application is deployed, the requirements expand and you're asked to add support for stock price transmission over an AMQP messaging system as well.

With Apache Thrift, the expanded capability will be fairly easy to implement. The new AMQP code can implement the existing Apache Thrift Transport interface, allowing the upper layers of code to use either the Socket solution or the AMQP solution without knowing the difference (see figure 2.3).

The modular nature of Apache Thrift transports allows them to be selected and changed at compile time or runtime, giving applications plug-in support for a range of devices (see figure 2.4).

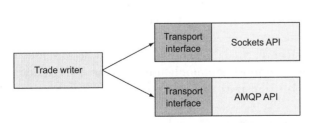

Figure 2.3   Multiple I/O targets can be used interchangeably if they expose a common interface, such as TTransport.

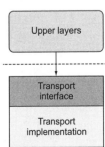

Figure 2.4   Abstract transport interface

2.1.1   *The transport interface*

The Apache Thrift transport layer exposes a simple byte-oriented I/O interface to upper layers of code. This interface is typically defined in an abstract base class called TTransport. Table 2.1 describes the TTransport methods present in most language implementations. Each Apache Thrift language implementation has its own subtleties. Apache Thrift language library implementations tend to play to the strengths of the language in question, making a level of variety across implementations the norm.

For example, certain languages define transport interfaces with additional methods for performance or other purposes. A case in point, the C++ language TTransport interface defines borrow() and consume() methods, which enable more efficient buffer processing. The examples here focus on the conceptual architecture of Apache Thrift.

Table 2.1   The TTransport interface

Method	Description
open()	Prepares the transport for I/O operations
close()	Shuts down the transport
isOpen()	Returns true if the transport is open, false otherwise
read()	Reads bytes from the transport
readAll()	Reads an exact number of bytes from the transport (blocking or erroring if they aren't available)
write()	Writes bytes to the transport (the transport may buffer the operation)
flush()	Forces any buffered bytes to be written to the underlying device

2.1.2   *Endpoint transports*

In this book we refer to Apache Thrift transports that write to a physical or logical device as "endpoint transports." Endpoint transports are always at the bottom of an Apache Thrift transport stack and most use cases require precisely one endpoint transport.

Apache Thrift languages supply endpoint transports for memory, file, and network devices. Memory-oriented transports, such as TMemoryBuffer, are often used to collect multiple small write operations that are later transmitted as a single block. File-based transports, such as TSimpleFileTransport, are often used for logging and state persistence.

The most important Apache Thrift Transport types are network-oriented and used to support RPC operations. The most commonly used Apache Thrift network transport is TSocket. The TSocket transport uses the Socket API to transmit bytes over TCP/IP (see figure 2.5).

Other devices and networking protocols can be exposed through the TTransport interface as well. For example, many Apache Thrift language libraries provide HTTP transports to read and write using the HTTP protocol. Building a custom transport for

Figure 2.5   Interprocess communications using the TSocket endpoint transport

an unsupported network protocol or device isn't typically difficult, and doing so enables the entire framework to operate over the new endpoint type.

2.1.3   *Layered transports*

Because Apache Thrift transports are defined by the generic TTransport interface, client code is independent of the underlying transport implementation. This gives transports the ability to overlay anything, even other transports. Layering allows generic transport behavior to be separated into interoperable and reusable components.

Imagine you're building a banking application that makes calls to a service hosted by another company and you need to encrypt all of the bytes traveling between your client and the RPC server. If you create a layered transport to provide the encryption, the client and server code could use your new encryption layer on top of the original network transport. The benefits of isolating this new encryption feature in a layered transport are several, not the least of which is that it can be inserted between the existing client code and old network transport with potentially no impact. The client code will see the encryption transport layer as another transport. The network endpoint transport will see the encryption transport as another client.

The encryption transport can be layered on top of any endpoint transport, allowing you to encrypt network I/O as well as file I/O and memory I/O. The layering approach allows the encryption concern to be separated from the device I/O concern.

In this book we refer to all Apache Thrift transports that aren't endpoint transports as "layered transports." Layered transports expose the standard Apache Thrift TTransport interface to clients and depend on the TTransport interface of the layer below. In this way one or more transport layers can be used to form a transport stack (see figure 2.6).

A commonly used Apache Thrift layered transport is the framing transport. This transport is called TFramedTransport in most language libraries and it adds a four-byte message size as a prefix to each

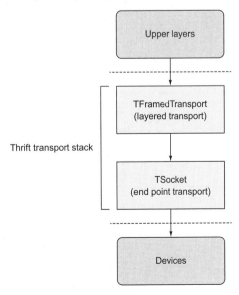

Figure 2.6   Layered transport stack

Apache Thrift message. This enables more efficient message processing in certain scenarios, allowing a receiver to read the frame size, and then provide buffers of the exact size needed by the frame.

> **NOTE** Clients and servers must use compatible transport stacks to communicate. If the server is using a TSocket transport, the client will need to use a TSocket transport. If the server is using a TFramedTransport layer on top of a TSocket, the client will have to use a TFramedTransport layer on top of a TSocket. Apache Thrift doesn't have a built-in runtime transport or protocol discovery mechanism, though custom discovery systems can be created on top of Apache Thrift.

Another important feature offered by layered transports is buffering. The TFramedTransport implicitly buffers writes until the `flush()` method is called, at which point the frame size and data are written to the layer below. The TBufferedTransport is an alternative to the TFramedTransport that can provide buffering when framing isn't needed. Several languages build buffering into the endpoint solution and don't provide a TBufferedTransport (Java is an example).

2.1.4 Server transports

When two processes connect over a network to facilitate communications, the server must listen for clients to connect, accepting new connections as they arrive. The abstract interface for the server's connection acceptor is usually named TServerTransport. The most popular implementation of TServerTransport is TServerSocket, used for TCP/IP networking. The server transport wires each new connection to a TTransport implementation to handle the individual connection's I/O. Server transports follow the factory pattern with TServerSockets manufacturing TSockets, TServerPipes manufacturing TPipes, and so on (see figure 2.7).

Server transports typically have only four methods (see table 2.2). The `listen()` and `close()` methods prepare the server transport for use and shut it down, respectively. Clients cannot connect before `listen()` is invoked or after `close()` is invoked. The

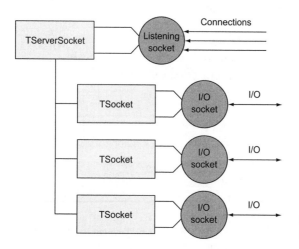

Figure 2.7 Server transport and I/O transports

accept() method blocks until a client connection arrives. When a client initiates a connection, the server accept() method returns a TTransport wired to the connection that is then used to support normal RPC operations with the client. The interrupt() method breaks the server transport out of the blocking accept() call, causing it to return.

Table 2.2 The TServerTransport interface

Method	Description
accept()	Accepts a waiting connection and returns an I/O transport wired to the new connection
close()	Stops listening and closes down the server transport
interrupt()	Breaks the server transport out of a blocking accept() call
listen()	Enables the server transport to accept connections

2.2 *Protocols*

In the context of Apache Thrift, a protocol is a means for serializing types. Apache Thrift RPC doesn't support every type defined in every language. Rather, the Apache Thrift type system includes all the important base types found in most languages (int, double, string, and so on), as well as a few heavily used and widely supported container types (map, set, list). All protocols must be capable of reading and writing all the types in the Apache Thrift type system.

Protocols sit on top of a transport stack (see figure 2.8). Labor is divided between the transport that's responsible for manipulating bytes and the protocol that's responsible for working with data types. Transports see only opaque byte streams; protocols turn data types into byte streams (see figure 2.9) and vice versa.

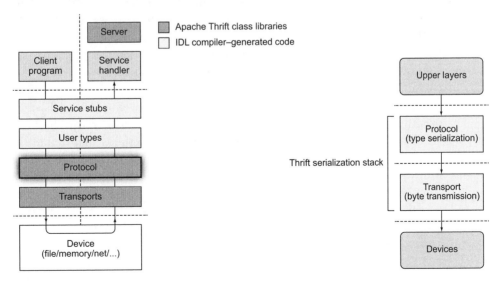

Figure 2.8 Apache Thrift protocols

Figure 2.9 Serialization stack

For example, if you want to store an integer into a disk file on one system and make it readable on another system, you need to ensure that the integer is stored in an agreed-upon byte order. Either the most significant or least significant byte must be first. The choice between these two options is made by the serialization protocol. The transport simply writes the bytes supplied to disk in the order presented.

Apache Thrift provides several serialization protocols, each with its own goals:

- *The Binary Protocol*—Simple and fast
- *The Compact Protocol*—Smaller data size without excessive overhead
- *The JSON Protocol*—Standards-based, human-readable, broad interoperability

The Binary Protocol is the default Apache Thrift protocol, and at the time of initial release, it was the only protocol. The Binary Protocol requires minimal CPU overhead, essentially writing the desired types into the byte stream as they are, after attending to byte ordering, type normalization, and a few other tasks. Thus, a 64-bit integer is going to take up about 64 bits on the wire when using the Binary Protocol.

The Compact Protocol is designed to minimize the size of the serialized representation of data. The Compact Protocol is fairly simple but does use more CPU in the process of shuffling bits into smaller spaces. In cases where I/O is the bottleneck and CPU abounds (a common situation), this is a good protocol to consider.

The JSON Protocol converts inputs into JSON formatted text. Of the three common Apache Thrift protocols, JSON is likely to produce the largest representation on the wire and consume the most CPU. The advantages of JSON are broad interoperability and human readability.

Apache Thrift languages typically provide an abstract protocol interface, called TProtocol, adhered to by all concrete protocol implementations. This interface defines methods for reading and writing each of the Apache Thrift types as well as compositional methods used to serialize containers, user-defined types, and RPC messages.

A key feature of the Apache Thrift type system is its support for user-defined types in the form of structs. Apache Thrift structs are IDL-based composite types built from a set of fields. The fields can be of any legal Apache Thrift type, including base types, containers, and other structs.

Apache Thrift messages are the envelopes used to deliver RPC calls and responses over transports. These messages are implemented as specialized Apache Thrift structs.

Table 2.3 lists several of the typical TProtocol methods that define the Apache Thrift type system. Each write method listed here has a corresponding read method with the same suffix (for example, `writeBool()`/`readBool()`). (See chapter 5 for a complete TProtocol listing.)

Table 2.3 Abbreviated TProtocol interface

Method	Description
writeBool()	Serializes a Boolean value
writeByte()	Serializes a byte value
writeI16()	Serializes a 16-bit integer value
writeI32()	Serializes a 32-bit integer value
writeI64()	Serializes a 64-bit integer value
writeDouble()	Serializes a double precision floating point value
writeString()	Serializes a string value
...	

2.3 *Apache Thrift IDL*

Combining Apache Thrift Protocols and Transports provides a way to serialize doubles, lists of strings, and other such generic data representations. While useful, most applications also deal in user-defined data types. For example, a stock trading application may deal in trade reports, a social platform may deal in status updates, and a flight simulator may deal in telemetry.

Interface Definition Languages (IDLs) can be used to define application-level types and service interfaces, enabling tools to generate code to automate serialization for these types. Rather than hand-coding the serialization of a Trade Report for a stock trading program, you can describe the trade type in IDL and let the Apache Thrift IDL Compiler generate the serialization code for you.

Apache Thrift IDL is implementation language independent. The IDL compiler reads IDL files and can output serialization code and RPC client/server stubs in any of the Apache Thrift target languages (see figure 2.10).

Imagine you're writing a program for the California Fisheries Bureau in Python and you want to call a server maintained by the Seattle Ocean Research Center to retrieve Halibut catch levels, but you discover the server is written in Java. If the server was coded with an Apache Thrift API you could compile the server interface IDL for Python and then use the Python stubs to call the Java server directly.

The following listing shows an example of what such an interface definition might look like.

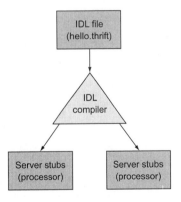

Figure 2.10 IDL compilation

Listing 2.1   ~/thriftbook/arch/halibut.thrift

```
struct Date {          ❶
    1: i16  year
    2: i16  month
    3: i16  day
}

service HalibutTracking {              ❷
    i32 get_catch_in_pounds_today()
    i32 get_catch_in_pounds_by_date(1: Date dt, 2: double tm)
}
```

The service defined in the IDL file above is called `HalibutTracking` ❷. This service depends on the user-defined type `Date` ❶. To compile the IDL into language-specific code, the IDL compiler is invoked with a switch indicating the target language to generate code for. The command `thrift --gen java halibut.thrift` will output a set of Java files designed to enable serialization of the `Date` type and client/server RPC stubs to support the `HalibutTracking` service. The command `thrift --gen py halibut.thrift` would generate stubs for the same interface in Python.

2.3.1 *User-defined types and serialization*

User-defined types (UDTs) are an important aspect of external interfaces. While it's possible to compose the `get_catch_in_pounds_by_date()` method in our above example with discrete year/month/day parameters, the `Date` type is much more expressive, reusable, and concise. Apache Thrift IDL allows user-defined types to be created with the "struct" keyword.

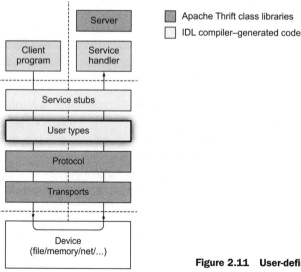

Figure 2.11   **User-defined types**

The IDL compiler generates language-specific types from IDL types; for example, the struct keyword will cause the IDL compiler to produce a class in C++, a record in Erlang, and a package in Perl. These generated types have built-in serialization capabilities, making it easy to serialize them using any Apache Thrift protocol/transport stack (see figure 2.11). To keep things generic, the IDL compiler code output examples below use pseudo code, approximating the output you might see for any given language.

The following listing shows a pseudo code example of what an IDL compiler-generated UDT for the example `Date` type might look like in some languages.

Listing 2.2 Thrift-generated user-defined type

```
class Date {            ❶
 public:
   short year;
   short month;
   short day;

   read(TProtocol protocol) {…};         ❷
   write(TProtocol protocol) {…};  ⟵
};                                          ❸
```

The trivial `Date` type ❶ illustrated in pseudo code above has the exact fields described in the IDL and is organized into a class with the same name as the IDL struct. The Apache Thrift compiler creates `read()` ❷ and `write()` ❸ methods to automate the process of serializing the type through the Apache Thrift TProtocol interface. This makes transmitting a complex data structure as easy as calling `read` or `write` on the structure with the target Apache Thrift Protocol as a parameter.

Apache Thrift structs are used internally within the Apache Thrift Framework as the means to package all RPC data transmissions. The argument list of each Apache Thrift Service method is defined in an "args" struct. This allows Apache Thrift to use the same convenient struct `read()` and `write()` methods to send and receive RPC parameter lists.

The implementation of a struct's `write` method is a simple sequential invocation of the appropriate TProtocol methods. The following listing shows the pseudo code for the `write` method of the `Date` struct.

Listing 2.3 Thrift-generated struct `write()` method

```
Date::write(TProtocol protocol) {
  protocol.writeStructBegin("Date");

  protocol.writeFieldBegin("year", T_I16, 1);
  protocol.writeI16(this.year);
  protocol.writeFieldEnd();

  protocol.writeFieldBegin("month", T_I16, 2);
  protocol.writeI16(this.month);
```

```
    protocol.writeFieldEnd();

    protocol.writeFieldBegin("day", T_I16, 3);
    protocol.writeI16(this.day);
    protocol.writeFieldEnd();

    protocol.writeFieldStop();
    protocol.writeStructEnd();
}
```

The ability to compose serializable, language-agnostic types is a key feature of the Apache Thrift IDL. Types can be serialized to memory and then sent over messaging systems, types can be used directly in RPC methods, and types can be serialized to files.

2.3.2 *RPC services*

For many programmers, building cross-language RPC services is the primary reason for using Apache Thrift. Defining services in Apache Thrift IDL allows the IDL compiler to generate client and server stubs that supply all of the plumbing necessary to call a function remotely (see figure 2.12).

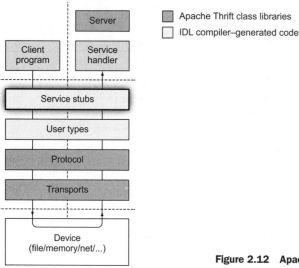

Figure 2.12   **Apache Thrift RPC services**

The following listing shows pseudo code for the compiler-generated `HalibutTrack-`
ing service interface.

Listing 2.4   Thrift-generated service interface

```
interface HalibutTracking {
    int32 get_catch_in_pounds_today();
    int32 get_catch_in_pounds_by_date(Date dt, double tm);
};
```

This service has two methods, both of which return a 32-bit integer and one that takes a `Date` struct and a `double` as input. In addition to defining the interface in the target language, the IDL compiler will generate a pair of classes to support RPC on this interface: a client stub for use in the client process and a server stub, called a processor, for use in the server process. The client class is used as a proxy for the remote service. The processor is used to invoke the user-defined service implementation on behalf of the remote client.

THE CLIENT STUB

A client interested in calling a service in a remote server can call the desired method on the client proxy object. Under the covers the client proxy sends a message to the server, including information regarding the method to invoke and any parameters. Typically, the client proxy then waits to receive the result of the call from the server (see figure 2.13). Using the generated client proxy makes developing software utilizing RPC services as natural as coding to local functions.

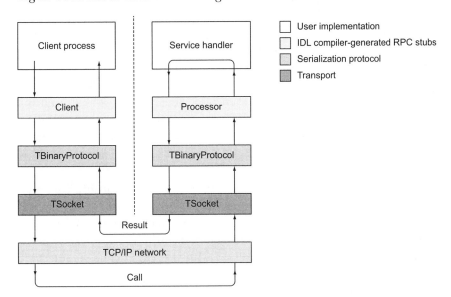

Figure 2.13   Thrift RPC call processing

The following listing shows pseudo code for the IDL compiler-generated client implementation of the `HalibutTracking` service `get_catch_in_pounds_by_date()` method.

Listing 2.5   Thrift-generated client code

```
int32 HalibutTrackingClient::get_catch_in_pounds_by_date(Date dt,double tm)
{
    send_get_catch_in_pounds_by_date(dt, tm);        ❶
    return recv_get_catch_in_pounds_by_date();       ❷
}
```

```
void HalibutTrackingClient::send_get_catch_in_pounds_by_date(Date dt, double tm)
{
    protocol.writeMessageBegin("get_catch_in_pounds_by_date", T_CALL, 0);      ❸

    HalibutTracking_get_catch_in_pounds_by_date_args args;
    args.dt = dt;
    args.tm = tm;
    args.write(protocol);        ❹

    protocol.writeMessageEnd();
    protocol.getTransport().flush();        ❺
}
```

In this example, the client implementation of get_catch_in_pounds_by_date() calls an internal "send_" method ❶ to send a message to the server. This is followed by a call to a second "recv_" method ❷ to receive the results. This is the basis of the Apache Thrift RPC protocol. Clients send messages to servers to invoke methods, and servers send results back.

The second method in the listing is the pseudo code for the send method. The send method creates a message to send to the server. The message begins with the protocol writeMessageBegin() call ❸. This serializes the T_CALL constant that informs the server that this is an "RPC call"-type message. The string "get_catch_in_pounds_by_date" is serialized to indicate which method we want to invoke. The 0 passed here indicates we won't use sequence numbers. Message sequence numbers are useful in certain applications but aren't employed in most normal Apache Thrift RPC (for more information on the use of Apache Thrift messages, see chapter 8, "Implementing services").

As we discovered in the previous section, the Apache Thrift IDL compiler can generate read() and write() serialization methods for any struct defined in IDL. Rather than reinvent the wheel, Apache Thrift generates an internal struct for each method's argument list, called args. To add the method's arguments to the byte stream, the args struct is instantiated and initialized with the parameters for the method call. Calling the args object's write() method ❹ serializes all the parameters required to invoke the get_catch_in_pounds_by_date() method.

The message serialization is completed by calling writeMessageEnd() to bookend the writeMessageBegin() call. Once the message has been completely serialized, the transport stack is asked to flush() the bytes out to the network (in case they have been buffered) ❺.

The client follows the send_get_catch_in_pounds_by_date() call ❶ with the complimentary recv_get_catch_in_pounds_by_date() call ❷ (omitted in the example for brevity). The server may respond to an RPC invocation with one of two messages. The first is a normal T_REPLY and the second is a T_EXCEPTION. Consistent with the creation of the args class, the Thrift Compiler generates a result class for each service method to package the method's results. The recv_get_catch_in_pounds_by_date() method performs the same operations as the send_get_catch_in_pounds_by_date() method but in reverse, using the result object read()

method to recover the server's response. If the `recv_get_catch_in_pounds_by_` `date()` method decodes a normal result, it's returned. If an exception is decoded, language-specific processing occurs, such as throwing the exception.

While high level, this is a fairly concise summary of the function of Apache Thrift RPC from the client's perspective. There are additional considerations on the server side of the equation.

SERVICE PROCESSORS

The server side of an RPC call consists of two code elements. The processor is the server side IDL-generated stub, the counterpart of the client stub. The Thrift compiler generates a client and processor pair for each IDL-defined service. The processor uses the protocol stack to deserialize service method call requests, invoking the appropriate local function. The result of the local function call is packaged into a result structure by the processor and sent back to the client. The processor is essentially a dispatcher, receiving requests from the client and then dispatching them to the appropriate internal function.

SERVICE HANDLERS

Processors depend on a user-coded service "handler" to implement the service interface (hey, you gotta do some work around here). The handler is supplied to the processor to complete the RPC support chain. The service handler is the only code you need to write to implement a complete Apache Thrift service.

2.4 Servers

In the context of Apache Thrift, a server is a program specifically designed to host one or more Apache Thrift Services. As it turns out, the job of an Apache Thrift RPC server is fairly formulaic. Servers listen for client connections, dispatch calls to services using generated processors, and get shut down by admins on occasion (see figure 2.14).

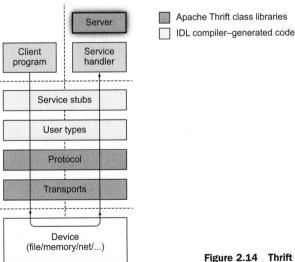

Figure 2.14   Thrift servers

The boilerplate nature of server operation allows Thrift to supply a library of server classes with a wide range of implementations. Different language libraries support different server classes based on the community's needs and the capabilities of the language. For example, Java offers single and multithreaded servers, as well as servers that use dedicated client threads and servers that use thread pools to process requests, while Go servers use go routines. Concurrency models are the key distinction between the various servers offered (for more server details see chapter 10).

Most production needs can be met with an existing library server. Apache Thrift is open source, so even unique requirements can be met by customizing an existing server. Let's look at a simplified Java program in the following listing that uses an Apache Thrift library server to support the HalibutTracking service.

Listing 2.6 Psuedo Java server

```
public class JavaServer {
    public static void main(String[] args) {
        TServerTransport svrTransport = new TServerSocket(8585);          ❶
        HalibutTrackingHandler handler = new HalibutTrackingHandler();    ❷
        HalibutTracking.Processor<HalibutTrackingHandler> processor =
            new HalibutTracking.Processor<>(handler);        ◁
        TServer server = new TSimpleServer(                   ❸
            new Args(svrTransport).processor(processor));     ◁
        server.serve();                                        ❹
    }
}
```

This simple Java server begins by creating a TServerSocket server transport ❶ that will listen on port 8585 for new client connections. A HalibutTrackingHandler object is created ❷ to implement the service (handler code not shown; it will contain whatever logic your implementation requires). Next we create a processor ❸ to manage RPC call dispatching. A TSimpleServer object is then constructed with the server transport and the processor/handler pair as input ❹. We specified no protocol, so the default Binary Protocol will be used. As a final step we call the server's serve() method, at which point the server begins accepting connections and processing calls to the HalibutTracking service.

Using the TSimpleServer class from the Apache Thrift Java language library we can create a full-featured server in about five lines of code. Complex services may require many lines of Handler code; however, the server shell doesn't get much more complicated than what you see above. A multithreaded async server can be implemented in about the same footprint.

2.5 Security

Apache Thrift doesn't make explicit provisions for security at the framework level. By making security an external concern, Apache Thrift allows the appropriate security mechanisms to be applied without complicating Thrift or impacting its performance unnecessarily.

Many Apache Thrift implementations are housed entirely in private data centers. In these scenarios, much of the required security may come in the form of isolation, including firewalls, DMZs, and other schemes. Microservice orchestration platforms often implement interservice security and policy through service meshes like Istio. Various Apache Thrift language libraries include degrees of support for security features such as SASL (Simple Authentication and Security Layer) and SSL/TLS. Custom security mechanisms can be integrated into Apache Thrift using the layering model discussed previously. The Apache Thrift architecture leaves the door open to many possibilities.

In the next chapter, we'll look at various ways to set up a working Apache Thrift development environment and cover several general RPC debugging techniques.

Summary

Key points from this chapter

- Transports provide device independence for the rest of the Apache Thrift framework.
- Endpoint transports perform byte I/O on physical or logical devices, such as networks, files, and memory.
- Layered transports add functionality to existing transports in a modular fashion, such as message framing and buffering.
- Any number of layered transports can be stacked on top of a single endpoint transport to create a transport stack.
- Server transports aren't true transports; rather they are factories, accepting client connections and manufacturing new transports for each connecting client.
- Protocols are modular serialization engines. The primary Apache Thrift protocols are
    - Binary: Simple and fast binary representations of data
    - Compact: Trades CPU overhead for a smaller data footprint
    - JSON: Trades speed and size for readability and broad interoperability
- Apache Thrift IDL allows user-defined types and service interfaces to be defined.
- The Apache Thrift IDL compiler generates self-serializing representations of IDL user-defined types in various output languages.
- The Apache Thrift IDL compiler generates client and server stubs for IDL-defined service interfaces in various output languages.
- The Apache Thrift Server library allows IDL-defined services to be deployed with minimal coding effort and a range of concurrency models.

3

Building,
testing, and debugging

This chapter covers

- Acquiring a prebuilt Apache Thrift IDL compiler
- Building the Apache Thrift IDL compiler and language libraries from source
- Reviewing the Apache Thrift source tree and project structure
- Running language and cross-language tests
- Debugging RPC applications

To build programs using Apache Thrift we'll need the Apache Thrift IDL compiler, and, for certain languages, we'll also need compiled runtime libraries. To build "working" programs we'll need familiarity with testing and debugging techniques as well.

One of the most challenging things about open source software can be getting started, as in: how do I build this thing so that I can use it?! This chapter will get you started quickly and provide an orientation to the overall Apache Thrift development environment. We'll look at different ways to acquire and/or build the

Apache Thrift IDL compiler and libraries. We'll also examine the Apache Thrift source tree and build systems, including Apache Thrift language libraries, the Apache Thrift tutorial, and the Apache Thrift test suite. The final sections of this chapter look at a few useful techniques for debugging RPC applications. This is an overview chapter and remains language-agnostic where possible, focusing on the Apache Thrift framework as a whole.

3.1   *Installing the Apache Thrift IDL compiler*

Apache Thrift-based RPC programs depend on two things: Apache Thrift libraries and IDL-generated code. Because Apache Thrift is a cross-language framework, there is no "one" Apache thrift library. Rather, the general constructs of Apache Thrift are implemented in each supported language as a standalone library for that specific language.

Apache Thrift language libraries can be installed in a variety of ways, depending on the target programming language. Many programming languages have package managers with versions of the Apache Thrift library directly available. Language libraries are also available as source through the Apache Thrift source code repository. Part 3 of this book provides jump-starts for several of the most popular Apache Thrift languages. These jump-starts describe the process for installing the necessary Apache Thrift libraries for the language in question.

The Apache Thrift IDL compiler is the tool used to generate application-specific code from your interface definitions. Internally, the Apache Thrift compiler is divided into an IDL parser and language-specific generators. The parser builds an abstract syntax tree (AST) from the IDL, and then one or more generators turn the AST into code for the target programming language(s). For more information on the Apache Thrift Interface Definition Language, see chapter 6, "Apache Thrift IDL."

To demonstrate what the IDL compiler does for us, consider the following command line session:

```
$ echo "const i32 x = 42" > test.thrift          ❶
$ thrift --gen cpp test.thrift                ❷
$ ls -l
drwxrwxr-x  2 randy randy 4096 Feb  7 18:10 gen-cpp/
-rw-rw-r--  1 randy randy   17 Feb  7 18:10 test.thrift
$ ls -l gen-cpp
-rw-rw-r-- 1 randy randy 261 Feb  7 18:10 test_constants.cpp
-rw-rw-r-- 1 randy randy 343 Feb  7 18:10 test_constants.h
-rw-rw-r-- 1 randy randy 242 Feb  7 18:10 test_types.cpp
-rw-rw-r-- 1 randy randy 401 Feb  7 18:10 test_types.h
$ cat gen-cpp/test_constants.h
/**
 * Autogenerated by Thrift Compiler (1.0.0-dev)
 *
 * DO NOT EDIT UNLESS YOU ARE SURE THAT YOU KNOW WHAT YOU ARE DOING
 *   @generated
 */
#ifndef test_CONSTANTS_H
#define test_CONSTANTS_H
```

```
#include "test_types.h"

class testConstants {
 public:
  testConstants();

   int32_t x;
};

extern const testConstants g_test_constants;           ❸

#endif
$ cat gen-cpp/test_constants.cpp
/**
 * Autogenerated by Thrift Compiler (1.0.0-dev)
 *
 * DO NOT EDIT UNLESS YOU ARE SURE THAT YOU KNOW WHAT YOU ARE DOING
 *  @generated
 */
#include "test_constants.h"

const testConstants g_test_constants;

testConstants::testConstants() {
  x = 42;

}
```

The first command in this session echoes a trivial Apache Thrift interface definition to the file test.thrift ❶. The second command parses the IDL and generates C++ code to implement the IDL ❷. With a single line of IDL and one compiler command, the Thrift IDL compiler has created many lines of code for us.

In the C++ case, the IDL constant "x" is placed within a singleton object identified by the global variable g_test_constants ❸. The "g" prefix stands for global, "test" is the name of the IDL file, and "constants" indicates that this is the singleton wrapper class that will house all the constants for this Thrift IDL file. Not only did the complier save us the typing but it also built us a global constant construct with minimal global namespace impact and the ability to support built-in types and collections. Perhaps most importantly, it can do this for any number of popular programming languages, respecting the syntax of each.

You don't need to understand C++ to see the value added here. The IDL compiler takes the drudgery out of coding interfaces and guarantees that the interface will be implemented consistently and with best practices across a wide range of languages.

There are several ways to acquire a working Apache Thrift IDL compiler:

- Platform installers
- VMs and containers
- Source
- Internet binaries

We'll look at each option in turn.

> **TIP** Never download executable code or code you plan to compile into executable code from an untrusted source.

3.1.1 *Platform installers*

Many operating system distributions provide package managers with Apache Thrift packages supplied by the default package repositories. Package names vary and packages can contain the Apache Thrift compiler as well as one or more libraries.

UBUNTU 14.04 AND 16.04 LTS

On Ubuntu 14.04, 16.04, and 18.04 LTS, you can install the Apache Thrift compiler with apt-get. The following command line session displays all the Thrift-related packages available from the native Ubuntu 14.04 repositories (you may need to run these commands as root by prefixing them with "sudo"):

```
$ apt-get update                    ❶
$ apt-cache search thrift                        ❷
python-thrift - Python library for Thrift
python-txamqp - AMPQ client library using Twisted
golang-thrift-dev - Go library for linking against Thrift clients
libthrift-java - Java language support for Thrift
php-horde-thrift - Thrift
thrift-compiler - code generator/compiler for Thrift definitions
$ apt-get install -y thrift-compiler    ◁──┐
...                                         ❸
$ thrift --version
Thrift version 0.9.0
```

In the previous example, the first command updates the repository indexes with the latest package listings. This is an important step, because several Ubuntu base package lists don't include the Apache Thrift compiler ❶. The second command shows that several Apache Thrift language library packages are available, as well as the IDL compiler package ❷. The third command installs the thrift-compiler package ❸. As you can see, the example Ubuntu Thrift-compiler package installed version 0.9.0 of the IDL compiler, which is a few years old at the time of this writing.

Ubuntu 16.04 and 18.04 provide Apache Thrift compiler version 0.9.1 at the time of this writing.

CENTOS 7

CentOS and other flavors of Enterprise Linux (EL) don't have Apache Thrift in the base repositories; however, the Extra Packages for Enterprise Linux (EPEL) repository provides several Apache Thrift packages. Here is a session on a base CentOS 7 server that adds EPEL repository support, lists the Thrift-related packages, and then installs the Apache Thrift compiler:

```
# wget http://dl.fedoraproject.org/pub/epel/7/x86_64/e/
➥ epel-release-7-6.noarch.rpm                         ❶
...
```

```
2016-06-15 01:35:12 (396 KB/s) - 'epel-release-7-6.noarch.rpm'
⮡ saved [14432/14432]

# rpm -ivh epel-release-7-6.noarch.rpm          ◄─❷
warning: epel-release-7-6.noarch.rpm: Header V3 RSA/SHA256 Signature, key ID
⮡ 352c64e5: NOKEY
Preparing...                      ################################ [100%]
Updating / installing...
   1:epel-release-7-6             ################################ [100%]
# yum search thrift       ❸
...
======================================================================
libthrift-java.noarch : Java support for thrift
libthrift-javadoc.noarch : API documentation for java-thrift
perl-thrift.noarch : Perl support for thrift
php-horde-Horde-Thrift.noarch : Thrift
python-thrift.x86_64 : Python support for thrift
thrift-devel.x86_64 : Development files for thrift
fb303.x86_64 : Basic interface for Thrift services
thrift.x86_64 : Software framework for cross-language services development

   Name and summary matches only, use "search all" for everything.
# yum install -y thrift.x86_64       ◄─┐
...                                     ❹
# thrift --version
Thrift version 0.9.1
```

The wget command in the previous session downloads the EPEL repository information
rpm ❶ (on a base CentOS install you may need to use yum install wget), and the second command installs the rpm ❷, updating the yum repository indexes. The third command displays all of the Thrift-related packages ❸. The EPEL repository offers
thrift.x86_64, a v0.9.1 Thrift package. This package includes the compiler and also
the C++ libraries for Thrift. The fourth command installs the Apache Thrift package ❹.

WINDOWS

Several individuals have posted Thrift compilers on the Nuget platform. You can
install Nuget packages from the Visual Studio Package Manager prompt using the
Install-Package command (PM> Install-Package Thrift). The Apache Thrift community also typically offers a Windows build of the latest Apache Thrift compiler in
the download area of the official website (https://thrift.apache.org/download).

OS X

On OS X, both MacPorts and Homebrew have current versions of Apache Thrift available through the "thrift" package/formula. In the past, these solutions essentially
downloaded the Apache Thrift source and built it locally. More recently the Thrift
binary is installed directly, making installation fast and easy.

OTHER PLATFORMS

Other platforms may also provide Apache Thrift packages. Linux systems, in particular, are prone to offering Apache Thrift support, largely because Apache Thrift is integral to other tools, for example Hive, Cassandra, and HBase.

3.1.2　*VMs and containers*

Prefabricated virtual machines and containers can be used to build or run an Apache Thrift IDL compiler.

VAGRANT

Vagrant is a devops tool that makes it easy to boot a local virtual machine, provision it, use it, and destroy it. The Apache Thrift source tree contains a "contrib" folder, which is the home to several Vagrantfiles. These Vagrantfiles instruct Vagrant to boot a virtual machine and build the entire Apache Thrift platform. While this can take a good 20–30 minutes, it's a reliable way to build a Thrift compiler. Vagrant files for Ubuntu 14.04 and CentOS 6.5 are provided.

To use the Vagrantfiles you must have Vagrant and Oracle VirtualBox installed. The following shows an example session running the Apache Thrift CentOS 6.5 Vagrantfile on a Windows host from within a Git Bash shell (Git Bash can be installed on Windows/OSX and Linux from git-scm.com):

```
thrift@RONAM ~
$ git clone http://github.com/apache/thrift
Cloning into 'thrift'...
remote: Counting objects: 41123, done.
remote: Compressing objects: 100% (4/4), done.
remote: Total 41123 (delta 0), reused 0 (delta 0), pack-reused 41119
Receiving objects: 100% (41123/41123), 11.65 MiB | 7.61 MiB/s, done.
Resolving deltas: 100% (28724/28724), done.
Checking connectivity... done.
Checking out files: 100% (1774/1774), done.


thrift@RONAM ~
$ cd thrift/contrib/vagrant/centos-6.5/

thrift@RONAM ~/thrift/contrib/vagrant/centos-6.5 (master)
$ vagrant up
...
==> default: Use "make install" to install the compiler and libraries.

Randy@RONAM ~/thrift/contrib/vagrant/centos-6.5 (master)
$ vagrant ssh
Last login: Sat Sep 27 23:39:13 2014

# /thrift/compiler/cpp/thrift --version
Thrift version 1.0.0-dev
# exit
```

The vagrant up command boots a virtual machine, configures and builds the entire Apache Thrift system (the compiler and libraries for more than 20 languages), and runs unit tests for each based on the instructions in the working directory's Vagrantfile. The process involves downloading, configuring, and building packages, sources, and libraries for various tools and languages. When the configuration completes you can ssh into the VM and inspect the build results. For more information on Vagrant, see www.vagrantup.com. For more information on building Apache Thrift from source, see section 3.1.3.

DOCKER

Another solution for those in need of the latest Apache Thrift IDL compiler is Docker. Docker can be installed on Linux, Windows, and OS X. Docker containers are lightweight, isolated environments that use minimal resources and can be started faster than virtual machines. Most Apache Thrift images are Linux-based and will only run on Linux systems or within a Linux VM on a non-Linux host.

Docker Hub (https://hub.docker.com) is a cloud-based registry hosting many Docker images with several Apache Thrift repositories. If you have Docker installed you can use the Docker search command to find Docker Hub-hosted Thrift images:

```
$ docker search thrift
NAME                                 DESCRIPTION                               STARS
thrift                               Thrift is a framework for generating clien...  66
evarga/thrift                        This is a Docker image for Apache Thrift. ...   4
apache/thrift                        Apache Thrift                                   4
whiteworld/thrift                                                                    1
thrift/thrift-compiler               Apache Thrift Compiler                          1
randyabernethy/thrift-book           Companion container image for the Programm...   1
jimdo/thrift                         Mirror of Apache Thrift                         0
lulichn/thrift                       Thrift                                          0
bufferoverflow/thrift                Apache Thrift - *make cross*                    0
thrift/thrift-compiler-test          thrift-compiler test run to verify https:/...   0
cjmay/thrift                         thrift builds                                   0
saltside/thrift                      Our thrift fork as docker image used to ge...   0
nsuke/thrift                         Temporary docker images for Apache Thrift CI    0
iwan0/hbase-thrift-standalone        hbase-thrift-standalone                         0
foxwoods/thrift                      Thrift 0.8                                      0
itzg/thrift                          Provides the Apache Thrift generator tool       0
thrift/ubuntu                                                                        0
cjmay/thrift-4042                    MWE of THRIFT-4042 (egg extraction error)       0
thrift/debian                        build/docker/debian                             0
zezuladp/thrift                                                                      0
thrift/thrift-build                  Apache Thrift build environment.                0
rzhilkibaev/spark-standalone-thrift  Standalone Spark with Thrift                    0
andyfactual/jenkins-dind-thrift      Jenkins server with thrift compiler installed   0
reecerobinson/spark-thrift-server    Docker container based on spark-nosql that...   0
zhoumingjun/thrift                                                                   0
```

If you have Docker installed, you can download a repository image, with the Thrift compiler already built and installed, and use it like an executable to compile your IDL files with the Docker run command. For example, to compile the IDL file hello.thrift in the /src directory for C++, you could use the following command:

```
docker run -v "/src:/src" apache/thrift:latest \
        -o /src --gen cpp /src/hello.thrift
```

The –v switch mounts the host /src directory with your IDL files into the Docker container. The apache/thrift:latest argument causes a container to be created from the latest tagged image from the Thrift repository in the Apache namespace. If the image isn't found locally it will be automatically downloaded from Docker Hub. The apache prefix in the name "apache/thrift" indicates that the image is maintained by the Apache Software Foundation. There is an "official" image simply called "thrift" maintained by the Docker community, among several others. The Apache image and the Docker official image are similar but maintained separately.

The second line of arguments in the `docker` run command make up a normal set of thrift IDL arguments, using the `-o` switch to emit the generated code into the mounted host /src directory so that the output will be accessible after the container run completes.

This is convenient because you never need to build or install the Thrift compiler and you can run it anywhere you have Docker installed. But if you don't use Docker this may not be a great solution.

The Apache Thrift source tree also includes Dockerfiles that can be used to create preconfigured Docker Debian, Ubuntu, and CentOS containers that have all of the packages necessary to build the entire Apache Thrift platform. You'll find the Dockerfiles and a README.md in the Apache Thrift source repository build/docker directory.

This book has a companion Docker image configured with a version of Apache Thrift built with C++, Java, and Python support. The image includes all the examples from the book and can be run with a command something like:

```
docker run -it randyabernethy/thrift-book
```

3.1.3 Building from source

Apache Thrift is an open source framework, so you can always download the source and build it yourself. The Apache Thrift website documents the source tree build process at https://thrift.apache.org/docs/BuildingFromSource. Build dependencies for various systems are listed at https://thrift.apache.org/docs/install.

Building the compiler for Apache Thrift isn't too complicated, but it does have several prerequisites. To build the Apache Thrift IDL compiler your system needs to have the following tools installed:

- A C++ compiler
- GNU Flex v2.5+ (a Lex clone used to generate the Thrift lexical scanner)
- GNU Bison v2.5+ (a Yacc clone used to generate the Thrift parser)
- A supported build system

Apache Thrift builds with the native C++ compilers on three main target environments: GCC/G++ on *nix, XCode/Clang on OS X, and Visual Studio for C++ on Windows. You can also use MinGW or Cygwin to treat Windows like a Linux system; however, I would recommend sticking with Visual Studio for simplicity and reliability. If you need to use MinGW or Cygwin, they're fine for experienced users.

The Apache Thrift IDL compiler is written in C++98, and it uses the flex tool to generate the lexer code that turns IDL into tokens and the Bison tool to generate the parser code that applies the parser rules to the tokens. All the generated C++ code is then compiled to create the "thrift" binary executable (thrift.exe on Windows).

BUILDING ON LINUX, *NIX, AND OS X WITH AUTOTOOLS

On Linux platforms, either Autotools (the GNU build system) or CMake can be used. To use Autotools, the older Apache Thrift build system, you must have both Autoconf 2.6+ and Automake 1.14+ installed.

With all the required dependencies in place you can build the Apache Thrift compiler on a Linux system something like this:

```
$ git clone http://github/apache/thrift      ❶
$ cd thrift                                    ❷
$ git checkout 0.11.0   ❸
$ ./bootstrap.sh                               ❹
$ ./configure --disable-libs      ❺
$ make                                         ❻
$ sudo make install       ❼
```

The git clone command makes a local copy of the current Apache Thrift development source ❶. Once copied, you can change into the repository root ❷ and check out the version you want to use ❸. The Apache Thrift source has tags for each released version, so you can check out any prior version from the development repository. Taking this approach requires that you have git installed on your system (http://git-scm.com/). You can also download the most recently released source in tar.gz format from the Apache Thrift website (https://thrift.apache.org/download).

Once the correct source files are in the working directory you must run boot-strap.sh, which runs Autoconf and Automake to generate various build files ❹. The configure program is run next ❺. This tool detects the resources installed on your system and then determines what to build. For example, if your system has appropriate versions of Python, Ruby, and Go installed, configure will prepare the build to build and test these Apache Thrift libraries. This example just builds the IDL compiler by using the --disable-libs switch, which causes configure to leave all of the language libraries out of the build.

The make command runs flex and bison to generate lexer/parser code, and then compiles all the C++ source with G++ (the GNU C++ compiler) ❻. Assuming everything builds correctly, you can then run make install to copy the compiler, which the build creates at compiler/cpp/thrift, to /usr/local/bin/thrift, which is typically on the system path ❼.

What can go wrong? Well, many things. Apache Thrift is a complex fabric of tools and software in a wide variety of languages. Fortunately, when building the compiler, the list of dependencies is manageable and getting the system to build isn't too challenging.

BUILDING WITH CMAKE

Apache Thrift 0.9.2 added partial support for the CMake build system. If you choose to use CMake instead of Autotools, you won't need the Autotools dependencies but you will need to have CMake installed.

CMake is widely supported and easy to use on *nix systems. Here are several ways to install CMake in various environments:

- Ubuntu: `$ sudo apt-get install cmake`
- CentOS: `$ sudo yum install cmake`
- Windows: Download from http://www.cmake.org/download/
- OS X: Download from http://www.cmake.org/download/ or `$ brew install cmake`

CMake simplifies the compiler build process and relaxes several of the Autotools dependencies not supported by older OSes such as Ubuntu 12 or CentOS 6. For example, on a newly installed CentOS 7 minimal configuration system you can build the Thrift compiler with the following commands:

```
$ sudo yum groupinstall "Development Tools"    ❶
$ sudo yum install cmake                        ❷
$ git clone http://github.com/apache/thrift     ❸
$ cd thrift                                      ❹
$ git checkout 0.9.2        ❺
$ cmake .                                        ❻
$ make            ❼
```

The first step installs a broad range of development tools, including GCC-C++, Flex, Bison, and git ❶. The second step installs CMake ❷.

With all the dependencies installed, we can clone the Apache Thrift repository ❸, change into the root of the source tree ❹, and check out the version we'd like to build ❺. Finally, we can request that CMake generate make files suitable for building Thrift ❻ and then build Apache Thrift with them ❼. In early versions, the build step places the compiler in the bin folder (bin/thrift) within the Thrift source tree; in later versions cmake is configured to emit the Thrift compiler in the same directory as autotools (compiler/cpp/bin).

Running the Thrift `--version` command will report the compiler version built. The CMake configuration was not present prior to 0.9.2 and therefore you cannot use CMake to build older versions of Thrift.

Using CMake is similar on most platforms. For example, to build the IDL compiler with CMake on a fresh, minimal Ubuntu 14.04 system, the steps shown in the following command line session will work:

```
$ sudo apt-get install build-essential
$ sudo apt-get install flex
$ sudo apt-get install bison
$ sudo apt-get install git
$ sudo apt-get install cmake
$ git clone http://github.com/apache/thrift
$ cd thrift
$ git checkout 0.9.2 .
$ cmake .
$ make
$ sudo make install
```

The CMake suite also provides the `CPack` command for creating platform installers. You can run `CPack` after a successful make to generate installer support for the current platform. For example, here's a `CPack` run on Ubuntu:

```
thriftusr@ubuntu:~/thrift$ cpack
CPack: Create package using DEB
CPack: Install projects
CPack: - Run preinstall target for: thrift
CPack: - Install project: thrift
CPack: Create package
CPack: - package: /home/randy/thrift/thrift-1.0.0-dev-Linux.deb generated.
```

The previous `CPack` session generates a Debian package which can be used to install the Thrift compiler on any Debian-based system.

BUILDING ON WINDOWS

The Apache Thrift source tree contains a Visual Studio project in the compiler/cpp directory that you can use to build the IDL compiler on Windows. This sidesteps Autotools and CMake. If you're building only the compiler, the Visual Studio project is fairly straightforward to use, with the exception of the dependency on Flex and Bison, which are rarely preinstalled on Windows.

You can download Flex and Bison binaries for Windows from various sources. Two of note are

- Win-Flex-Bison: http://sourceforge.net/projects/winflexbison
- Flex/Bison for Windows: http://gnuwin32.sourceforge.net/packages/flex.htm and http://gnuwin32.sourceforge.net/packages/bison.htm

Once Flex and Bison are on the path, you can start Visual Studio and build the Apache Thrift compiler project to generate a thrift.exe. The Visual Studio project file depends on a program called "flex.exe" and a program called "bison.exe" being on the path. If you install Flex and/or Bison under a different name (for example, win-flex.exe) or in a folder not on the path, you'll need to update the project file appropriately before building.

3.2   *The Apache Thrift source tree*

The Apache Thrift source tree is organized into several important top-level directories:

- *aclocal*—Houses Autoconf local macros used in Autotools builds.
- *build*—CMake-, Docker-, and Travis CI-specific support files.
- *compiler*—The IDL compiler source files.
- *contrib*—Support files that aren't part of the core Apache Thrift platform but are broadly useful to the Apache Thrift community (for example, Vagrantfiles, ZeroMQ examples, etc.).
- *debian*—Debian packaging support.

- *doc*—Documents covering the language-independent aspects of Apache Thrift are housed here. This is a sparse folder but it does have a few items of interest (beware: some may be out of date).
- *lib*—The root folder for all of the supported language libraries and their test suites and examples.
- *test*—The cross-language test suite.
- *tutorial*—The cross-platform tutorial.

Of particular interest is the lib directory. At the time of this writing there were more than 20 language libraries in the lib tree. Each of these languages has its own way of organizing code, testing its code, and packaging code or binaries. While it's beyond the scope of this book to cover them all, if you're comfortable programming in a particular language you'll likely find yourself at home digging into your language's lib directory. For example, a Java programmer would probably expect to find the TBinaryProtocol.java source file in "lib/java/src/org/apache/thrift/protocol/", and that's where it is.

The most commonly used Apache Thrift languages are covered in part 3 of this book. The part 3 chapters provide a jump-start for the target languages, showing you how to install the necessary Apache Thrift libraries and build starter Apache Thrift clients and servers in that language's style.

The Apache Thrift ./tutorial directory is worth a look for those new to Apache Thrift. The tutorial is based around a simple calculator interface. New language contributions are generally expected to provide a calculator server and client. All the calculator clients can call any of the calculator servers to perform calculations, demonstrating the cross-language nature of Apache Thrift. The IDL and source code in this directory will give you a primer on the basics of building an Apache Thrift client and/or server in any language.

3.3 *Apache Thrift tests*

The ./test directory houses cross-language/platform tests and shared test files. Originally all tests were here, so you may find remnants of individual language tests. Going forward, all language-specific tests should be placed in the language's lib directory (for example, lib/nodejs/test). Of particular importance is the IDL file ./test/ThriftTest .thrift. This interface is designed to test the proper functionality of an Apache Thrift language implementation. It's the interface used by the core Apache Thrift test suite and it includes nearly every possible Apache Thrift IDL construct, including some particularly complex, nested types.

A language that doesn't pass client/server testing using this interface and all of its complex types is considered either broken or incomplete. The Apache Thrift committers try to ensure that all code added to the platform either improves upon, or at least doesn't worsen, the test results associated with the ThriftTest.thrift interface.

Apache Thrift includes two main batteries of tests:

- Language-specific tests
- Cross-language tests

The language tests should be located in the lib/<lang>/test directory (for example, lib/nodejs/test). Such tests are executed when make check is run after a successful build. You can also run make check in a particular language directory to run the tests for only that language. A full make check from the Thrift root can take well over 15 minutes to complete.

For example, to run the nodejs tests, you'd run make check in the Nodejs library directory, as shown in the following session:

```
randy@ubuntu:~/thrift/lib/nodejs$ make check
/usr/bin/npm install --no-bin-links ../../
cd ../.. && /usr/bin/npm test && cd lib/nodejs
> thrift@1.0.0-dev test /home/randy/thrift
> lib/nodejs/test/testAll.sh
binary.test.js
✓ Should read signed byte
✓ Should write byte
✓ Should read I16
✓ Should write I16
✓ Should read I32
✓ Should write I32
✓ Should read doubles
✓ Should write doubles

OK: 50 assertions (9ms)
  Testing Client/Server with protocol compact and transport buffered
...
```

The cross-language tests run tests with various pairs of languages to ensure that a client from one language can talk to a server from another. The C++ and Java languages are the most commonly used reference languages.

You can run the cross-language test suite from the root of the Thrift repository with the make cross command. This includes all the tests from make check and takes quite a while. After make cross has generated all the necessary support files, you can run follow-on cross tests directly using the Python test driver. For example

```
randy@ubuntu:~/thrift/test$ ./test.py --client cpp --server java
Apache Thrift - Integration Test Suite
Wed Jun 15 06:33:09 2016
========================================================================
server-client:      protocol:    transport:                    result:
java-cpp            compact      framed-ip                      success
java-cpp            compact      buffered-ip-ssl                success
java-cpp            compact      framed-ip-ssl                  success
java-cpp            compact      buffered-ip                    success
java-cpp            compact      fastframed-framed-ip           success
java-cpp            compact      fastframed-framed-ip-ssl       success
java-cpp            binary       framed-ip                      success
java-cpp            binary       framed-ip-ssl                  success
java-cpp            binary       buffered-ip-ssl                success
java-cpp            binary       buffered-ip                    success
java-cpp            binary       fastframed-framed-ip-ssl       success
```

```
java-cpp            binary        fastframed-framed-ip        success
java-cpp            json          framed-ip-ssl               success
java-cpp            json          framed-ip                   success
java-cpp            json          buffered-ip-ssl             success
java-cpp            json          buffered-ip                 success
java-cpp            json          fastframed-framed-ip-ssl success
java-cpp            json          fastframed-framed-ip        success
========================================================================
No unexpected failures.
You can browse results at:
    file:///thrift/test/index.html
# If you use Chrome, run:
#    cd /thrift
#    python -m SimpleHTTPServer 8001
# then browse:
#    http://localhost:8001/test/
Full log for each test is here:
    test/log/client_server_protocol_transport_client.log
    test/log/client_server_protocol_transport_server.log
0 failed of 18 tests in total.
Test execution took 18.7 seconds.
Wed Jun 15 06:33:28 2016
```

You can use test.py --help for more details on command line options.

3.4 *Debugging RPC services*

Debugging networked applications can be tricky. When you want to debug a single process, you can attach to it with a debugger and look at everything. The entire process is there on your system and the debugger (a good one, anyway) can inspect every bit of memory and control all the threads of execution.

Dealing with multiple communicating processes on the same system complicates matters, and separating those processes across a network greatly complicates matters. For example, it's possible to have an RPC client and server that each run perfectly with other systems but blow up when connected together. In such cases, both the client and server may be correct but the interface they expect may be inconsistent. Nonfunctional requirements, particularly those relating to performance, are another area requiring networking knowledge and other tangential skill sets.

Debugging processes written in specific languages is something we'll leave to those using the respective languages and the many books covering debugging in these languages. RPC-specific debugging techniques are, however, worth special treatment. How do you track down network and interface problems?

Due to the range of possible problems, there's no "one" way to perform networked RPC service debugging. However, there are several key tools and techniques we can use in different situations to zero in on problems. We'll look at several of those in the next few sections.

3.4.1 *Examining packets on the wire*

Imagine a scenario where you're providing services in the cloud to third parties using Apache Thrift. Maybe you're a shoe wholesaler and retailers call into your API to get products and pricing. You might have an SDK that customers use that internally calls your Apache Thrift services, or perhaps you share your IDL with them and they build their own clients directly.

Now imagine that as you grow your business, you begin to have scaling problems. You can't support enough clients per server and people are complaining that the number of calls per second they can make is too low. When you load test the system in your lab with your test code, everything looks great. What to do?

One of the most important things to understand when it comes to the performance and scaling of a distributed system is what your network traffic looks like. Our scaling problem could be caused by many things, but one of the first diagnostic steps to take is to look at the network directly. In fact, I'd go so far as to say that it's worth getting familiar with the normal traffic patterns of any distributed application. Fortunately, this is easy to do with one of the several network *sniffers* available. In this section, we'll use WireShark (https://www.wireshark.org/), a free open source packet sniffer that runs on Windows, OS X, and Linux. WireShark and sniffers like it are powerful tools and a useful addition to the kit of any RPC programmer.

Before we start sniffing, let's consider the code for the service we'll examine. Our service is simple; here's the IDL, as shown in the following listing.

Listing 3.1   ~thriftbook/part1/debugging/sniffing/hello_name.thrift

```
service HelloSvc {
    string hello_func(1: string fname, 2: string lname)
}
```

The `HelloSvc::hello_func()` takes two string parameters and returns a string (see listing 3.1). Let's assume we host this service using a Python server and our problem client is written in C++. To generate stubs for these two languages we can use the Thrift compiler as follows:

```
$ thrift --gen py --gen cpp hello_name.thrift
$ ls -1
total 20
drwxrwxr-x 2 randy randy 4096 Feb  8 17:04 gen-cpp
drwxrwxr-x 3 randy randy 4096 Feb  8 17:04 gen-py
-rw-rw-r-- 1 randy randy  722 Feb  8 17:02 hello_client.cpp
-rw-rw-r-- 1 randy randy   78 Feb  8 17:01 hello_name.thrift
-rw-rw-r-- 1 randy randy  488 Feb  8 17:04 hello_server.py
```

With Python stubs in "gen-py" and C++ stubs in "gen-cpp", let's look at the hypothetical server involved in this problem (see the following listing).

```
import logging
logging.basicConfig()
import sys
sys.path.append("gen-py")

from thrift.transport import TTransport
from thrift.transport import TSocket
from thrift.protocol import TBinaryProtocol
from thrift.server import TProcessPoolServer
from hello_name import HelloSvc

class HelloHandler:
    def hello_func(self, fname, lname):
        print("[Server] Handling client request")
        return "Hello " + fname + " " + lname

handler = HelloHandler()
proc = HelloSvc.Processor(handler)
trans_ep = TSocket.TServerSocket(port=9095)              ❶
trans_fac = TTransport.TBufferedTransportFactory()
proto_fac = TBinaryProtocol.TBinaryProtocolFactory()
server = TProcessPoolServer.TProcessPoolServer(proc,
                                               trans_ep,
                                               trans_fac,
                                               proto_fac)

print("[Server] Started")
server.serve()
```

This is a simple server and hard to find fault with. The server listens on port 9095 for clients ❶, which will be important when we start sniffing. We want to filter out uninteresting traffic, and all the packets destined for this server will be targeting port 9095. Python server details are discussed in the Python section of the scripting chapter in part 3, but for now we'll ignore the implementation details and focus on RPC debugging concepts that apply to any language.

Imagine we run our Python server on an Ubuntu cloud instance. We'd need to add the Python `dev` and `pip` packages to set up Apache Thrift for Python on our build server. The Python `pip` installer will build the Apache Thrift Python "C" extensions that speed up Python protocol operations during the install. Here's an example set of commands we might use to configure the cloud instance and run the Python server:

```
$ sudo apt-get install python-dev
$ sudo apt-get install python-pip
$ sudo pip install thrift
$ python hello_server.py
[Server] Started
```

Next let's look at a hypothetical C++ test client used to benchmark the Python server in the lab. Using this client, everything runs smoothly.

Listing 3.3   ~thriftbook/part1/debugging/sniffing/hello_client.cpp

```cpp
#include "gen-cpp/HelloSvc.h"
#include <thrift/transport/TSocket.h>
#include <thrift/transport/TBufferTransports.h>
#include <thrift/protocol/TBinaryProtocol.h>
#include <boost/make_shared.hpp>
#include <iostream>
#include <string>

using namespace apache::thrift::transport;
using namespace apache::thrift::protocol;
using boost::make_shared;

int main() {
    auto trans_ep = make_shared<TSocket>("localhost", 9095);
    auto trans_buf = make_shared<TBufferedTransport>(trans_ep);
    auto proto = make_shared<TBinaryProtocol>(trans_buf);
    auto client = make_shared<HelloSvcClient>(proto);

    trans_buf->open();
    std::string msg;
    client->hello_func(msg, "Zaphod", "Beeblebrox");
    std::cout << "[Client] received: " << msg << std::endl;
    trans_buf->close();
}
```

This code is textbook as well. The client is connecting to the server on port 9095 and sending a couple of name strings to the server (Zaphod and Beeblebrox), then displaying the response string. C++ details are covered in the C++ chapter of part 3. Here's how we could build and test the C++ client:

```
$ g++ --std=c++11 hello_client.cpp gen-cpp/HelloSvc.cpp -lthrift
$ ./a.out
[Client] received: Hello Zaphod Beeblebrox
```

From the output shown, we can tell that, functionally, this client/server pair works. We received the correct message from the server. What about the nonfunctional requirements associated with performance? Let's look at what's happening on the wire to see if things are going as expected (figure 3.1).

A WireShark capture from a session with our client calling our server once and then shutting down appears in figure 3.1. This capture displays 11 packets in the top pane. Our test server and client are binding to the localhost IP address 127.0.0.1. Also, we know the server is running on port 9095.

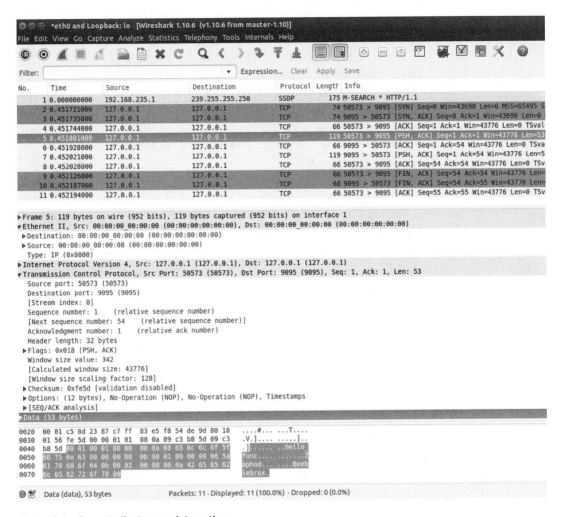

Figure 3.1   Correct client server interaction

Let's walk through the packets displayed one by one. The following numbers correspond to the packet numbers in the WireShark listing:

1. This isn't our packet (neither to nor from 127.0.0.1:9095). WireShark provides powerful filtering that you can use to show only the packet to/from ports you're interested in. For more WireShark information, see the excellent online WireShark documentation (https://www.wireshark.org/docs/).

2. The client connects to the server. In the Info column, you can see that the traffic is bound for port 9095 (our server) and the message type is SYN, for synchronize, TCP shorthand for "I would like to connect."

3. The server accepts (ACKs) the client and sends its own SYN back in one go.

4. The client ACKs the server SYN. Now a TCP connection is established.

5 As expected, the client passes the request and the input strings to the server. You can see the data length is 53 bytes (Len=53), which includes our two input strings "Zaphod" and "Beeblebrox", as well as the method call overhead. The data is highlighted and displayed in the bottom WireShark pane. Note that the client sends this data with the push (PSH) flag. This tells the server TCP/IP stack not to buffer the data, but rather to pass it up to the application (our Python server) immediately. Otherwise, the data would sit in the network buffer and our client would wonder why the server wasn't responding. Every RPC call should end with a PSH packet.

6 The server ACKs our RPC call. As inefficient as this sounds, TCP provides guaranteed delivery; every packet must be acknowledged or it will be resent. We're using the TSocket transport that's built on TCP, thus every packet sent from either side requires its own ACK. Notice that the ACK data length is 0 (Len=0).

7 This is the server's response. The data length is 53 and the payload contains Apache Thrift RPC response info and your response string. This packet and the client request packet are the only two in our 10-packet run that contain data (Len > 0).

8 This is the client ACK for the server RPC response.

9 The last three packets handle the TCP connection close protocol. First the client tells the server it's finished (FIN), after which it can send no data.

10 The server ACKs the client's FIN and sends its own FIN to indicate it will also send no more data.

11 The client ACKs the server FIN and the connection ends.

Everything looks good in the above RPC test. The packet inspection insight leads us to expect 10 packets at most for a client/server RPC call. If the connection stayed open for multiple calls, we could ignore the six packets of TCP setup and tear down, making it four packets per RPC call.

3.4.2 *Unbuffered interfaces*

If our lab test looks good, what could go wrong in production? As it turns out, many problems specific to networked services can plague unsuspecting RPC developers. A particularly common issue has to do with unbuffered interfaces.

For example, imagine we attach our sniffer to the production network running the real client production code (as opposed to the lab test client code shown above). When you make a WireShark capture you discover the output in figure 3.2.

Believe it or not, this is a trace for the same exact RPC call against the same exact server. The only thing that has changed is the client. Our simple RPC call now took 34 packets; 28 if you don't count the connect/disconnect overhead. That's a 750% increase in packet flow. ACKs take up 66 bytes on the wire, and 14 of them are associated with our RPC request, instead of one. Only 16 characters are passed to the server. What's wrong?

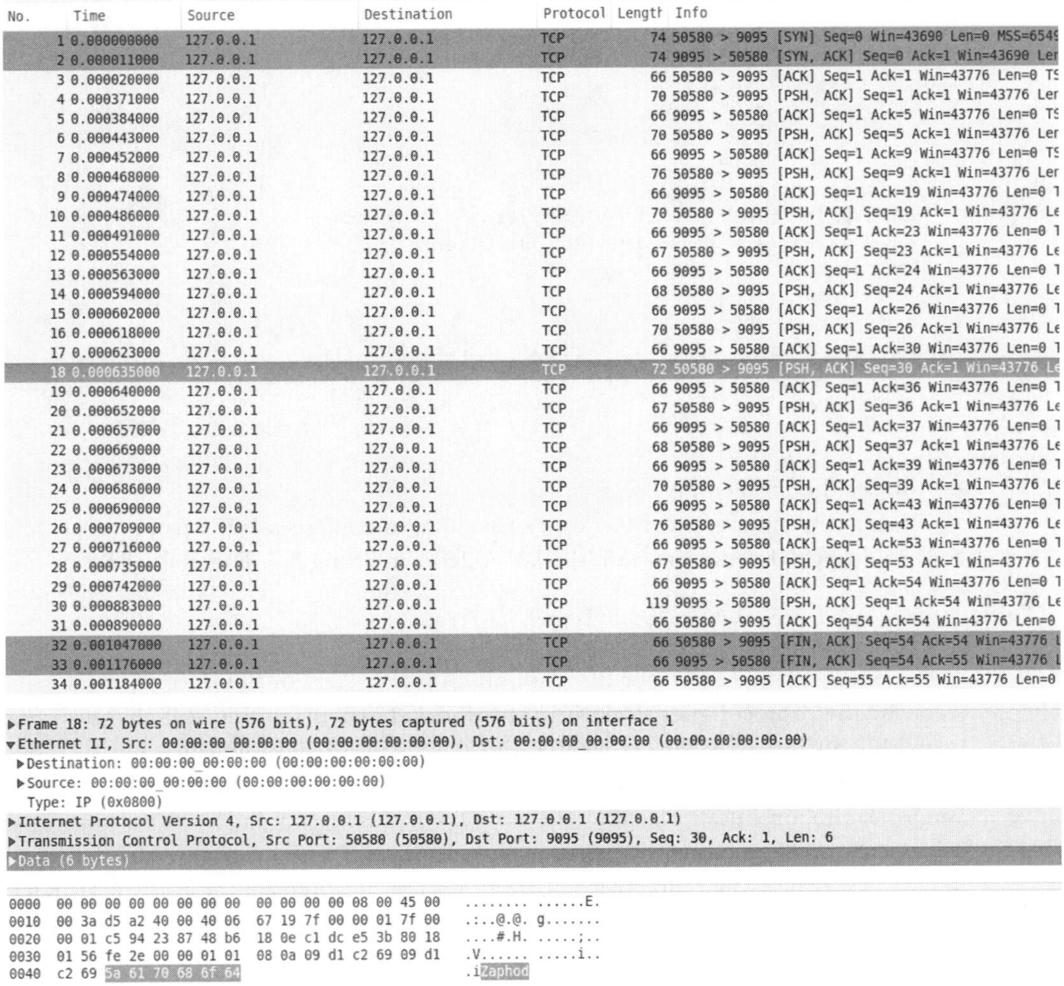

No.	Time	Source	Destination	Protocol	Length	Info
1	0.000000000	127.0.0.1	127.0.0.1	TCP	74	50580 > 9095 [SYN] Seq=0 Win=43690 Len=0 MSS=6549
2	0.000011000	127.0.0.1	127.0.0.1	TCP	74	9095 > 50580 [SYN, ACK] Seq=0 Ack=1 Win=43690 Ler
3	0.000020000	127.0.0.1	127.0.0.1	TCP	66	50580 > 9095 [ACK] Seq=1 Ack=1 Win=43776 Len=0 TS
4	0.000371000	127.0.0.1	127.0.0.1	TCP	70	50580 > 9095 [PSH, ACK] Seq=1 Ack=1 Win=43776 Ler
5	0.000384000	127.0.0.1	127.0.0.1	TCP	66	9095 > 50580 [ACK] Seq=1 Ack=5 Win=43776 Len=0 TS
6	0.000443000	127.0.0.1	127.0.0.1	TCP	70	50580 > 9095 [PSH, ACK] Seq=5 Ack=1 Win=43776 Ler
7	0.000452000	127.0.0.1	127.0.0.1	TCP	66	9095 > 50580 [ACK] Seq=1 Ack=9 Win=43776 Len=0 TS
8	0.000468000	127.0.0.1	127.0.0.1	TCP	76	50580 > 9095 [PSH, ACK] Seq=9 Ack=1 Win=43776 Ler
9	0.000474000	127.0.0.1	127.0.0.1	TCP	66	9095 > 50580 [ACK] Seq=1 Ack=19 Win=43776 Len=0 T
10	0.000486000	127.0.0.1	127.0.0.1	TCP	70	50580 > 9095 [PSH, ACK] Seq=19 Ack=1 Win=43776 Le
11	0.000491000	127.0.0.1	127.0.0.1	TCP	66	9095 > 50580 [ACK] Seq=1 Ack=23 Win=43776 Len=0 T
12	0.000554000	127.0.0.1	127.0.0.1	TCP	67	50580 > 9095 [PSH, ACK] Seq=23 Ack=1 Win=43776 Le
13	0.000563000	127.0.0.1	127.0.0.1	TCP	66	9095 > 50580 [ACK] Seq=1 Ack=24 Win=43776 Len=0 T
14	0.000594000	127.0.0.1	127.0.0.1	TCP	68	50580 > 9095 [PSH, ACK] Seq=24 Ack=1 Win=43776 Le
15	0.000602000	127.0.0.1	127.0.0.1	TCP	66	9095 > 50580 [ACK] Seq=1 Ack=26 Win=43776 Len=0 T
16	0.000618000	127.0.0.1	127.0.0.1	TCP	70	50580 > 9095 [PSH, ACK] Seq=26 Ack=1 Win=43776 Le
17	0.000623000	127.0.0.1	127.0.0.1	TCP	66	9095 > 50580 [ACK] Seq=1 Ack=30 Win=43776 Len=0 T
18	0.000635000	127.0.0.1	127.0.0.1	TCP	72	50580 > 9095 [PSH, ACK] Seq=30 Ack=1 Win=43776 Le
19	0.000640000	127.0.0.1	127.0.0.1	TCP	66	9095 > 50580 [ACK] Seq=1 Ack=36 Win=43776 Len=0 T
20	0.000652000	127.0.0.1	127.0.0.1	TCP	67	50580 > 9095 [PSH, ACK] Seq=36 Ack=1 Win=43776 Le
21	0.000657000	127.0.0.1	127.0.0.1	TCP	66	9095 > 50580 [ACK] Seq=1 Ack=37 Win=43776 Len=0 T
22	0.000669000	127.0.0.1	127.0.0.1	TCP	68	50580 > 9095 [PSH, ACK] Seq=37 Ack=1 Win=43776 Le
23	0.000673000	127.0.0.1	127.0.0.1	TCP	66	9095 > 50580 [ACK] Seq=1 Ack=39 Win=43776 Len=0 T
24	0.000686000	127.0.0.1	127.0.0.1	TCP	70	50580 > 9095 [PSH, ACK] Seq=39 Ack=1 Win=43776 Le
25	0.000690000	127.0.0.1	127.0.0.1	TCP	66	9095 > 50580 [ACK] Seq=1 Ack=43 Win=43776 Len=0 T
26	0.000709000	127.0.0.1	127.0.0.1	TCP	76	50580 > 9095 [PSH, ACK] Seq=43 Ack=1 Win=43776 Le
27	0.000716000	127.0.0.1	127.0.0.1	TCP	66	9095 > 50580 [ACK] Seq=1 Ack=53 Win=43776 Len=0 T
28	0.000735000	127.0.0.1	127.0.0.1	TCP	67	50580 > 9095 [PSH, ACK] Seq=53 Ack=1 Win=43776 Le
29	0.000742000	127.0.0.1	127.0.0.1	TCP	66	9095 > 50580 [ACK] Seq=1 Ack=54 Win=43776 Len=0 T
30	0.000883000	127.0.0.1	127.0.0.1	TCP	119	9095 > 50580 [PSH, ACK] Seq=1 Ack=54 Win=43776 Le
31	0.000890000	127.0.0.1	127.0.0.1	TCP	66	50580 > 9095 [ACK] Seq=54 Ack=54 Win=43776 Len=0
32	0.001047000	127.0.0.1	127.0.0.1	TCP	66	50580 > 9095 [FIN, ACK] Seq=54 Ack=54 Win=43776
33	0.001176000	127.0.0.1	127.0.0.1	TCP	66	9095 > 50580 [FIN, ACK] Seq=54 Ack=55 Win=43776 L
34	0.001184000	127.0.0.1	127.0.0.1	TCP	66	50580 > 9095 [ACK] Seq=55 Ack=55 Win=43776 Len=0

```
▶Frame 18: 72 bytes on wire (576 bits), 72 bytes captured (576 bits) on interface 1
▼Ethernet II, Src: 00:00:00_00:00:00 (00:00:00:00:00:00), Dst: 00:00:00_00:00:00 (00:00:00:00:00:00)
 ▶Destination: 00:00:00_00:00:00 (00:00:00:00:00:00)
 ▶Source: 00:00:00_00:00:00 (00:00:00:00:00:00)
  Type: IP (0x0800)
▶Internet Protocol Version 4, Src: 127.0.0.1 (127.0.0.1), Dst: 127.0.0.1 (127.0.0.1)
▶Transmission Control Protocol, Src Port: 50580 (50580), Dst Port: 9095 (9095), Seq: 30, Ack: 1, Len: 6
▶Data (6 bytes)
```

```
0000  00 00 00 00 00 00 00 00  00 00 00 00 08 00 45 00   ........ ......E.
0010  00 3a d5 a2 40 00 40 06  67 19 7f 00 00 01 7f 00   .:..@.@. g.......
0020  00 01 c5 94 23 87 48 b6  18 0e c1 dc e5 3b 80 18   ....#.H. .....;..
0030  01 56 fe 2e 00 00 01 01  08 0a 09 d1 c2 69 09 d1   .V...... .....i..
0040  c2 69 5a 61 70 68 6f 64                            .iZaphod
```

Figure 3.2   Problematic client server interaction

The following listing shows the customer code that caused this traffic pattern.

Listing 3.4   ~thriftbook/part1/debugging/sniffing/hello_client_bad.cpp

```cpp
#include "gen-cpp/HelloSvc.h"
#include <thrift/transport/TSocket.h>
#include <thrift/transport/TBufferTransports.h>
#include <thrift/protocol/TBinaryProtocol.h>
#include <boost/make_shared.hpp>
#include <iostream>
#include <string>
```

```
using namespace apache::thrift::transport;
using namespace apache::thrift::protocol;
using boost::shared_ptr;
using boost::make_shared;

int main() {
    shared_ptr<TTransport> trans = make_shared<TSocket>("localhost", 9095);
    auto proto = make_shared<TBinaryProtocol>(trans);
    auto client = make_shared<HelloSvcClient>(proto);

    trans->open();
    std::string msg;
    client->hello_func(msg, "Zaphod", "Beeblebrox");
    std::cout << "[Client] received: " << msg << std::endl;
    trans->close();
}
```

Do you see the problem?

Even if you cannot read C++, you can see that one line is missing from the client's code in listing 3.4 compared with the lab code from listing 3.3. This is the line:

```
trans = make_shared<TBufferedTransport>(trans);
```

The client has failed to buffer the endpoint TSocket. Without buffering, every write made by the protocol goes straight to the TSocket and on to the TCP/IP stack. The network layer has no way to know that this data is part of a larger message and so it sends the data out immediately. Apache Thrift Protocols are designed to be modular and work with any interface you might design. For this reason, Protocols serialize individual types; each number or string in the interface is serialized individually. In an RPC call the protocol serializes several, if not tens or hundreds of these elements, such as the name of the function to call, the first parameter, the second parameter, and so on. If you look at figure 3.2 you'll see that the packet highlighted has a Len of 6 and the payload is "Zaphod". Our first parameter was sent out in its own private packet.

Also note that each individual interface value is sent with the PSH flag, meaning that the network stack will push the data up to the Apache Thrift server, forcing it to read this traffic, realize that it's incomplete, and go back to waiting for the next set of bytes. In a server with many clients, we changed the server load tremendously. The server used to perform one task per client call. In this example, the server receives 14 PSH packets, likely cutting the server's capacity by a factor of 14 or more.

It's important to realize that "functionally" the two clients are the same, because they both work and return the correct result. Typical unit tests and integration tests won't uncover this kind of problem. This is a nonfunctional problem, but as you can see, it's debilitating. The obvious takeaway here is to make sure that all clients and servers buffer RPC requests and responses. The broader takeaway is that if you're going to build distributed systems of any sort, it's well worth getting acquainted with the networks and traffic patterns your application depends on for its operation. A sniffer such as WireShark is an invaluable tool.

TIP   Get familiar with your RPC application traffic patterns and check them occasionally in production to uncover issues before they become problems. Use baselines and compare traffic patterns for new builds against these baselines to detect problems early.

3.4.3   Interface misalignment

Let's consider another common RPC problem scenario. Assume we've run an upgrade on several of your production services. Immediately after the upgrade several users begin complaining about service errors. If our code works well in tests with new clients, it's likely that we've broken the interface contract we have with old clients.

One of the most important features of Apache Thrift is its ability to evolve interfaces without breaking backward compatibility (more on this in the service design chapter in part 2). However, it's also possible to change aspects of the interface that will, sometimes subtly, break backwards compatibility.

Imagine we're using essentially the same server code from listing 3.2. After the upgrade, when our clients make calls we occasionally see the following server output:

```
$ python hello_server.py
[Server] Started
[Server] Handling client request
ERROR:thrift.server.TProcessPoolServer:[Errno 104] Connection reset by peer
Traceback (most recent call last):
  File "/usr/local/lib/python2.7/dist-packages/thrift/server/
➥ TProcessPoolServer.py", line 78, in serveClient
    self.processor.process(iprot, oprot)
  File "gen-py/hello_name/HelloSvc.py", line 78, in process
    (name, type, seqid) = iprot.readMessageBegin()
  File "/usr/local/lib/python2.7/dist-packages/thrift/protocol/
➥ TJSONProtocol.py", line 318, in readMessageBegin
    self.readJSONArrayStart()
  File "/usr/local/lib/python2.7/dist-packages/thrift/protocol/
➥ TJSONProtocol.py", line 306, in readJSONArrayStart
    self.readJSONSyntaxChar(LBRACKET)
  File "/usr/local/lib/python2.7/dist-packages/thrift/protocol/
➥ TJSONProtocol.py", line 211, in readJSONSyntaxChar
    current = self.reader.read()
  File "/usr/local/lib/python2.7/dist-packages/thrift/protocol/
➥ TJSONProtocol.py", line 140, in read
    self.data = self.protocol.trans.read(1)
  File "/usr/local/lib/python2.7/dist-packages/thrift/transport/
➥ TTransport.py", line 159, in read
    self.__rbuf = StringIO(self.__trans.read(max(sz, self.__rbuf_size)))
  File "/usr/local/lib/python2.7/dist-packages/thrift/transport/TSocket.py",
➥ line 105, in read
    buff = self.handle.recv(sz)
error: [Errno 104] Connection reset by peer
```

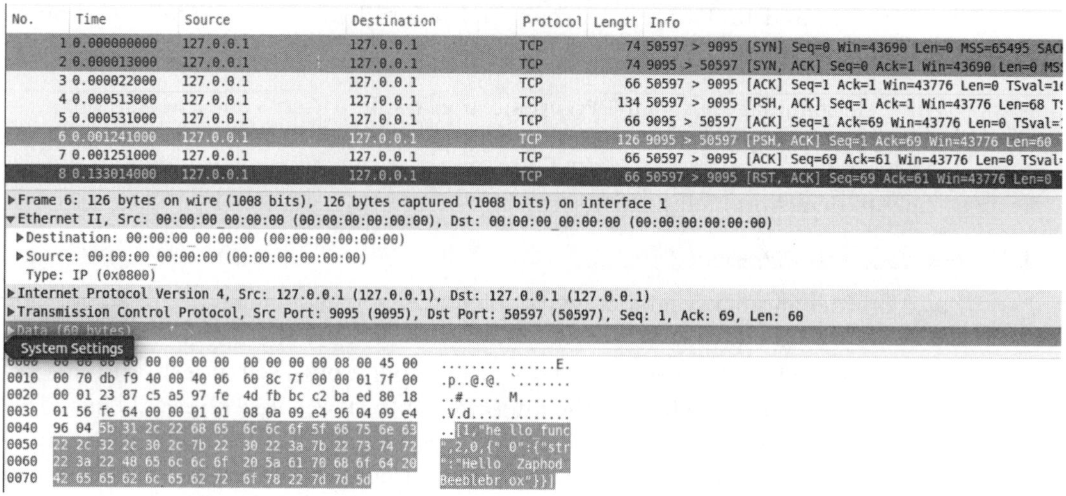

No.	Time	Source	Destination	Protocol	Length	Info
1	0.000000000	127.0.0.1	127.0.0.1	TCP	74	50597 > 9095 [SYN] Seq=0 Win=43690 Len=0 MSS=65495 SAC
2	0.000013000	127.0.0.1	127.0.0.1	TCP	74	9095 > 50597 [SYN, ACK] Seq=0 Ack=1 Win=43690 Len=0 MS
3	0.000022000	127.0.0.1	127.0.0.1	TCP	66	50597 > 9095 [ACK] Seq=1 Ack=1 Win=43776 Len=0 TSval=1
4	0.000513000	127.0.0.1	127.0.0.1	TCP	134	50597 > 9095 [PSH, ACK] Seq=1 Ack=1 Win=43776 Len=68 T
5	0.000531000	127.0.0.1	127.0.0.1	TCP	66	9095 > 50597 [ACK] Seq=1 Ack=69 Win=43776 Len=0 TSval=
6	0.001241000	127.0.0.1	127.0.0.1	TCP	126	9095 > 50597 [PSH, ACK] Seq=1 Ack=69 Win=43776 Len=60
7	0.001251000	127.0.0.1	127.0.0.1	TCP	66	50597 > 9095 [ACK] Seq=69 Ack=61 Win=43776 Len=0 TSval
8	0.133014000	127.0.0.1	127.0.0.1	TCP	66	50597 > 9095 [RST, ACK] Seq=69 Ack=61 Win=43776 Len=0

```
▶Frame 6: 126 bytes on wire (1008 bits), 126 bytes captured (1008 bits) on interface 1
▼Ethernet II, Src: 00:00:00_00:00:00 (00:00:00:00:00:00), Dst: 00:00:00_00:00:00 (00:00:00:00:00:00)
 ▶Destination: 00:00:00_00:00:00 (00:00:00:00:00:00)
 ▶Source: 00:00:00_00:00:00 (00:00:00:00:00:00)
  Type: IP (0x0800)
▶Internet Protocol Version 4, Src: 127.0.0.1 (127.0.0.1), Dst: 127.0.0.1 (127.0.0.1)
▶Transmission Control Protocol, Src Port: 9095 (9095), Dst Port: 50597 (50597), Seq: 1, Ack: 69, Len: 60
▶Data (60 bytes)
```
System Settings
```
0000  00 00 00 00 00 00  00 00 00 00 00 08 00 45 00   ........ .....E.
0010  00 70 db f9 40 00 40 06  60 8c 7f 00 00 01 7f 00   .p..@.@. `.......
0020  00 01 23 87 c5 a5 97 fe  4d fb bc c2 ba ed 80 18   ..#..... M.......
0030  01 56 fe 64 00 00 01 01  08 0a 09 e4 96 04 09 e4   .V.d.... ........
0040  96 04 5b 31 2c 22 68 65  6c 6f 5f 66 75 6e 63   ..[1,"he llo func
0050  22 2c 32 2c 30 2c 7b 22  30 22 3a 7b 22 73 74 72   ",2,0,{" 0":{"str
0060  22 3a 22 48 65 6c 6c 6f  20 5a 61 70 68 6f 64 20   ":"Hello  Zaphod
0070  42 65 65 62 6c 65 62 72  6f 78 22 7d 7d 5d         Beeblebr ox"}}]
```

Figure 3.3   Client RPC connection reset

The server output contains noise, but the essential information here is the final line, "Connection reset by peer". This is network speak for "the client hung up on me." In this case, the server did exactly as it was told, but, at the network level, the client failed to acknowledge the response to the RPC call and hung up.

We can again turn to a packet sniffer for help. Figure 3.3 displays a capture of the packets that caused the above server complaint.

Let's consider this situation rationally. What do we know about normal packet exchanges between a client and a server for a single RPC request? Several things

- We know that the client should send one PSH packet to complete the request per RPC call (there could be several packets before the PSH if the payload is large).
- We know that the server should send one PSH packet to complete the response per RPC call.

In the figure 3.3 packet list the request looks fine, one PSH to the server (packet 4). The response also looks fine, one PSH to the client (packet 5). We can see that the client's network stack ACKed the response (packet 6), meaning the data was received. We know the server sent a response, and we know the client's network stack (TCP/IP) received it. TCP provides a checksum supporting basic data integrity, but it certainly doesn't guarantee that the data is correct semantically.

When the Apache Thrift I/O stack cannot interpret input, the typical response is to hang up the connection. This is exactly what the client does in packet 8, using the RST flag to reset, aborting the connection. Seeing RSTs in the trace is rarely good. This almost always indicates that the sender could no longer understand the data stream. Often the only sensible way to recover from this sort of failure is to start over, disconnecting and reconnecting. If we execute this same code path with the same data again in the future, we're likely to produce the same error.

In the age of digital networks and high fidelity, we rarely see packet corruption. Errors like this one almost always point to the two programs using a different interface. In fact, we can surmise that the calling interface was agreeable to both parties. The server accepted the parameters passed and returned a normal response ("Hello Zaphod Beeblebrox"). The client, however, didn't like the response from the server and killed the connection upon receiving it.

In this debugging session, the server code found in listing 3.2 and the client code found in listing 3.3 were used with a different protocol. Rather than using the TBinary-Protocol on both sides, the TJSONProtocol is used on both sides. The Apache Thrift TJSONProtocol encodes RPC requests in JavaScript Object Notation (JSON), which is essentially text. This makes traces much easier to read. You may not always be at liberty to make such a protocol switch, but in testing scenarios it can be helpful. For example, the data pane in figure 3.3 shows the return data in JSON, making it clear that we're returning a "str", or string type.

TIP When debugging RPC packet exchanges, consider using the JSON protocol to make interpreting data in network traces simpler.

At this point we know the server returned the string "Hello Zaphod Beeblebrox". This is clearly not what the client was expecting.

Imagine our customer having this problem emails you the output from their end, which looks like this:

```
$ ./a.out
terminate called after throwing an instance of
➡ 'apache::thrift::TApplicationException'
  what():  hello_func failed: unknown result
Aborted (core dumped)
```

The client reports an "unknown result". The most likely cause here is that the IDL the client used to generate their calling code expects a different return type than the string sent by our server.

In this example, the server IDL is that found in listing 3.1. The client, on the other hand, is using an older IDL, shown in the following listing.

> **Listing 3.5** **~thriftbook/part1/debugging/iferror/hello_name_old.idl**

```
service HelloSvc {
    i32 hello_func(1: string fname, 2: string lname)
}
```

The IDL in listing 3.1 says `hello_func()` returns a string, and the IDL in listing 3.5 says `hello_func()` returns an i32. As you can see, this is disasterous. The rules of interface evolution are clearly laid out in part 2 of this book. Under no circumstances should you ever change the return type of a given function in a given service. One correct approach would be to add a new function with the desired return type and deprecate or even delete the old function. Another approach would be to deprecate the entire old `HelloSvc` service and create a new service, `HelloSvc2`.

When clients call functions that don't exist, servers return a `TApplication-Exception`, indicating that no such function exists. Compared to our current situation, this would be an improvement, with better feedback for the would-be debugger and reduced load on the server (the server ignoring the bad call rather than fulfilling it). An even better solution, and a best practice, would be to return a struct. Structs can have members added and removed without breaking backward compatibility. For more information on using structs, see the user-defined types chapter in part 2.

> **TIP** Suspect an interface mismatch when clients and servers that test successfully cannot communicate and/or when RST packets are found in traces.

In this example, all the information needed to get to the bottom of things is supplied in the listings above. In production settings, it may be much more difficult to know which server is compiled with which IDL. Looking at logs and code check-ins can help, but seeing the data in the packet is definitive. Even when binary protocols are used you can easily reverse-engineer the packet data to get to the bottom of things quickly.

This scenario demonstrates only one of many possible interface misalignments, but the approach described can be applied universally to this type of problem.

3.4.4 *I/O stack misalignment*

Another common problem in Apache Thrift RPC is I/O stack misalignment. Each Apache Thrift RPC call uses an I/O stack consisting of precisely one Protocol (`TBinaryProtocol`/`TCompactProtocol`/`TJSONProtocol`) and a transport stack. Clients and servers must use compatible (usually the exact same) I/O stacks.

For example, a server using `TSocket` and `TBinaryProtocol` cannot communicate with a client using `TSocket` and `TCompactProtocol`.

A common error in this category involves non-blocking servers. Servers that use non-blocking I/O (for example, the C++ and Java `TNonblockingServer` type) automatically apply a framing layer that prepends every message with the 4-byte message size. Such a server's I/O stack looks like this: `TSocket/TFramedTransport/TBinaryTransport`. A client using an I/O stack without the framing layer (`TSocket/TBinaryProtocol`) will fail to communicate with the server.

> **TIP** Verify that clients and servers are using compatible I/O stacks when clients and servers cannot communicate in any way.

A packet sniffer will clearly show one side sending 4-byte prefixes with every packet and/or the other side failing to do so. Adding a `TFramedTransport` layer will repair this problem. Mismatched protocols (such as `TCompactProtocol` trying to communicate with `TBinaryProtocol`) and mismatched endpoint transports (such as `TSocket` trying to communicate with `TPipe`) will also cause total communications failure.

Not all dissimilar I/O stacks are incompatible. Certain layered transports are non-mutating—they don't modify the data passing through them. Non-mutating transports can be added to either the server or the client without the counterparty noticing. For example, the `TBufferedTransport` is non-mutating; it doesn't change the application data stream. It does, however, have a large impact on the packet structure of client/server exchanges (see the "Unbuffered interfaces" topic earlier in this chapter). Non-mutating transport layers can be added for logging or monitoring without impacting the functional operation of the system, though these layers may create nonfunctional performance issues.

3.4.5 *Instrumenting code*

Let's consider one final scenario. Imagine you manage Apache Thrift services that run in the cloud and you have no access to the client or their code. Now imagine several of your clients begin reporting intermittent problems such as, "everything works when I test, but two or three times a day in production we have a call fail." Errors that don't reproduce in the lab and that are nondeterministic in production are tricky to isolate. These errors are often load-related but they can also be attributed to faulty client or server logic, triggered only on occasion.

Load balancing and auto scaling systems typically produce logs indicating the performance (that is, round trip latency) and start/stop times of target servers in the load balancing group. Examining latency patterns from load balancers can provide insight into server capacity and performance boundaries.

Another tool you can use to corner intermittent failures is a packet capture system. Packet capturing systems log every packet in and out of a network or host. WireShark is great for small captures or for inspecting large captures from other sources, but we need a different tool, for example TCPDump, to log general network activity all day long.

This approach has several caveats. If you use a production server for packet logging, you'll impact its performance, perhaps greatly. Also, the logger will likely require terabytes of free storage space. Even quiescent servers can easily exchange many gigabytes of data in a day.

In many settings, packet capture systems may already be installed on the network. Network security professionals often have a form of packet capture operating in their networks. If not, you might configure a simple standalone solution, such as the Security Onion (securityonion.net). Tools of this sort require a machine with a promiscuous network adapter, one configured to pick up packets even if they aren't destined for that adapter. You also need the proper network configuration. Switches must be set up to send all traffic to the packet capture node, where normally they only send traffic to the target machine. Most cloud vendors will not allow such activity, which may constrain you to logging on the target server. Software-defined networks and service meshes provide another logging possibility in the cloud.

If you do have access to packet capture data, sifting through a terabyte of packets can be complex. Searching for RST packets and the like is a Big Data chore. To exacerbate the problem, often the information you need is spread across multiple perfectly acceptable packets. It's only when you put them together that they reveal a problem. If your environment doesn't have efficient support for the kind of data searches you require, there are other more focused options.

Many of the more robust Apache Thrift server platforms (C++, Java, C#, and others) support server events. Server events provide developers with a way to hook critical server state changes independent of the services running on the server so you can write one set of server event handlers and use it with all of your services. The server events fired by Apache Thrift are as follows:

- Server boot
- Client connect
- Client RPC call
- Client disconnect

Your event handler can therefore log every call and every client connection and disconnection. The RPC call handler is passed the transport interface associated with the call, allowing the data to be inspected by the handler.

This gives you the ability to log the methods called, their parameters, and other useful details. This application level log may help you identify problems much faster than sifting through large sets of network packets.

> **TIP**   Consider using server events to produce application-level logs to help track down intermittent RPC errors.

For more information on server events, see the `TServerEventHandler` interface section of chapter 10.

3.4.6   *Additional techniques*

If you're facing a resilient RPC problem, one approach you may find helpful is narrowing the focus by isolating the issue within a particular part of the Apache Thrift I/O stack (for more details on the Apache Thrift architecture, see chapter 2). Each layer may involve different debugging techniques.

- *Apache Thrift server code*—TSimpleServer, TThreadedServer, and so on
- *Client proxies and server stubs*—IDL compiler code for client and processor classes
- *Generated type serializers*—IDL compiler code for your structs, unions, and so on
- *Apache Thrift protocols*—`TBinaryProtocol`, `TCompactProtocol`, and `TJSONProtocol`
- *Apache Thrift layered transports*—`TBufferedTransport`, `TFramedTransport`, and so on
- *Apache Thrift endpoint transports*—`TSocket`, `TNamedPipe`, and so on
- *Programming language interface*—`Sockets`, `Python Twisted`, and so on
- *System networking stack*—TCP/IP, named pipes, and so on
- *Physical network intermediaries*—Switches, routers, firewalls, load balancers, and so on

Because Apache Thrift provides a pluggable transport and protocol model, transports and protocols can easily be swapped in and out to test configurations and code interactions. No code base is bug-free; this includes Apache Thrift. If everything works when you use the `TBinaryProtocol` but not when you use the `TCompactProtocol`, perhaps you've discovered a bug in Apache Thrift. On the other hand, you may have discovered a bug in your code that only manifests when `TCompactProtocol` is used. Regardless, Apache Thrift makes it easy to test each individual layer when the circumstances demand it, and, because Apache Thrift is open source, you can debug the entire system at the source-code level.

You may also find useful debugging tools on the internet. For example, Pinterest has put together a particularly handy Apache Thrift RPC introspection toolkit called thrift-tools (https://github.com/pinterest/thrift-tools). The Kubernetes-centered cloud native movement has introduced a host of new debugging challenges with the dynamic orchestration of services; however, many new tools for observability have been created for these environments, such as ZipKin, LightStep, Jagger, OpenTracing, Istio/Envoy and more.

While this section offers useful tools, it's far from comprehensive. As you peruse the chapters in parts 2 and 3 of this book, you'll no doubt discover other Apache Thrift features and architectural insights that will help you zero in on problems and design better services and tests.

Summary

Key chapter takeaways

- You can download prebuilt Apache Thrift IDL compilers for Windows from the Apache Thrift website and you can acquire Apache Thrift container images on Docker Hub.
- You can build the Apache Thrift IDL compiler from source using Autotools or CMake.
- The Apache Thrift source tree offers a wealth of example code in the test and tutorial directories, as well as add-ons in the contrib directory.
- The Apache Thrift language library source is found with unit tests beneath the /lib directory.
- Cross-language tests allow you to test the interaction of any language client with any language server.
- Network and RPC introspection tools can help you debug the most common Apache Thrift interoperability problems, including I/O stack misalignment, interface incompatibilities, and lack of message buffering.

Part 2

Programming Apache Thrift

Apache Thrift is a modular, cross-language serialization and RPC framework based on a powerful, exstensible, plugable, layered architecture. One of the things that sets Apache Thrift apart is the end-to-end nature of the solution it provides, bringing support for more than 20 languages together in a single complete RPC system.

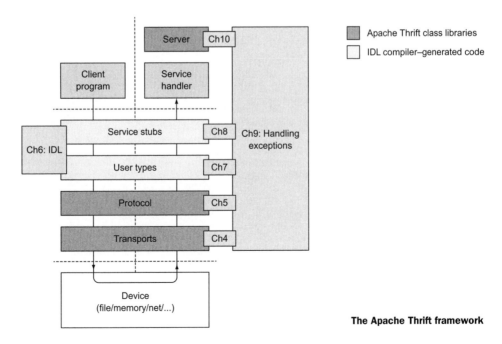

The Apache Thrift framework

Part 2 of this book takes you on a comprehensive guided programming tour of the entire framework, layer by layer. From the foundational plug-in transport layer to the full-featured RPC server library, Part 2 will give you the tools you need to get the most out of Apache Thrift.

You can read Part 2 straight through or pick and choose chapters associated with the parts of Apache Thrift you want to know more about.

Moving
bytes with transports

This chapter covers

- Understanding the role transports play in the Apache Thrift Framework
- Coding endpoint-independent read and write operations using transports
- Using memory, disk, and network transports
- Using server transports in network servers
- Building a transport stack with layered transports

This chapter explores the Apache Thrift transport layer (see figure 4.1). Transports are the bottom layer of the Apache Thrift framework, and they are foundational to everything else you'll do with Apache Thrift. Transports aren't typically used in a standalone setting, rather they're the final link in the chain for Apache Thrift serialization and RPC applications. However, by building simple "transport only" programs, we can learn much about one of the most important parts of the Apache Thrift platform.

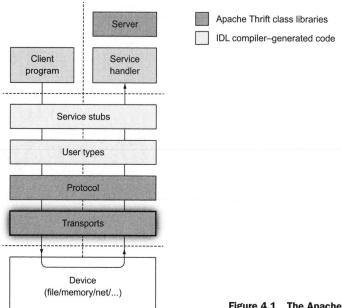

Figure 4.1   **The Apache Thrift transport layer**

Keep in mind that Apache Thrift protocols and transports are designed to work together as a layered stack. In the first few examples of this chapter you'll see that each of our demonstration languages generates different bits for the same object. As we'll see in chapter 5, Apache Thrift protocols normalize the bits transported by all of the supported languages.

The Apache Thrift Transport Library is a collection of code elements (classes in most languages) providing a standard way to read and write bytes from endpoints. An endpoint can be a chunk of memory, a file on disk, a network socket, or any other physical or logical device. Apache Thrift transports all support the same interface, making it easy to switch underlying endpoints without impacting other code.

For example, imagine a stock price feed program that writes trade records out to a memory buffer using an Apache Thrift transport. The Apache Thrift transport interface shields the price feed program from the actual device being written to. If the memory transport is swapped for a disk transport to redirect the data to a file on disk, the price feed application won't be impacted.

Transports usually support both read and write operations but need not. For example, a file transport might allow reading but disallow writing when connected to a file located on a CDROM. Often it may make sense to use one transport instance for reading and another instance for writing. For example, certain transports have a single internal buffer, which isn't suitable for scenarios where outbound data is written to the buffer at the same time that inbound data is written to the buffer.

The Thrift class library provides an assortment of transports that can be used to move bytes around in different ways. All of these transports implement a shared interface,

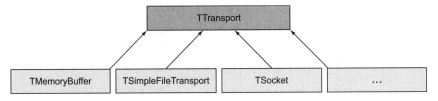

Figure 4.2   Example `TTransport` hierarchy

defined by the `TTransport` class (see figure 4.2). Certain languages use a different name for the interface; for example it's `TTransportBase` in Python.

Apache Thrift language implementations may offer a unique set of transports. Several backend biased languages, such as C++ and Java, provide a wide array of transports with a variety of buffering features and device support. Other languages provide a more modest set of transports focusing on Socket or HTTP interactions. When necessary, custom transports can be created easily.

In this chapter, we'll look at a representative subset of the many transports available. By the end of the chapter, we'll have described how transports work and how to take advantage of the key transport features in code.

4.1   *Endpoint transports, part 1: Memory & disk*

Apache Thrift transports that read or write physical or logical devices are referred to in this book as endpoint transports. Most Apache Thrift language libraries offer three important endpoint transport types:

- *Memory transports*—Read/write blocks of memory, used for buffering and caching
- *File transports*—Read/write disk files, used for logging and object storage
- *Network transports*—Read/write network devices, used for RPC

For example, `TSocket` is an endpoint transport used to read from and write to a TCP/IP network socket. Certain Apache Thrift language implementations offer more than one transport for a given endpoint type, while others may be missing support for an endpoint type completely. For example, the C++ library provides several disk transports, but JavaScript supplies one. Each Apache Thrift language library has evolved to suit the needs of the people using it, which has created a diverse, but typically pragmatic, range of transports on a language-by-language basis.

The principal benefit provided by endpoint transports is their ability to decouple the rest of an application from the actual underlying device. We gain the ability to reuse the extensive library of pre-coded and tested Apache Thrift transports and the ability to build custom transports without impacting higher layers of code.

To develop a better understanding of endpoint transports and how they work, we'll build a simple example program that writes a stock trade report to an Apache Thrift transport in each of the three demonstration languages, C++, Java, and Python. We'll try out this program with each of the three main endpoint types: memory, disk, and network.

As you look over the code examples, take note of the similarities and differences between the various languages. Apache Thrift language libraries generally stay true to their language's style and idioms; however, the shared Apache Thrift transport interfaces are conceptually identical across languages, making it easy for polyglot programmers to switch languages.

4.1.1   *Programming with memory transports*

One of the simplest transports found in most Thrift Language libraries is TMemory-Buffer (figure 4.3). This transport provides support for reading and writing to a block of memory. Let's look at a version of the stock trade writer that writes trades to memory in each of the three demonstration languages.

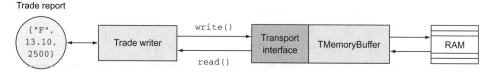

Figure 4.3   Simple Apache Thrift memory transport client

C++ TMEMORYBUFFER

The following C++ program listing creates a struct to house a stock trade report and uses the Apache Thrift C++ TMemoryBuffer transport to read and write the trade to memory.

```
Listing 4.1   ~/thriftbook/part2/transports/memory/mem_trans.cpp

#include <thrift/transport/TBufferTransports.h>        ❶
#include <iostream>

struct Trade {               ❷
   char symbol[16];
   double price;
   int size;
};

int main() {
    apache::thrift::transport::TMemoryBuffer trans(4096);        ❸

    Trade t{"F", 13.10, 2500};
    trans.write(reinterpret_cast<const uint8_t *>(&t), sizeof(t));        ❹

    Trade tin;
    int n = trans.read(reinterpret_cast<uint8_t *>(&tin), sizeof(tin));        ❺

    std::cout << "Trade(" << n << "): " << tin.symbol << " "
            << tin.size << " @ " << tin.price << std::endl;
}
```

The sample program begins by including the TBufferTransports.h header ❶, which provides the declaration for TMemoryBuffer, and the iostream header, which supports the std::cout C++ console output object. Next it declares a Trade struct ❷, to house the trade report data we plan to read and write.

The main function creates a TMemoryBuffer transport initialized with 4K of memory to use for reading and writing ❸. The TMemoryBuffer allocation will grow automatically if the data written exceeds the current size. TMemoryBuffer exports the standard Apache Thrift TTransport interface, allowing us to use it like any other transport. Note the namespace prefix used to scope the TMemoryBuffer class. All of the C++ Thrift Library elements live within the apache::thrift namespace. Transport-specific elements are housed within the transport sub-namespace, apache::thrift::transport. Many other Apache Thrift language libraries follow a similar pattern. The namespace typically matches the path to the header file containing the class declaration.

We can read ❺ and write ❹ trade objects as binary chunks using the read and write methods of the TTransport interface. Both the read and write methods accept a pointer to the memory bytes to send/receive and a length parameter to indicate how many bytes should be written or read. The transport is disinterested in our data types, dealing only in raw pointers to uint8_t (byte pointers). The write method returns void (nothing) and the read method returns the number of bytes read.

Transport read() and write() methods are conceptually the same across languages; however, the actual syntax varies to fit the style of the language in question. Low-level C and C++ code often use pointers and raw memory for device I/O, as demonstrated here. Java and Python don't support pointers and use their own language-specific objects for byte-level reads and writes.

Here's a sample session building and running the C++ stock writer program from listing 4.1:

```
$ ls -l
-rw-r--r-- 1 randy randy   646 Apr 11 23:19 mem_trans.cpp
$ g++ mem_trans.cpp -Wall -std=c++11 -lthrift
$ ./a.out
Trade(32): F 2500 @ 13.1
```

Compiling Apache Thrift C++ code

The examples in this book build C++ code with GCC 4.8 in a 64-bit Ubuntu container. The G++ command is a wrapper around GCC (the GNU Compiler Collection), with C++ sensibilities. The GCC compiler is readily available on OS X and Linux systems and widely used elsewhere. The LLVM-based Clang C++ compiler and Microsoft's C++ compiler are also frequently used with Apache Thrift.

Executable programs must be linked with the Apache Thrift C++ library code. This can be done by including the source files directly in your project, but more commonly the Apache Thrift library sources are built into a library object and linked to directly. On Unix-like systems, the Apache Thrift C++ library is typically located at /usr/local/lib/libthrift.a. The "-Wall" switch turns on all warnings in GCC. The "-std=c++11" switch enables C++11 support. The lowercase "l" switch adds our library name (the lib prefix and the extension are assumed and must not be supplied with g++). If you're building on a different platform or using a different tool chain, you'll need to make the appropriate adjustments to your command line.

> **(continued)**
> If you receive errors when trying to compile this example, the good news is that this is a simple program and a great test case for debugging your build process. Look at the C++ chapter in part III for more C++ development environment setup information.

You may have noticed that our struct contains 16 bytes of characters, an 8-byte double and a 4-byte integer for a total of 28 bytes, yet the output suggests 32 bytes were read. This example was compiled and executed on a 64-bit machine; the compiler has therefore defaulted to 64-bit memory alignment. This caused the 28-byte struct we declared to be padded by the compiler to 32 bytes (see figure 4.4). This ensures that sequential structures begin on 64-bit boundaries, potentially making access to such structures faster for the memory hardware. Increasing the size of our struct by 15% for fast memory operations might be a good tradeoff. On the other hand, if the primary purpose of this struct is to be transmitted en masse to remote computers, we're probably better off with 28 bytes. Most compilers support pragmas and command line switches to explicitly specify how to pad structs. Here's an example build where our struct is "packed" on 4-byte boundaries during compilation:

```
$ g++ -fpack-struct=4 mem_trans.cpp -Wall -std=c++11 -lthrift
$ ./a.out
Trade(28): F 2500 @ 13.1
```

Symbol					Price							Size				Padding			
F	\0			...	1	3.1	0					2	5 0	0					
0	1	2	3	15	16	17	18	19	20	21	22	23	24	25	26	27	28	29	30 31

Figure 4.4 Trade data memory layout

This run reduces the memory footprint to the expected 28 bytes (this is a Linux example and may need to be modified to work on other platforms). As you can see, padding must be standardized across platforms and languages to make these bytes readable on another machine or in another language.

JAVA TMEMORYBUFFER

Apache Thrift is a cross-language framework. If something can be done in one language, it can typically be done in most other languages. Let's look at the following listing to see what writing our stock trade to memory looks like in Java.

Listing 4.2   ~/thriftbook/part2/transports/memory/MemTrans.java

```java
import java.io.ByteArrayInputStream;
import java.io.ByteArrayOutputStream;
import java.io.IOException;
import java.io.ObjectInputStream;
```

```java
import java.io.ObjectOutputStream;
import java.io.Serializable;
import org.apache.thrift.transport.TMemoryBuffer;
import org.apache.thrift.transport.TTransportException;

public class MemTrans {

    static private class Trade implements Serializable {      ❶
        public String symbol;
        public double price;
        public int size;
    };

    public static void main(String[] args)
            throws IOException, TTransportException, ClassNotFoundException {
        TMemoryBuffer transport = new TMemoryBuffer(4096);      ◁━┐
                                                                 ❷
        Trade trade = new Trade();
        trade.symbol = "F";
        trade.price = 13.10;
        trade.size = 2500;
        ByteArrayOutputStream baos = new ByteArrayOutputStream();
        ObjectOutputStream oos = new ObjectOutputStream(baos);
        oos.writeObject(trade);
        transport.write(baos.toByteArray());          ❸

        byte[] buf = new byte[4096];
        int bytes_read = transport.read(buf, 0, buf.length);     ❹
        ByteArrayInputStream bais = new ByteArrayInputStream(buf);
        ObjectInputStream ois = new ObjectInputStream(bais);
        Trade trade_read = (Trade) ois.readObject();
        System.out.println("Trade(" + bytes_read + "): " +
                            trade_read.symbol + " " + trade_read.size +
                            " @ " + trade_read.price);
    }
}
```

This Java example illustrates many of the hallmarks of the Java language: extensive use of objects, no pointers, and a comprehensive language library used to isolate Java code from hardware details. That said, Java and C++ are both object-oriented languages, so the program looks fairly similar in both languages.

The Java code imports a number of Java and Apache Thrift classes that will be used to read and write the Trade message. The Java io library supports object serialization, accounting for several of these library imports. The only two direct Apache Thrift dependencies are TMemoryBuffer and TTransportException. TMemoryBuffer supplies the same memory-based storage for the transport read/write operations we examined in the C++ example. TTransportException is an Apache Thrift library exception type, which may be thrown by several of the TMemoryBuffer methods. As it turns out, the C++ example may throw the C++ version of TTransportException as well; however, unlike Java, C++ doesn't require us to declare or catch all possible exceptions to sucessfully compile. We'll take a more complete look at Apache Thrift exceptions in chapter 9, "Handling Exceptions."

All of our code must live in a class in Java so a `MemTrans` class is used to house this trivial program. We declare a `Trade` structure as a data-only static nested class ❶. This class is declared to implement `Serializable`. `Serializable` is a Java marker interface with no methods; declaring the class `Serializable` makes it, well, serializable. The `ObjectOutputStream` and `ObjectInputStream` classes know how to move the bits of Java `Serializable` objects to and from byte arrays.

Our `main()` method declares all of the exceptions we might throw, including the Apache Thrift `TTransportException`. Unlike C++, Java doesn't allow us to create objects on the stack, so the program begins by constructing a `TMemoryBuffer` on the heap with a buffer size of 4K ❷. The code also instantiates and initializes a `Trade` object to write to the transport.

Because accessing the bytes of our object entangles us with machine-specific information (padding, endianess, and so on), we must use Java libraries to ensure we gain the JVM "write once run anywhere" benefit. Here we use `ByteArrayOutputStream` and `ObjectOutputStream` to turn our object into a byte array, which can then be written to our `TMemoryBuffer` ❸. Both of these java.io classes are part of the system-specific libraries available with all Java runtimes.

Reading the bytes is more or less the same process in reverse ❹. Begin by allocating a byte array to receive the bytes, and then read the bytes back in from the `TMemory-Buffer`. Finally, we reconstitute the `Trade` object from the bytes and display its data.

The following snippet shows a sample session building and running the Java trade writer:

```
$ ls -l
-rwxr-xr-x 1 randy randy 40398 Apr 11 23:31 a.out
-rw-r--r-- 1 randy randy   646 Apr 11 23:19 mem_trans.cpp
-rw-r--r-- 1 randy randy  1429 Apr 11 23:41 MemTrans.java          ❶
$ javac -cp /usr/local/lib/libthrift-1.0.0.jar MemTrans.java       ❷
$ ls -l
-rwxr-xr-x 1 randy randy 40398 Apr 11 23:31 a.out
-rw-r--r-- 1 randy randy  1730 Apr 11 23:41 MemTrans.class          ❸
-rw-r--r-- 1 randy randy   646 Apr 11 23:19 mem_trans.cpp
-rw-r--r-- 1 randy randy  1429 Apr 11 23:41 MemTrans.java
-rw-r--r-- 1 randy randy   449 Apr 11 23:41 MemTrans$Trade.class    ❹
$ java -cp /usr/local/lib/libthrift-1.0.0.jar:. MemTrans   ←┐
Trade(96): F 2500 @ 13.1          ←┐                        ❺
                                   ❻
```

The entire program is contained in the MemTrans.java ❶ file, so we can compile this into byte code with the Java compiler, javac ❷. Compilation generates class bytecode files for all of our classes ❸❹. In a production setting we'd package the class files into an appropriate Java archive and use a build system to automate the process. To keep things platform-neutral and to illustrate the actual steps, we'll run the tools directly throughout this book.

Compiling Apache Thrift Java code

The Java examples in this book are compiled with the Java SE7 javac compiler. On our demonstration system, the Apache Thrift Java library isn't installed on the default class path. We use the javac "-cp /usr/local/lib/libthrift-1.0.0.jar" switch to add the Apache Thrift Java library to the class path during compilation. If your installed version of Thrift is not the development edge, you may need to change the lib name (for example, a recent version of the Thrift-book container on Docker Hub uses libthrift-0.11.0.jar).

After building the class files we start the Java virtual machine (java) with the same class path switch. We also typically add the current directory to the class path on the command line (multiple paths are seperated by ":", the "." represents the current directory) to enable the JVM to find the startup class in the current directory.

Take a look at chapter 12 in part 3 for Java development environment setup information.

We can run our newly compiled program under the Java Virtual Machine using the `java` command ❺. While our program compiles and runs without incident, notice that our C++ `Trade` objects ranged between 28 and 32 bytes, but our Java `Trade` object is 96 bytes ❻. The serialized Java object contains a great deal more information than our raw C++ struct. To restore the C++ struct we must not only know the layout of the struct, but we must also know system-dependent things, such as what the original byte ordering was and whether the structure was packed on 4-byte or 8-byte boundaries. The serialized Java object contains all of the information needed to restore the object on any JVM running on any hardware. Even so, a 3X size increase could be a problem for some applications.

PYTHON TMEMORYBUFFER

To round out our transport examples, let's try writing the stock trade reports to memory in Python, as shown in the following listing.

Listing 4.3 ~/thriftbook/part2/transports/memory/mem_trans.py

```
import pickle
from thrift.transport import TTransport

class Trade:                          ❶
    def __init__(self):
        symbol=""
        price=0.0
        size=0

trans = TTransport.TMemoryBuffer()    ❷
trade = Trade()
trade.symbol = "F"
trade.price = 13.10
trade.size = 2500
trans.write(pickle.dumps(trade))      ❸
```

```
trans.cstringio_buf.seek(0)                    ❹
bstr = trans.read(4096)
trade_read = pickle.loads(bstr)
print("Trade(%d): %s %d @ %f" %
      (len(bstr), trade_read.symbol, trade_read.size, trade_read.price))
```

This Python program begins with an import of the standard Python pickle library, perhaps the most common way to serialize objects in Python. Next we import the TTransport module that defines TMemoryBuffer. As in our prior examples, we then create our Trade message type ❶.

The main program body begins by initializing a TMemoryBuffer object ❷ and a trade object. We then write the pickled trade object to the transport endpoint ❸. The pickle.dumps() method serializes the Trade object, returning a binary string, which is written by the TMemoryBuffer to an internal StringIO object. The standard Python 2.7 StringIO class implements the Python File Object interface for a memory buffer, allowing our TMemoryBuffer to grow as large as we might need within the bounds of memory available. The Python implementation doesn't require us to indicate how large the memory buffer will be initially, a subtle variation from the C++ and Java implementations.

TMemoryBuffer and Python 2/3

Under Python 2.x, Apache Thrift uses the StringIO module to perform binary buffering. In Python 3.x, the old StringIO module is merged with the io module and a new class, io.BytesIO, is used to handle byte I/O. The Apache Thrift Python libraries are designed to work with either Python 2.x or Python 3.x, insulating users from the different byte-level APIs. While examples in this book use Python 2.7, either Python 2 or 3 can be used. Look at the scripting chapter in part III for Python development environment setup information.

You may note that the Python read code block includes a seek call ❹, inconsistent with the C++ and Java examples. This is an implementation issue within the Python TMemoryBuffer class. Because StringIO/BytesIO objects act like memory files, they have only one file pointer and it moves to the end of the file as writes append to the file. To read from the object we need to move the file pointer back to the beginning of the file. The TMemoryBuffer offers a cstringio_buf property that we can use to directly access the Python buffer. In Python 2 this buffer is a StringIO object; in Python 3 it's a BytesIO object; however, both offer the seek method.

Here is a sample session running the Python program:

```
$ python mem_trans.py
Trade(86): F 2500 @ 13.100000
```

The Python version of our memory transport read/write test works as expected; however, we now have another unique serialization size to consider: the Python code reports a `Trade` size of 86 bytes pickled. While this serialization works fine for Python readers and writers, it's not compatible with our prior Java and C++ examples.

MEMORY TRANSPORT TAKEAWAY

The three previous examples exposed the fundamental compile time, link time, and runtime dependencies of Apache Thrift programs and provided a look at how to use Apache Thrift library classes in our code. The command line build and execution commands allowed us to get a sense for the practical operation of the tools needed to run simple Apache Thrift programs in each of the demonstration languages. It also gave us a chance to see that different programming languages may have slightly different Apache Thrift implementations and library features.

Another important insight is the range of sizes found in our serialized `trade` objects. The `Trade` in C++ was 28 or 32 bytes, in Java it was 96 bytes, and in Python it was 86 bytes. All three languages offer additional built-in and third-party serialization options that would increase this diversity further. It's clear that there's no way we could send a trade between languages and expect it to be recognizable with transports only. To communicate across languages we need a standard means to serialize messages. In the next chapter we'll see how Apache Thrift protocols ensure consistent serialization across languages.

Now that you know how to read and write with Apache Thrift memory transports, let's take a look at how Apache Thrift uses transports for file I/O.

4.1.2 *Programming with file transports*

In addition to memory-based endpoints, most Thrift language libraries provide one or more file transports. File transports can be useful in scenarios where objects must be serialized to disk for archival, logging, or testing puposes. In the listings in this section we'll change each of our previous `TMemoryBuffer`-based trade reporting programs to record trades to disk. Because we used the generic Apache Thrift transport interface to read and write trade reports, we can swap the memory transport for a file transport without changing any of our other code (see figure 4.5).

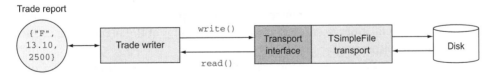

Figure 4.5   Simple Apache Thrift file transport client

C++ TSIMPLEFILETRANSPORT

The C++ Apache Thrift library provides a `TSimpleFileTransport` class that supports basic file I/O. In listing 4.4 we update our C++ Trade writer to write our trade messages to disk. As you examine the code, notice that the I/O operations are identical to those found in the `TMemoryBuffer` example, only the transport in use has changed.

Listing 4.4   ~/thriftbook/part2/transports/disk/file_trans.cpp

```cpp
#include <thrift/transport/TSimpleFileTransport.h>
#include <iostream>
#include <cstring>

using namespace apache::thrift::transport;

struct Trade {
    char symbol[16];
    double price;
    int size;
};

int main() {
    TSimpleFileTransport trans_out("data", false, true);       ❶
    Trade trade{ "F", 13.10, 2500 };
    trans_out.write((const uint8_t *)&trade, sizeof(trade));    ❷
❸  trans_out.close();

    TSimpleFileTransport trans_in("data", true, false);        ❹
    std::memset(&trade, 0, sizeof(trade));
    int bytes_read = trans_in.read((uint8_t *)&trade, sizeof(trade));   ❺

    std::cout << "Trade(" << bytes_read << "): " << trade.symbol
              << " " << trade.size << " @ " << trade.price
              << std::endl;
}
```

Transport constructors require the information needed to connect the transport to its endpoint. For the previous memory transport, we provided the number of bytes to initially allocate for the buffer. File transport constructors require the file name to open and the file access mode.

In this example, we created two `TSimpleFileTransport` objects, one for writing ❶ and one for reading ❹. The two Boolean values supplied in the constructors are the read and write flags, respectively. After we write to our write-only file transport ❷, we use a read-only transport to read the bytes back ❺. Two transports are required, because the `TSimpleFileTransport` is that simple. It's easy to use but it doesn't have file-seeking facilities, so to read from the beginning of the file we must reopen the file with a fresh transport.

Note also that we closed the write file transport before trying to read from the read file transport ❸. Closing a file typically forces lower layers to flush buffers to disk.

Here's a sample session building and running the file transport example:

```
$ g++ --std=c++11 -Wall file_trans.cpp -lthrift
$ ./a.out
Trade(32): F 2500 @ 13.1
$ ls -l
-rwxr-xr-x 1 randy randy 33667 Feb 10 14:19 a.out
-rw-r--r-- 1 randy randy    32 Feb 10 14:30 data
-rw-r--r-- 1 randy randy   764 Feb 10 14:18 filetrans.cpp
```

The file transport example creates a file called "data" that stores the same 32-byte object that our memory transport received in the previous C++ example.

JAVA TSIMPLEFILETRANSPORT

This Java listing modifies our prior Java memory writer to write trades to a disk file using the Apache Thrift TSimpleFileTransport Java class, as shown in the following listing.

Listing 4.5   ~/thriftbook/part2/transports/disk/FileTrans.java

```java
import java.io.ByteArrayInputStream;
import java.io.ByteArrayOutputStream;
import java.io.IOException;
import java.io.ObjectInputStream;
import java.io.ObjectOutputStream;
import java.io.Serializable;
import org.apache.thrift.transport.TSimpleFileTransport;
import org.apache.thrift.transport.TTransportException;

public class FileTrans {

    static private class Trade implements Serializable {
        public String symbol;
        public double price;
        public int size;
    };

    public static void main(String[] args)
        throws IOException, TTransportException, ClassNotFoundException {
        Trade trade = new Trade();
        trade.symbol = "F";
        trade.price = 13.10;
        trade.size = 2500;

        TSimpleFileTransport trans_out =
                        new TSimpleFileTransport("data",false,true);
        ByteArrayOutputStream baos = new ByteArrayOutputStream();
        ObjectOutputStream oos = new ObjectOutputStream(baos);
        oos.writeObject(trade);
        trans_out.write(baos.toByteArray());
        trans_out.close();

        TSimpleFileTransport trans_in =
                        new TSimpleFileTransport("data",true,false);
        byte[] buf = new byte[128];
        int iBytesRead = trans_in.read(buf, 0, buf.length);
        ByteArrayInputStream bais = new ByteArrayInputStream(buf);
        ObjectInputStream ois = new ObjectInputStream(bais);
        trade = (Trade) ois.readObject();

        System.out.println("Trade(" + iBytesRead + "): " + trade.symbol
                + " " + trade.size + " @ " + trade.price);
    }
}
```

This code is nearly identical to the C++ version with respect to the Thrift operations. We have the Java language-specific imports and exception lists as well as the Java object serialization code, but the TSimpleFileTransport construction and the read/write calls are in direct corespondence with the C++ example. The following code snippet is a sample session building and running the Java trade writer:

```
$ ls -l
-rw-r--r-- 1 randy randy 1513 Feb 15 02:05 FileTrans.java
$ javac -cp /usr/local/lib/libthrift-1.0.0.jar FileTrans.java
$ java -cp /usr/local/lib/libthrift-1.0.0.jar:. FileTrans
Trade(97): F 2500 @ 13.1
$ ls -l
-rw-r--r-- 1 randy randy   97 May 24 01:54 data
-rw-r--r-- 1 randy randy 1812 Feb 15 02:12 FileTrans.class
-rw-r--r-- 1 randy randy 1513 Feb 15 02:05 FileTrans.java
-rw-r--r-- 1 randy randy  494 Feb 15 02:12 FileTrans$Trade.class
```

PYTHON TFILEOBJECTTRANSPORT

As a final example let's look at the code changes needed to write our trades to disk with Python in the following listing.

Listing 4.6   ~/thriftbook/part2/transports/disk/file_trans.py

```python
import pickle
from thrift.transport import TTransport

class Trade:
    def __init__(self):
        symbol=""
        price=0.0
        size=0

trans_out = TTransport.TFileObjectTransport(open("data","wb"))   ❶
trade = Trade()
trade.symbol = "F"
trade.price = 13.10
trade.size = 2500
trans_out.write(pickle.dumps(trade));
trans_out.close()

trans_in = TTransport.TFileObjectTransport(open("data","rb"))    ❷
bstr = trans_in.read(4096)
trade = pickle.loads(bstr)
print("Trade(%d): %s %d @ %f" % (len(bstr), trade.symbol, trade.size,
                                 trade.price))
```

The Python Apache Thrift library has no TSimpleFileTransport; rather it has TFileObjectTransport, which is a wrapper around a standard Python FileObject. We supply each TFileObjectTransport with a Python FileObject to use via the Python open() system function ❶❷. In the first case, we specify a writable binary file ("wb") and in the second case we specify a readable binary file ("rb").

Here's a sample run session with our new Python code:

```
$ python file_trans.py
Trade(86): F 2500 @ 13.100000
```

4.2 The transport interface

Section 4.1 gave us a look at the most basic aspects of Apache Thrift using memory and disk-based endpoint transports. Before we jump into network transports it's worth taking a closer look at the abstract transport interface shared by all transports. Each Apache Thrift language library implements the transport interface slightly differently, though the core concepts are consistent across languages. The abstract transport interface is defined in a class called TTransport in most languages, as shown in table 4.1.

Table 4.1 The TTransport interface

Returns	Method	Parameters	Behavior
void	close	-	Disconnect the transport endpoint.
void	flush	-	Transmit any buffered write bytes to the endpoint.
bool	isOpen	-	Return true if the transport is open.
void	open	-	Connect to the transport endpoint.
bool	peek	-	Return true if transport is readable.
i32	read	Buffer, Len	Read up to Len bytes into Buffer and return number of bytes read.
i32	readAll	Buffer, Len	Read exactly Len bytes or fail with TTransportException type END_OF_FILE; return bytes read (always the same as Len).
i32	readEnd	-	Called to signal the end of a multipart read and returns total bytes read or 0.
void	write	Buffer, Len	Write Len bytes from buffer.
i32	writeEnd	-	Signal the end of a multipart write; return total bytes written or 0.

In many languages, several of the TTransport methods are nops for certain transport implementations. For example, open() is often a nop because many of the transports open their endpoint at construction time, as was the case with the TMemoryBuffer.

Though in practice you will not find yourself coding against transports very often, if you do it's best to code to the TTransport abstraction rather than a specific implementation, making your code portable across transport types. For example, you may develop against a transport that doesn't need a call to open(); however, if you code defensively and call open() anyway, this ensures that your code will work with other transports down the road.

NOTE The Apache Thrift Framework may use different types in different languages for a parameter or return value depending on the type most appropriate for the language in question. The buffers in the transport interface are an example. In C++ these buffers are byte pointers, in Java they're byte arrays, and in Python they're dynamically typed (StringIO in Python 2 and BytesIO in Python 3).

Most of the transport methods will throw a `TTransportException` when faced with difficulty. Apache Thrift makes no guarantees that language-specific lower layers will not throw their own language-specific or system-level exceptions. Java supports a range of unchecked exceptions that need not be declared and can go uncaught. We'll look more closely at Apache Thrift exception processing later in this part of the book.

4.2.1 *Basic transport operations*

Five of the `TTransport` operations are at the core of most Apache Thrift operations:

- `open()`—Enable the transport for I/O.
- `write()`—Move bytes into the transport.
- `read()`—Move bytes out of the transport.
- `flush()`—Move buffered bytes to the endpoint.
- `close()`—Flush and disable the transport for I/O.

A transport must be open before I/O can take place, thus `open()` should be called before any I/O is attempted. The `close()` method is the bookend to `open()` and should be called upon completion of all transport I/O. Transports generally close themselves on deallocation; however, garbage-collected systems make object cleanup non-deterministic, potentially leaving system resources tied up for an extended period. Well-designed code should generally make explicit calls to `open()` and `close()` at the appropriate points.

The `read()` and `write()` methods are simplistic conceptually but can have a wide range of behavior in practice. For example, when no data is available, the `read()` method may block the calling thread until data arrives, return immediately with a length of 0, or even throw an exception, depending on the transport type and language.

The `write()` method also has a range of implementations. For example, writing to a `TMemoryBuffer` will store the data in memory and return immediately in most languages. In the context of a file or network based transport, write operations may not send bytes to the endpoint immediately. Most operating systems supply complex I/O buffering to optimize device I/O. For example, writing to a file-based transport doesn't typically ensure that the data has been pushed to the disk. Certain transports also supply their own internal buffers.

In normal Apache Thrift programming you'll `open()` and `close()` transports in your code, but the read and write operations will be performed by the serialization protocols (`TBinaryProtocol`, and so on). Protocols don't, however, know when a particular RPC message is complete, serializing the call parameters one by one. For this reason it's left to the higher-level IDL compiler-generated RPC stub code to call the transport flush() method when an RPC operation is complete.

4.3   *Endpoint transports, part 2: Networks*

There are a number of Apache Thrift network transports implemented in various languages. Examples include TCP/IP sockets, named pipes, and HTTP. The TCP/IP socket transport is at the heart of most RPC applications.

Network transports implement the abstract transport interface in much the same way as memory and file transports. For example, assume you need to write a simple program to read and display files; however, you don't know if the files will be on the local filesystem or on the web. You could solve this problem in code with Apache Thrift transports. By developing your reader to use the abstract transport interface, you could isolate the reader from the endpoint type, providing a disk transport or a network transport as required dynamically.

4.3.1   *Network programming with TSocket*

To get a better understanding of transport plugability we'll build a simple file reader that works with disk and network transports. The read_trans() method in this program will read from any object supporting the TTransport interface. The program will supply the reader with a network transport connected to a web page for reading and a disk-based transport connected to a file for reading.

Network transports usually don't open their endpoints on construction as did the memory and disk transports we tried. The open() method on a network transport typically connects the network transport to the network peer. Before reading from the network-attached web server, we'll need to send a GET request for a particular page; the index page of the Apache Thrift website is used in the examples.

C++ TSOCKET

The C++ code in the following listing uses TSocket to read a web page from a web server and a TSimpleFileTransport to read a file from disk. The function that does the reading doesn't care which transport type it receives.

> **Listing 4.7**   ~/thriftbook/part2/transports/net/sock_trans.cpp

```cpp
#include <thrift/transport/TSimpleFileTransport.h>      ❶
#include <thrift/transport/TSocket.h>
#include <iostream>
#include <memory>

using namespace apache::thrift::transport;

void read_trans(TTransport * trans) {          ❷
    const int buf_size = 1024*8;
    char buf[buf_size];
```

```
    while (true) {
        int bytes_read = trans->read(reinterpret_cast<uint8_t *>(buf),
                                     buf_size-1);
        if (bytes_read <= 0 || buf_size <= bytes_read)
            break;
        buf[bytes_read] = '\0';
        std::cout << buf << std::endl;
    }
}

int main()
{
    //Display web page          ③
    std::unique_ptr<TTransport> trans(new TSocket("thrift.apache.org",80));
④   trans->open();
    trans->write(reinterpret_cast<const uint8_t *>("GET / \n"),7);       ⑤
⑥   trans->flush();
    read_trans(trans.get());
    trans->close();                   ⑦
    //Display file
    trans.reset(new TSimpleFileTransport("sock_trans.cpp"));             ⑧
    trans->open();
    read_trans(trans.get());    ⑨
    trans->close();
}
```

The above listing includes the `TSocket` and `TSimpleFileTransport` headers to declare our network and file transports, as well as the standard C++ `iostream` and memory headers for `std::cout` and `std::unique_ptr` support ❶.

In `main()` we create a `unique_ptr<TTransport>` and initialize it with a `TSocket` created on the heap ❸. The `TSocket` is constructed with the endpoint for the Apache Thrift website. Note that the `unique_ptr<TTransport>` ensures that our code depends only on the `TTransport` abstraction, allowing us to switch to other transports later in the code ❽.

To connect the socket to the endpoint we call the `open()` method ❹; this connects the socket to the Apache Foundation website. The open call may take a moment while the system resolves the host name and sets up the connection. The `write()` call simply sends a generic GET / request to the web server, which should respond with the HTML for the index page ❺. Note that the `TTransport` C++ `read()`/`write()` methods deal in `uint8_t` pointers, so we must reinterpret the `char` string pointer before passing it to `write()`.

The `write()` call raises a question: Did we write to a local buffer or did we write to the Apache web server on the other end of our TCP connection? In this case the C++ `TSocket` is a thin layer on top of the Sockets Networking API, and the write goes to the network immediately. Other implementations, such as Java, buffer this write in a local write buffer. Calling `flush()` ❻ on the transport ensures that any buffered data is pushed out to the endpoint (in this case the C++ `flush()` call is a nop).

What if the server doesn't respond even `after` it receives the request, perhaps due to a crash or other malfunction? The C++ `TSocket` interface provides access to a wide range of underlying socket features. If you've written network software in C or C++, most of these features will be familier. For example the `TSocket::setRecvTimeout(int ms)` method sets the receive timeout. This limits the time to block while waiting for a `read()` operation to complete. A `TTransportException::TIMED_OUT` will be thrown if a `read()` method times out.

The `read_trans()` function ❷ supplies the reading logic for our program. It will accept any `TTransport` type of object to read from; we use it here with both network and file transports. Web servers (and other endpoints) often respond in chunks rather than in one large transfer. For this reason we need to read continuously until we've received the entire web page.

Upon completion of the `read_trans()` function we close the transport ❼ and perform the second read with a file transport that's been set to read the sock_trans.cpp source file ❽. The `read_trans()` function reads from the file transport in the same way that it reads from the network transport ❾.

Here's a code snippet that shows a session building and running the code:

```
$ g++ -std=c++11 sock_trans.cpp -lthrift
$ ./a.out | head
<!DOCTYPE HTML PUBLIC "-//W3C//DTD HTML 4.01 Transitional//EN">
<html lang="en">
  <head>
    <title>Welcome to The Apache Software Foundation!</title>

    <meta http-equiv="Content-Type" content="text/html;charset=UTF-8">
    <meta property="og:image"
     content="http://www.apache.org/images/asf_logo.gif" />

    <link rel="stylesheet" type="text/css" media="screen"
     href="/css/style.css">
    <link rel="stylesheet" type="text/css" media="screen"
     href="/css/code.css">
```

NOTE The Apache Thrift web server has gotten picky lately, returning an error when presented with this crude, not particularly standard, web request ("GET /"). As long as you get a response, you know your socket is working.

JAVA TSOCKET

The Apache Thrift Java transport library also provides a `TSocket` transport to connect to TCP endpoints. The following listing shows the same simple `TSocket` program in Java.

> **Listing 4.8 ~/thriftbook/part2/transports/net/SockTrans.java**

```
import org.apache.thrift.transport.TSocket;
import org.apache.thrift.transport.TSimpleFileTransport;
import org.apache.thrift.transport.TTransport;
```

```
import org.apache.thrift.transport.TTransportException;

public class SockTrans {

    public static void main(String[] args) throws TTransportException {
        //Display web page
        TTransport trans = new TSocket("thrift.apache.org", 80);
        final String msg = "GET / \n";
        trans.open();
        trans.write(msg.getBytes());
        trans.flush();                          ❶
        read_trans(trans);
        trans.close();
        //Display file
        trans = new TSimpleFileTransport("SockTrans.java");
        trans.open();
        read_trans(trans);
        trans.close();
    }

    public static void read_trans(TTransport trans) {
        final int buf_size = 1024*8;
        byte[] buf = new byte[buf_size];

        while (true) {
    ❷      try {
                int bytes_read = trans.read(buf, 0, buf_size);
                if (bytes_read <= 0 || buf_size < bytes_read) {
                    break;
                }
                System.out.print(new String(buf, 0, bytes_read, "UTF-8"));
            } catch (Throwable t) {
                break;
            }
        }
    }
}
```

The Java version of the TSocket example reads almost exactly like the C++ version with a couple of differences. First the TSocket flush() call is mandatory in Java ❶. The Java TSocket implementation uses java.io BufferedInputStream and BufferedOutputStream objects to manage socket I/O. The streams are created with 1024-byte buffers by default. Writes to the socket go into the buffer and are only delivered over the network when the buffer is full and/or when flush() is called. It's mandatory that we call flush() before starting our read operation to ensure the server has received our request.

The second implementation difference is the way in which the BufferedInputStream handles the loss of connection. In C++ the TSocket::read() method returns 0 upon connection close. In Java the TSocket::read() method throws an END_OF_FILE type TTransportException in response to closure. The code example traps any exceptions in the read_trans() method and exits ❷.

Here's a sample build and run session with the Java file/web reader:

```
$ javac -cp /usr/local/lib/libthrift-0.10.0.jar SockTrans.java
$ java -cp /usr/local/lib/libthrift-0.10.0.jar:\
> /usr/share/java/slf4j-api.jar:\                    ❶
> /usr/share/java/slf4j-simple.jar:\
> . \
> SockTrans | head

<!DOCTYPE HTML PUBLIC "-//W3C//DTD HTML 4.01 Transitional//EN">
<html lang="en">
  <head>
    <title>Welcome to The Apache Software Foundation!</title>

    <meta http-equiv="Content-Type" content="text/html;charset=UTF-8">
    <meta property="og:image"
➥ content="http://www.apache.org/images/asf_logo.gif" />

    <link rel="stylesheet" type="text/css" media="screen"
➥ href="/css/style.css">
    <link rel="stylesheet" type="text/css" media="screen"
➥ href="/css/code.css">

$
```

The Java `TSocket` implementation is the first, but not the last, of the Java library classes we'll use that rely on SLF4J. The Simple Logging Facade for Java (SLF4J) is a commonly used logging interface that dynamically loads an appropriate underlying logging system at application startup. It's difficult to write an Apache Thrift Java application without it depending on SLF4J.

In this example we use two JARs from SLF4J to support the Thrift `TSocket` dependencies ❶. The first is the API (`slf4j-api.jar`) and the second is the simple logger (`slf4j-simple.jar`), that outputs to `stderr`. Another option is to use the nop logger (`slf4j-nop.jar`), which ignores all logging. For more information on setting up SLF4J, see the Java chapter in part 3.

PYTHON TSOCKET

The Apache Thrift Python transport library also provides a `TSocket` transport to connect to TCP endpoints. The following listing shows the same web page/file reader in Python.

Listing 4.9   ~/thriftbook/part2/transports/net/sock_trans.py

```python
from thrift.transport import TSocket
from thrift.transport import TTransport

def read_trans(t):
    while (True):
        try:
            data = t.read(4096)
```

```
            if len(data) > 0:
                print(data)
            else:
                break
        except:
            break

#read network
trans = TSocket.TSocket("thrift.apache.org", 80)
trans.open()
trans.write("GET /\n")
trans.flush()
read_trans(trans)
trans.close()
#Read file
trans = TTransport.TFileObjectTransport(open("sock_trans.py","rb"))
trans.open()
read_trans(trans)
trans.close()
```

In this program the Python TSocket and TTransport modules are imported to give us access to the TSocket and TFileObjectTransport classes. We create, open, write, and flush the socket and file transports in much the same way that we did in C++ and Java.

Like the Java implementation, the Python TSocket.read() method throws an exception when the connection is closed. Interestingly the TFileObjectTransport.read() returns an empty string upon read failure. Variations like this are important to test for; at the time of this writing the Apache Thrift code itself is the only real documentation at this level of detail.

The following code snippet shows a run of the Python TSocket example:

```
$ python sock_trans.py | head

<!DOCTYPE HTML PUBLIC "-//W3C//DTD HTML 4.01 Transitional//EN">
<html lang="en">
  <head>
    <title>Welcome to The Apache Software Foundation!</title>

    <meta http-equiv="Content-Type" content="text/html;charset=UTF-8">
    <meta property="og:image"
      content="http://www.apache.org/images/asf_logo.gif" />

    <link rel="stylesheet" type="text/css" media="screen"
      href="/css/style.css">
    <link rel="stylesheet" type="text/css" media="screen"
      href="/css/code.css">

Traceback (most recent call last):
  File "sock_trans.py", line 11, in <module>
    print data,
IOError: [Errno 32] Broken pipe
```

4.4   *Server transports*

The previous TSocket network transport examples gave us a look at client-side transport code. Servers are similar to clients in many ways but have the added responsibility of listening for and accepting inbound connections. Apache Thrift supplies a TServer-Transport class in most languages to take care of accepting new client connections.

End users don't typically interact with TServerTransports. To create a fully functional Apache Thrift server, you select a server transport type for use by a prebuilt server and Apache Thrift does the rest. We'll look at the prebuilt Apache Thrift servers in detail in chapter 10. However, to get a better understanding of the network functions implemented by server transports we'll build a simple server by hand here using an Apache Thrift server transport.

Server transports aren't servers and they aren't transports; rather they're a specialization of the factory pattern, manufacturing new endpoint transports in response to client connections. Java and other languages call this type of class an acceptor. In Apache Thrift, the most common type of server transport is TServerSocket.

A TServerSocket object listens for new connections on a TCP port. When a client connects, the TServerSocket accepts the connection and manufactures a new TSocket wired to the client (see figure 4.6). Often the accepting thread will then go back to waiting for the next connection, while other threads manage the client I/O traffic.

To put server transports into perspective, imagine that we need to generalize our trade report writer from the last example to create a trade report server, the goal being to accept client network connections, read requests for various stock symbols, and then write the appropriate trade message back to the client. To build this simple server we need a server transport to accept new client connections.

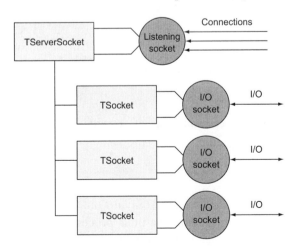

Figure 4.6   Server transports manufacture endpoint transports.

4.4.1 *Programming network servers with server transports*

Several server transport implementations exist, but the most common is TServer-Socket, the implementation that works with TCP/IP.

C++ TSERVERSOCKET

The following listing shows a simple Apache Thrift TServerSocket network server written in C++.

> **Listing 4.10 ~/thriftbook/part2/transports/server/server_trans.cpp**

```
#include <thrift/transport/TServerSocket.h>
#include <boost/shared_ptr.hpp>                         ❶
#include <string>
#include <iostream>
#include <memory>

using namespace apache::thrift::transport;
using boost::shared_ptr;

int main()
{
  const std::string msg("Hello Thrift!\n");
  const std::string stop_cmd("STOP");
  const int buf_size = 1024*8;
  char buf[buf_size] = "";
  auto port = 9090;                                                    ❷

    std::unique_ptr<TServerTransport> acceptor(new TServerSocket(port));
❸  acceptor->listen();
    std::cout << "[Server] listening on port " << port << std::endl;

  do {                                            ❹
    shared_ptr<TTransport> trans = acceptor->accept();    ◁┘
    auto len = trans->read(reinterpret_cast<uint8_t *>(buf), buf_size);
    buf[(0 < len && len < buf_size) ? len : 0] = '\0';
    std::cout << "[Server] handling request: " << buf << std::endl;
    trans->write(reinterpret_cast<const uint8_t *>(msg.c_str()),
                 msg.length());
    trans->flush();
    trans->close();
  } while (0 != stop_cmd.compare(0, std::string::npos, buf, 4));

  std::cout << "[Server] exiting" << std::endl;
  acceptor->close();
}
```

This program is single-threaded and can therefore only do one thing at a time. As designed, it will accept a single client connection at a time, process one message from the client, hang up, and wait for the next client to connect.

The server socket is initialized with port 9090 ❷, however clients cannot begin to connect until the listen() method is called ❸. Once in listening mode the TCP/IP port will backlog client connections until they're accepted.

The server transport `accept()` method blocks until a client connects and then returns a `boost::shared_ptr<TTransport>` ❹, a shared ownership smart pointer for the client-connected `TSocket`. The `boost/shared_ptr.hpp` header defines this shared pointer type ❶. The `boost::shared_ptr` class is used throughout the Apache Thrift C++ library to keep track of framework objects, like the `TSocket` in this example.

> **BOOST C++ LIBRARIES** The Boost C++ Libraries are a popular collection of open source C++ libraries, almost essential to modern C++ programming prior to C++11. The Apache Thrift C++ libraries predate C++11 and at present don't use C++11 features; instead, they rely heavily on Boost. The `boost::shared_ptr` offers identical functionally to the `std::shared_ptr` in C++11. Shared pointers are a style of smart pointer that use reference counting to ensure objects are destroyed after all references to the object are released. The C++ chapter in part 3 provides details related to installing the necessary C++ Boost libraries for Apache Thrift development.

This program spends most of its life in a loop, accepting new connections, reading messages, and sending responses. If a client sends the "STOP" message, the server breaks out of the loop, closes the listening socket, and exits.

Let's look at a sample build and run of the server:

```
$ g++ -std=c++11 server_trans.cpp -lthrift
$ ./a.out
[Server] listening on port 9090
[Server] handling request HELLO
[Server] handling request STOP
[Server] exiting
```

This server test run is responding to a telnet client sending messages from another shell. Here's the session log from the telnet client shell:

```
$ telnet localhost 9090
Trying 127.0.0.1...
Connected to localhost.
Escape character is '^]'.
HELLO
Hello Thrift!
Connection closed by foreign host.
$ telnet localhost 9090
Trying 127.0.0.1...
Connected to localhost.
Escape character is '^]'.
STOP
Connection closed by foreign host.
```

Server socket examples in Java and Python are included in the source code for the book and offer no surprises, following the C++ example with the exception of normal language-specific variations.

4.4.2   *The server transport interface*

Now that we've seen a server transport in action, let's step back and look at the abstract Thrift `TServerTransport` interface, shown in Table 4.2.

Table 4.2   TServerTransport Abstract Interface

Returns	Method	Parameters	Behavior
TTransport	accept	-	Return a `TTransport` for each inbound connection.
void	close	-	Disconnect the server listening endpoint.
void	interrupt	-	Break out of a blocking `accept()` call [optional].
void	listen	-	Begin listening to the endpoint for connections.

The server transport interface consists of four methods. The `listen()` method is analogous to the `open()` method of a normal `TTransport`. The `listen()` method causes the server transport to register interest in receiving new connections over the configured endpoint. In the previous examples, our endpoint was the TCP port 9090 on the local host.

Once the server transport is listening, new connections are backlogged (made to wait) until the `accept()` method is called. Calling `accept()` completes a client connection request and returns a `TTransport` wired to the client. This `TTransport` can then be used to perform I/O with the client. If a thread calls the `accept()` method and no client connections are waiting, the thread will block until a client connection arrives.

You have several ways around indefinite accept blocking. One is to call the `interrupt()` method from another thread, though not all `TServerTransport` implementations support `interrupt()`.

Server transports may also offer timeout settings for accept operations. If the accept timeout value is set to 0, the `accept()` call will generate an error immediately (usually in the form of an exception) if no client connections are waiting. The C++ `TServerSocket` class provides the `setAcceptTimeout()` method to set an accept timeout. The Java `TServerSocket` implementation provides access to the underlying Java listening socket through `getServerSocket()`, which in turn provides a `setSoTimeout()` method. In Python, you can set the timeout directly on the Python socket (which is called "handle") using the Python socket `settimeout()` method. Note that these language-specific features are not part of the `TServerTransport` interface.

Here are timeout examples in each of the demonstration languages, where the timeout is set to 10 seconds:

- *C++*: acceptor->setAcceptTimeout(10000)
- *Java*: acceptor.getServerSocket().setSoTimeout(10000)
- *Python*: acceptor.handle.settimeout(10)

Changing the timeout to 0 essentially makes the accept operation non-blocking. However, accepted socket connections will still produce blocking TSocket objects for new client connections. We'll look into non-blocking I/O on TSockets in more detail in later chapters.

The final server transport method is close(). The close() method shuts down the endpoint, acting as the bookend to listen(). Clients attempting to connect before listen() or after close() will fail. Client connections waiting in the backlog when the server crashes or closes the listening socket will also fail. The nature of the client failure is language-specific.

4.5   *Layered transports*

As we discussed in chapter 2, transports can be layered. When a feature needs to be added to an endpoint transport it may be easier to create a layer on top of an existing endpoint transport, rather than rewriting the endpoint transport. This layered model increases code reuse and makes it easier to separate concerns. Layered transports can be applied on top of endpoint transports as well as other layered transports, making them stackable and particularly flexible.

Layered transports expose the TTransport interface to clients just like endpoint transports, but unlike endpoint transports, they perform their I/O on a lower-level TTransport interface rather than a device.

For example, consider a hypothetical TTeeTransport. Such a transport could copy all write() data to two underlying transports. This would allow one copy of all messages written to be delivered to a TSocket for RPC operations and a second copy to be written to a TSimpleFileTransport for logging (see figure 4.7). Multiple TTee-Transports could be stacked to copy messages to an unlimited number of endpoints. This pattern is extensible, making custom layered transports a reasonable option when new low-level, application-specific functionality is required (tracing, debugging, logging, and so on).

Each Apache Thrift language library supplies its own set of layered transports. In most languages TFramedTransport and TBufferedTransport are the most important.

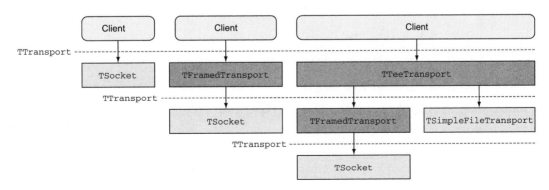

Figure 4.7   Layered transport examples

Both transports provide a buffering layer on top of underlying transports. Writing to either of these transports places data in a buffer until the buffer is filled or the client calls `flush()`. This can improve performance by buffering several small writes locally within the process (inexpensive), then making a single system call (expensive) to transmit the buffered data with `flush()`.

4.5.1   *Message framing*

The `TFramedTransport` is a particularly important layered transport. In Apache Thrift terms, a frame is a message transmitted with a four-byte prefix recording the size of the message. Using this framing technique enables read optimizations. For example, transports normally have no idea how much data will ultimately be available for reading. The frame size provides a means to determine the number of bytes to read with each read operation. Framing is required by all of the Apache Thrift nonblocking servers.

Let's update the `TServerSocket` example with a framing layer to see how transport layering works.

C++ TFRAMEDTRANSPORT

The following listing shows the C++ `TServerTransport` example with a `TFramedTransport` layer added.

> **Listing 4.11   ~/thriftbook/part2/transports/layers/server_frame.cpp**

```cpp
#include <thrift/transport/TServerSocket.h>
#include <thrift/transport/TBufferTransports.h>      ❶
#include <boost/shared_ptr.hpp>
#include <boost/make_shared.hpp>
#include <string>
#include <iostream>
#include <memory>

using namespace apache::thrift::transport;
using boost::shared_ptr;
using boost::make_shared;

int main()
{
  const std::string msg("Hello Thrift!\n");
  const std::string stop_cmd("STOP");
  const int buf_size = 1024*8;
  char buf[buf_size] = "";
  auto port = 9090;

  auto acceptor = std::make_shared<TServerSocket>(port);
  acceptor->listen();
  std::cout << "[Server] listening on port "
            << port << std::endl;

  do {
    auto trans_ep = acceptor->accept();
```

```
    auto trans =
        make_shared<TFramedTransport>(trans_ep);        ❷
    auto len =
        trans->read(reinterpret_cast<uint8_t *>(buf),
                    buf_size);
    buf[(0 < len && len < buf_size) ? len : 0] = '\0';
    std::cout << "[Server] handling request: "
                << buf << std::endl;
    trans->write(
        reinterpret_cast<const uint8_t *>(msg.c_str()),
        msg.length());
    trans->flush();
    trans->close();
  } while (0 != stop_cmd.compare(0,
                                    std::string::npos,
                                    buf,
                                    4));

  std::cout << "[Server] exiting" << std::endl;
  acceptor->close();
}
```

This listing has two differences from the prior C++ server. The first is the inclusion of the TBufferTransports.h header ❶. The TFramedTransport is defined in the buffer header because it buffers all writes until flush() is called. In fact, the call to flush() defines a frame boundary. When flush() is called, the framed transport determines the number of bytes in the frame buffer, then sends the frame size followed by the buffered bytes.

The second and only other change is that the endpoint transport returned by acceptor->accept() is wrapped in a TFramedTransport ❷. Because TFramedTransport supplies the TTransport interface the rest of the code sees no difference between TSocket and TFramedTransport. The code uses a Boost TTransport shared smart pointer in both cases.

Communicating with our server in the presence of the framing layer will be difficult with telnet. To test our server and to see how framing operations work under the covers, we'll build a C++ manual framing client to communicate with the server. The C++ client takes a command line string and sends it to the framed server, computing and sending the frame size manually for demonstration purposes.

> **Listing 4.12   ~/thriftbook/part2/transports/layers/client_frame.cpp**

```
#include <thrift/transport/TSocket.h>
#include <string>
#include <iostream>
#include <memory>

using namespace apache::thrift::transport;

int main(int argv, char **argc)
```

```
{
    std::unique_ptr<TTransport> trans(new TSocket("localhost", 9090));
    trans->open();

    const std::string msg(argc[1]);
    uint32_t frame_size = htonl(msg.length());
    trans->write(reinterpret_cast<const uint8_t *>(&frame_size), 4);    ❶
    trans->write(reinterpret_cast<const uint8_t *>(msg.c_str()),
                 msg.length());
    trans->flush();

    trans->read(reinterpret_cast<uint8_t *>(&frame_size), 4);    ❷
    frame_size = ntohl(frame_size);
❸  std::unique_ptr<char[]> upBuf(new char[frame_size+1]);
    int bytes_read =
            trans->read(reinterpret_cast<uint8_t *>(upBuf.get()),
                        frame_size);
    if (frame_size == bytes_read) {
        upBuf[bytes_read] = '\0';
        std::cout << upBuf.get() << std::endl;
    }
    trans->close();
}
```

This client is similar to the TSocket program we used to get the http://thrift
.apache.org index page earlier in this chapter. We use a TSocket to connect to the
local host on port 8585. Next we determine the frame size for our message. The message
is recovered from the command line and saved as a std::string.

One of the issues we need to consider when building our frame size is that various
platforms use different byte orders in memory. The Apache Thrift framing system uses
big endian order, placing the most significant byte first in the stream. Because C++ uses
whatever endianness the underlying platform uses, we use a standard socket networking
macro to change our frame size from host byte ordering to TCP/IP network byte
ordering (which is always big endian). The call to htonl() (host to network long) takes
care of this, either swapping our byte ordering or leaving it intact as appropriate. Once
we have the frame size prepared, we can send it and the message ❶.

The read side is similar. We read the frame size from the socket, convert it to the
host's byte order, and then allocate a buffer to house the frame ❷. This is a nice optimization,
allowing us to allocate the exact number of bytes needed, as opposed to the
8K buffer we used in the web reader ❸. Next we read the rest of the frame and display
the message received.

Here's a sample build and run on the server side:

```
$ g++ -std=c++11 server_frame.cpp -lthrift -oserver
$ ./server
[Server] listening on port 9090
[Server] handling request Hello
[Server] handling request STOP
[Server] exiting
```

We built our server using the -o switch to name the executable "server". The server received two requests; the second was a STOP, causing the server to exit. Here's the session log from the client side:

```
$ g++ -std=c++11 client_frame.cpp -lthrift -oclient
$ ./client Hello
Hello Thrift!

$ ./client STOP
```

The first client run sends the frame size and five bytes of data ("Hello"). The response is 18 bytes containing a 4-byte frame size and 14 bytes of data ("Hello Thrift!\n"). On the second call the server successfully decodes our "STOP" message and exits.

The source code for the book includes Java and Python versions of the above framed server if you want to look at the experiment in another language. You can use the C++ client to test both the Java and Python framed servers, or write your own clients in another language!

Summary

Practical Apache Thrift applications rarely restrict their use of the framework to the transport layer. However, transports underlie every Apache Thrift application and are a foundational part of Apache Thrift programming. In this chapter, we wrote sample programs exploring all of the key aspects of the Apache Thrift transport layer.

Key points in this chapter

- Transports are the lowest layer of the Apache Thrift software stack.
- All Apache Thrift features depend on transports.
- Transports implement the TTransport interface.
- The TTransport interface defines device-independent, byte-level read and write operations.
- Endpoint transports implement TTransport and perform read/write operations against a device.
- Endpoint transports are offered in most languages for memory, disk, and network devices.
- Server transports use the factory pattern to manufacture network transports as client connections are accepted.
- Layered transports implement TTransport and provide additional features on top of an underlying transport.
- Layered transports enable separation of concerns and reuse in the transport stack.
- The TFramedTransport is a commonly used layered transport and is required to connect to non-blocking servers.
- A transport stack may include any number of layered transports but must always lead to endpoint transports at the bottom of the stack.

Serializing
data with protocols
5

This chapter covers

- Understanding the Apache Thrift serialization protocol layer
- Serializing language-based types
- Programming with the Apache Thrift Binary, Compact, and JSON protocols
- Selecting the most appropriate protocol for an application

In chapter 4, the Transport chapter, we saw how the Apache Thrift transport layer provides a byte-level interface used to perform I/O against a range of physical and logical devices. We also noted that different languages typically produce different representations of data when built-in serialization is used. To communicate across languages, we need a layer to create standard serialized representations for data. Apache Thrift protocols (see figure 5.1) provide this functionality.

Protocols create and consume a single, central representation of logically equivalent structures across languages. Using Apache Thrift protocols, a C++ object can be

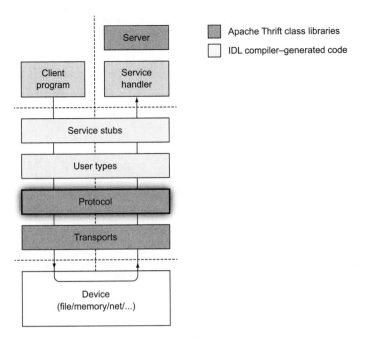

Figure 5.1 The Apache Thrift protocol layer

serialized into a common format, sent to a Ruby program, and reconstituted as a Ruby object (see figure 5.2). Protocols also support communications between dissimilar hardware platforms where byte ordering, padding, and pointer width may vary. For example, Apache Thrift supports communicating between 32-bit and 64-bit C++ applications without incompatibilities. The Apache Thrift protocols stan-

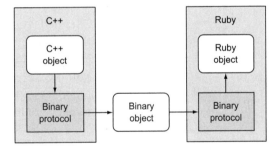

Figure 5.2 Apache Thrift cross-language serialization with the binary protocol

dardize the representation of serialized objects independent of language, operating system, or hardware platform.

Many distributed applications use XML or JSON to provide a central data representation; however, these formats only supply part of the solution. Much work must be done to produce a standardized XML or JSON format that can be used to serialize native types across languages. For example, how will binary blocks of data be handled, what will happen when data fields are missing or unexpected data fields are present, what complex types will be supported, and how will they be represented? Several classes of serialization problems are solved by the Apache Thrift framework, not the least of which is the code needed to perform the serialization.

Many serialization frameworks support only one serialization format; Apache Thrift allows you to choose from several. Each serialization protocol exports the standard Apache Thrift protocol interface, allowing custom protocol implementations to plug in easily. Protocols can be selected at compile time or runtime, making it possible to change protocols as needs change without changing the code that uses the protocol.

The abstract protocol interface is typically defined in a class called `TProtocol`. `TProtocol` implementations keep a reference to a `TTransport` used as the target for all protocol read and write operations (see figure 5.3). This transport reference is typically set at protocol construction time for the life of the protocol, binding the protocol and transport together into an I/O stack. Any protocol can use any transport because protocols depend only upon the abstract `TTransport` interface, not the underlying implementation. Thus, a given protocol can serialize to memory, disk, or over a network.

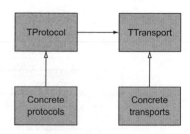

Figure 5.3   Transport/protocol dependency

The Apache Thrift framework has three primary protocols:

- *Binary*—Usually named `TBinaryProtocol`, this protocol serializes data in binary form, much as it's typically laid out in memory. The `TBinaryProtocol` is the "default" Apache Thrift protocol. All language implementations support `TBinaryProtocol`.
- *Compact*—Usually named `TCompactProtocol`, this protocol is supported by fewer languages than `TBinaryProtocol`, though most support it. The compact protocol produces binary output with smaller serialized data representations than the binary protocol.
- *JSON*—Usually named `TJSONProtocol`, this protocol uses the JSON text-based format, trading larger serialized size for broad interoperability and human readability.

In normal scenarios, you use the Apache Thrift IDL compiler to generate serialization code; however, in this chapter, we'll hand code several simple serialization examples. The examples are designed to help you understand the under-the-hood mechanics, as well as how to choose the appropriate protocol for a given application.

5.1   *Basic serialization with the binary protocol*

The `TBinaryProtocol` serializes base types in a format nearly identical to their representation in memory. The protocol also adds metadata to the serialization stream to enable features such as interface evolution, allowing serialized types to change incrementally over time without breaking existing programs.

Like all Apache Thrift protocols, `TBinaryProtocol` must be layered on top of a `TTransport` object. Invoking a protocol `write` method serializes the data provided and calls the `write` method of the transport with the resulting bytes (see figure 5.4).

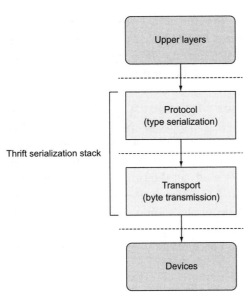

Figure 5.4   The protocol/transport stack

5.1.1   *Using the C++ TBinaryProtocol*

To get an understanding of protocols from the C++ perspective, we'll build a simple
Apache Thrift C++ program to serialize a string, as shown in the following listing.

Listing 5.1   ~/ThriftBook/part2/protocols/bin_mem.cpp

```
#include <thrift/transport/TBufferTransports.h>
#include <thrift/protocol/TBinaryProtocol.h>
#include <boost/make_shared.hpp>
#include <iostream>
#include <string>

using namespace apache::thrift::transport;
using namespace apache::thrift::protocol;
using boost::make_shared;

int main()
{
    auto trans = make_shared<TMemoryBuffer>(4096);      ❶
    TBinaryProtocol proto(trans);    ❷

❸  int i = proto.writeString(std::string("Hello Thrift Serialization"));
    std::cout << "Wrote " << i << " bytes to the TMemoryBuffer"
            << std::endl;

    std::string msg;                          ❹
    i = proto.readString(msg);      ⟵—
    std::cout << "Read " << i << " bytes from the TMemoryBuffer"
            << std::endl;
    std::cout << "Recovered string: " << msg << std::endl;
}
```

The include block at the top of the file adds support for the Boost library make_shared<> template, which creates Boost shared pointers used throughout the Apache Thrift library. The program also uses the TMemoryBuffer endpoint transport defined in the TBufferTransports.h header file and the TBinaryProtocol from the TBinaryProtocol.h file.

The first bit of code in the main function constructs a TBinaryProtocol object ❷, initializing it with the shared_ptr to our transport ❶. Notice that the TMemoryBuffer smart pointer satisfies the TBinaryProtocol constructor, which requires only a TTransport interface and doesn't have any knowledge of the actual transport implementation. Once constructed, the protocol object sends all the bytes it serializes to this transport by calling the transport write() method. Conversely, the protocol reads all of the bytes it's asked to deserialize from this transport by calling the transport read() method. The remainder of the code uses the binary protocol to write a string to the memory buffer ❸ and then reads it back ❹. Here's a sample session using the program:

```
$ g++ -o bin_mem bin_mem.cpp -Wall -std=c++11 -lthrift
$ ./bin_mem
Wrote 30 bytes to the TMemoryBuffer
Read 30 bytes from the TMemoryBuffer
Recovered string: Hello Thrift Serialization
```

As you can see, the binary protocol has taken our 26-character string and stored it in a block of memory 30 bytes long. The additional 4 bytes of metadata are consumed by a 32-bit integer prefix that specifies the length of our string.

5.1.2 *Using the Java TBinaryProtocol*

The following listing shows a Java version of the same TBinaryProtocol program.

> Listing 5.2   ~/ThriftBook/part2/protocols/BinMem.java

```java
import org.apache.thrift.TException;
import org.apache.thrift.protocol.TProtocol;
import org.apache.thrift.protocol.TBinaryProtocol;
import org.apache.thrift.transport.TMemoryBuffer;

public class BinMem {

    public static void main(String[] args) throws TException {
        TMemoryBuffer trans = new TMemoryBuffer(4096);
        TProtocol proto = new TBinaryProtocol(trans);

        proto.writeString("Hello Thrift Serialization");
        System.out.println("Wrote " + trans.length() +
                        " bytes to the TMemoryBuffer");

        String strMsg = proto.readString();
        System.out.println("Recovered string: " + strMsg);
    }
}
```

A few differences exist between the C++ and Java versions of this program, one of which is that the Java TBinaryProtocol read/write methods don't return the number of bytes read/written. As an alternative, we can use the length() member of the TMemoryBuffer to discern the number of bytes written. Here's a sample session using the Java program:

```
$ javac -cp /usr/local/lib/libthrift-1.0.0.jar BinMem.java
$ java -cp /usr/local/lib/libthrift-1.0.0.jar:. BinMem
Wrote 30 bytes to the TMemoryBuffer
Recovered string: Hello Thrift Serialization
```

As you can see, the Java implementation wrote the same 30 bytes that our C++ program wrote. This is the key to Apache Thrift portability; no matter which language you use, the serialized representation of equivalent objects is identical for a given Apache Thrift protocol.

5.1.3 Using the Python TBinaryProtocol

The following listing shows the Python version of the TBinaryProtocol example.

Listing 5.3 ~/ThriftBook/part2/protocols/bin_mem.py

```
from thrift.transport import TTransport
from thrift.protocol import TBinaryProtocol

trans = TTransport.TMemoryBuffer()
proto = TBinaryProtocol.TBinaryProtocol(trans)        ❶
proto.writeString("Hello Thrift Serialization")
print ("Wrote %d bytes to the TMemoryBuffer" % (trans.cstringio_buf.tell()))

trans.cstringio_buf.seek(0)          ❷
msg = proto.readString()
print("Recovered string: %s" % (msg))
```

Much like the other two examples, we create the TMemoryBuffer transport, and then hand it to the TBinaryProtocol constructor ❶. Like Java, the Python protocol read() and write() methods don't return the size of the I/O operation. Here we access the TMemoryBuffer object's underlying IO object (a StringIO object in Python2, a BytesIO object in Python3) and use the tell() method to see how many bytes have been consumed at the storage level. As you may recall from our brush with TMemoryBuffer in chapter 4, memory-based IO objects act like files, so we must go back to the beginning of the "file" before we begin reading ❷. Here's a run:

```
$ python bin_mem.py
Wrote 30 bytes to the TMemoryBuffer
Recovered string: Hello Thrift Serialization
```

The Python program has written the same 30 bytes that the C++ and Java equivalents wrote.

NOTE   The examples in part 2 of this book use Python 2.7; however, properly written Apache Thrift Python code will also run under Python 3. See chapter 16 in part 3 for more Python language-specific details.

5.1.4   *Takeaway*

Programs written in all three of these languages serialized their data in an identical fashion, creating 30-byte strings with the length housed in the first four bytes. A program in any of these languages could have de-serialized the string. Given only the Apache Thrift transport and protocol tools, we can now read and write a comprehensive range of data types across any group of Apache Thrift-supported languages. These serialized objects can be transmitted over RPC interfaces, passed through message queues, or written to NoSQL databases—all with full support for any Apache Thrift language or platform.

The examples above assume that the serialized object is a string. Practical serialization tasks require more robust metadata. For example, when de-serializing an object we need to know what type of object we encountered and we need tools to serialize complex object types, such as containers and structures. The TProtocol interface provides this along with other features.

5.2   *The TProtocol interface*

The TProtocol interface provides a generic set of methods implemented by concrete serialization protocols. The interface is organized into a set of write methods and a set of read methods supporting serialization of the various Apache Thrift IDL types. To write a double to the serialization stream you call writeDouble(), to read a double you call readDouble(), and so on. Table 5.1 presents a list of the TProtocol methods.

Table 5.1   TProtocol interface

Base type serialization	
writeBool()	readBool()
writeByte()	readByte()
writeI16()	readI16()
writeI32()	readI32()
writeI64()	readI64()
writeDouble()	readDouble()
writeString()	readString()
writeBinary()	readBinary()
Container serialization	
writeMapBegin()	readMapBegin()
writeMapEnd()	readMapEnd()
writeListBegin()	readListBegin()
writeListEnd()	readListEnd()

Table 5.1 TProtocol interface *(continued)*

Container serialization *(continued)*	
`writeSetBegin()`	`readSetBegin()`
`writeSetEnd()`	`readSetEnd()`
RPC message methods	
`writeMessageBegin()`	`readMessageBegin()`
`writeMessageEnd()`	`readMessageEnd()`
Structure methods	
`writeStructBegin()`	`readStructBegin()`
`writeStructEnd()`	`readStructEnd()`
`writeFieldBegin()`	`readFieldBegin()`
`writeFieldEnd()`	`readFieldEnd()`
`writeFieldStop()`	
Utility methods	
`getTransport()`	

5.2.1 Apache Thrift serialization

The `TProtocol` interface defines several groups of serialization methods. In most languages, any of the methods in these groups can potentially throw a `TProtocolException` when faced with an error condition. For more information on exception management in Apache Thrift, see chapter 9 on Handling Exceptions.

SERIALIZING VALUES

Each base type supported by Apache Thrift IDL has a pair of read/write methods, for example, the `readString()` and `writeString()` methods from the `TBinaryProtocol` examples earlier in this chapter. The Apache Thrift type system is defined by what `TProtocol` allows you to serialize. All data communicated through RPC must decompose to one of these base types. As you can see from the methods in table 5.1, Apache Thrift protocols support serialization of Boolean values, signed 8-bit (byte/i8), 16-bit (i16), 32-bit (i32), and 64-bit (i64) integers, double-precision floating point values, strings of UTF8 characters, and binary chunks.

> **NOTE** Much discussion has taken place around adding support for a 4-byte float base type. This addition wouldn't be backward compatible and the new type would need to be added to every protocol in every language in the Apache Thrift tree for fully integrated language support. While this would allow use cases not needing 8-byte doubles to cut size on the wire to 4 bytes, the lack of compatibility and big bang workload appears to have stalled the initiative at the time of this writing.

STRINGS

Two value types deserve discussion. These are the string and binary types.

The string IDL type is designed to represent an array of characters. Characters can be encoded in a variety of ways depending on the language and the needs of the program. The Apache Thrift Binary, Compact, and JSON protocols use UTF-8 encoded characters as their exchange format for strings (see figure 5.5). UTF-8 is an 8-bit Unicode format that overlays the ASCII character set. Escape sequences are used for characters that require multiple bytes to represent.

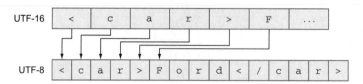

Figure 5.5   Apache Thrift protocols convert language-specific string encodings into UTF-8 for serialization.

Systems such as the native Windows API, OS X Cocoa, Qt, Java, and .NET use UTF-16 characters, which are 16-bit Unicode with support for extended characters spanning more than 16 bits.

Strings that aren't UTF-8 will be converted when serialized with an Apache Thrift protocol. Two Java programs communicating over Apache Thrift RPC will have to serialize their UTF-16 strings using UTF-8, then convert the UTF-8 data back to UFT-16 to de-serialize. While this may sound grim to the performance-conscious, keep in mind that the lion's share of characters used to describe HTML pages and other computer-oriented documents in any language fit in 8 bits. Many UTF-16 to UTF-8 conversions will cut the serialized size of strings representing XML or HTML documents in half. There are pros and cons to all encoding schemes; however, UTF-8 offers the combination of full Unicode support, compact size, and no byte-ordering overhead. These factors underlie UTF-8's dominance as the character encoding of choice of the internet.

> **NOTE** In 2016, W3Techs reported that 87.5% of websites used UTF-8 character encoding.

Certain languages, such as C++, don't have a standard character encoding. C++ supports the `std::string` type, which can contain ASCII, UTF-8, or any other encoding. Whatever you put in a `std::string`, the `size()` method will return the number of bytes, which will not be the same as the number of characters if multi-byte characters are present. C++ also supports `std::wstring` characters for wide (16- or 32-bit) string representations. Only 8-bit UTF-8 or ASCII strings should be passed to Apache Thrift protocols for string serialization in C++.

Python offers support for a vast range of character encodings. General Python 2.x use of quoted strings ("hello" + "world") produces 8-bit ASCII data. The Python protocols serialize and de-serialize strings without translation by default. If your application uses Unicode strings (u'Mot' + unichr(246) + u'rhead'), which are 16-bit in Python, you'll need to force these strings to serialize using UTF-8. An IDL compiler directive can be used to force generated Python code to convert all strings to and from UTF-8 during serialization:

```
$ thrift -gen py:utf8strings hello.thrift
```

This directive causes generated code to serialize a string called myString as myString.encode(utf-8), and to de-serialize it as "myString = result.decode('utf-8')".

Due to the convoluted evolution of string storage in computing, it's worth taking time to understand the way your language of choice handles characters and to verify that the appropriate Apache Thrift string handling features are being used in your code.

BINARY

The binary IDL type is designed to represent an array of bytes. Binary data isn't tampered with during serialization. This allows you to serialize anything: a text document, a bitmap, a raw memory snapshot, and so on. Apache Thrift protocols allow the party de-serializing a binary object to determine its size in bytes but nothing more. The de-serializing party must have out-of-band knowledge of the binary object to manipulate it.

SERIALIZING CONTAINERS

Apache Thrift supports serialization of three container types: lists, sets, and maps. Each has a begin and an end method between which the elements contained are serialized. The writeXXXBegin() method stores the number of elements in the container and the readXXXBegin() method recovers the number of elements in the container. Containers can contain any base type, as well as other containers and structs.

Maps contain key value pairs, while lists and sets contain elements of a single type. Lists and sets are distinguished conceptually in that sets don't allow duplicate values and lists do. The Apache Thrift serialization system avoids adding unnecessary overhead to the serialization process and makes no checks for set element or map key uniqueness. IDL maps and sets translate into container types in implementation languages, such as std::set in C++, set() in Python, and java.util.Set in Java.

CONTAINERS AND DUCK TYPING

Languages that support duck typing, such as Python, may allow types to be supplied for serialization that don't match the type specified in the IDL. For example, a Python list provides the features required by a serializer to encode a Python set. However, the list isn't a set and can contain duplicates.

Consider the following example IDL and Python client code:

```
#IDL:
service HelloSvc { string hello_func(1: set<i32> s) }      ❶

#Client:
client = HelloSvc.Client(protocol)
❷  s = set()
[s.add(x) for x in [1,2,3]]
client.hello_func(s)
print("Python Client: calling with " + str(s))
```

❸
```
l = list()
[l.append(x) for x in [1,1,1]]
client.hello_func(l)
print("Python Client: calling with " + str(l))
```

Because Python uses duck typing, any container supplying the iteration features used by the serialization layer will work when calling the `hello_func()` ❶ method. The above code passes muster with the Python interpreter because both sets ❷ and lists ❸ can be iterated as required by the serialization code. Here's a sample server's Hello service handler implementation for the `hello_func()`:

```
class HelloHandler:
    def hello_func(self, s):
        print("Python Server: handling client request: " + str(s))
        return "Hello thrift, from the python server"
```

The server displays the string representation of the set received. When we run the client, everything looks fine:

```
$ python hello_client.py
Python Client: calling with set([1, 2, 3])
Python Client: calling with [1, 1, 1]
```

Yet on the server side, the data is different:

```
$ python hello_server.py
Python Server: started
Python Server: handling client request: set([1, 2, 3])
Python Server: handling client request: set([1])
```

The result here shows that the first "set" of three values arrived intact, but the second "list" of three values didn't. In Python, as in many languages, adding a duplicate to a set isn't an error; duplicates are silently ignored. The Apache Thrift client serialized all three elements in both calls, but when the server recovered the elements in the second call and added them into a local set container, the duplicates were ignored. We end up with only one of the three duplicate values on the server (as desired with sets), but we pay the price for serializing, transmitting, and de-serializing all three.

> **NOTE** IDL container types define the language container type that will be created when de-serializing a collection, but not necessarily the type of container provided during serialization.

Statically typed languages will not allow a list to be supplied when a set is required. However, in dynamic languages it's worth trying to match IDL types or at least understand the consequences of not doing so.

SERIALIZING STRUCTS

Apache Thrift supports user-defined types in the form of structs. Serializing a struct requires that you begin the struct with `writeStructBegin()` and end it with `write-StructEnd()`. The fields within the struct must be serialized within the field begin and end calls, `writeFieldBegin()` and `writeFieldEnd()`. Struct fields can be base types, containers, or other structs.

> **NOTE** The IDL compiler has limited support for forward or partial type declarations. A struct can only contain a type that's been fully defined previously in IDL in most cases. With the exception of experimental features in C++, self-referential structs aren't supported and all type graphs must be acyclic (if struct A contains struct B, B cannot contain A directly or indirectly).

When the field list for a struct is completely serialized, the `writeFieldStop()` method is called. The read process follows the same pattern to de-serialize a struct. The `skip()` method allows readers to skip fields they aren't interested in or don't recognize.

The Apache Thrift IDL compiler automatically generates struct serialization code for every struct defined in IDL, meaning normal Apache Thrift projects don't require any hand-coded struct serialization logic. We will, however, build struct serialization examples later in this chapter to develop a better understanding of the workings of protocols and Apache Thrift RPC.

SERIALIZING MESSAGES

Apache Thrift remote procedure calls are composed of messages sent between the client and the server. Clients make calls by sending CALL Messages and servers send responses by sending REPLY Messages. Thrift Messages are wrappers for structs transmitted between the client and the server. The IDL compiler generates an `args` struct to contain the parameters for function call requests sent to servers. The IDL compiler also creates a `result` struct to contain the return values sent back in reply messages to the caller (see figure 5.6).

Messages have a name, a type, and a sequence ID. In Apache Thrift RPC, the message name is the method to be called on the server. Sequence IDs provide a place for a unique message sequence number, used in certain asynchronous callback systems but set to 0 in most cases. The server must reply with the same sequence ID received in the associated `T_CALL`.

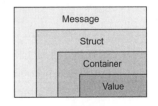

Figure 5.6 Messages are the unit of communication in Apache Thrift RPC, packaging structs, containers, and values passed between clients and servers.

The message type is one of the four values in table 5.2.

The `T_CALL` message type embodies a normal RPC call sent from a client to a server (see figure 5.7). A `T_REPLY` message is a normal server reply to a `T_CALL`. The `T_EXCEPTION` message is an abnormal server reply to a `T_CALL`. The `T_ONEWAY` message is a client call that will not receive a response of any kind, neither `T_REPLY` nor `T_EXCEPTION`. Apache Thrift

Table 5.2   Apache Thrift RPC message types

Value	Message type	Purpose
1	T_CALL	Sent by clients to servers to call RPC functions.
2	T_REPLY	Sent by servers to clients in response to RPC function calls.
3	T_EXCEPTION	Sent by servers to clients when RPC function calls fail.
4	T_ONEWAY	Sent by clients to servers to call RPC functions with no reply.

protocols provide `writeMessageBegin()` and `writeMessageEnd()` methods to serialize messages. Read versions of these methods de-serialize messages.

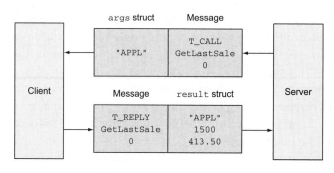

Figure 5.7   **Apache Thrift RPC clients send T_CALL messages to call methods on servers, and servers send T_REPLY messages to clients with function call results.**

TRANSPORT STACK ACCESS

The `TProtocol` interface provides one method that isn't used for serialization, `getTransport()`. The `getTransport()` method returns a reference to the underlying transport stack, which is principally useful in allowing users to flush the transport buffers when desired.

5.2.2   C++ TProtocol

Each Apache Thrift implementation language defines `TProtocol` with its own specific sensibilities. The following listing is a digest of the `TProtocol` method prototypes found in the Apache Thrift C++ library.

Listing 5.4   TProtocol.h

```
class TProtocol [C++]
  uint32_t writeMessageBegin(const std::string& name,
                             const TMessageType messageType,
                             const int32_t seqid)
  uint32_t writeMessageEnd()
  uint32_t writeStructBegin(const char* name)
  uint32_t writeStructEnd()
  uint32_t writeFieldBegin(const char* name,
                           const TType fieldType,
                           const int16_t fieldId)
  uint32_t writeFieldEnd()
```

```
uint32_t writeFieldStop()
uint32_t writeMapBegin(const TType keyType,
                       const TType valType,
                       const uint32_t size)
uint32_t writeMapEnd()
uint32_t writeListBegin(const TType elemType, const uint32_t size)
uint32_t writeListEnd()
uint32_t writeSetBegin(const TType elemType, const uint32_t size)
uint32_t writeSetEnd()
uint32_t writeBool(const bool value)
uint32_t writeByte(const int8_t byte)
uint32_t writeI16(const int16_t i16)
uint32_t writeI32(const int32_t i32)
uint32_t writeI64(const int64_t i64)
uint32_t writeDouble(const double dub)
uint32_t writeString(const std::string& str)
uint32_t writeBinary(const std::string& str)

uint32_t readMessageBegin(std::string& name,
                          TMessageType& messageType,
                          int32_t& seqid)
uint32_t readMessageEnd()
uint32_t readStructBegin(std::string& name)
uint32_t readStructEnd()
uint32_t readFieldBegin(std::string& name,
                        TType& fieldType,
                        int16_t& fieldId)
uint32_t readFieldEnd()
uint32_t skip(TType type)
uint32_t readMapBegin(TType& keyType, TType& valType, uint32_t& size)
uint32_t readMapEnd()
uint32_t readListBegin(TType& elemType, uint32_t& size)
uint32_t readListEnd()
uint32_t readSetBegin(TType& elemType, uint32_t& size)
uint32_t readSetEnd()
uint32_t readBool(bool& value)
uint32_t readByte(int8_t& byte)
uint32_t readI16(int16_t& i16)
uint32_t readI32(int32_t& i32)
uint32_t readI64(int64_t& i64)
uint32_t readDouble(double& dub)
uint32_t readString(std::string& str)
uint32_t readBinary(std::string& str)

boost::shared_ptr<TTransport> getTransport()
```

As you can see, the C++ methods accept the identifiers to serialize or de-serialize as parameters and return the bytes read or written as a result. Errors are typically thrown as TProtocolExceptions, though the current code base may also throw the C++ standard library exception bad_alloc when failing to allocate internal buffers.

The only new features introduced here are TType and TMessageType. TMessageType is an enumeration defining the values from table 5.2, and TType is an enumeration declaring all the supported serialization types (T_LIST, T_I64, T_DOUBLE, and so on).

5.2.3 Java TProtocol

The Java TProtocol interface is nearly identical to the C++ interface. The most
important difference is that the Java TProtocol interface doesn't return the number
of bytes involved in the underlying I/O. Instead the write operations return nothing
and the read operations return the object read.

The TProtocol methods report the possibility of throwing TException. TProtocol-
Exceptions are generated for protocol processing issues occurring in the protocol
library, such as failure to parse the bytes for a certain type during a read. Underlying JVM
issues are usually reported as TExceptions.

The following listing shows the Java TProtocol methods.

Listing 5.5   TProtocol.java

```
public abstract class TProtocol [Java]
  public abstract void writeMessageBegin(TMessage message)
                                        throws TException;
  public abstract void writeMessageEnd() throws TException;
  public abstract void writeStructBegin(TStruct struct) throws TException;
  public abstract void writeStructEnd() throws TException;
  public abstract void writeFieldBegin(TField field) throws TException;
  public abstract void writeFieldEnd() throws TException;
  public abstract void writeFieldStop() throws TException;
  public abstract void writeMapBegin(TMap map) throws TException;
  public abstract void writeMapEnd() throws TException;
  public abstract void writeListBegin(TList list) throws TException;
  public abstract void writeListEnd() throws TException;
  public abstract void writeSetBegin(TSet set) throws TException;
  public abstract void writeSetEnd() throws TException;
  public abstract void writeBool(boolean b) throws TException;
  public abstract void writeByte(byte b) throws TException;
  public abstract void writeI16(short i16) throws TException;
  public abstract void writeI32(int i32) throws TException;
  public abstract void writeI64(long i64) throws TException;
  public abstract void writeDouble(double dub) throws TException;
  public abstract void writeString(String str) throws TException;
  public abstract void writeBinary(ByteBuffer buf) throws TException;

  public abstract TMessage readMessageBegin() throws TException;
  public abstract void readMessageEnd() throws TException;
  public abstract TStruct readStructBegin() throws TException;
  public abstract void readStructEnd() throws TException;
  public abstract TField readFieldBegin() throws TException;
  public abstract void readFieldEnd() throws TException;
  public abstract TMap readMapBegin() throws TException;
  public abstract void readMapEnd() throws TException;
  public abstract TList readListBegin() throws TException;
  public abstract void readListEnd() throws TException;
  public abstract TSet readSetBegin() throws TException;
```

```
public abstract void readSetEnd() throws TException;
public abstract boolean readBool() throws TException;
public abstract byte readByte() throws TException;
public abstract short readI16() throws TException;
public abstract int readI32() throws TException;
public abstract long readI64() throws TException;
public abstract double readDouble() throws TException;
public abstract String readString() throws TException;
public abstract ByteBuffer readBinary() throws TException;

public TTransport getTransport()
```

Note that the Java methods use Plain Old Data (POD) types for multi-element reads and writes. For example, rather than passing a name, type, and sequence ID to the `writeMessageBegin()` method, you pass a `TMessage` parameter in Java. The `TMessage` class looks like this:

```
public final class TMessage {
  public TMessage()…
  public TMessage(String n, byte t, int s) …

  public final String name;
  public final byte type;
  public final int seqid;

  public String toString()…
  public boolean equals(Object other) …
  public boolean equals(TMessage other) …
}
```

Correspondingly, the `readMessageBegin()` method returns a `TMessage` object. The other POD types defined for use with Java protocol methods are `TStruct`, `TField`, `TList`, `TMap`, and `TSet`. The Java implementation of `TProtocol` lacks a `skip()` method. However, the Apache Thrift Java protocol library has a static `skip()` implemented in the helper class `org.apache.thrift.protocol.TProtocolUtil`. Because `skip()` isn't a member of `TProtocol` you must pass it the protocol to perform the skip on. Here's the signature of the `TProtocolUtil.skip()` method:

```
public static void skip(TProtocol prot, byte type)
```

5.2.4   Python TProtocolBase

The Python `TProtocol` interface has a few minor differences from the previous examples. The most obvious is the fact that it's called `TProtocolBase` rather than `TProtocol`. In Python, class access control is always public, so you have no function to return the underlying transport; you can grab it directly through the "trans" attribute. `TProtocolBase` has several helper functions but is otherwise consistent with C++ and Java.

The following listing shows the Python TProtocolBase interface.

Listing 5.6   TProtocol.py

```
class TProtocolBase:
  def writeMessageBegin(self, name, ttype, seqid):
  def writeMessageEnd(self):
  def writeStructBegin(self, name):
  def writeStructEnd(self):
  def writeFieldBegin(self, name, ttype, fid):
  def writeFieldEnd(self):
  def writeFieldStop(self):
  def writeMapBegin(self, ktype, vtype, size):
  def writeMapEnd(self):
  def writeListBegin(self, etype, size):
  def writeListEnd(self):
  def writeSetBegin(self, etype, size):
  def writeSetEnd(self):
  def writeBool(self, bool_val):
  def writeByte(self, byte):
  def writeI16(self, i16):
  def writeI32(self, i32):
  def writeI64(self, i64):
  def writeDouble(self, dub):
  def writeString(self, str_val):
  def writeBinary(self, str_val):

  def readMessageBegin(self):
  def readMessageEnd(self):
  def readStructBegin(self):
  def readStructEnd(self):
  def readFieldBegin(self):
  def readFieldEnd(self):
  def readMapBegin(self):
  def readMapEnd(self):
  def readListBegin(self):
  def readListEnd(self):
  def readSetBegin(self):
  def readSetEnd(self):
  def readBool(self):
  def readByte(self):
  def readI16(self):
  def readI32(self):
  def readI64(self):
  def readDouble(self):
  def readString(self):
  def readBinary(self):

  def skip(self, ttype):
  trans
```

The Python TProtocolBase class trans attribute is a reference to the underlying transport stack.

5.3   Serializing objects

In the prior sections, we saw how Apache Thrift can portably read and write data using serialization protocols. Next, we'll build a few simple programs that read and write the user-defined trade type from the Transport chapter. These programs mimic the way Apache Thrift serializes types during RPC operations, giving you a good under-the-hood understanding of serialization in Apache Thrift. You'll also use these simple programs to benchmark the three Apache Thrift protocols at the end of the chapter.

The simple string serialization examples shown previously gave us a chance to look at the basic syntax associated with protocol I/O. In practice, most Apache Thrift serialization tasks involve serializing structures. For example, a Trade type might look like this in C++:

```
struct Trade {
    char symbol[16];
    double price;
    int size;
};
```

When serializing a string, the TBinaryProtocol prefixes the string with metadata, the string length. Metadata is also used to identify each field in a structure, allowing the reader to choose the fields they're interested in and skip the rest. The following example programs demonstrate the structure serialization process and how Apache Thrift uses serialization metadata.

Keep in mind that 99% of the time you won't write serialization code. Rather, you'll describe your interface in Apache Thrift IDL and the IDL compiler will automatically generate serialization code for all the types you define. These examples are here to help you understand the workings of the serialization process so that you can debug real-world problems and choose the best protocol for a given task.

5.3.1   Struct serialization

The following listing shows a C++ example that serializes a trade struct to disk.

> **Listing 5.7   ~/ThriftBook/part2/protocols/bin_file_write.cpp**

```
#include <thrift/transport/TSimpleFileTransport.h>
#include <thrift/protocol/TProtocol.h>
#include <thrift/protocol/TBinaryProtocol.h>
#include <boost/make_shared.hpp>
#include <iostream>
#include <string>


using namespace apache::thrift::transport;
using namespace apache::thrift::protocol;
using boost::make_shared;

struct Trade {
```

```
    char symbol [16];
    double price;
    int size;
};

int main()
{
    auto path_name = "data";
    auto trans = make_shared<TSimpleFileTransport>(path_name,false,true);    ❶
    auto proto = make_shared<TBinaryProtocol>(trans);          ⟵┐
                                                                ❷
    Trade trade{"F", 13.10, 2500};
    int i = 0;
    i += proto->writeStructBegin("Trade");        ❸

    i += proto->writeFieldBegin("symbol", T_STRING, 1);        ❹
❺  i += proto->writeString(std::string(trade.symbol));
    i += proto->writeFieldEnd();                      ⟵┐
                                                        ❻
    i += proto->writeFieldBegin("price", T_DOUBLE, 2);
    i += proto->writeDouble(trade.price);
    i += proto->writeFieldEnd();

    i += proto->writeFieldBegin("size", T_I32, 3);
    i += proto->writeI32(trade.size);
    i += proto->writeFieldEnd();

    i += proto->writeFieldStop();          ❼
❽  i += proto->writeStructEnd();

    std::cout << "Wrote " << i << " bytes to " << path_name << std::endl;
}
```

This example uses a TSimpleFileTransport wired to a file called "data" as the serialization endpoint ❶. After initializing the TSimpleFileTransport, all the interactions with the transport are managed by the protocol. The TBinaryProtocol is used for serialization ❷.

Not all Apache Thrift protocols require an implementation for all TProtocol methods; however, calling each of the methods in order is important for portability, allowing us to swap out protocols without modifying the calling code. The sequence of writes used to serialize a structure starts with the writeStructBegin() call, which is passed the struct name ❸. Fields are then written with the writeFieldBegin() call ❹, a write data call to write the actual value of the field ❺, and a writeFieldEnd() call to finalize the field ❻. The writeFieldBegin() call takes the name of the field, the type of the field, and the identifier for the field. The field identifier should be a unique positive value within the scope of the other fields in the struct. When we've written all the fields, the protocol requires us to call writeFieldStop() ❼ and then writeStructEnd() ❽. Each of the write calls returns the number of bytes written, which is accumulated in the integer variable "i" for this example.

While serializing a struct is more work than serializing the data alone, it provides a framework for field discovery and versioning which we'll find invaluable later.

Here's a sample session running the program:

```
$ g++ -o bin_file_write bin_file_write.cpp -Wall -std=c++11 -lthrift
$ ./bin_file_write
Wrote 27 bytes to data
$ ls -l data
-rw-r--r-- 1 randy randy 27 Feb 18 10:25 data
```

In the Transport chapter, our C++ trade struct took up a minimum of 28 bytes in memory. Even with the structure and field metadata, the Thrift TBinaryProtocol has managed to serialize our object in 27 bytes, because TBinaryProtocol only stores the characters used from our symbol field. Let's use a debugger to get a little more information about what's happening under the hood. The following session log uses the GNU debugger to examine the size of the serialized output from our program after each protocol write call:

```
$ g++ -g -o bin_file_write bin_file_write.cpp -Wall -std=c++11 -lthrift   ❶
$ gdb bin_file_write                                                       ❷
...
Reading symbols from bin_file_write...done.
(gdb) b 28                                                                 ❸
Breakpoint 1 at 0x4024dd: file bin_file_write.cpp, line 28.
(gdb) run                                                                  ❹
Starting program: /ThriftBook/part2/protocols/bin_file_write
[Thread debugging using libthread_db enabled]
Using host libthread_db library "/lib/x86_64-linux-gnu/libthread_db.so.1".
Breakpoint 1, main () at bin_file_write.cpp:28
28    i += proto->writeStructBegin("Trade");
(gdb) next                                                                 ❺
30      i += proto->writeFieldBegin("symbol ", T_STRING, 1);
(gdb) print i                                                              ❻
$1 = 0
(gdb) next                                                                 ❼
31      i += proto->writeString(std::string(trade.symbol));
(gdb) print i                                                              ❽
$2 = 3
(gdb) next                                                                 ❾
32      i += proto->writeFieldEnd();
(gdb) print i                                                              ❿
$3 = 8
(gdb) next
34        i += proto->writeFieldBegin("price ", T_DOUBLE, 2);
(gdb) print i                                                              ⓫
$4 = 8
(gdb) quit
A debugging session is active. Inferior 1 [process 20764] will be killed.
Quit anyway? (y or n) y
```

> **NOTE** If you get errors trying to run gdb within a container you may need to run the container with the `--privileged` flag.

Our first step is to rebuild the program with debugging information (we use the -g switch with G++) **❶**. Next we load the program into the gdb debugger **❷**, set a break point at line 28 **❸**, and run the program **❹**. The program stops at our break point and, at each step, gdb displays the next unexecuted line. The next command executes the previously displayed next line, and again displays the next unexecuted line **❺**. The print command allows us to display the contents of variable i, which is 0 after the call to writeStructBegin() **❻**. The TBinaryProtocol doesn't require a structure header in its serialization process, so writeStructBegin() is a nop in this particular protocol.

The next call is to writeFieldBegin() for the "symbol" field **❼**. This call emits three bytes into the stream **❽**. TBinaryProtocol uses one byte to store the type of the field and two bytes to store the field ID. As you read the debug output, keep in mind that next is displaying the next unexecuted line **❾**, so print statements show the state prior to execution of the most recent line displayed. The call to writeString() adds 5 bytes to the stream **⓫**. This is consistent with our experience; the string length prefix is 4 bytes and the string itself, "F" in this case, is 1 byte. The writeFieldEnd() call, like writeStructBegin(), adds no bytes to the stream when using TBinaryProtocol **❿**.

TBinaryProtocol doesn't write the field names ("symbol", "price", "size") to the serialization stream. The metadata for TBinaryProtocol fields includes only the field type and ID. This highlights the importance of field IDs and the relative unimportance of field names in TBinaryProtocol use. Transmission efficiency is greatly improved by using 16-bit IDs to track fields rather than arbitrarily long string names. While certainly not recommended, the binary protocol allows a serializing program to use one set of struct field names and a de-serializing program to use another set of field names, as long as the field IDs and types align.

5.3.2   *Struct de-serialization*

Now that we have our struct bytes serialized to disk and a basic understanding of how the binary protocol works, let's look at the reverse process. To demonstrate the cross-language nature of Apache Thrift, we'll build a struct reader in Java and read the data written by the C++ writer program, as shown in the following listing.

Listing 5.8   ~/ThriftBook/part2/protocols/BinFileRead.java

```
import org.apache.thrift.TException;
import org.apache.thrift.protocol.TProtocol;
import org.apache.thrift.protocol.TBinaryProtocol;
import org.apache.thrift.protocol.TField;
import org.apache.thrift.protocol.TStruct;
import org.apache.thrift.protocol.TType;
import org.apache.thrift.protocol.TProtocolUtil;
import org.apache.thrift.transport.TTransport;
import org.apache.thrift.transport.TSimpleFileTransport;

public class BinFileRead {
```

```
static private class Trade {

    public String symbol;
    public double price;
    public int size;
};

public static void main(String[] args) throws TException {
    TTransport trans = new TSimpleFileTransport("data", true, false);   ❶
    TProtocol proto = new TBinaryProtocol(trans);          ⟵┐
                                                            ❷
    Trade trade_read = new Trade();
    TField field = new TField();

    TStruct struct_obj = proto.readStructBegin();
    while(true) {
        field = proto.readFieldBegin();
        if (field.id == TType.STOP) {
            break;
        }
        switch(field.id) {
        case 1:
            trade_read.symbol = proto.readString();
            break;
        case 2:
            trade_read.price = proto.readDouble();
            break;
        case 3:
            trade_read.size = proto.readI32();
            break;
        default:
            TProtocolUtil.skip(proto,field.type);     ❹
            break;
        }
        proto.readFieldEnd();
    }
    proto.readStructEnd();

    System.out.println("Trade: " + trade_read.symbol + " " +
                        trade_read.size + " @ " + trade_read.price);
    }
}
```

❸ marks the `while(true) {` line.

The struct deserialization code in listing 5.8 begins much like the write code. We import the necessary classes and set up the transport and protocol at the top of the file, but this time the file transport is configured for reading ❶. We must always read with the same protocol used to write ❷.

The field reading process is different from the field writing process. In this simple example, it would be perfectly valid to replace every write call in the trade writer with a read call in the trade reader. However, we can simplify the read side by reading fields in a loop ❸. This does several things. First, it makes our reader ambivalent to the field order discovered in the stream. We can read field 2, then 1, then 3, or any other pattern.

Another important feature is that we can ignore fields we don't recognize. For example, imagine that the program writing these trades decides to add a timestamp as field 4. Our current reader can still read the struct, but it will skip fields it doesn't recognize ❹. The ability to extend structs and parameter lists without breaking existing code is one of the key interface evolution features provided by Apache Thrift.

The Apache Thrift IDL compiler generates serialization code for structs similarly to the previous write and read examples. One notable difference is that the IDL compiler-generated read code also makes sure that the type is as expected before de-serializing a field. In this trivial program, we assume the size field will be an int, the symbol field will be a string, and the price field will be a double.

Here's a session running the C++ writer and then the Java reader:

```
$ rm data
$ g++ -o bin_file_write bin_file_write.cpp -Wall -std=c++11 -lthrift
$ ./bin_file_write
Wrote 27 bytes to data
$ javac -cp /usr/local/lib/libthrift-1.0.0.jar BinFileRead.java
$ java -cp /usr/local/lib/libthrift-1.0.0.jar:. BinFileRead
Trade: F 2500 @ 13.1
```

The writer emits 27 bytes and the reader consumes the same 27 bytes, handily recovering our structure from the disk file.

5.3.3   *Struct evolution*

Finally, let's look at a Python version of the `trade` writer program. To make things interesting, we'll demonstrate one of the key features of interface evolution by adding a `timestamp` field to the `trade` struct in the following listing.

> **Listing 5.9   ~/ThriftBook/part2/protocols/bin_file_write.py**

```python
from thrift.transport import TTransport
from thrift.protocol import TBinaryProtocol
from thrift import Thrift

class Trade:
    def __init__(self):
        symbol=""
        price=0.0
        size=0
        timestamp=0.0          ❶

trans = TTransport.TFileObjectTransport(open("data","wb"))
proto = TBinaryProtocol.TBinaryProtocol(trans)

trade = Trade()
trade.symbol = "GE"
```

```
trade.price = 27.25
trade.size = 1700
trade.timestamp = 9.5

proto.writeStructBegin("Trade")

proto.writeFieldBegin("symbol", Thrift.TType.STRING, 1)
proto.writeString(trade.symbol)
proto.writeFieldEnd()

proto.writeFieldBegin("price", Thrift.TType.DOUBLE, 2)
proto.writeDouble(trade.price)
proto.writeFieldEnd()

proto.writeFieldBegin("size", Thrift.TType.I32, 3)
proto.writeI32(trade.size)
proto.writeFieldEnd()

proto.writeFieldBegin("timestamp", Thrift.TType.DOUBLE, 4)        ❷
proto.writeDouble(trade.timestamp)
proto.writeFieldEnd()

proto.writeFieldStop()
proto.writeStructEnd()

print("Wrote Trade: %s %d @ %f  tm: %f" %
      (trade.symbol, trade.size, trade.price, trade.timestamp))
```

With the exception of the fact that the TType enumeration is located in the Thrift.py module rather than the protocol package, as in the Java and C++ examples, the Python code is similar to both prior examples.

Note that in our Python example, we've added the timestamp double field to the trade struct serialization ❶ ❷. This won't be a problem for our Java reader because it will skip any fields it doesn't recognize. This allows us to deploy our improved Python program immediately without breaking the Java program. The Java programmers can take their time adding support for the timestamp field or ignore it altogether if it isn't important to their users. The ability to incrementally update parts of a distributed application without impacting other parts is a key requirement for tools used by teams applying continuous integration and continuous delivery.

Here's a sample run using the Python writer and the Java reader:

```
$ rm data
$ python bin_file_write.py
Wrote Trade: GE 1700 @ 27.250000  tm: 9.500000
$ java -cp /usr/local/lib/libthrift-1.0.0.jar:. BinFileRead
Trade: GE 1700 @ 27.25
$ ls -l data
-rw-r--r-- 1 randy randy 39 Jun 23 03:51 data
```

The Python writer has serialized 39 bytes of data but the Java program has no problem ignoring the unknown added field.

We used the TBinaryProtocol in all the previous examples. However, two additional, widely supported protocols are available: TCompactProtocol and TJSONProtocol. We'll look at each in the next several pages.

5.4 *TCompactProtocol*

The compact protocol is a simple and efficient protocol that trades a small amount of compute overhead for reduced data size after serialization. The amount of compression provided varies based on application data patterns, though a 20–50% size reduction is common.

> **NOTE** TCompactProtocol preserves all the information in the input stream but only outputs the bits that are in use by integers. This typically reduces the size of the resultant serialized output. The compact protocol must store additional information with the serialized data to identify the end of each serialized integer, because the actual serialized length will vary. For example, a 64-bit integer will result in a serialized object of 1–10 bytes. The worst-case scenario for the compact protocol is positive or negative integers of large size (using bits in the highest order byte will require 10 bytes of storage). The best-case scenario is small values; for example, anything between –64 and 64 will produce only one byte in the output stream.

Like all protocols, the TCompactProtocol uses the TTransport interface to write out its serialized data and exposes the TProtocol interface to its users. This makes it a snap to replace any other Apache Thrift protocol with the TCompactProtocol. The following listing shows a Java version of the trade writer using the TCompactProtocol.

Listing 5.10   ~/ThriftBook/part2/protocols/CompFileWrite.java

```java
import org.apache.thrift.TException;
import org.apache.thrift.protocol.TProtocol;
import org.apache.thrift.protocol.TCompactProtocol;
import org.apache.thrift.protocol.TField;
import org.apache.thrift.protocol.TStruct;
import org.apache.thrift.transport.TTransport;
import org.apache.thrift.transport.TSimpleFileTransport;
import org.apache.thrift.protocol.TType;

public class CompFileWrite {

    static private class Trade {
        public String symbol;
        public double price;
        public int size;
    };

    public static void main(String[] args) throws TException {
        TTransport trans = new TSimpleFileTransport("data", false, true);
        TProtocol proto = new TCompactProtocol(trans);        ◁─── ❶
```

```
            Trade trade = new Trade();
            trade.symbol = "F";
            trade.price = 13.10;
            trade.size = 2500;

            proto.writeStructBegin(new TStruct());

            proto.writeFieldBegin(new TField("symbol",
                                           TType.STRING,
                                           (short) 1));
            proto.writeString(trade.symbol);
            proto.writeFieldEnd();

            proto.writeFieldBegin(new TField("price",
                                           TType.DOUBLE,
                                           (short) 2));
            proto.writeDouble(trade.price);
            proto.writeFieldEnd();

            proto.writeFieldBegin(new TField("size",
                                           TType.I32,
                                           (short) 3));
            proto.writeI32(trade.size);
            proto.writeFieldEnd();

            proto.writeFieldStop();
            proto.writeStructEnd();

            System.out.println("Wrote trade to file");
    }
}
```

The main code body here is virtually identical to the C++ `TBinaryProtocol` writer example with one exception: we created a `TCompactProtocol` object instead of a `TBinaryProtocol` object ❶. The protocol still depends on the `TTransport` interface and still exposes the `TProtocol` interface, so neither its dependents nor dependencies are impacted by the change.

Here's a sample session that involves building and running the `TCompactProtocol` trade writer program:

```
$ rm data
$ javac -cp /usr/local/lib/libthrift-1.0.0.jar CompFileWrite.java
$ java -cp /usr/local/lib/libthrift-1.0.0.jar:. CompFileWrite
Wrote trade to file
$ ls -l data
-rw-r--r-- 1 randy randy 16 Jun 23 14:45 data
```

The `compact` protocol took our serialized `trade` image from 27 bytes, in the prior example with `TBinaryProtocol`, to 16 bytes. The compact image is less than 60% of the size of the straightforward binary image. Different data profiles will garner different results.

Thus, by coding to the abstract `TProtocol` interface we can substitute any Apache Thrift protocol. Here are examples instantiating a `compact` protocol instance in C++, Java, and Python:

- C++

```
#include <thrift/protocol/TCompactProtocol.h>
apache::thrift::protocol::TCompactProtocol proto(trans);
```

- Java

```
import org.apache.thrift.protocol.TCompactProtocol;
TProtocol proto = new TCompactProtocol(trans);
```

- Python

```
from thrift.protocol import TCompactProtocol
proto = TCompactProtocol.TCompactProtocol(trans)
```

5.5   *TJSONProtocol*

JavaScript Object Notation (JSON) is a simple text-based alternative to XML for human readable data exchange. While native to JavaScript, many languages and frameworks use JSON to exchange data. Much like the `compact` protocol example, changing our code to use JSON involves changing the protocol type constructed and little more. The following listing shows a Python `trade` writer adapted for JSON.

Listing 5.11   ~/ThriftBook/part2/protocols/json_file_write.py

```
from thrift.transport import TTransport
from thrift.protocol import TJSONProtocol
from thrift import Thrift

class Trade:
    def __init__(self):
        symbol=""
        price=0.0
        size=0

trans = TTransport.TFileObjectTransport(open("data","wb"))
proto = TJSONProtocol.TJSONProtocol(trans)              <──┐
                                                           ❶
trade = Trade()
trade.symbol = "F"
trade.price = 13.10
trade.size = 2500

proto.writeStructBegin("Trade")

proto.writeFieldBegin("symbol", Thrift.TType.STRING, 1)
proto.writeString(trade.symbol)
proto.writeFieldEnd()

proto.writeFieldBegin("price", Thrift.TType.DOUBLE, 2)
proto.writeDouble(trade.price)
proto.writeFieldEnd()
```

```
proto.writeFieldBegin("size", Thrift.TType.I32, 3)
proto.writeI32(trade.size)
proto.writeFieldEnd()

proto.writeFieldStop()
proto.writeStructEnd()

print("Wrote Trade: %s %d @ %f" % (trade.symbol, trade.size, trade.price))
```

The Python JSON protocol implementation is located in the `TJSONProtocol` module that we import at the top of the listing. With the exception of the `TJSONProtocol` instantiation ❶, the code here follows the same pattern as the previous `TBinary-Protocol` and `TCompactProtocol` examples. Here's a sample run:

```
$ rm data
$ python json_file_write.py
Wrote Trade: F 2500 @ 13.100000
$ ls -l data
-rw-r--r-- 1 randy randy 51 Jun 23 15:01 data
$ cat data
{"1":{"str":"F"},"2":{"dbl":13.1},"3":{"i32":2500}}
```

JSON is a text-based protocol, so we can display the contents of the file written. The output is easy enough to read, though the size of the generated file is the largest of these examples. Apache Thrift emits the field ordinals rather than the field names in the serialized output, saving space but making the data a little harder to interpret directly. However, the upside is that JavaScript and other JSON-enabled platforms can easily communicate with any language using the JSON protocol.

Here are the `TJSONProtocol` dependencies and construction syntax for each of our three demonstration languages:

- C++
  ```
  #include <thrift/protocol/TJSONProtocol.h>
  TJSONProtocol proto(trans);
  ```
- Java
  ```
  import org.apache.thrift.protocol.TJSONProtocol;
  TProtocol proto = new TJSONProtocol(trans);
  ```
- Python
  ```
  from thrift.protocol import TJSONProtocol
  proto = TJSONProtocol.TJSONProtocol(trans)
  ```

5.6 *Selecting a protocol*

At this point, you may wonder which protocol is the best choice for your application. The standard software development answer is: it depends. The `TBinaryProtocol` has the widest support among Apache Thrift languages, so it might make the most sense as a default choice.

The `TCompactProtocol` is simple, fairly fast, and does a good job of reducing the size of most payloads. The actual serialization code associated with `TBinaryProtocol` will typically run slightly faster than that of TCompactProtocol, however most systems are I/O-bound not compute-bound, making the smaller footprint of TCompactProtocol capable of higher throughput than TBinaryProtocol in many situations. If you're interested in performance, the best advice is to test your code in your languages on your platform under a range of real-world load profiles using the various protocols. Only then can you make a completely objective decision.

JSON encoding also has its benefits. It's the easiest format for third-party tools to parse, and Apache Thrift IDL types serialized to JSON can be represented directly in JSON-based document stores such as MongoDB. JSON also has the benefit of being easy for humans to read.

Given the ease with which protocols can be swapped in and out, there's little sense in not performing a direct comparison in cases where performance is critical. Listing 5.12 is a sample C++-based timing test built around our trivial struct serialization process. While this is the most generic of examples, it may help you develop intuition about protocol and transport interaction. The program allows you to select a transport, optional buffering layer, and a protocol. It then proceeds to write 1,000,000 Trade structs through the protocol, reporting write size and timing at the end of the process.

Listing 5.12   ~/ThriftBook/part2/protocols/proto_write_times.cpp

```cpp
#include <iostream>
#include <string>
#include <chrono>
#include <memory>
#include <boost/shared_ptr.hpp>
#include <thrift/transport/TSimpleFileTransport.h>
#include <thrift/transport/TBufferTransports.h>
#include <thrift/protocol/TCompactProtocol.h>
#include <thrift/protocol/TBinaryProtocol.h>
#include <thrift/protocol/TJSONProtocol.h>

using namespace apache::thrift::transport;
using namespace apache::thrift::protocol;

struct Trade {
    char symbol[16];
    double price;
    int size;
};

int main(int argc, char *argv[]) {
    std::string usage("usage: " + std::string(argv[0]) +
        " (m[emory]|f[ile]) (b[inary]|c[ompact]|j[son]) [b[uffering]]");
    if (argc != 3 && argc != 4) {
        std::cout << usage << std::endl;
        return -1;
    }

    boost::shared_ptr<TTransport> trans;                    ❶
```

```
if (argv[1][0] == 'm' || argv[1][0] == 'M') {
    const int mem_size = 64*1024*1024;
    trans.reset(new TMemoryBuffer(mem_size));
    std::cout << "TMemoryBuffer(" << mem_size << ")/";
}
else if (argv[1][0] == 'f' || argv[1][0] == 'F') {
    const std::string path_name("/tmp/thrift_data");
    trans.reset(new TSimpleFileTransport(path_name, false, true));
    std::cout << "TSimpleFileTransport(" << path_name << ")/";
}
else {
    std::cout << usage << std::endl;
    return -1;
}

if (argc == 4 && (argv[3][0] == 'b' || argv[3][0] == 'B')) {    ❷
    std::cout << "TBufferedTransport/";
    trans.reset(new TBufferedTransport(trans));
}
else if (argc == 4) {
    std::cout << usage << std::endl;
    return -1;
}

std::unique_ptr<TProtocol> proto;    ❸
if (argv[2][0] == 'b' || argv[2][0] == 'B') {
    std::cout << "TBinaryProtocol" << std::endl;
    proto.reset(new TBinaryProtocol(trans));
}
else if (argv[2][0] == 'c' || argv[2][0] == 'C') {
    std::cout << "TCompactProtocol" << std::endl;
    proto.reset(new TCompactProtocol(trans));
}
else if (argv[2][0] == 'j' || argv[2][0] == 'J') {
    std::cout << "TJSONProtocol" << std::endl;
    proto.reset(new TJSONProtocol(trans));
}
else {
    std::cout << usage << std::endl;
    return -1;
}

Trade trade;
trade.symbol[0] = 'F'; trade.symbol[1] = '\0';
trade.price = 13.10;
trade.size = 2500;

auto start = std::chrono::steady_clock::now();    ❹
int i = 0;
for (int loop_count = 0; loop_count < 1000000; ++loop_count) {
    i += proto->writeStructBegin("Trade");

    i += proto->writeFieldBegin("symbol", T_STRING, 1);
    i += proto->writeString(std::string(trade.symbol));
```

```
            i += proto->writeFieldEnd();

            i += proto->writeFieldBegin("price", T_DOUBLE, 2);
            i += proto->writeDouble(trade.price);
            i += proto->writeFieldEnd();

            i += proto->writeFieldBegin("size", T_I32, 3);
            i += proto->writeI32(trade.size);
            i += proto->writeFieldEnd();

            i += proto->writeFieldStop();
            i += proto->writeStructEnd();
            proto->getTransport()->flush();          ❺
        }
    auto stop = std::chrono::steady_clock::now();          ❻
    std::cout << "Bytes: " << i << ", seconds: "
              << std::chrono::duration<double>(stop - start).count()
              << std::endl;
}
```

Pointers to the abstract bases `TTransport` ❶ and `TProtocol` ❸ are used throughout the code, allowing us to select the type of transport and protocol at runtime. The user sets the transport and protocol via the command line.

A buffering transport layer can be added optionally ❷. This will have little effect on the memory transport, but it will make a big difference in the performance of the disk-based transport. The buffering layer will aggregate the many small data writes made by the protocol and, when `flush` is called ❺, write a single larger block to disk. This will improve disk-based write performance on most platforms by reducing the number of system calls by an order of magnitude.

The C++ chrono library is used to perform the timing. The `steady_clock::now()` method returns a time point in the specified clock ❹. Fine-grained timing has many subtle issues. Clocks have a range of precision and can be unsteady (jumping around as they're synched with outside sources). Even though the code asks for a steady clock, the system may not support such a thing. The std::chrono library can be queried for precision and steady clock data ❻. If you're interested in digging deeper, see *The C++ Standard Library: A Tutorial and Reference, 2nd Edition* (Josuttis, 2012), or check the web for std::chrono references.

Each struct write is flushed to the endpoint ❺. If we were serializing large numbers of structs to disk, flushing each struct individually might not be optimal. However, if we're performing RPC message exchanges with other systems, this would be mandatory. The `flush` call has no effect on the raw endpoint transports (it's a nop); however, the buffered transport writes its buffer to the endpoint in response to the call. The buffered transport and `flush` call effectively turn the 12 protocol writes required to serialize the struct into a single underlying endpoint transport write.

```
Listing 5.13   part2/protocols/ts.sh
```

```
#!/bin/sh
./proto_write_times
./proto_write_times m b
./proto_write_times m c
./proto_write_times m j
rm /tmp/thrift_data
./proto_write_times f b
rm /tmp/thrift_data
./proto_write_times f b b
rm /tmp/thrift_data
./proto_write_times f c
rm /tmp/thrift_data
./proto_write_times f c b
rm /tmp/thrift_data
./proto_write_times f j
rm /tmp/thrift_data
./proto_write_times f j b
```

Here's the output from a run of the ts.sh shell script (listing 5.13) that tests each of the combinations of transport and protocol, deleting the temporary file prior to each file transport run for consistency:

```
$ g++ -std=c++11 proto_write_times.cpp -lthrift
$ source ts.sh
usage: ./proto_write_times (m[emory]|f[ile]) (b[inary]|c[ompact]|j[son])
➥ [b[uffering]]
TMemoryBuffer(67108864)/TBinaryProtocol
Bytes: 27000000, seconds: 0.643162
TMemoryBuffer(67108864)/TCompactProtocol
Bytes: 16000000, seconds: 0.704852
TMemoryBuffer(67108864)/TJSONProtocol
Bytes: 51000000, seconds: 2.91436
rm: cannot remove `/tmp/thrift_data': No such file or directory
TSimpleFileTransport(/tmp/thrift_data)/TBinaryProtocol
Bytes: 27000000, seconds: 12.4693
TSimpleFileTransport(/tmp/thrift_data)/TBufferedTransport/TBinaryProtocol
Bytes: 27000000, seconds: 2.14986
TSimpleFileTransport(/tmp/thrift_data)/TCompactProtocol
Bytes: 16000000, seconds: 9.60298
TSimpleFileTransport(/tmp/thrift_data)/TBufferedTransport/TCompactProtocol
Bytes: 16000000, seconds: 2.08301
TSimpleFileTransport(/tmp/thrift_data)/TJSONProtocol
Bytes: 51000000, seconds: 52.9839
TSimpleFileTransport(/tmp/thrift_data)/TBufferedTransport/TJSONProtocol
Bytes: 51000000, seconds: 5.42823
```

When I/O bound (writing to disk with TSimpleFileTransport), the compact protocol is noticably faster than the binary protocol because we're storing 40% fewer bytes, reducing the run time by about 25% unbuffered and a few percent when buffered. For memory operations (using the TMemoryBuffer transport) the binary protocol is marginally faster than the compact protocol. In this case the reduced size doesn't make up for the computational overhead necessary to compact the serialized objects. JSON has advantages associated with human readability and a high degree of interoperability, but it isn't a competitor in the performance or size departments.

Performance over sockets adds many variables, for example, client and server system load, languages used, flush() patterns, network and counterparty latency, among others factors. If performance is a concern, testing the actual system under consideration will give you the most pragmatic insight.

Summary

Apache Thrift protocols serialize application data into a standard format readable by any Apache Thrift language library supporting that protocol. The combination of transports and protocols creates a plug-in style architecture making Apache Thrift an extensible platform for data serialization, supporting a choice of protocols and the possible addition of new serialization protocols over time.

- Apache Thrift protocols provide cross-language serialization.
- The TProtocol interface provides the abstract interface for all Apache Thrift serialization formats.
- Protocols depend on the transport layer TTransport interface to read and write serialized bytes.
- One serialization protocol can be substituted for another with little or no impact on upper layers of software.
- The TProtocol interface defines the Apache Thrift type system exposed through Apache Thrift IDL.
- Protocols support the serialization of
  - *RPC messages*
  - *Structs*
  - *Collections*—List, set, and map
  - *Base types*—Ints, doubles, strings, and so on
- Apache Thrift supplies three main protocols:
  - *Binary*—The default protocol, supported by the most languages, is fast and efficient.
  - *Compact*—Trades CPU overhead for reduced serialization size.
  - *JSON*—A text-based, widely interoperable, human-readable protocol with higher CPU overhead and relatively large serialization size.

Apache Thrift IDL

In this chapter, we'll examine the features of the Apache Thrift Interface Definition Language (IDL) and learn how to use the Apache Thrift compiler to generate cross-language type serialization and RPC support code (see figure 6.1). We'll begin by exploring the syntax of the IDL itself and then cover compiler operation, trying out various bits of IDL along the way.

6.1 Interfaces

Interfaces exist in hardware and software, defining interactions between components running on a single system as well as components interoperating across networks. The power of abstraction delivered by interfaces is one of the most basic and critical tools in computer science for managing complexity.

Most developers design and use interfaces daily. In object-oriented programming, each class created has its own interface, allowing state and other implementation

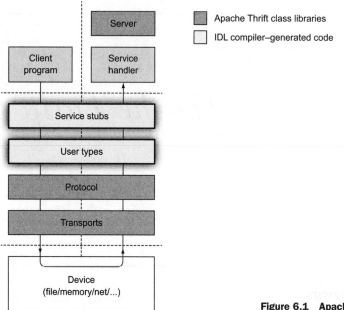

Figure 6.1   Apache Thrift IDL

details to be encapsulated. When clients are isolated from implementation details, as long as the interface is preserved, object internals can change as needed. The implementation can even be moved to another computer if the client has a local proxy for the remote object that supports the same interface.

The Apache Thrift framework is entirely focused on enabling programmers to design and construct cross-language, distributed computing interfaces. Interfaces consist of two principle parts:

- *User-defined types (UDTs)*—The things exchanged between systems
- *Services*—Sets of methods exposing cohesive functionality

Interface Definition Languages are designed to allow programmers to define interface contracts in an abstract fashion, independent of any programming language or system platform. IDL contracts ensure that all parties communicating over an interface know exactly what will be exchanged and how to exchange it. This allows tools to do the busy work of generating code to interoperate over the interface. IDLs allow developers to focus on the problem domain, not the mechanics of remote procedure calls or cross-language serialization.

NOTE It has been suggested that modern interaction styles, such as REST, and extensible encoding schemes, such as JSON and XML, obviate the need to explicitly describe interfaces. This is a mistake. For a client and a server to have a meaningful interaction, schema and semantics must be in place. IDLs provide an explicit and concise language with which to describe mechanical interface contracts. The interface semantics not explicit in the IDL can be addressed in IDL doc strings. Whether exchanges are based on IDLs or verbs, URIs, and media types, undocumented interfaces leave contracts unclear and defined only in the code using them, making systems hard to maintain and easy to break.

Mechanical and semantic contract elements

Most IDL contracts ensure mechanical interoperability but can only imply part of the full interface semantics. For example, consider the following interface used to record sailboat race times:

```
service BoatRaceTimes {
    i16 BeginRace(1: i32 CourseID, 2: map<i32,i32> BoatsAndTeams),
    void ReportFinish(1: i16 RaceNumber, 2: i32 Boat, 3: bool DNF=false),
}
```

Syntactically this interface can ensure that a 32-bit `CourseID` is supplied when `BeginRace` is called. However, it cannot ensure that the course ID is a positive number less than 100,000, or that the `ReportFinish()` method is called for each boat represented in the `BoatsAndTeams` map of the `BeginRace()` call.

Interfaces should include documentation declaring the mechanical and semantic aspects of the interface contract that aren't explicit in the IDL. For example, the `BoatRaceTimes` interface might carry the following documentation in comment form:

`/** BeginRace` method returns a race number and registers the `BoatIDs` of the boats beginning the race in the key component of the `BoatsAndTeams` map. Each `BoatID` supplied to `BeginRace` should be reported by the `ReportFinish()` method for a given `RaceNumber. */`

Note that interface documentation should be devoid of implementation details, describing only the contractual semantics. Nowhere do we suggest how boat IDs are stored, cached, or linked to other elements. This is important because implementations are typically volatile and multiple implementations of a single interface contract may exist.

Semantics should be made explicit in the interface syntax when possible. This minimizes the need for documentation and allows the compiler to enforce the semantics. Descriptive names and wise use of types and type definitions contribute greatly to highly explicit interfaces. For example, if a timing function for a boat race accepts a collection of boats to time, but the list must contain no boat more than once, the interface should prefer a declaration such as `set<i32> boats` over `list<i32> boats`. The `set` container type makes the unique requirement explicit. Great interfaces are hard to use incorrectly.

Often decisions around interface semantics represent many hours of careful consideration, yet these decisions are easily lost over time or as interfaces propagate through an organization if not documented. An experienced programmer should be able to build a working service with nothing more for guidance than a well-documented IDL.

IDL best practices

- Represent as much of the interface contract explicitly in IDL as possible.
- Clearly document semantics that cannot be made explicit in IDL.

Keep interfaces abstract and free of implementation details.

User-defined types and services are the principal components of Apache Thrift IDL interfaces. To get a better feel for interface definition in Apache Thrift IDL, let's look at a sample IDL in the following listing that defines a trade reporting interface for the hypothetical "Pacific Northwest Fish Market."

Listing 6.1   ~/ThriftBook/part2/IDL/fish_trade.thrift

```
/** Apache Thrift IDL definition for the Fish Market TradeHistory service
 */

namespace * FishTrade

enum Market {
    Unknown      = 0
    Portland     = 1
    Seattle      = 2
    SanFrancisco = 3
    Vancouver    = 4
    Anchorage    = 5
}

typedef double USD

struct TimeStamp {
    1: i16  year
    2: i16  month
    3: i16  day
    4: i16  hour
    5: i16  minute
    6: i16  second
    7: optional i32 micros
}

union FishSizeUnit {
    1: i32  pounds
    2: i32  kilograms
    3: i16  standard_crates
    4: double  metric_tons
}

struct Trade {
    1: string       fish                    //The symbol for the fish traded
    2: USD          price                   //Price per size unit
    3: FishSizeUnit amount                  //Amount traded
    4: TimeStamp    date_time               //Date/time trade occured
    5: Market       market=Market.Unknown//Market where trade occured
}

exception BadFish {
    1: string       fish       //The problem fish
    2: i16          error_code //The service specific error code
}
```

```
exception BadFishes {
    1: map<string, i16>  fish_errors //The problem fish:error pairs
}


service TradeHistory {
    /**
     * Return most recent trade report for a fish type
     *
     * @param fish the symbol for the fish traded
     * @return the most recent trade report for the fish
     * @throws BadFish if fish has no trade history or is invalid
     */
    Trade GetLastSale(1: string fish)
        throws (1: BadFish bf)


    /**
     * Return most recent trade report for multiple fish types
     *
     * @param fish the symbols for the fish to return trades for
     * @param fail_fast if set true the first invalid fish symbol is thrown
     *                 as a BadFish exception, if set false all of the bad
     *                 fish symbols are thrown using the BadFishes
     *                 exception. If no bad fish are passed this parameter
     *                 is ignored.
     * @return list of trades cooresponding to the fish supplied, the list
     *         returned need not be in the same order as the input set and
     *         a given input fish type may have multiple trades in the
     *         output list due to simultanious transactions
     * @throws BadFish first fish discovered to be invalid or without a
     *                 trade history (only occurs if fail_fast=true)
     * @throws BadFishes all fish discovered to be invalid or without a
     *                 trade history (only occurs if fail_fast=false)
     */
    list<Trade> GetLastSaleList(1: set<string> fish
                                2: bool fail_fast=false)
        throws (1: BadFish bf  2: BadFishes bfs)
}
```

This sample IDL illustrates many of the common features of the Apache Thrift IDL. We'll refer to this IDL listing as we progress through the IDL features in the pages ahead.

The focus of this IDL file is the definition of the TradeHistory service. The Trade-History service has two functions, GetLastSale() and GetLastSaleList(). These two functions aren't complete without the rest of the definitions in the file. For example, both functions use the trade struct that has several attributes, including a Time-Stamp struct and a Market enumeration. Each of these user-defined elements must be defined before use.

Thrift IDL looks like C++ language source with a few differences. Two, in particular, stand out. One is the lack of an element separator in enum, struct, union, exception, and function field/parameter lists. Apache Thrift allows comma or semi-colon element terminators, but they aren't required. All three of the following declarations are equivalent:

```
struct Date1 {1: i16 year   2: i16 month  3: i16  day}
struct Date2 {1: i16 year,  2: i16 month, 3: i16  day,}
struct Date3 {1: i16 year;  2: i16 month; 3: i16  day;}
```

The first of the previous examples, using whitespace separators, is preferred by many.

The second key difference is the numeric IDs assigned to each field and parameter. These numeric field IDs are particularly important; we'll take a deeper look at them shortly.

The Apache Thrift IDL compiler reads IDL files and outputs code in one or more languages to support serializing the types and calling the service functions defined in the IDL. The compiler-generated code uses Apache Thrift protocols and transports. The user can supply any protocol or transport, enabling a choice of serialization schemes and transport endpoints. Apache Thrift servers can be implemented in a few lines of code with the help of the Apache Thrift libraries and IDL compiler output.

6.2   *Apache Thrift IDL*

Learning a particular IDL is similar to learning the declarative part of a normal programming language. Familiarity with the features of the language allows you to write the most direct and expressive code. To make sure that you have the tools necessary to code highly effective Apache Thrift interfaces, we'll take a brief IDL tour using the fish_trade.thrift listing as a guide.

> **NOTE**   Many editors offer syntax highlighting and auto-completion features. Such features can help coders avoid syntax errors and speed the coding process. Apache Thrift IDL is a language, and syntax highlighting extensions have been built for it. The ItelliJ Thrift add-on is particularly good (https://plugins .jetbrains.com/plugin/7331). Eclipse has a plugin (http://thrift4eclipse .sourceforge.net/en/index.html), as does Vim (https://github.com/apache/ thrift/blob/master/contrib/thrift.vim), GEdit (https://github.com/Randy-Abernethy/ThriftBook/blob/master/tools/thrift.lang), and other editors. If your favorite editor doesn't have Apache Thrift IDL support, extensions are often easy (and instructive!) to create.

6.2.1   *IDL file names*

The example IDL file in listing 6.1 is named fish_trade.thrift. Apache Thrift IDL files are given a ".thrift" extension by convention. While this extension isn't strictly required in all scenarios, some tools require it.

Apache Thrift IDL file names, up to but not including the ".thrift" extension, are used in the generation of identifiers in certain languages. For example, if your Thrift IDL file is named "abc%def.thrift" and you declare a constant, the Thrift compiler will generate a constant class named "abc%defConstants" in C++. This isn't a legal identifier in most languages and causes a compiler error in C++. An important takeaway here is that successful

IDL code generation doesn't imply compliable/linkable/interpretable code. While the IDL compiler tries to ensure that generated code is always buildable, problems can arise, and they're usually related to poorly named or conflicting identifiers created by the user.

BEST PRACTICE Always use alphanumeric IDL file names and always use the ".thrift" file name extension.

6.2.2 *Element names*

All of the interface elements defined in the fish_trade.thrift IDL file are given names. Services, structs, unions, enumerations, fields, parameters, exceptions, and all other interface elements must have a name. All top-level IDL element names must be unique, regardless of type. For example, it's an error to create a service with the name "abc" and a struct with the name "abc". Fields, methods, and other attribute elements must have names that are unique within their containing element. For example, two separate services can each have methods named "abc", but the method "abc" may only appear once in a service.

In the example IDL file in listing 6.1, the enumeration at the top of the file is named Market, the first field of the "Trade" struct is named fish, the first exception type defined is named BadFish, and the first method of the TradeHistory service is named GetLastSale. Thrift IDL is case-sensitive; thus "abc" and "ABC" are different names. Names must begin with a letter or an underscore and can be followed by any sequence of letters, numbers, underscores, or periods. The lexer pattern for Thrift IDL names looks like this:

```
[a-zA-Z_][\.a-zA-Z_0-9]*
```

Apache Thrift IDL keywords and reserved words may not be used as element names.

6.2.3 *Keywords*

Thrift IDL has 30 active keywords, as shown in table 6.1. These character sequences cannot be used as element names and each has specific meaning to the Thrift IDL compiler.

Table 6.1 Apache Thrift IDL keywords

Keyword	Description
binary	Base type supporting an array of bytes.
bool	Base type for Boolean (Thrift: true/false).
const	Constant modifier used to declare interface constants.
cpp_include	Adds a #include line for the given literal in C++ output.
cpp_type	Allows the container implementation type to be selected in C++.
double	Base type for double-precision floating-point values (typically 8 bytes).

Table 6.1   Apache Thrift IDL keywords *(continued)*

Keyword	Description
enum	Enumeration type.
exception	Exception type (like `struct`s but returned in error scenarios).
extends	Used to designate interface inheritance.
false	False value for `bool` types.
i8	Base type for 8-bit signed integers.
i16	Base type for 16-bit signed integers.
i32	Base type for 32-bit signed integers.
i64	Base type for 64-bit signed integers.
include	Used to include definitions from another IDL file during processing of this file.
List	Container type housing zero or more elements of <elementType>.
Map	Container type housing zero or more pairs of <keyType, valueType>.
Namespace	Defines language-specific namespaces and similar code organization directives.
Oneway	Modifier designating a service method that doesn't return.
Optional	Field modifier designating members that need not be supplied.
Required	Field modifier designating members that must be supplied.
Service	Keyword used to declare an RPC interface.
Set	Container type housing a unique `set` of <elementType>.
String	Base type for sequence of characters.
Struct	Keyword used to declare a packaged set of fields as a user-defined type.
Throws	Clause used to declare the exception types thrown by a service method.
True	The `Boolean` true value for `bool`.
Typedef	Keyword enabling aliases to be assigned to type names.
Union	Keyword used to declare a packaged set of fields where only one is valid at a time.
Void	Base type for "empty." Allowed only as the return type for a service method.

DEPRECATED KEYWORDS

Table 6.2 shows an additional 20 keywords that are now deprecated. Most of these represent the old way to specify a namespace for a particular language target. The keywords beginning with xsd were used internally at Facebook and are no longer maintained by Apache Thrift. Several of these keywords were still operable at the time of this writing but they shouldn't be used in new code as keywords or identifiers.

Table 6.2 Deprecated keywords

Keyword	Description
async	Deprecated (changed to `oneway`)
byte	Superseded by i8
cocoa_prefix	Deprecated
cpp_namespace	Deprecated
csharp_namespace	Deprecated
delphi_namespace	Deprecated
java_package	Deprecated
perl_package	Deprecated
php_namespace	Deprecated
py_module	Deprecated
ruby_namespace	Deprecated
senum	Deprecated
smalltalk_category	Deprecated
slist	Deprecated
smalltalk_prefix	Deprecated
xsd_all	Deprecated
xsd_attrs	Deprecated
xsd_namespace	Deprecated
xsd_nillable	Deprecated
xsd_optional	Deprecated

RESERVED WORDS

The following lexically sorted list of symbols aren't part of Thrift IDL syntax but may not be used in Thrift IDL for various reasons, many of which are related to output language conflicts:

```
BEGIN, END, __CLASS__, __DIR__, __FILE__, __FUNCTION__, __LINE__, __METHOD__,
__NAMESPACE__, abstract, alias, and, args, as, assert, begin, break, case,
catch, class, clone, continue, declare, def, default, del, delete, do,
dynamic, elif, else, elseif, elsif, end, enddeclare, endfor, endforeach,
endif, endswitch, endwhile, ensure, except, exec, finally, float, for,
foreach, from, function, global, goto, if, implements, import, in, inline,
instanceof, interface, is, lambda, module, native, new, next, nil, not, or,
package, pass, print, private, protected, public, raise, redo, rescue, retry,
register, return, self, sizeof, static, super, switch, synchronized, then,
this, throw, transient, try, undef, unless, unsigned, until, use, var,
virtual, volatile, when, while, with, xor, yield
```

6.3   *The IDL compiler*

The Apache Thrift IDL compiler is an executable program that reads IDL files and generates code in one or more target languages to support the constructs described in the IDL (services, types, and so on). The IDL compiler operates in phases, each of which can generate errors when problems are encountered.

6.3.1   *Compilation phases and error messages*

The IDL compiler generates application-specific code from an IDL file in three phases. In phase one, the IDL is scanned for tokens, such as keywords, names, operators, and the like. In phase two, the tokens are parsed into program element vectors using grammar rules; for example, a "{" character must be followed by a matching "}" character. In phase three, the language generator converts the element vectors into language-specific code (see figure 6.2).

The element vectors include lists of all the typedefs defined, all the constants defined, all the structs defined, and so on. Bad IDL will generate compiler errors

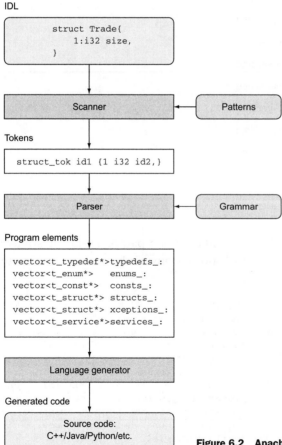

Figure 6.2   Apache Thrift IDL compiler compilation phases

originating from the compilation phase that discovers the problem. Understanding the basic nature of these three phases may help you to identify the source of problems during compilation failure.

The Apache Thrift IDL compiler is called thrift (thrift.exe on Windows) and is invoked with the IDL file to compile and with switches indicating one or more output languages to generate code for. Here is an example compilation of the `fish_trade` `.thrift` IDL:

```
$ thrift -v -gen cpp -gen java -gen py fish_trade.thrift              ❶
Scanning /home/randy/thriftbook/test/fish_trade.thrift for includes   ❷
Parsing /home/randy/thriftbook/test/fish_trade.thrift for types       ❸
Program: /home/randy/thriftbook/test/fish_trade.thrift                ❹
Generating "cpp"            ❺
Generating "java"
Generating "py"
```

The -v compiler switch causes the compiler to emit verbose logging information ❶. IDL files can include other IDL files, so the compiler begins by scanning for any included IDL files that need to be parsed in addition to the current file (this is separate and distinct from the scanning process which turns the file text into tokens) ❷.

The parser runs the lexical scanner first (SCANNER PHASE), to turn the file text into tokens, and then builds a set of program element vectors (PARSER PHASE) representing the types and services defined within the IDL (this line therefore logs the scanning and parsing phases) ❸.

The next line signals the beginning of the LANGUAGE GENERATOR PHASE ❹. Each -gen switch on the command line emits a log line for the output language before the compiler runs the code generator for that language ❺.

In the SCANNER PHASE, the Thrift compiler uses a Lex-based scanner (generated with GNU Flex by default) to break IDL into atomic elements called tokens. Tokens come in the form of Apache Thrift IDL keywords, literal values, element names, sets of braces, and the like. Because the scanner code used in the Apache Thrift compiler is generated from a generic Lex-style patterns file, the error messages from this phase are fairly generic. Any reports of the following types come from the scanner:

- Token too large
- Cannot use reserved language keyword: *xxxx*
- This integer is too big: *xxxx*
- Unexpected token in input: *xxxx*
- Input in flex scanner failed
- Out of dynamic memory in yy *xxxx*
- End of file while read string at *xxxx*
- Bad escape character
- Fatal flex scanner internal error—no action found
- Input buffer overflow; can't enlarge buffer because scanner uses REJECT

Such errors are usually indicative of typos, bad characters in the file, and other basic syntax issues.

The PARSER PHASE of the Thrift compilation process parses the tokens using grammar rules defined in a Yacc (Yet Another Compiler Compiler) rules file. The parser code in the Apache Thrift compiler is typically generated by Bison (the GNU Yacc clone). The Yacc grammar rules file allows bad grammar to be flagged with custom error messages so errors generated by the parser may be more informative than those from the lexical scanner. Example parser errors include

- Syntax error, unexpected xxxx, expecting xxxx.
- Warning: "ruby_namespace" is deprecated. Use "namespace rb" instead.
- Warning: Negative value supplied for enum xxxx.
- Warning: 64-bit constant xxxx may not work in all languages.
- Error: Service xxxx has not been defined.
- Error: Throws clause may not contain non-exception types.
- Error: Implicit field keys are deprecated and not allowed with -strict.
- Error: xxxx - field identifier/name has already been used.

The error reports generated by the parser involve syntax that can be scanned into legal tokens but that violates IDL grammar rules. As the examples show, the messages associated with rule violation are usually easy to interpret. The parser doesn't know anything about the output languages and will make no comment regarding suitability beyond generic IDL grammar conformance.

The third phase of IDL compilation, the LANGUAGE GENERATER PHASE, involves generating output code from the internal element vectors produced by the scanner and parser. Each language specified receives the same read-only copy of the program elements to work from. At this point the compile should succeed unless something fairly nasty occurs, such as running out of memory. If the IDL was scanned against the legal patterns and parsed against the legal grammar, it should be possible for the language generator to create code to implement the IDL.

6.3.2 Command line switches

The IDL compiler has several command line switches, the most important of which is the -gen switch that is used to specify output languages. Command line switches can be prefixed with one or two hyphens. Table 6.3 contains a list of the top-level command-line switches supported by the Apache Thrift IDL compiler.

Table 6.3 Apache Thrift IDL compiler command-line switches

Switch name	Description
-allow-neg-keys	Enables negative field IDs (strongly discouraged).
-allow-64bit-consts	Do not warn when encountering 64-bit constants.
-audit oldFile	Specifies an "old" IDL file to use for output comparison.

Table 6.3   Apache Thrift IDL compiler command-line switches *(continued)*

Switch name	Description
-audit-nofatal	Causes thrift to return 0 even if the audit fails.
-debug	Builds code with debug messages directed at stdout.
-gen lang	Specifies a language to generate code for; lang may be any one of the supported output languages.
-help	Displays the command line help message.
-I path	Includes path when searching for included IDL.
-Iold path	Defines an include path for the old audit IDL file.
-Inew path	Defines an include path for the new audit IDL file.
-nowarn	Suppress compiler warnings.
-o path	Specifies the path to use for code output (creates gen-* folders within).
-out path	Specifies the path to use for code output (does not create gen-* folders).
-r or -recurse	Generates code for included IDL files (see Including External Files).
-strict	Strict mode; full compiler warnings.
-v or -verbose	Verbose mode.
-version	Displays compiler version number.

LANGUAGE GENERATORS

The -gen switch specifies which output languages to generate code for. Table 6.4 shows the language options supported.

Table 6.4   Supported output languages flags

Language option	Description
as3	ActionScript 3
c_glib	C-dependent on GNU glib library (a portable object-oriented framework for C)
cl	Common Lisp
Cocoa	Cocoa (Apple's native object-oriented API for OS X and iOS directly supporting Objective-C and other languages)
Cpp	C++
Csharp	C#
D	D
Dart	Dart
Delphi	Delphi

Table 6.4 Supported output languages flags *(continued)*

Language option	Description
Erl	Erlang
Go	Go (golang)
Gv	Graphviz (generates a visual model of the input IDL)
Haxe	Haxe
hs	Haskell
html	HTML (generates documentation for the input IDL)
java	Java
javame	Java Micro Edition
js	Java Script
json	JSON (generates a JSON version of the IDL)
lua	Lua
netcore	C# for .net core
ocaml	OCaml
perl	Perl
php	PHP
py	Python 2.x with old style classes (class A)
rb	Ruby
rs	Rust
st	Smalltalk
swift	Swift
xml	XML (generates an XML version of the IDL)

The most basic compiler examples involve compiling an IDL file and outputting code in a single language. For example, if we want to compile our `fish_trade.thrift` from listing 6.1 and create output for Graphviz, we could use a command like this:

```
$ thrift -gen gv fish_trade.thrift        ❶
$ ls -l
drwxr-xr-x 2 randy randy 4096 Jun  2 20:11 gen-gv        ❷
$ ls -l gen-gv
-rw-r--r-- 1 randy randy 1482 Jun  2 21:19 fish_trade.gv        ❸
```

The -gen switch specifies the output language, in this case "gv" for Graphviz ❶.

By default, all output code is placed in a directory with the name "gen-*lang*", where lang is replaced with the language abbreviation ❷.

The IDL compiler output is the fish_trade.gv code file in the previous example ❸. Typical compiler output files take the form of source code generated for a particular programming language. However, in this example we asked the compiler to produce a graphical model of our IDL definitions in Graphviz format. Graphviz is an open source graph visualization program available for Windows, Mac, Linux, Solaris, and other platforms (www.graphviz.org). Loading our generated .gv file into GVEdit produces the image in figure 6.3.

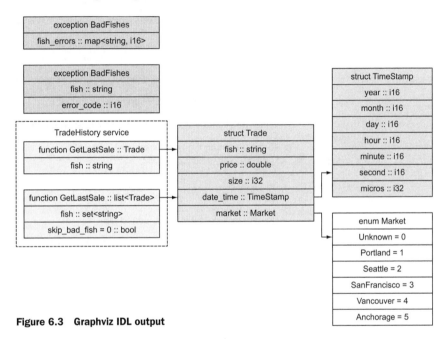

Figure 6.3   Graphviz IDL output

LANGUAGE GENERATOR OPTIONS

Many of the language generators have additional options that can be invoked as follows:

```
thrift -gen gv:exceptions fish_trade.thrift
```

In this case, gv is the language followed by a colon and exceptions is the option flag. This option changes the output graphic so that service methods show connections to the exceptions they throw.

Several options can be listed, separated by commas. For example

```
thrift  -gen php:inlined,server  myservice.thrift
```

Options can also have values, for example

```
thrift  -gen py:dynbase=MyBaseClass  myservice.thrift
```

Table 6.5 shows the language-specific options supported by the current version of Apache Thrift.

Table 6.5 Language-specific IDL compiler options

Option	Description
as3	
bindable	Add [bindable] metadata to all the struct classes.
Cocoa	
async_clients	Generate clients which invoke asynchronously via block syntax.
debug_descriptions	Allow use of debugDescription so the app can add description via a category/extension.
log_unexpected	Log every time an unexpected field ID or type is encountered.
pods	Generate imports in Cocopods framework format.
promise_kit	Generate clients which invoke asynchronously via promises.
validate_required	Throw exception if any required field isn't set.
C++	
cob_style	Generate "Continuation OBject"-style classes.
include_prefix	Use full include paths in generated files.
moveable_types	Generate move constructors and assignment operators.
no_client_completion	Omit calls to completion__() in CobClient class.
no_default_operators	Omit generation of default operators (==, !=, and <).
no_ostream_operators	Omit generation of ostream definitions.
pure_enums	Generate pure enums instead of wrapper classes.
templates	Generate templatized reader/writer methods.
C#	
async	Adds async support using Task.Run.
hashcode	Generate a hashcode and equals implementation for classes.
nullable	Use nullable types for optional properties.
serial	Add serialization support to generated classes.
union	Use new union typing, which includes a static read function for union types.
Wcf	Adds bindings for WCF to generated classes.
Dart	
library_name	Optional override for library name.

Table 6.5   Language-specific IDL compiler options *(continued)*

Option	Description
library_prefix	Generate code that can be used within an existing library. Use a dot-separated string (that is, my_parent_lib.src.gen).
pubspec_lib	Optional override for thrift lib dependency in pubspec.yaml (that is, thrift: 0.x.x). Use a pipe delimiter to separate lines (that is, \thrift:| git:| url: git@foo.com).
Delphi	
ansistr_binary	Use AnsiString for binary properties.
constprefix	Name TConstants classes after IDL to reduce ambiguities.
events	Enable and use processing events in the generated code.
register_types	Enable TypeRegistry; allows for creation of struct, union, and container instances by interface or TypeInfo().
xmldoc	Enable XMLDoc comments for Help Insight, and so on.
Erl	
legacynames	Output files retain naming conventions of Thrift 0.9.1 and earlier.
maps	Generate maps instead of dicts.
otp16	Generate non-namespaced dict and set instead of dict:dict and sets:set.
Go	
ignore_initialisms	Disable automatic spelling correction of initialisms (that is, "URL").
legacy_context	Use legacy x/net/context instead of context in go<1.7.
package=	Package name (default: inferred from Thrift file name).
package_prefix=	Package prefix for generated files.
read_write_private	Make read/write methods private; default is public read/write.
thrift_import=	Override Thrift package import path.
Gv	
buildmacro=my.macros.Class.method(args)	Add @:build macro calls to generated classes and interfaces.
callbacks	Use onError()/onSuccess() callbacks for service methods (such as AS3).
exceptions	Draw arrows from methods to exceptions.
rtti	Enable @:rtti for generated classes and interfaces.

Table 6.5   Language-specific IDL compiler options *(continued)*

Option	Description
HTML	
noescape	Don't escape HTML in doc text.
standalone	Self-contained mode (CSS embedded in HTML).
Java	
android	Generated structures are parcelable.
android_legacy	Don't use `java.io.IOException` (throwable).
beans	Members will be private, and setter methods will return `void`.
fullcamel	Convert underscored_accessor_or_service_names to camelCase.
generated_annotations= [undated|suppress]	undated: suppress the date at @Generatedannotations; suppress: suppress @Generated annotations entirely.
handle_runtime_exceptions	Send `TApplicationException` to the client when `RuntimeException` occurs on the server. (Default behavior is to close the connection instead.)
hashcode	Generate `hashcode` methods.
java5	Generate Java 1.5-compliant code (includes `android_legacy` flag).
nocamel	Do not use camelCase field accessors with beans.
option_type	Wrap optional fields in an `Option` type.
private-members	Members will be private; setter methods return "this" as usual.
reuse-objects	Data objects will not be allocated, but existing instances will be used (read and write).
sorted_containers	Use `TreeSet/TreeMap` instead of `HashSet/HashMap` as implementation for `set/map`.
JS	
jquery	Generate jQuery-compatible code.
node	Generate node.js-compatible code.
ts	Generate TypeScript definition files.
with_ns	Create global namespace objects when using node.js.
JSON	
merge	Generate output with included files merged.
Lua	
omit_requires	Suppress generation of requiring "somefile".

Table 6.5 Language-specific IDL compiler options *(continued)*

Option	Description
Netcore	
hashcode	Generate a hashcode and equals implementation for classes.
nullable	Use nullable types for properties.
serial	Add serialization support to generated classes.
union	Use new union typing, which includes a static read function for union types.
wcf	Adds bindings for WCF to generated classes.
PHP	
inlined	Generate PHP inlined files.
json	Generate JsonSerializable classes (requires PHP >= 5.4).
nsglobal=NAME	Set `global` namespace.
psr4	Generate each PHP class in a separate file (allows PSR4 autoloading).
oop	Generate PHP with object-oriented subclasses.
rest	Generate PHP REST processors.
server	Generate PHP server stubs.
validate	Generate PHP validator methods.
Py	
coding=CODING	Add file encoding declare in generated file.
dynamic	Generate dynamic code; less code generated but slower.
dynbase=CLS	Derive generated classes from class `CLS` instead of `TBase`.
dynexc=CLS	Derive generated exceptions from `CLS` instead of `TExceptionBase`.
dynfrozen=CL S	Derive generated immutable classes from class `CLS` instead of `TFrozenBase`.
dynimport='from foo.bar import CLS' no_utf8strings	Add import line to code; typically used to find `dynbase` class.
old_style	Do not encode/decode strings using utf8 in the [Deprecated]. Generate `old-style` classes.
package_prefix='top.package.'	`Package` prefix for generated files.
slots	Generate code using `slots` for instance members.

Table 6.5   Language-specific IDL compiler options *(continued)*

Option	Description
`tornado`	Generate code for use with the Tornado async web-framework-generated code (https://github.com/tornadoweb/tornado). Basically no effect for Python 3.
`twisted`	Generate Twisted-friendly RPC services.
Rb	
`namespaced`	Generate files in idiomatic namespaced directories.
`rubygems`	Add a "require 'rubygems'" line to the top of each generated file.
Swift	
`async_clients`	Generate clients that invoke asynchronously via `block` syntax.
`debug_descriptions`	Allow use of `debugDescription` so the app can add description via a category/extension.
`log_unexpected`	Log every time an unexpected field ID or type is encountered.
`promise_kit`	Generate clients that invoke asynchronously via promises.
XML	
`merge`	Generate output with included files merged.
`no_default_ns`	Omit default `xmlns` and add `idl:` prefix to all elements.
`no_namespaces`	Do not add namespace definitions to the XML model.

Covering each of these language-specific options in detail is outside the scope of this book. That said, many of the most important options are demonstrated within the part 3 chapters covering the language in question. As new languages are added and as the languages supported mature, new switches are often added to the IDL compiler. Use the "thrift –help" command to see the latest.

6.4   *Comments and documentation*

Apache Thrift IDL supports an assortment of commenting conventions. Often, important aspects of an interface cannot be described in IDL syntax. For example, "never pass 0 to the SetDivisor() method". The addition of appropriate comments can make semantic elements of an interface clear, allowing the interface to be fully described, mechanically and semantically, within the Apache Thrift IDL source.

Apache Thrift supports the following comment styles:

- /* multiline comment */
- /** multiline doc string comment */
- // rest of line comment
- # rest of line comment

Many tools can pick up doc string comments for automatic documentation generation. The Apache Thrift IDL compiler includes an HTML generator that creates an HTML file set capturing IDL elements and their doc strings (see figure 6.4). To generate HTML documentation for the fish_trade.thrift IDL file use the following command:

```
$ thrift -gen html fish_trade.thrift
```

This will create a gen-html subdirectory with HTML output files including each of the IDL elements and any associated doc strings.

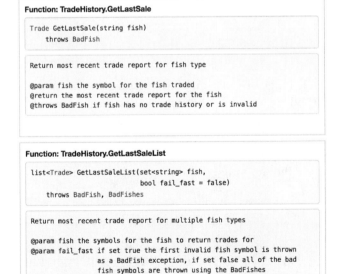

Figure 6.4　IDL
compiler HTML output

6.5   *Namespaces*

The IDL compiler places IDL-defined services and types into the global scope by default in most languages. This leaves the identifiers for these elements open to name collisions with other globally-scoped objects. Namespaces are named scopes within which identifiers can be declared independent of global and other scopes. Apache Thrift IDL supports namespaces across a variety of languages.

Placing Apache Thrift IDL definitions within a namespace is a good practice. Defining a namespace within an IDL file causes the IDL compiler to generate all the IDL elements within the namespace scope in the specified language, exporting only the namespace name into the output language's global scope.

Here are several namespace examples:

```
namespace cpp FishTrade
namespace java FishTrade
namespace py FishTrade
```

The namespace keyword is followed by a "namespace-scope" and a namespace name. The scope defines the generated language to apply the namespace to. This allows developers to specify different namespace names for different languages. For example, this is a C++ namespace directive:

```
namespace cpp FishTrade
```

It will generate the following compiler output in C++:

```
namespace FishTrade {
        . . .
}
```

Target languages use a wide range of syntax and file structures to represent namespace scopes. For example, Java and Python have the concept of a package, represented on disk as a subdirectory. When generating namespaces for Java and Python, the Apache Thrift compiler creates a subdirectory with the namespace name for all the IDL elements. The list of supported namespace scopes expands as new languages and features are added to the IDL compiler. These are the supported namespace scopes as of this writing:

```
*, as3, c_glib, cocoa, cpp, csharp, d, dart, delphi, erl, go, haxe, java, js,
lua, netcore, perl, php, php.path, py, py.twisted, rb, rs, smalltalk.prefix,
smalltalk.category, xml
```

The "*" namespace scope is particularly useful. Using the * applies the namespace identifier to all generated languages capable of implementing a namespace. This is the approach taken in our sample fish_trade.thrift IDL listing:

```
namespace * FishTrade
```

The namespace keywords must appear before any IDL definitions in the IDL source. Subsequent namespace definitions mask prior namespace definitions. This feature can be useful if you want all languages to use FishTrade except C++. For example

```
namespace * FishTrade
namespace cpp FishTrade1
```

This IDL places code for all languages within the FishTrade namespace, with the exception of C++, which will use the FishTrade1 namespace.

Providing a namespace with the "*" scope is a best practice. Consistency and avoiding global scope pollution are both desirable software traits.

6.6   Built-in types

Most of the Apache Thrift IDL keywords are used to define the type of an element. Apache Thrift IDL types can be broken up into three categories: base types, containers, and user-defined types (UDTs).

6.6.1   Base types

The base types in Thrift IDL supply a minimal but broadly useful set of built-in types commonly found in nearly all programming languages, shown in table 6.6.

Table 6.6   Apache Thrift IDL base types

Keyword	Description
binary	Base type supporting an array of bytes
bool	Base type for Boolean (Thrift: true/false)
double	Base type for double-precision floating point (8 bytes)
i8	Base type for 8-bit integers (the "byte" keyword was used for this type in older versions)
i16	Base type for 16-bit integers
i32	Base type for 32-bit integers
i64	Base type for 64-bit integers
string	Base type for sequence of characters
void	Base type allowed only as the return type for a service method

These types are all self-explanatory; however, there are a few points worth mentioning.

The first thing you may note is that Apache Thrift IDL defines only signed integers, available in 1, 2, 4, and 8-byte sizes (i8, i16, i32, i64, respectively). When using unsigned values in your programs you need to take care that they don't overrun the capacity of the signed ints used by Apache Thrift.

String and binary types in Apache Thrift are closely related. The string type is defined as a sequence of characters in IDL, and the binary type is defined as a sequence of bytes. The primary difference between the two arises in the language-specific representation of each. For example, Java uses `java.nio.ByteBuffer` for IDL binary and `java.lang.String` for IDL string. Wire representations are defined by the protocol used. On the wire, strings are serialized as a sequence of UTF-8 characters when using the Binary, Compact, or JSON protocols. Languages based on the JVM or .Net platforms will have to convert back and forth from their native UTF-16 character types.

The `bool` type has two possible values represented by the IDL keywords "true" and "false". Certain target languages may represent IDL `true` and `false` constants as 1 and 0, while others may have their own `True` and `False` keywords.

The double type is the only floating point type. It's treated as an IEEE-754 formatted 8-byte floating point. Apache Thrift has no equivalent to the defined precision "DECIMAL" or "NUMERIC" types found in languages like SQL or the 4-byte float type found in many languages.

The void type expresses the absence of type/value. The void type is special in that it can only define the return type of a function, indicating that a function returns no value. Normal functions of the void type still generate reply messages when they complete and may throw exceptions.

6.6.2 *Container types*

Apache Thrift IDL supports three container types, as seen in table 6.7.

Table 6.7 Apache Thrift IDL container types

Keyword	Description
List<>	Container type housing zero or more <elementType>
Map<,>	Container type housing zero or more pairs of <keyType, valueType>
Set<>	Container type housing a unique collection of zero or more <elementType>

Containers are common in most languages today and offer prebuilt data structures for a specific contained type. The Apache Thrift IDL adopts the angle bracket syntax used by C++ templates and Java Generics to distinguish the container from the type contained (such as `set<double>`). Here are container examples from our fish_trade .thrift IDL file:

```
exception BadFishes {
    1: map<string, i16>  fish_errors          ❶
}

...

list<Trade> ❷ GetLastSaleList(1: set<string> fish              ❸
                        2: bool skip_bad_fish=false)
```

The first example, `fish_errors` ❶, is a mapping container with string keys and 16-bit integer values. Maps cannot contain duplicate keys. The `fish_errors` definition would cause the IDL compiler's C++ generator to emit a `std::map<std::string, int16_t>` to represent the element in C++. The Java language generator would emit a Hash-Map<>, the Python and Ruby generators would emit `Dictionaries`, the PHP generator would emit an associative array, and so on. Map containers are ordered in certain languages (such as `std::map<>` in C++), but not in others (such as HashMap<> in Java). Best practice: don't depend on ordering in IDL map and set containers.

The second container example is the list returned by the `GetLastSaleList` function ❷. Lists are ordered and can contain duplicates. The example list container will generate a `std::vector<Trade>` type in C++, an ArrayList<Trade> in Java, and a dynamic array in scripting languages.

The third example container, `fish` ❸, is a set of strings. Sets cannot contain duplicates. This set example would emit a `std::set<std::string>` in C++, a HashSet<> in Java, a set in Python, a `dictionary` in PHP/Ruby, and so on. Like maps, sets aren't always ordered depending on the language, and should therefore be considered unordered.

Containers may house any valid Thrift type, including other containers and structs. Certain languages cannot support complex map keys. For this reason, it's often best to use a base type for map keys unless you have a strong motivation to do otherwise.

CUSTOM C++ CONTAINERS

The C++ generator allows you to change the C++ implementation types used to represent Apache Thrift IDL containers. For example, C++98 did not have a hash table implementation of the map type until Technical Report 1, wherein the hash map was called `std::tr1::unordered_map<>`. C++11 provides `std::unordered_map<>`. The hash table implementation is typically faster than `std::map`'s binary tree implementation. By using the Apache Thrift IDL "cpp_type" directive you can change the C++ container implementation type used for any particular IDL object, giving you the ability to use the faster `unordered_map` type when desirable. The following code demonstrates generating IDL for the default C++ map<> type:

```
exception BadFishes {
    1: map<string, i16>  fish_errors          ❶
}

$ thrift -gen cpp fish_trade.thrift

>>  std::map<std::string, int16_t>  fish_errors;          ❷
```

Here's a modified version of the same IDL that generates a C++ unordered map:

```
cpp_include "<unordered_map>"          ❶

exception BadFishes {
```

```
    1: map cpp_type "std::unordered_map<string, int16_t>" <string, i16>
       fish_errors                          ←─┐
}                                             ❷
```

```
$ thrift -gen cpp fish_trade.thrift
```

```
>>   #include <unordered_map>
>>   ...
>>   std::unordered_map<string, int16_t> fish_errors;     ❸
```

In the first example, a standard IDL map type is defined ❶, causing the IDL compiler to emit a standard C++ map implementation ❷.

The second example IDL is modified in two places. The first line causes the C++ generator to add an `include` statement for the `unordered_map` header ❶. The second modification uses the `cpp_type` keyword to set a new implementation type for the container ❷. The C++ generator uses the type requested when emitting C++ code for the map ❸.

This feature allows programmers to choose the best implementation for the task involved. For example, given three maps in your IDL, you could make the first an `unordered_map`, let the second use the default, and use a custom map type for the third. The `cpp_type` IDL modifier is ignored by other language generators.

Defining custom container types can create dependencies in your code unforeseen by the IDL compiler, such as the dependence on the `unordered_map` header in the previous listing. The `cpp_include` keyword allows you to include the necessary headers in your generated C++ code. This feature is also ignored by other language generators. See the "Including external files" section later in this chapter for more `cpp_include` details.

SORTED JAVA CONTAINERS

Java also offers a special container implementation feature through the `sorted _containers` IDL compiler switch:

```
$ thrift -gen java fish_trade.thrift
```

```
>>   fish_errors = new HashMap<String,Short>();     ❶
```

```
--------------------------------------------------------
```

```
$ thrift -gen java:sorted_containers fish_trade.thrift     ❷
```

```
>>   fish_errors = new TreeMap<String,Short>();     ❸
```

When the `sorted_containers` switch is enabled ❷, the Apache Thrift IDL elements set and map are implemented with `TreeSet<>` and `TreeMap<>` ❸, respectively, rather than `HashSet<>` and `HashMap<>` ❶. The hash implementations are unordered, whereas the tree implementations order the elements in the container by key in the case of maps and by value in the case of sets.

Note that the C++ approach to container customization is per object and the Java approach is global for a particular IDL compilation. It's unfortunate that these features are implemented inconsistently, one with a command line switch and fixed type substitution and the other with IDL keywords. It's likely that a future iteration of the Apache Thrift IDL will clean this up, standardizing language-specific type implementations using IDL annotations.

6.6.3   *Literals*

Apache Thrift supports interface constants and default values for base and container types. Literals are required to represent these constant and default values. The following listing shows IDL code demonstrating the various literal value representations for the various Apache Thrift IDL types.

```
Listing 6.2   ~/ThriftBook/part2/IDL/literals.thrift

const bool b0 = 0//same as false           ❶
const bool b1 = 1//same as true
const bool b2 = false
const bool b3 = true

const i8 i1 = 42            ❷
const i16 i2 = -42
const i32 i3 = +42
const i64 i4 = 0x4f//Hex (lower case x only)
const i64 i5 = 0x4F
const i64 i6 = 042//Decimal 42(!), no octal support
const i32 i7 = i6//A const can be initialized with another const

const double d1 = 123.456          ❸
const double d2 = -123.456
const double d3 = 123.456e6
const double d4 = -123.456E-6 //Expressions (e.g. 4.5/7.2) not supported
const double d5 = +123.456e+6

const string s1 = "hello"          ❹
const string s2 = 'hello'
const string s3 = "\"Thrift\\hello\tworld\'\r\n" //6 escape sequences
const binary s4 = 'hello world\n'  //Binaries are initialized like strings

❺ const list<i16> lc = [ 42, 24, 42 ]
const set<i32> sc = [ 42, 24, 42 ]//Duplicates not detected by IDL Compiler
const map<i16,string> mc = { 42:"hello", 24:"world" }
```

Boolean values can be initialized with the keywords `true` or `false` ❶. Boolean values can also be initialized with any integer literal. The C programming language and others have made 0 and 1 traditional representations of `false` and `true` respectively. Be advised that any positive value will be represented as `true`, and 0 or a negative value will be represented as `false` in Apache Thrift IDL. This will certainly surprise C programmers (such as -34 == `false` !!!).

BEST PRACTICE   Use the explicit "true" and "false" literals when initializing IDL Booleans.

Integer literals can be in decimal form (such as 42), prefixed with a + or -, or represented as a hexadecimal value prefixed with "0x" (such as 0xFF42) ❷. Octal constants aren't supported, and the value "042" will be interpreted as 42-decimal. The last integer example shows that a const can be initialized with an existing const. In the example i7, a 32-bit integer, is initialized with i6, a 64-bit integer. While this could cause an overflow, the IDL compiler will not warn you. Even an obvious overflow, such as const i8 b = 999, will not generate a warning. Best practice is to ensure constants and defaults use literals of the appropriate size. Most language compilers will complain when encountering such overflows, but the Apache Thrift IDL compiler will happily generate code with overflows.

Floating point literals can be represented in decimal form or using scientific notation with + or − signs allowed before the coefficient and/or exponent ❸. Fractional exponents aren't allowed.

String and binary literals are collected within single (') or double (") quotes ❹. The backslash (\) is reserved as an escape character. There are six possible escape sequences:

- \\—A backslash
- \'—A single quote
- \"—A double quote
- \t—A tab
- \r—A carriage return
- \n—A line feed

Container literals are also possible ❺. Lists and sets are collected between square brackets and maps are collected between curly braces. Container elements are provided sequentially separated by commas. Map elements are provided in pairs with the key and value components separated by a colon (such as { key1 : value1, key2 : value2 }). Note that while set and map containers don't support duplicate keys, the IDL compiler makes no checks for duplicates. The code generated will initialize the language container implementation with the literal values exactly as listed. In certain implementations, this will cause an old key to be replaced with the new key and in others it will generate a compile or runtime error. Best practice is to ensure set literals don't have duplicate elements and that map literals don't have duplicate keys.

6.7   *Constants*

As listing 6.2 illustrates, Apache Thrift IDL allows you to declare interface constants. Keep in mind that everything defined within an IDL file should represent an element integral to the contract between clients and servers. If a constant is an important part of the interface contract, then it belongs in IDL. This will give it a representation in all the generated output languages and make it accessible within the IDL itself. Constants that are associated with an implementation don't belong in IDL.

The following listing shows a trivial IDL file with a single constant definition.

Listing 6.3   ~/ThriftBook/part2/IDL/const.thrift

```
const i32 MAX_TRADE_SIZE = 100000
```

The IDL file in listing 6.3 creates a 32-bit integer constant called `MAX_TRADE_SIZE` and sets it to the value `100,000`. To compile this IDL file for our three demonstration languages we could do the following:

```
$ ls -1
total 4
-rw-r--r-- 1 randy randy 33 Feb 24 20:46 const.thrift
$ cat const.thrift
const i32 MAX_TRADE_SIZE = 100000
$ thrift -gen cpp -gen py -gen java const.thrift
$ ls -1
-rw-r--r-- 1 randy randy   33 Feb 24 20:46 const.thrift
drwxr-xr-x 2 randy randy 4096 Feb 24 20:48 gen-cpp
drwxr-xr-x 2 randy randy 4096 Feb 24 20:48 gen-java
drwxr-xr-x 3 randy randy 4096 Feb 24 20:48 gen-py
```

The previous session generates language-specific code for our constant in C++, Java, and Python. Let's examine each in turn.

6.7.1   C++ interface constant implementation

Basic IDL compilation targeting C++ always emits a pair of files for constants: the constant .h header and .cpp source file. The source IDL is named const.thrift, which causes the output files to be named "const_constants.xxx":

```
$ ls -1 gen-cpp
-rw-r--r-- 1 randy randy 282 Feb 24 20:48 const_constants.cpp
-rw-r--r-- 1 randy randy 363 Feb 24 20:48 const_constants.h
-rw-r--r-- 1 randy randy 193 Feb 24 20:48 const_types.cpp
-rw-r--r-- 1 randy randy 350 Feb 24 20:48 const_types.h
```

Listings 6.4 and 6.5 show the generated C++ constants files.

Listing 6.4   const_constants.h

```
#ifndef const_CONSTANTS_H
#define const_CONSTANTS_H

#include "const_types.h"

class constConstants {
```

```
  public:
   constConstants();
   int32_t MAX_TRADE_SIZE;
};

extern const constConstants g_const_constants;

#endif
```

Listing 6.5   const_constants.cpp

```
#include "const_constants.h"

const constConstants g_const_constants;

constConstants::constConstants() {
  MAX_TRADE_SIZE = 100000;
}
```

In the C++ context, a Thrift IDL constant is implemented as a member of a class with a single global instance g_XXX_constants (where XXX is the name of the IDL file). Any C++ source may use this global by including the header and linking against the compiled image of the XXX_constants.cpp. The C++ source file (const_constants.cpp in this case) initializes the constant values.

6.7.2   *Java interface constant implementation*

The Thrift compiler generates a single Java file for our const.thrift IDL. In Java, IDL constants are represented as static final attributes within the XXXConstants class, where XXX is the name of the IDL file, as shown in the following listing.

Listing 6.6   constConstants.java

```
...
public class constConstants {

  public static final int MAX_TRADE_SIZE = 100000;
}
```

6.7.3   *Python interface constant implementation*

The Python output for the const.thrift IDL emits a Python package directory structure with a constants.py module. The constant ends up in the constants.py file defined directly at the top level of the file, as shown in the following listing.

Listing 6.7   constants.py

```
...
MAX_TRADE_SIZE = 100000
```

The diverse implementations illustrated here give insight into the range of syntax and sensibilities associated with different programming languages. This also highlights the value of cross-language tools like Apache Thrift and the complexity of cross-language interoperability.

6.8 Typedefs

Using custom type names when defining interfaces can add clarity to the IDL and help make it more self-describing. For example, if we use a map container throughout an IDL file for fish lookups, creating a map type named FISH_MAP might not only be more readable, but it might also help us to use consistent key and value types throughout a long IDL file.

The following listing demonstrates the use of the typedef keyword.

Listing 6.8 ~/ThriftBook/part2/IDL/typedef.thrift

```
typedef double USD
typedef i16 SHORT
typedef i32 INT
typedef i32 LONG
typedef map<i16, string> FISH_MAP
typedef FISH_MAP FISH_LOOKUP

const SHORT shrt = 89
const FISH_MAP fm = { 1:"Halibut", 2:"Salmon" }
```

This example IDL defines several new type names. The syntax for a typedef involves listing the source type followed by the new type name. typedef type names can be used to define other types, as exemplified in the FISH_LOOKUP typedef, where FISH_LOOKUP is defined as FISH_MAP type, which, in turn, is defined as map<i16,string>.

Once defined, user-defined type names can be used anywhere a normal Apache Thrift IDL type can be used. The previous example creates two constants, shrt and fm, using typedef type names SHORT and FISH_MAP.

The C++ code generator produces C++ typedef statements matching those in the IDL. These typedefs are emitted in the XXX_types.h header. Other language generators tend to replace the IDL-defined type names with the underlying language types when generating code.

6.9 Enum

Like typedef, the enum keyword allows you to create a new IDL type. Apache Thrift IDL enums provide a convenient way to represent a constant set of discrete values. IDL enum types are frequently, but not always, represented as enums in generated code. For example, C++ represents IDL enums as C++ language enums in generated code; however Python uses a class for enums, Ruby uses a module, PHP uses a class, and Haskell creates a new "data" type for enums.

IDL elements such as method parameters, struct fields, and constants, can be declared of enum type. Here's an example enum in Apache Thrift IDL:

```
enum WestCoast {          ❶
    CA = 1      ❷
    OR = 2
    WA = 3
}

const WestCoast PRIMARY_FISH_HATCHERY = WestCoast.OR        ❸
const WestCoast SECONDARY_FISH_HATCHERY = 3        ❹
```

In this example, the new enum type WestCoast is defined ❶ to include three possible values: CA, OR, and WA ❷. Elements of the WestCoast type should never hold any other value than those listed in the IDL. This covenant can be violated in generated code if the target language doesn't provide the proper assurances. For example, certain languages may allow a WestCoast type object to be assigned a value of 42. Passing a West-Coast object over RPC with an out-of-range value can cause undefined behavior.

In the previous example, two enum constants are defined. PRIMARY_FISH_HATCHERY is set to the value 2 using the enumeration constant WestCoast.OR ❸. The constant SECONDARY_FISH_HATCHERY is set to the value 3 ❹, synonymous with the enumeration constant WestCoast.WA. The Apache Thrift IDL compiler generates an error if an out-of-range value is assigned to an enum type object within an IDL file.

BEST PRACTICE   Use the enumeration form for initializing values, because it's more readable and sidesteps an entire class of possible errors.

Enumeration constant values can be declared explicitly, as in the previous example where CA is set to 1, OR is set to 2, and WA is set to 3. Explicit values can be supplied in any order. If explicit values aren't supplied, the IDL compiler will assign an integer value automatically. For example, the following IDL will generate values for CA, OR, and WA of 0, 1, and 2, respectively:

```
enum WestCoast {
    CA
    OR
    WA
}
```

It isn't good practice to mix automatic and explicit value assignments. The IDL compiler simply increments the prior enumeration value when assigning an automatic value. For example, the following IDL will give both CA and WA the value 2:

```
enum WestCoast {
    CA = 2
    OR = 1//Sets the IDL Compiler's internal counter to 1
    WA//IDL Compiler assigns the value 2 (1++)
}
```

Enum constants should be non-negative integers. The IDL compiler will produce a warning if negative enumeration values are encountered, though most language generators will use them.

> **BEST PRACTICE** Explicitly assign positive values to enumeration constants. This avoids compatibility problems associated with changing value generation across compiler or IDL source file versions, among other problems.

6.10 *Structures, unions, exceptions, and argument-lists*

Structures, unions, exceptions, and argument-lists all allow a set of elements to be collected together into an affinity group. Services contain a set of functions. Each function has an argument-list composed of a set of fields. Structs, unions, and exceptions also contain a set of fields. Internally the Apache Thrift IDL compiler uses the same data structure to represent sets of fields in structs, unions, exceptions, and argument-lists.

The following listing shows example declarations of a struct, union, exception, and argument-list. Notice the similarities.

Listing 6.9 Compound types

```
struct stTimeStamp {
    1: i16   year
    2: i16   month
    3: i16   day
}
union unTimeStamp {
    1: i16   year
    2: i16   month
    3: i16   day
}
exception exTimeStamp {
    1: i16   year
    2: i16   month
    3: i16   day
}
service svTimeStamp {
    void fnTimeStamp (1: i16   year
                      2: i16   month
                      3: i16   day)
}
```

Fields may be of any valid type, including base types, structs, unions, exceptions, and containers. Each of the groups of fields in listing 6.9 are compiled into language-specific classes with `read()` and `write()` methods. The `read()` method reads an instance of the struct, union, exception, or argument-list. The `write()` method writes the struct, union, exception, or argument-list. The read and write operations take a protocol as the argument to read from or write to.

6.10.1 *Structs*

Structs are perhaps the simplest of the field grouping types and the principle way users build IDL-based UDTs. Structs provide a convenient way to collect a set of related fields together into a single manageable program element:

```
struct TimeStamp {
    1: i16   year
    2: i16   month
    3: i16   day
}
```

Each struct defined in IDL creates a type and must be given a name. In the previous example IDL, the struct type declared is named `TimeStamp`. All the interesting aspects of a struct are described by the fields it contains. Fields are discussed in the next topic. The next chapter describes building serialization applications with UDTs in detail.

6.10.2 *Fields*

Most of the details associated with fields are universal to structs, unions, exceptions, and argument-lists. Fields are described here using structs in the examples, but the principals apply to unions, exceptions, and argument-lists unless otherwise noted.

Field lists take the following form:

```
[id:] [requiredness] type FieldName [=default] [,|;]
...
```

Each field has a type, a name, and an identifier (ID). Fields may not use undefined or partially defined types. For example, struct "A" may not contain a field of type "A". IDL types other than services don't support inheritance and cannot be organized into type hierarchies.

> **NOTE** At the time of this writing, an experimental initiative designed to enable self-referential types in Apache Thrift IDL is in progress. For example, a struct type named "Node" could have attributes of "Node &" (Node reference) type. This makes it possible to create DAGs (Directed Acyclic Graphs), such as trees and singly linked lists. This feature is only implemented in C++ at the time of this writing and isn't heavily tested.

IDs

Field IDs, occasionally called keys, are 16-bit integers that can be explicit or implicit. The Thrift framework uses the field ID to uniquely identify fields in many situations. For example, when calling an RPC function, arguments can be passed in any order. The receiving side will use the field IDs to match the parameters passed with the correct arguments.

Explicit field IDs must be positive integers. In the `TimeStamp` example struct in listing 6.9, the field IDs are 1, 2, and 3. It's almost always advantageous to define field IDs explicitly. Implicit field identifiers are assigned by the IDL compiler when explicit IDs aren't provided. Implicit IDs are negative (beginning at -1 and decrementing). Changing the order of fields in a struct without explicit IDs will almost always break compatibility with existing code because the implicit IDs generated for the new order will likely be different from the previous implicit IDs. For example, given struct {i16 a, i16 b} the IDL compiler will generate IDs -1 and -2 for a and b, respectively. However, given struct {i16 b, i16 a}, the IDL compiler will generate IDs -2 and -1 for a and b, respectively.

The IDL compiler provides the -allow-neg-keys switch to allow negative IDs to be assigned explicitly. This should only be used to solve interoperability problems with existing Apache Thrift systems reliant on predefined negative IDs.

REQUIREDNESS

Each field has a requiredness attribute that defines how Apache Thrift reads and writes the field. Fields can be given one of three requiredness values: required, default, and optional. However, a fourth possibility arises when a program discovers a field it doesn't know in a serialized struct, referred to here as 'undefined'. Struct readers ignore these undefined fields.

Three possible requiredness scenarios exist for a program writing an IDL struct (required, default, and optional), and four possible requiredness scenarios can be encountered by a program reading fields from a serialized struct (the prior three plus undefined fields). Table 6.8 displays the set of requiredness possibilities.

Table 6.8 Field requiredness

Field requiredness	Write behavior	Read behavior
Required	Always written	Must be read or error
<default>	Always written	Read if present
Optional	Written if set .	Read if present
<undefined>	N/A	Ignored

Consider the following struct:

```
struct Trade {
    1: required string      fish     ❶
❷  2:            double      price
    3: optional i32          size     ❸
}
```

This simple struct illustrates all of the possible IDL requiredness values. The first field is marked required ❶. The second field has no requiredness designation, making it default requiredness ❷. The third field has the optional designation ❸. Table 6.8 also has a fourth row, listing <undefined> requiredness. Undefined requiredness refers to the scenario where a reader discovers a field it doesn't have a definition for. For example, imagine you're working with the above IDL and while reading a trade struct you discover a fourth field called `time_stamp`. This field isn't defined in your version of IDL (perhaps the data was sent by an application with a new extended version of the `trade` struct). Undefined fields not represented in the reader's version of the struct IDL are ignored.

The first field, `fish`, is required ❶. This field will always be written when the struct is serialized and must also be read when the struct is being de-serialized. If the struct `read()` method fails to find a `required` field when reading the structure, a `TProtocolException` will be raised. Take care when defining `required` fields, because they're the least flexible of the requiredness types. For example, when you remove or add a `required` field, every program communicating that struct must be updated to avoid raising exceptions.

It's worth noting that many languages use an `isset` struct internally to track whether fields have been set or not. However, `required` fields in C++ and other implementations don't have the added overhead of the `isset` mechanism. Being `required` fields, they are implicitly always set. The `isset` Boolean flags typically consume 4 bytes in C++ implementations, adding 4 bytes of memory consumption per field to `default` and `optional` requiredness fields. The size of the struct on the wire is unchanged, so this is only a concern for the program's in-memory footprint in extreme cases.

The second field, `price`, uses `default` requiredness ❷. The `price` field will always be written but need not be found during read operations. This makes it possible for struct definitions to evolve incrementally over time.

For example, imagine two systems, one in a Portland Market and the other in a Seattle Market, which communicate using Apache Thrift RPC. Assume that the team working in Portland needs to add a `TimeStamp` field to the previous `trade` struct. This can be done without burdening the Seattle team with the change. If the `TimeStamp` is given `default` requiredness, it will always be transmitted by the Portland system and it will always be read if present by the Portland system. This allows the Portland system to make use of the new `TimeStamp` field immediately. On the other hand, when the Portland Market transmits the `trade` struct to the Seattle system, Seattle will ignore the `TimeStamp` field, which in the Seattle IDL is undefined. When the Seattle system transmits a `trade` struct to the Portland System without the `TimeStamp` field, Portland will tolerate the absence of the `TimeStamp` field because it isn't required.

The third field in the previous `trade` struct is optional ❸. Optional fields are only written if they've been set. The IDL compiler generates "setter" methods for `optional` fields in most languages. You should set `optional` fields through the setter method to enable the set flag, which tells the Apache Thrift platform to serialize the value. Certain languages implement the setter behavior implicitly when the field is assigned a value, but you should check the code generated for your language to be sure.

For the optional `size` field in the previous `trade` struct, C++ would generate the following set method:

```
void __set_size(const int32_t val) {
    size = val;
    __isset.size = true;
}
```

The Java language generator provides a full collection of methods to manipulate fields. The following code shows the Java code associated with the optional size field:

```
public int getSize() {
  return this.size;
}

public Trade setSize(int size) {
  this.size = size;
  setSizeIsSet(true);
  return this;
}


public void setSizeIsSet(boolean value) {
  __isset_bitfield = EncodingUtils.setBit(__isset_bitfield,
                                    __SIZE_ISSET_ID, value);
}

public void unsetSize() {
  __isset_bitfield = EncodingUtils.clearBit(__isset_bitfield,
                                    __SIZE_ISSET_ID);
}

public boolean isSetSize() {
  return EncodingUtils.testBit(__isset_bitfield, __SIZE_ISSET_ID);
}
```

The Python language treatment of the optional size field is different still. Because Python is dynamically typed, any field can be set to the special built-in None value. Fields set to None aren't written during serialization. To unset a field in Python, you assign None to it. The subtlety here is that the Python language allows all(!) fields to be set to None, making it possible to set even a required field to None. Because fields set to None will not be serialized this makes it possible to violate the field's requiredness contract. Care on the part of the user must be taken in dynamic programming languages to adhere to the requiredness semantics.

Optional fields are similar to default requiredness fields; however, optional fields can add value in scenarios where bandwidth is critical. For example, imagine a client which sends a struct to a server with 40 possible fields, but only 7 or 8 of them are used for any given call. If all these fields are optional, the client will only transmit the fields that have been set. The server can in turn use the language-specific isset feature to determine which fields have been passed. The struct on both sides will have 40 fields, but the transmission will only contain the optional fields that have been set.

DEFAULT VALUES

The final attribute that can be associated with a field is the `default` value:

```
struct Trade {
    1: string        fish
    2: double        price
    3: i32           size = 100        ❶
}
```

The previous IDL example provides a `default` value of 100 for the `size` field ❶. This has the effect of initializing the `size` field to 100. Thus, unless you change the value, it will always be serialized as 100.

Structs, unions, and exceptions cannot be assigned to in Apache Thrift IDL. You cannot create struct constants or literals. For example, the following IDL is illegal:

```
struct Point {
    1: i32    x
    2: i32    y
}
struct Square {
    1: Point  origin = {0, 0} //IDL Compiler error here
    2: i32    side = 1
}
```

`Default` values assigned to fields with either `default` or `required` requiredness are set by both the struct writer and the struct reader. Thus, if a `default` requiredness field isn't present when reading a struct, the field's `default` value is used by the reader. Conversely, if a writer and a reader have different `default` values for a `default`/`required` requiredness field, the writer's transmitted value will overwrite the reader's. This is easiest to remember by thinking of the simple two-step process that takes place:

- The reader and writer both initialize their struct fields with their respective `default` values.
- The writer transmits its final values to the reader, while the reader replaces `default` values for fields received with the received values.

Fields with `optional` requiredness can be assigned `default` values. However, unlike `required` and `default` requiredness fields, `optional` fields holding their `default` value need not be transmitted. The `default` field value will not take up space on the wire, leaving the reader's locally initialized `default` value intact.

Note two important points regarding `optional` fields with `default` values. First, not all language implementations elide `default` values when `optional` fields are serialized. This implies that certain languages, when faced with a `struct` having 100 `optional` fields, all with `default` values, will transmit all 100 fields. This is likely not what you want. Removing the `default` values would cause these fields to be serialized only when set.

The second point is that by transmitting the default value from the writer to the reader, we assure that both parties see the same value. Eliding default values associated with optional fields allows the writer and reader to see different values in some cases. For example, imagine the writer has a version of IDL specifying an optional field default value of "4", but the reader has a version of the IDL with a default value of "5" for the same field. If the default isn't transmitted, the reader will assume a value of 5 and the writer will assume a value of 4. This can cause undefined behavior.

Optimizations are often garnered in trade for safety. Eliding default values for optional fields is designed to trade functional correctness in certain (perhaps corner) cases for reduced serialization size and therefore reduced transmission. It's advisable to carefully consider the language implementation and general implications associated with optional fields combined with default values prior to use. In most cases, it's best to avoid default values for optional fields.

6.10.3 *Exceptions*

Exceptions are defined exactly like structs but are declared with the exception keyword. Here are the two exceptions declared in our fish_trade.thrift IDL file:

```
exception BadFish {
    1: string       fish        //The problem fish
    2: i16          error_code //The service specific error code
}

exception BadFishes {
    1: map<string, i16>  fish_errors, //The problem fish:error pairs
}
```

Unlike structs, IDL compiler code generators integrate exception types into the Apache Thrift exception class hierarchy of the target language. Also unlike structs, exceptions may be declared as throwable by service methods using the throws clause. Here's an example of the throws clause from our fish_trade.thrift IDL:

```
    list<Trade> GetLastSaleList(1: set<string> fish
                                2: bool fail_fast=false)
        throws (1: BadFish bf 2: BadFishes bfs)
```

For a detailed description of IDL exceptions and sample programs see chapter 9, "Handling exceptions."

6.10.4 *Unions*

Unions are designed to create single-value elements that can be represented with multiple types. Unions are declared like structs, except that they may only have one field set at a time. In keeping with the design of a single, type-flexible value, unions cannot have required fields and can only have one default value. Because only one of the union fields is ever set at a time, unions only ever serialize or deserialize one value.

Unions aren't fully supported in all Apache Thrift languages at the time of this writing. Target languages that don't implement union semantics treat IDL union declarations as structs with all `optional` fields. Unions are serialized under the covers as structs. This allows languages with union support to communicate with languages representing unions as structs. Programmers must be careful to respect union semantics in cases where only one of the languages enforces these semantics, making sure that no more than one field is set at a time. While many target languages allow code to set more than one union field, this can cause undefined behavior if the union is serialized.

6.11 Services

Services are exactly like interfaces in many programming languages—they define a set of related functions but provide no implementation. One of the primary goals of the Apache Thrift framework is to allow users to define services in IDL, whereupon the IDL compiler can generate all the serialization and RPC code required to support the service in a cross-language RPC setting.

The `service` keyword is used to define a new service. Services contain a set of one or more functions, also known as methods. Here's a simple `service` definition with a single function:

```
service svTimeStamp {
    double fnTimeStamp()
}
```

Services are the only construct in Apache Thrift IDL supporting inheritance. The `extends` keyword is used to implicitly include all of the methods from another service into the current service. A service may extend at most one other service; multiple inheritance isn't supported:

```
service svDateTime extends svTimeStamp {
    i64 fnDate()
    string fnDateString()
}
```

In the previous example, the `svDateTime` service has three methods: the `fnTimeStamp()` method inherited from the `svTimeStamp` service, and the two locally defined methods, `fnDate()` and `fnDateString()`. Method implementations can not be inherited or overloaded; each service implementation must provide a single version of all methods it declares or inherits.

The full syntax for IDL service definitions has the following form:

```
service name [extends base_name] {
    [oneway] return_type func_name(field [,|;] ...)
        [throws (field [,|;] ...)]
    ...
}
```

FUNCTIONS

Services are sets of functions. Functions are a way to invoke functionality and option-ally receive a result. The simplest function definition involves a return type, a function name, and an empty parameter list. For example

```
i64 fnDate()
```

Functions can return any legal non-exception IDL type, including base types, contain-ers, and structs. Functions can also return void, which implies no value is returned.

Functions can be provided with arguments in the form of a field list. For example

```
void fnSetDate (1: i16  year 2: i16  month 3: i16  day = 1)
```

Argument-lists are sets of fields similar to struct fields. Arguments can have default values; however, they always have default requiredness and cannot be flagged as optional or required. At a minimum, each argument should have an ID, a type, and a name. Function arguments can be added and removed like struct fields to support interface evolution. Servers receiving requests with missing arguments will use default values (language-defined or user-defined), and servers receiving unknown parameters will ignore them.

Functions can be declared oneway. For example

```
oneway void fnSetDate (1: i16  year 2: i16  month 3: i16  day)
```

Oneway functions don't supply a return message to the caller. This can remove as much as half of the RPC overhead associated with a remote call. It also means that the caller doesn't wait for the server to respond and will have no way to know when or if the operation succeeded on the server side.

The previous fnSetDate function without the oneway keyword will require one message from the client to communicate the call to the server, then another message from the server to the client to communicate the result. Even a void function requires the response message. If the server succeeds, the response message will inform the RPC stub to return from a blocking client call. If the server throws an exception des-tined for the client, the response message will carry the exception information.

Service functions may throw exceptions; however, only RPC framework exceptions (of type TApplicationException) and user-defined exceptions declared in a throws list will be propagated back to the calling client. The following code shows an example function declaration with an exception specification:

```
exception Bad {
    1: i16 problem
}

exception Worse {
    1: i64 big_problem
}
```

```
service svTimeStamp {
    void fnTimeStamp (1: i16  year 2: i16  month 3: i16  day)
        throws (1: Bad b 2: Worse w)
}
```

In the previous IDL, the fnTimeStamp function declares that it may throw either the Bad exception type or the Worse exception type. The throws list elements are similar to fields and have an ID, a type, and a name, though requiredness and default values aren't supported. Only user-defined IDL exception types may be listed in a throws list. For further discussion and examples of user-defined exception use, see chapter 9, "Handling exceptions." Detailed Apache Thrift service examples are provided throughout the remaining chapters of this book.

6.12 *Including external files*

As projects get larger, managing all the necessary interface types and services in a single IDL file may become challenging. Apache Thrift IDL addresses this issue by allowing IDL files to include other IDL files.

For example, imagine our software team has defined types associated with individual music tracks in the IDL file track.thrift to support a music database. If a separate development team needs to create interface elements associated with complete albums based on our track elements, we have an opportunity for reuse. The album developers could add their interface elements to the track.thrift file; however, it might be more convenient for the new album interface features to be defined within a separate album.thrift IDL file. This avoids adding interface elements to the track.thrift file that aren't needed by other parts of the system. In this situation the album.thrift IDL file can include the track .thrift IDL file to resolve the album interface dependencies. See figure 6.5. The track.thrift IDL file might look something like the following listing.

Figure 6.5   The album.thrift IDL file includes the track.thrift IDL file.

Listing 6.10   ~/ThriftBook/part2/IDL/track.thrift

```
namespace * music

enum PerfRightsOrg {
    ASCAP = 1
    BMI  = 2
    SESAC = 3
    Other = 4
}

typedef double Minutes
```

```
struct MusicTrack {
    1: string title
    2: string artist
    3: string publisher
    4: string composer
    5: Minutes duration
    6: PerfRightsOrg pro
}
```

The track.thrift interface elements can be made available in the album.thrift IDL file, as shown in the following listing.

Listing 6.11 ~/ThriftBook/part2/IDL/album.thrift

```
include "track.thrift"        ❶

namespace * music             ❷

struct Album {
    1: list<track.MusicTrack> tracks     ❸
    2: track.Minutes duration
    3: string UPC_code
}
```

The album.thrift IDL file includes the track.thrift IDL file at the top of the listing ❶. Apache Thrift IDL files are conceptually organized into header and body sections. The header section of an IDL file contains `include` statements and `namespace` statements which don't define new interface elements. The header section is followed by the body that contains all the interface definitions.

Note that the MusicTrack and Minutes types from the track.thrift IDL are used in the album.thrift file but must be "scoped" so that the IDL compiler can resolve them ❸. To access interface elements from external IDL files, the element name is prefixed with the name of the IDL source file. In the album.thrift examples, the `MusicTrack` type from the track.thrift file is accessed using the `track.MusicTrack` notation.

It's important to distinguish between IDL source file scoping and `namespace` scoping ❷. These features are completely separate. The IDL compiler grammar processor treats IDL `namespace` declarations as opaque program elements to be passed on to language-specific generators. Namespaces have no bearing on the success or failure of IDL lexing and parsing. Conversely, the IDL compiler requires external IDL elements to be scoped by filename or parsing will fail. The output code generated by the IDL compiler shows no trace of the IDL file scoping prefixes. In the example here, both the elements from the track.thrift file and the elements from the album.thrift file will be placed within the same "music" namespace by most language generators; generated file types will have no trace of the "track." scoping prefixes used in the IDL.

Including an external IDL file will typically generate the appropriate #include, #import, require, or other dependency resolution statements in generated code for target languages. For example, in the album.thrift IDL, we include the track.thrift IDL file; if generating C++ code, the types from track.thrift will end up in a track_types.h header. The C++ code generator will add this dependency to the album_types.h file in the form of a #include track_types.h statement. The IDL compiler code generator does "the right thing" to ensure the generated code will compile/run in the target language.

The process of compiling a dependent IDL file is similar to compiling any other IDL file, as shown in the following session:

```
$ ls -l
-rw-r--r-- 1 randy randy 151 Jun  5 00:01 album.thrift
-rw-r--r-- 1 randy randy 294 Jun  5 00:31 track.thrift
$ thrift -gen java album.thrift
$ ls -l
-rw-r--r-- 1 randy randy  151 Jun  5 00:01 album.thrift
drwxr-xr-x 3 randy randy 4096 Jun  5 00:43 gen-java
-rw-r--r-- 1 randy randy  294 Jun  5 00:31 track.thrift
$ ls -l gen-java
drwxr-xr-x 2 randy randy 4096 Jun  5 00:43 music
$ ls -l gen-java/music
-rw-r--r-- 1 randy randy 19546 Jun  5 00:43 Album.java
```

In the previous session, the album.thrift IDL is compiled as usual. The output listing demonstrates one important point. When compiling a dependent IDL file, the IDL compiler scans and parses the dependencies, but does not generate code for the dependencies. Here we generated Java output for only our album IDL file, producing only the Album.java file. To force the compiler to generate code for dependencies you can use the -r recurse switch:

```
$ ls -l
-rw-r--r-- 1 randy randy 151 Jun  5 00:01 album.thrift
-rw-r--r-- 1 randy randy 294 Jun  5 00:31 track.thrift
$ thrift -r -gen java album.thrift
$ ls -l gen-java/music
-rw-r--r-- 1 randy randy 19546 Jun  5 00:49 Album.java
-rw-r--r-- 1 randy randy 27164 Jun  5 00:49 MusicTrack.java
-rw-r--r-- 1 randy randy   980 Jun  5 00:49 PerfRightsOrg.java
```

Adding the -r switch causes the IDL compiler to generate code for all the included IDL files. This compile produced the expected Album.java file but also files for the two types in the track.thrift IDL source, MusicTrack.java and PerfRightsOrg.java.

Let's look at a more complex example. Imagine a store interface was added to our system for handling online music purchases. Assume a radio interface was also added to support internet radio operations. Next, our promoter adds requirements that introduce the radio contest interface. The radio contest interface depends on the store and the radio interfaces creating a dependency tree similar to that in figure 6.6.

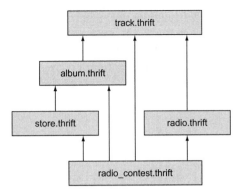

Figure 6.6   IDL include hierarchy

Here are the listings for the three new IDL files introduced in figure 6.6.

Listing 6.12   ~/ThriftBook/part2/IDL/store.thrift

```
include "album.thrift"

service Store {
    album.Album buyAlbum( 1: string UPC_code, 2: string acct )
    list<album.Album> similar( 1: string UPC_code )
}
```

Listing 6.13   ~/ThriftBook/part2/IDL/radio.thrift

```
include "track.thrift"

service Radio {
    list<track.MusicTrack> getPlayList( 1: i16 hour )
    void makeRequest( 1: track.MusicTrack track )
}
```

Listing 6.14   ~/ThriftBook/part2/IDL/radio_contest.thrift

```
include "radio.thrift"
include "store.thrift"
include "album.thrift"
include "track.thrift"

service RadioContest {
    album.Album RedeemPrize( 1: string callerNumber
                             2:
```

Apache Thrift IDL files can only access elements from IDL files that have been directly included in the current file. For example, the radio_contest.thrift file cannot access the MusicTrack type in track.thrift by including radio.thrift or store.thrift. If radio_contest depends on type elements from track.thrift, it must include track.thrift directly. While this keeps things simple, it also requires you to ensure IDL name collisions don't take place. No notational means exist for distinguishing between two separate files with the same name; for example, ~/build/music/track.thrift and ~/build/radio/track.thrift are indistinguishable.

Here's a command line session showing the output generated by compiling the radio_contest.thrift IDL recursively:

```
$ ls -l
-rw-r--r-- 1 randy randy 151 Jun  5 00:54 album.thrift
-rw-r--r-- 1 randy randy 205 Jun  5 01:07 radio_contest.thrift
-rw-r--r-- 1 randy randy 148 Jun  4 23:35 radio.thrift
-rw-r--r-- 1 randy randy 149 Jun  5 01:03 store.thrift
-rw-r--r-- 1 randy randy 294 Jun  5 00:31 track.thrift
$ thrift -r -gen java radio_contest.thrift
$ ls -l
-rw-r--r-- 1 randy randy  151 Jun  5 00:54 album.thrift
drwxr-xr-x 3 randy randy 4096 Jun  5 01:21 gen-java
-rw-r--r-- 1 randy randy  205 Jun  5 01:07 radio_contest.thrift
-rw-r--r-- 1 randy randy  148 Jun  4 23:35 radio.thrift
-rw-r--r-- 1 randy randy  149 Jun  5 01:03 store.thrift
-rw-r--r-- 1 randy randy  294 Jun  5 00:31 track.thrift
$ ls -l gen-java
drwxr-xr-x 2 randy randy  4096 Jun  5 01:21 music
-rw-r--r-- 1 randy randy 34567 Jun  5 01:21 RadioContest.java
-rw-r--r-- 1 randy randy 54784 Jun  5 01:21 Radio.java
-rw-r--r-- 1 randy randy 60453 Jun  5 01:21 Store.java
$ ls -l gen-java/music
-rw-r--r-- 1 randy randy 19546 Jun  5 01:21 Album.java
-rw-r--r-- 1 randy randy 27164 Jun  5 01:21 MusicTrack.java
-rw-r--r-- 1 randy randy   980 Jun  5 01:21 PerfRightsOrg.java
```

In this example the `track.thrift` and `album.thrift` types are placed in the music namespace, and the other classes, having no namespace, are generated directly in the gen-java directory. Up to this point all the included IDL files have been in the current directory. As the number of IDL files grows it may be more convenient to place IDL files in separate subdirectories. The IDL compiler `-I` switch allows include directories to be added to the compiler's search path. The first `-I` switch overrides the default current directory search. You can provide as many search directories as you like by repeating the `-I` switch. The following code shows an example compiling our IDL tree with the radio.thrift IDL file located in a separate subdirectory:

```
$ ls -l
-rw-r--r-- 1 randy randy  151 Jun  5 00:54 album.thrift
drwxr-xr-x 2 randy randy 4096 Jun  5 01:25 rad
-rw-r--r-- 1 randy randy  205 Jun  5 01:07 radio_contest.thrift
-rw-r--r-- 1 randy randy  149 Jun  5 01:03 store.thrift
-rw-r--r-- 1 randy randy  294 Jun  5 00:31 track.thrift
$ ls -l rad
-rw-r--r-- 1 randy randy 148 Jun  4 23:35 radio.thrift
$ thrift -r -I ./rad -I . -gen java radio_contest.thrift
$ ls -l
-rw-r--r-- 1 randy randy  151 Jun  5 00:54 album.thrift
```

```
drwxr-xr-x 3 randy randy 4096 Jun  5 01:34 gen-java
drwxr-xr-x 2 randy randy 4096 Jun  5 01:25 rad
-rw-r--r-- 1 randy randy  205 Jun  5 01:07 radio_contest.thrift
-rw-r--r-- 1 randy randy  149 Jun  5 01:03 store.thrift
-rw-r--r-- 1 randy randy  294 Jun  5 00:31 track.thrift
```

Two -I switches are supplied in the previous compiler line to allow the Thrift compiler to locate files in the "./rad" directory as well as the current directory (".").

6.13 *Annotations*

Apache Thrift IDL is intentionally generic. By defining constructs supported by most modern programming languages, the Apache Thrift IDL has a high probability of being directly implementable in your programming language of choice.

There are, however, times when special cases for a given language come into play. The Apache Thrift IDL generally handles these situations with annotations. Annotations are special key/value pairs added to IDL files that have meaning to selected code generators within the IDL compiler.

For example, suppose you're generating C++ code on a platform where it's important that all the integer types generated stick to the traditional short, int, and long type names. Using the cpp.type annotation, you can override the type emitted for a particular field or parameter:

```
struct  anno  {
  1: i32 (cpp.type = "long") counter
}
```

This annotation causes the C++ code generator to declare the counter field as type long, rather than the normal int32_t. All the other (non-CPP) code generators will ignore this annotation. Unfortunately, at present the cpp.type annotation only works for base types. Container types must be replaced using the cpp_type keyword; see the "Custom C++ containers" section earlier in this chapter for more details.

Annotations can be applied to any type, function, enum value, or field (including struct fields, union fields, exception fields, and function parameters). Annotations are always enclosed in parentheses and contain the annotation key and an assigned value string. The string isn't optional, although it may be empty. Commas within the parentheses may separate multiple annotations.

There are only two operable annotations as of this writing, the cpp.type annotation and the final annotation. In supported languages, the final annotation restricts the output class from being used as a base class for subclasses:

```
struct  anno  {
  1: i32 (cpp.type = "long") counter
} (final="true")
```

The previous example specifies that the `anno` struct should be "final" in supported languages. Table 6.9 shows the actual actions taken by various code generators in response to `final`.

Table 6.9   Final annotation behavior

Code generator	Action
AS3	Marks the class `final`
C++	Suppresses the virtual destructor normally generated for structs
C#	Makes classes generated for structs sealed
Delphi	Makes classes generated for structs sealed
Java/JavaME	Makes classes generated for structs and unions final

In the case of the `final` annotation, the value ("true" in the previous example) is ignored, the string can be anything, and the presence of the "final" key is what the code generators are looking for.

While only two annotations exist now, the annotation feature ensures that future target language-specific customizations have an outlet that will not involve polluting the generic Apache Thrift IDL.

Summary

Apache Thrift IDL is an expressive yet compact interface definition language. It provides modern features while supporting a wide range of implementation languages.

- IDLs support the process of developing explicit mechanical contracts between clients and servers.
- Apache Thrift supports a selection of commenting styles, including `doc` strings, that can be used to generate documentation with the Apache Thrift IDL compiler and other tools (such as Doxygen).
- Apache Thrift IDL supports a small but flexible set of base types:
  - `binary`
  - `bool`
  - `byte`
  - `double`
  - `i16`
  - `i32`
  - `i64`
  - `string`
  - `void`
- Apache Thrift IDL supports three container types:
  - `list`
  - `set`
  - `map`

- Apache Thrift IDL supports interface constants.
- Apache Thrift IDL supports several user-defined types:
  - `typedef`
  - `enum`
  - `struct`
  - `union`
  - `exception`
- Apache Thrift IDL doesn't support type inheritance.
- Apache Thrift IDL doesn't support self-referential types or forward definitions (with experimental exceptions).
- The `service` keyword allows RPC `service` interfaces to be defined.
- Apache Thrift supports interface inheritance but not overloading or overriding.
- IDL files can include other IDL files, allowing large interfaces to be organized across files.
- The `namespace` keyword supports namespace and package generation in various target languages.

User-defined types

This chapter covers

- Designing effective cross-platform data types
- Serializing objects
- Designing for type evolution
- Looking inside type serialization
- Using Zlib compression

At this point we've covered the foundational elements of the Apache Thrift framework. Chapter 4 exposed us to the transport layer and demonstrated its ability to provide device independence, chapter 5 covered the serialization capabilities of the plug-in protocol layer, and chapter 6 took us on a comprehensive tour of the Apache Thrift IDL syntax.

As discussed in chapter 6, Apache Thrift interfaces have three key facets:

- *User-Defined Types (UDTs)*—Data types that define the structure of data shared and exchanged by Apache Thrift programs
- *Constants*—Immutable instances of types
- *Services*—Collections of functions implemented by servers that can be called remotely by clients (covered in chapter 8)

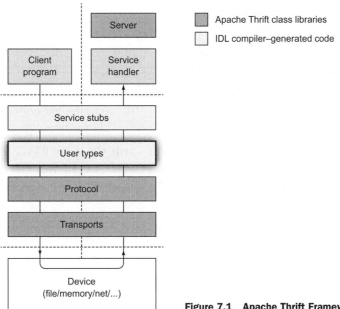

Figure 7.1   Apache Thrift Framework user-defined types

In this chapter, we'll focus on the design and use of cross-language user-defined types (see figure 7.1). The Apache Thrift IDL makes it fairly effortless to declare complex types that can then be easily exchanged across a wide range of languages.

Apache Thrift UDTs have built-in serialization features that leverage the Apache Thrift Protocol and Transport libraries. Using these serialization features, UDTs can be passed to RPC functions and returned as result values across languages. UDTs can also be serialized for transmission over messaging systems and for storage in disk files or databases.

IDL-declared UDTs are important aspects of many interfaces. For example, a service that allows you to look up tweets might have a Tweet UDT that it returns. A stock market trading service might have an Order UDT that it accepts to initiate a trade. Apache Thrift also makes it possible for interfaces, including UDTs, to evolve over time without breaking existing users of the interface. The ability to change UDTs without impacting compatibility with older applications is a marquee feature of Apache Thrift.

Certain Apache Thrift users use UDTs in the sole context of RPC services. However, several use cases involve serializing types to disk, message queues, databases, HDFS, and other non-RPC targets. This chapter examines Apache Thrift UDT best practices that will be useful in any context.

We will begin by building a trivial Apache Thrift UDT to get familiar with the mechanics of declaring and serializing custom types.

7.1   *A simple user-defined type example*

Creating and working with UDTs in Apache Thrift is straightforward:

1 Describe the UDT in Apache Thrift IDL.
2 Compile the IDL to generate native language code for the UDT.
3 Use the UDT as you would any other type in the target language.
4 Serialize/de-serialize the UDT using the IDL compiler-generated `read()`/ `write()` methods to exchange the type with other platforms and languages.

To demonstrate the creation and use of Apache Thrift UDTs, we'll create a simple struct to capture the position of a satellite in orbit around the Earth. The following listing defines the type in IDL with a latitude and a longitude as well as an elevation.

Listing 7.1   ~/ThriftBook/part2/types/simple/simple_udt.thrift

```
struct EarthRelPosition {
    1: double latitude
    2: double longitude
    3: double elevation
}
```

This `EarthRelPosition` type is declared as an IDL struct. When compiled, it will produce a language-specific type definition appropriately implemented in the target language. For example, in C++, Java, and Python, the IDL compiler will generate a class called `EarthRelPosition`. However, in C this UDT will be represented as a struct, in Perl as a package, in Haskell as a data type, and so on.

All three fields have been declared as type double and given an ID. IDs are an important part of field declarations. Every field should have a positive integer ID, unique within the struct. Serialization protocols use these IDs to identify the fields of a UDT during serialization and de-serialization, not the field names.

We'll build our first UDT serialization program in C++. Keep in mind that the concepts described here carry over to any Apache Thrift language implementation. The following command line session completes step #2 of our process, compiling the IDL and generating C++ code for the `EarthRelPosition` UDT:

```
$ thrift --gen cpp simple_udt.thrift
$ ls -l
drwxr-xr-x 2 randy randy   4096 Jul  5 15:14 gen-cpp
-rw-r--r-- 1 randy randy    102 Jul  5 15:02 simple_udt.thrift
$ ls -l gen-cpp
-rw-r--r-- 1 randy randy    280 Jul  5 15:49 simple_udt_constants.cpp
-rw-r--r-- 1 randy randy    372 Jul  5 15:49 simple_udt_constants.h
-rw-r--r-- 1 randy randy   2761 Jul  5 15:49 simple_udt_types.cpp
-rw-r--r-- 1 randy randy   1828 Jul  5 15:49 simple_udt_types.h
```

The Apache Thrift compiler requires the `--gen` switch followed by a language to compile for and an IDL file to compile. For a full IDL reference, see chapter 6.

In this example, we're compiling the simple_udt.thrift IDL source for C++. The compiler emits a directory named gen-cpp containing the output files. The compiler's C++ output has two pairs of files: one pair to house the IDL constants and one pair to house the IDL types. The header files (.h) provide declarations and the source files (.cpp) provide implementation. The constants files are always generated, even when no constants are declared. Because we didn't declare any constants, the constants files contain only empty boilerplate code and can be ignored.

The simple_udt_types.h header contains the C++ declaration for the EarthRel-Position type. The compiler has created a C++ class named EarthRelPosition to support operations on this type. Take a minute to look through these two types files if you like. Don't worry if part of the code doesn't make sense at present; we'll spend the rest of this chapter describing the features of Apache Thrift-generated UDTs. The following is an abbreviated version of the IDL compiler-generated C++ class:

```cpp
class EarthRelPosition {
 public:
  EarthRelPosition() : latitude(0), longitude(0), elevation(0) {}
  virtual ~EarthRelPosition() throw() {}
  double latitude;
  double longitude;
  double elevation;
  uint32_t read(::apache::thrift::protocol::TProtocol* iprot);
  uint32_t write(::apache::thrift::protocol::TProtocol* oprot) const;
};
```

The class provides public attributes for each of our three IDL struct fields, along with a default constructor and a virtual destructor. The interesting bits are the read() and write() methods. These methods are backed with code to de-serialize and serialize the UDT using any Apache Thrift Protocol.

To see how this generated EarthRelPosition class works, let's build a short C++ program that serializes and de-serializes the UDT, which is shown in the following listing.

Listing 7.2 ~/ThriftBook/part2/types/simple/simple_udt.cpp

```cpp
#include "gen-cpp/simple_udt_types.h"
#include <thrift/transport/TBufferTransports.h>
#include <thrift/protocol/TBinaryProtocol.h>
#include <boost/make_shared.hpp>
#include <iostream>
#include <iomanip>

using namespace apache::thrift::transport;
using namespace apache::thrift::protocol;
using boost::make_shared;

int main() {
    auto trans = make_shared<TMemoryBuffer>(1024);        ❶
    auto proto = make_shared<TBinaryProtocol>(trans);     ❷
```

```
     EarthRelPosition ep;              ❸
     ep.latitude = 0.0;
     ep.longitude = 180.0;
     ep.elevation = 42164.0;

     proto->getTransport()->open();        ❹
❺   ep.write(proto.get());
     proto->getTransport()->flush();           ❻

     std::cout << "Wrote Position: " << std::setprecision(2) << std::fixed
               << std::setw(8) << ep.latitude
               << ", " << std::setw(8) << ep.longitude
               << ", " << std::setw(8) << ep.elevation << std::endl;

     EarthRelPosition epRead;                 ❼
     epRead.read(proto.get());
❽   proto->getTransport()->close();

     std::cout << "Read  Position: " << std::setprecision(2) << std::fixed
               << std::setw(8) << epRead.latitude
               << ", " << std::setw(8) << epRead.longitude
               << ", " << std::setw(8) << epRead.elevation << std::endl;
}
```

This program creates an instance of our UDT ❸, initializes it, and then serializes it ❺. We use the `TBinaryProtocol` serialization scheme ❷ and the `TMemoryBuffer` endpoint transport ❶ in this example. However, because the Apache Thrift I/O stack is modular and pluggable, we can easily change out either the protocol, the transport, or both.

To test the serialization round trip, the program also reads the data back into a second instance of the UDT ❼. A call to flush the transport stack is inserted between the write operations and the read operations to ensure that the write data is pushed to the endpoint before we try to read ❻. Code should also always `open()` the transport stack before using it ❹ and `close()` the transport stack after I/O is complete ❽.

Note that the protocol object has a pointer to the transport that can be recovered using the `getTransport()` method ❹. In this example, we could have used the transport directly (through the trans pointer), but in many applications, isolated functions may only have access to the protocol object. The `TProtocol` `getTransport()` method ensures that I/O code with only a protocol reference can always access the `TTransport` interface to `open()`, `close()` and `flush()` buffered bytes.

Here's a sample build and run of listing 7.2:

```
$ g++ --std=c++11 simple_udt.cpp gen-cpp/simple_udt_types.cpp -lthrift
$ ./a.out
Wrote Position:     0.00,   180.00,  42164.00
Read  Position:     0.00,   180.00,  42164.00
```

While this is a trivial example, it illustrates the ease with which any UDT can be serialized using Apache Thrift. We could hand-code custom logic to write these three fields to memory or disk fairly easily. However, Apache Thrift makes the process of serializing complex types with nested collections, subtypes, and a variety of other features as easy as this trivial example. With support for a range of languages and the ability to seamlessly plug in different transports and protocols, Apache Thrift is a good choice for a host of serialization chores.

7.2 Type design

In Apache Thrift terms, types describe the logical structure of the things exchanged through interfaces. In many applications, user-defined types are the most important part of the interface. In fact, certain interfaces consist of nothing but UDT declarations. Apache Thrift IDL supplies a number of type design tools:

- struct
- union
- enum
- typedef
- Base types
- Collections

To get familiar with each of these tools, we'll create a UDT that applies all of them in an effective way. This UDT will support a software system that records celestial observations made by astronomers. The astronomers use radio telescopes to study pulsars, quasars, and other celestial features. We'll need a UDT to store each observation made by several different radio telescopes.

Let's assume that our radio astronomy observations consist of the following fields:

- The position of the object observed
- The time of the observation
- The number of telescopes used to make the observation
- The magnitude of radio waves detected over each of several frequencies
- The telescope system recording the measurement (see figure 7.2)
- A visible spectrum bitmap of the sky at the time of the observation

Several possible schemes can be used to define the position of an object observed by a radio telescope. To capture data from all the radio telescope sources, we'll need to accommodate positions that have various types.

Figure 7.2   The Arecibo Radio Telescope is an example RadioObservationSystem that might contribute RadioObservation data for use with the radio_observation.cpp program. Photo from https://en.wikipedia.org/wiki/Arecibo_Observatory and used under https://creativecommons.org/licenses/by-sa/4.0/deed.en.

This is a complex list of features for a type; however, we can easily model all of them with Apache Thrift IDL. The following listing shows one possible approach.

> **Listing 7.3   ~/ThriftBook/part2/types/complex/radio_observation.thrift**

```
//Radio Telescope Observation Types
//////////////////////////////////////////////////////////////
namespace * radio_observation
const string Version = "1.0.0"

//There are 3 different position types used
//  by the radio telescopes we support
struct EarthRelPosition {
    1: double latitude
    2: double longitude
    3: double elevation
}
struct RelVector {
    1: EarthRelPosition pos
    2: double declination
    3: double azimuth
}
struct ICRFPosition {
    1: double right_ascension
    2: double declination
    3: optional i16 ecliptic_year
}

/**
 * Position: The focal point of an observation. This union allows any
 * one of the three positon types to be used for position data.
 */
union Position {
    1: EarthRelPosition erpos
    2: RelVector rv
    3: ICRFPosition icrfpos
}

/** Time: the time in seconds and fractions of seconds since Jan 1, 1970 */
typedef double Time

/** RadioObservationSystem: Radio Telescopes/Arrays making observations */
enum RadioObservationSystem {
    Parkes  = 1
    Arecibo = 2
    GMRT    = 17
    LOFAR   = 18
    Socorro = 25
    VLBA    = 51
}

/**
 * RadioObservation: Data related to an observation made by a radio
 * telescope.
```

```
* - telescope_count: the number of telescopes in the array (0 if unknown)
* - time: time of the observation
* - researcher: this field is deprecated
* - system: the radio telescope capturing the observation
* - freq_amp: frequency(i64 Hz) amplitude(double Watts) observations
* - pos: the position of the object or area observed
* - sky_bmp: optional bitmap image of the area of the sky observed
*/
struct RadioObservation {
    1: i32 telescope_count
    2: Time time
    //3: string researcher; retired
    4: RadioObservationSystem system
    5: map<i64, double> freq_amp
    6: Position pos
    7: optional binary sky_bmp
}
```

The IDL in listing 7.3 is one possible solution to the interface requirements for radio telescope observations. The degenerate case might be a single struct containing all the needed fields with only base types, such as i16 and double. Such an interface would be hard to use, hard to reuse, and hard to evolve. By using the right tools for each feature of the UDT, we can build a type from components that communicates intent, semantics, and structure. A well-designed UDT can also evolve over time as requirements change and new features are added.

To get a visual picture of the types in our IDL and their relationships, look at the Graphviz model in figure 7.3. The Apache Thrift IDL compiler will generate interface

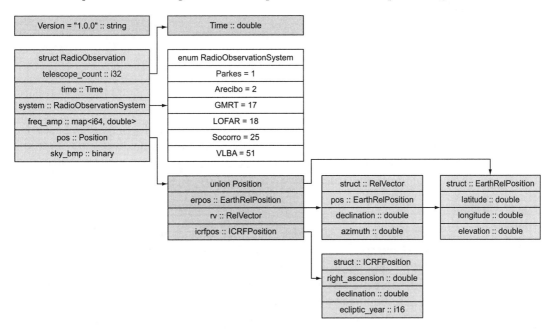

Figure 7.3 A Graphviz diagram of the `radio_observation` type interface

models for any IDL with the `--gen gv` switch (`thrift --gen gv radio_observation .thrift`). The resulting `gv` output file can be displayed with the free open source Graphviz viewer (http://www.graphviz.org/).

The types provided in our IDL capture several important design decisions. Many of these decisions are driven by a desire to ensure that the interface supports requirements in a way that allows the UDT to be efficient and flexible. Let's look at each of the design choices in detail.

7.2.1   Namespaces

The first non-comment line of the IDL declares the wildcard (*) namespace scope `radio_observation`. Namespace declarations must be listed before any services, types, or constants are declared. The asterisk indicates that the namespace should be used for all output languages generated by the IDL compiler. For more information on namespace syntax, see the namespace section in chapter 6:

```
namespace * radio_observation
```

It's a good idea to place all your interface definitions in a descriptive namespace. The IDL compiler language generators handle namespaces in different ways. Most commonly, a namespace is a scope subordinate to the global scope within which all the IDL declarations are listed. Specifying a namespace keeps all the names created in your IDL out of the global scope when you generate code in most languages, reducing the opportunity for name collisions.

7.2.2   Constants

The second IDL statement in our file is a `const string` named `Version`:

```
const string Version = "1.0.0"
```

Many developers find version strings like this useful even though Apache Thrift IDL allows multiple versions of an interface to interoperate. Knowing which interface version each program is using can help when planning upgrades or assessing program capabilities. This version string can be accessed programmatically through the `Version` name and displayed in startup logs and the like. This `Version` constant is purely a user-defined construct; the Apache Thrift framework takes no notice of it.

7.2.3   Structs

Apache Thrift IDL structs are used to define new types represented by a packaged group of fields. Conceptually, structs are the tool used to represent messages, objects, records, and any other affinity group needed by an interface. The `RadioObservation` struct is the focus of the radio_observation.thrift interface definition file. The next several topics describe the features of this struct.

7.2.4 Base types

The first field in the `RadioObservation` struct is `telescope_count`. Simple value fields are typically represented with base types:

```
struct RadioObservation {
    1: i32 telescope_count
    ...
}
```

This field will store the number of radio telescopes used to make the observation. An integer type is a good fit for the telescope count, and i32 strikes a good balance between size (4 bytes) and assurance that we can capture the count of even the largest telescope array (i32 has a range of +/- approximately 2Bn). Apache Thrift IDL doesn't support unsigned integers, so semantics such as (0==unknown) and (< 0 is illegal) should be documented in the IDL doc strings (as demonstrated in the example code).

7.2.5 Typedefs

Typedefs allow a new type to be created from a preexisting type. The `Time` type in the `radio_observation` IDL is an example:

```
typedef double Time

struct RadioObservation {
    ...
    2: Time time
    ...
}
```

The time field in the `RadioObservation` struct records the time of the observation. The time is a double recording the number of seconds from some epoch. Elevations in meters might also be represented with doubles but you wouldn't pass an elevation to a function that requires a time.

If you're designing an interface with a semantic type implemented in terms of a base type, but the semantic type is particularly significant or widely used, it may be a good candidate for a typedef. Typedef types are self-documenting and, in statically typed languages, ensure that the underlying type isn't used accidentally in places where the typedef type is required.

7.2.6 Field IDs and retiring fields

All the fields defined in a struct or union should be given a positive 16-bit integer ID. Once assigned, the ID should never be reassigned for the life of that type:

```
struct RadioObservation {
    ...
    //3: string researcher; retired
    ...
}
```

In the type example, field number 3 has been retired. IDs can be retired safely but shouldn't be forgotten. The reason for this is that older code relying on prior versions of the interface will have semantic expectations associated with old IDs. Older versions of this interface used field number 3 to store a string with the Researcher name (as commented above). Deleting field 3 and then reusing it to describe something else would be confusing to an older program still expecting field number 3 to represent researcher.

IDs are i16 values (16-bit signed integers), giving us 32K positive IDs to work with. Running out of field IDs within a struct is hard to imagine, leaving little reason to do anything but comment out deleted fields, retiring the IDs permanently. By leaving the field comment in the IDL source, we can ensure that people extending the interface at a later time will not reuse the ID value.

7.2.7 *Enums*

Enums create a new type with a discrete set of possible values, usually more naturally described with human language rather than integers:

```
enum RadioObservationSystem {
    Parkes  = 1
    Arecibo = 2
    GMRT    = 17
    LOFAR   = 18
    Socorro = 25
    VLBA    = 51
}

struct RadioObservation {
    ...
    4: RadioObservationSystem system
    ...
}
```

The radio telescope IDL creates a new enum type to define the telescope system that generated each observation. An enumeration is used because the range of possibilities is small, fairly stable, and best expressed in human language. When you're dealing with stable sets, and the names of the elements are more important than the numbers used to represent them, an enum is often a good option.

Apache Thrift enum elements have explicit 32-bit integer values. These values shouldn't be reassigned for the life of the enum for the same reason ID values shouldn't be reused. New values can be added and old values can be commented out, but values shouldn't be re-purposed, to avoid incompatibilities with programs still using older versions of the interface.

To fully support interface evolution, the code making use of enum values should be prepared to handle unknown values gracefully. Such a situation might arise when a program using an older version of the interface uses an enumeration deleted in the current version of the IDL. For example, a program receiving a Radio Observation System unknown to it could print "unknown system" (rather than crashing!).

7.2.8 *Collections*

Apache Thrift IDL provides set, list, and map types to allow fields to represent repeating groups:

```
struct RadioObservation {
    ...
    5: map<i64,double> freq_amp
    ...
}
```

Our `RadioObservation` type uses a `freq_amp` attribute to capture the various frequency/ amplitude pairs associated with the observation. A map collection will allow zero or more frequencies with associated amplitudes to be captured. The map semantic suggests that the first value is a key and must be unique. We can iterate over the key/value pairs in the map or look up specific values using the key. The map type was selected to ensure that no frequency (represented by the i64 key) is entered twice and that each frequency has an associated amplitude (represented by the double).

We could have alternatively created a `struct FreqAmp{}` containing an i64 frequency and a double amplitude, then used a `list<FreqAmp>` to capture the observation data. However, this wouldn't have enforced our desire to have only one amplitude reading per frequency. Almost any conceptual data structure can be captured with various combinations of collections and structures. Choosing the most direct and expressive representation may require some thought, but it's almost always worth the effort.

Apache Thrift IDL allows any type to be used as a key in IDL maps and sets. Integers, strings, and enums are usually the best choice. Floating point values can be used; however, floating point processing can cause problems with key matching. Computationally, 0.999999 and 1.0 may be seen as the same, but they will represent separate keys. Using complex types for keys also typically leads to trouble; many languages don't support complex types (unions, structs, collections) as keys, making the generated code unusable in those languages.

7.2.9 *Unions*

Unions have a single purpose in Apache Thrift IDL, allowing a field's type to change:

```
union Position {
    1: EarthRelPosition erpos
    2: RelVector rv
    3: ICRFPosition icrfpos
}
```

```
struct RadioObservation {
    ...
    6: Position pos
    ...
}
```

Unions are declared like structs, but all fields are implicitly optional and only one field may be set at a time. The requiredness keywords "optional" and "required" aren't used with union fields. If you set field number 2, all other fields are implicitly unset.

Many programmers connect unions with a way to interpret the same bits in memory in different ways. Unions in Apache Thrift don't support this behavior. A single Apache Thrift Union will take on different configurations and sizes in memory depending on the field that's set. In Apache Thrift IDL terms, unions represent type flexibility. If you know that you need an attribute but you need to represent it with several possible types, a union is the right choice.

In the example, we're faced with supplying a position for the observation, but a position might be expressed several ways. By representing the position as a union, we can use any position type to capture the position of an observation, and, should the need arise, we can add new types in the future.

The presence of a union tells developers using this interface several things. First, it tells them that the type of the position field is not constant. This implies that they must supply support for various position types. Second, and more subtly, it tells them that new position types may be added, so it's possible that they may recover a position type they don't understand. This later insight will encourage union users to write code that degrades favorably in the face of unknown types and/or to support plugins that allow new type support to be added dynamically.

7.2.10 *Requiredness and optional fields*

Apache Thrift struct fields have a requiredness trait. Normal field declarations are said to have default requiredness. Fields can also be declared "required" or "optional". In the example, the optional modifier is applied to a bitmap field:

```
struct RadioObservation {
    ...
    7: optional binary sky_bmp
}
```

The sky_bmp field of the RadioObservation UDT is of binary type. Its purpose is to capture a bitmap image of the sky at the time of the radio telescope observation (see figure 7.4). Bitmaps can be small or large, but any bitmap will be comparatively large when contrasted with the size of the rest of our structure.

In scenarios where you want the ability to serialize a field, but only part of the time, making the field

Figure 7.4 The 25KB quasar.bmp used in the sky_bmp field of the RadioObservation test object created by DiskSer.java.

optional is a good choice. Transmitting the sky_bmp field could be performance pro-
hibitive in certain applications and mission critical in others. By making the field
optional, only those requiring it need serialize it. Large fields are good candidates for
optional requiredness.

> **TIP** In most situations, default requiredness is a good compromise. It's
> always serialized, but need not be present during de-serialization. If you want
> the flexibility to decide whether a field is serialized or not, choose optional
> requiredness. Required requiredness fields create runtime errors when not
> found during de-serialization, and they cannot evolve. They should be
> avoided unless you want to permanently enforce a field's presence.

7.3   *Serializing objects to disk*

Now that we've carefully designed our UDT, let's build a simple example program to
serialize the UDT to disk. The last program demonstrated type serialization to a memory buffer using C++. In this example, we'll serialize to disk using Java.

This program is trivial by design and meant to illustrate the type serializing features of a more advanced Apache Thrift UDT with as little distraction as possible. The
program serializes a RadioObservation to disk if the string "write" is supplied on the
command line, and de-serializes a RadioObservation if the string "read" is supplied
on the command line. The UDT is displayed to the console in both cases. Writes can
optionally include a sky_bmp image if the write parameter is followed by the string
"BMP". The file "quasar.bmp" from figure 7.4 is always used as the image source and
supplied with the sample code. See the following listing.

Listing 7.4   ~/ThriftBook/part2/types/complex/DiskSer.java

```java
import java.nio.file.Files;
import java.nio.file.Paths;
import java.io.IOException;
import java.util.HashMap;
import java.util.Map;
import org.apache.thrift.TException;
import org.apache.thrift.transport.TTransport;
import org.apache.thrift.transport.TSimpleFileTransport;
import org.apache.thrift.protocol.TBinaryProtocol;
import org.apache.thrift.protocol.TProtocol;
import radio_observation.ICRFPosition;
import radio_observation.Position;
import radio_observation.RadioObservation;
import radio_observation.RadioObservationSystem;
import radio_observation.radio_observationConstants;

public class DiskSer {
  public static void FakeInit(RadioObservation ro) {
      ro.telescope_count = 1;
      ro.system = RadioObservationSystem.Arecibo;
      ro.time = System.currentTimeMillis() / 1000.0;
```

```
        ICRFPosition pos = new ICRFPosition(270.3, 45.24);
        pos.setEcliptic_year((short)2000);
        ro.pos = new Position();
        ro.pos.setIcrfpos(pos);
        ro.freq_amp = new HashMap<>();
        ro.freq_amp.put(20500000L, 75.456);
        ro.freq_amp.put(50000000L, 29.321);
        ro.freq_amp.put(75000000L, 51.526);
    }

    public static void DumpICRFPosition(ICRFPosition pos) {
        System.out.println("Position        : " +
                    pos.declination + " dec - " +
                    pos.right_ascension + " ra [" +
                ((pos.isSetEcliptic_year())?pos.ecliptic_year:"") + "]");
    }

    public static void DumpObservation(RadioObservation ro) {
        System.out.println("Telescope Count: " + ro.telescope_count);
        System.out.println("System         : " + ro.system.name());
        System.out.println("Time           : " + ro.time);
        if (ro.pos.isSetIcrfpos()) {
          DumpICRFPosition(ro.pos.getIcrfpos());
        }
        System.out.println("Frequency   Magnitude");
        for (Map.Entry<Long, Double> entry : ro.freq_amp.entrySet()) {
            System.out.println("  "+entry.getKey()+"   "+entry.getValue());
        }
    }

    public static void WriteRadioObservation(TProtocol proto,
                                             boolean writeBMP,
                                             string bmpPath)
            throws TException, IOException {
        System.out.println("\nWriting Observations");
        System.out.println("-----------------------");
        RadioObservation ro = new RadioObservation();
        FakeInit(ro);
        if (writeBMP){
          ro.setSky_bmp(Files.readAllBytes(Paths.get(bmpPath)));
        }
        ro.write(proto);
        DumpObservation(ro);
    }

    public static void ReadRadioObservation(TProtocol proto)
            throws TException {
        System.out.println("\nReading Observations");
        System.out.println("-----------------------");
        RadioObservation ro = new RadioObservation();
        ro.read(proto);
        DumpObservation(ro);
    }
```

```
public static void main(String[] args) {
  TTransport trans = null;
  try {
    System.out.println("\nRadio Observation Disk Serializer " +
                    radio_observationConstants.Version);
    trans = new TSimpleFileTransport("data", true, true);
    trans.open();
    TProtocol proto = new TBinaryProtocol(trans);
    if (args.length > 0 && 0 == args[0].compareToIgnoreCase ("write")) {
      WriteRadioObservation(proto, args.length > 1, "quasar.bmp");
    } else if (args.length>0 && 0==args[0].compareToIgnoreCase("read")) {
      ReadRadioObservation(proto);
    }
    else {
        System.out.println("Usage: DiskSer (read | write [bmp])");
    }
  } catch (TException | IOException ex) {
    System.out.println("Error: " + ex.getMessage());
  }
  if (null != trans) {
    trans.close();
  }
}
}
```

We'll take this program apart function by function; however, first let's run the code to
see how it works. To begin, we'll need to generate Java code for the radio_observation
interface, as shown in the following session:

```
$ thrift -gen java radio_observation.thrift
$ ls -l
-rw-r--r-- 1 randy randy  3009 Jul  5 12:21 DiskSer.java
drwxr-xr-x 2 randy randy  4096 Jul  3 23:20 gen-java
-rwxrw-rw- 1 randy randy 25800 Jul  4 00:13 quasar.bmp
-rw-r--r-- 1 randy randy  1269 Jul  5 03:34 radio_observation.thrift
$ ls -l gen-java
drwxr-xr-x 2 randy randy 4096 Jul  6 04:06 radio_observation
$ ls -l gen-java/radio_observation/
-rw-rw-r-- 1 randy randy 19171 Mar 27 14:51 EarthRelPosition.java
-rw-rw-r-- 1 randy randy 20040 Mar 27 14:51 ICRFPosition.java
-rw-rw-r-- 1 randy randy 14143 Mar 27 14:51 Position.java
-rw-rw-r-- 1 randy randy  1203 Mar 27 14:51 radio_observationConstants.java
-rw-rw-r-- 1 randy randy 31864 Mar 27 14:51 RadioObservation.java
-rw-rw-r-- 1 randy randy  1197 Mar 27 14:51 RadioObservationSystem.java
-rw-rw-r-- 1 randy randy 18734 Mar 27 14:51 RelVector.java
```

Here we used the Apache Thrift IDL compiler to generate code for the UDT in Java.
The compiler places the output files in the gen-java directory. Because we specified
the radio_observation namespace in the IDL, the Java source files are located inside
the package subdirectory radio_observation. Now we can compile the disk serialization example:

```
$ javac -cp /usr/local/lib/libthrift-1.0.0.jar:\
            /usr/share/java/slf4j-api.jar:\
            /usr/share/java/slf4j-nop.jar \
            DiskSer.java  gen-java/radio_observation/*.java
$ ls -l
-rw-rw-r-- 1 randy randy  4903 Mar 27 15:35 DiskSer.class
-rw-rw-r-- 1 randy randy  3630 Mar 19 09:50 DiskSer.java
drwxrwxr-x 3 randy randy  4096 Mar 27 14:51 gen-java
-rwxrwxr-x 1 randy randy 25800 Mar 19 09:50 quasar.bmp
-rw-rw-r-- 1 randy randy  1330 Mar 19 09:50 radio_observation.thrift
```

In addition to adding the `libthrift` and `slf4j` jars to the class path, we must also compile the Java source for the various types defined in our IDL (gen-java/radio _observation/*.java) to support our main DiskSer.java program.

Once compiled, we can write the `RadioObservation` UDT to disk and read it back:

```
$ java -cp /usr/local/lib/libthrift-1.0.0.jar:\
           /usr/share/java/slf4j-api.jar:\
           /usr/share/java/slf4j-nop.jar:\
           gen-java:\
           .
           DiskSer
Usage: DiskSer (read | write [bmp])                  ❶
$ java -cp /usr/local/lib/libthrift-1.0.0.jar:\
           /usr/share/java/slf4j-api.jar:\
           /usr/share/java/slf4j-nop.jar:\
           gen-java:\
           .
           DiskSer write                             ❷

Writing Observations
------------------------
Telescope Count: 1
System       : Arecibo
Time         : 1.37305235312E9
Position     : 45.24 dec - 270.3 ra [2000]
Frequency    Magnitude
  50000000   29.321
  75000000   51.526
  20500000   75.456
$ ls -l data
-rw-r--r-- 1 randy randy   118 Jul  5 14:04 data          ❸
$ java -cp /usr/local/lib/libthrift-1.0.0.jar:\
           /usr/share/java/slf4j-api.jar:\
           /usr/share/java/slf4j-nop.jar:\
           gen-java:\
           .
           DiskSer read                              ❹

Reading Observations
------------------------
Telescope Count: 1
System       : Arecibo
Time         : 1.37305235312E9
```

```
Position        : 45.24 dec - 270.3 ra [2000]
Frequency   Magnitude
  50000000  29.321
  20500000  75.456
  75000000  51.526
$ rm data
$ java -cp /usr/local/lib/libthrift-1.0.0.jar:\
           /usr/share/java/slf4j-api.jar:\
           /usr/share/java/slf4j-nop.jar:\
           gen-java:\
           .
           DiskSer write bmp        ❺

Writting Observations
-----------------------
Telescope Count: 1
System          : Arecibo
Time            : 1.373058327153E9
Position        : 45.24 dec - 270.3 ra [2000]
Frequency   Magnitude
  50000000  29.321
  75000000  51.526
  20500000  75.456
$ ls -l data
-rw-r--r-- 1 randy randy 25925 Jul  5 14:05 data       ❻
```

The previous examples test all four code paths in the DiskSer.java program. In the first example ❶, we executed the program with no command line parameters to display a usage hint. The next run writes the RadioObservation UDT to disk ❷. The result is a 118-byte file ❸ containing a copy of the UDT.

Running the program with the read argument de-serializes the data structure from the file, and, as expected, outputs the same data ❹. As a last example, we deleted the data file and then requested that the program serialize the UDT with the optional bitmap field ❺. This saves the quasar.bmp file in the optional sky_bmp field and serializes the full UDT to disk. The new serialized object takes up 25,925 bytes on disk ❻.

Because this serialization program was created with Apache Thrift, we have several degrees of flexibility. We can easily switch protocols and serialize the Radio-Observations using JSON, or we could try to save disk space by using the Compact protocol. We can also use other transports, to serialize the UDT to memory or transmit it over a network connection. None of these changes would require any adjustment to the principle parts of this program.

For demonstration purposes, we've kept this program simple. It consists of a single DiskSer class with several static methods that implement the program's behavior. Let's take a quick look at each function, starting with main():

```java
public static void main(String[] args) {
  TTransport trans = null;
  try {
    System.out.println("\nRadio Observation Disk Serializer " +
```

```
                        radio_observationConstants.Version);
    trans = new TSimpleFileTransport("data", true, true);
    trans.open();
    TProtocol proto = new TBinaryProtocol(trans);
    if (args.length > 0 && 0 == args[0].compareToIgnoreCase ("write")) {
      WriteRadioObservation(proto, args.length > 1, "quasar.bmp");      ❶
    } else if (args.length>0 && 0==args[0].compareToIgnoreCase("read")) {
      ReadRadioObservation(proto);
    }
    else {
       System.out.println("Usage: DiskSer (read | write [bmp])");
    }
  } catch (TException | IOException ex) {
    System.out.println("Error: " + ex.getMessage());
  }
  if (null != trans) {
    trans.close();
  }
}
```

The main() function performs all of its logic in a protective try block. If the main() function body throws an exception, we log any failures, close the transport, and then exit. The function main() begins by printing out a masthead with the IDL version string and then opens a data file with read/write access. We then add a Binary Protocol to the I/O stack. If the user requested that we write to disk, we take the code path that calls the WriteRadioObservation() method. If the bmp suffix was also found, we pass Boolean True in the second parameter (the code tests for any third command line argument) ❶. We always pass the same bmp file path string, quasar.bmp:

```
public static void WriteRadioObservation(TProtocol proto,
                                          boolean writeBMP)
        throws TException, IOException {
    System.out.println("\nWritting Observations");
    System.out.println("------------------------");
    RadioObservation ro = new RadioObservation();
    FakeInit(ro);
    if (writeBMP){
      ro.setSky_bmp(Files.readAllBytes(Paths.get("quasar.bmp")));      ❶
    }
    ro.write(proto);
    DumpObservation(ro);
}
```

The WriteRadioObservation() method creates a new RadioObservation object and calls FakeInit() to initialize it. The RadioObservation type was generated by the IDL compiler with the same name used in the IDL. We import the class for this type at the top of the listing with the import radio_observation.RadioObservation statement, where radio_observation is the namespace and RadioObservation is the UDT.

Many languages provide setters, unsetters, and testers for optional fields. For example, this UDT offers the following methods:

- setSky_bmp()—Tells the UDT to serialize the sky_bmp field and sets its value
- unsetSky_bmp()—Tells the UDT not to serialize the sky_bmp field
- isSetSky_bmp()—Returns true if the sky_bmp field is set for serialization

If writeBMP was true we add the bitmap bytes to the binary sky_bmp field using the setSky_bmp() method ❶. This is important because the RadioObservation implementation must know that you want to enable this optional field. If you assign directly to the raw data member (sky_bmp), the UDT implementation may not know that you intend to serialize the field. Many language implementations use flags internal to the UDT to determine which optional fields are set. Calling the setSky_bmp() method ensures that the internal flag is set. While the optional field interface isn't consistent across language implementations (sadly), you should always use the UDT set method if one exists to set fields. It's worth looking over the code generated for any UDTs you design to get familiar with the implementation approach in the languages you're working with.

Once the UDT is properly initialized, we write it to the protocol using the UDT write() method. This takes care of serializing all the information required to store not only the data contained within the UDT, but also the metadata necessary to de-serialize the object (field IDs, types, and so on). The WriteRadioObservation() method dumps the contents of the UDT to the console for review:

```
public static void ReadRadioObservation(TProtocol proto)
        throws TException {
    System.out.println("\nReading Observations");
    System.out.println("------------------------");
    RadioObservation ro = new RadioObservation();
    ro.read(proto);
    DumpObservation(ro);
}
```

The ReadRadioObservation() method creates a new default instance of the Radio-Observation class, and then uses the read() method to de-serialize the byte stream, reconstituting the object. The ReadRadioObservation() method then dumps the UDT object to the console:

```
public static void FakeInit(RadioObservation ro) {
    ro.telescope_count = 1;
    ro.system = RadioObservationSystem.Arecibo;
    ro.time = System.currentTimeMillis() / 1000.0;
    ICRFPosition pos = new ICRFPosition(270.3, 45.24);
    pos.setEcliptic_year((short)2000);#A
    ro.pos = new Position();
    ro.pos.setIcrfpos(pos);
```

```
        ro.freq_amp = new HashMap<>();
        ro.freq_amp.put(20500000L, 75.456);
        ro.freq_amp.put(50000000L, 29.321);
        ro.freq_amp.put(75000000L, 51.526);
    }
```

The FakeInit() method initializes a new instance of the RadioObservation type with mocked up data. Note that the Java implementation of the RadioObservation type requires us to allocate instances of all the fields that are reference types. The telescope _count is an integer type and is directly assigned to. The RadioObservationSystem enum and typedef Time types are also base types under the covers and can be directly assigned to.

The pos field is a union and can take on several possible types. FakeInit() creates a new ICRFPosition object to use as the RadioObservation position. The generated ICRFPosition class has a constructor that accepts initial values for the declination and right_ascension. However, the ICRFPosition ecliptic_year field is optional and must be set using the setEcliptic_year() method to ensure that it's marked as set and therefore serialized ❶.

We must also set union fields using a set method. Here we use the setIcrfpos() method to set the active type and field value for the pos field. This implicitly unsets any prior field type that may have been enabled.

The last field initialized in FakeInit() is the frequency/amplitude map. Apache Thrift will support any map type implementing the standard Java Map interface. Here we've created a HashMap to house the three frequencies and amplitudes:

```
    public static void DumpICRFPosition(ICRFPosition pos) {
        System.out.println("Position      : " +
                    pos.declination + " dec - " +
                    pos.right_ascension + " ra [" +
                    ((pos.isSetEcliptic_year())?pos.ecliptic_year:"")+"]");   ❶
    }

    public static void DumpObservation(RadioObservation ro) {
        System.out.println("Telescope Count: " + ro.telescope_count);
        System.out.println("System        : " + ro.system.name());
        System.out.println("Time          : " + ro.time);
❷      if (ro.pos.isSetIcrfpos()) {
            DumpICRFPosition(ro.pos.getIcrfpos());
        }
        System.out.println("Frequency   Magnitude");
        for (Map.Entry<Long, Double> entry : ro.freq_amp.entrySet()) {
            System.out.println("  "+entry.getKey()+"  "+entry.getValue());
        }
    }
```

The last two functions are the Dump methods used to display the RadioObservation objects to the console. The DumpICRFPostition() method displays the ICRFPosition data. The method tests for the presence of the optional ecliptic_year before displaying it with the isSetEcliptic_year() method ❶.

The DumpObservation() method displays the various fields of the RadioObservation object. Before displaying the pos field, which is a union, the type in use must be determined. This program only supports the ICRFPosition type and uses the isSetIcrfpos() method to determine if the union is using the ICRFPosition type ❷. If the union is using another type, we skip displaying the position. This allows the dump to work with versions of the IDL that have Position types unknown to this IDL version. The loop at the bottom of the method displays the frequencies and amplitudes in the freq_amp map.

While this is a Java example, the key points illustrated here apply across the range of Apache Thrift implementations. In the next section, we'll look at the inner workings of the UDT.

7.4   *Under the type serialization hood*

At this point we have looked at the process of serializing a simple UDT and a complex UDT. To better understand the serialization process, let's take a look at the Apache Thrift code generated to support the radio observation UDT.

To start, we'll build a Python program to read and display RadioObservation UDTs from files on disk.

Listing 7.5   ~/ThriftBook/part2/types/complex/disk_ser.py

```python
import sys
sys.path.append("gen-py")

from thrift.transport import TTransport
from thrift.protocol import TBinaryProtocol
from radio_observation import ttypes

#Read in the serialized UDT
trans = TTransport.TFileObjectTransport(open("data","rb"))
trans.open()
proto = TBinaryProtocol.TBinaryProtocol(trans)
ro = ttypes.RadioObservation()
ro.read(proto)

#Display the contents of the UDT
print("\nReading Observations")
print("------------------------")
print("Telescope Count: %d" % ro.telescope_count)
print("System         : %s" %
      ttypes.RadioObservationSystem._VALUES_TO_NAMES[ro.system])
print("Time           : %f" % ro.time)
if None != ro.pos.icrfpos:
    print("Position       : %f dec - %f ra [%s]" %
          (ro.pos.icrfpos.declination,
           ro.pos.icrfpos.right_ascension,
           "" if None == ro.pos.icrfpos.ecliptic_year else
             str(ro.pos.icrfpos.ecliptic_year)))
```

```
print("Frequency   Magnitude")
for k,v in ro.freq_amp.items():
    print("  %d   %f" % (k,v))
print("Size of bmp: %d" % (0 if None == ro.sky_bmp else len(ro.sky_bmp)))

#Close the source file and write a copy of the UDT to a backup file
trans.close()
trans = TTransport.TFileObjectTransport(open("data.bak","wb"))
trans.open()
proto = TBinaryProtocol.TBinaryProtocol(trans)
ro.write(proto)
trans.close()
```

This Python program mirrors the RadioObservations read behavior of the previous Java program. It also writes a backup copy of the UDT to a new file without the bitmap. A key difference in the Python implementation is the absence of UDT set, unset, and isset methods for optional fields. The generated Python UDT code uses the None object to represent an unset field. Testing for None provides isset functionality, setting a field to a non-None value equates to set, and setting a field to None equates to unset.

The following session demonstrates using the Java program to serialize a Radio-Observation to disk, followed by using the previous Python program to de-serialize the RadioObservation:

```
$ ls -l
-rw-r--r-- 1 randy randy  3476 Jul  6 17:47 DiskSer.java
-rw-r--r-- 1 randy randy  1301 Jul  6 18:53 disk_ser.py
-rwxrw-rw- 1 randy randy 25800 Jul  4 00:13 quasar.bmp
-rw-r--r-- 1 randy randy  1430 Jul  6 14:32 radio_observation.thrift
$ thrift --gen java --gen py radio_observation.thrift
$ javac -cp /usr/local/lib/libthrift-1.0.0.jar:\
           /usr/share/java/slf4j-api.jar:\
           /usr/share/java/slf4j-nop.jar
           DiskSer.java
           gen-java/radio_observation/*.java
$ java -cp /usr/local/lib/libthrift-1.0.0.jar:\
           /usr/share/java/slf4j-api.jar:\
           /usr/share/java/slf4j-nop.jar:\
           gen-java:\
           .
           DiskSer write bmp

Writting Observations
-----------------------
Telescope Count: 1
System        : Arecibo
Time          : 1.3731621022E9
Position      : 45.24 dec - 270.3 ra [2000]
Frequency   Magnitude
  50000000  29.321
  75000000  51.526
  20500000  75.456
```

```
$ python disk_ser.py
Reading Observations
-----------------------
Telescope Count: 1
System      : Arecibo
Time        : 1373162102.200000
Position    : 45.240000 dec - 270.300000 ra [2000]
Frequency   Magnitude
  50000000  29.321000
  75000000  51.526000
  20500000  75.456000
Size of bmp: 25800
$ ls -l
-rw-r--r-- 1 randy randy 25925 Jul  6 18:55 data
-rw-r--r-- 1 randy randy   118 Jul  6 18:55 data.bak
-rw-r--r-- 1 randy randy  4846 Jul  6 18:54 DiskSer.class
-rw-r--r-- 1 randy randy  3476 Jul  6 17:47 DiskSer.java
-rw-r--r-- 1 randy randy  1301 Jul  6 18:53 disk_ser.py
drwxr-xr-x 3 randy randy  4096 Jul  6 18:54 gen-java
drwxr-xr-x 3 randy randy  4096 Jul  6 18:54 gen-py
-rwxrw-rw- 1 randy randy 25800 Jul  4 00:13 quasar.bmp
-rw-r--r-- 1 randy randy  1430 Jul  6 14:32 radio_observation.thrift
```

This session begins by generating code to support the radio observation IDL UDTs in both Java and Python. Next we build and run the Java program to serialize a sample `RadioObservation` to the file "data". The Python program is then used to read the object from the file and display its contents, also writing a backup of the UDT to a .bak file, but without the optional `sky_bmp`.

To begin the tour under the hood, let's look at the Python implementation of the `RadioObservation` type found in gen-py/radio_observation/ttypes.py, as shown in the following listing.

Listing 7.6 gen-py/radio_observation/ttypes.py A

```python
class RadioObservation:
  thrift_spec = (
    None, # 0
    (1, TType.I32, 'telescope_count', None, None, ), # 1
    (2, TType.DOUBLE, 'time', None, None, ), # 2
    None, # 3
    (4, TType.I32, 'system', None, None, ), # 4
    (5, TType.MAP, 'freq_amp', (TType.I64,None,TType.DOUBLE,None),None,),#5
    (6, TType.STRUCT, 'pos', (Position, Position.thrift_spec), None, ), # 6
    (7, TType.STRING, 'sky_bmp', None, None, ), # 7
  )

  def __init__(self, telescope_count=None, time=None, system=None,
               freq_amp=None, pos=None, sky_bmp=None,):
    self.telescope_count = telescope_count
    self.time = time
    self.system = system
```

```
        self.freq_amp = freq_amp
        self.pos = pos
        self.sky_bmp = sky_bmp

    def read(self, iprot): ...
    def write(self, oprot): ...
```

The Python implementation for the `RadioObservation` UDT comes in the form of a Python class. This class has four conceptual parts, which it shares with C++, Java, and most other Apache thrift language implementations:

- A *field database*—Provides metadata for each field used by the implementation
- A *default constructor*—Sets the fields to their initial default values
- A `read()` *method*—De-serializes the object using a provided protocol
- A `write()` *method*—Serializes the object using a provided protocol

In the previous Python code listing, the Field database comes in the form of the `thrift_spec RadioObservation` class attribute. This is a Python tuple containing a tuple for each field in the UDT. The field tuples contain the ID of the field, its IDL type, the field name, additional type information for complex field types, and, finally, a default value, if any.

The Python Default Constructor is the `__init__()` method. This method sets up an instance of the UDT with each of the fields initialized to a default value. Because none of the fields declared in the IDL have default values, all the fields are assigned the `None` object in Python, designating them as unset. As a rule, it's important to initialize all the non-optional fields in a UDT before serializing it. In languages with implementations similar to Python, even default requiredness fields will not be serialized unless initialized first.

In such implementations, you should also only read fields that you know to be set. This can be tricky when using languages like Python. For example, if we used our previous Python program to read in a `RadioObservation` file from a newer Java program that no longer emits the `telescope_count` field, this field would be left set to `None`. Attempting to print it (as in the example code) would raise an exception. Perhaps this is the behavior you want; if not, you should test the field prior to using it (if field == None: don't use). Another option would be to ensure fields have a default value in IDL. Whatever the approach, dynamically typed programs should use a consistent strategy to avoid accessing fields that might be set to `None` (or the equivalent) after de-serialization.

The UDT `read()` and `write()` methods encapsulate the serialization capability of the UDT. Let's look at each in turn.

7.4.1   *Serializing with write()*

The `write()` method performs the serialization task for a UDT. Though the Python implementation is satisfyingly compact, it's essentially the same logic provided by other languages. The following listing shows the `write()` method for the Radio-Observation UDT.

Listing 7.7 gen-py/radio_observation/ttypes.py B

```
    def write(self, oprot):
      oprot.writeStructBegin('RadioObservation')
❶    if self.telescope_count is not None:
        oprot.writeFieldBegin('telescope_count', TType.I32, 1)
        oprot.writeI32(self.telescope_count)
        oprot.writeFieldEnd()
      if self.time is not None:
        oprot.writeFieldBegin('time', TType.DOUBLE, 2)
        oprot.writeDouble(self.time)
        oprot.writeFieldEnd()
      if self.system is not None:
        oprot.writeFieldBegin('system', TType.I32, 4)
        oprot.writeI32(self.system)
        oprot.writeFieldEnd()
      if self.freq_amp is not None:
        oprot.writeFieldBegin('freq_amp', TType.MAP, 5)
        oprot.writeMapBegin(TType.I64, TType.DOUBLE, len(self.freq_amp))    ❷
        for kiter7,viter8 in self.freq_amp.items():
          oprot.writeI64(kiter7)
          oprot.writeDouble(viter8)
        oprot.writeMapEnd()
        oprot.writeFieldEnd()
      if self.pos is not None:
        oprot.writeFieldBegin('pos', TType.STRUCT, 6)
❸      self.pos.write(oprot)
        oprot.writeFieldEnd()
      if self.sky_bmp is not None:
        oprot.writeFieldBegin('sky_bmp', TType.STRING, 7)
        oprot.writeString(self.sky_bmp)
        oprot.writeFieldEnd()
      oprot.writeFieldStop()
      oprot.writeStructEnd()
```

The Python write() method serializes the UDT field-by-field. The fields happen to be serialized in order but need not be. The fields are written within the body of an Apache Thrift struct that's started with the Protocol writeStructBegin() method and ended with the writeFieldStop() and writeStructEnd() methods.

In the example, each field is tested for None before being written ❶. If the field exists, the writeFieldBegin() method is passed the name, type, and ID of the field, and then the field data is serialized. Note that, while the field name is passed to the writeFieldBegin() method, it's not serialized in any current Apache Thrift protocols, although the ID and type are.

The freq_amp field is a map requiring a loop to output all its key/value pairs ❷. The pos field is a Position union instance that is itself a complex type. To serialize an embedded complex type, the generated code calls the write() method for that type ❸.

7.4.2 De-serializing with read()

The read side of the equation is only slightly more complex. The side writing a data structure knows its layout in advance. However, when you're reading an Apache Thrift data structure, you're never sure what you'll find. Default requiredness fields may be missing if the object was serialized with a newer or older version of the IDL, optional fields may or may not be set, unions may contain any one of their possible types, collections may contain 0 or more elements, and fields may arrive in any order.

Here's a listing of the Python RadioObservation read() method.

Listing 7.8 gen-py/radio_observation/ttypes.py C

```
    def read(self, iprot):
      iprot.readStructBegin()
❶    while True:
        (fname, ftype, fid) = iprot.readFieldBegin()        ❷
        if ftype == TType.STOP:
❸        break
        if fid == 1:
          if ftype == TType.I32:
            self.telescope_count = iprot.readI32();         ❹
          else:
            iprot.skip(ftype)
        elif fid == 2:
          if ftype == TType.DOUBLE:
            self.time = iprot.readDouble();
          else:
            iprot.skip(ftype)
        elif fid == 4:
          if ftype == TType.I32:
            self.system = iprot.readI32();
          else:
            iprot.skip(ftype)
        elif fid == 5:
          if ftype == TType.MAP:
            self.freq_amp = {}
            (_ktype1, _vtype2, _size0 ) = iprot.readMapBegin()
❺          for _i4 in xrange(_size0):
              _key5 = iprot.readI64();
              _val6 = iprot.readDouble();
              self.freq_amp[_key5] = _val6
            iprot.readMapEnd()
          else:
            iprot.skip(ftype)
        elif fid == 6:
          if ftype == TType.STRUCT:
            self.pos = Position()
            self.pos.read(iprot)                            ❻
          else:
            iprot.skip(ftype)
        elif fid == 7:
          if ftype == TType.STRING:
            self.sky_bmp = iprot.readString();
          else:
```

```
      iprot.skip(ftype)
  else:
    iprot.skip(ftype)
  iprot.readFieldEnd()
iprot.readStructEnd()
```

The read() method begins with the readStructBegin() call and then proceeds to read fields in an endless loop ❶. The Protocol readFieldBegin() call returns the name (which is always "" in current protocol implementations), type, and ID of the next field in the serialization stream ❷. If this is the STOP field written by the writeFieldStop() call, we've finished de-serializing fields and exit the loop ❸. If the field ID isn't one we recognize, the field is skipped using the protocol's skip method. Given the field type, the skip() method can figure out how many bytes in the stream to discard.

If we recognize the field ID and the field type is the type we expect, the field value is de-serialized ❹. This provides motivation for never repurposing a field ID. Once a field ID is assigned and given a type, changing that type will cause programs using older versions of the IDL to ignore the field. If you need type flexibility for a field, you should make it of union type.

The map collection is de-serialized in a loop, much as it was serialized ❺. The complex union Position type is de-serialized using the Position class read() method ❻. When all fields have been read, the readStructEnd() method is called. The serialization stream is then ready for the next read operation.

7.5 *Type evolution*

Interface evolution, and therefore UDT evolution, is one of the most important features of Apache Thrift. Type evolution enables us to change types over time without breaking compatibility with preexisting programs. With proper planning, you can safely change almost any aspect of a UDT except IDs. How might a type evolve over time? Many possibilities exist:

- The name of a field may need to be changed.
- A new field may be required.
- An existing field may no longer be needed.
- The type of a field may need to be changed.
- The requiredness of the field may need to be changed.
- The default value of a field may need to be changed.

Let's consider each of these in turn. In our discussion, we'll look at the impact an IDL change has on programs on either side of the change. Programs using the old IDL before the change will be referred to as OLD and programs using the new IDL after the change will be referred to as NEW (see figure 7.5).

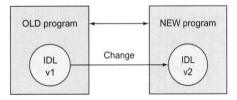

Figure 7.5 Programs using different versions of an interface can communicate with proper use of interface evolution in Apache Thrift.

7.5.1   *Renaming fields*

Apache Thrift fields can be renamed at any time without impacting interoperability using the current suite of protocols (binary/compact/json), because these Apache Thrift protocols don't serialize field names. Fields are identified in serialized form by the combination of the field ID and field type. The ID is the field's unique identifier. The type is used to ensure that the writer and the reader are using the same type. What each side calls the field in code is incidental.

Changing the semantics of a field is a breaking change under any circumstance. For example, changing field number 1 from "number of telescopes" to "number of frequency observations" will never work. However, changing the name of field number 1 from `telescope_count` to `num_tele` will always work. It doesn't matter what you call the value, as long as the semantic is number of telescopes, the type is i32, and the ID is 1.

> **TIP**   You can change Apache Thrift field names freely, but never change field semantics.

7.5.2   *Adding fields*

Perhaps the most common change facing evolving data types is the need to add more fields. Fortunately, adding a field to an Apache Thrift structure is almost always a backward-compatible operation. During de-serialization, fields that aren't recognized are ignored by default. This allows OLD programs to tolerate unknown newly added fields. New programs must also tolerate not receiving the new field when de-serializing data from old programs.

REQUIRED

Fields added after the initial API release shouldn't be made "required". Unless all systems using the UDT with the new "required" field are updated at once, missing required fields will cause exceptions in new programs when receiving copies of the UDT from old programs that don't provide the required field.

DEFAULT

Default requiredness is a good choice for new fields. However, because default fields are always serialized, it's easy to assume that they'll always be found in the serialization stream. This is not the case. If a struct is updated with a new field, old programs will not serialize the field, because they don't know about it. Giving new fields default values will ensure that the field is available and has a reasonable default, even when old programs don't serialize the field (see also "Changing a field's requiredness" in section 7.5.5).

OPTIONAL

Another good choice for new fields is optional requiredness. If you want to serialize optional fields, you can. If you want to suppress them, you can. When de-serializing, if the optional field is found, it's set; otherwise it's left unset. Optional tells us (explicitly) that this field may not always be there. The downside of optional fields, as you may have noticed from the examples above, is that they're the most complex to interact with. You must test for their presence before using them.

> **TIP** When adding new fields, give them a unique descriptive name and a unique, never-before-used ID. Make them default requiredness and give them a default value, or make them optional requiredness with no default value.

7.5.3 Deleting fields

As we saw in our `radio_observation.idl` example, the proper way to delete a field is to comment it out and retire its ID permanently. When new programs send UDTs to old programs, the old programs must tolerate the absence of fields that have been deleted in the new IDL. This often requires the field to have a default value assigned to it in old IDL versions.

If old programs cannot tolerate the absence of a deleted field, the field should be marked "required" (because it is). Required fields must never be deleted, because they're expected to be present at all times.

> **TIP** When deleting fields, comment out the field in the IDL to keep a record of its prior existence. Never reuse a deleted field ID and never delete required fields. Take care when deleting default requiredness fields without default values; old programs may (inappropriately) count on de-serializing a default requiredness value.

7.5.4 Changing a field's type

Changing the type of a field will cause the field to be ignored by programs expecting a different type. When a program reads a field, it checks the field ID *and* the field type. If these match a field that the program knows, the field is de-serialized. If these don't match, the field is skipped. Thus, changing the type of a field will cause old programs to no longer recognize the field when transmitted by new programs, and it will cause new programs to no longer recognize the field when transmitted by old programs. New programs can still share the field among themselves, and old programs can still share the field among themselves. While precarious, you may find this an acceptable way to migrate programs to a new field type.

A more effective option exists, but it requires preplanning. If you know that a field may have more than one type representation, it makes sense to make it of union type. Even if only one type is currently in use, a union will give you type flexibility going forward. For example, imagine you have to build a UDT with a temperature field. If your current sensors use 16 bits to capture the temperature, you might like to use an i16 to transmit it. However, if you know the requirements are likely to change, you could choose to initially create a union with only the i16 type:

```
union Temp {              //Temp union V1
    1: i16 ScalarCentTemp;
}
```

```
struct Data {
    1: Temp device_temperature_reading;
}
```

Later, as you deploy new devices that capture fractions of degrees, outputting data as doubles and strings from device to device, you can add these type options alongside the original i16. Old programs that only know about the union containing i16 will ignore the NEW types, but can still communicate with all parties using the i16 type, as shown in the following code:

```
union Temp {                      //Temp union V2
    1: i16 ScalarCentTemp;
    2: double FloatCentTemp;
    3: double FloatFarTemp;
    4: string asciiTemp;
}

struct Data {
    1: Temp device_temperature_reading;
}
```

Unions can also communicate separate type semantics using the same base data type. For example, several of our temperature devices may emit floating point Centigrade temperatures and others may emit floating point Fahrenheit temperatures. Using a union, you can capture these as separate fields using the same base type. Each union field is effectively a new typedef within the scope of the union.

> **TIP**   When faced with fields that may have more than one representation, use a union to allow the field to maintain its identity while taking on multiple types.

7.5.5   *Changing a field's requiredness*

Fields with "required" requiredness shouldn't be changed. Making a required field optional will cause exceptions when old programs find the field missing.

In situations where required fields need to be removed or made optional, changing the field from required to default can be a stepping stone. If you ensure that new programs using default requiredness always serialize the field, you won't break the old programs requiring the field. This can give you time to update the old programs to the new IDL gradually. Once all the programs are running the new IDL based on default requiredness, you can transition the field to optional or delete it altogether. To do this, you must have control over all the programs using the interface (rarely possible with public APIs).

Default and optional requiredness are similar (and identical in many language implementations). Changing between the two has little impact in most situations. It can make sense to make default requiredness fields optional to avoid serializing them in scenarios where this is critical. For more information on requiredness, see chapter 6.

> **TIP** Leave optional fields optional; it's the most flexible requiredness. Default fields can generally be changed to optional without impact if needed. Required fields should never be changed.

7.5.6 *Changing a field's default value*

Struct fields given default values in IDL are initialized with the default values in generated code. Consider the Data struct code snippets representing two different versions of an IDL interface:

```
struct Data {// V1
    1: i16 rating = 5
}

struct Data {// V2
    1: i16 rating = 10
}
```

If program A is built with V1 of the IDL, a default value of 5 will be assigned to its rating. If program B is built with V2, a default value of 10 will be assigned to its rating. Thus, if a third program de-serialized a default object from A, its rating would be 5; however, de-serializing an otherwise identical default object from B would provide a rating of 10. Finding two supposedly identical objects with different ratings could be surprising, even causing undefined behavior if the receiver uses 5 as a flag value for default configuration.

While Apache Thrift doesn't require default values associated with optional fields to be serialized, in practice, you must explicitly unset an optional field with a default value to avoid serializing it.

> **TIP** Changing a default value in IDL can produce subtle, application-defined effects and is therefore not always safe.

7.6 *Using Zlib compression*

Up to this point we've looked at a number of UDT examples and discussed the fine points of type design and evolution. To complete the type story, we need to look at data compression.

Often, storage size is a concern when serializing data to disk. Disk space is finite and, in many settings, it's faster to read and decompress a compressed image than it is to read the image uncompressed. It can be worth trading many CPU cycles for a smaller serialized image.

Apache Thrift protocols are designed to provide fast serialization of small units of data, making them suitable for many tasks, including streaming and RPC serialization. However, protocols aren't well suited for high-ratio, whole-object compression tasks.

Large objects, such as instances of our RadioObservation type with a sky_bmp attached, can benefit from whole object compression when the goal is long-term storage or disk optimization. To apply a compression algorithm to an entire UDT, we need to use a layered transport. Layered transports can buffer all the atomic pieces written by the protocol layer, and when the entire serialized object has been buffered, the transport layer can then compress the object as a unit and write it out to the underlying device (see figure 7.6).

Several Apache Thrift languages support the Zlib transport compression layer (see figure 7.6). Zlib is the open source compression library upon which pkzip, gzip, and many other compression tools are based (see zlib.net for more information on Zlib). All three of our demonstration languages, C++, Java, and Python, support Zlib compression.

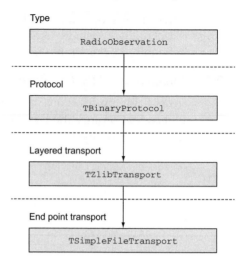

Figure 7.6   Type serialization Zlib compression stack

7.6.1   Using Zlib with C++

To demonstrate Zlib compression, we'll build a C++ program to convert uncompressed RadioObservation UDT files into compressed files. The program will read in the data file written by the Java program in the prior section and then write it back out using the Zlib compression layer, as shown in the following listing.

Listing 7.9   ~/ThriftBook/part2/types/zip/disk_ser_z.cpp

```cpp
#include "gen-cpp/radio_observation_types.h"
#include <thrift/transport/TSimpleFileTransport.h>
#include <thrift/transport/TZlibTransport.h>
#include <thrift/protocol/TBinaryProtocol.h>
#include <boost/shared_ptr.hpp>
#include <boost/make_shared.hpp>
#include <iostream>

using namespace apache::thrift::transport;
using namespace apache::thrift::protocol;
using namespace radio_observation;
using boost::make_shared;
using boost::shared_ptr;


void DumpRadioObservation(const RadioObservation & ro) {
    auto it0 = _RadioObservationSystem_VALUES_TO_NAMES.find(ro.system);
    auto psystem = (std::end(_RadioObservationSystem_VALUES_TO_NAMES) ==
```

```
                              it0) ? "" : it0->second;
    std::cout << "\nRadio Observation"
              << "\n------------------------"
              << "\nTelescope Count: " << ro.telescope_count
              << "\nSystem          : " << psystem
              << "\nTime            : " << ro.time
              << "\nPosition        : ";
    if (ro.pos.__isset.icrfpos) {
        std::cout << ro.pos.icrfpos.declination << " dec - "
                  << ro.pos.icrfpos.right_ascension << " ra [";
        if (ro.pos.icrfpos.__isset.ecliptic_year)
            std::cout << ro.pos.icrfpos.ecliptic_year;
        std::cout << "]";
    }
    std::cout << "\nFrequency   Magnitude\n";
    for (auto it : ro.freq_amp)
        std::cout << "  " << it.first << "  " << it.second << "\n";
    std::cout << "Size of bmp: " << ((ro.__isset.sky_bmp) ?          ❷
                                     ro.sky_bmp.length() : 0) << std::endl;
}

int main(int argc, char *argv[]) {
    if (argc != 2) {
        std::cout << "usage: " << argv[0] << " <filename>" << std::endl;
        return -1;
    }
    try {
        //Read the UDT in from the command line supplied filename
        std::cout << "Reading from uncompressed file: "
                  << argv[1] << std::endl;
        shared_ptr<TTransport> trans =
            make_shared<TSimpleFileTransport>(argv[1], true, true);
        auto proto = make_shared<TBinaryProtocol>(trans);               ❸
        trans->open();
        RadioObservation ro;
        ro.read(proto.get());
        trans->close();
        DumpRadioObservation(ro);

        //Write out the compressed version of the UDT
        std::string out_file(argv[1]); out_file += ".z";
        std::cout << "\nWritting to compressed file: "
                  << out_file << std::endl;
        Trans = make_shared<TSimpleFileTransport>(out_file, true, true);
❹      trans = make_shared<TZlibTransport>(trans);
        proto = make_shared<TBinaryProtocol>(trans);
        trans->open();
        ro.write(proto.get());
❺      trans->flush();
        trans->close();

        //Verify the compressed version of the UDT
        std::cout << "\nVerifying compressed file: "
                  << out_file << std::endl;
        trans = make_shared<TSimpleFileTransport>(out_file, true, true);
```

```
            trans = make_shared<TZlibTransport>(trans);
            proto = make_shared<TBinaryProtocol>(trans);
            trans->open();
            RadioObservation ro_check;
            ro_check.read(proto.get());
            trans->close();
            DumpRadioObservation(ro_check);
        } catch (std::exception ex) {
            std::cerr << "Error: " << ex.what() << std::endl;
        }
    }
```

This program illustrates several features associated with the IDL compiler-generated C++ UDT code. The first function in the listing, DumpRadioObservation(), displays the RadioObservation UDT much like the prior Java and Python examples. In the Java program, we used isSetXXX() methods to test for the presence of optional fields. In the Python example, we tested the field against the None object. The C++-generated code takes yet another route. Each C++ UDT contains an __isset struct that contains bools named after each field in the UDT. For example, in the Dump-RadioObservation() method, we test to see if the sky_bmp field is set by looking at ro.__isset.sky_bmp ❷.

Like Python, each IDL enumeration offers a lookup mechanism that allows a program to recover the enumeration name at runtime. The not-so-briefly named _RadioObservationSystem_VALUES_TO_NAMES map is generated by the IDL compiler to house the RadioObservationSystem enumeration names. We use the map find() method to test for the presence of the key we're looking for ❶. Keep in mind that the value passed could be arriving from a program using a different version of the IDL. We have no guarantee that the name will be found in the map. All such lookup results must be tested if we want to allow our interface to evolve seamlessly.

The main body of the program is straightforward. First, we de-serialize an existing RadioObservation using the binary protocol ❸. As always, we must de-serialize with the same protocol used in serialization. Next we create a new Apache Thrift I/O stack with the Zlib layered transport between the binary protocol and the file endpoint transport ❹. The protocol writes strings, integers, and doubles out to the Zlib layer that buffers the data, compressing only when a reasonable number of bytes are present. When the serialization is complete, we call the TZlibTransport's flush() method to complete the compression and flush the bytes out to the TSimpleFileTransport ❺.

The following code shows a sample session using the compression program:

```
$ ls -l
-rw-r--r-- 1 randy randy 25925 Jul  7 01:01 data                    ❶
-rw-r--r-- 1 randy randy  2950 Jul  7 01:07 disk_ser_z.cpp
-rw-r--r-- 1 randy randy  1330 Jul  7 01:01 radio_observation.thrift
❷ $ thrift -gen cpp radio_observation.thrift
  $ g++ -std=c++11 disk_ser_z.cpp gen-cpp/*.cpp -Wall -std=c++11 -lthrift
          -lthriftz -lz                    ⟵┐
❹ $ ./a.out data                               ❸
```

```
Reading from uncompressed file: data

Radio Observation
-------------------------
Telescope Count: 1
System        : Arecibo
Time          : 1.37316e+09
Position      : 45.24 dec - 270.3 ra [2000]
Frequency   Magnitude
  20500000   75.456
  50000000   29.321
  75000000   51.526
Size of bmp: 25800

Writting to compressed file: data.z
Verifying compressed file: data.z

Radio Observation
-------------------------
Telescope Count: 1
System        : Arecibo
Time          : 1.37316e+09
Position      : 45.24 dec - 270.3 ra [2000]
Frequency   Magnitude
  20500000   75.456
  50000000   29.321
  75000000   51.526
Size of bmp: 25800
$ ls -l
-rwxr-xr-x 1 randy randy 196212 Jul  7 01:42 a.out
-rw-r--r-- 1 randy randy  25925 Jul  7 01:01 data
-rw-r--r-- 1 randy randy   3640 Jul  7 01:42 data.z           ❺
-rw-r--r-- 1 randy randy   2950 Jul  7 01:07 disk_ser_z.cpp
drwxr-xr-x 2 randy randy   4096 Jul  7 01:42 gen-cpp
-rw-r--r-- 1 randy randy   1330 Jul  7 01:01 radio_observation.thrift
$ gzip -9 data
$ ls -l data.gz
-rw-r--r-- 1 randy randy   3636 Jul  7 01:01 data.gz          ❻
```

This example assumes that we have a "data" file on disk left over from a run of the previous radio observation Java program. Listing the files in the working directory, we can see that the data file is almost 26K ❶. Next, the session generates C++ code for the IDL types ❷ and compiles the C++ program ❸. We compile in the generated types from the gen-cpp directory and also include the thriftz library (which contains the TZLibTransport implementation) and the libz library (ZLib itself). The thriftz library is built automatically if Zlib is installed at the time Apache Thrift C++ is configured. Zlib support is supplied in a separate thrift library because it isn't typically used in RPC applications, and keeping it separate eliminates the Zlib dependency for those not using it. For more information on configuring your C++ development environment, see the C++ language chapter in part 3.

Running the C++ program on one of the data files generated by the previous RadioObservation Java program ❹ produces a compressed version of the file, which is under 4K in size ❺. This is less than 15% of the size of the original, essentially the same size produced by using gzip to compress the original file ❻. The C++ TZlibTransport uses the Zlib Z_DEFAULT_COMPRESSION compression level, which is 9. Level 0 is no compression (fast) and level 9 is best compression (slow). The TZlibTransport in C++ provides several default constructor parameters, the last of which allows the default compression level to be set.

7.6.2   *Using Zlib with Python*

To demonstrate Zlib interoperability across languages, we'll modify the Python program created earlier in the chapter to read the compressed file generated by the C++ program above. In the following listing, we read the data.z compressed file, display the UDT data, and then write out a new compressed data.z.bak version.

Listing 7.10   ~/ThriftBook/part2/types/zip/disk_ser_z.py

```python
import sys
sys.path.append("gen-py")

from thrift.transport import TTransport
from thrift.transport import TZlibTransport        ❶
from thrift.protocol import TBinaryProtocol
from radio_observation import ttypes

#Read in the serialized compressed UDT
ep_trans = TTransport.TFileObjectTransport(open("data.z","rb"))
trans = TZlibTransport.TZlibTransport(ep_trans)        ◁┄┄┄
trans.open()                                              ❷
proto = TBinaryProtocol.TBinaryProtocol(trans)
ro = ttypes.RadioObservation()
ro.read(proto)
trans.close()

#Display the contents of the UDT
print("\nReading Observations")
print("------------------------")
print("Telescope Count: %d" % ro.telescope_count)
print("System         : %s" %
    ttypes.RadioObservationSystem._VALUES_TO_NAMES[ro.system])
print("Time           : %f" % ro.time)
if None != ro.pos.icrfpos:
    print("Position         : %f dec - %f ra [%s]" %
      (ro.pos.icrfpos.declination,
       ro.pos.icrfpos.right_ascension,
       "" if None == ro.pos.icrfpos.ecliptic_year else
       str(ro.pos.icrfpos.ecliptic_year)))
print("Frequency   Magnitude")
for k,v in ro.freq_amp.items():
    print(" %d  %f" % (k,v))
print("Size of bmp: %d" % (0 if None == ro.sky_bmp else len(ro.sky_bmp)))
```

```
#Close source file and write a compressed copy of the UDT to a backup file
ep_trans = TTransport.TFileObjectTransport(open("data.z.bak","wb"))
trans = TZlibTransport.TZlibTransport(ep_trans)
trans.open()
proto = TBinaryProtocol.TBinaryProtocol(trans)
ro.write(proto)
trans.flush()          ❸
trans.close()
```

Like C++, the Python Zlib transport is called TZlibTransport and it's located in the
TZlibTransport.py module, which is added as an import at the top of the source ❶.
Other than adding the Zlib layer in between the endpoint transport and the protocol
❷, nothing is new here. The Python write side calls the TZlibTransport flush()
method ❸ to force all of the bytes out to the endpoint before closing the file.

Here is a sample session using the new Python program:

```
$ thrift -gen py radio_observation.thrift
$ python disk_ser_z.py
Reading Observations
------------------------
Telescope Count: 1
System         : Arecibo
Time           : 1373162102.200000
Position       : 45.240000 dec - 270.300000 ra [2000]
Frequency    Magnitude
  20500000   75.456000
  50000000   29.321000
  75000000   51.526000
Size of bmp: 25800
$ ls -l
total 256
-rw-r--r-- 1 randy randy   25925 Jul  7 03:36 data
-rw-r--r-- 1 randy randy    3640 Jul  7 03:47 data.z
-rw-r--r-- 1 randy randy    3640 Jul  7 04:15 data.z.bak
-rw-r--r-- 1 randy randy    2940 Jul  7 03:47 disk_ser_z.cpp
-rw-r--r-- 1 randy randy    1468 Jul  7 04:13 disk_ser_z.py
drwxr-xr-x 3 randy randy    4096 Jul  7 03:35 gen-py
-rw-r--r-- 1 randy randy    1330 Jul  7 01:01 radio_observation.thrift
```

Notice a few points of interest here. First, the Python program had no problem reading the C++ compressed file, data.z, because the Python zlib and C++ Zlib implementations are based on the same code base and are fully compatible. The version of
the compressed RadioObservation object written by the Python program (data.z.bak)
is identical to the C++ version (data.z). You can pass the Python TZlibTransport constructor an alternate compression level as the second parameter of the constructor.
For example

```
trans = TZlibTransport.TZlibTransport(ep_trans, 6)
```

Note that the compression level affects only compression output. Any proper Zlib transport can decode data at any level of compression.

The Java TZlibTransport is also implemented as a transport layer, much like the C++ and Python examples here. See the book website for Java versions of the above Zlib examples.

Summary

Apache Thrift IDL provides a rich set of tools for describing data types that can be exchanged across languages and platforms. The Apache Thrift framework also provides a flexible and comprehensive set of type serialization features:

- Structs are the Apache Thrift IDL mechanism for creating cross-language, user-defined types.
- Structs have one or more fields, each with a name, ID, type, requiredness, and, optionally, a default value.
- Optional requiredness fields offer the most serialization flexibility, allowing user code to decide whether to serialize them or not:
  - Optional fields are a good choice for any data that may not need to be serialized on all occasions, particularly data fields of large size.
  - Optional fields must typically be set with language-specific set methods to ensure that the UDT serializes them when the write() method is called.
  - Optional fields must be tested for existence after de-serialization and prior to access in case they were not found during the de-serialization process.
- Typedefs allow new semantic types to be created from existing types.
- Enums allow new enumeration types to be created.
- Unions are used to create fields that have more than one possible type or representation:
  - All union fields are optional.
  - Union values must be set with set methods in most languages.
  - Only one type should be set at a time within a union.
- UDTs can be serialized by calling their write() method and de-serialized by calling their read() method.
- Apache Thrift Interface Evolution features allow UDTs to change over time without breaking existing applications:
  - New fields can be added.
  - Old fields can be removed.
  - Fields can be represented with a selection of types when unions are used.
- The TZlibTransport can be layered on top of memory and file endpoint transports to compress serialized objects:
  - The TZlibTransport isn't supported by all languages.

Implementing services

This chapter covers

- Best practices for designing Apache Thrift RPC services
- Implementing and testing service handlers
- Taking advantage of service interface evolution
- Using service inheritance hierarchies

The prior part II chapters examined transports, protocols, Apache Thrift IDL, and IDL-based user-defined types. This brings us to the top-shelf feature of the Apache Thrift framework—RPC services.

As we saw in chapter 7, the Apache Thrift IDL compiler generates language-specific types for UDTs declared in IDL source files. These generated types can read and write themselves using any of the Apache Thrift serialization protocols. As we'll see in this chapter, UDT serialization is an integral part of Apache Thrift RPC (figure 8.1).

Apache Thrift RPC services allow developers to create backend functionality in their preferred language and then expose that functionality to clients in any of more than 20 supported languages with no more than a few lines of code. Service interfaces are declared in Apache Thrift IDL and then compiled by the IDL compiler, which generates RPC client and server stubs for each service. RPC stubs allow clients to call remote functions in other languages as if the functions were locally

227

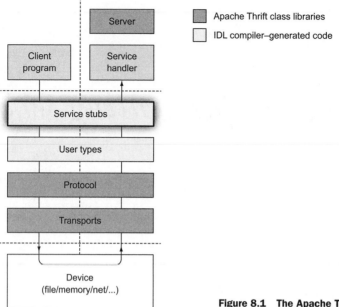

Figure 8.1   The Apache Thrift RPC service layer

defined. The required serialization and remote procedure call wiring is provided by
the Apache Thrift IDL compiler.

The two key components generated for each service by the IDL compiler are the
Client used in service client applications and the Processor used in server implementations. The service Client exposes the service interface locally and makes remote calls
to the peer service Processor. The Processor then calls implementations of the service
functions provided by a user-coded Handler (see figure 8.2).

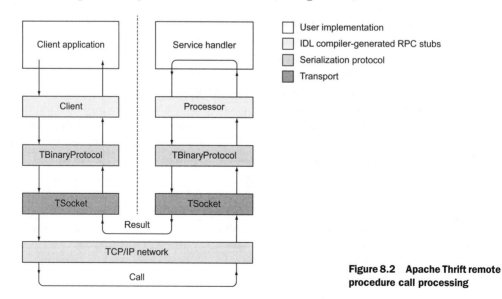

**Figure 8.2   Apache Thrift remote
procedure call processing**

While Apache Thrift RPC clients and servers typically run on separate machines, they need not. Clients and servers can run in separate processes on the same system or even within the same process, offering communication across threads. The Apache Thrift transport layer defines the communications channel used to connect clients and servers. Any inter-process communication mechanism supported by both the client and server languages can be used; for example, TCP/IP Sockets, Shared Memory, Named Pipes, or UNIX Domain Sockets, to name a few (see chapter 3 for more information on the transport layer).

In this chapter, we'll explore the features of Apache Thrift services and build several examples in our demonstration languages. This chapter focuses on IDL "services" and avoids digging into "server"–specific topics. Server specifics will be examined in the next chapter.

Over the next few pages we'll build a simple RPC application to demonstrate the fundamentals of Apache Thrift service construction. The service will have a simple interface allowing users to look up statistics for social networking sites. Building a basic Apache Thrift service can be boiled down to five simple steps:

1 Declare the service interface in Apache Thrift IDL.
2 Compile the IDL to generate RPC stubs in all the desired languages.
3 Create a handler that implements the service.
4 Use the IDL compiler-generated Processor and the Apache Thrift Transport, Protocol, and Server libraries to create a server to run the handler.
5 Use the IDL compiler-generated Client and the Apache Thrift Transport and Protocol libraries to build applications that use the IDL service.

We'll walk through each step in the following pages.

8.1 *Declaring IDL services*

The Apache Thrift IDL keyword "service" is used to declare a new service in an IDL file. Services have a name and a set of functions enclosed in braces. Each function within a service declaration is separated by white space, or, optionally, a comma or a semicolon. Functions have a return type, a name, and a set of parameters.

Here's a simple two-function service declaration that we'll use to complete step 1 in our example.

> **Listing 8.1   ~/ThriftBook/part2/services/simple/simple.thrift**

```
service SocialLookup {
    string GetSiteByRank( 1: i32 rank )
    i32 GetSiteRankByName( 1: string name )
}
```

The parameters of a function are declared in the same way as fields of a struct. Function parameters have an identifier, a requiredness, a type, a name, and a default value (see figure 8.3). While only the type and name are required, all parameters should be given a unique positive ID.

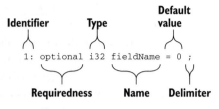

Each of these components is explained in the following sections.

Figure 8.3 Function parameter components

8.1.1 *Parameter identifiers*

Parameter identifiers (IDs) are used by the Apache Thrift framework to uniquely identify parameters during RPC processing. Identifiers are declared by placing an integer value followed by a colon at the beginning of a parameter declaration. Here's an example function with two parameters identified by the IDs 1 and 2:

```
i32 GetSiteRankByName(1: string name, 2: bool allowPartialMatch=false)
```

IDs are 16-bit integer values and must be unique within a parameter list. All IDs should be positive values; 0 and negative values are used internally by the Apache Thrift framework. Declaring identifiers (on both function parameters and struct fields) is optional. Leaving IDs out of an interface specification isn't recommended and greatly complicates the process of making incremental changes to the interface.

If an ID isn't supplied explicitly in IDL, the compiler will generate an ID internally. Compiler-generated IDs begin at -1 and decrement with each new parameter. If you change the parameter order or remove a parameter then recompile the IDL, the compiler will renumber all parameters without explicit IDs, and all programs using the old interface numbering scheme will misinterpret the new compiler-assigned field IDs.

> **TIP** Always assign a positive 16-bit integer ID (preferably sequential) to every function parameter and struct field. IDs must be unique within a struct or function parameter list. Consistent IDs are a critical enabler of interface evolution.

If you find yourself facing the chore of working with an existing Apache Thrift interface that failed to provide function parameter or struct field IDs, all isn't lost. You can update the IDL with negative parameter IDs matching those the compiler previously assigned (we'll see shortly that the compiler assigned numbers are easy to locate in generated source code). The IDL compiler will emit warnings when encountering negative IDs. To suppress these warnings, you can pass the IDL compiler the `-allow-neg-keys` command line switch.

8.1.2 *Parameter requiredness*

Parameter requiredness is similar to struct requiredness. Parameters can be assigned one of two requiredness levels:

- *required*—The parameter must always be present and can never be changed or removed without violating the interface contract:

```
void myFunc( 1: required i32 fieldName )
```

- *<default>*—The parameter is always supplied by the caller if it's known to the caller; however, the service providing the function cannot count on the parameter being supplied, thus providing support for clients which predate the addition of the parameter:

```
void myFunc( 1: i32 fieldName )
```

The `required` keyword makes interfaces rigid. The code generated for required parameters varies from language to language, though most implementations generate an exception if a required parameter isn't found on the server side.

Default requiredness implies that callers must supply the parameter, if known to them, but servers shouldn't require it. This allows such a parameter to be added or deleted at any point without breaking compatibility. Services should provide rational default values for newly added default requiredness parameters to support scenarios where the parameter isn't provided.

TIP Use default requiredness parameters with default values to maximize interface evolution flexibility.

Servers always ignore parameters that they don't recognize. This allows new parameters to be added to an interface without breaking older code. Apache Thrift's support for incrementally adding and deleting parameters allows you to update individual clients and services in a distributed application in isolation, avoiding the risk associated with updating all binaries across an entire enterprise. This incremental evolution is a key enabler of modern CI/CD and cloud native environments.

While Apache Thrift structs support optional requiredness, function parameters don't. In many settings, default requiredness is optimal for function parameters; however, optional requiredness does have advantages in certain scenarios. If the `optional` keyword is found in a parameter list, it's ignored and an IDL compiler warning is generated.

When optional parameters are needed, a UDT (struct) with default requiredness can be passed with optional fields inside it. In certain situations, it may make sense to design functions that take nothing but a single struct parameter containing the actual arguments, though this adds complexity to simple interfaces. For more information on requiredness, see chapter 6, "Apache Thrift IDL," and chapter 7, "Serializing user-defined types."

8.1.3 *Default parameter values*

Default parameter values provide a predefined value for a parameter. Default parameter values are declared by following the parameter name with an equal sign and the desired default value. The following code provides a default value of `false` for the `bool` parameter:

```
i32 GetSiteRankByName(1: string name, 2: bool allowPartialMatch=false)
```

Default values have no meaning and are effectively ignored in the context of required parameters. Required parameters must always be passed by the client and received by the server, so any initial default value is always overwritten by the value passed in the call. If no value is found in a call for a required parameter, an exception is raised, again making the default value of little use.

The only time default values come into play with normal requiredness parameters is when a client that doesn't know about a parameter calls a server that does. Parameters not supplied by the client retain their default values on the server side. This is a key feature, enabling servers to support clients with different versions of the interface.

For example, imagine you have a service with a function `f()` that takes no parameters. You have many client programs using this function, but you would like to slowly roll out a new version of function `f()`. The new version accepts a single i32 parameter called A. You could declare this new version of your function as follows: `f(1: i32 A=0);`. This will allow updated clients to call the function with the parameter A supplied, yet old clients will continue to work, because when function `f()` finds parameter A missing it will use the default value 0.

> **TIP** When adding new parameters to a service method, provide a default value. This allows the server to use the default value when processing calls from old programs that don't provide the new parameter.

Default parameter values have no effect on client-side code. A client using generated code for the RPC function prototype `f(1: i32 A=0)` cannot call the function f without supplying parameter A. Several languages (Python, C++, C#, among them) allow functions to be declared with default parameter values, making it possible for callers to leave out these parameters in native code. This behavior isn't supported by Apache Thrift; all clients must pass all parameters defined in their version of the interface when using Apache Thrift services.

8.1.4 *Function and parameter types*

Functions must be given a return type. Any legal IDL type can be returned by a function. The special void type is used to indicate that a function doesn't return a value. Function parameters can be of any valid IDL type other than void, including unions, typedefs, structs, and enums. Types must be declared prior to use. For this reason, services are usually the last items listed in an IDL source file.

8.2 *Building a simple service*

In chapter 1 we built a "Hello World" Python service to show how easy it is to create an Apache Thrift RPC solution. To begin the examples in this chapter, we'll construct a simple Java server to implement the `SocialLookup` service declared in listing 8.1.

8.2.1 *Interfaces*

Services specify an interface contract between clients and servers. This contract ensures that no matter what languages the client and server are written in, the calling conventions, parameters, and return values will be understood by both parties. Declaring a service in Apache Thrift IDL may require the definition of types and constants used by that service. Essentially, everything declared in an Apache Thrift IDL file is an element of the interface contract.

The IDL compiler typically generates an abstract interface for each service in target languages. This interface construct is a language-specific representation of the service, a set of function signatures with no implementation. Clients make calls using the interface and servers implement the interface. To build our `SocialLookup` example service we will need to implement the `SocialLookup` interface.

In C++, the `SocialLookup` service interface will be represented by a class called `SocialLookupIf` defined in the SocialLookup.h file. In Python, the `SocialLookup` service will be represented by a class called `Iface` in the SocialLookup.py file. In Java, this service is represented by the `Iface` interface nested within the `SocialLookup` class.

We'll build our first example service in Java. We can use the following IDL compiler command to generate Java code for the `SocialLookup` service:

```
$ thrift -gen java simple.thrift
```

This creates a `SocialLookup` class under the gen-java directory housing all the Apache Thrift RPC code required by the service. The following shows the section of code from the SocialLookup.java source that declares the `SocialLookup` `Iface` interface:

```
public class SocialLookup {
  public interface Iface {
    public String GetSiteByRank(int rank) throws TException;
    public int GetSiteRankByName(String name) throws TException;
  }
  ...
```

This is a Java representation of the IDL from listing 8.1. Unlike many other languages, the Java language requires that function declarations list all the exception types the function may throw. As you can see, Apache Thrift reserves the right to throw a `TException` (or derivative) from any function in an IDL service. For more information on exception processing in Apache Thrift, see chapter 9, "Handling exceptions."

Now that we have client/server stub code generated, the next step is to provide an implementation for the service interface.

8.2.2   *Coding service handlers and test harnesses*

To implement an Apache Thrift service, code must be provided for each of the methods of the interface generated for the service. The service implementation is called a handler by convention. The following listing demonstrates an implementation of the SocialLookup service handler.

Listing 8.2   ~/ThriftBook/part2/services/simple/SocialLookupHandler.java

```
import java.util.Collections;
import java.util.HashMap;
import java.util.Map;
import org.apache.thrift.TException;

public class SocialLookupHandler implements SocialLookup.Iface {     ❶
  private static class Site {
    public Site(String name, int visits) {
      this.name = name;
      this.visits = visits;
    }
    public String name;
    public int visits;
  };
  private static final Map<Integer, Site> siteRank;             ❷

  static {
    HashMap<Integer, Site> m = new HashMap<>();
    m.put(1, new Site("Facebook", 750000000));
    m.put(2, new Site("Twitter",  250000000));
    m.put(3, new Site("LinkedIn", 110000000));
    siteRank = Collections.unmodifiableMap(m);
  }

  @Override
  public String GetSiteByRank(int rank) throws TException {       ❸
    Site s = siteRank.get(rank);
    return (null == s) ? "" : s.name;
  }

  @Override
  public int GetSiteRankByName(String name) throws TException {
    for (Map.Entry<Integer, Site> entry : siteRank.entrySet()) {
      if (name.equalsIgnoreCase(entry.getValue().name)) {
        return entry.getKey();
      }
    }
    return 0;
  }
}
```

The SocialLookupHandler class implements the interface generated from the IDL service declaration ❶. Internally the handler class can have a constructor, static attributes, and initializers, along with any other feature supported by the language. In this case the handler creates a static `siteRank` map to contain the rank, site name, and unique visitors per month for the service ❷. Each of the methods from the service is annotated as an override of the interface function with the same signature ❸. This is a nice feature supported by several languages, enabling the compiler to produce an error if the override signature doesn't match that of the IDL-generated interface.

With the Handler complete, we can wire up an RPC server; however, RPC servers can be difficult to debug. Fortunately, we can test service handlers in-process without any RPC overhead. In-process tests are easier to construct and faster to run. In-process tests are also easier to debug. Services should certainly be tested using the same RPC scheme you plan to deploy to production, but adding in-process handler tests can reduce or even eliminate many problems that would be much harder to diagnose in a distributed setting. The following listing shows a class that tests the previous service handler.

Listing 8.3 ~/ThriftBook/part2/services/simple/StandAlone.java

```java
import org.apache.thrift.TException;

public class StandAlone {
  public static void main(String[] args) throws TException {
    SocialLookup.Iface socialLookup = new SocialLookupHandler();
    System.out.println("Number 1 site: " + socialLookup.GetSiteByRank(1));
    System.out.println("Twitter rank : " +
                   socialLookup.GetSiteRankByName("Twitter"));
  }
}
```
❶ (at `SocialLookup.Iface socialLookup = new SocialLookupHandler();`)
❷ (at `System.out.println("Twitter rank : " +`)

This example constructs a new instance of our service handler ❶, and then makes a few calls to its methods, printing out the results ❷. In this example, the client (`StandAlone`) and the service (`SocialLookupHandler`) communicate through the `socialLookup` service contract (`SocialLookup.Iface`). This standalone program will be far easier to debug than a two-process RPC solution. The following session shows a build and run:

```
$ ls -l
-rw-r--r-- 1 randy randy  111 Jul 10 22:30 simple.thrift
-rw-r--r-- 1 randy randy 1409 Jul  9 23:39 SocialLookupHandler.java
-rw-r--r-- 1 randy randy  365 Jul 10 22:23 StandAlone.java
$ thrift -gen java simple.thrift
$ javac -cp /usr/local/lib/libthrift-1.0.0.jar:\
/usr/share/java/slf4j-api.jar:\
/usr/share/java/slf4j-nop.jar
        StandAlone.java
        SocialLookupHandler.java
        gen-java/SocialLookup.java
$ java -cp /usr/local/lib/libthrift-1.0.0.jar:gen-java:. StandAlone
Number 1 site: Facebook
Twitter rank : 2
```
❶ (at `$ thrift -gen java simple.thrift`)
❷ (at `$ javac -cp /usr/local/lib/libthrift-1.0.0.jar:\`)
❸ (at `$ java -cp /usr/local/lib/libthrift-1.0.0.jar:gen-java:. StandAlone`)

In this session we use the IDL compiler to compile the `simple.thrift` service IDL ❶, generating the `gen-java/SocialLookup.java` source, which contains the interface declaration for the service. To build the application we must compile the generated interface definition, the service handler, and the standalone client ❷. Once built, we can run the standalone application, which causes the JVM to load the dependent handler and interface class files ❸. This approach can be used to build test harnesses for Apache Thrift service implementations in any language.

8.2.3   *Coding RPC servers*

The program demonstrated above runs as a single process; however, we can turn this standalone program into a distributed RPC application with almost no effort (see figure 8.4).

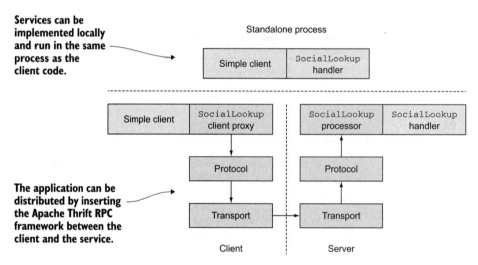

Figure 8.4   The Apache Thrift framework provides all the features required to seamlessly move embedded modules into standalone services.

To turn the service handler into a standalone server, we'll need to select a transport for clients to connect to, a protocol to serialize parameters and results, and a server component to manage client connections.

The IDL compiler creates a `Client` class which packages parameters and sends them to the server using the specified protocol/transport stack. The `Client` class is an in-process proxy for the out-of-process handler.

On the server side, the IDL compiler generates a `Processor` class. This class receives RPC messages from the client proxy and calls the handler on behalf of the client. To implement the server for our service we'll use the IDL-generated processor and a prebuilt Apache Thrift server class, as shown in the following listing.

```
Listing 8.4  ~/ThriftBook/part2/services/simple/SimpleServer.java
```

```java
import org.apache.thrift.TProcessor;
import org.apache.thrift.server.TServer;
import org.apache.thrift.server.TSimpleServer;
import org.apache.thrift.transport.TServerSocket;
import org.apache.thrift.transport.TTransportException;

public class SimpleServer {
  public static void main(String[] args) throws TTransportException {
    TServerSocket svrTrans = new TServerSocket(8585);            ❶
    TProcessor processor = new SocialLookup.Processor<>(
                                    new SocialLookupHandler());  ❷
    TServer server = new TSimpleServer(new TSimpleServer.Args(svrTrans)
                                    .processor(processor));      ❸

    server.serve();          ❹
  }
}
```

This simple server consists of four lines of Java code. The first thing required by an Apache Thrift RPC server is a server transport ❶. The server transport defines the mechanism used to connect to the server. In this case, we construct a TServerSocket to listen on TCP port 8585. Server transports are described in detail in chapter 4, "Moving bytes with transports."

The next line creates an instance of the IDL compiler-generated processor for the service ❷. The processor must be provided with a reference to a handler that implements the service interface, SocialLookup.Iface in this case.

The last object we need to create is a server that will take care of orchestrating the server transport connections and the processor for the service. Most Apache Thrift languages have several predefined servers to choose from. For our purposes, the TSimpleServer ❸ is a good choice, because as advertised, it's simple. Chapter 10, "Working with servers," covers the server library in depth.

The Java TSimpleServer constructor is initialized with an args object, a common pattern in Apache Thrift languages. The Args class must be provided with a server transport and service processor, at a minimum. The server transport is passed to the Args constructor and the processor is set using the processor() setter method.

The final line of code in the server is the server.serve() method call ❹. The serve() call causes the server transport to begin listening for and accepting client connections. Connected clients can then freely make RPC calls against the server's handler.

8.2.4 Coding RPC clients

Apache Thrift RPC clients are almost exactly like in-process service clients. To convert our standalone client into an RPC client, replace the in-process handler with the client proxy. The following listing shows an example RPC client for the server defined in the previous listing.

Listing 8.5   ~/ThriftBook/part2/services/simple/SimpleClient.java

```java
import org.apache.thrift.TException;
import org.apache.thrift.protocol.TBinaryProtocol;
import org.apache.thrift.protocol.TProtocol;
import org.apache.thrift.transport.TSocket;
import org.apache.thrift.transport.TTransport;

public class SimpleClient {
  public static void main(String[] args) throws TException {
    TTransport trans = new TSocket("localhost", 8585);        ❶
    trans.open();                                              ❸
    TProtocol proto = new TBinaryProtocol(trans);    ←┘
    SocialLookup.Iface socialLookup = new SocialLookup.Client(proto);     ❹

    System.out.println("Number 1 site: " + socialLookup.GetSiteByRank(1));
    System.out.println("Twitter rank : " +
                    socialLookup.GetSiteRankByName("Twitter"));           ❺
  }
}
```

❷ points to `trans.open();`

The code in the previous listing calls both functions supplied by the service handler and displays the results ❺. The IDL compiler-generated client class serves as the proxy for the out-of-process handler. The Java language service implementation organizes all the constituent classes required by a service within the service class, `SocialLookup` in this case. The client class for this service is therefore `SocialLookup.Client` ❹.

In this example, we use the binary protocol for serialization ❸. You may have noticed that no protocol was specified on the server side. An explicit server protocol can be specified through the server `args` object in Java; however, if no protocol is specified, the binary protocol is used as the server default. Clients must use the same protocol for serialization as the server.

Protocols depend on transports to perform the underlying byte transfers. Like the protocol, the endpoint transport used by the client must match the endpoint transport in place on the server. The server is using a `TServerSocket`, which requires us to use a `TSocket` on the client side ❶. `TSocket` uses TCP/IP for client/server communications, making it the most flexible and popular choice for RPC applications.

The client must configure the `TSocket` transport to connect to the server. The server was configured to listen on TCP port 8585 (by default, servers listen on all interfaces on the local host). If we run the simple client on a remote system, we need to supply a hostname or IP address to connect to the server. In this example, we run the client on the same system, so the "localhost" hostname is used to connect to the server ❶. The `TSocket` open() call connects the client to the server ❷.

The following session builds and runs the RPC client and server:

```
$ ls -l
drwxr-xr-x 2 randy randy 4096 Jul 11 00:36 gen-java
-rw-r--r-- 1 randy randy  685 Jul 11 00:16 SimpleClient.java
-rw-r--r-- 1 randy randy  590 Jul 10 22:17 SimpleServer.java
```

```
-rw-r--r-- 1 randy randy  111 Jul 10 22:30 simple.thrift
-rw-r--r-- 1 randy randy 1409 Jul  9 23:39 SocialLookupHandler.java
-rw-r--r-- 1 randy randy  365 Jul 10 22:23 StandAlone.java
$ javac -cp /usr/local/lib/libthrift-1.0.0.jar:\
           /usr/share/java/slf4j-api.jar:\
           /usr/share/java/slf4j-nop.jar \
           SimpleServer.java
           SocialLookupHandler.java
           gen-java/SocialLookup.java
$ java -cp /usr/local/lib/libthrift-1.0.0.jar:\
           /usr/share/java/slf4j-api.jar:\
           /usr/share/java/slf4j-nop.jar:\
           gen-java:\
           . \
           SimpleServer
```

At this point the server is waiting for connections. The following session builds and runs the client in a second shell:

```
$ javac -cp /usr/local/lib/libthrift-1.0.0.jar:\
           /usr/local/lib/slf4j-api-1.7.12.jar:\
           /usr/local/lib/slf4j-nop-1.7.12.jar \
           SimpleClient.java
           gen-java/SocialLookup.java
$ java -cp /usr/local/lib/libthrift-1.0.0.jar:\
           /usr/share/java/slf4j-api.jar:\
           /usr/share/java/slf4j-nop.jar:\
           gen-java:\
           . \
           SimpleClient

Number 1 site: Facebook
Twitter rank : 2
```

The output from this distributed RPC application is exactly the same as the output from the standalone application. The difference is that any number of clients written in any number of languages across any number of computers can now use the service via the Apache Thrift framework.

> **TIP** As you begin testing the examples, keep in mind that all the TCP-based RPC programs in this book use port 8585 or 9090. If you leave a server example running and move on to a new example, the new server cannot use port 8585 if it's already in use by an old server. If you have unexplained problems when trying to run an example server, use netstat ($ sudo netstat -nltp) or a similar tool to see if TCP port 8585 is already in use. You can either shut down the program using port 8585 or use a new port number for your server and clients.

8.3 Service interface evolution

One of the most important features of the Apache Thrift RPC system, from an operations standpoint, is the ability to incrementally change interfaces without breaking preexisting code. Cloud-based solutions and modern continuous integration and continuous deployment/delivery practices are confounded by rigid interfaces that require a global rebuild to make changes. The ability to evolve interfaces is a critical requirement in environments where changes are pushed to production frequently and in small increments.

Well-designed Apache Thrift interfaces can manage a wide range of incremental changes without breaking backward compatibility. Here are several of the common modifications supported by Apache Thrift interface evolution:

- Adding a parameter to a function
    - Old clients can call new servers if a default parameter value is provided for the new parameter.
    - New clients can call old servers; old servers will ignore the new parameter.
- Removing a parameter from a function
    - Old clients can call new servers that will ignore the deleted parameter.
    - New clients *cannot* safely call old servers unless the deleted parameter provided a default value in the old IDL.
- Adding functions
    - Old clients can call new servers.
    - New clients *cannot* call old servers, unless prepared to receive not implemented exceptions from old servers when calling unimplemented methods.
- Removing functions
    - Old clients *cannot* call new servers, unless prepared to receive not implemented exceptions when calling unimplemented methods.
    - New clients can call old servers.

Interface evolution is typically driven by the need for services to provide additional functionality. The Apache Thrift IDL gives services great latitude when it comes to making changes without breaking compatibility with older clients. The only server-side modification in the list above that's client-hostile is removing a function.

A common approach to removing functions is to deprecate them first. This provides a transition period during which the function is still supported, giving clients time to eliminate calls to the deprecated function, adopt the newer interface, or both.

Because old servers don't support new functions that new clients may depend upon, many enterprises incrementally upgrade servers over time when deploying new functions. New clients aren't supported until all servers have been upgraded to the new interface. Another approach is to partition the server space into old and new groups. Old clients can call either group, but new clients must use the new server group. This is easy to arrange in cloud-native orchestration systems such as Kubernetes.

User-defined types often comprise an important part of sophisticated interfaces. Apache Thrift IDL structs offer a wider range of evolution features than services and parameter lists. This gives functions making use of UDT parameters or UDT return types greater flexibility. For more information on UDT interface evolution, see chapter 7.

8.3.1 Adding features to a service

Let's look at a practical example to get a better feel for service interface evolution. Imagine we have a few new features we need to roll out for our SocialLookup service:

- Allow clients to retrieve all the sites with a unique user count within a given range.
- Allow rank lookups by partial name string.

These new features can both be handled directly by evolving our existing interface without breaking compatibility with old clients. The first new requirement can be satisfied by adding a new function to the service interface. Old clients won't know about the new function, but adding it won't impact their ability to use the preexisting functions.

Requirement number two involves a little more care to implement safely. Apache Thrift doesn't support overriding or overloading service functions. We cannot have two GetSiteRankByName() methods. To support the old functionality and the new functionality, we could add a new method with a new name. However, rather than supporting two functions with the same generalization, we can add a parameter to the existing function to toggle the string comparison mode. This is the approach we'll take next. To make sure that old clients can still call the function, we give the new parameter a default value that preserves the old functionality. The following listing shows the new updated IDL, evolved.thrift.

> **Listing 8.6 ~/ThriftBook/part2/services/evolution/evolved.thrift**

```
service SocialLookup {
    string GetSiteByRank( 1: i32 rank )
    i32 GetSiteRankByName(1: string name, 2: bool allowPartialMatch=false)
    list<string> GetSitesByUsers(1: i32 minUserCount, 2: i32 maxUserCount)
}
```

The GetSiteRankByName() method has a new allowPartialMatch parameter. This parameter has a default value of false. The function previously required a full match, so a default allowPartialMatch of false will cause the function to work as expected for old clients. New clients will have the option to pass a true value for allowPartial-Match. Interface evolution allows us to build just what we need, but keeps us from being locked in as requirements change and grow over time. The following listing implements the evolved interface in Python.

> **Listing 8.7 ~/ThriftBook/part2/services/evolution/evolved_server.py**

```
import sys
sys.path.append('gen-py')
from thrift.transport import TSocket          ❶
from thrift.server import TServer
❷ from evolved import SocialLookup
```

```
site_rank = {1 : ("Facebook", 750000000),
             2 : ("Twitter",  250000000),
             3 : ("LinkedIn", 110000000) }

class SocialLookupHandler(SocialLookup.Iface):          ❸
    def GetSiteByRank(self, rank):
        tup = site_rank[rank]
        return "" if (None==tup) else tup[0]

    def GetSiteRankByName(self, name, allowPartialMatch):     ❹
        for rank, value in site_rank.items():
            if allowPartialMatch:
                if value[0][:len(name)] == name:
                    return rank
            else:
                if value[0] == name:
                    return rank
        return 0

    def GetSitesByUsers(self, minUserCount, maxUserCount):    ❺
        return [v[0] for k, v in site_rank.items()
                if v[1] >= minUserCount and v[1] <= maxUserCount]

if __name__ == "__main__":
    svr_trans = TSocket.TServerSocket(port=8585)
    processor = SocialLookup.Processor(SocialLookupHandler())
    server = TServer.TSimpleServer(processor, svr_trans)
    server.serve()
```

This server is only slightly more complicated than the Hello World server from chapter 1. At the top of the file we import the `TSocket` and `TServer` modules ❶. These are the standard Apache Thrift Python library modules supporting socket transports and the `TSimpleServer`, respectively. To make the Python server a drop-in replacement for the older Java server we use the same transport (`TSocket`) and protocol (`TBinaryProtocol`). Changing either the transport or the protocol will require clients to make the same change.

The imported `SocialLookup` module will be generated by the IDL compiler for the `SocialLookup` service ❷. This module is generated in the "evolved" Python package (named after the IDL file name), which is a directory under the gen-py directory. The `SocialLookup` module contains the service interface definition (`SocialLookup.Iface`), the client proxy (`SocialLookup.Client`), and the server processor (`SocialLookup.Processor`).

As in the Java example, the service implementation comes in the form of a handler class that inherits from the service interface ❸. The `GetSiteRankByName()` method includes the new parameter `allowPartialMatch` ❹. Note that we don't specify the default value for `allowPartialMatch` in the handler code. The default is part of the interface, and the IDL-generated processor will pass the default to the handler if no value is sent by the client.

The new method in the interface ❺ is unknown to clients using the old `simple`.`thrift` interface, but doesn't impact them.

The following code shows a sample session generating Python code for the service with the IDL compiler and running the server:

```
$ ls -l
-rw-r--r-- 1 randy randy 1169 Jul 11 03:31 evolved_server.py
-rw-r--r-- 1 randy randy  219 Jul 11 02:10 evolved.thrift
$ thrift -gen py evolved.thrift
$ python evolved_server.py
```

While the server is up and running, we can test it with the old Java client in another shell:

```
$ java -cp /usr/local/lib/libthrift-1.0.0.jar:\
        /usr/share/java/slf4j-api.jar:\
        /usr/share/java/slf4j-nop.jar:\
        gen-java:\
        . \
        SimpleClient
Number 1 site: Facebook
Twitter rank : 2
```

Even though we've made multiple changes to the interface and changed server languages, the old client works as before. When the old client calls the `GetSiteRankByName()` method to recover the "Facebook" rank with only one parameter, the default `allowPartialMatch` value of `false` is supplied on the server side to make up for the missing parameter.

To complete the example, let's put together a simple Python client to test the evolved interface, as shown in the following listing.

Listing 8.8   ~/ThriftBook/part2/services/evolution/evolved_client.py

```
import sys
sys.path.append("gen-py")
from thrift.transport import TSocket
from thrift.protocol import TBinaryProtocol
from evolved import SocialLookup

socket = TSocket.TSocket("localhost", 8585)
socket.open()
protocol = TBinaryProtocol.TBinaryProtocol(socket)
client = SocialLookup.Client(protocol)                            ❶
print("Number 1 site: %s" % (client.GetSiteByRank(1)))            ❷
print("Twitter rank : %d" % (client.GetSiteRankByName("Twit", True)))   ❸
print("100-500mm Users : %s" % (str(client.GetSitesByUsers(100000000,   ❹
                                            500000000)))))
```

This Python client is almost exactly like the Hello World client from chapter 1. We import the required modules, connect the `TSocket` to the correct server host and port, set up a binary protocol, and create a client proxy for the `SocialLookup` service ❶. Here's a sample run of the new Python client with the new Python server:

```
$ python evolved_client.py
Number 1 site: Facebook
Twitter rank : 2
100-500mm Users : ['Twitter', 'LinkedIn']
```

The first method tested, `GetSiteByRank()`, hasn't changed and produces the same result that we acquired in the Java client ❷.

The second method, called `GetSiteRankByName()`, has a new parameter, `allow-PartialMatch`, which we supply a `True` value for ❸. The old Java client doesn't pass this parameter because the IDL it was built with doesn't have a second parameter. In Python we can pass `None` for any parameter we don't want transmitted; however, this will cause problems in cases where the server doesn't have a default to support the missing parameter. Best practice is to pass all parameters specified in a function's interface.

The final method, `GetSitesByUsers()`, is brand new and unknown to the old Java client, called here with the two required parameters ❹.

The output for the first two function calls is the same as that produced by the Java client. The third function call also produces the expected list of two sites.

What will happen if we run the new client against the old Java server? There's one good way to find out. With the old Java server running in another shell (requiring us to shut down the Python server), the following session shows the output from the new Python client:

```
$ python evolved_client.py
Number 1 site: Facebook              ❶
Twitter rank : 0                                  ❸
Traceback (most recent call last):          ◁──┘
  File "evolved_client.py", line 13, in <module>
    print("100-500mm Users : %s" %
➡    (str(client.GetSitesByUsers(100000000, 500000000))))
  File "gen-py/evolved/SocialLookup.py", line 121, in GetSitesByUsers
    return self.recv_GetSitesByUsers()
  File "gen-py/evolved/SocialLookup.py", line 138, in recv_GetSitesByUsers
    raise x
thrift.Thrift.TApplicationException: Invalid method name: 'GetSitesByUsers'
```

❷ appears at the "Twitter rank : 0" line.

Let's analyze this output. The first function hasn't changed between the old and the new interfaces, so, as expected, function call #1 is fine ❶.

The second function call has a new parameter in the new interface. Apache Thrift servers ignore parameters they don't recognize, so the old server receives a partial string from us, "Twit". Because the old server only matches on full strings, we get a rank of 0 back, indicating no match was found. This semantic failure may be a problem at the application layer, but, mechanically, function number two completed successfully and no exception was raised ❷.

The third function doesn't exist in the old service interface and raises an error ❸. In this case, the client proxy dutifully packaged up the parameters and called the server; however, the old server processor doesn't know the `GetSitesByUsers()` method and returned a `TApplicationException` back to the client with the text "Invalid method name: 'GetSitesByUsers'". In this situation, the client code can either trap the exception or fail. For more information on exception processing in the Apache Thrift framework, see chapter 9 later in this part. Note that the old Java server is still running. When a client calls a missing method, the server returns an exception and continues on about its business. The error is discovered on the server but thrown to the client.

As these examples show, it can be fairly easy to make seamless upgrades to servers, but because clients depend on server interfaces and semantics, upgrading clients in the face of older servers requires more caution and planning.

8.4 RPC services in depth

Having seen practical examples of services in action, it's worth taking a moment to poke around under the service hood to get a deeper understanding of the Apache Thrift RPC mechanisms.

8.4.1 Under the hood

As we've seen in the above IDL examples, the IDL compiler generates one or more target language files associated with the declarations in a given IDL source file. Constants typically end up in a separate constants file (or files) and UDTs end up in a separate types file (or files). However, services typically cause the IDL compiler to emit one file (or pair of files) per service. These service files contain several key elements across most Apache Thrift languages:

- *Iface*—An interface definition for the service in the target language.
- *IfFactory*—An abstract factory designed to manufacture implementations (handlers) of the `Iface`.
- *Client*—A client proxy used in client code to call the functions of the service.
- *Processor*—A server-based dispatcher which calls the correct service handler method in response to calls from the client.
- *ProcessorFactory*—A factory designed to manufacture instances of the processor.
- **_args structs*—Each function has a `funcName_args` struct that has fields for each function parameter. This struct is used to serialize parameters on the client side and de-serialize parameters on the processor side.
- **_result structs*—Each function has a `funcName_result` struct that has fields for the return value and each exception type found in the function's exception list. The processor uses this struct to serialize the function result and the client uses this struct to de-serialize the result.

We've used most of these features directly or indirectly in the previous pages. The `Iface` is the service interface in terms of the target language. The handlers we wrote to implement service behavior in Python and Java earlier in this chapter were derived from the service Iface. The name may vary a bit from language to language. For example, C++ prepends the name of the service and uses the If abbreviation (for example, SocialLookupIf), whereas Java and Python use the Iface identifier scoped by the class or module (for example, SocialLookup.Iface). Several languages, such as JavaScript, have no language support for interface constructs at all, leaving developers to carefully match implementations to the specification in the IDL.

Interface and processor factories are typically used by the classes in the server library to manufacture new handlers and processors for each client connection. We'll take a longer look at factories in chapter 10.

We've used the client and processor components of the RPC framework directly in each of our RPC examples. The client is the client-side stub, a proxy for the service itself, and the processor is the server-side stub, a dispatcher making calls to the user-coded handler on behalf of the remote client.

The _args and _result structs are used to pass parameters from the client to the server and return results from the server to the client, respectively (see figure 8.5). If you consider the ease with which we serialized a struct in chapter 7, you'll see why this is a compelling solution. Rather than serialize individual parameters, Apache Thrift organizes each function's parameters into a struct with the _args suffix. For example, the GetSiteByRank() method has a generated GetSiteByRank_args struct to house its parameters. This allows the framework to use the standard struct write method to serialize all the parameters on the client side (for example, GetSiteByRank_args .write(proto)) and then to call the struct's read method to de-serialize the parameters on the processor side (for example, GetSiteByRank_args.read(proto)). The same process is applied to the return result in the other direction, using the GetSiteByRank _result struct.

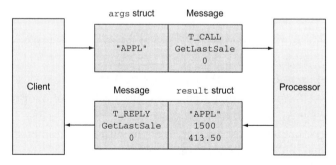

Figure 8.5   A typical RPC message exchange between a service client and service processor

The Apache Thrift RPC protocol boils down to the client sending a message to the server containing the args struct, and the server sending a reply back to the client containing the result struct. Table 8.1 illustrates the serialization protocol operations making up a message transmission in Apache Thrift RPC.

Table 8.1 Apache Thrift RPC messaging

Thrift sender	Thrift receiver
proto->writeMessageBegin(name, type, sn)	proto->readMessageBegin(name, type, sn)
args_msg->write(proto)	result_msg->read(proto)
proto->writeMessageEnd()	proto->readMessageEnd()
proto->getTransport()->writeEnd()	proto->getTransport()->readEnd()
proto->getTransport()->flush()	

RPC messages have a name, a type, and a sequence number (sn). The name is the name of the method to invoke. RPC messages come in four types:

- *T_CALL*—Used by the client to call a function on the server.
- *T_REPLY*—Used by the server to reply to a client call with a return value or a user-defined exception.
- *T_EXCEPTION*—Used by the server to reply to a client call with a TApplication-Exception.
- *T_ONEWAY*—Used by the client to call a one-way function.

Most RPC function calls involve the client sending a T_CALL message to the server with the _args struct for the function, and the server then sending a T_REPLY message back to the client with a _result struct. A T_REPLY message can return either the normal return value or a user-defined exception in the result struct.

The T_EXCEPTION message type is reserved for Apache Thrift framework errors resulting in TApplicationExceptions. These exceptions should only be generated by the framework and indicate a mechanical problem with the RPC mechanism; for example, calling a function that doesn't exist on the server. This type of error often signifies an interface version mismatch. We saw this in action when using the new Python SocialLookup client with the old Java SocialLookup server. In such a situation, no user-written code exists to throw an exception on the server; the error must be generated by the framework. The T_EXCEPTION message tells the client that the payload of the message will be a TApplicationException, not the otherwise expected _result struct.

The T_ONEWAY message type is used to call one-way functions on the server; it's otherwise exactly like the T_CALL message. T_ONEWAY messages don't receive a response message of any type.

8.4.2 One-way functions

One-way functions are exactly what they sound like, functions that send data to the server but do not receive anything back. This feature offers a way of providing server notifications or triggering an event on a server. Here's an example:

```
service SocialLookup {
    ...
    oneway void UpdateSiteUsers( 1: string name, 2: i32 users );
}
```

One-way functions are distinct from normal functions in that calling normal functions, such as void myFunc(1: i16 val); always results in a response message from the server. This may seem strange for a void function; however, while void functions don't return anything at the application level, the processor does send an RPC response back to the client proxy. When this response arrives, the client proxy returns from the call made by the user code in synchronous interfaces. One reason for this synchronization is that any normal function may throw an exception, even a void function. The user code must wait for the server response to know that the function, even a void function, completed successfully.

Because one-way functions don't receive a response of any type, it's impossible for a one-way function caller to know when or if the call completed. In cases where a client needs to notify a server, without regard to the result, one-way is a good option. One-way functions can have parameters like any other function, but should be declared void (the IDL compiler warns about non-void, one-way return types, which are ignored).

One-way functions have two benefits. The first is that one-way functions cut the message exchange count in half. The second is that they return on the client side as soon as the parameters have been written to the transport, allowing servers to process one-way calls while the client (even an otherwise synchronous one) continues with other work.

Consideration should be made before committing to one-way functions. First, migrating from a normal function to a one-way, or vice versa, is a breaking change. There is no way to evolve between the two types. Second, because one-way functions cannot return exceptions, you have no way of knowing if the server you're sending the one-way message to even implements the one-way function you're calling. Calling a missing normal function will raise a TApplicationException.

While the above cautions apply, in the right setting, one-way functions can be a useful asset. We'll demonstrate a one-way function in the next example.

8.4.3   *Service inheritance*

Apache Thrift services can inherit functions from previously declared services using the extends keyword. Apache Thrift doesn't support function overriding or overloading. Each service handler must provide implementations for all methods (though these can call shared helper functions, and so on). Also, no two methods may share the same name in an inheritance hierarchy.

To demonstrate inheritance, let's construct a new service based on the original simple service from the beginning of the chapter. Up to this point, we have built services in Java and Python, so we'll create this new implementation in C++.

Listing 8.9 ~/ThriftBook/part2/services/inherit/inherit.thrift

```
include "simple.thrift"       ❶

service SocialUpdate extends simple.SocialLookup {        ❷
    oneway void UpdateSiteUsers( 1: string name, 2: i32 users );      ❸
    i32 GetSiteUsersByName( 1: string name );
}
```

The IDL file in listing 8.9 defines the `SocialUpdate` service ❷. This service inherits all the functions found in the `SocialLookup` service. You can define as many services in a single file as you like; however, it's convenient to separate service definitions into multiple files. Using multiple files allows core interface components to be stored in one set of files and then included in various ancillary IDL files. This can be easier to manage than having one huge IDL file defining all interface components.

The example here includes the simple.thrift IDL file at the top of the listing ❶. This makes all of the declarations from simple.thrift available within inherit.thrift. To access elements from the simple.thrift IDL you must supply the file name as a prefix. For example, the `SocialUpdate` service extends simple.SocialLookup.

The `SocialUpdate` service adds two functions to the base service functions, `UpdateSiteUsers()` and `GetSiteUsersByName()`. `UpdateSiteUsers()` is a one-way function and will receive no response ❸. This function sends a social networking site name and the unique users per month for the site to the server. If this update takes the server a long time to complete, it will not impact the client, which will return from the function call as soon as the parameter bytes have been written to the network. The following session shows a sample IDL compile using the new inherit.thrift IDL:

```
$ ls -l
-rw-r--r-- 1 randy randy 143 Jul 11 08:56 inherit.thrift
-rw-r--r-- 1 randy randy 111 Jul 10 22:30 simple.thrift
$ thrift -r -gen cpp inherit.thrift          ❶
$ ls -l
drwxr-xr-x 2 randy randy 4096 Jul 11 08:58 gen-cpp
-rw-r--r-- 1 randy randy  143 Jul 11 08:56 inherit.thrift
-rw-r--r-- 1 randy randy  111 Jul 10 22:30 simple.thrift
$ ls -l gen-cpp
-rw-r--r-- 1 randy randy   265 Jul 11 08:58 inherit_constants.cpp
-rw-r--r-- 1 randy randy   351 Jul 11 08:58 inherit_constants.h
-rw-r--r-- 1 randy randy   195 Jul 11 08:58 inherit_types.cpp
-rw-r--r-- 1 randy randy   380 Jul 11 08:58 inherit_types.h
-rw-r--r-- 1 randy randy   260 Jul 11 08:58 simple_constants.cpp
-rw-r--r-- 1 randy randy   344 Jul 11 08:58 simple_constants.h
-rw-r--r-- 1 randy randy   194 Jul 11 08:58 simple_types.cpp
-rw-r--r-- 1 randy randy   352 Jul 11 08:58 simple_types.h
-rw-r--r-- 1 randy randy 16775 Jul 11 08:58 SocialLookup.cpp
-rw-r--r-- 1 randy randy 10566 Jul 11 08:58 SocialLookup.h                    ❷
-rw-r--r-- 1 randy randy  1497 Jul 11 08:58 SocialLookup_server.skelton.cpp
-rw-r--r-- 1 randy randy  5181 Jul 11 08:58 SocialUpdate.cpp
-rw-r--r-- 1 randy randy  5992 Jul 11 08:58 SocialUpdate.h                    ❸
-rw-r--r-- 1 randy randy  1373 Jul 11 08:58 SocialUpdate_server.skelton.cpp
```

In this example, we generate C++ code for the new service `SocialUpdate` ❶. Notice the use of the `-r` (recursive) switch. While the `include` statement within the IDL file will pull in all the declarations needed to generate code for the `SocialUpdate` service, it will not cause the IDL compiler to generate the code for the included IDL files. We need to compile simple.thrift and inherit.thrift before attempting to use the generated code. The `-r` switch requests that the compiler generate code for the current file and all include files encountered during processing, allowing us to compile inherit .thrift and all its dependencies in one go.

The output shows that both the `SocialLookup` ❷ and the `SocialUpdate` ❸ services have code generated for them. In the C++ language, extends relationships in IDL are carried over as C++ inheritance relationships. Here's the `SocialUpdate` interface as defined in the SocialUpdate.h file:

```cpp
#include "SocialLookup.h"

class SocialUpdateIf : virtual public  ::SocialLookupIf {        ❶
public:
  virtual ~SocialUpdateIf() {}
  virtual void UpdateSiteUsers(const string& name, const int32_t users)=0;
  virtual int32_t GetSiteUsersByName(const std::string& name)=0;
};
```

The `SocialUpdateIf` is derived from the `SocialLookupIf` in the C++ source ❶. Clients requiring the `SocialLookup` service can use the `SocialUpdate` service as well. The `SocialUpdate` service "is a" `SocialLookup` service. Let's take a look at a C++ server implementation for the `SocialUpdate` service.

Listing 8.10   ~/ThriftBook/part2/services/inherit/inherit_server.cpp

```cpp
#include "gen-cpp/SocialUpdate.h"
#include <thrift/transport/TBufferTransports.h>
#include <thrift/protocol/TBinaryProtocol.h>
#include <thrift/server/TSimpleServer.h>
#include <thrift/transport/TServerSocket.h>
#include <thrift/TProcessor.h>
#include <boost/make_shared.hpp>
#include <string>
#include <unordered_map>

using namespace ::apache::thrift::protocol;
using namespace ::apache::thrift::transport;
using namespace ::apache::thrift::server;
using boost::shared_ptr;

struct Site { std::string name; int users; };
std::unordered_map<int, Site> siteRank {        ❶
    {1, {"Facebook", 750000000}},
    {2, {"Twitter",  250000000}},
    {3, {"LinkedIn", 110000000}}
```

```
    };

    class SocialUpdateHandler : public SocialUpdateIf {            ➋
    public:
        //SocialUpdateIf
        virtual void UpdateSiteUsers(const std::string& name,
                                     const int32_t users) override {      ➌
            for (auto & it : siteRank)
                if (0 == it.second.name.compare(name))
                    it.second.users = users;
        }
        virtual int32_t GetSiteUsersByName(const std::string& name) override {
            for (auto it : siteRank)
                if (0 == it.second.name.compare(name))
                    return it.second.users;
            return 0;
        }
        //SocialLookupIf
        virtual void GetSiteByRank(std::string& _return,
                                   const int32_t rank) override {        ➍
            auto it = siteRank.find(rank);
            _return = (it == std::end(siteRank)) ? "" : it->second.name;
        }
        virtual int32_t GetSiteRankByName(const std::string& name) override {
            for (auto it : siteRank)
                if (0 == it.second.name.compare(name))
                    return it.first;
            return 0;
        }
    };

    int main(int argc, char **argv) {
        auto handler = make_shared<SocialUpdateHandler>();              ➎
➏      auto proc = make_shared<SocialUpdateProcessor>(handler);
        auto trans_svr = make_shared<TServerSocket>(9090);             ➐
➑      auto trans_fac = make_shared<TBufferedTransportFactory>();
        auto proto_fac = make_shared<TBinaryProtocolFactory>();        ➒
➓      TSimpleServer server(proc, trans_svr, trans_fac, proto_fac);
        server.serve();          ⟵
        return 0;                    ⓫
    }
```

This server has two principle components, the main() function and the Social-UpdateHandler class. The site rankings state used by the handler is stored in a global map ➊. Because this is a C++11 listing, we can statically initialize the map with the stock site data. By making the state global, we ensure that it won't be reinitialized each time the client connects. We'll investigate the way servers create and destroy handlers in chapter 10, "Working with servers."

A concern associated with all global state is the possibility that multiple clients will attempt to update it concurrently. This may lead to data corruption or logic errors. In this case, we're using TSimpleServer, which doesn't support concurrency. Server concurrency is another issue tackled in chapter 10, "Working with servers."

The `SocialUpdateHandler` class implements the `SocialUpdateIf` interface, which implicitly ensures that `SocialUpdateHandler` can service `SocialUpdate` clients and `SocialLookup` clients ❷. The first method defined is `UpdateSiteUsers()` ❸. This is the one-way method; notice that it looks no different from any other method. All the one-way mechanics are handled by the generated client and processor.

The `GetSiteByRank()` method may strike you as having a strange signature ❹. The function in the IDL is declared like this: `string GetSiteByRank( 1: i32 rank );`. In the C++ implementation, the return value is moved into the parameter list. This is an optimization associated with Apache Thrift support for pre-C++11 compilers.

The `main()` function creates several objects for use by `TSimpleServer`. The first statement in main creates an instance of the service handler which provides the service implementation ❺. Next we create an instance of the service processor, to dispatch RPC calls to the handler ❻. We then create a server transport to listen at port 9090 ❼. The next two statements create factories. The transport factory ❽ is used by the server to manufacture new `TSocket` transports each time a new client connects ❽. The protocol factory serves the same purpose but for serialization protocols ❾.

Servers use factories to manufacture the objects they need for each new connection. For example, if two clients are connected, the server will need two `TSocket` transports, one for each client. We'll cover factories in depth in chapter 10.

The next line constructs the server we'll use to run the RPC service. The `TSimpleServer` requires a server transport to handle listening for new clients, a protocol and transport factory to create a new socket and binary protocol for each new client, and a processor which fields inbound RPC messages from clients ❿. Once configured, we can run the simple server with the `serve()` method ⓫. Now that the server code is complete, let's look at a C++ client for the service.

Listing 8.11　~/ThriftBook/part2/services/inherit/inherit_client.cpp

```cpp
#include "gen-cpp/SocialUpdate.h"
#include <thrift/transport/TSocket.h>
#include <thrift/transport/TBufferTransports.h>
#include <thrift/protocol/TBinaryProtocol.h>
#include <boost/shared_ptr.hpp>
#include <boost/make_shared.hpp>
#include <iostream>

using namespace apache::thrift::transport;
using namespace apache::thrift::protocol;
using boost::make_shared;
using boost::shared_ptr;

int main() {
    shared_ptr<TTransport> trans;#1
    trans = make_shared<TSocket>("localhost", 8585);            ❶
    trans = make_shared<TBufferedTransport>(trans);
    trans->open();#1
```

```
    auto proto = boost::make_shared<TBinaryProtocol>(trans);          ❷
❸   SocialUpdateClient client(proto);

    std::string site_name;                              ❹
    client.GetSiteByRank(site_name, 1);       ◁⎯┘
    std::cout << "Number 1 site: " << site_name <<std::endl;
    std::cout << "Twitter rank : " << client.GetSiteRankByName("Twitter")
              <<std::endl;
    std::cout << "Twitter users: " << client.GetSiteUsersByName("Twitter")
              <<std::endl;
❺   client.UpdateSiteUsers("Twitter", 260000000);
    std::cout << "Twitter users: " << client.GetSiteUsersByName("Twitter")
              <<std::endl;
}
```

The client program is similar to the Java and Python clients in this chapter. We begin by setting up the transport stack ❶ using a TSocket pointed at the server's hostname and TCP port (8585). We add a message buffering layer for network efficiency and then open the connection.

Next the transport stack is wrapped in a TBinaryProtocol ❷, and a SocialUpdate-Client is constructed to perform I/O on the protocol ❸.

Once the client object is set up and the connection is open we can call remote functions. The first method called is GetSiteByRank(), which, as discussed previously, requires us to pass in the return buffer as the first call parameter ❹. This client also tests the new one-way method ❺ with calls which examine the user count before and after the one-way update. Note that while one-way methods are asynchronous in regard to execution on the server, they transmit requests synchronously. Thus, you can call normal methods and one-way methods interleaved (as long as the calls are made from the same thread), and the data transmitted to the server will be serialized, in order.

Here's a session building both the server and the client, and then running the server:

```
$ g++ -std=c++11 -Wall inherit_client.cpp gen-cpp/SocialUpdate.cpp
        gen-cpp/SocialLookup.cpp -lthrift -o client
$ g++ -std=c++11 -Wall inherit_server.cpp gen-cpp/SocialUpdate.cpp
        gen-cpp/SocialLookup.cpp -lthrift -o server
$ ./server
```

Our command line for the G++ compiler requires C++11, because we're using several C++11 features here, such as the ranged for statement (for(:)), auto type declarations, and an unordered_map (like a Java HashMap), to house the site-ranking data. We also must build both the SocialUpdate.cpp implementation and SocialLookup.cpp implementation files to manage RPC operations for the two interfaces we're implementing.

Here's the output when a client is run in a separate shell:

```
$ ./client
Number 1 site: Facebook
Twitter rank : 2
Twitter users: 250000000
Twitter users: 260000000
```

The first two lines are the same result we received when running the Java client against the Java server earlier in this chapter. The last two lines display the monthly user count before and after the one-way update.

By implementing the `SocialUpdate` interface, the server implicitly implements the `SocialLookup` interface. We can run the original `SocialLookup` Java client against our new C++ server. Here's an example:

```
$ java -cp /usr/local/lib/libthrift-1.0.0.jar:\
        /usr/share/java/slf4j-api.jar:\
        /usr/share/java/slf4j-nop.jar:\
        gen-java:\
        . \
        SimpleClient
Number 1 site: Facebook
Twitter rank : 2
```

Apache Thrift interface inheritance is an effective way to extend old service interfaces without tampering with the old service or its IDL in any way. Servers can implement the old interface and new interface and both can be active in the enterprise, supporting old and new clients contemporaneously.

8.4.4 *Asynchronous clients*

One-way messages are asynchronous in that they don't wait for a server response. As soon as the one-way message is completely written to the local endpoint transport, the one-way function call returns and the client is free to go on about its business.

Normal functions block until the server responds. This blocking behavior can defeat several of the benefits of distributed computing. For example, client and server systems each have CPU resources, yet in the context of a normal RPC call, either the client is running or the server is running, but not both. For example, the client runs, calls the server, and stops, blocking until the server response is received. The server receives the request and runs, returns the result, and waits for the next request. The client then receives the result and continues. This serial execution between the client and server simplifies application design in certain cases but may impair efficiency as well.

While a particular pair of client and server threads may be serialized, the CPU resources of both machines are likely busy with other client or server tasks during any session idle time. That said, in certain cases, allowing the client to continue doing other work while waiting for a server response can be a material performance benefit.

Synchronous operations on the server side aren't as much of a problem, because servers typically have many clients to serve and various concurrency means to ensure that CPUs are in continuous use.

Many Apache Thrift language implementations provide support for asynchronous clients. There are two common async client models:

- Callbacks
- Promises/futures

Callback models require the client to provide a callback function that will be invoked by the runtime when the RPC call completes. The second model involves promises, futures, or both. In this model, the RPC client returns an object (called a promise in certain implementations and a future in others) that acts as a proxy for the return value that hasn't yet been received. The client can test the "promise/future" to see if the result has been set, or even block until the result is received.

Async models typically make code more complex in languages where asynchronous behavior is not the norm (like Java and C++). On the other hand, in languages where everything is async anyway, such as JavaScript, this approach is natural and elegant.

Unless you have work that you can do while waiting for RPC calls to complete, using an asynchronous client in an otherwise synchronous language will only make code more complex. Also, not all languages provide asynchronous clients, and the implementations that do exist are fairly language-specific. For these reasons, we cover asynchronous client implementation in the language-specific chapters of part 3.

Summary

Apache Thrift services are collections of functions that can be called remotely using Apache Thrift RPC. The range of features provided by the Apache Thrift framework makes Apache Thrift RPC a good fit for modern, evolving, multi-language enterprises:

- Apache Thrift services are composed of sets of functions.
- Functions have a set of parameters and use parameter IDs, requiredness, and default values to enable interface evolution.
- Through interface evolution, multiple versions of a particular service interface can coexist in a production environment.
- Services are implemented by user-coded handlers.
- Handlers can be built into the client process and called directly for testing and debugging purposes.
- RPC operations are handled by an IDL-generated client object on the client side and a processor object on the server side.
- The client object exposes an interface identical to that of the handler implementing the service.
- The client object forwards RPC calls to the server-based processor that dispatches calls to the handler.

- RPC is implemented with messages (CALL, REPLY, EXCEPTION, and ONEWAY).
- Functions can be declared one-way in Apache Thrift IDL, which causes the function to transmit the parameters to the server without waiting for or receiving a reply of any kind.
- Services can inherit from other services using the extends keyword.
- Apache Thrift doesn't support overriding or overloading functions; a service handler must implement all the service methods, including those inherited, precisely once.
- Each programming language supported by Apache Thrift provides its own specific files for generated RPC code.

Handling exceptions 9

This chapter covers

- Understanding the Apache Thrift Exception Model
- Handling transport, protocol, and application exceptions
- Creating and working with user-defined exceptions
- Designing Apache Thrift programs with robust exception processing

The Apache Thrift framework can face a range of error conditions, including disk errors, network errors, and security violations. Many of these error conditions can occur completely independently of any coding flaws in user code or Apache Thrift. For example, consider a network client communicating with a server over a wireless connection that goes down. The failed wireless link will cause any attempt at communication between the client and server to result in an unexpected error.

Many programming languages support exception processing as a means for managing errors separately from an application's normal flow of control. Exception processing is often associated with object technology, but is supported by a variety of languages and platforms.

Apache Thrift adopts the exception processing model as its abstract model for managing errors. Languages that don't support exceptions, for example C and Go, return error values instead.

257

In previous chapters, our examples have largely ignored possible error conditions. As a rule, the code examples in part 2 of this book are focused on demonstrating features of Apache Thrift using the smallest amount of code. If you have a problem opening, closing, flushing, reading, or writing in these examples, your application will likely exit abruptly, because uncaught exceptions typically result in program termination. To make programs more robust, we can add statements to test for interface errors. This translates to trapping exceptions, testing return values, or handling error events, depending on the language.

In the sections ahead, we'll look briefly at the conceptual Apache Thrift exception hierarchy and examine practical examples of error processing in the three demonstration languages: C++, Java, and Python. We'll follow this with a look at user-defined exceptions in IDL and how to use them in code.

9.1   Apache Thrift exceptions

The Apache Thrift exception hierachy follows a similar pattern to that of the overall Apache Thrift framework. A base exception type, usually called TException, provides the abstraction used by all concrete Apache Thrift exceptions. Each layer of the Apache Thrift framework typically has its own exception type derived from TException (see figure 9.1).

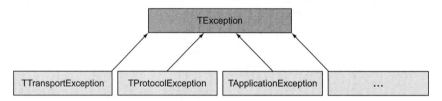

Figure 9.1   The Thrift exception hierarchy

Many Apache Thrift language implementations derive TException from the language's standard base exception, allowing Apache Thrift exceptions to work naturally within the language's error processing system. For example, the C++ TException is derived from std::exception, the Java TException is derived from java .lang.Exception, and the Python TException is derived from the Python built-in Exception class. This allows higher-level code, even code unaware of the presence of the Apache Thrift framework, to catch exceptions generated by framework code (see figure 9.2).

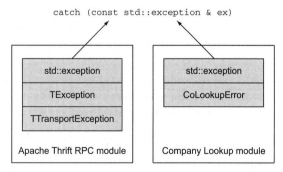

Figure 9.2   Generic language exception classes can be used to trap Apache Thrift exceptions.

TException is typically devoid of attributes and methods and provides a base class for all other Apache Thrift exceptions. The principle benefit of TException is that it can be used in catch blocks to catch any error originating from the Apache Thrift framework or Apache Thrift user-defined services.

Four concrete exception types are used throughout Apache Thrift. Each is typically derived from TException and each is associated with a particular layer of the Apache Thrift framework:

- *TTransportException*—Transport layer exceptions, associated with low-level byte read/write failures
- *TProtocolException*—Protocol layer exceptions, associated with serialization encoding/decoding failures
- *TApplicationException*—RPC layer exceptions, associated with a failure in IDL-generated RPC code on the client or server (often due to client/server interface or I/O stack mismatch)
- *User-defined exceptions*—Exceptions defined in IDL by the user, used to allow handlers on the server to throw errors back to the calling client

These principal exception types can be further specialized in derived classes. For example, the C++ TFileTransport library class can throw a TEOFException when a read request reaches the end of a file. The TEOFException type is derived from TTransportException. Specialization like this is uncommon, and these derived exception types can be caught using their base classes, making it less important for Apache Thrift users to have an exhaustive knowledge of the leaf exception classes.

It's also important to note that, of all of the exception types, users should only create and throw user-defined exceptions. User-defined exceptions are thrown by user-coded service handlers in the face of application-specific error conditions and are caught by client-side code. All other exception types are thrown by the framework, though users may, and often should, catch them in client code.

9.2 TTransportException

Endpoint transports often deal with hardware, exposing them to numerous types of exceptions. The TTransportException is used by the Apache Thrift transport library classes to report internal errors. It's also possible for software and system layers below Apache Thrift to raise non-Apache Thrift exceptions. In certain cases, Apache Thrift library and generated code will catch external exceptions and then raise a new TTransportException to throw to clients. In other cases, the low-level exceptions will flow directly to the client application.

> **TIP** The Apache Thrift framework may, in certain languages and platforms, raise exceptions not based on TException. In other words, Apache Thrift doesn't trap and rethrow all possible underlying system exceptions as TException types. Exceptions are most common, and should be planned for, when dealing with resources outside of the control of your process (network cards, memory, disk, and so on).

The `TTransportException` class has an exception type that can be retrieved using the `getType()` method in Java and C++, or by reading the "type" attribute directly in Python. The `TTransportException` exception types are defined as constants directly or through an enumeration, depending on the language. The possible types and their numeric representations aren't necessarily consistent across languages. Table 9.1 shows the `TTransportException` types defined in the three demonstration languages.

Table 9.1 TTransportException types

Value	C++ interpretation	Java interpretation	Python interpretation
0	UNKNOWN	UNKNOWN	UNKNOWN
1	NOT_OPEN	NOT_OPEN	NOT_OPEN
2	TIMED_OUT	ALREADY_OPEN	ALREADY_OPEN
3	END_OF_FILE	TIMED_OUT	TIMED_OUT
4	INTERRUPTED	END_OF_FILE	END_OF_FILE
5	BAD_ARGS		
6	CORRUPTED_DATA		
7	INTERNAL_ERROR		

The numeric divergence doesn't usually represent an interoperability problem, because `TTransportExceptions` don't typically cross process boundaries. Many sources of this exception leave the type value set to 0 (`UNKNOWN`) as well.

> **POLYGLOT NOTE** Apache Thrift `TTransportException` type values aren't consistent across all languages (see table 9.1). If you trap the `END_OF_FILE` type `TTransportException` in C++, with a value of 3, and pass it to a Java program, you may have problems, because the `TTransportException` type value 3 in Java is `TIMED_OUT`. Passing `TTransportException` "type" values across language boundaries is dangerous for this reason and can lead to undefined behavior.

To get more insight into `TTransportException` processing we'll add exception support to the `TSimpleFileTransport` example programs from chapter 4.

9.2.1   *C++ exception processing*

The following listing shows the C++ file transport example from chapter 4 with exception processing added. The program also includes command line-driven code to generate exceptions as a means to test the exception processing.

Listing 9.1 ~/ThriftBook/part2/exceptions/trans_excep.cpp

```
#include <thrift/Thrift.h>
#include <thrift/transport/TTransportException.h>
#include <thrift/transport/TSimpleFileTransport.h>
```

```
#include <iostream>
#include <exception>          ❸
#include <memory>
#include <cstring>

using namespace apache::thrift::transport;

struct Trade {
   char symbol[16];
   double price;
   int size;
};

int main(int argc, char ** argv)
{
   try {
      std::unique_ptr<TTransport> trans;
❹    if (argc > 1)
        trans.reset(new TSimpleFileTransport("data", false, false));
      else
        trans.reset(new TSimpleFileTransport("data", false, true));
      Trade trade{"F", 13.10, 2500};
      trans->write((const uint8_t *)&trade, sizeof(trade));
      trans->close();

      trans.reset(new TSimpleFileTransport("data",true,false));
      std::memset(&trade, 0, sizeof(trade));
      int bytes_read = trans->read((uint8_t *)&trade,sizeof(trade));

      std::cout << "Trade(" << bytes_read << "): " << trade.symbol
             << " " << trade.size << " @ " << trade.price
             << std::endl;
   } catch (const apache::thrift::transport::TTransportException & tte) {   ❺
      std::cout << "TTransportException(" << tte.getType() << "): "
             << tte.what() << std::endl;
   } catch (const apache::thrift::TException & te) {                    ❻
      std::cout << "TException: " << te.what() << std::endl;
❼ } catch (const std::exception & e) {
      std::cout << "exception: " << e.what() << std::endl;
❽ } catch (...) {
      std::cout << "Unknown Exception" << std::endl;
   }
}
```

The error handling code in this example is compartmentalized, leaving normal program flow unobstructed. The C++ "exception" header ❸ declares the C++ standard library exception class (std::exception). The "Thrift.h" header provides the TException declaration ❶ and the TTransportException.h header declares the TTransportException ❷.

This short program consists of a single main() function entirely contained within a try block. The catch clauses at the end of the try block trap exceptions in hierachical order, from the most specialized class to the most abstract (see figure 9.3). Apache

Thrift libraries throw `TTransportExcep-`
`tions` by value, and we catch them here by
reference ❺, enabling the `catch` clauses to
perform polymorphically. This is important
because C++ will process the first matching
`catch`, so if a base class is listed before a
derived class, the derived class `catch` will
never execute. Most compilers emit warnings associated with `catch` blocks that are
masked by earlier base class `catches`.

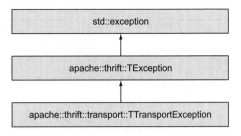

Figure 9.3   Apache Thrift C++ exception hierarchy

The `TTransportException` handler traps transport-specific issues; subsequently
the `TException` catch clause ❻ catches any other Thrift exceptions. The
`std::exception` catch ❼ will trap anything derived from the generic C++ standard
library exception, and finally the `catch-all` (...) ❽ will trap everything else that can
be caught. While this is a fairly robust exception processing regimen, it's important to
note that certain errors cannot be caught.

Note that the `catch` types are const. A const reference can catch a variable, but the
converse is not true. Best practice in C++ is to throw by value and catch by const reference where possible.

The code in this example has been configured to create an illegal file transport if
an argument is supplied on the command line ❹. Because `TSimpleFileTransports`
must be either readable or writable, the first branch of the `if` will throw a `TTransport-`
`Exception`. Here's an example run:

```
$ g++ -std=c++11 trans_excep.cpp -Wall -lthrift
$ rm data
$ ./a.out
Trade(32): F 2500 @ 13.1
$ rm data
$ ./a.out blowup
TTransportException(0): Neither READ nor WRITE specified
$
```

The session demonstrates a sucessful run and an unsuccessful run. The failed run
throws a `TTransportException` with a type of 0 and a message that the `catch` block
displays.

9.2.2   *Java exception processing*

The Java programming language provides an exception specification mechanism
fairly unique among its peer group. The Java compiler requires methods to catch or
declare any exception that might be raised. This makes the types of exceptions possible when calling a certain method easy to dertermine. The following listing shows the
Java version of the exception processing example.

Listing 9.2   ~/ThriftBook/part2/exceptions/TransExcep.java

```java
import java.io.ByteArrayInputStream;
import java.io.ByteArrayOutputStream;
import java.io.ObjectInputStream;
import java.io.ObjectOutputStream;
import java.io.Serializable;
import org.apache.thrift.TException;
import org.apache.thrift.transport.TSimpleFileTransport;
import org.apache.thrift.transport.TTransport;
import org.apache.thrift.transport.TTransportException;

public class TransExcep {

    static private class Trade implements Serializable {
        public String symbol;
        public double price;
        public int size;
    };

    public static void main(String[] args) {
        try {
            TTransport trans = new TSimpleFileTransport("data",false,true);
            Trade trade = new Trade();
            trade.symbol = "F";
            trade.price = 13.10;
            trade.size = 2500;
            ByteArrayOutputStream baos = new ByteArrayOutputStream();
            ObjectOutputStream oos = new ObjectOutputStream(baos);
            oos.writeObject(trade);
            trans.write(baos.toByteArray());
            trans.close();

            trans = new TSimpleFileTransport("data",
                                             (args.length==0),
                                             true);                    ❶
            byte[] buf = new byte[128];
            int iBytesRead = trans.read(buf, 0, buf.length);
            ByteArrayInputStream bais = new ByteArrayInputStream(buf);
            ObjectInputStream ois = new ObjectInputStream(bais);
            trade = (Trade) ois.readObject();
            System.out.println("Trade(" + iBytesRead + "): " + trade.symbol
                               + " " + trade.size + " @ " + trade.price);
    ❷  } catch (TTransportException tte) {
            System.out.println("TTransportException(" + tte.getType() +
                               "): " + tte);
        } catch (TException te) {                        ❸
            System.out.println("TException: " + te);
        } catch (Exception e) {
            System.out.println("Exception: " + e);
        } catch (Throwable t) {
            System.out.println("Throwable: " + t);       ❹
        }
    }
}
```

Java defines a small set of "unchecked exceptions," which need not be declared or caught; however, the lion's share of Java exceptions must be declared as thrown or caught within a given method. In the `main()` method in the previous listing, we provide `catch` clauses for all of the exceptions in the Java exception hierachy leading up to `TTransportException` (see figure 9.4). The Java compiler will complain if you provide a redundant or unnecessary catch clause. In this case, the `TException` class fits this cate-

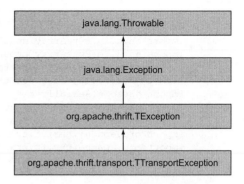

Figure 9.4   Thrift Java exception hierarchy

gory ❸ because the only exception thrown by the framework methods used here is `TTransportException` ❷. Though redundant, `TException` was left in place here to demonstrate `catch` clauses for the complete exception hierarchy.

The Java exception hierachy is rooted with the `java.lang.Throwable` class. The `Throwable` class catch in the Java example is equivalent to the C++ (...) catch. All things thrown in Java must be of type `Throwable`. User-defined Java exceptions should derive from `java.lang.Exception`, which is derived directly from `Throwable`. The Apache Thrift Java `TException` class is derived from `java.lang.Exception`, linking the Thrift exception hierarchy with the Java language exception hierarchy.

Most of the interesting information associated with exceptions in Java is found in the `Throwable` super class. The Java exception example uses the Throwable `toString()` method implicitly ❹ to produce string information when logging errors. The `TTransportException` "type" value is available through the `getType()` method and is usually the only additional piece of exception information of interest ❷.

Like our C++ example, this program has added a command line option that will cause an exception to be generated ❶. If an argument is supplied on the command line, this program will create the `read` transport with only the `write` flag set to `true`, causing the first read attempt to fail. The following code shows a sample session with the Java program:

```
$ javac -cp /usr/local/lib/libthrift-1.0.0.jar TransExcep.java
TransExcep.java:45: warning: unreachable catch clause
        } catch (TException te) {
          ^
  thrown type TTransportException has already been caught
1 warning
$ rm data
$ java -cp /usr/local/lib/libthrift-1.0.0.jar:./gen-java:. TransExcep
Trade(99): F 2500 @ 13.1
$ rm data
$java -cp /usr/local/lib/libthrift-1.0.0.jar:./gen-java:. TransExcep Crash
TTransportException(0): org.apache.thrift.transport.TTransportException:
    Read operation on write only file
$
```

In the example, we call methods which may throw a `TTransportException` but nothing which could throw an Apache Thrift `TException`, causing the compiler to generate a warning. The first run of the Java program is clean as expected, while the second run throws a `TTransportException` with a type of 0 and an appropriate error message.

9.2.3 *Python exception processing*

The following listing shows the Python version of the exception processing example.

Listing 9.3 ~/ThriftBook/part2/exceptions/trans_excep.py

```python
import pickle
import sys
from thrift import Thrift
from thrift.transport import TTransport

class Trade:
    def __init__(self):
        symbol=""
        price=0.0
        size=0

try:
    trans = TTransport.TFileObjectTransport(open("data","wb"))
    trade = Trade()
    trade.symbol = "F"
    trade.price = 13.10
    trade.size = 2500
    trans.write(pickle.dumps(trade));
    trans.close()

    if len(sys.argv) == 2:                          ❶
        raise TTransport.TTransportException(
                TTransport.TTransportException.NOT_OPEN, "cmd line ex")

❷  trans = TTransport.TFileObjectTransport(open("data",
                        ("wb" if len(sys.argv) > 2 else "rb")))
    bstr = trans.read(128)
    trade = pickle.loads(bstr)
    print("Trade(%d): %s %d @ %f" % (len(bstr), trade.symbol,
                        trade.size, trade.price))

except TTransport.TTransportException as tte:        ❸
    print("TTransportException(%d): %s" % (tte.type, tte))
except Thrift.TException as te:
    print("TException: %s" % te)
except Exception as e:                               ❹
    print("Exception: %s %s" % (type(e), e))
❺  except:
    print("BaseException: %s" % sys.exc_info()[0])
```

The Python exception hierachy is similar to the Java exception hierarchy. Python has an internal `BaseException` class from which all built-in exceptions are derived.

User-defined exceptions should be derived from the Exception class, which itself is derived from BaseException. The Apache Thrift TException class is derived from Exception and is the base for the transport library TTransportException class (see figure 9.5). In the example Python program, we have except blocks to catch all four of the exception classes in the hierarchy from TTransportException up.

This Python program is similar to the prior examples but also includes a block of code which demonstrates the way the

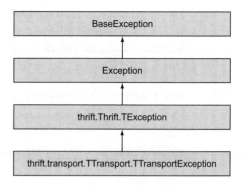

Figure 9.5   Apache Thrift Python exception hierarchy

Apache Thrift framework raises exceptions ❶. In Python the exception is constructed with a type and a message, then thrown with the raise statement. The Python TFileObjectTransport is a thin wrapper around a Python File object ❷. As such, all the exceptions generated in this example would come from the Python File object directly and therefore wouldn't be derived from TException.

The TTransportException except block ❸ displays the TTransportException type and any arguments supplied to the exception object when it was constructed. The type attribute is accessed directly and the exception construction arguments, in this case a string, are output as a result of the object's __str__() default string conversion method. Python offers a type() operator that will produce the string name of the class for the nested object. The Python type() function is used in the except block for Exception ❹. The Python sys module provides an exc_info() method that returns exception information associated with the current exception. This is useful in a default except block where no identifier is available to reference the current exception ❺.

The Python exception example has been coded to raise one of two exceptions in response to one or more command line arguments. If one command line argument is supplied, the program raises a TTransportException directly ❶. If two or more arguments are supplied, the code opens the read file in write-only mode, causing the first read to fail. Here's a sample session running the previous Python code:

```
$ rm data
$ python trans_excep.py
Trade(87): F 2500 @ 13.100000
$ rm data
$ python trans_excep.py crash
TTransportException(1): cmd line ex
$ rm data
$ python trans_excep.py crash burn
Exception: <type 'exceptions.IOError'> File not open for reading
```

9.2.4 *Error processing without exceptions*

Languages such as Go and C don't provide an exception processing mechanism. In such languages, errors are generally passed back with each function result. In many languages of this type, each function returns a success/failure code. In certain situations, you make a second call to gather error details. In other languages, a generic error structure or pointer is passed to every function call and populated with error data when the function fails.

To better understand non-exception-style error processing, we'll build a glib-based C example. Glib is a cross-platform C library providing various utilities, enabling object-oriented programming in C, among other things. It's used most heavily in Linux GUI development.

The Apache Thrift c_glib code generator doesn't emit straight C language code. Rather the c_glib libraries rely on g_lib and the GObject system it provides. Even if you cannot run the example in the following listing on your system, the code will give you an understanding of the way Apache Thrift error processing is handled in procedural languages.

Listing 9.4 ~/ThriftBook/part2/exceptions/trans_excep.c

```c
#include <stdio.h>
#include <thrift/c_glib/transport/thrift_memory_buffer.h>

struct Trade {
   char symbol[16];
   double price;
   int size;
};

int main(int argc, char ** argv) {
   GError *error = NULL;
   int result = 0;
   int size = (argc > 1) ? 5 : 1024;            ❶

   struct Trade trade;
   trade.symbol[0] = 'F'; trade.symbol[1] = '\0';
   trade.price = 13.10;
   trade.size = 2500;

   //Init glib type system and allocate an Apache Thrift Memory Transport
   g_type_init();
   ThriftMemoryBuffer *trans = g_object_new(THRIFT_TYPE_MEMORY_BUFFER,
                                            "buf_size", size, NULL);
❷ if (NULL == trans) {
      printf("Failed to create Memory Transport\n");
      return -1;
   }

   //Open the transport
   if (FALSE==thrift_memory_buffer_open(THRIFT_TRANSPORT(trans), &error)) {
❸    result = -1;
```

```
      printf("Open failed\n");
      if (NULL != error){
         printf(">> [%d]: %s\n", error->code, error->message);
         result = error->code;
         g_error_free(error);
      }
      g_object_unref(trans);
      return result;
   }

   //Write to the transport
   if (FALSE == thrift_memory_buffer_write(THRIFT_TRANSPORT(trans),
                                           (gpointer)&trade,
                                           sizeof(trade),
                                           &error)) {          ❹
      result = -1;
      printf("Write failed\n");
      if (NULL != error){
         printf(">> [%d]: %s\n", error->code, error->message);
         result = error->code;
         g_error_free(error);
      }
      g_object_unref(trans);
      return result;
   }
   printf("Wrote Trade(%zu): %s %d @ %lf\n",
          sizeof(trade), trade.symbol, trade.size, trade.price);

   //Flush the transport
   if (FALSE == thrift_memory_buffer_flush(THRIFT_TRANSPORT(trans),
                                           &error)) {      ⟵
      result = -1;                                         ❺
      printf("Flush failed\n");
      if (NULL != error){
         printf(">> [%d]: %s\n", error->code, error->message);
         result = error->code;
         g_error_free(error);
      }
      g_object_unref(trans);
      return result;
   }

   //Read a trade from the memory transport
   if (sizeof(trade) != thrift_memory_buffer_read(THRIFT_TRANSPORT(trans),
                                                  (gpointer)&trade,
                                                  sizeof(trade),
                                                  &error)) {    ❻
      result = -1;
      printf("Read failed\n");
      if (NULL != error){
         printf(">> [%d]: %s\n", error->code, error->message);
         result = error->code;
         g_error_free(error);
      }
      g_object_unref(trans);
```

```
        return result;
    }
    printf("Read  Trade(%zu): %s %d @ %lf\n",
           sizeof(trade), trade.symbol, trade.size, trade.price);

    //Clean up
    thrift_memory_buffer_close(THRIFT_TRANSPORT(trans), &error);
    g_object_unref(trans);
    return 0;
}
```

This simple program functions much like the prior exception examples. We create a memory transport ❷, open it ❸, write a trade to it ❹, flush the writes ❺, and then read the trade back ❻. The memory buffer will be sized at 1024 bytes by default; however, if one or more parameters are supplied on the command line, the buffer size will be made 5 bytes, causing the trade write to fail ❶.

Each library call must be tested for failure in this environment. Most of the Apache Thrift library functions used in this example accept a pointer to a pointer to a GError object. If the function fails, a GError is allocated and initialized with the error information and passed back using the GError ** supplied by the caller. The caller must then release the GError object when finished with it. To test the program, we run it normally once and then again with a parameter on the command line to cause an error:

```
$ pkg-config --cflags thrift_c_glib
-I/usr/local/include/thrift/c_glib
    -I/usr/include/glib-2.0
    -I/usr/lib/x86_64-linux-gnu/glib-2.0/include
$ pkg-config --libs thrift_c_glib
-L/usr/local/lib -lthrift_c_glib -lgobject-2.0 -lglib-2.0
$ gcc trans_excep.c `pkg-config --cflags thrift_c_glib --libs thrift_c_glib`
$ ./a.out
Wrote Trade(32): F 2500 @ 13.100000
Read  Trade(32): F 2500 @ 13.100000
$ ./a.out fail
Write failed
>> [4]: unable to write 32 bytes to buffer of length 5
```

We use the GNU C compiler (GCC) to build the program and also take advantage of the pkg-config command, which emits the necessary include and lib paths for build dependencies described in package files. The pkg-config utility originated on Linux but is available on most *nix systems as well as OS X and Windows. The Apache Thrift make install process prepares a /usr/local/lib/pkgconfig/thrift_c_glib.pc file that the pkg-config command uses to set the necessary include directories and libraries for Apache Thrift glib development.

The first run of the program completes normally. The second run is passed a command line parameter and subsequently allocates a small memory transport, causing the write operation to fail. The function returns false and passes back an initialized

GError object through the error parameter. We then use the error to report the details of the failure.

9.3 *TProtocolException*

The Thrift Protocol library throws TProtocolException objects when encountering errors. Most protocol error conditions involve reading rather than writing. For example, if a protocol is given a corrupted file to de-serialize or receives a message from a client using the wrong protocol or possibly a mismatched transport stack, a TProtocol-Exception will likely be raised.

The TProtocolException class is almost identical to the TTransportException class, supporting a message and a type. TProtocolExceptions are typically derived from TException in most languages. TProtocolExceptions have their own protocol-specific exception type values. Table 9.2 displays the types defined for TProtocol-Exceptions in the three demonstration languages.

Table 9.2   TProtocolException types

Value	C++	Java	Python
0	UNKNOWN	UNKNOWN	UNKNOWN
1	INVALID_DATA	INVALID_DATA	INVALID_DATA
2	NEGATIVE_SIZE	NEGATIVE_SIZE	NEGATIVE_SIZE
3	SIZE_LIMIT	SIZE_LIMIT	SIZE_LIMIT
4	BAD_VERSION	BAD_VERSION	BAD_VERSION
5	NOT_IMPLEMENTED	NOT_IMPLEMENTED	

TProtocolExceptions are raised, caught, and processed in the same way as TTrans-portExceptions. Application code interacting with Apache Thrift protocol classes should be prepared to handle TProtocolExceptions, particularly when reading. TProtocolExceptions may be trapped by catching the TProtocolException type directly or by catching TException, or through a language-specific base class.

TIP TTransportExceptions and TProtocolExceptions are always raised locally and never propagate from the server to the client.

9.4 *TApplicationException*

TTransportExceptions and TProtocolExceptions are generated locally and act much like normal language exceptions, propagating inside the process on the thread in which they occur until caught, and if uncaught they terminate the application. TApplicationExceptions behave differently from normal exceptions. The principle purpose of the TApplicationException class is to allow RPC layer processing errors to propagate from the server back to the client. As the name implies, these exceptions occur at the application layer. In network terms, the "application" layer includes the RPC system. User code operates at a higher layer and doesn't generate TApplication-Exceptions, rather making use of user-defined exceptions, which we cover next. TApplicationExceptions involve problems such as calling a method that isn't implemented or failing to provide the necessary arguments to a method.

TApplicationExceptions are typically produced by server processor library code and service-specific processor code generated by the Apache Thrift compiler. If an RPC error occurs on the server, a TApplicationException will automatically be sent to the client and then thrown or raised when recovered by the client proxy in the client process.

TApplicationExceptions have a type, a message, and are derived from TException, much like the TTransportException and TProtocolException classes. Table 9.3 contains a list of the TApplicationException types for each of the three demonstration languages.

Table 9.3 TApplicationException types

Value	C++	Java	Python
0	UNKNOWN	UNKNOWN	UNKNOWN
1	UNKNOWN_METHOD	UNKNOWN_METHOD	UNKNOWN_METHOD
2	INVALID_MESSAGE_TYPE	INVALID_MESSAGE_TYPE	INVALID_MESSAGE_TYPE
3	WRONG_METHOD_NAME	WRONG_METHOD_NAME	WRONG_METHOD_NAME
4	BAD_SEQUENCE_ID	BAD_SEQUENCE_ID	BAD_SEQUENCE_ID
5	MISSING_RESULT	MISSING_RESULT	MISSING_RESULT
6	INTERNAL_ERROR	INTERNAL_ERROR	INTERNAL_ERROR
7	PROTOCOL_ERROR	PROTOCOL_ERROR	PROTOCOL_ERROR
8	INVALID_TRANSFORM	INVALID_TRANSFORM	INVALID_TRANSFORM
9	INVALID_PROTOCOL	INVALID_PROTOCOL	INVALID_PROTOCOL
10	UNSUPPORTED_CLIENT_TYPE	UNSUPPORTED_CLIENT_TYPE	UNSUPPORTED_CLIENT_TYPE

TApplicationExceptions are caught and processed in the same way as the previously described exceptions, using normal language mechanisms. The Apache Thrift server-side code need not trap these exceptions, because they are always passed back to the calling client. All Apache Thrift RPC client code should be prepared to handle TApplicationExceptions. As we saw in the previous exception processing examples, TApplicationExceptions may be trapped by catching the TApplicationException type directly or by catching TException or a language-specific base class.

9.5   *User-defined exceptions*

In the previous sections, we looked at the exceptions thrown by the transport, protocol, and RPC layers of the Apache Thrift framework. This leaves the question: What happens when a user-defined service handler runs into trouble?

When an Apache Thrift service handler experiences an error (for example, not being able to find a customer database record, and so on), the service needs a way to report the problem. Raising a local exception, possibly killing the server process, isn't the desired approach. Service handlers need a way to report errors back to the calling client. In the RPC context, the client may be running on a separate computer and may be coded in a different language, making this process nontrivial.

Fortunately, the Apache Thrift framework makes propagating exceptions in a service handler back to a client seamless. Apache Thrift users can define custom exception types in IDL. Services defined in the IDL file can flag any method as capable of throwing these user-defined exceptions. The IDL compiler generates processor code that automatically catches user-defined exceptions raised by the service handler and passes them back to the client, where they're raised as normal client-side exceptions by the client proxy.

Like TApplicationExceptions, user-defined exceptions are derived from TException. The distinction is that TApplicationExceptions are raised by the Apache Thrift framework and user-defined exceptions are raised by user code.

For example, if a program used by a seafood distributor calls an Apache Thrift fish market server to retrieve the price of halibut, but halibut isn't in the database, the service handler can raise a user-defined BadFish exception. The Apache Thrift framework will then pass the BadFish exception back to the client automatically (see figure 9.6). It's important to recognize that user-defined exceptions are an integral part of a service's interface and therefore are defined within the IDL.

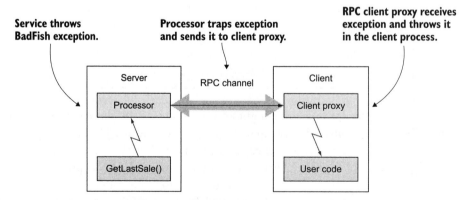

Figure 9.6   User-defined exceptions specified in the Apache Thrift IDL can be automatically transferred from the service handler to the calling client.

9.5.1 *User-defined exception IDL example*

To get a better feel for how user-defined exceptions work, let's build an exception-enabled RPC application. The `TradeHistory` service example in the following listing provides a `GetLastSale()` method that returns the going price for fish. However, if an unsupported fish type is requested, such as halibut, an exception will be generated. Here's the IDL that declares the exception for bad fish requests and then associates it with the `GetLastSale()` method.

> **Listing 9.5   ~/ThriftBook/part2/exceptions/excep.thrift**

❶
```
exception BadFish {
    1: string       fish,       //The problem fish
    2: i16          error_code, //The service specific error code
}

service TradeHistory {
    double GetLastSale(1: string fish)
        throws (1: BadFish bf),          ❷
}
```

Defining a custom exception in Apache Thrift IDL is exactly like defining a struct, but with the `exception` keyword ❶. In fact, Apache Thrift implements exceptions using structs internally.

The IDL "throws" keyword associates exceptions with the methods that might throw them ❷. Exception types are listed within parentheses and are separated by commas. Elements in the `throws` list are each given a unique positive ID value, like fields in an exception declaration and parameters in an argument list. In the previous example, the `GetLastSale()` method throws only one exception type, `BadFish`, with an ID of 1.

9.5.2 *C++ user-defined exception client*

A client program using the `TradeHistory` service `GetLastSale()` method should be prepared to handle the `BadFish` exception. The following listing shows a sample C++ client listing that calls `GetLastSale()` and processes the `BadFish` exception if thrown.

> **Listing 9.6   ~/ThriftBook/part2/exceptions/excep_client.cpp**

```
#include "gen-cpp/TradeHistory.h"
#include "gen-cpp/excep_types.h"
#include <thrift/transport/TSocket.h>
#include <thrift/transport/TBufferTransports.h>
#include <thrift/protocol/TBinaryProtocol.h>
#include <boost/shared_ptr.hpp>
#include <boost/make_shared.hpp>
#include <iostream>

using namespace apache::thrift::transport;
```

```
using namespace apache::thrift::protocol;
using boost::shared_ptr;
using boost::make_shared;

int main(int argv, char * argc[]) {
    shared_ptr<TTransport> trans;
    trans = make_shared<TSocket>("localhost", 8585);
    trans = make_shared<TBufferedTransport>(trans);

    auto proto = make_shared<TBinaryProtocol>(trans);
    TradeHistoryClient client(proto);

    try {
        trans->open();
        auto price = client.GetLastSale(argc[1]);
        std::cout << "[Client] received: " << price << std::endl;
    } catch (const BadFish & bf) {
        std::cout << "[Client] GetLastSale() call failed for fish: "
                        << bf.fish << ", error: " << bf.error_code
                        << std::endl;
    } catch (...) {
        std::cout << "[Client] GetLastSale() call failed" << std::endl;
    }
}
```

❶
❷

The sample program provides code to trap the user-defined exception ❶, as well as any other exceptions that may be raised ❷.

9.5.3   *C++ user-defined exception server*

User-defined exceptions are raised on the server by using the native language exception mechanism in the service handler. For example, to raise the BadFish exception in the GetLastSale() handler of a C++ TradeHistory implementation, you'd use the C++ throw statement with a BadFish object.

> **WARNING**   Nothing stops a service handler from throwing an exception type not listed in the IDL throws clause. However, the processor that dispatches RPC calls to the service handler will only trap exceptions listed in the throws list. Other exceptions will not be caught by the processor, and instead of being passed back to the client, they will likely kill the server thread, or possibly the entire server.

To get a complete picture of the user-defined exception process, we'll build a simple RPC server example using our excep.thrift IDL. The session below compiles the excep.thrift IDL, generating C++ RPC stubs used by our C++ client and RPC server:

```
$ thrift -gen cpp excep.thrift
$ ls -l
-rw-r--r-- 1 randy randy  240 Jun  5 17:28 excep.thrift
drwxr-xr-x 2 randy randy 4096 Jun  5 18:37 gen-cpp
$ ls -l gen-cpp
-rw-r--r-- 1 randy randy  251 Jun  5 18:37 excep_constants.cpp
```

```
-rw-r--r-- 1 randy randy  333 Jun  5 18:37 excep_constants.h
-rw-r--r-- 1 randy randy 2204 Jun  5 18:37 excep_types.cpp        ❶
-rw-r--r-- 1 randy randy 1534 Jun  5 18:37 excep_types.h
-rw-r--r-- 1 randy randy 9769 Jun  5 18:37 TradeHistory.cpp
-rw-r--r-- 1 randy randy 7113 Jun  5 18:37 TradeHistory.h
-rw-r--r-- 1 randy randy 1366 Jun  5 18:37 TradeHistory_server.skeleton.cpp   ❷
```

Compiling the IDL produces the standard *_types files which house our IDL types, including exception types ❶. The IDL compiler C++ code generator also creates a server skeleton for any services defined in the IDL source ❷. With a few lines of code, we can modify the skeleton for the TradeHistory service so that it throws the BadFish exception when the price of a fish we don't carry is requested. In the following listing, we throw a user-defined exception for any request other than halibut. It's a good idea to copy the server skeleton to a new filename before you modify it, because it will be overwritten each time you rerun the IDL compiler. Here's an example listing for the modified C++ server skeleton.

Listing 9.7   ~/ThriftBook/part2/exceptions/excep_server.cpp

```cpp
#include "gen-cpp/TradeHistory.h"
#include "gen-cpp/excep_types.h"               ❶
#include <thrift/protocol/TBinaryProtocol.h>
#include <thrift/server/TSimpleServer.h>
#include <thrift/transport/TServerSocket.h>
#include <thrift/transport/TBufferTransports.h>
#include <boost/shared_ptr.hpp>
#include <boost/make_shared.hpp>

using namespace ::apache::thrift::protocol;
using namespace ::apache::thrift::transport;
using namespace ::apache::thrift::server;

using boost::shared_ptr;
using boost::make_shared;

class TradeHistoryHandler : virtual public TradeHistoryIf {
public:
    double GetLastSale(const std::string& fish) {
        if (0 != fish.compare("Halibut")) {
            BadFish bf;
            bf.fish = fish;
            bf.error_code = 94;
❷          throw bf;
        }
        return 10.0;
    }
};

int main(int argc, char **argv) {
  int port = 8585;

  auto handler = make_shared<TradeHistoryHandler>();
```

```
    shared_ptr<TProcessor> proc =
      make_shared<TradeHistoryProcessor>(handler);
    shared_ptr<TServerTransport> svr_trans =
      make_shared<TServerSocket>(port);
    shared_ptr<TTransportFactory> trans_fac =
      make_shared<TBufferedTransportFactory>();
    shared_ptr<TProtocolFactory> proto_fac =
      make_shared<TBinaryProtocolFactory>();

    TSimpleServer server(proc, svr_trans, trans_fac, proto_fac);
    server.serve();
    return 0;
}
```

Because user-defined exceptions are another kind of user-defined type, we must include the IDL *_types.h header ❶ to provide exception definitions within our code. The exception can then be constructed, initialized, and thrown from the service handler ❷. This is exactly like throwing an exception in a standalone program. The following session compiles the example client and server, then runs the server:

```
$ g++ -o server excep_server.cpp \
          gen-cpp/TradeHistory.cpp gen-cpp/excep_types.cpp -lthrift
$ g++ -o client excep_client.cpp \
          gen-cpp/TradeHistory.cpp gen-cpp/excep_types.cpp -lthrift
$ ls -l
-rwxr-xr-x 1 randy randy 142841 Jun  5 18:54 client
-rw-r--r-- 1 randy randy    832 Jun  5 18:25 excep_client.cpp
-rw-r--r-- 1 randy randy   1388 Jun  5 18:52 excep_server.cpp
-rw-r--r-- 1 randy randy    240 Jun  5 17:28 excep.thrift
drwxr-xr-x 2 randy randy   4096 Jun  5 18:48 gen-cpp
-rwxr-xr-x 1 randy randy 202651 Jun  5 18:53 server
$ ./server
```

With the server running, we can start the client program in a separate shell to test normal and exceptional RPC responses:

```
$ ./client Halibut
[Client] received: 10
$ ./client Salmon
[Client] GetLastSale() call failed for fish: Salmon, error: 94
```

The completed example demonstrates a common scenario, that of a service running in one process detecting an error that needs to be passed back to a client. The Apache Thrift exception mechanism provides an elegant and seamless solution, wherein both the service code and the client code use their native (and potentially different) error processing mechanisms, with Apache Thrift generating the glue necessary to connect the two.

9.5.4   *Java user-defined exception client*

To illustrate cross-language exceptions, we can recreate the C++ exception client in Java.

Listing 9.8   ~/ThriftBook/part2/exceptions/ExcepClient.java

```java
import org.apache.thrift.protocol.TBinaryProtocol;
import org.apache.thrift.transport.TSocket;
import org.apache.thrift.TException;

public class ExcepClient {
    public static void main(String[] args) throws TException {
        TSocket socket = new TSocket("localhost", 8585);
        socket.open();
        TBinaryProtocol protocol = new TBinaryProtocol(socket);
        TradeHistory.Client client = new TradeHistory.Client(protocol);
        try {
            double price = client.GetLastSale(args[0]);
            System.out.println("[Client] received: " + price);
        } catch (BadFish bf) {
            System.out.println("[Client] GetLastSale()failed for fish: " +
                                      bf.fish + ", error " + bf.error_code);
        }
    }
}
```

The following code shows a sample session building and running the Java client against the C++ server (which must be running in another shell):

```
$ thrift -gen java excep.thrift
$ javac -cp /usr/local/lib/libthrift-1.0.0.jar:\
             /usr/share/java/slf4j-api.jar:\
             /usr/share/java/slf4j-nop.jar \
             ExcepClient.java \
         gen-java/TradeHistory.java \
         gen-java/BadFish.java
$ java -cp /usr/local/lib/libthrift-1.0.0.jar:\
             /usr/share/java/slf4j-api.jar:\
             /usr/share/java/slf4j-nop.jar:\
             ./gen-java:\
         . \
         ExcepClient Halibut
[Client] received: 10.0
$ java -cp /usr/local/lib/libthrift-1.0.0.jar:\
             /usr/share/java/slf4j-api.jar:\
             /usr/share/java/slf4j-nop.jar:\
             ./gen-java:\
         . \
         ExcepClient Salmon
[Client] GetLastSale() failed for fish: Salmon, error 94
```

This session runs much like the C++ client session. It's worth appreciating the fact that in this example, a C++ exception object was thrown in a C++ service, trapped by the Apache Thrift processor, serialized into a binary stream, transmitted to the Java client proxy, de-serialized into a Java exception object, and thrown in the Java client process. This is a lot of functionality in exchange for a few lines of IDL.

9.5.5   *Python user-defined exception client*

To round out the examples, the following listing demonstrates the exception client coded in Python.

> **Listing 9.9   ~/ThriftBook/part2/exceptions/excep_client.py**

```
import sys
sys.path.append("gen-py")

from thrift.transport import TSocket
from thrift.transport import TTransport
from thrift.protocol import TBinaryProtocol
from excep import TradeHistory
from excep.ttypes import BadFish

trans = TSocket.TSocket("localhost", 8585)
trans = TTransport.TBufferedTransport(trans)
trans.open()

proto = TBinaryProtocol.TBinaryProtocol(trans)
client = TradeHistory.Client(proto)
try:
    print("[Client] received: %f" % client.GetLastSale(sys.argv[1]))
except BadFish as bf:
    print("[Client] GetLastSale() call failed for fish: %s, error %d" %
              (bf.fish, bf.error_code))
```

Here's a session running the Python client with a normal and an exceptional call against the C++ server in the previous listing:

```
$ thrift -gen py excep.thrift
$ python excep_client.py Halibut
[Client] received: 10.000000
$ python excep_client.py Salmon
[Client] GetLastSale() call failed for fish: Salmon, error 94
```

Summary

This chapter has examined the exception processing features and components of the Apache Thrift framework. We looked at the predefined library exception classes used by Apache Thrift and also examined the features supporting user-defined exceptions in IDL and RPC services. These are the key points from this chapter:

- The Apache Thrift framework supports exception-based error processing semantics.
- Apache Thrift languages that don't support exceptions model exceptions by passing exception objects back to callers through return values, by using in/out parameters, or by raising error events, as appropriate to the language.
- Apache Thrift defines a shallow exception hierarchy, with TException as the base class for all Apache Thrift exception types.

- `TException` is typically derived from the target language's base exception type (that is, `std::exception` in C++, `java.lang.Exception` in Java, and `Exception` in Python).
- The Apache Thrift `TTransportException` type is the base class for all Apache Thrift transport layer exceptions.
- The Apache Thrift `TProtocolException` type is the base class for all Apache Thrift protocol layer exceptions.
- The Apache Thrift `TApplicationException` type is the base class for all Apache Thrift RPC layer exceptions generated by RPC `TProcessor` classes.
- User-defined exceptions are created in Apache Thrift IDL using the `exception` keyword.
- Service methods declare all UDEs thrown using a `throws` list.
- `TApplicationExceptions` and UDEs occurring on the server are passed back to the client for processing.
- `TTransportException`, `TProtocolException`, and `TApplicationException` classes have an integer "type" value that occasionally identifies the specific exception cause (usually accessed with the `getType()` method).
- Apache Thrift RPC exception processing support makes propagating exceptions in server handlers across process and language boundaries to clients as easy as raising exceptions locally.

10

Servers

This chapter covers

- Building RPC servers
- Understanding RPC server architecture
- Learning about server concurrency models
- Using factories to create per-connection handlers and custom I/O stacks
- Processing server events
- Using service multiplexing

This chapter is the culmination of part 2. At this point we've examined nearly all the moving parts within the Apache Thrift framework, from byte-level transport I/O all the way up to designing RPC Services. Our final framework topic is the Apache Thrift server (see figure 10.1).

Servers are the conductors of the Apache Thrift RPC symphony. Apache Thrift servers provide prebuilt and tested hosting for user-implemented services. Each Apache Thrift language provides a different set of servers based on the needs and capabilities of the language.

Using a server from the Apache Thrift server library can greatly reduce the effort associated with deploying cross-language services. Servers handle almost all

280

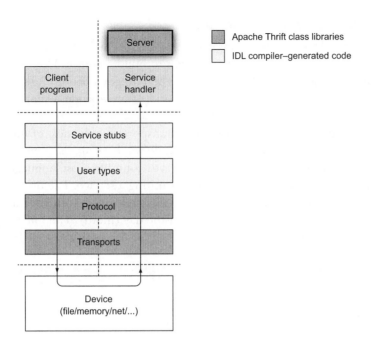

Figure 10.1 The Apache Thrift framework server library

the difficult issues involved in programming high performance RPC services, such as concurrency management, scalability, and cross-thread communications.

Apache Thrift servers have several features in common across languages. For example, they all host user-defined services and invoke them on behalf of remote client calls. They also have many differences, more so than any other layer of the framework. This is largely tied to the variety of concurrency features associated with the languages supported by Apache Thrift.

For example, the Node.js library provides a single threaded, event-driven server, while C++ and Java offer a variety of multithreaded servers. As modern cloud-native approaches to software development grow in popularity, scaling moves to the orchestration platform. Containerizing simple lightweight Apache Thrift servers written in Go or Python allows tools such as Kubernetes to scale them horizontally by creating new containerized instances across a cluster of hosts.

In the pages ahead, we'll take a high-level look at the principle mechanisms underpinning Apache Thrift servers across languages. We'll also look at the server profiles for the three demonstration languages and build servers exemplifying the various features and concurrency models they provide. At the end of the chapter you should have a clear understanding of what Apache Thrift servers are, how they work, and the key features implemented by Apache Thrift servers.

10.1   *Building a simple server from scratch*

Because almost every Apache Thrift language provides prebuilt RPC servers we can use out of the box, we almost never have a reason to build our own. However, we're going to build a simple server from scratch in C++ here to get a better understanding of Apache Thrift and how the prebuilt servers work. After we code a simple server, we'll try out several of the official Apache Thrift servers.

The Apache Thrift framework protocols and transports supply most of the wiring required to build a trivial server. The server we'll build will have almost identical functionality to the standard Apache Thrift TSimpleServer found in most language libs.

Servers are a means to an end, and the end is running a service. The first thing we need to do to create a working server is to define a service for it to host. For this example, we'll create a service that returns a message of the day (motd). The following listing shows the IDL for the service.

> Listing 10.1   ~thriftbook/part2/servers/simple/simple.thrift

```
service Message {
    string motd()
}
```

The following listing shows C++ source for a simple server hosting our Message service.

> Listing 10.2   ~thriftbook/part2/servers/simple/simple_server.cpp

```
#include "gen-cpp/Message.h"
#include <thrift/protocol/TBinaryProtocol.h>
#include <thrift/transport/TServerSocket.h>
#include <thrift/transport/TBufferTransports.h>
#include <thrift/TProcessor.h>
#include <memory>
#include <iostream>

using namespace ::apache::thrift::protocol;
using namespace ::apache::thrift::transport;
using namespace ::apache::thrift;
using std::shared_ptr;

const char * msgs[] = {"Apache Thrift!!",
                       "Childhood is a short season",
                       "'Twas brillig"};

class MessageHandler : public MessageIf {        ❶
public:
  MessageHandler() : msg_index(0) {;}
  virtual void motd(std::string& _return) override {
    std::cout << "Call count: " << ++msg_index << std::endl;
    _return = msgs[msg_index%3];
  }
private:
  unsigned int msg_index;
```

```
};

int main() {
    MessageProcessor proc(make_shared<MessageHandler>());       ❷
❸   TServerSocket trans_svr(9090);
    trans_svr.listen();                 ❹
    while (true) {
        auto trans = make_shared<TBufferedTransport>(trans_svr.accept());   ❺
        auto proto = make_shared<TBinaryProtocol>(trans);
        try{
            while(proc.process(proto, proto, nullptr)) {;}      ❻
        } catch (const TTransportException& ex) {
            std::cout << ex.what()
                        << ", waiting for next client" << std::endl;    ❼
        }
    }
}
```

The implementation for the Message service in this example is supplied by the MessageHandler class ❶. When we compile the simple.thrift IDL, the IDL compiler will create a Message.h header under the gen-cpp directory containing a C++ interface, MessageIf, modeled after our IDL Service. The MessageHandler is derived from the abstract MessageIf interface class. In this example, the service only has one function, motd(), which returns one of three messages. Each time the motd() method is called, the msg_index is incremented, rotating the message to return to the caller.

The main() function in this example implements the server behavior. The IDL compiler-generated Processor class takes care of reading network requests from clients and dispatching calls to the correct handler method. In the example, the Processor class, MessageProcessor, is constructed with an instance of the MessageHandler service implementation ❷. As always, the C++ framework wants all objects wrapped in a shared_ptr. The latest versions of Apache Thrift rely on C++11 std::shared_ptr; prior to version 0.11 this would need to be changed to a boost::shared_ptr for compatibility with C++98.

The next thing our server needs to do is listen for connections. To handle inbound client connections, we use a TServerSocket initialized to TCP port 9090 ❸. Calling the server socket's listen() method opens the socket, allowing client connections to queue up ❹.

The ubiquity of TSocket and TServerSocket

Multiple implementations of TServerTransport and TTransport exist. However, the dominance of TCP/IP and the socket-programming interface have made TServerSocket and the TSocket transport the preeminent, and often singular, solution for Apache Thrift RPC across implementation languages. Other transports such as TPipe, which supports NamedPipes, have benefits, but will also restrict the variety of clients that can connect to a given server. TPipe is efficient on Windows, but supported in few languages and on few platforms.

After setting the server transport to listen for connections, we begin a set of infinite loops. The outer loop accepts new connections ❺ and the inner loop processes requests on the current connection ❻.

The server transport accept() method returns a TTransport interface that we can use to perform I/O with the connected client. To gain cross-language benefits and integrate with the rest of the Apache Thrift RPC framework, we need to use a serialization protocol for all I/O. In this example, we select the TBinaryProtocol, which in turn wraps the accepted TSocket transport ❺.

The accept() method blocks the calling thread until a client connects. A call to accept() could last a microsecond if a client is already waiting or a few days if clients rarely connect.

Once a client does connect, we need to process RPC calls made over the connection. The inner while loop uses the processor process() method to process client RPC requests ❻. The process() method takes care of everything required to process one RPC request. The process() method will read the client's RPC message from the network, determine which handler method to call, unpack the parameters using the I/O stack, and call the handler. When the handler returns with a result, the processor serializes the result back to the client using the I/O stack. The inner loop breaks when the client disconnects, which causes the process() method to return 0 ❻.

Note that the TProcessor process() method takes three parameters, proc.process (proto, proto, and nullptr). In this example, we pass the protocol twice. The processor uses the first parameter for reading and the second for writing. We'll look at in/out protocol stacks in detail in section 10.4, "Using factories." The third parameter to the process() method is the Processor context, which we're not supporting in our simple server. This parameter works in conjunction with an optional TProcessorEvent-Handler. Processor event handlers allow us to hook processor events (pre/post I/O stack read/write operations) without hacking the Apache Thrift source code. You can find a processor event handler example in chapter 8, "Implementing services."

In this case the process() method, like the server transport accept() method, is a blocking call and won't return until it has read the next RPC message. If the client disconnects, the transport will throw a TTransportException, causing the program to exit the processing loop. Our server traps any TTransportExceptions inside the outer loop, reports the error message, and continues back around to the accept() call to wait for the next client to connect ❼.

Here's a session that builds and runs the simple server:

```
$ ls -l
-rw-r--r-- 1 randy randy 1148 Jul 15 06:46 simple_server.cpp
-rw-r--r-- 1 randy randy   35 Jul 15 04:47 simple.thrift
$ thrift -gen cpp simple.thrift
$ g++ -std=c++11 simple_server.cpp gen-cpp/Message.cpp -o server -lthrift
$ ./server
```

To test the server, we'll build a quick Python client. The Python client requests messages from the server in a loop until told to exit. The following listing shows the code.

Listing 10.3 ~thriftbook/part2/servers/simple/simple_client.py

```
import sys
sys.path.append("gen-py")
from thrift.transport import TSocket
from thrift.transport import TTransport
from thrift.protocol import TBinaryProtocol
from simple import Message

trans = TSocket.TSocket("localhost", 9090)
trans = TTransport.TBufferedTransport(trans)
proto = TBinaryProtocol.TBinaryProtocol(trans)
client = Message.Client(proto)

trans.open()
while True:
    print("[Client] received: %s" % client.motd())
    line = raw_input("Enter 'q' to exit, anything else to continue: ")
    if line == 'q':
        break

trans.close()
```

This client is almost identical to the hello world client in chapter 1. Here's a sample session running the client against the simple server:

```
$ thrift -gen py simple.thrift
$ python simple_client.py
[Client] received: Childhood is a short season
Enter 'q' to exit, anything else to continue: q
$ python simple_client.py
[Client] received: 'Twas brillig
Enter 'q' to exit, anything else to continue:
[Client] received: Apache Thrift!!
Enter 'q' to exit, anything else to continue: q
$
```

As simple as this client/server example is, it demonstrates several things we need to consider carefully as we build more complex servers. Notice the messages displayed on the client cycle across connections, indicating the msg_index increases with each call. Try disconnecting and reconnecting the client, and notice the count continues from the place it left off. This indicates the existence of a single stateful handler on the server supporting all connections.

The msg_index attribute of the MessageHandler class is an instance variable. Because we create a single handler on startup and reuse it for each new client, the message index is shared across connections and clients. For a trivial service like this, a single handler is fine. However, more sophisticated multiuser servers must be careful with shared mutable state. Any time multiple threads have concurrent access to mutable data, you have an opportunity for data corruption/loss unless a serialization mechanism is provided. Shared state can also present privacy concerns. If client data should be partitioned by connection, we should ensure that client A cannot access client B's data. Considering the relationship between handlers and connections is an important step in server concurrency design. We'll look at this topic in detail in section 10.4, "Using factories."

Another thing this trivial server demonstrates is the impact of concurrency on server design. The server is a single-threaded, single-connection solution. Figure 10.2 illustrates the processing model used by the simple server. The fact that the server is either waiting for connections or waiting for RPC requests defines its overall behavior. When running the Python client, the client connects, makes requests, and then disconnects when the end-user enters "q". If you attempt to connect with a second client while the first is still connected, the second client will hang, because the second client connection is received at the network layer, but won't be accepted by the server until the current client disconnects. The server only handles one client at a time. The second client is queued in the connection backlog at the network layer. If you exit the first client, the second will immediately respond as the server completes the processing loop from the first client and accepts the next waiting connection in the outer loop.

This simple server is almost exactly like the standard Apache Thrift `TSimpleServer` used in prior chapters. This processing model is the simplest and might be the fastest solution for a dedicated machine-to-machine connection; however, most servers must support many clients concurrently. To do this, the server must support a form of concurrency.

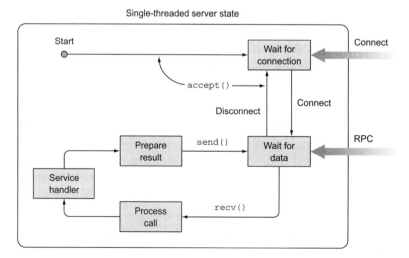

Figure 10.2   Connection-based, single-threaded server state diagram

10.2 *Using multithreaded servers*

One common way to manage multiple clients concurrently is to assign a separate thread of execution to each client connection. This approach places most of the concurrency management burden on the underlying operating system. The operating system must schedule threads for execution across the CPU resources available based on thread priority and workload. Because operating systems tend to be efficient thread schedulers, this model can be effective, scaling to thousands of clients depending on the hardware and load patterns.

As a next step, let's look at a Java server from the Apache Thrift server library that uses multiple threads to support multiple concurrent client connections. The Java language has a large selection of Apache Thrift servers, most of which are demonstrated in this book.

The examples from this chapter attempt to demonstrate generic Apache Thrift server features exhibited by all Apache Thrift language libraries. This goal is tempered by the fact that each language has its own syntax and concurrency features.

The first Apache Thrift server example uses the Java `TThreadPoolServer`. Unlike the hand-coded server, the thread pool server will allow multiple clients to connect concurrently. Client requests will each be processed on their own thread, making it possible to process client requests in parallel on multi-core hardware. We need to recode the C++ message service handler from listing 10.2 in Java to implement the new server, as demonstrated in the following listing.

Listing 10.4   ~/thriftbook/part2/servers/MessageHandler.java

```java
import java.util.Arrays;
import java.util.List;
import org.apache.thrift.TException;

public class MessageHandler implements Message.Iface {
  public MessageHandler() {
    msg_index = 0;
  }

  @Override
  public String motd() throws TException {
    System.out.println("Call count: " + ++msg_index);
    return msgs.get(Math.abs(msg_index%3));
  }

  private int msg_index;
  private static List<String> msgs = Arrays.asList("Apache Thrift!!",
                                    "Childhood is a short season",
                                    "'Twas brillig");
}
```

To complete the server, we need to build a Java class to house the `main()` function that will launch the application and create the `TThreadPoolServer` instance used to host the `message` service, as shown in the following listing.

Listing 10.5   ~/thriftbook/part2/servers/ThreadedServer.java

```java
import org.apache.thrift.TProcessor;
import org.apache.thrift.server.TServer;
import org.apache.thrift.server.TThreadPoolServer;
import org.apache.thrift.transport.TServerSocket;
import org.apache.thrift.transport.TTransportException;

public class ThreadedServer {
  public static void main(String[] args) throws TTransportException {
    TServerSocket svrTrans = new TServerSocket(9090);                      ❶
    TProcessor processor = new Message.Processor<>(new MessageHandler());  ❷
    TServer server = new TThreadPoolServer(                                ❸
                new TThreadPoolServer.Args(svrTrans).processor(processor));
    server.serve();                                                        ❹
  }
}
```

Remarkably, this multithreaded server is four lines of code. We set up a server socket with a listening port ❶, create a processor/handler stack for the service ❷, and then hand both to a new instance of the Java `TThreadPoolServer` ❸. To run the server, we call the `serve()` method ❹. This is all it takes to produce a highly scalable multi-threaded server in Apache Thrift. The process is as similar, and as compact, as those in any other languages.

We can use the Python client from listing 10.3 to test our server. Note that the service is still the same `Message` service, even though it's now coded in Java. One of the fantastic features of Apache Thrift is that the clients don't care what language hosts their service; they depend only on the service contract and the protocol/transport stack needed to connect to it. Should you decide that Erlang is the right platform for your server, you can switch at your leisure and your clients will be none the wiser.

The following example shows a build and run of the multithreaded server:

```
$ ls -l
drwxr-xr-x 2 randy randy 4096 Jul 15 07:33 gen-cpp
drwxr-xr-x 3 randy randy 4096 Jul 15 07:42 gen-py
-rw-r--r-- 1 randy randy  534 Jul 16 00:53 MessageHandler.java
-rw-r--r-- 1 randy randy  470 Jul 15 22:37 simple_client.py
-rw-r--r-- 1 randy randy 1148 Jul 15 06:46 simple_server.cpp
-rw-r--r-- 1 randy randy   35 Jul 15 04:47 simple.thrift
-rw-r--r-- 1 randy randy  590 Jul 16 00:53 ThreadedServer.java
$ thrift -gen java simple.thrift
$ javac -cp /usr/local/lib/libthrift-1.0.0.jar:\
            /usr/local/lib/slf4j-api-1.7.2.jar:\
            /usr/local/lib/slf4j-nop-1.7.2.jar
          ThreadedServer.java MessageHandler.java gen-java/*.java
```

```
Note: gen-java/Message.java uses unchecked or unsafe operations.
Note: Recompile with -Xlint:unchecked for details.
$ java -cp /usr/local/lib/libthrift-1.0.0.jar:\
        /usr/local/lib/slf4j-api-1.7.2.jar:\
        /usr/local/lib/slf4j-nop-1.7.2.jar:\
        gen-java:\
        .
        ThreadedServer
```

TIP Remember that if another server is already bound and listening to TCP port 9090 you can't launch a second server using that port. If you receive an error while trying to start a server, make sure to shut down any previous servers you may have started using the same port.

With the server now running, we can test it using the Python client. Here's a sample run of the client:

```
$ python simple_client.py
[Client] received: Childhood is a short season
Enter 'q' to exit, anything else to continue:
```

In the previous example the client connects to the server and immediately makes an RPC request for the message of the day. Running a second client in another shell will demonstrate the server's support for multiple connections. Here's the server output with two clients making interleaved requests:

```
Call count: 1
Call count: 2
Call count: 3
Call count: 4
```

Figure 10.3 illustrates the thread per connection processing model implemented by TThreadPoolServer. Upon calling serve(), the calling thread is conscripted to drive the server's accept() loop until the server exits (the top sub-state in figure 10.3). We'll refer to this thread as the acceptor thread. The acceptor thread calls the server transport's accept() method, which blocks the thread until a client connects. When a client connects, the accept() method returns a TTransport wired to the client. The acceptor thread then creates a new thread (or, in the case of the thread pool server, checks a thread out of a pre-created thread pool) and directs the thread to process I/O on the new TTransport. The acceptor thread then calls accept() again to wait for the next connection. The acceptor thread essentially provides the behavior of the outer processing loop from our hand-coded server example in listing 10.2.

The lower sub-state in figure 10.3 represents the processing model of the various client I/O threads. A client I/O thread spends its life processing RPC requests for the TTransport connection it was handed at startup. The I/O thread does nothing more than call the service processor's process() method, much like the inner processing loop demonstrated in our hand-coded server from listing 10.2.

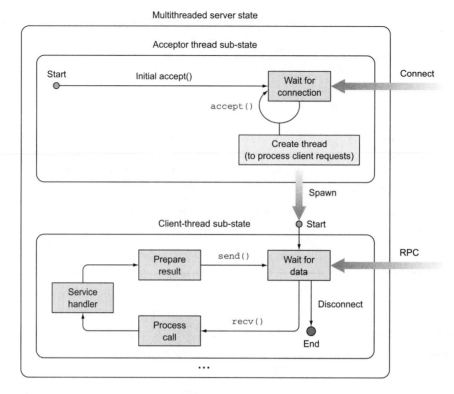

Figure 10.3   Connection-based, multithreaded server state diagram

As more connections come in, more client I/O threads are created (or checked out of the pool) to handle the connections. This gives the server the ability to process separate client requests concurrently on multiple CPUs.

This server will support large numbers of clients while running sophisticated services. The abstraction we've been building with transports, protocols, type serialization, RPC stubs, and now servers, creates tremendous leverage. We now have the tools to create low latency, highly concurrent servers with Apache Thrift in a few simple steps:

1   Code the service interface in Apache Thrift IDL.
2   Compile the IDL for the languages you require.
3   Code the service implementation in a handler.
4   Select a prebuilt server to run the service.

10.3   *Server concurrency models*

There are many ways to design a server that handles multiple clients at the same time. Two distinct processing models appear in the Apache Thrift server library:

- *Connection-Based Processing*—Each client's activity is processed in a loop driven by a single dedicated thread or coroutine (see figure 10.4).

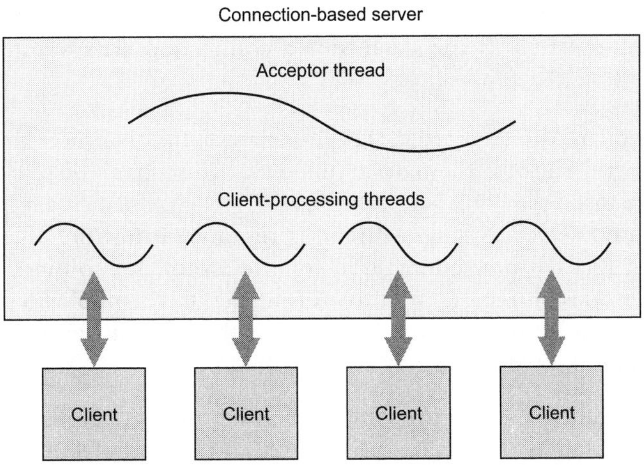

Connection-based server

Acceptor thread

Client-processing threads

Client   Client   Client   Client

Figure 10.4   Threading model for connection-based processing

- *Task-based processing*—Client activity is organized into tasks where each RPC request represents a task, or unit of work; worker threads are dispatched to execute tasks as they arrive, often with no concern for which thread processes which client's task (see figure 10.5).

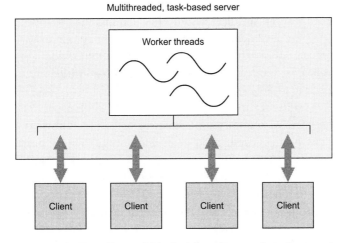

Multithreaded, task-based server

Worker threads

Client   Client   Client   Client

Figure 10.5   Threading model for task-based processing using a pool of worker threads; any thread may handle requests from any client.

10.3.1 *Connection-based processing*

Both servers created in this chapter have provided connection-based processing. The simple server handled one client at a time with a single thread, and the TThreadPool-Server created a thread pool and assigned one thread to each new client connection, returning threads to the pool when clients disconnect. Another common Apache

Thrift server, `TThreadedServer`, works exactly like `TThreadPoolServer` except that `TThreadedServer` creates a new thread each time a connection arrives and destroys the thread when the client disconnects.

> **TIP** The word "Pool" in the `TThreadPoolServer` name often confuses those new to Apache Thrift, causing them to assume that this server dispatches pooled threads on a task basis. This is not the case. The `TThreadPoolServer` is a connection-oriented server. A single thread is removed from the "thread pool" and assigned to each new connection for the life of the connection. Only when the client disconnects is the thread returned to the pool. To process 1,000 clients concurrently you will need 1,000 threads with either the threaded or thread pool server type.

Connection-based processing models are simple to code and easy to reason about. Threads in this model serve a single client for the life of a connection, processing requests from that client in the order submitted. This model also enables a system with 48 CPUs to service 48 connections in parallel.

This model also has drawbacks—consider a server with 1,000 connections. This connection-based server will create 1,000 threads, in the worst case, each with a call stack, a CPU context, and many other kernel and user mode resources. At most, 48 threads can run at any given time on the 48 CPU machine; therefore, at a minimum, 952 threads will be idle at any moment. At scale, thread-per-connection models have obvious shortcomings.

Languages with runtimes that simulate system threads, such as C# and Java, alleviate this problem to a degree by allocating runtime threads separately from (a usually smaller pool of) underlying system threads. Other languages that model concurrency using lightweight cooperative models, such as coroutines (goroutines in Go), nearly eliminate this concern altogether.

Another concern is locality. A thread that runs regularly will have all its resources (stack, registers, and so on) in memory and perhaps in cache. A thread that runs rarely is likely to have its resources relegated to slower storage. System hardware and operating systems collaborate to move high-traffic resources into cache and low-traffic resources to main memory or disk. If each of our 1,000 clients makes a request in sequence, the system has to schedule each of the 1,000 threads in turn, creating material system overhead and, in the worst case, memory thrashing (swapping data back and forth to cache and/or disk).

Modern operating systems are surprisingly good at managing high thread counts. For modest connection counts, connection-based processing can be a top performer. Many production environments use servers with connection-based processing, hosting thousands of connections. In certain settings, however, extreme load makes task-based processing a better choice for languages that otherwise make use of threads for concurrency.

10.3.2 *Task-based processing*

Task-based processing models are more complex than connection-based processing models, but typically deliver more efficient resource utilization. In task-driven systems, one or more system threads act as a processing pool, executing client RPC requests as they arrive, often with no consideration for which system thread handles a client's request (see figure 10.5).

Task-based processing doesn't ensure serialization on a given connection however. In connection-based processing everything associated with a connection will happen in order, because each connection is processed by a single dedicated thread. In the task-based model a client could send two messages sequentially, causing two threads to be dispatched on the server, one for each RPC call. This could potentially create a race condition for the connection's data or I/O resources. Clients must either wait for a response to each request before sending a second request, or servers must supply a mechanism to ensure that responses are written atomically. In the latter case, the client and server must also agree upon a mechanism that allows the client to determine which response goes with which request (such as a sequence number).

Task based servers, similar to connection-based servers, have two key responsibilities:

- Accepting connections
- Processing requests on accepted connections

The threading models associated with task-based servers are often divided across these two functions, handling each with a distinct set of threads. With this in mind let's examine each of the principal threading models implemented by Apache Thrift task-based servers.

SINGLE-THREADED TASK-BASED SERVERS

The simplest implementation of the task-based server is a single-threaded solution (see figure 10.6). A single thread can manage a moderate set of clients under many load profiles when using the task model. This is the native processing model in Node.js.

Single-threaded, task-based server

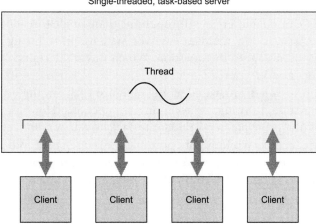

Figure 10.6 Threading model for task-based processing using a single system thread

A single-threaded, task-based server accepts new connections, processes RPC requests, and writes results back to clients—all on a single thread. While this single thread can only run on one CPU at a time, the model offers several advantages. First, because one thread is constantly handling client requests, operating systems will tend to ensure that the thread's resources are always in the ready state, improving thread performance.

This model also avoids context-switching overhead. When an operating system has to switch between system threads, it must save the registers and other context information for the old thread being suspended and then reinstate the context for the new thread to run. A single-threaded, task-based server never switches context internally; the single thread processes request after request, no matter the connection.

Such a single-threaded server also never dominates a multi-core system, because it can never consume more than 100% of a single CPU. This leaves all of the other cores free to run other services or operating system tasks. Also, single-threaded, task-based servers don't require internal synchronization; only one thread accesses data structures, avoiding contention and race conditions.

While seemingly simplistic, this single-threaded, task-based model has much to recommend it. The most concerning downside to this model is that if one client makes a request that takes a long time to complete, all of the other pending requests have to wait. Often, single-threaded, task-based servers post excellent throughput results (amount of work done over time) because of their low overhead. On the other hand, they may show the highest latency rates (average delay in response), due to their serialized request-processing model.

Another important benefit of this model is that it works well in cloud-native environments where containerized services can be scaled horizontally with ease. If you need 20 threads to handle a given workload, you can scale out, running 20 copies of a single-threaded, task-based server. Kubernetes and other systems work well with fine-grained services and can automate the scaling and HA functions elastically. The pure efficiency and low overhead of this model is largely responsible for the explosion of NodeJS-based, backend services in recent years.

HYBRID THREADING MODELS

Multithreaded models can enable greater throughput than single-threaded models within a single server process on multi-core server systems. Introducing multiple threads into the server model raises the question: Which threads accept connections and which threads process tasks?

In the abstract multithreaded, task-based model of figure 10.5, any thread can handle any task, whether reading, writing, or accepting connections. However, in many systems and languages, the principal networking interface used to wait for activity on a client connection is `select()`. While highly portable, `select()` isn't well suited to supporting multiple threads waiting to read from the same connection. This makes the ideal model illustrated in figure 10.5 difficult to implement in practice.

Connection-partitioned, task-based server

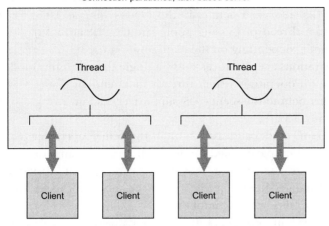

Figure 10.7   Threading model for task-based processing using connection partitioning

Many alternative models exist: for example, connections can be partitioned into groups (see figure 10.7). If a server has 1,000 active connections and 10 threads, each thread could be given 100 connections to manage.

While this solution allows the server to run in parallel on the available CPU resources, it still suffers from the key drawback of the single-threaded, task-based server: a long-running task will hold up all the other requests on connections assigned to that thread. This model is also generally implemented with statically assigned connections. Thus, if all the connections for thread 1 require service and none of the connections in any of the other threads are active, you lose the scale-out benefit.

In certain cases, a better solution is to handle connection I/O on an I/O thread and then hand off the service-processing burden to a processing thread pool (see figure 10.8). In this model a long-running task will only tie up one of the processing

Task-based server with processing pool

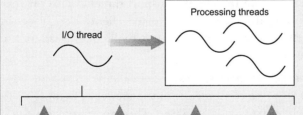

Figure 10.8   Threading model for task-based processing using separate I/O and processing threads

threads. The I/O thread performs short, deterministic I/O tasks, keeping the server responsive. The Java THsHaServer operates in this mode, using an I/O thread to dispatch RPC requests to a thread processing pool. The C++ TNonblockingServer can also operate in this mode, depending on the configuration used.

While the I/O operations are all processed by a single thread in this model, actual I/O often takes place on operating system threads independent of the server's user mode processing. This behind-the-scenes OS support can allow a single server I/O thread to handle high I/O loads.

This "processing pool" model addresses both of the principal concerns associated with the single-threaded and partitioned models of figures 10.6 and 10.7, CPU scale-out, and long-running task latency. However, the processing pool introduces significant complexity in exchange. Note that the I/O thread must now hand the inbound request off to one of several processing pool threads.

This brings up a critical question. How does a generic server I/O thread, which has no information about any particular Apache Thrift service, know what the boundaries of a "task" are? In the context of Apache Thrift RPC, a task is a client RPC request in the form of either a T_CALL or T_ONEWAY message. Without a shortcut, the I/O thread will need to de-serialize the entire message to figure out how much data to dispatch to the processing pool thread. This would defeat much of the purpose of using a processing pool, because de-serializing data can be a significant source of CPU overhead. Apache Thrift servers address this concern through message framing.

FRAMING AND TASK-BASED SERVERS

All of the Apache Thrift servers using task-based processing models require message framing, which is implemented by the TFramedTransport layer. The TFramedTransport places a 4-byte frame size at the front of each Apache Thrift RPC message. This allows the I/O thread to read the frame size, determine how large the RPC message is, and then read the entire RPC message into a TMemoryBuffer that can be handed off to a processing pool thread. This allows the I/O thread to process inbound requests quickly and completely, and independently of the service in question.

The processing thread receiving the data can then de-serialize it from the TMemory-Buffer as if it were reading from the client transport directly. This process works in reverse when the processing thread responds to the client. The processing thread writes the response to a TMemoryBuffer and returns it to the I/O thread for framing and transmission back to the client.

CONNECTION-PARTITIONED PROCESSING POOL SERVERS

The model in figure 10.8 can be combined with the model in figure 10.7 to improve I/O scaling on servers where I/O loads are large. This model replaces the single I/O thread of figure 10.8 with a set of threads using connection partitioning, as illustrated in figure 10.9. The C++ TNonblockingServer and the Java TThreadedSelectorServer both support one or more I/O threads, enabling connection partitioning.

Connection-partitioned, task-based server with processing pool

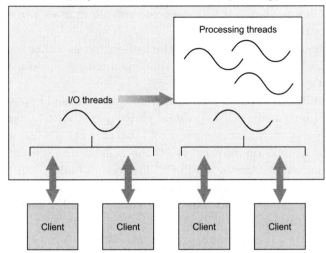

Figure 10.9 Threading model for task-based processing using connection-partitioned I/O and a processing pool

NON-BLOCKING I/O AND HIGH PERFORMANCE I/O APIS

The Apache Thrift connection-oriented servers use blocking I/O. Blocking I/O is simple to use, allowing a server thread to complete an RPC request and then immediately try to read from the connection again. The client may not send another request for hours, so the thread will block, waiting for the read to complete. The blocking I/O approach enables simple programming models, but doesn't usually maximize the processing potential of a thread.

Non-blocking I/O is an I/O mode where read and write I/O calls always return immediately, even if the I/O operation cannot be completed right away. In a non-blocking I/O scenario, a thread attempting to read from a connection with no data waiting would return with an error indicating that no data is present. Because the thread doesn't block, it's free to perform other work. While potentially more efficient, the thread now requires a way of discovering when connections are readable.

Threads can poll connections, reading occasionally until the connection has data; however, this is expensive. A better approach is to use a system-level API to detect I/O events. The select() system call provides a portable mechanism that will return a list of I/O events on a set of connections. While effective in some situations, select() isn't typically efficient when monitoring large quantities of connections. Most systems offer better interfaces for monitoring large collections of I/O endpoints. Unfortunately, top-shelf I/O APIs aren't portable. Windows offers I/O completion ports, Linux provides epoll, BSD has kqueue, and Solaris uses /dev/poll to provide optimal performance.

Java solves this problem to a degree in the JVM layer. Apache Thrift task-based Java servers (TNonblockingServer, THsHaServer, and TThreadedSelectorServer) use nio.selector.select() to handle I/O events. A Linux JVM is free to map the Java nio.selector.select() method to Linux epoll_wait(), and a BSD JVM is free to map nio.selector.select() to the kqueue kevent(). What happens depends on the JVM implementation. As always, the JVM is a large part of system-level performance in Java applications. Choose your JVM with care and test alternatives as part of any server performance measurements.

Python also provides a non-blocking server. The Python `TNonblockingServer` uses the Python `select.select()` method that's implemented as a normal native `select()` call on most systems.

C++ programs compile down to native binaries in most settings and have no virtual machine or interpreter intermediary. To maximize performance, the C++ `TNonblockingServer` uses the cross-platform `libevent` project (libevent.org). The `libevent` API uses the most efficient I/O API on most target platforms. Because `libevent` doesn't ship as part of most systems, the Apache Thrift C++ library only builds   `TNonblockingServer` support if `libevent` is present. The `TNonblockingServer` is compiled into a separate library called `thriftnb` and must be linked to directly (for example, -lthriftnb) if used in C++ programs.

I/O Completion Ports (IOCP) typically provide the fastest I/O API on Windows. Because the IOCP processing model is distinct, it's hard to map `select()`-based solutions to IOCP. No current in-trunk Apache Thrift servers use IOCP, though versions are available on the web.

MULTITHREADING PERFORMANCE CONSIDERATIONS

A common question asked by the performance conscious is: Does all the memory copying and synchronization incurred by the servers represented in figure 10.9 produce enough benefit to make it worth the complexity?

The answer is, in servers with modest connection counts, probably not. In most applications, a simple thread-per-connection server will outperform up to a point. Also, in cloud native systems running on clusters of commodity hardware where horizontal scale is the order of the day, probably not. Further, modern programming languages, such as Go, offer alternative concurrency mechanisms, such as goroutines, that preserve the simplicity of connection-based models while eliminating almost all the drawbacks.

In traditional server implementations where thousands of connections are handled by a single system, the task-based processing pool model can reduce the number of threads required to fully load a system by thousands, making it an important player in monolithic environments. A 48-CPU system can be fully loaded with a number of threads equivalent to a small multiple of the CPU count, somewhere between 98 and 192 threads, for example. A connection-based solution would use a thread per connection, thus requiring thousands of threads.

As always, the only way to determine the optimal server model is to test the available servers with your application, in your environment on your hardware, under real load. It's important to complete such testing with exposure to peak load scenarios. Peak load exposure is important because a server that runs fast enough 100% of the time is almost always preferable to a server that's much faster 99% of the time but melts down 1% of the time. Fortunately, Apache Thrift servers are easy to swap in and out of a given application, making testing a range of Apache Thrift servers a painless job.

10.3.3 *Multithreading vs. multiprocessing*

Early multiuser servers managed multiple clients by running a single listening process that forked off new copies of itself to handle newly accepted client connections (see figure 10.10). This model is called multiprocessing. It has benefits, but one drawback is that each new process has its own private address space, making it more expensive for a collection of connections to share resources.

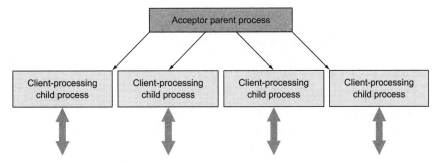

Figure 10.10   Multiprocessing server model

Threads were invented to allow parallel execution within the same process. Any thread in a process can read any memory address, socket, or other system resource the process holds. For this reason, most modern server models use multithreading (at some level) rather than multiprocessing.

The standard Python interpreter only allows one Python thread to run Python code within a single process at a given time. For this reason, multithreading on Python doesn't produce parallel execution. The same can be said of Ruby. To work around this issue, the Apache Thrift Python library offers two multiprocessing servers. These servers run multiple Python interpreter instances (processes), enabling parallel execution through multiprocessing rather than multithreading.

The Python TForkingServer is like the TThreadedServer except that it creates a new process for each inbound connection, rather than a new thread. The Python TProcessPoolServer is like the TThreadPoolServer except that it uses a fixed size set of processes to handle client connections (and thus can only handle process-pool-count many clients at one time).

10.3.4 *Server summary by language*

Each Apache Thrift language has its own set of servers. Choosing an appropriate server can be a challenge for developers new to Apache Thrift. The following is a complete list of the Apache Thrift servers available in C++, Java, and Python, along with notes regarding the server's concurrency model.

C++

Each Apache Thrift C++ Server offers a distinct set of tradeoffs. Table 10.1 summarizes the server processing models and threading options. Figure 10.11 shows the Apache Thrift C++ server hierarchy.

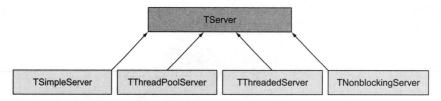

Figure 10.11   C++ server class hierarchy

Table 10.1   C++ server classes

Class	Processing model	I/O threads	Processing threads	Notes
TSimpleServer	Connection	1	-	One connection at a time. Processing is performed by the I/O thread.
TThreadedServer	Connection	1 acceptor thread + 1 thread per connection	-	A new thread is created for each new connection. The connection's thread handles I/O and processing on that connection.
TThreadPoolServer	Connection	1 acceptor thread + a configurable thread pool (connections backlog when the pool is exhausted)	-	A dedicated thread is assigned from the thread pool to each new connection. Threads return to the pool when clients disconnect (custom code can dynamically modify the pool size).
TNonblockingServer	Task	1+ (configurable)	0+ (configurable)	When configured with 0 processing threads, all processing takes place on the I/O thread reading the request; if more than 1 I/O threads is configured, connections are distributed statically across the set of I/O threads. The first I/O thread accepts all new connections; supports models illustrated in figures 10.6, 10.7, 10.8, and 10.9.

In scenarios where a client and server need a private channel for RPC, TSimpleServer is a good choice; it's often the fastest server model when it comes to processing requests from a single client. If the server must support multiple clients and the clients stay connected for long periods, TThreadedServer may be a good choice. If you need to support multiple clients and clients connect and disconnect often, TThread-PoolServer may be a better choice, because it avoids the overhead associated with creating and destroying threads.

If you need extreme scalability on a *nix platform, TNonblockingServer may be the best choice. This is the most complex server, but it uses libevent to provide cross-platform access to native I/O APIs and makes it possible to separately tune the I/O thread count and the processing thread pool size.

JAVA

The Apache Thrift Java server selection offers similar processing models to those found in the C++ library. However, Java doesn't provide a TThreadedServer. Also, the Java implementation defines three separate servers (TNonblockingServer, THsHaServer, and TThreadedSelectorServer) equating to the functionality of different configurations of the C++ TNonblockingServer. Figure 10.12 shows the Java server class hierarchy and table 10.2 lists the various Java servers and their concurrency models.

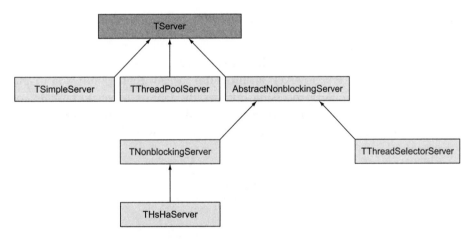

Figure 10.12   Java server class hierarchy

Table 10.2   Java server classes

Class	Processing model	I/O threads	Processing threads	Notes
TSimpleServer	Connection	1	-	One connection at a time. Processing is performed by the I/O thread.

Table 10.2   Java server classes *(continued)*

Class	Processing model	I/O threads	Processing threads	Notes
TThreadPoolServer	Connection	1 acceptor thread + a configurable thread pool (connections backlog when the pool is exhausted)	-	A dedicated thread is assigned from the thread pool to each new connection. Threads return to the pool when clients disconnect.
TNonblockingServer	Task	1	-	Supports model illustrated in figure 10.6.
THsHaServer	Task	1	1+ (configurable)	Supports model illustrated in figure 10.8.
TThreadedSelectorServer	Task	1+ (configurable)	1+ (configurable)	The first I/O thread accepts all new connections. Supports model illustrated in figure 10.9.

PYTHON

The Python server library provides the Simple, Threaded, ThreadPool, and Non-blocking style servers; however, all these use threads that Python won't run in parallel. To provide parallel processing options, the Python server library also offers two multiprocessing servers, TForkingServer and TProcessPoolServer (figure 10.10). Figure 10.13 shows the Python server class hierarchy and table 10.3 lists the Python servers and their concurrency models.

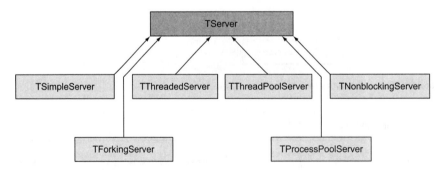

Figure 10.13   Python server class hierarchy

Table 10.3 Python server classes

Class	Processing model	I/O threads	Processing threads	Notes
`TSimpleServer`	Connection	1	-	One connection at a time. Processing is performed by the I/O thread.
`TThreadedServer`	Connection	1 acceptor thread + 1 thread per connection	-	A new thread is created for each new connection. The connection's thread handles I/O and processing on that connection.
`TThreadPoolServer`	Connection	1 acceptor thread + a configurable thread pool (connections backlog when the pool is exhausted)	-	A dedicated thread is assigned from the thread pool to each new connection. Threads return to the pool when clients disconnect.
`TNonblockingServer`	Task	1	1+ (configurable)	Supports model illustrated in figure 10.8.
`TForkingServer`	Connection	1 acceptor process + 1 process per connection	-	Uses Python `fork()` (not supported on Windows). Supports model illustrated in figure 10.10.
`TProcessPoolServer`	Connection	1 acceptor process + a configurable process pool (connections backlog when the pool is exhausted)	-	Uses Python multiprocessing module (supported on Windows). Supports model illustrated in figure 10.10.

10.4 Using factories

All of the servers discussed in this chapter so far have used the `TBinaryProtocol` for communication with clients. This raises the question: How do we configure a server to use a different protocol? And a related question: How do we add a layered transport to the server I/O stack? You may also wonder how to create a new handler instance for each client connection to keep client handler state separated. The answer to all these questions is by using factories.

The factory pattern is a creational software design pattern used heavily in the Apache Thrift framework. Factories allow application components to create objects without concern for the specific type of object manufactured. By supplying a server with different factories, we can customize many aspects of the overall server behavior.

In the following section, we'll use factories to create custom I/O stacks for client/server communication and use factories to define singleton and per-connection service processing models.

10.4.1 Building I/O stacks with factories

Apache Thrift servers associate a protocol object with each client connection accepted. Servers rely on a `TProtocolFactory` instance to manufacture protocol instances (see figure 10.14). This allows the user to provide a server with the factory that manufactures the desired concrete protocol type (JSON, Binary, Compact, and so on). The server depends only upon the abstract factory interface and the abstract protocol interface (`TProtocolFactory` and `TProtocol`, respectively).

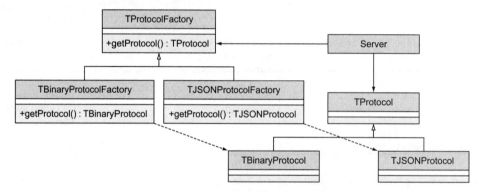

Figure 10.14   Apache Thrift servers depend on abstract protocol factories and abstract protocols. Users supply concrete protocol factories that manufacture concrete protocols.

Apache Thrift servers use factories to manufacture all of the per-connection resources required to communicate with a client. Factories typically provide a "factory method" that returns the manufactured object. Each time a connection arrives, Apache Thrift servers call three factory methods to create the support objects necessary to handle the connection I/O (see table 10.4). We call the resulting set of manufactured objects an I/O stack.

Table 10.4   Apache Thrift I/O stack factory classes

Abstract factory class	Factory method (pseudo code)	Product manufactured
TServerTransport	TTransport accept();	Endpoint transport
TTransportFactory	TTransport getTransport(TTransport trans);	Layered transport
TProtocolFactory	TProtocol getProtocol(TTransport trans);	Protocol

The `TServerTransport` class provides the `TServerTransport::accept()` factory method that manufactures an endpoint transport when a client connects. Unlike pure factories, the `TServerTransport` class also has additional responsibilities, such as managing the listening port.

The `TTransportFactory` class allows layered transports to be added above endpoint transport. The `getTransport()` factory method returns a layered transport applied to the transport passed in the parameter list. The trivial implementation of `TTransportFactory::getTransport()` returns the input transport without adding a layer.

The `TProtocolFactory::getProtocol()` factory method adds a serialization protocol to the top transport, completing the I/O stack.

Using these three factories we can configure Apache Thrift servers to create a customized I/O stack. An example I/O stack might include a `TServerSocket` factory to manufacture `TSockets`, a `TFramedTransportFactory` to add a framing layer, and a `TJSONProtocolFactory` to manufacture `TJSONProtocol` objects at the top of the stack (see figure 10.15). Each of these concrete factories implements the respective abstract factory type from table 10.4.

Most servers generate default factories when one or more of the three factories aren't specified at construction time. The exception is the endpoint transport factory, which must be defined by the user so that the server knows what port, pipe, or other device to listen on. The default layered transport factory is `TTransport-`

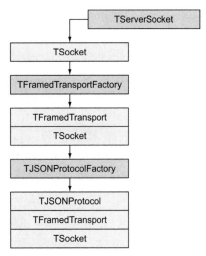

Figure 10.15 Building I/O stacks with factories

`Factory`, which returns the supplied underlying transport without adding any layers. The exception is the non-blocking servers, which use a `TFramedTransportFactory` by default. The default protocol factory is the `TBinaryProtocolFactory`.

To get a better understanding of factories and their operation, we'll build a new server in Python that uses factories to define a framing transport layer and JSON serialization, as illustrated in figure 10.15.

Listing 10.6   ~thriftbook/part2/servers/factory_server.py

```
import sys
sys.path.append("gen-py")
from thrift.transport import TSocket          ❶
from thrift.transport import TTransport        ❷
from thrift.protocol import TJSONProtocol        ❸
from thrift.server import TServer            ❹
from simple import Message

class MessageHandler(Message.Iface):        ❺
    msgs = ["Apache Thrift!!",
```

```
                "Childhood is a short season",
                "'Twas brillig"]
    def __init__(self):
        self.msg_index = 0
    def motd(self):
        self.msg_index += 1
        print("Call count: %s" % self.msg_index)
        return MessageHandler.msgs[self.msg_index%3]

if __name__ == "__main__":              ❻
    handler = MessageHandler()
    proc = Message.Processor(handler)
    svr_trans = TSocket.TServerSocket(port=9090)

    trans_fac = TTransport.TFramedTransportFactory()        ❼
❽  proto_fac = TJSONProtocol.TJSONProtocolFactory()

    server = TServer.TThreadedServer (proc, svr_trans,
                                      trans_fac, proto_fac)    ❾
    server.serve()
```

The code begins by importing the `TSocket` module that houses the `TServerSocket` class ❶ for our endpoint factory. `TServerSocket` is derived from `TServerTransport` and is used by the server to accept new connections and manufacture `TSocket` endpoints.

In many Apache Thrift language libraries, factory classes are located in the same source file as the type they manufacture. For example, in this program we import the `TTransport` module from the `thrift.transport` package which houses the `TFramedTransport` and `TFramedTransportFactory` classes ❷. The server will use the `TFramedTransportFactory` to add a `TFramedTransport` layer to the `TSocket` endpoint.

The `TJSONProtocol` module is imported to provide access to the `TJSONProtocolFactory` ❸. Constructing the server with a `TJSONProtocolFactory` will override the default `TBinaryProtocolFactory`, causing the server to use JSON serialization.

The `TServer` module, which defines most of the Python server classes, is included to give access to the `TThreadedServer` ❹. The `TThreadedServer` generates a new thread to handle each new client connection. This server is logically equivalent to the C++ server with the same name.

The `MessageHandler` class provides a Python implementation of the `Message` service ❺ and the main section ❻ provides the code to set up and run the server. In addition to the usual handler, processor, and server transport setup, the program creates a `TFramedTransportFactory` ❼ and a `TJSONProtocolFactory` ❽ to pass to the server constructor ❾.

Given the provided factories, our server will build an I/O stack including `TSocket`, `TFramedTransport`, and `TJSONProtocol` for each new client. To test the I/O stack, we'll build a simple C++ client using the same I/O stack. The following listing shows the code.

Listing 10.7 ~thriftbook/part2/servers/factory_client.cpp

```cpp
#include "gen-cpp/Message.h"
#include <thrift/transport/TSocket.h>
#include <thrift/protocol/TJSONProtocol.h>
#include <memory>
#include <iostream>
#include <string>

using namespace apache::thrift::transport;
using namespace apache::thrift::protocol;
using std::make_shared;
using std::shared_ptr;

int main(int argv, char * argc[]) {
    shared_ptr<TTransport> trans;
    trans = make_shared<TSocket>("localhost", 9090);        ❶
    trans = make_shared<TFramedTransport>(trans);    ❷
    auto proto = make_shared<TJSONProtocol>(trans);         ❸
    MessageClient client(proto);            ◁─┐
                                              ❹
    trans->open();
    std::string msg;
    do {
        client.motd(msg);
        std::cout << msg << std::endl;
        std::cout << "Enter to call motd, 'q' to quit" << std::endl;
        std::getline(std::cin, msg);
    } while (0 != msg.compare("q"));
    trans->close();
}
```

This is a boilerplate C++ client with a few exceptions. The I/O stack begins with
TSocket ❶, adds a framing transport layer ❷, and completes the stack with the JSON
protocol ❸. The I/O stack is passed to the MessageClient constructor ❹ to complete
the client setup.

Here's a session building and running the server:

```
$ ls -l
-rw-r--r-- 1 randy randy  827 Jul 19 00:40 factory_client.cpp
-rwxr-xr-x 1 randy randy  893 Jul 18 17:07 factory_server.py
-rw-r--r-- 1 randy randy   38 Jul 18 15:24 simple.thrift
$ thrift -gen py -gen cpp simple.thrift
$ python factory_server.py
```

...and a session building and running the client:

```
$ g++ factory_client.cpp gen-cpp/Message.cpp -Wall -std=c++11 -lthrift
$ ./a.out
Childhood is a short season
Enter to call motd, 'q' to quit
'Twas brillig
```

```
Enter to call motd, 'q' to quit
Apache Thrift!!
Enter to call motd, 'q' to quit
q
$
```

While outwardly the program appears to run as before, behind the scenes we have made significant changes to the I/O stack. RPC requests will now be formatted in JSON with frame headers on the wire.

Now that we've built a simple server and client with custom I/O stacks, it's worth reviewing each of the I/O stack factory types.

SERVER TRANSPORTS

We examined server transports in chapter 4. Connection-oriented endpoint transports, such as TSocket, offer a corresponding server transport, TServerSocket, to manufacture new endpoints when clients connect. The most common endpoint transport factories include

- TServerTransport (base class)
- TServerSocket
- TSSLServerSocket
- TPipeServer

LAYERED TRANSPORT FACTORIES

Layered transport factories produce layered transports on top of an existing transport. Servers pass endpoint transports to a transport factory method to acquire a fully layered transport stack. The transport factory method can return the original endpoint transport passed in (adding no layers), or it may return a stack with one or more layers added to the endpoint. Transport factories have the same name as the layered transport they produce with the "Factory" suffix. All transport factories are derived from TTransportFactory and offer the getTransport() factory method. The generic library TTransportFactory.getTransport() method returns the transport passed unaltered. The most common layered transport factories include

- TTransportFactory (base class)
- TBufferedTransportFactory
- TFramedTransportFactory
- TZlibTransportFactory

PROTOCOL FACTORIES

Protocol factories manufacture protocol objects wired to an underlying TTransport interface. All Apache Thrift I/O stacks must have precisely one concrete protocol object at the top of the stack. Each protocol has a factory with the protocol name and a "Factory" suffix. The four in-tree protocol factories are

- `TProtocolFactory` (base class)
- `TBinaryProtocolFactory`
- `TCompactProtocolFactory`
- `TJSONProtocolFactory`

10.4.2 *Processor and handler factories*

Handlers implement Apache Thrift IDL services. Handlers can be stateful, such as the `MessageHandler` in the previous server which has a single `msg_index` shared across all client connections. Any client calling `motd()` changes the `msg_index` for all clients. This occurs because servers use a single handler instance for all clients by default, as depicted in figure 10.16.

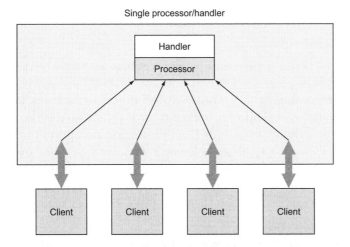

Figure 10.16   By default, servers use a single handler for service implementation.

When handlers are stateless, sharing them across all client connections is an effective approach.

In other cases, handlers share state on purpose. For example, a handler might capture server-wide statistics on call counts collected across all connections. In scenarios where handler state is shared by multiple concurrently executing clients, synchronization is warranted if state will be changed to ensure data corruption doesn't take place.

Another common handler pattern involves a handler that houses data associated with the client connection. For example, what if you wanted to use your `MessageHandler` from the previous examples, but needed each connection to maintain a private copy of the `msg_index`? This would require a handler factory capable of manufacturing a new handler for each new connection (see figure 10.17).

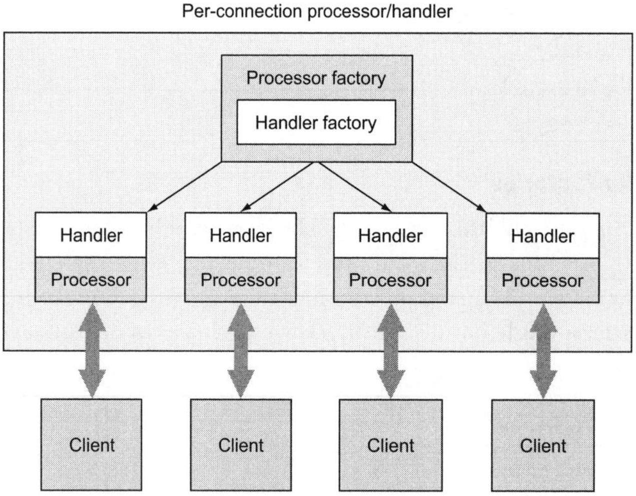

Per-connection processor/handler

Figure 10.17   Processor and handler factories allow servers to create per-connection handlers.

This feature is implemented in Apache Thrift through processor factories. Java, C++, Go, D, C#, and other languages support processor factories based on the TProcessor-Factory interface. Most scripting languages, like Python, don't support processor factories at the time of this writing (patches welcome!). Processor factories are used by servers that support them to manufacture a processor/handler pair for each client connection. By providing a server with a processor factory that creates a new handler for each connection, you can ensure each client has private handler state.

CREATING PER-CONNECTION HANDLERS

Let's create a server to demonstrate processor factory operation. The server in the following listing uses a processor factory to create a separate MessageHandler for each new client connection.

Listing 10.8   ~thriftbook/part2/servers/factories/factory_server.cpp

```cpp
#include "gen-cpp/Message.h"
#include <thrift/protocol/TJSONProtocol.h>
#include <thrift/server/TThreadedServer.h>
#include <thrift/transport/TServerSocket.h>
#include <thrift/transport/TTransport.h>
#include <thrift/TProcessor.h>
#include <memory>
#include <iostream>
#include <string>

using namespace ::apache::thrift::protocol;
using namespace ::apache::thrift::transport;
using namespace ::apache::thrift::server;
using namespace ::apache::thrift;
using std::make_shared;
```

```
using std::shared_ptr;

const char * msgs[] = {"Apache Thrift!!",
                       "Childhood is a short season",
                       "'Twas brillig"};

class MessageHandler : public MessageIf {          ❶
public:
    MessageHandler(int conn_no) :
        msg_index(0), connection_no(conn_no) {;}
    virtual void motd(std::string& _return) override {      ❷
        std::cout << "[" << connection_no << "] Call count: "
                  << ++msg_index << std::endl;
        _return = msgs[msg_index%3];
    }
private:
    unsigned int msg_index;
    unsigned int connection_no;
};


class MessageHandlerFactory : public MessageIfFactory {        ❸
public:
    MessageHandlerFactory() : connection_no(0) {;}
    virtual MessageIf* getHandler(const TConnectionInfo& connInfo) {
❹        return new MessageHandler(++connection_no);
    };
    virtual void releaseHandler(MessageIf* handler) {
❺        delete handler;
    };
private:
    unsigned int connection_no;
};


int main(int argc, char **argv) {
    auto handler_fac = make_shared<MessageHandlerFactory>();     ❻
    auto proc_fac = make_shared<MessageProcessorFactory>(handler_fac);    ❼

    auto trans_svr = make_shared<TServerSocket>(9090);
    auto trans_fac = make_shared<TFramedTransportFactory>();      ❽
    auto proto_fac = make_shared<TJSONProtocolFactory>();

    TThreadedServer server(proc_fac, trans_svr, trans_fac, proto_fac);    ❾
    server.serve();
}
```

This program uses factories to generate a tailored I/O stack and per-connection handlers. The MessageHandler class ❶ has a new constructor which accepts a connection number to display when outputting the call count. This will help verify the construction of independent handlers for each connection.

The implementation of the message service motd() method ❷ increments the msg_index as always; however, the per-connection handler implementation allows us to modify the handler state without synchronization concerns. Each connection will have its own private handler with its own private set of attributes. Because the `TThreadedServer` creates a single thread per connection, only one thread will access each handler, ensuring serial access to the handler state.

The next class in the listing is `MessageHandlerFactory` ❸. As you may guess, this is the factory the server will use to manufacture `MessageHandler` instances for each new connection. When you generate C++ code for an Apache Thrift service, the IDL compiler creates a client, a processor, and an interface (`serviceIF`) for the service. It also creates a `TProcessorFactory` subclass (`MessageProcessorFactory` in the example) and an interface factory for the service (`MessageIfFactory` in this example). The processor factory is implemented, but the interface factory is abstract and must be implemented by the user.

Handler factories are implemented by deriving from the interface factory and then implementing the two factory methods:

- `MessageIf* getHandler(const TConnectionInfo &connInfo);` ❹
- `releaseHandler(MessageIf *handler);` ❺

The `getHandler()` method is called by the server to manufacture a new handler for a connection. The `releaseHandler()` method is called by the server to dispose of a handler when a client disconnects.

The C++ language `HandlerFactory` implementations pass the `getHandler()` method a `TConnectionInfo` object, which looks like this:

```
struct TConnectionInfo {
  boost::shared_ptr<protocol::TProtocol> input;
  boost::shared_ptr<protocol::TProtocol> output;
  boost::shared_ptr<transport::TTransport> transport;
};
```

This structure contains the connection's input protocol, output protocol, and endpoint transport. The input and output protocols can be the same object; however, they're often separate protocol instances, as we'll see in the next section. The `TConnectionInfo` structure also contains the endpoint transport for the connection. The `TConnectionInfo` allows the handler factory to use protocol and transport information during the manufacturing process, if needed.

This factory method will construct a new handler instance with the incremented connection count ❹. The release handler receives the handler pointer the `getHandler()` factory method returned to the server and deletes the handler instance to free it ❺. Factories are always singular, meaning any factory state is shared by the entire server. The handler factory `connection_no` is therefore server-wide, allowing us to generate a unique connection count for each client by incrementing it with each call to `getHandler()`. Most servers use a single accept thread to call factory methods, making factories single-threaded, and thus free of internal synchronization concerns.

The first line of the `main()` function creates an instance of the handler factory **6**. The server doesn't use the handler factory directly; rather, it uses the processor factory that internally creates the handler. This requires us to pass the processor factory a handler factory instance to build handlers with **7**. In this server we also create an I/O stack compatible with the previous Python example, using the JSON protocol and a framing layer **8**.

The final line of code in `main()` creates a threaded server with all of the necessary factories **9**. This constructor accepts the factories for the processor, server transport, layered transport, and protocol, though each server implementation has its own set of constructors. Certain server constructors are minimalistic, accepting only a server transport and processor instance, and creating default factories for everything. Other server constructors are comprehensive, accepting explicit instances of all the factories. It's worth looking over the constructors of any server you plan to use to examine the range of possibilities.

The following code builds and runs the above server and shows the output produced when connecting two of the clients from listing 10.9 concurrently:

```
$ ls -l
-rw-r--r-- 1 randy randy  827 Jul 19 00:40 factory_client.cpp
-rw-r--r-- 1 randy randy 1890 Jul 19 21:36 factory_server.cpp
-rw-r--r-- 1 randy randy   38 Jul 18 15:24 simple.thrift
$ thrift -gen cpp simple.thrift
$ g++ -o client factory_client.cpp gen-cpp/Message.cpp -Wall -std=c++11\
      -lthrift
$ g++ -o server factory_server.cpp gen-cpp/Message.cpp -Wall -std=c++11\
      -lthrift
$ ./server
[1] Call count: 1
[1] Call count: 2
[2] Call count: 1
[2] Call count: 2
[1] Call count: 3
```

The previous session builds the client and server and runs the server. Next, clients connect from two separate shells. As you can see, each connection has its own handler with an independent connection number and `msg_index`.

Factories unlock a lot of power in Apache Thrift, but we've only scratched the surface.

10.4.3 *In/out factories*

Apache Thrift RPC clients and processors have separate protocol references for reading and writing. This allows application designers to create output stacks with different layers than those used by the input stack. For example, a server that returns large amounts of data might accept requests on the input side with a `TSocket/TFramedTransport/TBinaryProtocol` stack but return results using an additional `TZlibTransport` layer in the output stack.

This separate input/output protocol feature is easily overlooked because I/O stacks can be constructed with a single protocol, which is then used for both in and out operations (see figure 10.18).

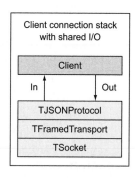

Figure 10.18 An Apache Thrift client using a shared I/O stack for input and output

In certain situations, it can be useful to have independent protocol stacks for input and output processing (see figure 10.19).

When you initialize a server with only one protocol factory and one transport factory, the server uses the same factory for both input and output. However, most servers have constructors that allow you to specify separate input and output protocol factories as well as separate input and output layered transport factories.

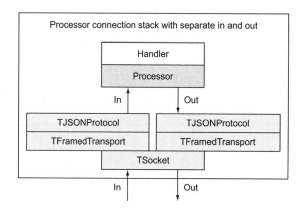

Figure 10.19 Servers create separate input and output protocol/transport stacks for use with processors.

10.4.4 *Building servers with custom factories and transports*

In general, providing the same protocol stack for input and output is simple and efficient. However, many otherwise difficult-to-implement arrangements can be coded easily by using distinct input and output protocol stacks.

For example, imagine that we'd like to log all JSON data transmitted to clients from our server. This could allow our auditing group to ensure that only appropriate data is leaving our server farm.

To build such a solution we could create a custom transport factory, `TWriteLogTransportFactory`, for use on the output protocol stack (see figure 10.20). This factory could manufacture the frame layer over the server-supplied endpoint to satisfy our existing clients, while also adding a custom `TTeeTransport` layer that will duplicate all write traffic, allowing us to send a second copy of the output to a `TSimpleFileTransport` for logging.

The modularity of the Apache Thrift I/O model makes these additions easy to implement. The only pieces we need to supply are the `TTeeTransport` and the `TWriteLogTransportFactory` to assemble the output stack.

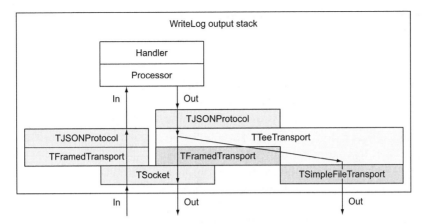

In   Out

Figure 10.20   Using separate input and output I/O stacks to provide custom output behavior

Before we examine the code, let's look at a sample session running the custom in/out server stack from figure 10.20 with everything built in Java:

```
$ thrift -gen java simple.thrift                              ❶
$ javac -cp /usr/local/lib/libthrift-1.0.0.jar:\
           /usr/local/lib/slf4j-api-1.7.2.jar:\
           /usr/local/lib/slf4j-nop-1.7.2.jar                 ❷
           *.java gen-java/*.java                        ↩
Note: gen-java/Message.java uses unchecked or unsafe operations.
Note: Recompile with -Xlint:unchecked for details.
$ java -cp /usr/local/lib/libthrift-1.0.0.jar:\
           /usr/local/lib/slf4j-api-1.7.2.jar:\
           /usr/local/lib/slf4j-nop-1.7.2.jar:\
           gen-java:\
           .
           FactoryServer                                      ❸
Call count: 1
Call count: 2
Call count: 3
^C                                                            ❹
$ ls -l
-rw-r--r-- 1 randy randy 1541 Jul 20 02:47 FactoryClient.class
-rw-r--r-- 1 randy randy  823 Jul 20 02:33 FactoryClient.java
-rw-r--r-- 1 randy randy 1823 Jul 20 02:47 FactoryServer.class
-rw-r--r-- 1 randy randy 1003 Jul 20 02:41 FactoryServer.java
drwxr-xr-x 2 randy randy 4096 Jul 20 02:47 gen-java
-rw-r--r-- 1 randy randy 1276 Jul 20 02:47 MessageHandler.class
-rw-r--r-- 1 randy randy  601 Jul 20 02:40 MessageHandler.java
-rw-r--r-- 1 randy randy   38 Jul 18 15:24 simple.thrift
-rw-r--r-- 1 randy randy  148 Jul 20 02:47 svr_log_101
-rw-r--r-- 1 randy randy 1053 Jul 20 02:47 TTeeTransport.class
-rw-r--r-- 1 randy randy 1031 Jul 20 02:40 TTeeTransport.java
-rw-r--r-- 1 randy randy 1149 Jul 20 02:47 TWritelogTransportFactory.class
-rw-r--r-- 1 randy randy  808 Jul 20 02:41 TWritelogTransportFactory.java
❺ $ cat svr_log_101
```

```
[1,"motd",2,1,{"0":{"str":"Childhood is a short season"}}]
[1,"motd",2,2,{"0":{"str":"'Twas brillig"}}]
[1,"motd",2,3,{"0":{"str":"Apache Thrift!!"}}]
$
```

As always, we use the IDL compiler to generate RPC stubs for the message service ❶. Next, we compile all the Java classes for the client and server ❷. Then we run the server and connect with a client running in another shell ❸. The server is killed after handling a few sample requests ❹. The file listing also shows the log file, which contains the JSON data shipped to the client ❺.

Now let's look at the code for the custom factory and I/O stack used by this new server. The following listing shows the main server class.

Listing 10.9   ~/thriftbook/part2/servers/factories/FactoryServer.java

```
import org.apache.thrift.TProcessor;
import org.apache.thrift.server.TServer;
import org.apache.thrift.server.TThreadPoolServer;
import org.apache.thrift.transport.TServerSocket;
import org.apache.thrift.transport.TTransportException;
import org.apache.thrift.protocol.TJSONProtocol;
import org.apache.thrift.transport.TFramedTransport;

public class FactoryServer {

  public static void main(String[] args) throws TTransportException {
    TServerSocket svrTrans = new TServerSocket(8585);
    TProcessor processor = new Message.Processor<>(new MessageHandler());

    TServer server = new TThreadPoolServer (           ❶
            new TThreadPoolServer.Args(svrTrans)       ❷
      ❸    .processor(processor)
      ❹    .protocolFactory(new TJSONProtocol.Factory())
            .inputTransportFactory(new TFramedTransport.Factory())       ❺
            .outputTransportFactory(new TWritelogTransportFactory(100)));
    server.serve();
  }
}
```

This program uses the service handler class from listing 10.4. The server itself is a Java TThreadPoolServer, which provides multi-client support ❶. Rather than taking all construction parameters in parameter lists, Java servers use Args classes for initialization. The Args object here is constructed with a server transport ❷. The service processor must be set, but the server will use default factories if no other Args settings are configured. In this example we use the various setter methods of the Args class to configure the factories needed ❸.

This server uses a single JSON protocol factory ❹ for input and output, but uses two distinct layered transport factories, one for input and another for output ❺. On the input side, we use a simple framing layer. On the output side, we use a custom

TWritelogTransportFactory; this factory creates a framing layer over the server-provided endpoint (a TSocket, in this case) and then uses a custom Tee transport to copy all output to a TSimpleFileTransport as well. The following listing shows the code for the TWritelogTransportFactory.

Listing 10.10 ~/thriftbook/part2/servers/factories/TWritelogTransportFactory.java

```
import org.apache.thrift.transport.TFramedTransport;
import org.apache.thrift.transport.TSimpleFileTransport;
import org.apache.thrift.transport.TTransport;
import org.apache.thrift.transport.TTransportException;
import org.apache.thrift.transport.TTransportFactory;

public class TWritelogTransportFactory extends TTransportFactory {    ❶

  private int clientID = 0;

  public TWritelogTransportFactory(int clientStartID) {
    clientID = clientStartID;
  }

  @Override
  public TTransport getTransport(TTransport trans) {    ❷
    TSimpleFileTransport log;                                  ❸
    try {
      log = new TSimpleFileTransport ("svr_log_" + ++clientID, false, true);
      log.open();
    } catch (TTransportException ex) {
      log = null;
    }
    TFramedTransport frame = new TFramedTransport(trans);    ❹
    return new TTeeTransport (frame, log);                   ❺
  }
}
```

This custom transport factory builds the transport stack components depicted in gray in figure 10.20. Essentially, we want all writes to get framed and sent out to the socket but also to get copied to the log file. To achieve this, we create a custom TTeeTransport that writes all bytes to two separate underlying transports.

To function as a transport factory for Apache Thrift Servers, a class must implement the TTransportFactory interface ❶. The only method required is the factory method, getTransport() ❷, which receives the endpoint transport from the server, wraps the endpoint in a framed transport ❹, then sets it as the left side of the Tee transport ❺. We also create a TSimpleFileTransport ❸ and open it using the file name svr_log_ followed by a sequential number initialized at construction.

The following listing shows the last piece of the server, the TTeeTransport.

```
import org.apache.thrift.transport.TTransport;
import org.apache.thrift.transport.TTransportException;

public class TTeeTransport extends TTransport {              ❶

  private TTransport left;                    ❷
  private TTransport right;

  public TTeeTransport (TTransport left, TTransport right) {        ❸
    this.left = left;
    this.right = right;
  }
  @Override
  public void flush() throws TTransportException {         ❹
    left.flush();
    right.flush();
  }
  @Override
  public boolean isOpen() {
    return true;
  }
  @Override
  public void open() throws TTransportException {             ❺
    throw new TTransportException("open not supported");
  }
  @Override
  public void close() {            ❻
    left.close();
    right.close();
  }
  @Override
  public int read(byte[] bytes, int i, int i1) throws TTransportException {
    throw new TTransportException("read not supported");
  }
  @Override
  public void write(byte[] bytes,int i,int i1) throws TTransportException {
    left.write(bytes, i, i1);          ❼
    right.write(bytes, i, i1);
  }
}
```

This simple layered transport overlays two transports ❷ and writes all output to both
❼. TTeeTransport is derived from the TTransport base ❶ and implements all the
required methods to serve as a proper layered transport. The internal left and right
transports are set at construction time ❸, and both are assumed to already be open.

   The flush() ❹, write() ❼, and close() ❻ methods all pass their calls on to the
left and right transports. We've made the open() and read() methods illegal ❺,
throwing an exception if they're called.

A Java client is listed here for completeness, though any of the JSON/framed/
TSocket message service clients we've built previously will talk to the new Java server.

```
import org.apache.thrift.TException;
import org.apache.thrift.protocol.TProtocol;
import org.apache.thrift.protocol.TJSONProtocol;
import org.apache.thrift.transport.TFramedTransport;
import org.apache.thrift.transport.TSocket;
import org.apache.thrift.transport.TTransport;

public class FactoryClient {
  public static void main(String[] args) throws TException {
    TTransport trans=new TFramedTransport(new TSocket("localhost", 8585));
    TProtocol proto = new TJSONProtocol (trans);
    Message.Iface client = new Message.Client(proto);
    trans.open();
    String line;
    do {
      System.out.println("Message from server: " + client.motd());
      System.out.println("Enter to continue, 'q' to quit: ");
      line = System.console().readLine();
    } while (0 != line.compareToIgnoreCase("q"));
  }
}
```

As demonstrated in the preceding pages, factories offer a range of integration points
in the Apache Thrift framework for configuring servers. Factories allow us to return
the same service handler for every connection or a new distinct handler for each connection. Factories also allow us to choose a desired protocol and layered transport
stack for input, output, or both.

While factories allow us to provide custom RPC processing, there may be times
where you aren't interested in modifying the processing of an RPC request but would
like to perform some side effect. To do this, you can hook code to various events taking place on the server.

10.5 *Server interfaces and event processing*

In this section, we'll look at server event processing. Server events allow you to monitor server activity independent of any service implementation. Server events are fired
when the server accepts a connection, deletes a connection, or processes a request on
a connection.

This can be useful in many scenarios. For example, imagine you're interested in
logging all the connections accepted by a server. Server events would be a good fit
here because server events are independent of any service, making server event handlers useful with any server regardless of the service or services it supports.

Server event processing isn't supported by all Apache Thrift language servers
(patches welcome!) Of the three demonstration languages, both C++ and Java support

server event processing but Python doesn't yet. In languages where it's supported, server event handlers are set through the TServer interface.

10.5.1 *TServer*

In much the same way that transports implement the TTransport interface and protocols implement the TProtocol interface, Apache Thrift servers typically implement the TServer interface. The TServer interface varies a bit from language to language. Here are four of the more important methods generally present:

```
TServer:
  void serve();
  void stop();
  void setServerEventHandler(TServerEventHandler eventHandler);
  TServerEventHandler getServerEventHandler();
```

We've used the serve() method to run servers since chapter 1. The serve() method returns only when the server is shut down. In the examples we've used so far, we call serve() on the main program thread and thus give up control to the serve() method until the user stops the server by sending SIGINT (typically by pressing Ctrl+C). In the next example, we'll run the server's serve() method on a background thread, giving us the ability to call the stop() method to shut down the server.

The stop() method doesn't always produce an immediate shutdown. Certain servers exit immediately, and others stop receiving new connections but wait until all current clients disconnect on their own before exiting. All C++ and Java servers provide a stop() method. Of all the Python servers, only the TProcessPoolServer and TNonblocking-Server provide a stop() method; the rest must be stopped with SIGINT.

The last two TServer methods set and get the server's event handler. At the time of this writing, only C++, Java, Haxe, C#, Delphi, and D support server events.

10.5.2 *TServerEventHandler*

Apache Thrift servers generate events at several key points in their lifecycle. The TServerEventHandler class defines a callback interface which applications can implement to receive notifications when server events take place. Here is the TServerEvent-Handler interface:

```
TServerEventHandler:
  void preServe();
  ServerContext createContext(TProtocol input,
                              TProtocol output);
  void processContext(ServerContext serverContext,
                      TTransport inputTransport,
                      TTransport outputTransport);
  void deleteContext( ServerContext serverContext,
                      TProtocol input,
                      TProtocol output);
```

To implement a server event handler, you must derive a new class from TServerEvent-Handler and then pass an instance of this class to the server's setServerEvent-Handler() method.

The preServe() method is called by servers before they begin servicing clients. This is a good place to do any expensive initialization, because it's called outside of the context of a client interaction.

The createContext() and deleteContext() methods are called after a client connects and after a client disconnects, respectively. These methods allow an application to perform pre- and post-client connection activities. For example, a program could log the client connection time in createContext() and log the disconnect time in deleteContext(), tracking the client's total connection time.

The processContext() method is called every time a client makes an RPC call. Each call to a Thrift service invokes processContext() prior to being processed by the processor and interface handler.

The serverContext parameter is a void pointer in C++ and an empty interface reference called ServerContext in Java. The server keeps track of this context on a client-by-client basis. You can allocate any type of object in createContext() and return it to the server as the current connection's serverContext. The server will then pass that object pointer to deleteContext() and processContext() any time the client associated with that object is involved. For example, createContext() could allocate a usage statistics record and return it to the server. Each call to processContext() could then compute the Thrift RPC calls per minute consumed by the client and store the result in the usage record, perhaps rejecting clients making excessive calls (circuit breaking), logging their activity, setting off an alarm, and so on.

When the client disconnects, the deleteContext() method could write the session statistics to disk or stdout. The deleteContext() method should delete any server-Context allocated by createContext().

The createContext() and deleteContext() methods both receive a pointer to the input and output protocols associated with the connected client. The event handler is free to read and write through the protocol pointers, though care must be taken to coordinate such activity with any client programs used. The processContext() method is called with the endpoint transport for the connection.

SERVER EVENT HANDLERS VERSUS SERVICE HANDLERS

Server event handlers and factory-generated service handlers are invoked for similar events. For example, if a handler factory is used, a service handler gets created when a client connects, calling the handler constructor. When the client disconnects, the service handler gets destroyed, calling the handler destructor. The server event handler receives events when clients connect and disconnect, as well. The distinction is that server event handlers are service-independent. A server event handler can be used with a server serving any service or group of services. Server event handlers are therefore best suited to service-independent server tasks, while factory-generated service handlers are often more appropriate for service-specific connect/disconnect logic.

10.5.3 *Building a C++ thread pool server with server events*

To gain practical experience with server event handlers we'll build a new multi-threaded server in C++ to handle `message` service requests. This server will use the C++ `TThreadPoolServer` class. The C++ `TThreadPoolServer` has a configurable thread pool size. However, should more connections than the server has threads arrive, the excess client connections will backlog. Backlogged connections get no service until an active connection disconnects, freeing a thread to service the next connection in the backlog (see figure 10.21).

What if we like the ability to reuse threads over and over as connections come and go, but don't like the possibility that clients might get backlogged? In this case, we can add threads to the thread pool dynamically by writing some custom code. To do this we'll need to be notified as clients connect and disconnect.

The server event processing facility is a perfect fit for this challenge. The `createContext()` event will allow us to monitor new connections and subsequently decide if we need to add worker threads. The `deleteContext()` event will allow us to scale down the thread pool if too many threads are idle.

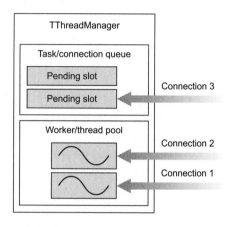

Figure 10.21   `TThreadManager` task queue and worker thread pool

USING THE THREADMANAGER CLASS TO CREATE THREAD POOLS

The C++ `TNonblockingServer` and `TThreadPoolServer` both use pools of threads to process work. The `TNonblockingServer` is task-based, so work equates to an individual RPC request. The `TThreadPoolServer` is connection-based, so work equates to a connection.

The Apache Thrift C++ framework implementation provides a `ThreadManager` class (one of the rare framework classes not prefixed with "T"). The `ThreadManager` class essentially manages a pool of threads that can be dispatched. The following code shows the interface exposed by the `ThreadManager` class declared in `ThreadManager.h`:

```
ThreadManager:
  //Thread manager methods
  virtual void start() = 0;
  virtual void stop() = 0;
  virtual void join() = 0;
  virtual STATE state() const = 0;
  //Thread (i.e. Worker) methods
  virtual void addWorker(size_t value=1) = 0;
  virtual void removeWorker(size_t value=1) = 0;
  virtual size_t idleWorkerCount() const = 0;
  virtual size_t workerCount() const = 0;
  virtual std::shared_ptr<ThreadFactory> threadFactory() const = 0;
```

```
virtual void threadFactory(std::shared_ptr<ThreadFactory> value) = 0;
//Task (connections in the TThreadPoolServer context) methods
virtual size_t pendingTaskCount() const  = 0;
virtual size_t totalTaskCount() const = 0;
virtual size_t pendingTaskCountMax() const = 0;
virtual size_t expiredTaskCount() = 0;
virtual void add(std::shared_ptr<Runnable> task,
                 int64_t timeout=0LL,
                 int64_t expiration=0LL) = 0;
virtual void remove(std::shared_ptr<Runnable> task) = 0;
virtual std::shared_ptr<Runnable> removeNextPending() = 0;
virtual void removeExpiredTasks() = 0;
virtual void setExpireCallback(ExpireCallback expireCallback) = 0;
//Static TheadManager creation method
static std::shared_ptr<ThreadManager> newSimpleThreadManager(
                      size_t count=4, size_t pendingTaskCountMax=0);
```

To create a TThreadPoolServer, we'll need to provide a ThreadManager. The static ThreadManager::newSimpleThreadManager() method generates a new Thread-Manager and allows us to set the thread pool size (count) and the maximum number of connections allowed to be waiting for a thread (pendingTaskCountMax).

The thread pool server will use the ThreadManager Task methods internally to assign new connections to threads in the pool. We'll use the thread methods to track the threads in use and create new threads when the pool is close to exhaustion. The workerCount() method returns the total number of threads in the pool and the idleWorkerCount() method returns the number of threads waiting in the pool for work. If the idle thread count reaches zero, we'll add worker threads to the pool using the addWorker() method. We can also use the removeWorker() method to eliminate threads if the idle thread count is too high.

USING THE THREADFACTORY CLASS TO CREATE THREADS

System threads are implemented by operating systems. This makes threads inherently non-portable. Language runtimes and interpreters solve this problem by creating a thread abstraction on top of the underlying operating system. For this reason, Python and Java threads are represented in code the same way on any platform. C++ uses native interfaces and other options, making threading a little more complex. The Apache Thrift library uses the PlatformThreadFactory abstraction to support different thread implementations (see the following sidebar for details).

> ### Apache Thrift C++ threading
> C++ environments have several prevalent threading APIs available. The 2011 C++11 standard introduced a library class that provided a portable thread abstraction, std::thread. Apache Thrift is backward-compatible with C++99, however, making C++11 std::thread an optional feature. Most *nix systems support POSIX pthreads; however, Windows doesn't. Boost is a third-party library providing a cross-platform boost::thread implementation, the base for the C++11 standard.

Because of the range of possibilities, Apache Thrift uses factories to create threads. The following thread APIs are supported:

- Boost
- C++11STD
- Posix

C++ servers use the generic `PlatformThreadFactory` type to provide threads for pools and other purposes. `PlatformThreadFactory` is a typedef for one of the three supported thread interfaces. Here's a snippet from the `PlatformThreadFactory.h` header:

```
#ifdef USE_BOOST_THREAD
   typedef BoostThreadFactory PlatformThreadFactory;
#elif USE_STD_THREAD
   typedef StdThreadFactory PlatformThreadFactory;
#else
   typedef PosixThreadFactory PlatformThreadFactory;
#endif
```

Posix is the default thread factory; however, on Windows installations, USE_BOOST_THREAD or USE_STD_THREAD will be defined, depending on your compiler version. You can also explicitly define a particular platform factory (for example, "new StdThreadFactory()"). All the `PlatformThreadFactory` classes implement the abstract `ThreadFactory` interface:

```
ThreadFactory:
boost::shared_ptr<Thread>
   newThread(boost::shared_ptr<Runnable> runnable);
Thread::id_t getCurrentThreadId();
```

The `newThread()` method is the factory method, used to generate new threads for thread pools and other purposes. The `getCurrentThreadId()` method returns the current running thread's platform-specific unique ID.

Let's look at the source for the `TThreadPoolServer` program. The main routine and server event handler are declared in separate files. The following listing shows the code for the main file.

Listing 10.13 ~/thriftbook/part2/servers/events/event_server.cpp

```
#include "server_event_handler.h"          ❶
#include "gen-cpp/Message.h"
#include <thrift/transport/TServerSocket.h>
#include <thrift/transport/TBufferTransports.h>
#include <thrift/protocol/TCompactProtocol.h>
#include <thrift/concurrency/ThreadManager.h>
#include <thrift/concurrency/PlatformThreadFactory.h>
#include <thrift/server/TServer.h>
#include <thrift/server/TThreadPoolServer.h>
```

```cpp
#include <iostream>
#include <string>
#include <thread>
#include <functional>
#include <memory>

using namespace ::apache::thrift;
using namespace ::apache::thrift::protocol;
using namespace ::apache::thrift::transport;
using namespace ::apache::thrift::server;
using namespace ::apache::thrift::concurrency;
using std::shared_ptr;
using std::make_shared;

const char * msgs[] = {"Apache Thrift!!",
                       "Childhood is a short season",
                       "'Twas brillig"};

class MessageHandler : public MessageIf {          ❷
public:
    MessageHandler() : msg_index(0) {;}
    virtual void motd(std::string& _return) override {
        _return = msgs[++msg_index%3];
    }
private:
    unsigned int msg_index;
};

int main(int argc, char **argv) {
  //Setup the socket server and the service processor and handler
  const int port = 8585;#3
  auto handler = make_shared<MessageHandler>();
  auto proc = make_shared<MessageProcessor>(handler);           ❸
  auto svr_trans = make_shared<TServerSocket>(port);

  //Setup the protocol and layered transport factories
  auto trans_fac = make_shared<TBufferedTransportFactory>();    ❹
  auto proto_fac = make_shared<TCompactProtocolFactory>();

  //Setup the thread manager and thread factory, then create the threads
❺ auto t_man = ThreadManager::newSimpleThreadManager(2,1);
  auto t_fac = make_shared<PlatformThreadFactory>();     ❻
❼ t_man->threadFactory(t_fac);
  t_man->start();              ❽

  //Setup the server and run it on a background thread
  TThreadPoolServer server(proc, svr_trans, trans_fac, proto_fac, t_man);   ❾
❿ server.setTimeout(3000);
  server.setServerEventHandler(make_shared<SvrEvtHandler>(t_man,2,4));   ⓫
⓬ std::thread server_thread(std::bind(&TThreadPoolServer::serve, &server));

  //Wait for the user to quit
  std::string str;                                                         ⓭
  std::cout << "[Server:" << port << "] enter to quit" << std::endl;
  std::getline(std::cin, str);#13
```

```
        //Stop accepting new connections (thread manager stops when tasks end)
⑭    server.stop();
     std::cout   << "Waiting for current("
                 << t_man->workerCount() - t_man->idleWorkerCount()
                 << ") and queued(" << t_man->pendingTaskCount()
                 << ") client tasks to exit..." << std::endl;
⑮    server_thread.join();
     std::cout << "service complete, exiting." << std::endl;
}
```

This program is divided into two parts, the server_event_handler.h header ❶ and the previous event_server.cpp. The main server source displayed in the previous listing supplies the message service handler used throughout this chapter ❷.

The main() function is responsible for assembling the necessary objects and then running the TThreadPoolServer. The first few lines of code in main() create a processor/handler stack for our message service and a server transport to listen at port 8585 ❸.

The next two lines create the protocol and transport factories for the server to use ❹. We selected the compact protocol for this server. If our server is typically I/O bound, the compact protocol can help reduce the size of RPC messages.

The server uses the TBufferedTransport layer to buffer the underlying endpoint until flushed. The buffered layer is transparent to clients because it adds nothing to the data stream transmitted between the client and server, unlike the framed transport. Java doesn't have a TBufferedTransport because TSocket is self-buffered in Java.

TIP I/O stacks in C++ and Python should always use either a TFramed-Transport or TBufferedTransport layer for efficiency when writing to non-memory-based endpoints. These layers buffer the many small writes made by the protocol layer, avoiding many small writes to network or disk devices.

The next block of code sets up the ThreadManager for the server ❺. We use the new-SimpleThreadManager(2,1) call to create a ThreadManager with two startup threads and a task queue that will support one waiting task (task means connection in this context).

NOTE The network stack has its own backlog, separate and distinct from the ThreadManager task queue. The acceptor thread provided by the TThread-PoolServer will accept all inbound connections and add them to the Thread-Manager task queue. The ThreadManager will throw a TooManyPendingTasks-Exception if the task queue is full, causing the acceptor thread to close the accepted connection immediately (hanging up on the client). The acceptor will then continue accepting new connections under the assumption that the ThreadManager threads will drain the queue over time.

The ThreadManager doesn't have a default thread factory, so we must explicitly create one ❻ and assign it to the ThreadManager instance ❼. The ThreadManager threads don't start automatically, so we must call the start() method to launch the worker pool threads ❽.

The next block of code creates the TThreadPoolServer. The server instance is created like simpler servers with the usual factories and the addition of the ThreadManager ❾. Next we set the task timeout in milliseconds to 3000 ❿. This causes the server to configure the ThreadManager tasks (new client connections) with a timeout of three seconds. If a task waiting in the task queue is found to be older than three seconds, the ThreadManager will close the connection and discard it (see figure 10.22).

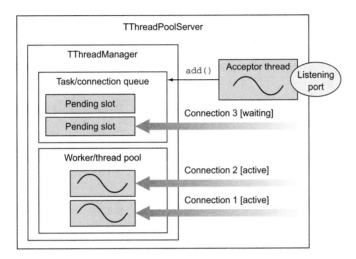

Figure 10.22 `ThreadPoolServer` connection processing

Before running the server, we set the server event handler. The server wants a std::shared_ptr to a TServerEventHandler. The code in main constructs a SvrEvt-Handler on the heap with make_shared<>, which wraps it in a std::shared_ptr ⓫.

Rather than calling the server's serve() method directly, this program runs the server on a background thread ⓬. This allows the main() thread to continue to be responsive to console input. Here we create a standard C++11 thread, std::thread. If you aren't using C++11, you can use a boost::thread with the same code. The thread needs an entry point and it expects a normal f(void)-style function. To pass the server's serve() method, which takes an implicit "this" pointer as a parameter, we must bind the server instance (this) to the serve() method. Here we use the std::bind utility from the C++11 functional header to create a wrapper which will make the correct call. Again if you aren't using C++11, you can use boost::bind() or std::tr1::bind().

Now that the server is running in the background we can interact with the user. The next block of code waits for the user to press Enter ⓭. When the user presses Enter we invoke the server stop() method ⓮. Each server responds differently to this request. The TThreadPoolServer stops accepting new connections, but the Thread-Manager continues processing requests on existing connections until the connections close. The main() function uses the server join() method to wait for any remaining threads to exit ⓯.

When all of the connections are closed, the ThreadManager threads will exit and the join call will return, allowing the program to shut down.

Before testing the server let's look at the event processor listing.

Listing 10.14   ~/thriftbook/part2/servers/events/server_event_handler.h

```
#ifndef _MY_SERVER_EVENT_HANDLER_H_
#define _MY_SERVER_EVENT_HANDLER_H_ 1

#include <thrift/transport/TTransport.h>
#include <thrift/protocol/TProtocol.h>
#include <thrift/concurrency/ThreadManager.h>
#include <thrift/concurrency/PlatformThreadFactory.h>
#include <thrift/server/TServer.h>
#include <sstream>
#include <string>
#include <memory>

class SvrEvtHandler :                                                    ❶
                public apache::thrift::server::TServerEventHandler
{
public:
  PoolSvrEvtHandler(                          ❷
    std::shared_ptr<apache::thrift::concurrency::ThreadManager> th_man,
    unsigned int thread_min,
    unsigned int thread_max) :
        t_man(th_man), t_min(thread_min), t_max(thread_max)
  {;}

  std::string stats(int reduce_in_use_by=0) {        ❸
    std::stringstream ss;
    ss << "(threads in use: "
      << t_man->workerCount() - t_man->idleWorkerCount() - reduce_in_use_by
      << "/" << t_man->workerCount() << " - connections waiting: "
      << t_man->pendingTaskCount() << ")";
    return ss.str();
  }

❹ virtual void preServe() override {
    std::cout << "  preServe " << stats() << std::endl;
  }

❺ virtual void* createContext(
    std::shared_ptr<apache::thrift::protocol::TProtocol> in,
    std::shared_ptr<apache::thrift::protocol::TProtocol> out) override
  {
    std::cout << "  create   " << stats() << std::endl;
    if (t_man->idleWorkerCount() == 0 && t_man->workerCount() < t_max) {
      t_man->addWorker();
      std::cout << "    No idle threads, added a new worker thread\n"
                << stats() << std::endl;
```

```
        }
        return new int(0);
    }

❻  virtual void deleteContext(void* svr_ctx,
        std::shared_ptr<apache::thrift::protocol::TProtocol> in,
        std::shared_ptr<apache::thrift::protocol::TProtocol> out) override
    {
        std::cout << "  delete   " << stats(1) << std::endl;
        if (t_man->idleWorkerCount() >= t_man->workerCount()/2 &&
            t_man->workerCount() > t_min) {
          t_man->removeWorker();
          std::cout << "     Too many idle threads, deleted a worker thread\n"
                    << stats(1) << std::endl;
        }
        int * pCallCount = reinterpret_cast<int *>(svr_ctx);
        delete pCallCount;
    }

❼  virtual void processContext(void* svr_ctx,
        std::shared_ptr<apache::thrift::transport::TTransport> trans)
        override
    {
        int * call_count = reinterpret_cast<int *>(svr_ctx);
        std::cout << "     Client call #" << ++(*call_count) << std::endl;
    }

private:
    std::shared_ptr<apache::thrift::concurrency::ThreadManager> t_man;
    unsigned int t_min;
    unsigned int t_max;
};

#endif //_MY_SERVER_EVENT_HANDLER_H_
```

Because this is a header file, we don't use "using" statements, to avoid polluting the global namespace of the source files, including the header. As a consequence, the namespace prefixes make the code more verbose than usual.

This server event handler demonstrates the creation and use of server event handlers, but also shows how you can dynamically manage the available threads in a thread manager. SvrEvtHandler is responsible for ensuring that the TThreadPoolServer's thread pool grows as connections come in.

SvrEvtHandler is the sole class declared in this header and it's derived from TServerEventHandler ❶. The constructor for the class requires a reference to the ThreadManager we'll monitor and a minimum and maximum thread count to grow the thread manager's thread pool between ❷. The stats() method displays the number of threads currently assigned to connections, the total number of threads, and the number of connections waiting for service ❸. The balance of the listing provides bodies for all the TServerEventHandler virtual functions.

The `preServe()` method is called before any clients connect and displays the stats ❹.

The `createContext()` method is called immediately after a client connects but before any RPC messages are processed ❺. Each connection drains a thread from the pool, assigning it to the connection until the client closes the connection. Because the thread pool status has changed we check to make sure that idle threads are still available to process connections. If we're out of threads and not at the max, we add a new thread by calling the `ThreadManager addWorker()` method.

We also have the opportunity to create a context object as the return value of `createContext()`. We can return `nullptr` or any other pointer. In this case, we're going to keep track of the client call count, so we allocate an integer on the heap, initialize it to `0`, and return the `int` pointer as the context for this connection. The server will keep track of this pointer and pass it back to us on subsequent calls associated with this connection.

The `deleteContext()` method is the reciprocal of `createContext()` ❻. Here we check to see if the thread pool is too large, knowing that a thread is about to be freed from service. Because `deleteContext()` is called before the thread is returned to the pool, we subtract 1 from the active thread count to get correct `status()` output. The `removeWorker()` method is used to remove a `ThreadManager` thread if we have excess threads and are above the minimum. The `deleteContext()` method also has the responsibility of releasing any memory associated with the connection context allocated in `createContext()`. In this case, we delete the integer context pointer as the last statement in `deleteContext()`.

The `processContext()` call is straightforward—recovering the connection context integer, incrementing it, and displaying it ❼.

The following code shows a session building and running the server with several clients connecting and disconnecting:

```
$ thrift -gen cpp simple.thrift
$ g++ -o server event_server.cpp gen-cpp/Message.cpp -Wall -std=c++11
        -lthrift
$ ./server
[Server:8585] Enter to quit
  preServe (threads in use: 0/2 - connections waiting: 0)
  create   (threads in use: 1/2 - connections waiting: 0)
    Client call
  create   (threads in use: 2/2 - connections waiting: 0)
    No idle threads, added a new worker thread
          (threads in use: 2/3 - connections waiting: 0)
    Client call
  create   (threads in use: 3/3 - connections waiting: 0)
    No idle threads, added a new worker thread
          (threads in use: 3/4 - connections waiting: 0)
    Client call
  create   (threads in use: 4/4 - connections waiting: 0)
    Client call
    Client call
```

```
    Client call
Thrift: Sun Jul 21 01:17:25 2013 TThreadPoolServer: Caught TException:
➥ TimedOutException
    Client call

  delete    (threads in use: 3/4 - connections waiting: 1)
  create    (threads in use: 4/4 - connections waiting: 0)
    Client call #1
Thrift: Sun Jul 21 01:20:18 2013 TSocket::write_partial() send()
➥ <Host: ::ffff:127.0.0.1 Port: 36931>Connection reset by peer
  delete    (threads in use: 3/4 - connections waiting: 0)
    Client call
  delete    (threads in use: 2/4 - connections waiting: 0)
  delete    (threads in use: 1/4 - connections waiting: 0)
   Too many idle threads, deleted a worker thread
          (threads in use: 1/3 - connections waiting: 0)
  delete    (threads in use: 0/3 - connections waiting: 0)
   Too many idle threads, deleted a worker thread
          (threads in use: 0/2 - connections waiting: 0)

Waiting for current(0) and queued(0) client tasks to exit...
service complete, exiting.
$
```

7 (next to TimedOutException line)

8 (next to Client call #1 block)

9 (next to delete threads in use: 2/4 line)

10 (next to Waiting for current line)

In this example session, the server is started on a background thread, allowing us to shut down the server by pressing Enter **1**. The server starts, as configured, with two worker threads **2**. The first client to connect reduces the idle thread count to 1 **3**. The second client to connect reduces the idle thread count to 0, causing the create-Context() server event handler method to add a worker thread **4**. The third connection also causes a thread to be added to the worker pool **5**.

The fifth connection arrives immediately after the fourth connection **6**; however, the server event processor was initialized with a thread pool max size of 4, which causes the fifth connection to be added to the task queue without expanding the thread pool. The createContext() event won't be fired for this connection until it's assigned a thread, which explains why connection number 5 isn't logged. Because the task timeout was set to 3,000 milliseconds, and no existing connections close during this time, the fifth connection times out after waiting for 3 seconds and is closed by the ThreadManager **7**.

Shortly thereafter a sixth connection arrives and is placed in the task queue. This connection has no thread on the server, yet is connected at the network level, and the client makes an RPC request, which arrives at the server but remains in the network buffer. The client decides not to wait for the server and closes the connection. The server still has the connection queued, and the socket buffer contains the RPC request and the connection close request.

Next an existing connection closes, making room for the queued connection **8**. The server assigns the free thread to the queued connection, which processes the buffered RPC request and then finds the connection closed. The server event processing of this complex sequence looks something like this:

- *Delete*—An existing client closes; status is 3 connections working and 1 in the queue.
- *Create*—The queued connection is handed to a thread; status is 4 connections working.
- *Process*—The client request is processed.
- *Error*—The processor tries to read the next message, but the client has closed the connection.
- *Delete*—The connection (already closed) is deleted and the thread is returned to the pool; status 3 threads working.

Finally, the clients begin to close out, causing the deleteContext() method to reduce the thread count progressively ❾. When all of the clients have closed, Enter is pressed and the server exits in an orderly fashion in response to our TServer stop() ❿. The following listing shows the C++ client used to test the server in the previous listing.

Listing 10.15   ~/thriftbook/part2/servers/events/event_client.cpp

```
#include <iostream>
#include <string>
#include <boost/shared_ptr.hpp>
#include <thrift/transport/TSocket.h>
#include <thrift/transport/TBufferTransports.h>
#include <thrift/protocol/TCompactProtocol.h>
#include "gen-cpp/Message.h"

using namespace apache::thrift::transport;
using namespace apache::thrift::protocol;

int main(int argv, char * argc[]) {
    boost::shared_ptr<TTransport> trans(new TSocket("localhost", 8585));
    trans.reset(new TBufferedTransport(trans));
    boost::shared_ptr<TProtocol> proto(new TCompactProtocol(trans));
    MessageClient client(proto);
    trans->open();

    std::string msg;
    do {
        client.motd(msg);
        std::cout << msg << std::endl;
        std::cout << "Enter to call motd, 'q' to quit" << std::endl;
        std::getline(std::cin, msg);
    } while (0 != msg.compare("q"));
    trans->close();
}
```

This client program is fairly run of the mill. The client spends its time calling the message service motd() method, exiting at the user's request.

The server example in this section has demonstrated several important Apache Thrift server features:

- *Server event processing*—While this is a C++ example, the server event processing functionality is identical in Java and other languages, with the obvious language adjustments for pointers and threads.
- C++ *ThreadManager use*—The `ThreadManager` is used with `TThreadPoolServer` and `TNonblockingServer` classes to provide connection and task processing thread pools, respectively.
- *Running servers on background threads*—Calling the `serve()` method on a background thread allows the main thread to optionally launch multiple servers on multiple background threads and to continue responding to the user.

10.6 Servers and services

Apache Thrift servers host Apache Thrift services. Services provide no logic to define how to wait for clients to connect or how to process RPC requests across multiple client connections. As we've seen in the preceding pages, listening for new connections, accepting connections, dispatching RPC calls, and closing client connections are the responsibility of the Apache Thrift server.

Consider the IDL shown in the following listing.

Listing 10.16 Sample multiservice IDL

```
include "mtypes.thrift"
namespace * music

service Radio {
  list<mtypes.MusicTrack> getPlayList(1: i16 hour)
  void makeRequest(1: mtypes.MusicTrack track)
}

service RadioContest {
  mtypes.Album RedeemPrize(1: string callerNumber
                           2: mtypes.MusicTrack bonusTrack)
}

service Store {
  mtypes.Album buyAlbum(1: string ASIN
                        2: string acct)
  list<mtypes.Album> similar(1: string ASIN)
}
```

This IDL declares three services: `Radio`, `RadioContest`, and `Store`. To place any of these services into production, we'll need to provide a server.

While servers and services are often in one-to-one correspondence, they need not be. Figure 10.23 depicts three servers. The first (top) program shown has one Apache Thrift server hosting the `Radio` service. This is the service deployment model we have used in prior RPC examples. In the illustration, the top program has a server listening on TCP port 8501, and when connections from clients arrive at that port, they're wired to the `Radio` service.

The second (middle) example in figure 10.23 depicts a program that hosts two Apache Thrift servers. The first server is listening on port 8502, dispatching requests for the `Radio` service. This program also hosts a second Apache Thrift server listening on port 8503, which is dispatching requests for the `RadioContest` service. The main entry point for this program may have created two background threads, executing the 8502 server on the first thread and the 8503 server on the second thread, using multithreading to allow both servers to run in parallel within the same process.

Another possibility is depicted in the third (bottom) program of figure 10.23. This program hosts a single server listening on port 8505, but the server accepts requests for three different services over this single port. This example uses service multiplexing. The benefit of service multiplexing is that it allows you to partition functions into manageably sized services without having to run many servers listening on many ports to host them. With service multiplexing a single server and port can provide many services to clients over a single connection, sharing threads and other resources.

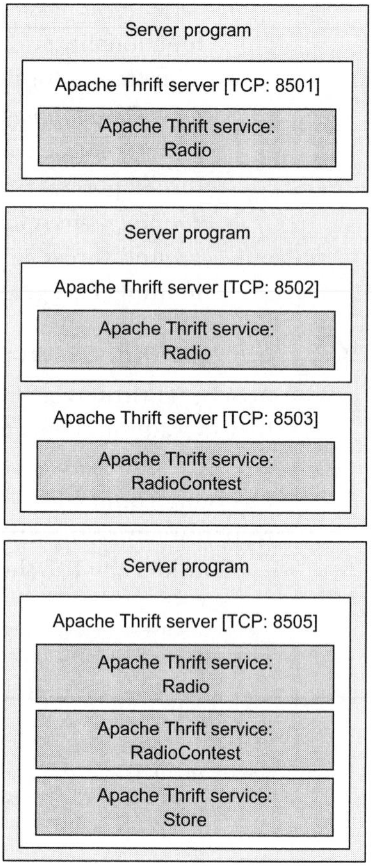

10.6.1 *Building multiservice servers*

Service multiplexing allows services to share a single port, and therefore transport. By allowing many services to operate over a single port, Apache Thrift can reduce the number of client network connections required.

Figure 10.23 Programs, servers, and services

Like most components of the Apache Thrift framework, the multiplexing feature is modular and plugs into the existing I/O stacks of clients and servers. To configure a server for multiplexing, a multiplexed processor is placed between the protocol and a set of service processors. The example in figure 10.24 shows a single server hosting two services: `Message` and `ServerTime`. The multiplexed processor calls the `Message-Processor` or the `ServerTimeProcessor`, based on the service information encoded in client requests.

The multiplexed protocol on the client side adds the service name to any RPC call made, allowing the multiplexed processor to use the service name to invoke the correct service. Service multiplexing requires both the client and the server to add multiplexing support to their respective I/O stacks. Multiplexed clients can only communicate with multiplexed servers, and vice versa.

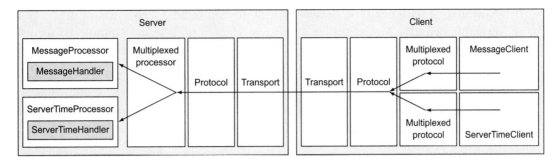

Figure 10.24 Multiplexed processors and multiplexed protocols allow a single server to host multiple services.

10.6.2 *Building a multiplexed Java threaded selector server*

To demonstrate multiplexed service operation, we'll build the example illustrated in figure 10.24. For this example, we'll use the Java TThreadedSelectorServer as the host for our services.

The first thing we need to do to create a multiplexed server is to define multiple services. We'll use the Message service from listing 10.4 as well as the new ServerTime service from listing 10.17. The server time service returns the server's time in string form, adjusted by a user-supplied number of hours.

Listing 10.17 ~/thriftbook/part2/servers/multiservice/time.thrift

```
service ServerTime {
    string time_at_server(1: i16 HourOffset)
}
```

The implementation for ServerTime is structurally identical to the message service implementation. The following listing shows the Java handler class for the ServerTime service.

Listing 10.18 ~/thriftbook/part2/servers/multiservice/ServerTimeHandler.java

```
import org.apache.thrift.TException;

public class ServerTimeHandler implements ServerTime.Iface {

  @Override
  public String time_at_server(short HourOffset) throws TException {
    long theTime = System.currentTimeMillis();
    long mils = theTime % 1000;  theTime /= 1000;
    long seconds = theTime % 60;  theTime /= 60;
    long minutes = theTime % 60;  theTime /= 60;
    long hours = (theTime + HourOffset) % 24;
    return "server time: " + hours + ":" + minutes + ":" + seconds;
  }
}
```

Now that we have two services to work with, we can build a server to host them. This example defines a Java `MultiServiceServer` class to provide the multiplexed service support. The program uses a `TThreadedSelector` server configured with three I/O threads and six task-processing threads.

Listing 10.19 `~/thriftbook/part2/servers/multiservice/MultiServiceServer.java`

```java
import java.io.BufferedReader;
import java.io.IOException;
import java.io.InputStreamReader;
import org.apache.thrift.TMultiplexedProcessor;
import org.apache.thrift.server.TServer;
import org.apache.thrift.transport.TTransportException;
import org.apache.thrift.protocol.TJSONProtocol;
import org.apache.thrift.server.TThreadedSelectorServer;
import org.apache.thrift.transport.TNonblockingServerSocket;

public class MultiServiceServer {

  static class RunnableServer implements Runnable {          ❶
    public RunnableServer(TServer svr) {
      this.svr = svr;
    }
    @Override
    public void run() {
      svr.serve();
    }
    private TServer svr;
  }

  public static void main(String[] args)
        throws TTransportException, IOException, InterruptedException {
    TNonblockingServerSocket svrTrans = new TNonblockingServerSocket(8585); ❷
    TMultiplexedProcessor proc = new TMultiplexedProcessor();   ❸
    proc.registerProcessor("Message",
        new Message.Processor<>(new MessageHandler()));          ❹
    proc.registerProcessor("ServerTime",
        new ServerTime.Processor<>(new ServerTimeHandler()));

    TServer server = new TThreadedSelectorServer(              ❺
            new TThreadedSelectorServer.Args(svrTrans)
            .processor(proc)
            .protocolFactory(new TJSONProtocol.Factory())
            .workerThreads(6)
            .selectorThreads(3));
    Thread server_thread =                                     ❻
        new Thread(new RunnableServer(server), "server_thread");
    server_thread.start();

    System.out.println("[Server] press enter to shutdown> ");
    BufferedReader br =
        new BufferedReader(new InputStreamReader(System.in));  ❼
    br.readLine();
```

```
      System.out.println("[Server] shutting down...");
❽     server.stop();
      server_thread.join();
      System.out.println("[Server] down, exiting");
  }
}
```

The MultiServiceServer class has two components, the RunnableServer inner class and the main() method. The RunnableServer class implements Java's Runnable interface and allows us to run the Apache Thrift server on a background thread. The RunnableServer class accepts a TServer object at construction time and calls the TServer serve() method when a Java Thread calls the run() method ❶.

The main() function of the program begins by creating the server transport which will be used with all of the multiplexed services ❷. All the Java non-blocking servers (TNonblockingServer, THsHAServer, and TThreadedSelectorServer) require TNonblockingServerSocket as the server transport. The TNonblockingServerSocket creates TNonblockingSockets rather than TSockets. It also provides an implicit framing layer. Clients of the Java non-blocking servers must use a TFramedTransport layer to communicate with the non-blocking servers.

The next step in building the multiplexed server is to create and initialize the TMultiplexedProcessor ❸. The multiplexed processor acts as a wrapper around all of the other service processors that will be supported by the server. New services are added to the multiplexed processor's processing list with the registerProcessor() method. This program registers both the Message and ServerTime services ❹.

The next block of code creates the TThreadedSelectorServer ❺. The server Args are initialized with the non-blocking server transport, the JSON protocol, and the multiplexed processor. We also set the worker (task) thread pool size to 6 and the selector (I/O) thread pool size to 3. The TThreadedSelectorServer has a dedicated connection acceptor thread. The selector thread pool handles all of the socket I/O, passing processing tasks off to the worker pool of threads. If the worker pool size is set to 0, the Selector pool will perform the I/O and task processing itself. Much like the C++ TNonblockingServer, this enables a wide range of tuning options.

Next the main() function creates a thread to run the server and then calls the thread start() method to start the thread, and thereby the server ❻. The RunnableServer run() method called in response to the thread start() call invokes the server serve() method.

Once the server is running, the foreground thread waits for the user to press Enter ❼ and then shuts down. The call to the server stop() method requests that all of the server threads shut down ❽. The call to join waits for all of the threads to exit before exiting the main() thread. Unlike some servers, the call to the TThreaded-SelectorServer stop() method shuts down the server threads regardless of current client connections.

The following code shows a build and run of the multiservice server:

```
$ ls -l
-rw-r--r-- 1 randy randy  601 Jul 21 05:20 MessageHandler.java
-rw-r--r-- 1 randy randy 1227 Jul 21 04:27 MultiServiceClient.java
-rw-r--r-- 1 randy randy 1761 Jul 21 05:37 MultiServiceServer.java
-rw-r--r-- 1 randy randy  497 Jul 21 05:20 ServerTimeHandler.java
-rw-r--r-- 1 randy randy   38 Jul 21 03:51 simple.thrift
-rw-r--r-- 1 randy randy   68 Jul 21 04:05 time.thrift
$ thrift -gen java simple.thrift
$ thrift -gen java time.thrift
$ javac -cp /usr/local/lib/libthrift-1.0.0.jar:\
            /usr/local/lib/slf4j-api-1.7.2.jar:\
            /usr/local/lib/slf4j-nop-1.7.2.jar
            *.java gen-java/*.java
Note: Some input files use unchecked or unsafe operations.
Note: Recompile with -Xlint:unchecked for details.
$ java -cp /usr/local/lib/libthrift-1.0.0.jar:\
            /usr/local/lib/slf4j-api-1.7.2.jar:\
            /usr/local/lib/slf4j-nop-1.7.2.jar:\
            gen-java:\
            .
            MultiServiceServer
[Server] press enter to shutdown>
Call count: 1
Call count: 2
Call count: 3

[Server] shutting down...
[Server] down, exiting
$
```

Clients using multiplexed servers must be modified to support multiplexing. The following listing demonstrates a simple client for our multiplexed server.

Listing 10.20 ~/thriftbook/part2/servers/multiservice/MultiServiceClient.java

```
import org.apache.thrift.TException;
import org.apache.thrift.protocol.TProtocol;
import org.apache.thrift.protocol.TJSONProtocol;
import org.apache.thrift.protocol.TMultiplexedProtocol;
import org.apache.thrift.transport.TSocket;
import org.apache.thrift.transport.TFramedTransport;
import org.apache.thrift.transport.TTransport;

public class MultiServiceClient {
  public static void main(String[] args) throws TException {
    TTransport trans =
        new TFramedTransport(new TSocket("localhost", 8585));    ❶
    TProtocol proto = new TJSONProtocol (trans);

    TMultiplexedProtocol msgMProto =
        new TMultiplexedProtocol(proto, "Message");
    Message.Client msgClient = new Message.Client(msgMProto);    ❷
    TMultiplexedProtocol timeMProto =
        new TMultiplexedProtocol(proto, "ServerTime");
    ServerTime.Client timeClient = new ServerTime.Client(timeMProto);
```

```
      trans.open();
      String line;
      do {
         System.out.println("Message from server: " + msgClient.motd());
         System.out.println("Time at server: " +
                          timeClient.time_at_server((short)-1));
         System.out.println("Enter to continue, 'q' to quit: ");
         line = System.console().readLine();
      } while (0 != line.compareToIgnoreCase("q"));
   }
}
```
❸

This client is like most clients, with a few differences. The first adjustment is the addition of the TFramedTransport to the I/O stack ❶. Non-blocking server clients must always use a framing layer.

The next adjustment relates to the multiplexing feature ❷. Here we wrap the normal protocol (TJSONProtocol in this case, corresponding to the server's protocol selection) in a multiplexed protocol for each of the services we want to reach. Multiplexed clients can only communicate with multiplexed servers. By the same token, normal clients cannot communicate with multiplexed servers. However, a multiplexed client need only support the services it's interested in. For example, if the server supports 50 multiplexed services and the client is only interested in three of them, the client only needs to create multiplexed protocols for the services it will call.

Once the multiplexed protocols are created, a standard service client can be created using the appropriate multiplexed protocol. As you may have noticed during the server code review, the multiplexed processor and protocol objects are given string names representing the service in question. These strings, Message and ServerTime in this case, are the service keys and may not be duplicated on a given server. Best practice is to use the service name as the string key; however, anything will work as long as it's unique on the server and the client and server keys match exactly. These names are passed on the wire with each request, so many users prefer to make them short.

The final bit of code in the client calls the functions of the two services and displays the results ❸. The following code shows a client session with the previous server:

```
$ java -cp /usr/local/lib/libthrift-1.0.0.jar:\
          /usr/local/lib/slf4j-api-1.7.2.jar:\
          /usr/local/lib/slf4j-nop-1.7.2.jar:\
          gen-java:\
          .
          MultiServiceClient
Message from server: Childhood is a short season
Time at server: server time: 12:28:35
Enter to continue, 'q' to quit:
q
$
```

Summary

This chapter covered the most important Apache Thrift server features and concepts. Part 3 of this book extends the server discussion to include language-specific servers and features.

Here are the key points from this chapter:

- Each language has its own strengths and weaknesses impacting server design and implementation.
- Server concurrency is a complex subject and many processing models are represented by the Apache Thrift server library.
- Apache Thrift servers supply either connection-based or task-based (RPC call) processing models.
- Factories are used by servers to generate transports, protocols, processors, handlers, and threads in response to client requests.
- RPC clients and servers maintain separate input and output protocols and transport layers above the network endpoint.
- Users can define many possible I/O processing paths using built-in and custom transports and factories.
- Handlers are per server by default but can be generated per connection by supplying servers with a processor and handler factory.
- Server events allow user code to intercept client connect, disconnect, and processing events in a service-independent fashion.
- Non-blocking servers require clients to use a framing transport layer.
- A single server and port can host many services by using multiplexed processors.
- Multiplexed services can only communicate with clients that use multiplexed protocols.

Part 3

Apache Thrift languages

Apache Thrift provides native support for a wide range of programming languages, making it possible to connect clients and servers from almost any language seamlessly. However, every programming language has its own unique characteristics and ecosystem.

Part 3 of this book provides a jumpstart for a wide range of languages and environments commonly used with Apache Thrift. Each chapter provides everything you need to get going with the language(s) in question, including instructions for installing the necessary Apache Thrift language libraries and guidelines for building a basic client and server. This part opens with the big three backend languages: C++, Java/JVM, and C#/.Net. These are followed by JavaScript coverage for the server side and the browser side. The scripting chapter covers Python, Perl, PHP, and Ruby. The final chapter provides an overarching retrospective that considers Apache Thrift's place in modern cloud-based enterprise development, exploring messaging, performance, best practices, and more.

This part of the book is augmented on the web with web chapters covering additional languages such as Haxe, Rust, and Go.

Building clients
and servers with C++

This chapter covers

- Configuring Apache Thrift for C++ development
- Building C++ RPC clients and servers with Apache Thrift
- Understanding the features of the Apache Thrift C++ library
- Maximizing Apache Thrift C++ performance

The C++ programming language is one of the core Apache Thrift languages, generally considered the reference implementation for cross-language compatibility testing. Many developers use C++ due to the performance of the executables it produces. Apache Thrift makes it easy to build distributed applications that integrate the performance of C++ services with clients coded in a variety of languages.

In this chapter, we'll begin our Apache Thrift C++ exploration with a look at the C++ library's dependencies and build process on several platforms. Next we'll look at a simple RPC client and server to get familiar with the basics. Then we'll review the features of the Apache Thrift C++ library and its architecture, and finish up with an advanced non-blocking server example.

11.1 Setting up Apache Thrift for C++ development

Apache Thrift C++ setup is a little more complex than configuration for other languages. We pay this price in trade for the ability to create fast, memory-efficient, native programs.

As a first step in the setup process we need to decide how to use the Apache Thrift C++ library code. We have three options:

- Shared libraries
- Static libraries
- Source

The Apache Thrift C++ source code can be built into shared or static libraries and then dynamically or statically linked with an application. The Apache Thrift build system emits `.so` shared libraries and `.a` static libraries on *nix systems. On Windows, only static library support is supplied. If you're containerizing your services, static libraries are probably best because you probably can't (or won't want to) share the shared `lib` across containers, and the shared `lib` contains all of the core C++ library code, whether you're using it or not.

Another possible approach is to include the necessary Apache Thrift C++ sources in your project build, compiling them directly into your executable. The end result is a statically linked executable, much like the static library case. The difference is that you'll need to configure, include, and compile the Apache Thrift sources in every new project you create. This is more effort than building a static or dynamic library, but it does simplify source debugging and linking because you don't need to configure tools to locate libs and sources external to your project, nor do you need to create separate debug and release versions of the Apache Thrift libraries. Compiling the required sources into your project is a good option if you want to dig into the Apache Thrift source or if you're at an impasse trying to build libs on a particular platform. In this chapter, we'll focus on building the Apache Thrift C++ sources into libraries.

Apache Thrift tries to avoid dependencies whenever possible. Each additional dependency creates a burden for all users, whether they directly require the dependency or not. For this reason, the base Apache Thrift C++ library doesn't include support for event-based, non-blocking I/O, zlib compression, or Qt servers. These features can be built into their own extension libraries if required. Here's a list of the full suite of Apache Thrift C++ libraries as of v0.11:

- *libthrift*—Base features (complete solutions can be built with this)
- *libthriftnb*—Non-blocking support via `libevent`, used by the `TNonblocking-Server`
- *libthriftz*—Compression support via `zlib`, used by `TZlibTransport`
- *libthriftqt*—Qt4 server support used by the `TQTcpServer`
- *libthriftqt5*—Qt5 server support used by the `TQTcpServer`

The Apache Thrift build system will create all the libraries for which the dependencies are met on the build machine. For example, those who want to use the Apache Thrift non-blocking server need to have the `libevent` framework installed prior to building. In our build discussion, we'll create each of these libraries in turn.

11.1.1 Apache Thrift C++ versions and Boost

At the time of this writing, most Apache Thrift C++ libraries have migrated from the original C++98 code to C++11 (typically with backward-compatible support). To make C++98 workable, the Apache Thrift libraries depended on Boost, a robust set of extensions to core C++. Therefore, to build C++ applications with Apache Thrift 0.10.0 and earlier you'll need to install Boost:

- Apache Thrift <= 0.10.0: C++98, Boost required
- Apache Thrift >= 0.11.0: C++11, Boost not required

The most prevalent Boost dependency in Apache Thrift <= v0.10.0 is `boost::shared_ptr`, which is header-based. Multithreaded Apache Thrift servers may use `boost::thread` as well, which requires a compiled Boost library.

Boost is a feeder platform for the C++ standards body. The second C++ standard, C++11, includes virtual replicas of `boost::shared_ptr` and `boost::thread` in the form of `std::shared_ptr` and `std::thread`. If you're using the latest version of Apache Thrift, you can safely skip Boost installation if you like and use the `std lib` versions of things.

INSTALLING BOOST

Many platforms provide package managers that make installing Boost easy; however, package managers frequently provide older versions of Boost. Apache Thrift 0.9.2, 0.9.3, and 0.10.0 require Boost 1.53.0+, though older versions of Apache Thrift will work with older versions of Boost. If you're going to install Boost, you might as well install the latest version unless you have a specific reason not to. The Boost website (boost.org) lists the current Boost version, and the big red "Get Boost" button will allow you to download the latest.

> **NOTE** The Apache Thrift IDL compiler, though written in C++, has never had a dependency on Boost and can be built without installing Boost, regardless of your Apache Thrift version.

The following is a brief example session setting up Boost 1.65.1 from source on a new install Ubuntu 16.04 system:

```
thrift@ubuntu:~$ sudo apt-get update; sudo apt-get install g++ wget      ❶
thrift@ubuntu:~$ wget
➥ http://sourceforge.net/projects/boost/files/boost/1.65.1/boost_1_65_1.tar.gz ❷
...
thrift@ubuntu:~$ tar xvf boost_1_65_1.tar.gz      ❸
...
thrift@ubuntu:~$ cd boost_1_65_1
```

```
thrift@ubuntu:~/boost_1_65_1$ ./bootstrap.sh
...
thrift@ubuntu:~/boost_1_65_1$ sudo ./b2 install
...
```

To set up Boost, first update the package indexes and install a couple of tools, wget to download the Boost archive and the GNU C++ compiler (G++) to build the Boost libraries ❶. Next we download ❷ and extract ❸ the Boost archive. Finally, we build and install Boost ❹ using the b2 Boost build tool. The boost libraries are installed in /usr/local/lib and the headers (.hpp) are installed in the /usr/local/include/boost directory on Ubuntu 14.04 and 16.04. An approach similar to this will work on most systems, including Windows. See the Boost website for more information.

If you prefer to install from packages, as of the time of this writing, you can install Boost 1.55 from packages on Ubuntu 14.04:

```
thrift@ubuntu:~$ sudo apt-get install libboost1.55-all-dev
```

On Ubuntu 16.04 you can install 1.58 from packages:

```
thrift@ubuntu:~$ sudo apt-get install libboost1.58-all-dev
```

On RHEL/Centos 7 systems you can install Boost 1.53 from packages with Yum:

```
[thrift@localhost ~]$ sudo yum install boost-devel
```

On 64-bit RHEL/Centos 7 systems, Boost libraries are installed in /usr/lib64 and headers are installed in /usr/include/boost.

11.1.2 *Building Apache Thrift C++ libraries*

Before we can create our first Apache Thrift application in C++ we need to build at least the libthrift library. The standard way to build Apache Thrift C++ libraries depends on the version of Apache Thrift you're using. Prior to version 0.11.0, the GNU build system (also known as Autotools) was the standard build system. After Apache Thrift v0.11.0, the CMake platform became the preferred build system. The next few examples build the Apache Thrift C++ libraries using Autotools, supported by all Apache Thrift versions as of this writing. We'll also demonstrate a CMake build at the end of this section for users working with newer versions of Apache Thrift.

BUILDING APACHE THRIFT C++ LIBRARIES ON UBUNTU 14.04 AND 16.04

The Apache Thrift C++ library build process is similar on most *nix systems. The following code builds Apache Thrift C++ libraries on a base Ubuntu 14.04 or 16.04 system:

```
thrift@ubuntu:~$ sudo apt-get install git libtool flex bison pkg-config
                                g++ libssl-dev automake make          ❶
...
thrift@ubuntu:~$ git clone https://github.com/apache/thrift          ❷
```

```
...
thrift@ubuntu:~$ cd thrift
thrift@ubuntu:~/thrift$ ./bootstrap.sh          ❸
...
thrift@ubuntu:~/thrift$ ./configure CPPFLAGS='-O2' CFLAGS='' CXXFLAGS=''      ❹
...
thrift@ubuntu:~/thrift$ make          ❺
...
thrift@ubuntu:~/thrift$ sudo make install      ❻
...
```

The previous session begins by installing the Git source code control system and the necessary build tools ❶. Next you use Git to copy the Apache Thrift source tree from GitHub to the local machine ❷. The Apache Thrift github.com source repository is a mirror of the official ASF hosted repository; however, it's the primary work place used by the community and is almost always current. You can also download the most recent release of the source in tarball format from the Apache Thrift website download page (thrift.apache.org/download).

The `bootstrap.sh` script prepares the build tools for use ❸, and the configure command customizes the make files based on settings and the local system configuration ❹. The `make` command ❺ builds the Apache Thrift libraries in thrift/lib/ cpp/.libs and `sudo make install` ❻ installs the libraries in /usr/local/lib. The install also copies Apache Thrift headers to /usr/local/include/thrift.

The configure command used here optimizes the libraries for release using the -O2 switch. The CPPFLAGS (C preprocessor) settings apply to all build operations. Adding empty strings for CFLAGS (C compiler flags) and CXXFLAGS (C++ compiler flags) turns off default switches for C and C++ compilations.

This build generates the base Apache Thrift C++ libthrift.a static library and the libthrift.so shared library. Also, because this distribution includes zlib support in the base OS install, the libthriftz.a and libthriftz.so libraries will be generated.

GENERATING DEBUGGING INFORMATION
To generate libraries for debugging, you can change to the debugging optimization level and enable debugging symbols with a configure command something like this:

```
thrift@ubuntu:~/thrift$ ./configure CPPFLAGS='-Og -g' CFLAGS='' CXXFLAGS=''
```

USING ALTERNATE COMPILERS
The examples here use the GNU Compiler Collection (GCC), though you can select your preferred compiler using the CC and CXX variables. For example, to use Clang (clang.llvm.org) you might add the following configure switches (along with the desired optimization switches):

```
thrift@ubuntu:~/thrift$ ./configure CC=/usr/bin/clang CXX=/usr/bin/clang++
```

BUILDING APACHE THRIFT C++ LIBRARIES ON CENTOS 7

Building Apache Thrift on other Linux flavors is essentially the same as the Ubuntu process. Packages often have different names across package managers however. For example, the following code shows a session building Apache Thrift libraries on a base Centos 7 system:

```
[thrift@localhost ~]$ sudo yum -y groupinstall "Development Tools"
...
[thrift@localhost ~]$ sudo yum -y install openssl-devel
...
[thrift@localhost ~]$ git clone https://github.com/apache/thrift
...
[thrift@localhost ~]$ cd thrift
[thrift@localhost thrift]$ ./bootstrap.sh
...
[thrift@localhost thrift]$ ./configure CPPFLAGS='-O2' CFLAGS='' CXXFLAGS=''
...
[thrift@localhost thrift]$ make
...
[thrift@localhost thrift]$ sudo make install
...
```

This session follows the same steps as the Ubuntu session, though with different packages. RHEL-based systems offer a Developer Tools group install that installs a wide array of common developer tools, including the GNU build system, g++, Git, and many other packages. If installation size or download time is a concern, you can slim the installation down considerably by installing only the packages you need. The Developer Tools bundle doesn't include openssl, which is added separately here.

> **NOTE** Few Apache Thrift C++ sources use openssl (for example, TSSLSocket and TSSLServerSocket). If you're not using SSL-specific features you can eliminate the SSL dependency by removing the TSSL* sources from the build.

BUILDING APACHE THRIFT C++ LIBRARIES WITH CMAKE

Building the Apache Thrift C++ libraries with CMake is much like building with Autotools. To use the CMake build system, you'll need to install the appropriate dependencies and the CMake package. The following shows an example session building Apache Thrift on a newly installed Ubuntu 16.04 base server:

```
thrift@ubuntu:~$ sudo apt-get install git cmake flex bison g++ libssl-dev
                                       libboost1.58-all-dev libevent-dev
...
thrift@ubuntu:~$ git clone https://github.com/apache/thrift
...
thrift@ubuntu:~$ cd thrift
thrift@ubuntu:~/thrift$ cmake .
...
thrift@ubuntu:~/thrift$ make
...
thrift@ubuntu:~/thrift$ sudo make install
...
```

The make command builds the C++ libraries in the thrift/lib directory and the make install command copies headers to /usr/local/include and libraries to /usr/local/lib, as in the Autotools build.

At the time of this writing, Centos 7 default package repositories install CMake 2.8.11; however Apache Thrift requires 2.8.12. To install version 2.8.12 you can use the following commands:

```
$ wget http://www.cmake.org/files/v2.8/cmake-2.8.12.tar.gz
$ tar xzf cmake-2.8.12.tar.gz
$ cd cmake-2.8.12
$ ./configure
$ make
$ sudo make install
```

If an older version of CMake is installed you may want to uninstall it first to avoid version conflicts. You'll need to yum install wget if it isn't present prior to executing the previous commands.

ADDING NON-BLOCKING SERVER SUPPORT
Perhaps the most scalable prebuilt server in the Apache Thrift C++ library is the TNonblockingServer. This server is built into the libthriftnb library that depends on libevent (libevent.org). To install libevent on Ubuntu 14.04 and 16.04:

```
thrift@ubuntu:~/thrift$ sudo apt-get install -y libevent-dev
```

To install libevent on Centos 7:

```
[thrift@localhost ~]$ sudo yum -y install libevent-devel
```

> **NOTE** You'll need to rerun the configure command to generate a new configuration any time you add system components that will impact the build (such as libevent). You should also run make clean before running make install on successive builds to ensure that sources are completely rebuilt following any configuration changes.

ADDING QT SUPPORT
Qt is a cross-platform C++ application and UI development framework. Apache Thrift provides a Qt-based server implementation that depends on the Qt libraries.

On Ubuntu 14.04 and 16.04 you can install the "qt-sdk" package to enable Qt 4 and 5 support. On Centos 7 you can install the "qt-devel" package to enable Qt 4 support.

COMPLETE LIBRARY LISTING
While few require all the Apache Thrift C++ libraries, it's possible to build the full suite on a single system, as shown in the following session. A complete C++ library build will install the following library files:

```
  881863 /usr/local/lib/libthrift-1.0.0-dev.so
 1952480 /usr/local/lib/libthrift.a
    1022 /usr/local/lib/libthrift.la
  170927 /usr/local/lib/libthriftnb-1.0.0-dev.so
  363992 /usr/local/lib/libthriftnb.a
    1036 /usr/local/lib/libthriftnb.la
      24 /usr/local/lib/libthriftnb.so -> libthriftnb-1.0.0-dev.so
   76641 /usr/local/lib/libthriftqt-1.0.0-dev.so
   81320 /usr/local/lib/libthriftqt5-1.0.0-dev.so
  115598 /usr/local/lib/libthriftqt5.a
    1066 /usr/local/lib/libthriftqt5.la
      25 /usr/local/lib/libthriftqt5.so -> libthriftqt5-1.0.0-dev.so
  110720 /usr/local/lib/libthriftqt.a
    1057 /usr/local/lib/libthriftqt.la
      24 /usr/local/lib/libthriftqt.so -> libthriftqt-1.0.0-dev.so
      22 /usr/local/lib/libthrift.so -> libthrift-1.0.0-dev.so
   63263 /usr/local/lib/libthriftz-1.0.0-dev.so
   92152 /usr/local/lib/libthriftz.a
    1029 /usr/local/lib/libthriftz.la
      23 /usr/local/lib/libthriftz.so -> libthriftz-1.0.0-dev.so
```

APACHE THRIFT LIB VERSIONS

The code session in the previous section was built using the latest commit at the time on the master branch of the Apache Thrift source tree, evident by the -dev suffix on all the libraries. The make install process creates unversioned links to the last installation added to the system, allowing users to link to "thrift" rather than "thrift-1.0.0-dev". As new installations are performed, the symbolic links are automatically updated.

Multiple versions of Apache Thrift can be installed; however, only the shared libraries of previous versions will persist. For example, the following code snippet shows a system where v1.0 dev libraries were installed, followed by the installation of v0.9.2 libraries:

```
thrift@ubuntu:~/thrift$ ls -l /usr/local/lib/libthrift*
-rwxr-xr-x   872068 Jun 22 06:54 libthrift-0.9.2.so
-rwxr-xr-x   857893 Jun 20 01:43 libthrift-1.0.0-dev.so
-rw-r--r-- 1973190 Jun 22 06:54 libthrift.a
-rwxr-xr-x     1010 Jun 22 06:54 libthrift.la
lrwxrwxrwx       18 Jun 22 06:54 libthrift.so -> libthrift-0.9.2.so
```

This installation offers both 0.9.2 and 1.0.0-dev shared libraries, but new application builds will link with libthrift-0.9.2. You can examine the library's .la file for more details; for example:

```
$ cat /usr/local/lib/libthrift.la | grep -B1 dlname
# The name that we can dlopen(3).
dlname='libthrift-0.9.2.so'
```

You can use the ldd command to see which shared libraries an existing executable is linked to, as shown in the following code:

```
thrift@ubuntu:~/ThriftBook/part3/cpp/simple$ ldd client
    linux-vdso.so.1 =>  (0x00007fff4e1fe000)
    libthrift-0.9.2.so => /usr/local/lib/libthrift-0.9.2.so
    libstdc++.so.6 => /usr/lib/x86_64-linux-gnu/libstdc++.so.6
    libgcc_s.so.1 => /lib/x86_64-linux-gnu/libgcc_s.so.1
    libc.so.6 => /lib/x86_64-linux-gnu/libc.so.6
    libssl.so.1.0.0 => /lib/x86_64-linux-gnu/libssl.so.1.0.0
    libcrypto.so.1.0.0 => /lib/x86_64-linux-gnu/libcrypto.so.1.0.0
    libpthread.so.0 => /lib/x86_64-linux-gnu/libpthread.so.0
    libm.so.6 => /lib/x86_64-linux-gnu/libm.so.6
                /lib64/ld-linux-x86-64.so.2
    libdl.so.2 => /lib/x86_64-linux-gnu/libdl.so.2
```

NOTE   If you receive an error of the form, "error while loading shared libraries: libthrift-0.9.2.so: cannot open shared object file: No such file or directory" on a Linux system, it may be because the build process failed to update the shared library cache. This can be fixed in most cases by rerunning the dynamic linker configuration tool:

```
thrift@ubuntu:~ $ sudo ldconfig
```

In production scenarios, you may want to use a specific release of Apache Thrift for stability. To build a version other than the development tip, you can check out the desired version of the source before building. For example, to display the tagged versions and then check out code to build Apache Thrift libraries for v0.9.2, you would use the `git` commands shown in the following code:

```
thrift@ubuntu:~/thrift$ git tag
0.10.0
0.2.0
0.3.0
0.4.0
0.5.0
0.6.0
0.6.1
0.7.0
0.8.0
0.9.0
0.9.1
0.9.2
0.9.3
thrift@ubuntu:~/thrift$ git checkout 0.9.2 .
```

The `git tag` command displays the defined tags and the `git checkout` command allows you to check out the files at the desired commit. Once checked out you can build the source tree as normal. To switch back to the most recent commit (-dev), check out the master branch (for example, $ `git checkout master .`). Note that the "." supplied at the end of the `checkout` command tells `git` to update the current working directory and its subdirectories with the files at the desired commit; this command must be executed from the root directory of the thrift tree and will overwrite existing changes. For more help with Git see the Git website (git-scm.com).

APACHE THRIFT C++ LIBRARY TESTS

In either an Autotools or CMake environment, you can build and run the Apache Thrift internal unit tests with the `make check` command. When run from the Thrift root, this command will test all configured libraries. To test only the C++ library, you can change directories to thrift/lib/cpp in the source tree and then run `make check`. To run the cross-language test suite you can use the `make  cross` command from the root of the source tree.

11.1.3 *Building Apache Thrift C++ libraries on Windows*

There are several ways to build Apache Thrift C++ libraries on Windows. The preferred approach is to use Visual Studio. Optionally, you can build the C++ libraries under Cygwin or MinGW. The Apache Thrift website has fairly complete instructions for Cygwin and MinGW builds. This section outlines the Visual Studio build process.

The Apache Thrift source tree includes a Visual Studio solution file (see figure 11.1) to build the Apache Thrift libs on Windows. The solution file is located in the thrift/lib/cpp directory and is called thrift.sln. You can open the solution file in Visual Studio using the File > Open > Project/Solution… command.

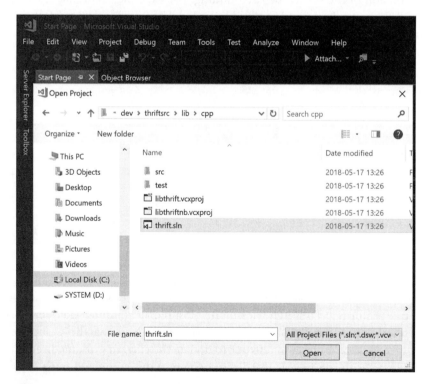

Figure 11.1   Visual Studio Thrift solutions file

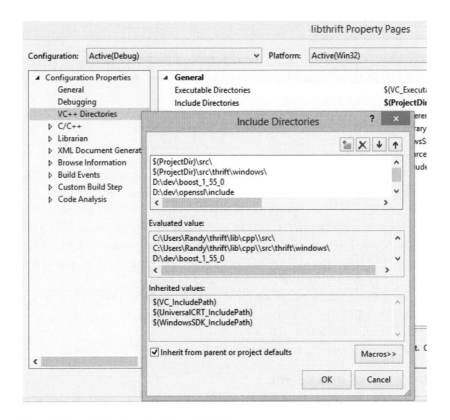

Figure 11.2   Adding Boost and OpenSSL paths

Before you can build the libthrift.lib C++ library you'll need to install Boost (>=1.53), unless you're building version 0.11.0+. If you require SSL support, you'll also need to install OpenSSL. If you won't need SSL, you can remove the corresponding .h and .cpp SSL files from the source folders in the project explorer and build the library without OpenSSL.

Visual Studio needs to know where to find any required external libraries. You can configure the Boost and OpenSSL include paths in the project properties dialog (see figure 11.2) by right-clicking the libthrift project in the Solution Explorer and choosing Properties. You can configure these settings per configuration (Debug/Release) and platform (Win32/x64) or for all configurations and platforms by adjusting the combo boxes at the top of the dialog box.

When properly configured you can right click the libthrift project in the Solution Explorer and choose "Build" to create the libthrift.lib static library (see figure 11.3). The library will be written to disk in the appropriate directory for the configuration and platform type selected. For example, an x64 Release build will create thrift\lib\cpp\x64\Release\libthrift.lib. The libthrift project properties dialog allows the configuration type to be changed to DLL, but no exports support packaging the Apache Thrift library as a DLL at present.

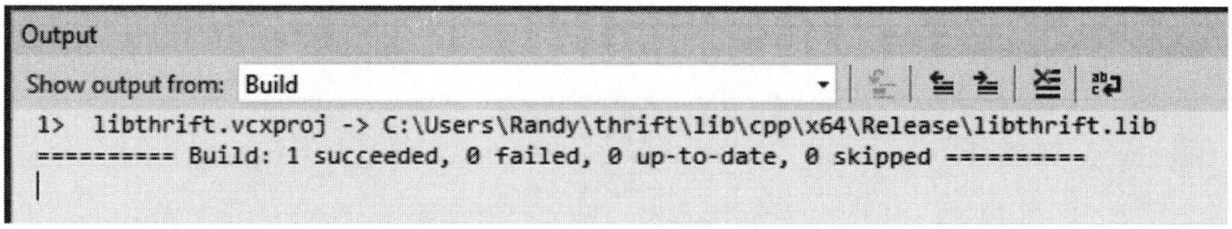

Figure 11.3   Building libthrift.lib on Windows

The Visual Studio solution also includes a project to build libthriftnb.lib, housing the TNonblockingServer. Before building libthriftnb.lib you'll need to install and build Libevent (libevent.org), which the non-blocking server uses to manage socket events. Libevent provides excellent performance in cross-platform *nix settings, but falls back to the select API on Windows. If you're interested in extreme scale and performance on Windows, you might consider writing a custom Windows server using IO Completion Ports. Otherwise, the stock non-blocking server running on Windows is no slouch and is probably the best choice for highly scaled loads.

The provided Visual Studio solution doesn't include projects for libthriftz or the Qt libraries. Both libraries can be built on Windows, but you have to create your own Visual Studio project configs at present.

Now that you have Apache Thrift set up for C++ development, let's get to it.

11.2   A simple client and server

In part 3 of this book we begin each chapter with a simple Hello World RPC application. All part 3 chapters share the same Hello World IDL, allowing us to test any Hello World client with any Hello World server, regardless of programming language.

11.2.1   The Hello IDL

The helloSvc interface used with the Hello World application accepts a name string and returns a greeting. The IDL source appears in the following listing.

> **Listing 11.1   ~/ThriftBook/part3/cpp/simple/hello.thrift**

```
service helloSvc {
    string getMessage(1: string name)
}
```

To generate C++ client/server stubs for our helloSvc IDL, we can use the thrift compiler with the following command line:

```
thrift@ubuntu:~/ThriftBook/part3/cpp/simple$ thrift --gen cpp hello.thrift
```

Compiling the hello IDL file produces several C++ source files in the gen-cpp directory:

```
thrift@ubuntu:~/ThriftBook/part3/cpp/simple$ ls -l gen-cpp
total 44
-rw-rw-r-- 1 thrift thrift  251 Jun 22 09:19 hello_constants.cpp        ❶
-rw-rw-r-- 1 thrift thrift  333 Jun 22 09:19 hello_constants.h
-rw-rw-r-- 1 thrift thrift 9328 Jun 22 09:19 helloSvc.cpp
-rw-rw-r-- 1 thrift thrift 8432 Jun 22 09:19 helloSvc.h
-rw-rw-r-- 1 thrift thrift 1336 Jun 22 09:19 helloSvc_server.skeleton.cpp   ❸
-rw-rw-r-- 1 thrift thrift  239 Jun 22 09:19 hello_types.cpp
-rw-rw-r-- 1 thrift thrift  399 Jun 22 09:19 hello_types.h
```

❷
❹

The *_constants.* files ❶ house all of the constants defined within the IDL. We didn't
define any IDL constants, so these files will contain only boilerplate code. The
helloSvc.* files contain the support code required to build clients and servers using
the helloSvc interface ❷. The *_server.skeleton.cpp ❸ is a simple test server generated to give you a starting point when building your own servers. The *_types.* files ❹
house any user-defined types (UDTs) from the IDL; these will also contain boilerplate
code, because the IDL doesn't declare any UDTs. For complete coverage of the Apache
Thrift IDL, see chapter 6.

11.2.2 Building a simple C++ client

Now that we have our helloSvc client and server stubs generated, we can create a simple RPC client program to use the interface. The Apache Thrift C++ generator has created a skeleton server for our service that we can test our client against. The code for
our C++ RPC client appears in the following listing.

Listing 11.2   ~/ThriftBook/part3/cpp/simple/hello_client.cpp

```cpp
❶ #include "gen-cpp/helloSvc.h"                            ❷
  #include <thrift/transport/TSocket.h>           ◄───┘
  #include <thrift/transport/TBufferTransports.h>              ❸
  #include <thrift/protocol/TBinaryProtocol.h>            ❹
❺ #include <memory>
  #include <iostream>              ❻

  using namespace apache::thrift::transport;      ❼
  using namespace apache::thrift::protocol;
❽ using std::shared_ptr;
  using std::make_shared;

  int main() {
      shared_ptr<TTransport> trans;
      trans = make_shared<TSocket>("localhost", 9090);       ❾
      trans = make_shared<TBufferedTransport>(trans);
❿     auto proto = make_shared<TBinaryProtocol>(trans);
      helloSvcClient client(proto);        ◄───┐
                                               ⓫
⓬     try {
          trans->open();          ⓭
⓮         std::string msg;
```

```
        client.getMessage(msg, "world!");        ⑮
        std::cout << msg << std::endl;
⑯   } catch(...) {
        std::cout << "Client caught an exception" << std::endl;
    }
    trans->close();              ⑰
}
```

The code begins by including various dependencies listed in most local to most global order. Listing headers in this order ensures that local headers are independent and don't nondeterministically rely on features included (or not included) by previously included headers. An Apache Thrift application will commonly have several distinct groups of headers:

- Hand-coded, application-specific headers
- IDL-generated, application-specific headers
- Apache Thrift-specific headers
- Third-party library headers (for example, Boost headers)
- C++ standard headers

We haven't created any project-specific headers, so the first header in the list is the Thrift-generated header for the hello service interface ❶. The hello world example demonstrates the use of an I/O stack consisting of

- TSocket
- TBufferedTransport
- TBinaryProtocol

The Apache Thrift TSocket transport provides TCP communications and is defined in TSocket.h ❷. The C++ implementation of the TSocket transport writes bytes directly to the network as it receives them. To ensure that we only write complete messages to the network, we need to add a buffering layer, implemented by TBufferredTransport in the TBufferTransports.h header ❸. The TBinaryProtocol is the default Apache Thrift protocol for most servers, performing cross-platform/language serialization ❹. Apache Thrift headers are installed on the system's standard header path under a directory called Thrift by default. Subdirectories are used to segregate headers by transport, protocol, server, and so on.

This application is coded for Apache Thrift >= 0.11.0 and uses std shared_ptr and make_shared smart pointer templates, which are defined in the standard memory header ❺. The final header, iostream, allows us to log output to the console ❻.

The next block of code includes several using statements. Apache Thrift C++ components are housed in namespaces that reflect the path to the sources. The first two using statements are directives which make Apache Thrift transport and protocol namespaces available in the current scope ❼. This allows us to refer to TSocket directly, without the apache::thrift::transport namespace prefix.

The second pair of using statements are declarations specifying the source for shared_ptr and make_shared in the current scope ❽. By writing all our code with unscoped `shared_ptr` and `make_shared` templates, we can easily switch from Boost to std `shared_ptr` and `make_shared`.

The `main()` function in our client program creates an Apache Thrift I/O stack, constructs a `helloSvc` client with the I/O stack, and then calls the `getMessage()` function on the server. The transport stack consists of a `TSocket` and a `TBufferedTransport` ❾. In this example, the `trans` identifier is a smart pointer to the top of the transport stack. The endpoint transport, a `TSocket`, gets initialized with the host and port to connect to, though the connection isn't established until we call `open()` on the transport stack ⓭. See chapter 4 for detailed information on Apache Thrift transports.

The serialization protocol always sits at the top of the I/O stack. In this example, a `TBinaryProtocol` instance is initialized with the top of the transport stack ❿. For detailed information on protocols, see chapter 5.

The completed I/O stack is used to initialize our `helloSvc` client ⓫. The `helloSvcClient` class is found in the `helloSvc.h` header and was generated from the `helloSvc` service declaration in our hello.thrift IDL file.

Up to this point the code hasn't done anything particularly dangerous; however, the next block of code opens the transport stack ⓭. This will cause the socket transport to attempt to connect to the designated host, which involves networking, a great source of nondeterministic behavior. To protect networking code from unforeseen network issues, it's a good idea to use `try` blocks and appropriate `catch` statements ⓬.

The operable block of code in this example is the bit that makes the RPC call to the server ⓯. The first thing you may notice about the RPC call is that the service definition for `getMessage()` indicates that it returns a `string`, but the code expects `void`. What gives?

C++ functions cannot safely return references to temporary objects, and copying objects housing dynamically managed resources, like `strings`, can be expensive in C++98. The Apache Thrift code generator builds stubs that require complex return types to be passed as out parameters, avoiding the performance hit. The code here passes in an empty `string` called `msg` to receive the response from the `get-Message()` call ⓮.

The `catch`-all statement at the end of the `main()` function ⓰ will trap any exceptions that might be raised should the `open()` or `getMessage()` calls fail. Following the success or failure of the program, we close the transport, which closes the TCP connection ⓱.

To test the client, we can build and run the `hello_client.cpp` source and the generated skeleton server. Here's an example session building both the client and the skeleton server:

```
thrift@ubuntu:~/ThriftBook/part3/cpp/simple$ g++ -o client        ❶
                              hello_client.cpp gen-cpp/helloSvc.cpp    ❷
                    ❸        -Wall -std=c++11
                              -lthrift            ❹
```

```
thrift@ubuntu:~/ThriftBook/part3/cpp/simple$ g++ -o server
              gen-cpp/helloSvc_server.skeleton.cpp gen-cpp/helloSvc.cpp
              -Wall -std=c++11
              -lthrift
```

The client build line uses the GNU G++ C++ compiler to compile an executable named `client` ❶. The build includes the source for the client and the generated client stub code for the `helloSvc` ❷. The `-Wall` switch turns on all warnings and the `-std` switch specifies that this source should be compiled as C++11 ❸.

> **NOTE**   Both C++98 and C++11 Apache Thrift library sources will compile without difficulty when using a C++11 compliant compiler and user code.

The build command requires information regarding library dependencies; passing the `-l` switch with the `thrift` parameter tells the linker to link the program with the installed version of libthrift.so ❹.

The skeleton server build command is nearly identical, substituting the skeleton server source for the client source. To test the application, we can run the server in one shell and then launch the client in another. For example, to run the server:

```
thrift@ubuntu:~/ThriftBook/part3/cpp/simple$ ./server
getMessage
```

Running the client in another shell will cause the server to output the name of the method called, `getMessage`:

```
thrift@ubuntu:~/ThriftBook/part3/cpp/simple$ ./client
```

While this session isn't super informative, we can determine that the client did call the server and didn't throw an exception. If you review the source code for the skeleton server, you'll see that it's in fact a skeleton, accepting calls but implementing no behavior. Let's build a more complete hello server.

11.2.3 *Creating a simple RPC server*

Using the generated skeleton server as a guide, we can easily build a simple server that receives a name from the client and returns a greeting string. An example C++ hello world server appears in the following listing.

> **Listing 11.3   ~/ThriftBook/part3/cpp/simple/hello_server.cpp**

```cpp
#include "gen-cpp/helloSvc.h"
#include <thrift/server/TSimpleServer.h>
#include <thrift/transport/TServerSocket.h>
#include <thrift/transport/TBufferTransports.h>
#include <thrift/protocol/TBinaryProtocol.h>
#include <memory>
#include <iostream>
```

```
using namespace ::apache::thrift::server;
using namespace ::apache::thrift::protocol;
using namespace ::apache::thrift::transport;
using std::shared_ptr;
using std::make_shared;

class helloSvcHandler : public helloSvcIf {           ❶
public:
    virtual void getMessage(std::string& _return,
                            const std::string& name) override {     ❷
        std::cout << "Server received: " << name          ❸
                  << ", from client" << std::endl;
        _return = "Hello " + name;
    }
};

int main() {
    auto handler = make_shared<helloSvcHandler>();        ❹
    auto proc = make_shared<helloSvcProcessor>(handler);   ❺

      auto trans_svr = make_shared<TServerSocket>(9090);          ❻
❼   auto trans_fac = make_shared<TBufferedTransportFactory>();
    auto proto_fac = make_shared<TBinaryProtocolFactory>();    ❽

    TSimpleServer server(proc, trans_svr, trans_fac, proto_fac);    ❾
    server.serve();
    return 0;
}
```

The server code begins with `include` and `using` statements similar to those found in the client. The first interesting bit of code is the `helloSvcHandler` declaration ❶. This class is the actual implementation of the `helloSvc`. The handler class is derived from the generated pure virtual `helloSvcIf` class. In this case, the handler implements the one method defined for the service, `getMessage()` ❷. Note that the C++11 "override" specifier is used here to ensure that we match the base class prototype. This is important because the generated server processor will not invoke the method in response to an RPC call if the signature isn't a match. Every IDL-defined method must be implemented by the handler. In this case the implementation for `getMessage()` is trivial ❸, printing out a console message on the server and returning a greeting string.

The `main()` function body configures the server instance. Apache Thrift server classes provide connection management and RPC request dispatch through IDL-generated server stubs. As demonstrated here, the Apache Thrift C++ code uses smart pointers to manage all the principal objects constructed to support RPC operations.

Most of the identifiers in the `main` function are declared with the `auto` keyword, alleviating the need to declare the long type names involved. The first object created is an instance of the handler defined to process client requests ❹. The second object declared is the IDL-generated processor for the `helloSvc` ❺. The processor is constructed with a reference to the handler it will invoke in response to client requests.

The next three lines of code set up the server's I/O stack. Because the I/O stack on the server and the client must be compatible, we must use the same endpoint and protocol that we used in the client program, TSocket and TBinaryProtocol, respectively. Because servers typically manage many client connections, the server needs a way to generate many I/O stacks. To meet this requirement Apache Thrift provides server-specific endpoint factories such as TServerSocket ❻. TServerSocket isn't an endpoint transport; rather, it's a listener/factory that generates new TSocket endpoints for each connecting client.

The server will also use a transport factory ❼ to generate all the layered transports to apply to the new client endpoint. The layered transport factory used here creates a TBufferedTransport for each new client TSocket.

The I/O stack is completed with a protocol generated by a protocol factory ❽. Every Apache Thrift C++ endpoint transport has a corresponding server transport, and every layered transport/protocol has a corresponding factory.

With the I/O stack defined, we can create a server instance. We have several C++ server types to choose from. In this example, we're using the TSimpleServer ❾, a basic, but suitable, server for testing. The server.serve() method places the server in an endless loop waiting for and servicing connections.

Here's a session building the new server and testing it with the existing client. The server side

```
thrift@ubuntu:~/ThriftBook/part3/cpp/simple$ g++ -o server
                            hello_server.cpp gen-cpp/helloSvc.cpp
                            -Wall -std=c++11 -lthrift
thrift@ubuntu:~/ThriftBook/part3/cpp/simple$ ./server
Server received: world!, from client
```

The client side

```
thrift@ubuntu:~/ThriftBook/part3/cpp/simple$ ./client
Hello world!
thrift@ubuntu:~/ThriftBook/part3/cpp/simple$
```

Now that we have a basic C++ client and server built, we can take a deeper look at the full range of features provided by the Apache Thrift C++ library.

11.3   *C++ transports, protocols, and servers*

As one of the original Apache Thrift supported languages, C++ has perhaps the most complete set of transports, protocols, and servers. In this section, we'll take a brief look at the various server components available to users.

11.3.1   *C++ transports*

Apache Thrift transports move bytes from one place to another. The TTransport class provides the base interface for all transport implementations (essentially the methods: open, close, read, write, and flush). The headers and implementation files for all C++ transports can be found in thrift/lib/cpp/src/thrift/transport. Each transport class, with several exceptions, has its own .h and .cpp files; for example, the source for TSocket can be found in TSocket.h and TSocket.cpp. Transports can be divided into endpoints and layers. We examine both types here.

C++ ENDPOINT TRANSPORTS

Apache Thrift endpoint transports perform I/O with a physical or logical device. Endpoint transports can be organized into three categories: those performing I/O with peers over a network, those performing I/O with files, and those performing I/O with memory. The C++ endpoint transports are summarized in table 11.1.

Table 11.1 C++ endpoint transports

Endpoint	Type	Factory	Base
TSocket	Network	TServerSocket	TVirtualTransport<TSocket>
TSSLSocket	Network	TSSLServerSocket	TSocket
TPipe	Network	TPipeServer	TVirtualTransport<TPipe>
TFDTransport	File		TVirtualTransport<TFDTransport>
TSimpleFileTransport	File		TFDTransport
TMemoryBuffer	Memory		TVirtualTransport<TMemoryBuffer, TBufferBase>

Table 11.1 lists the principle C++ endpoint transports. Each endpoint is listed with its type, its factory (if any), and its base class. We'll talk more about the TVirtualTransport and the transport class hierarchy shortly. For now, let's focus on the various concrete endpoint transports and their functions.

The first half of the endpoint transports listed in table 11.1 are network transports. Network transports are generally created directly on the client side, one for each desired connection, and indirectly on the server side. The classes that manage the allocation of network resources on a server (for example, TServerSocket, TPipeServer, and TSSLServerSocket) are tasked with the responsibility of generating endpoint transports for each new client connection the server receives. A single TServerSocket can generate a new TSocket for potentially thousands of clients on a busy server.

TSocket is the most used and interoperable endpoint transport for RPC. TSocket can connect over TCP network sockets and domain sockets on *nix systems.

The TSSLSocket endpoint adds TLS (Transport Layer Security) encryption to the basic socket functionality provided by TSocket. The TPipe endpoint performs I/O over named pipes on Windows. Windows-named pipes can be used for inter-process communications (IPC) and network communications. On non-Windows systems, TPipe is a typedef for TSocket. This causes TPipe on Linux to work but to be incompatible with

TPipe systems on Windows. It's perhaps clearer to avoid TPipe on non-Windows systems, using TSocket directly if that's what you mean to do.

The next two endpoint transports are file based. The TFDTransport will perform I/O against any provided file descriptor. The TSimpleFileTransport performs I/O against a named file system file. These transports don't have factories because they aren't designed for client/server RPC. Their principle purpose is serializing UDTs to and from disk.

The last transport is the TMemoryBuffer transport. Like the file transports it's not designed for direct client/server RPC. The memory transport is typically used to store a serialized message that can then be passed between threads or sent over a messaging system.

C++ endpoint transports often have additional transports layered on top of them. The next section introduces the various C++ layered transports.

C++ LAYERED TRANSPORTS

Layered transports are designed to overlay an existing transport or transport stack. Each layer above the endpoint performs an additional service during I/O processing. Certain layered transports mutate the data stream but others don't.

Non-mutating transport layers make no changes to the data stream. For example, the TBufferedTransport is a non-mutating transport; it buffers writes between message transmissions but doesn't change the data written. Non-mutating transports can be applied freely on a client or a server without impacting the peer system.

Mutating transports change the data stream. For a client to communicate successfully with a server, both parties must use the same endpoint and the same set of mutating layered transports, stacked in the same order. For example, the TFramedTransport adds a 32-bit message size prefix to each RPC message. If a server uses the TFramedTransport, all clients wishing to interact with that server must also use the TFramedTransport.

Table 11.2 lists the layered transports available, and their types, factories, and base classes.

Table 11.2   C++ layered transports

Layer	Type	Factory	Base
TBufferedTransport	NonM	TBufferedTransportFactory	TVirtualTransport<TBuffered Transport, TBufferBase>
TFramedTransport	Mut	TFramedTransportFactory	TVirtualTransport<TFramed Transport, TBufferBase>
THttpServer	Mut	THttpServerTransportFactory	THttpTransport
TZlibTransport	Mut	TZlibTransportFactory	TVirtualTransport<TZlibTran sport>

We used the `TBufferedTransport` in the hello world RPC program earlier in this chapter. If no other buffer is present, this class can be used to perform the critical task of buffering the many protocol writes necessary to create a single message.

The `TFramedTransport` is required when interacting with a `NonblockingServer`. The `TFramedTransport` adds a frame size (also known as message size) to the front of every message, making it possible for I/O threads reading from the network to dispatch entire messages to worker threads. This allows I/O threads to focus on network I/O, leaving worker threads to perform the expensive tasks of de-serializing and processing requests. The `TFramedTransport` layer provides its own buffering and shouldn't be used with the `TBufferedTransport` layer.

All the transports listed in table 11.2 can be found in .h/.cpp files named after the transport in the thrift/lib/cpp/src/thrift/transport directory. The exception is that the `TBufferedTransport`, `TFramedTransport`, and `TMemoryBuffer` transport are all found in the TBufferTransports.h/.cpp files.

The `THttpTransport` is a base class for the `THttpClient` and the `THttpServer` classes. This family of classes supports the HTTP client/server protocol layered over `TSocket`. The `THttpServerTransportFactory` can be passed to an Apache Thrift server as a layered transport factory to produce `THttpServer`-wrapped `TSockets`. Clients can connect to such a server using the `THttpClient` class (which also wraps a `TSocket`). The client/server asymmetry of HTTP requires separate layered transports for clients and servers. Due to the added overhead of HTTP, C++ applications tend only to use this set of transports when interfacing with preexisting HTTP-centric infrastructure. While there are no examples in the printed book, you can find a helloSvc HTTP client and server example in the book's GitHub repo here: Thrift-Book/part3/cpp/simple/ (http_client.cpp and http_server.cpp).

The `Zlib` transport provides high ratio compression in the I/O stack. Due to the overhead required to perform the compression, this is generally only valuable in scenarios where the size of a single message is large, many kilobytes to megabytes. This transport layer can be effective when serializing large UDTs to disk files or to memory buffers for transmission over messaging systems.

For more information on Apache Thrift transports and Zlib examples, see chapter 4.

11.3.2 C++ protocols

Protocols provide the means to serialize and de-serialize IDL types. Three principal protocols are supported across the Apache Thrift framework, all of which are available in the C++ library:

- *TBinaryProtocol*—Represents data fairly directly in binary form
- *TCompactProtocol*—Represents data in binary form compressing integer types
- *TJSONProtocol*—Represents data using JavaScript Object Notation

The reader and the writer in an Apache Thrift exchange must use the same serialization protocol. For more information on Apache Thrift protocols see chapter 5.

11.3.3 *Runtime versus compile time polymorphism*

The Apache Thrift C++ library provides two distinct ways for protocols to perform I/O against the transport stack. The first is dynamic (runtime) polymorphism. This approach involves the protocol calling TTransport class methods that then virtually call the correct implementation. The second is static polymorphism, wherein the protocol calls the correct transport method directly at runtime.

When a protocol writes to TTransport, the virtual call expense is paid with each write. To put this in perspective, a normal RPC call could involve as few as ten or as many as hundreds of incremental serialization operations involving the protocol reading/writing the transport stack. Though C++ compilers are good at function call optimization, they have almost no capacity to optimize virtual function calls. Such calls invoke functions through pointers and lookup tables (vtables) associated with types defined at runtime.

To address this issue, both the TBinaryProtocol and TCompactProtocol are implemented as templates, TBinaryProtocolT<Transport_> and TCompactProtocolT <Transport_>, respectively. These templates are parameterized at compile time with the transport type that they'll read/write. This allows the protocol to be statically bound to the correct transport type, avoiding virtual function calls and allowing the compiler to optimize the read and write operations more effectively.

In the hello world example, we used the TBinaryProtocol type, which is a typedef for TBinaryProtocolT<TTransport>. I/O calls invoking TTransport require a virtual function call at runtime. If the code used a TBinaryProtocolT<TBufferedTransport> protocol type, the write() calls would have invoked the correct TBufferedTransport implementation directly without a virtual call.

Figure 11.4 illustrates the different call paths taken by protocols using a two-layer transport stack, TBufferedTransport over TSocket. The figure shows the inheritance hierarchy for each transport in the transport stack. The second (bottom) protocol is statically bound to the TBufferedTransport, and the other (top) protocol is statically bound to the root TTransport implementation.

In this example, the NVI (Non-Virtual Interface) calls are handled directly by the type referenced by the protocol template, and the VI (Virtual Interface) calls use a *_virt() function to invoke the concrete implementation virtually. Protocols always call the NVI interface. However, if they're statically bound to TTransport, the TTransport NVI implementation calls the corresponding virtual method.

The TVirtualTransport class template provides all the necessary *_virt implementations, each of which calls the derived NVI method. Concrete transports can inherit from the TVirtualTransport template. The TVirtualTransport is parameterized with the type instantiating it. This is an example of the Curiously Reoccurring Template Pattern (google CRTP for more information), commonly used to implement static polymorphism behind an NVI.

As figure 11.4 illustrates, declaring your protocol as type TBinaryProtocol (which typedefs to TBinaryProtocolT<TTransport>) causes write requests to take the dashed

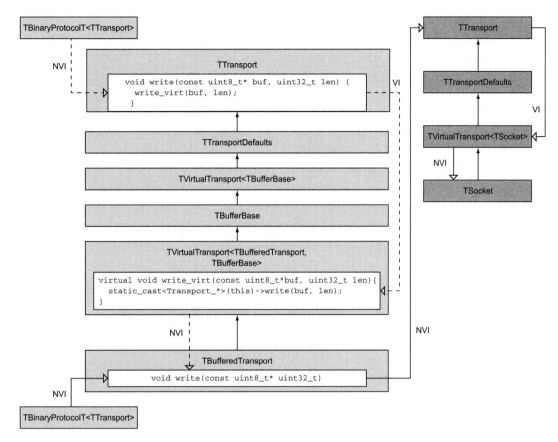

Figure 11.4 Comparing static binding (NVI) and dynamic binding (VI) call paths

path, which involves a hard-to-optimize virtual function call to `TVirtualTrans-port::write_virt`, before we finally get to `TBufferedTransport::write()`. Calls made by a `TBinaryProtocolT<TBufferedTransport>` type protocol will always be made directly to `TBufferedTransport::write()`.

Referring to figure 11.4, you may be wondering about the VI calls between `TBufferedTransport` and `TSocket`. Why aren't these calls using static binding? The short answer is that turning all the layered transports into templates would increase the complexity of the I/O stack considerably. Also, the buffering layer will only write to the underlying transport when the message is complete. Thus 200 protocol writes to the NVI buffer may require only one virtual write to the endpoint. This makes the added complexity that would be required to implement an intra-transport NVI hard to justify.

What kind of performance increase will compile time binding buy us? It depends on the nature of the implementation. A system performing huge numbers of serialization operations per RPC call might see significant gains; other applications might not notice the difference. To give you a sense for the potential, the protocol write times example at the end of chapter 5 shows a 0–20% shorter runtime when static polymorphism is used on a test system, depending on the endpoint and protocol selected. This is hardly a proxy for your practical application, however. The only way to assess the impact static binding will have on your application is to measure it in your application.

Both the binary and compact protocols offer factory templates with support for compile time binding on the server side, `TBinaryProtocolFactoryT` and `TCompact-ProtocolFactoryT`, respectively.

We'll use static polymorphism on the client and server side in the non-blocking server example later in this chapter. With a solid understanding of the I/O stack facilities provided by C++, it's time to turn our attention to the RPC server library.

11.3.4 C++ servers

The Apache Thrift C++ library offers a full range of server options. The following are the server types available:

- *TSimpleServer*—Simple, single-threaded, single-client server
- *TThreadedServer*—Multithreaded server creating a new thread for each connection
- *TThreadPoolServer*—Multithreaded server assigning threads from a pool to connections; when clients disconnect, threads are returned to the pool
- *TNonblockingServer*—Multithreaded server that dynamically feeds requests to a pool of worker threads

With the exception of the `TSimpleServer`, each of these server types requires the ability to create threads within the server process. The Apache Thrift C++ library supports three thread APIs:

- *pthread*—*nix native threads (default)
- *std::thread*—standard C++11 threads
- *boost::thread*—Boost cross-platform threads

The build system will use the `pthread` API on *nix platforms. Windows builds are configured to define `USE_STD_THREAD` if `std::thread` is supported, and otherwise define `USE_BOOST_THREAD` and the `boost::thread` implementation. Future implementations may rely purely on `std::thread`, to simplify cross-platform development.

The first example in this chapter demonstrated the `TSimpleServer`. Chapter 10 provides C++ examples of `TThreadedServer` and `TThreadPoolServer`. In the next section, we'll explore the final C++ server type, `TNonblockingServer`.

11.4 The C++ TNonBlockingServer

The Apache Thrift C++ `TNonblockingServer` is the most complex of the C++ servers, with numerous settings and several unique dependencies. However, if performance is the goal, the non-blocking server is a contender for fastest all-around RPC server in the Apache Thrift fleet.

As you may recall from chapter 10, both `TThreadedServer` and `TThreadPoolServer` use one thread per client connection. Each server thread is assigned to a client and handles all of that client's requests exclusively. Upon completing a request, threads immediately try to read from the underlying transport. This will normally block the thread, putting it into a wait state until data is sent by the client and the read can complete. Thus, if the client doesn't write and doesn't disconnect, the server thread managing the client connection will block forever. This blocking I/O model often requires far more threads than are needed to keep the CPUs running at full capacity.

Dispatching threads from a pool to complete work can be a more efficient approach. Such a pool, dispatched on a per-task (RPC request) basis, can be sized large enough to keep the hardware saturated. This is the model provided by the `TNon-BlockingServer`. When input arrives from any client on any socket, any available worker thread can be dispatched to process the task. A small number of constantly active threads creates a greater likelihood that each thread will have its required resources at the ready, and because threads can handle requests from multiple clients, you have fewer context switches, improving efficiency. Scheduling a thread that hasn't run in a while, or switching between hundreds of threads, creates significant system overhead, delaying client responses.

The Apache Thrift `TNonblockingServer` uses event-driven thread pools to process work. Non-blocking server threading can be configured in two ways. The first way uses a single thread pool for all work. The second way uses an I/O thread pool to read and write network messages and a separate worker thread pool to process RPC requests.

In this section, we'll create a non-blocking server to host a high-performance stock trade reporting service. The server will accept requests for stock quotes from clients and return trade reports with relevant data. The IDL for the service appears in the following listing.

Listing 11.4   ~/ThriftBook/part3/cpp/nbsvr/trade_report.thrift

```
/** Stock Trade Reporting interface */

namespace * TradeReporting              ❶

struct TradeReport {                     ❷
    1: string   symbol,
    2: double   price,
    3: i32      size,
    4: i32      seq_num
}
                                ❸
service TradeHistory {          ⟵
    TradeReport get_last_sale(1: string Symbol)
}
```

The `TradeHistory` service ❸ defined in the IDL provides a single method, `get_last_sale()`, which returns a `TradeReport` struct ❷. Both the `TradeReport` UDT and the `TradeHistory` service will be generated within the `TradeReporting` namespace ❶.

The server implementation for this service will have three main parts:

- *TradeHistoryHandler*—This class will implement the `TradeHistory` service logic.
- *TradeHistoryIfInstanceFactory*—This is the factory that will generate a new `Trade-HistoryHandler` for each connection.
- *main()*—The application entry point which will configure and launch the RPC server.

We'll examine each section in turn. The complete server source can be found in listing 11.8. To begin, let's look at the `TradeHistoryHandler` in the following listing.

Listing 11.5 `TradeHistoryHandler`

```
class TradeHistoryHandler : virtual public TradeHistoryIf {          ❶
public:
    TradeHistoryHandler(const TConnectionInfo & ci, int con_count) :   ❷
            con_id(con_count), call_count(0) {
        auto sock = dynamic_pointer_cast<TSocket>(ci.transport);       ❸
        std::string soc_info;
        if (sock) {
            soc_info = sock->getSocketInfo();                          ❹
        }
        std::cout << "[Server] ConCreate : "
                << std::this_thread::get_id()
                << ':' << con_id << ':' << call_count               ❺
                << " (" << soc_info << ')' << std::endl;
    }

    virtual ~TradeHistoryHandler() {                      ❻
        std::cout << "[Server] ConDelete : " << std::this_thread::get_id()
                << ':' << con_id << ':' << call_count << std::endl;
    }

    void get_last_sale(TradeReport& trade,                       ❼
                    const std::string& symbol) override {
        trade.seq_num = (con_id * 10000) + (++call_count);
        trade.symbol = symbol;
        if (0 == symbol.compare("APPL")) {
            trade.price = 127.61;
            trade.size = 500;
        } else if (0 == symbol.compare("MSFT")) {
            trade.price = 46.23;
            trade.size = 400;
        } else {
            trade.price = 0.0;
            trade.size = 0;
        }
    }
```

```
        std::cout << "[Server] GetLastSale(" << std::this_thread::get_id()
                << ':' << con_id << ':' << call_count << ") returning: "
                << trade.seq_num << "> "
                << trade.symbol << " - " << trade.size << " @ "
                << trade.price << std::endl;
    }

private:
    const int con_id;
    int call_count;
};
```

In this program, the only required handler element is the implementation of the get
_last_sale() method. However, to demonstrate the relationship between the handler
and the threads invoking it at runtime, we have added additional features and logging.

The TradeHistoryHandler class is derived from TradeHistoryIf, the IDL-generated
service interface ❶. The server will use a handler factory to generate a new instance of
this handler for each inbound connection. This allows us to use calls to the handler constructor ❷ to identify new connections. Like all other Apache Thrift C++ library servers,
the non-blocking server will not call a connection's handler instance concurrently.
While we may not know which thread will be used to call the handler for any given task,
the design of TNonblockingServer ensures that only one task (RPC request) can be
active at a time for a given connection, so we can safely change the handler's state during
processing without locks.

In scenarios where a singleton handler is used for all connections in a multithreaded server, the handler's attributes cannot be changed safely. In such cases, concurrency countermeasures (such as std::atomic<>, std::mutex<>) are required to
avoid data races.

Apache Thrift servers pass handler factories a TConnectionInfo object each time
they ask the factory to provide a new handler. The TConnectionInfo class, defined in
the thrift/TProcessor.h header, includes TProtocol smart pointers to the input and
output protocols, as well as a TTransport smart pointer to the endpoint transport for
the connection.

Because we know the endpoint will be a TSocket, we can dynamically cast the
TTransport down to a TSocket ❸, and then use the getSocketInfo() method to
recover the connected host and port ❹. The TSocket class offers several other useful
methods for recovering connection information (for example, getPeerAddress(),
getPeerHost(), and so on); refer to the thrift/transport/TSocket.h header for more
details. The handler constructor logs the socket information, a connection ID, the call
count, and the ID of the current thread to the console ❺.

Note that the thread ID cannot be safely used as a unique identifier for the connection, because non-blocking servers configured with a pool of worker threads may use
any worker to call the handler. The opposite is true of TSimpleServer, TThreadPool-
Server, and TThreadedServer—all three assign a thread to a connection and use only
that thread to service the connection.

The handler class destructor will be invoked when the associated client connection terminates. By having the destructor output the same information displayed in the constructor (sans the socket info) ❻, we can identify the number of calls made over the life of the connection, among other things.

The implementation for the sole RPC method in this service, get_last_sale(), returns a dummy quote for either of the two stock tickers it knows, APPL and MSFT ❼. The method increments the handler's integer call_count attribute, which again is safe because the handler cannot be invoked concurrently.

Now that we have a service handler implemented, let's examine the handler factory needed to create instances of it, as shown in the following listing.

Listing 11.6   TradeHistoryFactory

```
class TradeHistoryFactory : virtual public TradeHistoryIfFactory {
public:
  TradeHistoryFactory() : con_count(0) {;}
  virtual TradeHistoryIf* getHandler(const TConnectionInfo & ci) override {
❶    return new TradeHistoryHandler(ci, ++con_count);
  }
  virtual void releaseHandler(TradeHistoryIf * handler) override  {
❷    delete handler;
  }
private:
  int con_count;        ❸
};
```

The handler factory in listing 11.6 is a simple class implementing the IDL compiler-generated TradeHistoryIfFactory interface. Each time the server accepts a new connection, it will call the factory getHandler() method to acquire a handler ❶. The getHandler() method is passed the TConnectionInfo for the connection in question, which in our case we pass on to the newly created handler. Our get-Handler() method also increments a connection counter, con_count ❸. This is safe because the TNonblockingServer only accepts new connections and creates handlers for them on the listening thread, I/O thread 0. All other Apache Thrift servers at the time of this writing also accept connections, and generate I/O stacks and handlers on a single thread.

When an existing connection disconnects, the handler factory releaseHandler() method is called ❷. In our case, we delete the handler object, causing its destructor to be called, logging its demise. This will only be called once, but can be called by any worker thread in a non-blocking server configured with a worker thread pool.

If your handler is stateless, using a single handler instance for all connections will typically be more efficient than creating a new instance of the handler for each connection. The IDL compiler generates a singleton handler factory for every IDL service automatically. This singleton handler factory is ready to use and perfect for situations where a single handler will service all connections. For example, the TradeHistory.h file generated for our `TradeHistory` service contains a predefined `TradeHistoryIf-SingletonFactory` class. This handler factory is constructed with a smart pointer to a handler instance. The factory `getHandler()` method then returns this same handler instance every time it's called by the framework.

The final block of server code covers the construction of the `TNonblockingServer` itself, as shown in the following listing.

Listing 11.7   Nonblocking Server `main()`

```cpp
int main() {
    //Setup server parameters
    auto port = 9090;
    auto hw_threads = std::thread::hardware_concurrency();
    int io_threads = hw_threads / 2 + 1;
    int worker_threads = hw_threads * 1.5 + 1;
    auto trans = make_shared<TNonblockingServerSocket>(port);

    //Create I/O factories
    auto handler_fac = make_shared<TradeHistoryFactory>();
    auto proc_fac =
        make_shared<TradeHistoryProcessorFactory>(handler_fac);
    auto proto_fac =
        make_shared<TCompactProtocolFactoryT<TMemoryBuffer>>();

    //Setup the worker-thread manager
    auto thread_man =
        ThreadManager::newSimpleThreadManager(worker_threads);
    thread_man->threadFactory(make_shared<PlatformThreadFactory>());
    thread_man->start();

    //Start the server on a background thread
    TNonblockingServer server(proc_fac, proto_fac, trans, thread_man);
    server.setNumIOThreads(io_threads);
    std::thread server_thread([&server](){server.serve();});

    //Log status and wait for user to quit
    std::string str;
    do {
        std::cout << "[Server (" << hw_threads << ", "
                  << server.getNumIOThreads() << '/'
                  << thread_man->workerCount() << "):"
                  << port << "] Enter 'q' to quit" << std::endl;
        std::getline(std::cin, str);
    } while (str[0] != 'q');

    //Stop the server, wait for I/O and worker threads then exit
    server.stop();
    std::cout   << "waiting for server to exit..." << std::endl;
    server_thread.join();
    std::cout << "service complete, exiting." << std::endl;
    return 0;
}
```

❶
❷
❸
❹
❺
❻

The main() entry point begins with a block of code which sets the port number to listen on and defines the number of threads to use in the I/O and worker pools ❶. The TNonblockingServer always creates an I/O thread pool and can optionally make use of a worker pool as well. The last line in this block creates a non-blocking server socket initialized with the port to listen on.

The first phase of processing in a non-blocking server involves reading RPC requests from the network. The I/O pool is designed to handle network read and write operations. The TNonblockingServer always uses built-in framing logic, requiring all clients to use the TFramedTransport layer. The framing layer adds a 4-byte frame size to every RPC request and response. This allows the TNonblockingServer I/O threads to read the first 4 bytes of a transmission and then directly read the exact number of bytes containing the balance of the request without de-serializing the message.

The second phase of processing involves de-serializing the message and using it to invoke the appropriate service handler. This can be performed by the I/O thread that reads the message, though this isn't optimal in most settings. The I/O threads are statically assigned to connections in a round robin fashion. If the sockets associated with a single I/O thread become busy, that thread may become an I/O bottleneck. While an I/O thread is processing an RPC request, it cannot perform I/O on any of the sockets it's responsible for. Moving the RPC request processing to a background thread can improve the responsiveness of the I/O thread pool if the RPC operation is nontrivial.

Often TNonblockingServers are configured with a worker thread pool dedicated to receiving and processing RPC messages from the I/O threads (see figure 11.5). In this model the I/O threads read the raw bytes from the network directly into TMemoryBuffers. The I/O threads then add "tasks" containing TMemoryBuffers to the worker queue for processing. Any worker thread can process any task (RPC request). The libevent library is used to synchronize the various threads in the TNonBlockingServer.

Optimally configured servers have enough threads to keep all the available processors busy. A key piece of information when seeking the optimal thread count is the number of processors available. The main() function here uses the std::thread ::hardware_concurrency() function to discover the number of CPUs on the current machine, then uses the CPU count to size the I/O and worker thread pools ❶. Note that handler implementations that block on cross server or disk I/O may require a worker pool much larger than the number of CPUs.

Consider a server with an average of 50 requests in progress, all blocking while waiting for responses from other servers. The blocking threads cannot handle new requests. You would need more than 50 worker threads to ensure new requests can be processed immediately in this case. In our example server we arbitrarily set the I/O pool size to half the number of CPUs and the worker pool size to 50% more than the number of CPUs. Choosing optimal tread pool sizes can only be done in the context of the specific server, services, and load in question.

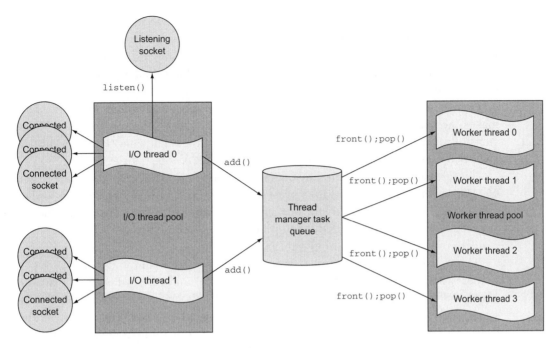

Figure 11.5 Non-blocking server threading model

The second block of code in the `main()` function ❷ creates the handler, processor, and protocol factories we'll provide to the server. As you may notice, we selected the Compact protocol for this server and also chose to statically bind the protocol factory template to the `TMemoryBuffer` transport. You may have been expecting `TFramedTransport` as the template parameter. This would be correct for a normal server using `TFramedTransport` at the top of the transport stack. In the case of the `TNonblockingServer`, however, the I/O thread uses custom framing code that reads the frame information but doesn't de-serialize the request bytes. Instead the I/O thread copies the RPC message into a `TMemoryBuffer` and adds it as a task to the worker queue. The selected protocol will then read directly from the `TMemoryBuffer`.

Choosing the wrong static binding target for a protocol factory will not break your build; the `xxxProtocolFactoryT<>::getProtocol()` method will silently return a `xxx-ProtocolT<TTransport>` if the server-supplied transport type doesn't match the template parameter type. While the virtual call back is convenient, it may hide the fact that static binding is not in place. Note that this is only the case for factories; should you create a protocol class template for `TFramedTransport` (`TBinaryProtocolT<TFramed-Transport>`) and try to give it a `TBufferedTransport`, the code will not compile.

The next block of code ❸ creates a thread manager for the `TNonblockingServer`. The non-blocking server provides its own I/O thread management but requires an external manager for the worker thread pool. The `ThreadManager` class is defined in the ThreadManager.h/.cpp files in thrift/lib/cpp/src/thrift/concurrency. The simple thread manager implementation created by newSimpleThreadManager() is the only predefined implementation. The newSimpleThreadManager() method takes the number of threads to allocate for the worker pool as a parameter. A second parameter can be supplied to set a task queue limit. The default value (0) allows the task queue to grow unbounded.

Once constructed, the ThreadManager must be supplied with a Thread factory. This makes the ThreadManager code independent of the thread API used. The Platform-ThreadFactory defined in thrift/lib/cpp/src/thrift/concurrency/PlatformThread-Factory.h uses the API defined in the build settings (STD, BOOST, or PTHREAD).

The last block of code before the operational loop sets up our TNonblockingServer ❹. The server is constructed with a processor factory and a protocol factory, as well as a transport to listen on and the worker thread manager. The server's setNumIO-Threads() method is used to set the number of I/O threads to use. When the server is ready to run, we use a standard C++ thread to run the server in the background.

The user input loop ❺ displays basic server information and waits for the user to request a server shutdown. When the user presses "q" and Enter, the server exits the read loop and calls the server.stop() method ❻. This causes the server to send messages to all the worker and I/O threads, shutting down the thread pools. When all the NonblockingServer threads have terminated, the background thread running the server, server_thread, will exit, causing the server_thread.join() call to return and allowing the main thread to exit.

While not overly complex, this example server demonstrates many of the key features of the TNonblockingServer class. The TNonblockingServer provides many other tunable features, such as default buffer sizes and more. See the TNonblocking-Server source in thrift/lib/cpp/src/thrift/server for more configuration details.

The complete server code appears in the following listing.

Listing 11.8   ~/ThriftBook/part3/cpp/nbsvr/nb_server.cpp

```cpp
#include "gen-cpp/trade_report_types.h"
#include "gen-cpp/TradeHistory.h"
#include <thrift/TProcessor.h>
#include <thrift/transport/TBufferTransports.h>
#include <thrift/transport/TNonblockingServerSocket.h>
#include <thrift/protocol/TCompactProtocol.h>
#include <thrift/server/TNonblockingServer.h>
#include <thrift/concurrency/ThreadManager.h>
#include <thrift/concurrency/PlatformThreadFactory.h>
#include <memory>
#include <thread>
#include <iostream>
#include <string>
#include <atomic>

using namespace ::apache::thrift::transport;
using namespace ::apache::thrift::protocol;
using namespace ::apache::thrift::server;
```

```cpp
using namespace ::apache::thrift::concurrency;
using namespace ::apache::thrift;
using namespace TradeReporting;
using std::shared_ptr;
using std::make_shared;

class TradeHistoryHandler : virtual public TradeHistoryIf {
public:
    TradeHistoryHandler(const TConnectionInfo & ci, int con_count) :
            con_id(con_count), call_count(0) {
        auto sock = dynamic_pointer_cast<TSocket>(ci.transport);
        std::string soc_info;
        if (sock) {
            soc_info = sock->getSocketInfo();
        }
        std::cout << "[Server] ConCreate : " <<  std::this_thread::get_id()
                << ':' << con_id << ':' << call_count
                << " (" << soc_info << ')' << std::endl;
    }
    virtual ~TradeHistoryHandler() {
        std::cout << "[Server] ConDelete : " <<  std::this_thread::get_id()
                << ':' << con_id << ':' << call_count << std::endl;
    }
    void get_last_sale(TradeReport& trade,
                       const std::string& symbol) override {
        trade.seq_num = (con_id * 10000) + (++call_count);
        trade.symbol = symbol;
        if (0 == symbol.compare("APPL")) {
            trade.price = 127.61;
            trade.size = 500;
        } else if (0 == symbol.compare("MSFT")) {
            trade.price = 46.23;
            trade.size = 400;
        } else {
            trade.price = 0.0;
            trade.size = 0;
        }

        std::cout << "[Server] GetLastSale(" <<  std::this_thread::get_id()
                << ':' << con_id << ':' << call_count << ") returning: "
                << trade.seq_num << "> "
                << trade.symbol << " - " << trade.size << " @ "
                << trade.price << std::endl;
    }
private:
    const int con_id;
    int call_count;
};


class TradeHistoryFactory : virtual public TradeHistoryIfFactory {
public:
    TradeHistoryFactory() : con_count(0) {;}
    virtual TradeHistoryIf* getHandler(const TConnectionInfo & ci) override
    {
```

```cpp
            return new TradeHistoryHandler(ci, ++con_count);
        }
        virtual void releaseHandler(TradeHistoryIf * handler) override {
            delete handler;
        }
private:
    int con_count;
};


int main() {
    //Setup server parameters
    auto port = 9090;
    auto hw_threads = std::thread::hardware_concurrency();
    int io_threads = hw_threads / 2 + 1;
    int worker_threads = hw_threads * 1.5 + 1;
    auto trans = make_shared<TNonblockingServerSocket>(port);

    //Create I/O factories
    auto handler_fac = make_shared<TradeHistoryFactory>();
    auto proc_fac = make_shared<TradeHistoryProcessorFactory>(handler_fac);
    auto proto_fac =
        make_shared<TCompactProtocolFactoryT<TFramedTransport>>();

    //Setup the worker-thread manager
    auto thread_man =
        ThreadManager::newSimpleThreadManager(worker_threads);
    thread_man->threadFactory(make_shared<PlatformThreadFactory>());
    thread_man->start();

    //Start the server on a background thread
    TNonblockingServer server(proc_fac, proto_fac, trans, thread_man);
    server.setNumIOThreads(io_threads);
    std::thread server_thread([&server](){server.serve();});

    //Log status and wait for user to quit
    std::string str;
    do {
        std::cout << "[Server (" << hw_threads << ", "
                  << server.getNumIOThreads() << '/'
                  << thread_man->workerCount() << "):"
                  << port << "] Enter 'q' to quit" << std::endl;
        std::getline(std::cin, str);
    } while (str[0] != 'q');

    //Stop the server, wait for I/O and worker threads then exit
    server.stop();
    std::cout   << "waiting for server to exit..." << std::endl;
    server_thread.join();
    std::cout << "service complete, exiting." << std::endl;
    return 0;
}
```

To test the non-blocking server example, we need to create a matched client. The following listing shows the source for a simple client that connects, makes a stock quote request, and exits.

Listing 11.9 ~/ThriftBook/part3/cpp/nbsvr/nb_client.cpp

```cpp
#include "gen-cpp/trade_report_types.h"          ❶
#include "gen-cpp/TradeHistory.h"
#include <thrift/Thrift.h>
#include <thrift/transport/TSocket.h>
#include <thrift/transport/TBufferTransports.h>
#include <thrift/protocol/TCompactProtocol.h>
#include <memory>
#include <iostream>

using namespace apache::thrift;
using namespace apache::thrift::transport;
using namespace apache::thrift::protocol;
using namespace TradeReporting;                   ❷
using std::shared_ptr;
using std::make_shared;

int main() {
    auto trans_ep = make_shared<TSocket>("localhost", 9090);     ❸
    auto trans = make_shared<TFramedTransport>(trans_ep);
    auto proto = make_shared<TCompactProtocolT<TFramedTransport>>(trans);   ❹
❺   TradeHistoryClient client(proto);

    try {
        trans->open();
        std::string input;
        std::string symbol("APPL");
        TradeReport trade;
        do {
            client.get_last_sale(trade, symbol);
            std::cout << std::boolalpha
                      << "[Client] trade(" << symbol << "): "
                      << trade.seq_num << ">  "
                      << trade.symbol << " "
                      << trade.size  << " @ "
                      << trade.price <<  std::endl;
            std::cout << "enter 'q' to quit, anything else to GetLastSale"
                      << std::endl;
            std::getline(std::cin, input);
        } while (input[0] != 'q');
    } catch(const TTransportException& te) {
        std::cout << "Client caught a TTransportException: "
                  << te.what() << std::endl;
    } catch(const TException& e) {
        std::cout << "Client caught a TException: "
                  << e.what() << std::endl;
    } catch(...) {
        std::cout << "Client caught an exception" << std::endl;
    }
    trans->close();
}
```

The client program in the previous listing shares many of the same header dependencies as the server it's paired with. In particular, the `types` header and the `TradeHistory` service header emitted from the `trade_report.thrift` IDL are required ❶. We also use the IDL namespace, `TradeReporting`, to simplify references to the IDL-generated classes ❷.

Non-blocking server clients must use a `TSocket` (or `TSSLSocket`) endpoint and a `TFramedTransport` layer ❸. The server was also configured with the `TCompactProtocol`, so the client must use this as well. In the client example, we statically bind the compact protocol to the framed transport layer ❹. Finally, we create a `TradeHistory` client to use the I/O stack ❺.

The remaining client code is much like other simple clients. The main function makes RPC calls to the server using the `get_last_sale()` method, prints out the results, and continues until the user indicates it's time to quit. The exception block at the end of the main function traps transport exceptions, which are the most common exception type, given that they report network errors. `catch` blocks are also provided for generic Apache Thrift exceptions, and finally a `catch all` block (see chapter 9 for more information on Apache Thrift exceptions).

To build the client and server, we can use commands something like the ones shown in the following command line session:

```
thrift@ubuntu:~/ThriftBook/part3/cpp/nbsvr$ thrift -gen cpp
                                 trade_report.thrift

thrift@ubuntu:~/ThriftBook/part3/cpp/nbsvr$ g++ -o server nb_server.cpp
            gen-cpp/TradeHistory.cpp gen-cpp/trade_report_types.cpp
            -Wall -std=c++11 -lthrift -lthriftnb -levent -pthread

thrift@ubuntu:~/ThriftBook/part3/cpp/nbsvr$ g++ -o client nb_client.cpp
            gen-cpp/TradeHistory.cpp gen-cpp/trade_report_types.cpp
            -Wall -std=c++11 -lthrift
```

The first line in the build session compiles the IDL as usual. The second line builds the non-blocking server. Note the addition of the `-lthriftnb`, `-levent`, and `-lpthread` switches. These inform the linker to link against the non-blocking thrift library, the `libevent` library, and the `pthread` library, respectively. All libraries must be present to create a working non-blocking server.

By default, g++ will link to the `.so` shared libraries for each of the `-l` dependencies listed. You can specify libraries you'd like to statically link to using the `-Wl,-Bstatic` switch. To return to dynamic linking you can use the `-Wl,-Bdynamic` switch. For example, to statically link to `libthrift.a` and `libthriftnb.a` you could use the following build command:

```
thrift@ubuntu:~/ThriftBook/part3/cpp/nbsvr$ g++ -o server nb_server.cpp
            gen-cpp/TradeHistory.cpp gen-cpp/trade_report_types.cpp
            -Wall -std=c++11
            -Wl,-Bstatic -lthrift -lthriftnb
```

The C++ TNonBlockingServer   379

```
                     -Wl,-Bdynamic -levent -lpthread
thrift@ubuntu:~/ThriftBook/part3/cpp/nbsvr$ ldd ./server
linux-vdso.so.1 =>  (0x00007fff27565000)
libevent-2.0.so.5 => /usr/lib/x86_64-linux-gnu/libevent-2.0.so.5
libpthread.so.0 => /lib/x86_64-linux-gnu/libpthread.so.0
libstdc++.so.6 => /usr/lib/x86_64-linux-gnu/libstdc++.so.6
libgcc_s.so.1 => /lib/x86_64-linux-gnu/libgcc_s.so.1
libc.so.6 => /lib/x86_64-linux-gnu/libc.so.6
/lib64/ld-linux-x86-64.so.2
libm.so.6 => /lib/x86_64-linux-gnu/libm.so.6
```

The g++ build command in the previous code uses the static flag to statically link the
Thrift libraries and then uses the dynamic flag to switch back to dynamically linking
for the `libevent` and `pthread` libraries. Once built, you can use `ldd` to verify the
absence of the statically linked libraries in the shared library dependencies list.

　　With everything built we can give the server a test run, executing the client binary
in another shell. The following shows a sample server session with two clients connected concurrently:

```
thrift@ubuntu:~/ThriftBook/part3/cpp/nbsvr$ ./server
[Server (2, 2/4):9090] Enter 'q' to quit
Thrift: Tue Jun 23 07:55:46 2015 TNonblockingServer: Serving on port 9090,
⇥ 2 io threads.
Thrift: Tue Jun 23 07:55:46 2015 TNonblockingServer using libevent 2.0.21-
⇥ stable method epoll
Thrift: Tue Jun 23 07:55:46 2015 TNonblocking: IO thread #0 registered for
⇥ listen.
Thrift: Tue Jun 23 07:55:46 2015 TNonblocking: IO thread #0 registered for
⇥ notify.
Thrift: Tue Jun 23 07:55:46 2015 TNonblocking: IO thread #1 registered for
⇥ notify.
Thrift: Tue Jun 23 07:55:46 2015 TNonblockingServer: IO thread #1 entering
⇥ loop...
Thrift: Tue Jun 23 07:55:46 2015 TNonblockingServer: IO thread #0 entering
⇥ loop...
[Server] ConCreate : 140360398878464:1:0 (<Host: ::ffff:127.0.0.1 Port:
⇥ 58512>)
[Server] GetLastSale(140360434870016:1:1) returning: 10001> APPL - 500 @
⇥ 127.61
[Server] ConCreate : 140360398878464:2:0 (<Host: ::ffff:127.0.0.1 Port:
⇥ 58513>)
[Server] GetLastSale(140360402036480:2:1) returning: 20001> APPL - 500 @
⇥ 127.61
[Server] GetLastSale(140360400983808:2:2) returning: 20002> APPL - 500 @
⇥ 127.61
[Server] GetLastSale(140360399931136:1:2) returning: 10002> APPL - 500 @
⇥ 127.61
[Server] ConDelete : 140360398878464:1:2
[Server] GetLastSale(140360434870016:2:3) returning: 20003> APPL - 500 @
⇥ 127.61
[Server] ConDelete : 140360390485760:2:3
q
waiting for server to exit...
```

```
Thrift: Tue Jun 23 07:56:10 2015 TNonblockingServer: IO thread #0 run()
↪ done!
Thrift: Tue Jun 23 07:56:10 2015 TNonblocking: join done for IO thread #0
Thrift: Tue Jun 23 07:56:10 2015 TNonblockingServer: IO thread #1 run()
↪ done!
Thrift: Tue Jun 23 07:56:10 2015 TNonblocking: join done for IO thread #1
↪ service complete, exiting.
```

You can see that the server reports two CPUs (an accurate picture of the VM that the code was running on) and that it has created 2 I/O threads and four worker threads (2, 2/4) ❶. You can also see that all connections are created by the thread with ID 140360398878464. This is the non-blocking server's sole listening thread (I/O thread 0). Once accepted, connections 1 and 2 (identified by the number after the thread ID) are handled by different threads on each subsequent request.

The following code shows a capture of the session from one of the clients in the server session shown above:

```
thrift@ubuntu:~/ThriftBook/part3/cpp/nbsvr$ ./client
[Client] trade(APPL): 20001>  APPL 500 @ 127.61
enter 'q' to quit, anything else to GetLastSale

[Client] trade(APPL): 20002>  APPL 500 @ 127.61
enter 'q' to quit, anything else to GetLastSale

[Client] trade(APPL): 20003>  APPL 500 @ 127.61
enter 'q' to quit, anything else to GetLastSale
q
```

If you've started your Apache Thrift journey here, there is much more to discover in part 2 of this book, where the Apache Thrift IDL and each of the layers of the framework are examined in detail.

Summary

This chapter has covered

- How to set up an Apache Thrift C++ development environment
- How the Apache Thrift C++ library is organized
- How to build C++ clients and servers
- An overview of Apache Thrift C++ library transports, protocols, and servers
- How to take advantage of static protocol/transport binding
- How to use handler factories to recover client connection information
- How to build and use non-blocking servers

*Building clients
and servers with Java*

This chapter covers

- Configuring Apache Thrift for Java and other JVM-based development environments
- Building Java RPC clients and servers with Apache Thrift
- Understanding the features of the Apache Thrift Java library
- Creating synchronous and asynchronous Java RPC clients and servers

Java as a language is a pillar of the open source world. Perhaps even more important than Java is the platform the Java language is based upon, the Java Virtual Machine (JVM). The JVM is the enabler of the marquee "write once run everywhere" feature promoted by the original Java developers. The JVM also provides a base for innovative new languages such as Scala, Groovy, and Clojure to build upon. Even languages popular as standalone interpreters, such as Python, Node.js, and Ruby, have been ported to the JVM to leverage its inherent interoperability and portability.

A language that can be compiled into JVM byte code can interact with byte code generated by any other JVM language. This makes it possible for any JVM language to take advantage of the vast array of JVM-based libraries, including Apache Thrift.

In this chapter, we'll examine the Apache Thrift Java library in detail. The chapter will walk you through building the Apache Thrift Java library JAR, as well as the steps required to create native Java projects using Ant and Maven. We'll also look at using Apache Thrift on the JVM from non-Java languages. After building a starter RPC application, the chapter examines the various parts of the Apache Thrift Java and will walk you through the construction of asynchronous Java clients and servers.

Let's begin by setting up a JVM-oriented development environment for Apache Thrift.

12.1   Setting up Apache Thrift for Java development

Users can set up Apache Thrift for Java/JVM application development in several different ways. One common approach involves simply downloading a pre-compiled Apache Thrift library JAR file for the version of Apache Thrift that you require. The Apache Thrift release process includes publishing the Java library JAR to the Maven 2 Central Repository. You can find JAR files for all releases since v0.6.0 at http://repo1.maven.org/maven2/org/apache/thrift/libthrift.

Alternatively, you can build the Apache Thrift Java library into a JAR file from the development source. The Apache Thrift development trunk can be cloned from github.com. To build the Apache Thrift Java sources, you'll need to have a system with Java 7+ and Ant for Apache Thrift version 0.10 and earlier, or Java 8+ and Gradle for Apache Thrift 0.11 and later.

There has been discussion around moving the Java build to Maven, though this has only been discussion to present. Regardless, the build process would be nearly identical for both, with the Ant build process requiring you to execute ant in the thrift/lib/java directory and the Maven build process requiring you to invoke mvn package in the thrift/lib/java directory.

The following example session clones a copy of the Apache Thrift source and then uses Gradle to build the Apache Thrift library JAR on an Ubuntu 16.04 system:

```
thrift@ubuntu:~$ git clone http://github.com/apache/thrift
...
thrift@ubuntu:~$ cd thrift
thrift@ubuntu:~/thrift$ cd lib/java
thrift@ubuntu:~/thrift/lib/java$ ./gradlew assemble
...
BUILD SUCCESSFUL in 42s
7 actionable tasks: 7 executed
user@ubuntu:~/thrift/lib/java$ ls -l build
total 24
drwxrwxr-x 3 user user 4096 Nov 19 11:37 classes
drwxrwxr-x 2 user user 4096 Nov 19 11:37 deps
drwxrwxr-x 3 user user 4096 Nov 19 11:37 docs
drwxrwxr-x 2 user user 4096 Nov 19 11:37 libs
drwxrwxr-x 3 user user 4096 Nov 19 11:37 resources
```

```
drwxrwxr-x 7 user user 4096 Nov 19 11:37 tmp
user@ubuntu:~/thrift/lib/java$ ls -l build/libs/
total 976
-rw-rw-r-- 1 user user 246457 Nov 19 11:37 libthrift-1.0.0-SNAPSHOT.jar
-rw-rw-r-- 1 user user 568073 Nov 19 11:37 libthrift-1.0.0-SNAPSHOT-javadoc.jar
-rw-rw-r-- 1 user user 178052 Nov 19 11:37 libthrift-1.0.0-SNAPSHOT-sources.jar
user@ubuntu:~/thrift/lib/java$
```

The end result of the previous session is the libthrift-1.0.0-SNAPSHOT.jar. This JAR includes up-to-the-minute patches from the development branch. If you want to create a JAR for a previously released version of Apache Thrift, you can check out the desired version by `git tag` before you build. The Apache Thrift source repository includes tags for each released version. The following session shows an example of checking out and building version 0.9.0 with ant:

```
thrift@ubuntu:~/thrift/lib/java$ git tag
0.10.0
0.2.0
0.3.0
0.4.0
0.5.0
0.6.0
0.6.1
0.7.0
0.8.0
0.9.0
0.9.1
0.9.2
0.9.3
thrift@ubuntu:~/thrift/lib/java$ git checkout 0.9.0
Note: checking out '0.9.0'.
...
thrift@ubuntu:~/thrift/lib/java$ ant
thrift@ubuntu:~/thrift/lib/java$ ls -l build
total 1172
drwxr-xr-x 11 root root   4096 Mar  5 18:54 ./
drwxr-xr-x  9 root root   4096 Mar  5 18:54 ../
drwxr-xr-x  2 root root   4096 Mar  5 18:54 META-INF/
drwxr-xr-x  4 root root   4096 Feb 13 02:51 javadoc/
drwxr-xr-x  2 root root   4096 Mar  5 18:54 lib/
-rw-r--r--  1 root root 379626 Mar  5 18:54 libthrift-0.9.0.jar
-rw-r--r--  1 root root   3293 Mar  5 18:54 libthrift-0.9.0.pom
-rw-r--r--  1 root root 537458 Feb 13 02:51 libthrift-1.0.0-javadoc.jar
-rw-r--r--  1 root root 236844 Feb 13 02:50 libthrift-1.0.0.jar
-rw-r--r--  1 root root   3341 Mar  5 18:34 libthrift-1.0.0.pom
drwxr-xr-x  4 root root   4096 Mar  5 18:54 org/
drwxr-xr-x  2 root root   4096 Feb 13 02:50 test/
drwxr-xr-x  2 root root   4096 Feb 13 02:50 tools/
```

Once built, you can add the libthrift jar to your class path or copy it to a directory on your system class path. If you don't have access to Git, it can be installed from packages on most systems, or you can install the latest version of Git from the git-scm.com website.

12.1.1 *Apache Thrift and SLF4J*

The Apache Thrift Java library uses the Simple Logging Facade for Java (SLF4J). SLF4J is designed to provide a stable application logging interface that can be connected to a range of implementations at runtime without disturbing application code. Code using SLF4J makes calls to the `slf4j-api`, which in turn makes calls to the desired backend at runtime. SLF4J connectors are used to interface with the desired backend. For example, to use SLF4J with Log4J, you'd include `slf4j-api`, the `slf4j-log4j12` connector, and the actual `log4j` logging implementation jar. If you'd rather not provide a logging backend, you can use the `slf4j-nop` connector jar to ignore logging. The examples in this book all use the `slf4j-nop` implementation.

When using SLF4J, be sure that precisely one implementation is provided on the class path. A missing implementation will produce runtime errors, as will multiple implementations. Apache Thrift requires version 1.5.8 of SLF4J, though newer versions all work fine in my experience. For more information on SLF4J or to download the latest version, see its website: www.slf4j.org.

Now that we have an Apache Thrift library JAR and SLF4J dependencies covered, let's build a simple Java RPC client and server.

12.2   *A simple client and server*

In part III of this book we begin each chapter with a simple Hello World RPC application. All the part III chapters share the same Hello World IDL, allowing us to test any Hello World client with any Hello World server, regardless of programming language.

12.2.1 *The Hello IDL*

The `helloSvc` interface contains a single `getMessage()` method that accepts a name string and returns a greeting. The IDL source appears in the following listing.

> **Listing 12.1   ~/ThriftBook/part3/java/simple/hello.thrift**

```
service helloSvc {
    string getMessage(1: string name)
}
```

To generate Java client/server stubs from our `helloSvc` IDL, we can use the Thrift compiler with the following command line:

```
thrift@ubuntu: $ thrift --gen java hello.thrift
```

The Thrift IDL compiler `--gen` switch is used to specify the output language produced for the IDL. The IDL compiler offers other useful switches, and several are Java-specific. For more information on the Thrift IDL compiler, see chapter 6, Apache Thrift IDL. Compiling the hello IDL file produces a single Java source file in the gen-cpp directory:

```
thrift@ubuntu: $ ls -l gen-java
total 36
-rw-rw-r-- 1 thrift thrift 33030 Jul  6 22:10 helloSvc.java
```

The Apache Thrift implementation in the Java language captures all of the client-side and server-side stub code within a single class named after the service, helloSvc in this case. Apache Thrift–generated service classes have several nested elements:

- Client
- Processor
- Iface

The helloSvc.Client class implements the client side of helloSvc. Client programs instantiate this class and invoke its methods to make RPC calls to a connected server. The helloSvc.Processor class is used by servers to process calls to helloSvc. Users create services by deriving a handler class from the helloSvc.Iface interface and implementing its methods.

Asynchronous versions of the client/server stubs and the interface are also generated for each service:

- AsyncClient
- AsyncProcessor
- AsyncIface

We'll use both the synchronous and asynchronous versions of the Java service classes at various points in this chapter. Let's start with the synchronous client for our first simple service.

12.2.2 Building a simple Java client

Creating a simple RPC client program in Java is fairly straightforward. A sample RPC client for hellosvc appears in the following listing.

Listing 12.2 ~/ThriftBook/part3/java/simple/HelloClient.java

```
import org.apache.thrift.protocol.TBinaryProtocol;        ❶
import org.apache.thrift.transport.TSocket;               ❷
import org.apache.thrift.TException;                       ❸

public class HelloClient {

    public static void main(String[] args) {               ❹
        TSocket trans = new TSocket("localhost", 9090);     ❺
        TBinaryProtocol proto = new TBinaryProtocol(trans); ❻
        helloSvc.Client client = new helloSvc.Client(proto);  ❼

        try {
            trans.open();                                   ❽
            String str = client.getMessage("world");        ❾
            System.out.println("[Client] received: " + str);
```

```
        } catch (TException ex) {                              ⑩
            System.out.println("Error: " + ex.toString());
        }
        trans.close();            ⑪
    }
}
```

Like most Apache Thrift programs, we begin by importing the transport and protocol libraries necessary to create the I/O stack used to communicate with the server. In this listing, we import the `TBinaryProtocol` ❶ to provide serialization and the `TSocket` ❷ transport to provide byte-level I/O over TCP.

The Java language exception specification requires programs catch or declare almost all exceptions that may be raised within a block. The Apache Thrift Java library throws exceptions when faced with certain errors. The Apache Thrift base exception class in Java is named `org.apache.thrift.TException`. All Apache Thrift–specific exceptions are either `TException` instances or derived class instances. Importing the `TException` class ❸ will allow us to trap all errors raised by the Apache Thrift library in our exception handler.

Transports perform byte-level I/O and are particularly exposed to exceptional situations such as network disconnects, file read/write errors, and so on. The Apache Thrift Java transport package defines its own `org.apache.thrift.transport` `.TTransportException` class to flag transport-specific errors.

Another important `TException`-derived class is `org.apache.thrift` `.TApplicationException`. This exception type is used to describe exceptions involving the misuse of an interface; for example, a client calling a function that doesn't exist on the server. This can happen when the client you're using doesn't match the processor the server is using. `TApplicationExceptions` are typically raised on the server and passed back to the client. For more information on exception processing in Apache Thrift, see chapter 9, "Handling exceptions."

The entire operational portion of this client program is contained within the `HelloClient` class `main()` method ❹. The `TSocket` ❺ is constructed with the hostname and port of the server to connect to, and the binary protocol ❻ wraps the transport, providing a serialization layer. The IDL-generated client class is constructed with the protocol to complete the stack ❼.

If you're familiar with other Apache Thrift language implementations, you may wonder why we haven't added a buffering layer between the protocol and the endpoint transport. The Java library implementation of `TSocket` is self-buffering, making an additional buffering layer both unnecessary and undesirable.

Up to this point the code hasn't interacted with the server. To connect to the server we invoke the `open()` method on the transport ❽. Once connected we call the `getMessage()` method and display the result ❾.

In this example, all the client code interacting with the Apache Thrift server is included in a `try` block. Any `TException` or derived exceptions raised are caught and logged in the `catch` block ⑩. The client closes the connection with the server following successful execution (or exception handling), using the transport close() method ⑪.

The complete RPC client required nothing more than a few import statements and three or four lines of communications stack setup code. Before we can test the client, we need to build a server.

12.2.3 *Creating a simple RPC server*

For the server implementation, we'll code a server which returns a message to callers invoking the helloSvc getMessage() function. The server code appears in the following listing.

Listing 12.3   ~/ThriftBook/part3/java/simple/HelloServer.java

```java
import org.apache.thrift.TProcessor;
import org.apache.thrift.server.TSimpleServer;
import org.apache.thrift.transport.TServerSocket;
import org.apache.thrift.transport.TTransportException;
import org.apache.thrift.TException;

public class HelloServer {                              ❶

    public static class MessageHandler implements helloSvc.Iface {     ❷

        @Override                                                       ❸
        public String getMessage(String name) throws TException {
            System.out.println("[Server] received: " + name);
            return "Hello " + name;
        }
    }

    public static void main(String[] args) throws TTransportException {   ❹
❺      TServerSocket trans_svr = new TServerSocket(9090);
        TProcessor proc = new helloSvc.Processor<>(new MessageHandler());  ❻
        TSimpleServer server =
            new TSimpleServer(
                new TSimpleServer.Args(trans_svr)                          ❼
                    .processor(proc)
            );
        System.out.println("[Server] waiting for connections");
❽      server.serve();
    }
}
```

Like the simple client, the server code is completely contained within a minimal Java class, HelloServer ❶. The HelloServer class includes a main function ❹ to launch the server and a nested handler class called MessageHandler ❷ that implements the service interface.

The getMessage() method implementation ❸ logs the client-supplied input string and then returns a simple greeting. Even though the getMessage() implementation doesn't throw, it declares that it throws. This is required to provide an exact interface override. The Apache Thrift IDL compiler always adds throws TException to Java interface methods to enable servers to throw user-defined exceptions back to clients. When a server-based handler method throws an appropriate TException, the processor that called the handler catches the exception and transmits it back to the client stub so that it can be raised on the client.

The main() function ❹ also provides an exception specification, throws TTransportException. This is required because the TServerSocket constructor ❺ can throw a TTransportException if network initialization fails. Once started, Apache Thrift servers generally trap and log runtime client networking errors and move on, processing the next connection or request.

The TServerSocket class is derived from the abstract TServerTransport class. The server transport listens for connections on the specified port (9090 in this example) and creates new endpoint transports for each connected client.

The next line of code creates a processor ❻ to convert network input into calls to the service handler. The processor is an interface-specific, server-side stub generated by the IDL compiler.

The next block of code initializes the server ❼. The server class used here is the simple server, a single-threaded, single-client server implementation. Java RPC server classes are generally initialized with a server-specific Args class. In this example we construct the args object with the server transport to use and then add the desired processor with a chaining call to the Args processor() method. We didn't specify a protocol in this example, which causes the server to choose the default TBinaryProtocol. As always, ensuring that the client and server have compatible I/O stacks is required for proper interoperability.

The final line of server code invokes the serve() method on the initialized server object ❽. The serve() method places the server in an endless loop, waiting for and servicing connections.

To test this code with the client we need to build both the client and server.

12.2.4 Building with Ant

Most Java projects use one of several build systems; Ant and Maven are particularly important when using Apache Thrift.

Ant is a Java-based replacement for the make build system. Ant has been a part of many Java projects for more than a decade and enjoys widespread support in IDEs and integration with a host of tools, such as the Ivy dependency management system.

To build our simple project with Ant, we can create a build.xml script to detail the build steps required. Ant build files are straightforward XML files organized into targets, much like Makefiles used with make. One or more configured targets can be executed on the Ant command line. An example build.xml for the simple client and server above appears in the following listing.

```
<project default="all">                    ❶
    <target name="clean">                   ❷
        <delete dir="gen-java"/>
        <delete>
            <fileset dir="." includes="*.class"/>
        </delete>
    </target>

    <target name="compile">                 ❸
        <exec executable="thrift">
            <arg line="-gen java"/>
            <arg value="hello.thrift"/>
        </exec>
        <javac includeantruntime="false"
        ➥ classpath="/usr/local/lib/libthrift-1.0.0.jar:/usr/share/java/
        ➥ slf4j-api.jar:/usr/share/java/slf4j-nop.jar" srcdir="gen-java"
        ➥ destdir="gen-java"/>
        <javac includeantruntime="false"
        ➥ classpath="/usr/local/lib/libthrift-1.0.0.jar:gen-java" srcdir="."
        ➥ destdir="."/>
    </target>

    <target name="runServer">                    ❹
        <java classname="HelloServer" classpath="/usr/local/lib/libthrift-
        ➥ 1.0.0.jar:/usr/share/java/slf4j-api.jar:/usr/share/java/slf4j-
        ➥ nop.jar:gen-java:."/>
    </target>

    <target name="runClient">                    ❺
        <java classname="HelloClient" classpath="/usr/local/lib/libthrift-
        ➥ 1.0.0.jar:/usr/share/java/slf4j-api.jar:/usr/share/java/slf4j-
        ➥ nop.jar:gen-java:."/>
    </target>

    <target name="all" depends="clean,compile"/>      ❻
</project>
```

Build.xml scripts are formatted-XML documents containing a single element, the project ❶. The project tag typically includes a default attribute set to all, which causes the "all" target to run when no other target is specified. This allows us to execute ant with no parameters in the build.xml directory to execute the "all" target.

Targets are the top-level elements within the project element. Targets define executable build processes that Ant can perform. The first target in the listing is the clean target ❷. We use the clean target to delete the IDL compiler-generated gen-java directory and to delete any class files in the projects working directory.

The next target is the compile target ❸. This target invokes the IDL compiler using an exec element and compiles the Java sources in the gen-java and project directories using separate javac elements. The javac elements include classpath attributes that include the jars depended upon by the .java files being built.

The build script also includes targets to run the RPC server ❹ and the RPC client ❺. These also include the necessary `classpath` attributes.

The final target is the "all" target which causes the clean and compile targets to run in order ❻. A run of the "all" target should look something like the following:

```
thrift@ubuntu:~/ThriftBook/part3/java/simple$ ant
Buildfile: /home/thrift/ThriftBook/part3/java/simple/build.xml

clean:
    [delete] Deleting directory /home/thrift/ThriftBook/part3/java/simple/gen-
        java

compile:
    [javac] Compiling 1 source file to
    /home/thrift/ThriftBook/part3/java/simple/gen-java
    [javac] Compiling 2 source files to
    /home/thrift/ThriftBook/part3/java/simple

all:

BUILD SUCCESSFUL
Total time: 1 second
```

Now that all the class files have been generated, we can run the server in one shell and the client in another using the appropriate build targets. Here's a sample run of the server:

```
thrift@ubuntu:~/ThriftBook/part3/java/simple$ ant runServer
Buildfile: /home/thrift/ThriftBook/part3/java/simple/build.xml

runServer:
    [java] [Server] waiting for connections
    [java] [Server] received: world
```

Here's a sample run of the client:

```
thrift@ubuntu:~/ThriftBook/part3/java/simple$ ant runClient
Buildfile: /home/thrift/ThriftBook/part3/java/simple/build.xml

runClient:
    [java] [Client] received: Hello world

BUILD SUCCESSFUL
Total time: 0 seconds
```

Using Ant allows us to lay out our project any way we choose. In exchange, we must imperatively describe each step of the build process to Ant in our build.xml. Some developers make Ant their first choice when it comes to build tools, but other systems are also popular. In the next section, we'll look at building a simple RPC client and server using a Maven project.

12.2.5 *Building with Maven*

Maven is the counterpoint to Ant. Maven uses convention over configuration and provides complete application lifecycle management, whereas Ant focuses on imperative build automation. For example, with Ant you must configure the directory to build, while with Maven a standard project directory is defined by convention. On the lifecycle front, Maven includes a broader set of features, including a comprehensive dependency resolution system, and a standard central repository for JAR files. Ant focuses on build automation, leaving dependency management up to a sister tool called Ivy. Both tools work well with Apache Thrift.

Maven defines projects within a standard pom.xml file. Predefined targets perform compilation and packaging. Maven's ability to resolve dependencies dynamically by downloading Java libraries makes it convenient for projects that use many third-party libraries. Java projects using Apache Thrift can automatically download the desired Apache Thrift JAR files from the Maven 2 Central Repository by supplying the correct dependency element in the Maven pom.xml.

To build the simple RPC client and server with Maven, we need to move our source files into the standard Maven project structure. You can open/import a Maven project using any of the major Java IDEs, including NetBeans, Eclipse, and IntelliJ IDEA.

To reorganize our simple RPC project to suit Maven, we need to create a project directory with a pom.xml file. Next we need a src/main/java directory under our project folder to host our .java files. In addition, we need to create a src/main/thrift directory to host our IDL source, as shown in the following command line session:

```
thrift@ubuntu:~/ThriftBook/part3/java/simple_mvn$ ls -l
-rw-rw-r-- 1 thrift thrift 2395 Jul 19 11:47 pom.xml
drwxrwxr-x 3 thrift thrift 4096 Jul 19 04:28 src
thrift@ubuntu:~/ThriftBook/part3/java/simple_mvn$ ls -l src/main/java
-rw-rw-r-- 1 thrift thrift  714 Jul 19 03:34 HelloClient.java
-rw-rw-r-- 1 thrift thrift 1050 Jul 19 04:12 HelloServer.java
thrift@ubuntu:~/ThriftBook/part3/java/simple_mvn$ ls -l src/main/thrift
-rw-rw-r-- 1 thrift thrift 59 Jul 19 04:58 hello.thrift
```

A simple pom.xml project file for the RPC application might look something like the following.

Listing 12.5 ~/ThriftBook/part3/java/simple_mvn/pom.xml

```xml
<?xml version="1.0" encoding="UTF-8"?>
<project xmlns="http://maven.apache.org/POM/4.0.0"
         xmlns:xsi="http://www.w3.org/2001/XMLSchema-instance"
         xsi:schemaLocation="http://maven.apache.org/POM/4.0.0
         ➥ http://maven.apache.org/xsd/maven-4.0.0.xsd">
    <modelVersion>4.0.0</modelVersion>

    <name>Simple Apache Thrift Maven Project</name>
    <groupId>thriftbook</groupId>
    <artifactId>simple</artifactId>
    <version>1.0-SNAPSHOT</version>
```

❶

❷

```
    <properties>                                                ❸
        <project.build.sourceEncoding>UTF-8</project.build.sourceEncoding>
    </properties>

    <build>                        ❹
        <plugins>           ❺
❻          <plugin>
                <groupId>org.apache.maven.plugins</groupId>
                <artifactId>maven-compiler-plugin</artifactId>
                <version>3.3</version>
                <configuration>
                    <source>1.7</source>
                    <target>1.7</target>
                </configuration>
            </plugin>
❼          <plugin>
                <groupId>org.apache.thrift</groupId>
                <artifactId>thrift-maven-plugin</artifactId>
                <version>0.10.0</version>
                <configuration>

  <thriftExecutable>/usr/local/bin/thrift</thriftExecutable>
                </configuration>
                <executions>
                    <execution>
                        <id>thrift-sources</id>
                        <phase>generate-sources</phase>
                        <goals>
                            <goal>compile</goal>
                        </goals>
                    </execution>
                </executions>
            </plugin>
❽          <plugin>
                <artifactId>maven-assembly-plugin</artifactId>
                <configuration>
                    <descriptorRefs>
                        <descriptorRef>jar-with-dependencies</descriptorRef>
                    </descriptorRefs>
                </configuration>
            </plugin>
        </plugins>
    </build>

❾  <dependencies>
        <dependency>
            <groupId>org.apache.thrift</groupId>
            <artifactId>libthrift</artifactId>
            <version>0.10.0</version>
        </dependency>
        <dependency>
            <groupId>org.slf4j</groupId>
            <artifactId>slf4j-nop</artifactId>
            <version>1.7.2</version>
```

```
        </dependency>
    </dependencies>
</project>
```

The first several lines of the pom.xml are boilerplate and define the file as a Maven Project Object Model (POM) source file ❶. The next four lines of the pom.xml define the project name and coordinates ❷. Maven identifies projects by coordinates, which include the `groupId`, `artifactId`, and `version` tags. The coordinates should form a globally unique identifier for the project's artifact, generally a JAR. To achieve this, almost all projects use a reverse domain name as the group ID.

The properties section of the pom.xml defines an explicit character encoding for source files processed ❸. Leaving this out will cause the build system to use platform-specific encoding and also produces a warning.

The build element ❹ houses the bulk of the project specification and is broken down into two primary sub-elements, plugins ❺ and dependencies ❻.

Maven is essentially a plugin runner. Compilation, packaging, and other features are all performed by plugins; Maven's task is to orchestrate them. Goals such as compiling and packaging invoke the plugins necessary to perform the tasks required to achieve the goal. Many Maven plugins are available; you can even have Maven drive Ant build targets with the Ant plugin. This example project configures three plugins.

The first plugin configured in the pom.xml is the `maven-compiler-plugin` ❻. The Maven Java compiler plugin is used automatically by Maven and it uses Java language version 1.5 by convention. Because Apache Thrift uses features such as diamond generic notation, we need to increase the language version to 1.7, which we can do by providing the compiler plugin with configuration settings for source and target versions in the pom.xml.

The second plugin configured is the `thrift-maven-plugin` ❼. This plugin invokes the Apache Thrift compiler as part of the build process. The plugin was originally written and distributed by David Trott, but as of Apache Thrift version 0.9.3 it has become a part of the Apache Thrift source in the contrib section (thanks David!). The example uses the v0.10.0 plugin to match the version of the Apache Thrift lib used in the dependencies section. It's important to use the same version of the `thrift-maven-plugin`, compiler (/usr/bin/thrift), and `libthrift`. Mismatches may work but often don't.

At the time of this writing, two versions of the `thrift-maven-plugin` were available under the org.apache.thrift group in the Maven Central Repository (https://mvnrepository.com/artifact/org.apache.thrift/thrift-maven-plugin). See table 12.1.

Table 12.1 Thrift-maven-plugin versions

Version	Repository	Usages	Date
0.10.0	Central	0	(Jan 2017)
0.9.3	Central	0	(Oct 2015)

Older versions of Apache Thrift (see table 12.2) can be used with the original artifact created by David. In contrast to the Apache version, David's version uses a `groupId` of `org.apache.thrift.tools` and an `artifactId` of `maven-thrift-plugin`.

Table 12.2   Older Thrift versions available

Version	Repository	Usages	Date
0.1.11	Central	0	(Aug 2013)
0.1.10	Twitter	0	(May 2012)

The following listing shows a sample pom stanza including the original thrift plugin for use with Apache Thrift versions 0.9.2 and earlier.

Listing 12.6   POM stanza for old Maven Thrift plugin

```
<plugin>
    <groupId>org.apache.thrift.tools</groupId>
    <artifactId>maven-thrift-plugin</artifactId>
    <version>0.1.11</version>
    <configuration>

<thriftExecutable>/usr/local/bin/thrift</thriftExecutable>
    </configuration>
    <executions>
        <execution>
            <id>thrift-sources</id>
            <phase>generate-sources</phase>
            <goals>
                <goal>compile</goal>
            </goals>
        </execution>
    </executions>
</plugin>
```

The Thrift plugin can optionally be configured with an IDL compiler executable path using the `thriftExecutable` tag. If this tag isn't supplied, the thrift executable must be available on the path. The `thrift` plugin looks for .thrift files in the project src/main/thrift directory. Generated code is emitted into the target/generated-sources/thrift directory.

The final plugin is the `maven-assembly-plugin` **8**. The assembly plugin makes it easy to build a JAR file including the project class files and all the class files from the project's dependencies. The resulting JAR supplies everything needed to run the application.

The last section of the pom.xml, the dependencies element, declares the direct dependencies of the project source **9**. This section begins with the dependency on Apache Thrift (org.apache.thrift/libthrift). Conveniently, all artifacts hosted by

Maven Central have their own pom.xml files describing their dependencies, so we only need to list our direct dependencies, and Maven will automatically download any jars required by the libraries we use.

The second dependency defined is `org.slf4j/slf4j-nop`. This provides a non-operational logger for the slf4j-api library used by `libthrift`.

With a pom.xml and a proper project structure in place, building an Apache Thrift RPC application with Maven is easy:

```
thrift@ubuntu:~/ThriftBook/part3/java/simple_mvn$ mvn package
...
thrift@ubuntu:~/ThriftBook/part3/java/simple_mvn$ ls -l target
total 56
drwxrwxr-x 2 thrift thrift  4096 Jul 19 21:02 classes
drwxrwxr-x 4 thrift thrift  4096 Jul 19 20:53 generated-sources
drwxrwxr-x 2 thrift thrift  4096 Jul 19 20:53 maven-archiver
drwxrwxr-x 3 thrift thrift  4096 Jul 19 20:53 maven-status
-rw-rw-r-- 1 thrift thrift 35483 Jul 19 21:02 simple-1.0-SNAPSHOT.jar
drwxrwxr-x 2 thrift thrift  4096 Jul 19 21:02 surefire
```

The Maven `mvn` command accepts a goal, `package` in this case, and then executes all the necessary plugins to achieve that goal. In this example, Maven compiles, tests, and packages the project, producing a JAR file with all the project classes. We haven't defined any tests, so the test phase doesn't do anything.

To package the project into a JAR that also includes all the project dependencies, we can use the assembly plugin. The following code shows a session that builds an application JAR including our RPC client, server, and all the required dependencies:

```
thrift@ubuntu:~/ThriftBook/part3/java/simple_mvn$ mvn assembly:assembly
...
thrift@ubuntu:~/ThriftBook/part3/java/simple_mvn$ ls -l target
total 1256
drwxrwxr-x 2 thrift thrift     4096 Jul 19 21:07 archive-tmp
drwxrwxr-x 2 thrift thrift     4096 Jul 19 21:07 classes
drwxrwxr-x 4 thrift thrift     4096 Jul 19 20:53 generated-sources
drwxrwxr-x 2 thrift thrift     4096 Jul 19 20:53 maven-archiver
drwxrwxr-x 3 thrift thrift     4096 Jul 19 20:53 maven-status
-rw-rw-r-- 1 thrift thrift    35483 Jul 19 21:07 simple-1.0-SNAPSHOT.jar
-rw-rw-r-- 1 thrift thrift 1221722 Jul 19 21:07 simple-1.0-SNAPSHOT-jar-
➥ with-dependencies.jar
drwxrwxr-x 2 thrift thrift     4096 Jul 19 21:07 surefire
```

Now we can run the client and server using the assembly JAR. Here's an example:

```
thrift@ubuntu:~/ThriftBook/part3/java/simple_mvn$ java -cp target/simple-1.0-
➥ SNAPSHOT-jar-with-dependencies.jar HelloServer
[Server] waiting for connections
[Server] received: world
```

Here's a run of the client:

```
thrift@ubuntu:~/ThriftBook/part3/java/simple_mvn$ java -cp target/simple-
➥ 1.0-SNAPSHOT-jar-with-dependencies.jar HelloClient
[Client] received: Hello world
```

As you can see, both Maven and Ant are easy to use, yet each has its own style. Other build systems, such as Gradle, also have their fan bases. You'll find Ant scripts for each of the Java projects demonstrated in this book in the book's associated GitHub repository.

12.3   *Using Apache Thrift in other JVM languages*

At the beginning of this chapter we discussed the fact that Java libraries, such as Apache Thrift, are compiled down to standard JVM bytecode before being executed. Bytecode .class files are therefore programming language agnostic. This makes it possible for any JVM language to use libraries coded in any other JVM language.

While Apache Thrift can be used to build RPC applications in Java, it can also be used by other JVM languages such as Scala, Clojure, and Groovy. We can also use the Apache Thrift IDL compiler to generate Java stubs for an interface, and then the Java stubs can be compiled to byte code for use by non-Java JVM programs. To demonstrate this, we'll rewrite the hello world Java client in Clojure using the same Java IDL stubs we used in the Java example.

Our Clojure client can be tested against any Apache Thrift helloSvc server. The following listing shows an example session run against the Java server from listing 12.3:

```
thrift@ubuntu:~$ java -cp ~/clojure-1.7.0/clojure-1.7.0.jar:\
➥ /usr/local/lib/libthrift-1.0.0.jar:\
➥ /usr/share/java/slf4j-api.jar:\
➥ /usr/share/java/slf4j-nop.jar:\
➥ gen-java \
                  ➥ clojure.main
Clojure 1.7.0
user=> (let [trans (org.apache.thrift.transport.TSocket. "localhost" 9090)]
          (.open trans)
          (let [proto (org.apache.thrift.protocol.TBinaryProtocol. trans)]
              (let [client (helloSvc$Client. proto)]
              (.getMessage client "world"))))
"Hello world"
```

The previous session starts the Clojure interpreter under the JVM (launched with the java command), and then executes a simple Clojure RPC client that approximates the previous hello world program. The example uses the Apache Thrift Java library TSocket and TBinaryProtocol and the IDL compiler-generated Java helloSvc$Client to call the getMessage RPC method. The result, as always, is "Hello world".

To try this example on your own machine, all you need to do is download the Clojure JAR from http://clojure.org/getting_started.

While the Apache Thrift Java classes make polyglot JVM development fairly easy, some users prefer to use idiomatic interfaces more in tune with the languages they're coding in rather than those provided by the Apache Thrift IDL compiler. For example, Java is an object-oriented language, while Scala has a more functional bent. Twitter uses the Scala language for many projects and subsequently developed the open source Scrooge system, which generates native idiomatic Scala code for Apache Thrift (https://twitter.github.io/scrooge/).

12.4 Java transports, protocols, and servers

As one of the original Apache Thrift supported languages, Java has a complete set of transports, protocols, and servers. In this section, we'll see a brief overview of the various servers and I/O stack classes available to users.

12.4.1 Java transports

Apache Thrift transports move bytes from one place to another. The TTransport class provides the base interface for all transport implementations (essentially the methods open, close, read, write, and flush). The Java source files for all transports can be found in thrift/lib/java/src/org/apache/thrift/transport. Transports can be divided into endpoints and layers. We examine both types here.

JAVA ENDPOINT TRANSPORTS

Apache Thrift endpoint transports perform I/O with facilities external to Apache Thrift. Endpoint transports can be organized into three categories: those performing I/O with peers over a network, those performing I/O with files, and those performing I/O with memory. Table 12.3 lists the endpoint transports provided by the Apache Thrift Java library.

Table 12.3   Java endpoint transports

Endpoint	Type	Factory	Base
TSocket	Network	TServerSocket	TIOStreamTransport
TNonblockingSocket	Network	TNonblockingServerSocket	TNonBlockingTransport
TSimpleFileTransport	File		TTransport
TMemoryBuffer	Memory		TTransport

Each endpoint is listed with its type, its factory (if any), and its base class. The network endpoint transports implemented by the Java library are TSocket and TNonblocking-Socket. The TNonblockingSocket is wire compatible with TSocket and only used on the server side with non-blocking servers and on the client side with async clients.

TSocket and TNonblockingSocket transports are created directly on the client side, one for each desired connection, and indirectly on the server side, in response to inbound client connections. RPC servers use factories to accept network connections and generate TSocket/TNonblockingSocket instances to handle each new connection's traffic.

The next endpoint transport, TSimpleFileTransport, is file-based, performing I/O against a named file system file. This transport doesn't have a factory because it isn't designed for client/server RPC. Its principle purpose is serializing UDTs to and from disk.

The last transport is the TMemoryBuffer memory transport. Like the file transports, it isn't designed for client/server RPC. The memory transport is typically used to store a serialized message that can then be passed between threads or sent over a messaging system.

Endpoint transports often have additional transports layered on top of them. The next section introduces the Java layered transports.

JAVA LAYERED TRANSPORTS

Layered transports are designed to overlay an existing transport or transport stack. Each layer above the endpoint performs an additional service during I/O processing.

Table 12.4 lists the layered transports available, their factories, and base classes.

Table 12.4   Java layered transports

Layer	Factory	Base class
TFramedTransport	TFramedTransport.Factory	TTransport
TFastFramedTransport	TFastFramedTransport.Factory	TTransport
THttpClient	THttpClient.Factory	TTransport
TZlibTransport	TZlibTransport.Factory	TTransport

The TFramedTransport "frames" each message by adding a frame size (also known as message size) to the front of every message. Framing is only required when interacting with a non-blocking type server; in Java this includes the TNonblockingServer, THsHaServer, and TThreadedSelectorServer. Framing makes it possible for non-blocking server I/O threads to dispatch entire messages to worker threads without de-serializing the message to find out where it ends.

The Java TFramedTransport allocates a new 1K internal memory buffer for each inbound frame, growing the buffer if the message size requires. The TFast-FramedTransport is wire compatible with the TFramedTransport but reuses a single inbound buffer for all frames. This buffer grows as needed but never shrinks and is never reallocated. Therefore the "at rest" buffer allocation of TFramed-Transport is NumConnections * 1K and the at rest buffer allocation for TFastFramed-Transport is sum (largest message written on each connection). Depending on usage patterns and host environments, TFastFramedTransport may be faster or slower than TFramedTransport.

The THttpClient is a client-side implementation of HTTP. Adding this layer to a TSocket allows Apache Thrift RPC to take place over HTTP. HTTP adds additional over-head to normal TCP-based RPC, so this should only be used if HTTP is required; for example, when network intermediaries require specific HTTP headers to manage traffic. The Java TServlet server implements the Apache Thrift HTTP server-side in Java.

The Zlib transport provides high ratio compression in the I/O stack. Due to the overhead required to perform the compression, this is generally only valuable in scenarios where the size of a single message is very large, many kilobytes to megabytes. This transport layer can be effective when serializing large UDTs to disk files or to memory buffers for transmission over messaging systems.

For more on Apache Thrift transports see chapter 4.

12.4.2 *Java protocols*

Protocols provide the means to serialize and de-serialize IDL types. Three principal protocols are supported across the Apache Thrift framework, all of which are available in the Java library:

- *TBinaryProtocol*—Represents data in binary form
- *TCompactProtocol*—Represents data in binary form compressing integer types
- *TJSONProtocol*—Represents data using JavaScript Object Notation

The reader and the writer in an Apache Thrift exchange must use the same serialization protocol. For more information on Apache Thrift protocols, see chapter 5.

12.4.3 *Java servers*

The Apache Thrift Java library offers several server options:

- *TSimpleServer*—Simple, single-threaded, single-client server.
- *TThreadPoolServer*—Multithreaded server assigning threads from a pool to process connections; when clients disconnect, threads are returned to the pool.
- *TNonblockingServer*—Single-threaded, task-based server; messages from all connections are processed sequentially by a single thread (requires clients to use a framed transport).
- *THsHaServer*—Single I/O thread reads frames and queues them to a processing pool of configurable size (requires clients to use a framed transport).
- *TThreadedSelectorServer*—Multiple I/O threads read frames; frames are queued to a processing pool of configurable size (requires clients to use a framed transport).
- *TServlet*—Extends javax.servlet.http.HttpServlet to provide a Java Servlet-compatible Apache Thrift server using the HTTP protocol.

The first example in this chapter demonstrated the TSimpleServer. Chapter 10 provides Java examples of TThreadedSelectorServer and TThreadPoolServer. Chapter 17 provides a TServlet example. We'll complete the Java examples with a look at asynchronous clients and an asynchronous THsHaServer implementation in the next section.

12.5   *Asynchronous Java RPC*

In a world of distributed software systems, uncertainty around the length of time an operation may take is the norm. Call a server on a calm Sunday night and it may respond instantly. Call the same server on a busy Friday afternoon and it may take minutes to process your request. Synchronous systems attempt to perform processing in a predefined order. For example, imagine you want to run an RPC request and do the laundry; you could do these things synchronously like this:

- RPC Call (5 min)
  - Make request
  - Receive response
- Do laundry (20 min)

If the response takes a long time to arrive it might be a while before you get to start the laundry. In the previous example it takes 25 minutes to complete the work. Asynchronous systems allow us to break up the request/response pair into separate operations, making it possible to do the laundry while the server is working on our request:

- RPC request (instantaneous)
- Do laundry (20 min)
- RPC response (ready any time after the laundry is done)

In the asynchronous model we ignore the RPC response until we've completed the laundry, causing the completion of all tasks to take only 20 minutes. The durations a software program deals with are orders of magnitude smaller, but the effect is the same.

All the examples we've built in this chapter so far have used synchronous code of the "make a request, receive the response, do the laundry" variety. If the response isn't ready right away the code blocks, halting execution until the response arrives. Blocking allows code to execute in a predefined order, making it simpler and easy to reason about. These are valuable features not lightly cast aside.

However, it's worth noting that blocking is one of the most costly things you can do in a high-performance system. When a thread blocks, the operating system scheduler must switch in a new thread to the CPU the blocking thread was using. This context switch is relatively expensive and does nothing to advance the cause of any of the user applications running on the system. Worse, you must pay this toll twice, the second time when your thread is ready to run again. The longer your thread is blocking, the more of its precious resources are evicted from the various caches that make execution efficient. At the end of the day, if you can use up the entire CPU time slice granted you by the operating system, minimizing the number of context switches, your ratio of actual work done to system overhead will benefit. In short, don't block when you have laundry to do.

Let's consider a practical example. Imagine we need to write a program to produce stock quotations. Several of the quotations will be provided electronically, but others will be provided by humans on the floor of the stock exchange. If we tie up a processing thread waiting for each quote request sent to a floor broker, we'll need many threads to keep the application alive. It might be more efficient to send the quote requests to the humans asynchronously, and then return to processing electronic quotes, letting the humans run in the background.

An asynchronous server processor will allow us to handle user requests in any order we like. For example, we might receive a request for an electronic quote, a floor quote, and another electronic quote. Using asynchronous processing on the server, we can process the first electronic quote, dispatch the floor quote to a broker, and then, instead of blocking, process the second electronic quote. The floor broker quote will be processed when it finally arrives, but we can keep all the threads busy working in the meantime.

The code that appears in listing 12.8 implements such a stock quote server using Apache Thrift Java server-side async features. Before we jump into the server code, let's take a quick look at the stock quote interface in the following listing.

Listing 12.7   ~/ ThriftBook/part3/java/async /trade_report.thrift

```
namespace * TradeReporting

struct TradeReport {
    1: string   symbol,
    2: double   price,
    3: i32      size,
    4: i32      seq_num
}

service TradeHistory {
    TradeReport get_last_sale(1: string Symbol)
}
```

This interface is identical to the one used in chapter 11 with the C++ non-blocking server. In Java the IDL compiler will emit all of our code within the `TradeReporting` package. The `TradeHistory` service will allow clients to call the `get_last_sale()` method with a stock symbol, retrieving an appropriate `TradeReport`.

The server will need several parts. We'll create a `FloorBroker` class to run in the background, simulating slow floor broker quotations. We'll also need an async handler for the `TradeHistory` service and a `main` function to set up the Apache Thrift I/O stack and server. The source for our async server appears in the following listing.

Listing 12.8   ~/ ThriftBook/part3/java/async/AsyncServer.java

```
import java.io.IOException;
import java.util.concurrent.atomic.AtomicInteger;
import java.util.concurrent.BlockingQueue;
import java.util.concurrent.LinkedBlockingQueue;
import org.apache.thrift.TProcessor;
```

```
import org.apache.thrift.protocol.TBinaryProtocol;
import org.apache.thrift.server.TServer;
import org.apache.thrift.server.TThreadedSelectorServer;
import org.apache.thrift.transport.TNonblockingServerSocket;
import org.apache.thrift.transport.TTransportException;
import org.apache.thrift.async.AsyncMethodCallback;


public class AsyncServer {

    private static AtomicInteger seq = new AtomicInteger(0);    ❶

    private static class FloorQuoteReq {    ❷
        public String symbol;
        public AsyncMethodCallback callback;

        public FloorQuoteReq(String s, AsyncMethodCallback amc) {
            symbol = s;
            callback = amc;
        }
    }

    private static class FloorBroker implements Runnable {    ❸

        private BlockingQueue<FloorQuoteReq> manualQuoteQ;

        public FloorBroker() {
            manualQuoteQ = new LinkedBlockingQueue<FloorQuoteReq>();    ❹
        }

        public BlockingQueue<FloorQuoteReq> getQ() { return manualQuoteQ; }

        @Override
        public void run() {    ❺
            try {
                while (true) {
                    FloorQuoteReq fqr = manualQuoteQ.take();
                    Thread.sleep(10000);
        ❻          fqr.callback.onComplete(
                        new TradeReporting.TradeReport(fqr.symbol,
                                               50.25, 1500,
                                               seq.incrementAndGet()));
                }
            } catch (InterruptedException ex) {
                System.out.println("[Server] Floor broker thread exiting");
            }
        }
    }

    public static class TradeHistoryHandler    ❼
            implements TradeReporting.TradeHistory.Iface {

        @Override
        public TradeReporting.TradeReport get_last_sale(String symbol) {
            return new TradeReporting.TradeReport(symbol, 76.50, 500,
```

```
                                                  seq.incrementAndGet());
        }
    }

    private static class AsyncTradeHistoryHandler          ⑧
            implements TradeReporting.TradeHistory.AsyncIface {

        private TradeHistoryHandler electronic;            ⑨
        private BlockingQueue<FloorQuoteReq> manual;       ⑩

        public AsyncTradeHistoryHandler(BlockingQueue<FloorQuoteReq> q) {
            manual = q;
            electronic = new TradeHistoryHandler();
        }

        @Override                                          ⑪
        public void get_last_sale(String symbol,
                                  AsyncMethodCallback callback)
                throws org.apache.thrift.TException {
            if (symbol.length() < 3) {
                manual.add(new FloorQuoteReq(symbol, callback));
            } else {
                callback.onComplete(electronic.get_last_sale(symbol));
            }
        }
    }

    public static void main(String[] args)                ⑫
            throws TTransportException, IOException, InterruptedException {

        FloorBroker floor = new FloorBroker();             ⑬
        (new Thread(floor)).start();

        TProcessor proc = new TradeReporting.TradeHistory.AsyncProcessor(   ⑭
            new AsyncTradeHistoryHandler(floor.getQ()));
        TNonblockingServerSocket trans_svr =               ⑮
            new TNonblockingServerSocket(9090);
        TServer server =
            new THsHaServer(
                new THsHaServer.Args(trans_svr)                              ⑯
                .processor(proc)
                .protocolFactory(new TBinaryProtocol.Factory())
                .workerThreads(4));
        System.out.println("[Server] listening of port 9090");
⑰      server.serve();
    }
}
```

The server listing is almost completely contained within the AsyncServer class. The class begins by creating an atomic, and therefore thread-safe, integer called seq ❶ that allows us to provide a unique sequence number for each trade report. Next the FloorQuoteReq class is declared ❷. This class captures floor broker quote requests, including the symbol to quote and the callback object used to return the result to the caller when the quote is finally available.

The next nested class is `FloorBroker` ❸. This class simulates the slow floor broker quote process. A concurrent blocking queue ❹ is used to hold the pending quote requests. A background thread will be used to execute the `run()` function ❺, which simulates the floor broker by processing 1 quote every 10 seconds. The Apache Thrift `AsyncMethodCallback` object `onComplete()` method ❻ allows us to asynchronously respond to the client when their quote is ready. Event processing loops like this are a hallmark of asynchronous systems, though often hidden within a framework or inside a language runtime.

The `TradeHistory` handler class ❼ is a straightforward Apache Thrift service handler implementing the `TradeReporting.TradeHistory.Iface` generated from the IDL. Because we're building an asynchronous service implementation, the actual handler provided to the server for processing is an `AsyncTradeHistoryHandler` ❽. This handler implements the `AsyncIface` version of the service. We invoke the synchronous `TradeHistory` handler for electronic quotation requests ❾ and queue slower floor traded stock requests for asynchronous execution ❿. The asynchronous `get_last_sale()` method ⓫ (arbitrarily) queues requests for stocks with less than three characters in their symbol for async execution and processes the rest synchronously using the synchronous handler.

The `main()` function handles the server startup ⓬. The `main()` function begins by creating the `FloorBroker` instance used to process quotes asynchronously and then starts a background thread to run the queue processing loop ⓭.

Next the `main()` function creates an `AsyncProcessor` for the `TradeHistory` service and initializes it with an instance of the async `TradeHistory` handler ⓮. We construct the handler with a reference to the `FloorBroker` queue so that the handler can queue up deferred floor broker quote requests.

Asynchronous clients and servers require the non-blocking socket transport. On the server side the endpoint transport must be `TNonblockingServerSocket` ⓯. The server transport is configured to listen on port 9090.

For the server class, we selected `THsHaServer` ⓰. This server uses a single I/O thread to dispatch messages from the network to a pool of worker threads. Any of the non-blocking-type Java servers can be used in async applications, which also includes the `TThreadedSelectorServer` and the `TNonblockingServer`. All these servers internally implement the `TFramedTransport` layer on top of a `TNonblockingSocket` for each client connection. Clients typically use a `TFramedTransport` over a `TSocket` to connect to asynchronous servers; however clients can be async as well by using the async `TNonblockingSocket` endpoint on the client side. The server is configured to use the `TBinaryProtocol` for serialization. Once configured, we start the server using the `serve()` method ⓱.

The key difference between the Apache Thrift async server and a synchronous server is the use of the service-specific `AsyncProcessor`. When using this processor, the async handler interface is invoked with an `AsyncMethodCallback` that we use to return results to the client at some point in the future.

Async servers are a good fit in many situations but are particularly effective for long-polling interfaces where responses are returned well after the original request was made. For more on long polling and a code example, see chapter 13.

Now that we have a stock quote server ready, we can turn our attention to building a client to test it with. Client programs can benefit from asynchronous RPC in much the same way as servers, so while we're on the subject, we may as well build a stock quote client using the Apache Thrift async `client` interface. A simple async client appears in the following listing.

Listing 12.9 ~/ ThriftBook/part3/java/async/AsyncClient.java

```java
import java.io.IOException;
import java.util.concurrent.CountDownLatch;
import java.util.concurrent.TimeUnit;
import java.util.concurrent.TimeoutException;
import org.apache.thrift.protocol.TBinaryProtocol;
import org.apache.thrift.transport.TNonblockingSocket;
import org.apache.thrift.TException;
import org.apache.thrift.async.TAsyncMethodCall;
import org.apache.thrift.async.TAsyncClientManager;
import org.apache.thrift.async.AsyncMethodCallback;
import TradeReporting.TradeReport;

public class AsyncClient {

    //Class template supporting async wait and timeout
    private static abstract class WaitableCallback<T>            ❶
            implements AsyncMethodCallback<T> {

        private CountDownLatch latch = new CountDownLatch(1);

        //Synchronization Interface
        public void reset() { latch = new CountDownLatch(1); }
        public void complete() { latch.countDown(); }
        public boolean wait(int i) {
            boolean b = false;
            try {                                                ❷
                b = latch.await(i, TimeUnit.MILLISECONDS);
            }
            catch(Exception e) {
                System.out.println("[Client] await error");
            }
            return b;
        }

        //AsyncMethodCallback<T> interface
        @Override
        public void onError(Exception ex) {            ❸
            if (ex instanceof TimeoutException) {
                System.out.println("[Client] Async call timed out");
            } else {
                System.out.println("[Client] Async call error");
```

```
                }
            complete();
        }
    }

    //Application entry point
    public static void main(String[] args)          ④
            throws IOException, InterruptedException, TException {

        //Async client and I/O stack setup
        TAsyncClientManager client_man = new TAsyncClientManager();
        TNonblockingSocket trans_ep =
            new TNonblockingSocket("localhost", 9090);           ⑤
        TradeReporting.TradeHistory.AsyncClient client =
            new TradeReporting.TradeHistory.AsyncClient(
                new TBinaryProtocol.Factory(),client_man, trans_ep);

        //get_last_sale() async callback handler
        WaitableCallback<TradeReport> wc =                   ⑥
                new WaitableCallback<TradeReport>() {

            @Override
            public void onComplete(TradeReport tr) {       ⑦
                try {
                    System.out.println("[Client] received [" +
                                    tr.seq_num + "] " + tr.symbol +
                                    " : " + tr.size + " @ " + tr.price);
                } finally {
                    complete();
                }
            }
        };

        //Make a couple of async calls (one electronic one manual)
        wc.reset();
        client.get_last_sale("IBM", wc);                               ⑦
        System.out.println("[Client] get_last_sale() executing async");
    ⑧  wc.wait(500);
        wc.reset();
        client.get_last_sale("F", wc);        ⑨
        wc.wait(25000);

        //Make an async call which will time out
    ⑩  client.setTimeout(1000);
        wc.reset();
        client.get_last_sale("GE", wc);
        wc.wait(5000);

        //Shutdown async client manager and close network socket
    ⑪  client_man.stop();
        trans_ep.close();
    }
}
```

The async client code begins by creating a class named `WaitableCallback` ❶. This generic class is designed to be parameterized with the return type of a given service method, in this case a `TradeReport`. This helper class could be used with any number of async methods; however, in our case we have only a single service method to manage: `get_last_sale_call`.

Using asynchronous calls allows the client code to make server requests and then go about other work. The async client API doesn't currently support multiple outstanding calls on the wire. A way is needed to determine whether a given call is complete or not before we can make further calls to the server. The `WaitableCallback` class uses a Java `CountDownLatch` to synchronize successive server calls when necessary ❷.

The `WaitableCallback` class `reset()` function reinitializes the latch, the `complete()` function decrements the latch, and the `wait()` function blocks until the latch is reduced to zero. The async handlers invoke the `complete()` method to signal other program elements when it's safe to make further calls to the server.

The `WaitableCallback` class implements the `AsyncMethodCallback` generic interface. This interface has two methods, `onComplete()` and `onError()`. The `onComplete()` method is invoked when a server replies to an RPC request. The `onError()` callback ❸ is invoked in error conditions. The `WaitableCallback` generic is a helper class and only provides a partial implementation, supplying a definition for `onError()` but not `onComplete()`. This will allow us to create instances of `WaitableCallback` with custom implementations of `onComplete()` throughout our code, while sharing one standard `onError()` handler.

The `AsyncMethodCallback` class changed its interface in a breaking way before Thrift v0.10.0 was released. Older versions were parameterized with the method call object (for example, `get_last_sale_call` here) rather than the method return type. You can find an example source file that works with older versions of Apache Thrift in the book's Git history.

The client `main()` function ❹ provides the setup for the server connection as well as several asynchronous calls to the stock quote server. The first block of code in the `main()` function configures the Apache Thrift I/O stack and the `TAsyncClient-Manager` ❺. The `TAsyncClientManager` instance provides an event loop responsible for invoking callbacks and timeouts in the asynchronous framework.

Async clients must use the `TNonblockingSocket` endpoint transport with implicit message framing, as we've done here. Async clients can only connect to servers that use a `TSocket`/`TFramedTransport`-compatible server stack. We also create an `Async-Client` instance, which allows us to invoke RPC methods asynchronously. The client is initialized with the `TBinaryProtocol` for serialization, matching the server.

The next block of code creates a `WaitableCallback` instance used to handle async callback processing for the `get_last_sale()` method. The `onComplete()` override provides our normal response processing behavior ❼.

With the setup out of the way, we can begin to make calls to the server. In the first RPC invocation we reset the `WaitableCallback` latch, request a quote for IBM, print out a message, and then wait for the call to complete before making the next call ❽. Note that because the call to get_last_sale() is asynchronous, the "...executing async" message will typically display before the callback prints out the server response. You could easily run any other code you like here (do the laundry) while the quotation request is processed in the background.

The wait() method is called here with a value of 500 milliseconds. This causes the wait to timeout if the server doesn't respond within 500 milliseconds. The wait will return when the server callback completes or when the timeout elapses.

When the first wait completes, we make a second call requesting a quote for Ford ("F") ❾. This symbol is less than 3 characters long, so it will go to the floor on the server, taking 10 seconds to process. To support this, we allow a wait of up to 25 seconds.

Prior to making the final request, we set the async timeout to one second ❿. The next request will be routed to the floor on the server, causing this third RPC call to timeout after one second, before the five-second wait completes.

The final bit of code performs clean up, stopping the client manager and closing the transport ⓫.

The GitHub source for this project includes a build.xml ant script that we can use to test run the client and server, as shown in the following command line session:

```
thrift@ubuntu:~/ThriftBook/part3/java/async$ ant
Buildfile: /home/thrift/ThriftBook/part3/java/async/build.xml

clean:

compile:
    [javac] Compiling 2 source files to
    ➥ /home/thrift/ThriftBook/part3/java/async/gen-java
    [javac] Compiling 2 source files to
    ➥ /home/thrift/ThriftBook/part3/java/async
    [javac] Note: /home/thrift/ThriftBook/part3/java/async/AsyncServer.java
    ➥ uses unchecked or unsafe operations.
    [javac] Note: Recompile with -Xlint:unchecked for details.

all:

BUILD SUCCESSFUL
Total time: 1 second
```

The following session shows a sample run of the client:

```
thrift@ubuntu:~/ThriftBook/part3/java/async$ ant runClient
Buildfile: /home/thrift/ThriftBook/part3/java/async/build.xml

runClient:
    [java] [Client] get_last_sale() executing async
    [java] [Client] received [1] IBM : 500 @ 76.5
    [java] [Client] received [2] F : 1500 @ 50.25
    [java] [Client] Async call timed out
```

```
BUILD SUCCESSFUL
Total time: 11 seconds
```

...and the server:

```
thrift@ubuntu:~/ThriftBook/part3/java/async$ ant runServer
Buildfile: /home/thrift/ThriftBook/part3/java/async/build.xml

runServer:
     [java] [Server] listening of port 9090
```

As you can see from the client session, the "...executing async" message appears before the server response to the RPC call, which was invoked first. Also, the quote for symbol F took approximately 10 seconds to return and the final request timed out after 1 second, as expected.

   While we've covered a fair amount of Apache Thrift Java in this chapter, Java is one of our three demonstration languages in part 2 of this book. You'll see (or have seen) many more interesting Apache Thrift Java code snippets in chapters 4–10.

Summary

This chapter covered

- How to set up Apache Thrift for Java and JVM-based development
- How to use Ant and Maven with Apache Thrift
- How to build Java RPC clients and servers
- An overview of Apache Thrift Java transports, protocols, and servers
- How to build asynchronous RPC clients and servers

13

Building C# clients and servers with .NET Core and Windows

This chapter covers

- Configuring Apache Thrift for use with .NET Core on Windows
- Building C# RPC clients and servers with Apache Thrift
- Creating Apache Thrift applications with Visual Studio
- Using C#-supported transports, protocols, and servers

The .NET Core framework and CLR virtual machine provide a distinct and parallel alternative to the Java/JVM ecosystem in enterprise application development, yet often applications from these two environments need to collaborate. Apache Thrift can play an important role in such polyglot settings, providing a unified communication framework that works effectively with C# and other .NET development languages, as well as more than 20 non-.NET languages, including Java.

This chapter walks you through the process of building Apache Thrift clients and servers using C#. While C# is often thought of as a Windows-based language, it's also widely used on UNIX-like systems, and many developers also use C# in iOS and Android mobile environments. Apache Thrift integrates well with C# and .NET Core in all these settings. In this chapter, we'll focus on the Windows implementation of .NET Core and C#, though C# developers in other environments should find it easy to adopt the code examples to their preferred platform.

.NET disambiguation

Microsoft introduced C# and the .NET Framework in 2000, at which time the .NET virtual machine (known as the CLR or Common Language Runtime) operated on Windows only, though it was designed to be platform portable. The .NET Framework is often used for desktop development, due to its rich GUI toolkits and other Windows-specific features.

In 2001, Ximian (later acquired by Novell) open sourced the Mono Project, a Linux-based CLR which allowed .NET-based applications to run on Linux, Android, and other systems. In 2010 Apache Thrift 0.1.0 was released with built in support for C# on Mono 1.2.6 for Linux users and .NET Framework 3.5 for Windows users.

After leaving Novell in 2011, the Mono founders formed a company to support and extend Mono called Xamarin. Xamarin was acquired by Microsoft in 2016, and much of their work has turned into tooling within Visual Studio with support for Xamarin Mono environments for iOS and Android mobile devices.

In 2014 Microsoft announced .NET Core to include cross-platform support for .NET directly and to embrace the open source model under the mantle of the .NET Foundation. The .NET Core is a redesigned version of .NET with simplified class libraries and full support for NuGet package-based updates, perfect for building modern cross-platform microservices. Support for .NET Core 2.0 was added in Apache Thrift 0.11 in late 2017.

In 2016 Microsoft introduced the .NET Standard to define a single set of requirements all .NET offerings must support. This allows developers to code to the .NET Standard and then run on any .NET platform. Modern .NET Framework (4.6.1+), .NET Core (2.0+), Mono (5.4), and the latest Xamarin environments all support the 2017 .NET Standard 2.0.

We begin this chapter with a look at the process of setting up an Apache Thrift development environment on Windows, while at the same time covering the general coding techniques used to build RPC applications with the C# language.

NOTE Each chapter in part 3 of this book is designed to get you up and running with a particular language, platform, or both. While there's much more Apache Thrift .NET to see, hopefully this chapter prepares you for serious C# RPC development. For more information on Apache Thrift transports, protocols, IDL, and servers, see part 2 of this book. Part 2 code examples are written in C++, Java, and Python, but the features are fairly easy to translate back to C#, given the overview presented here.

13.1   *Setting up Apache Thrift on Windows*

To set up a basic C# development environment for Apache Thrift on Windows, developers need to have the following resources at hand:

1   Build tools (compilers, linkers, interpreters, and so on) for the languages to be used
2   The Apache Thrift IDL compiler
3   Apache Thrift libraries for the programming languages that will be used

The Microsoft Visual Studio IDE is a powerful development platform used extensively for Windows-based development in a range of programming languages. The Community (formerly Express) version of Visual Studio for Windows Desktop is available on Microsoft's website as a free download. We use the "Visual Studio Community 2017 edition; .NET desktop development" system in this chapter to build C# RPC clients and servers (older versions of Visual Studio should also work fine). You can either download and install Visual Studio Community or follow along with your favorite IDE/Editor. Apache Thrift requires .NET Framework v3.5+ or .NET Core 2.0 as of Apache Thrift version 0.11.0; the examples below use .NET Framework 4.5.

The Apache Thrift website provides a precompiled thrift.exe IDL compiler for download, making building the compiler from source unnecessary on Windows. The compiler can be found on the Apache Thrift download page (http://thrift.apache.org/download). Placing the compiler on the path makes it easy to access (though perhaps inelegant; I usually drop thrift.exe into the C:\Windows directory):

```
C:\Users\Randy>dir C:\Windows\thrift.exe
 Volume in drive C is OS
 Volume Serial Number is D023-5174

 Directory of C:\Windows

2017-03-12  09:30 PM         5,642,240 thrift.exe
               1 File(s)      5,642,240 bytes
               0 Dir(s)   317,772,148,736 bytes free
```

The last step in preparing a system for Apache Thrift C# development is acquiring the Apache Thrift C# library. Much like Java, C# programs are compiled down to byte code, which is then interpreted by a platform-specific virtual machine or runtime environment. The Visual Studio platform installs the .NET Framework that includes the Microsoft Common Language Runtime (CLR). One advantage offered by runtime environments is that programs and libraries can be compiled to byte code once on any platform and then used on any other system supporting the runtime.

This allows us to download a precompiled version of the Apache Thrift C# library and use it on any system that supports the CLR. Later in this chapter (section 13.4.2), we'll use the Windows-centric NuGet package manager to install a pre-built Apache Thrift library.

Another benefit common to runtime platforms is that no matter what language you use, the byte code format is the same, so libraries written in one language can be readily used by programs written in another language. In the .NET world this means that F#, VisualBasic, and Visual C++ applications can use the Apache Thrift C# library for RPC as easily as C# programs can.

For our initial C# development environment, we'll build the Apache Thrift C# library from source. Even if you choose to use a prepackaged library later, it's worth building the library from source once or twice to understand the process, should you ever need to source debug a problem or make use of an as-yet-unreleased patch.

To build the Apache Thrift C# library we'll need a copy of the Apache Thrift sources. A compressed version of the source tree can be found on the same download page as the IDL compiler, or the source code repository can be cloned from GitHub if you have Git installed. In these examples, we have the Thrift source installed in the directory C:\dev\thriftsrc. Support for the .NET Framework is in thriftsrc/lib/csharp, and support for .NET Core is in thriftsrc/lib/netcore.

Once we have a copy of the Apache Thrift source code, we can build the C# support library with Visual Studio. To build the Apache Thrift .NET Framework C# library follow these steps:

1 Run Visual Studio.
2 Choose [File] > Open Project and open the Visual Studio solution file for the C# library: C:\dev\thriftsrc\lib\csharp\src\Thrift.sln (if prompted, install .NET Framework 3.5 support).
3 When the solution is loaded, right-click the Thrift project in the Solution Explorer pane and choose Build (see figure 13.1).

This will build a debug version of the Apache Thrift C# library. The runtime library in our example is created at C:\dev\thriftsrc\lib\csharp\src\bin\Debug\Thrift.dll.

To build a release version of the library you can change the solution configuration from "Debug" to "Release" in the Solution Configurations combo box (in the Visual Studio toolbar) and then rebuild the Thrift project.

Now that we have an IDL compiler and the Apache Thrift C# library ready, we can begin building .NET RPC applications.

> **NOTE** You can also build the Thrift.dll on Linux platforms using the Mono framework. For example, on Ubuntu Linux you would use the following command to build the release version of the Thrift.dll:

```
~/thrift/lib/csharp/src$ xbuild /p:Configuration=Release
    /p:TargetFrameworkVersion="v4.5" Thrift.csproj
```

For this to work, the Mono framework supporting v4.5 and tools must be installed. For example, on Ubuntu you can install the latest Mono platform with the following command:

```
$ sudo apt-get install mono-complete
```

You may need to adjust the `TargetFrameworkVersion` build parameter to match your framework version. Similar instructions work on OSX, and you can "brew install mono" to add Mono support.

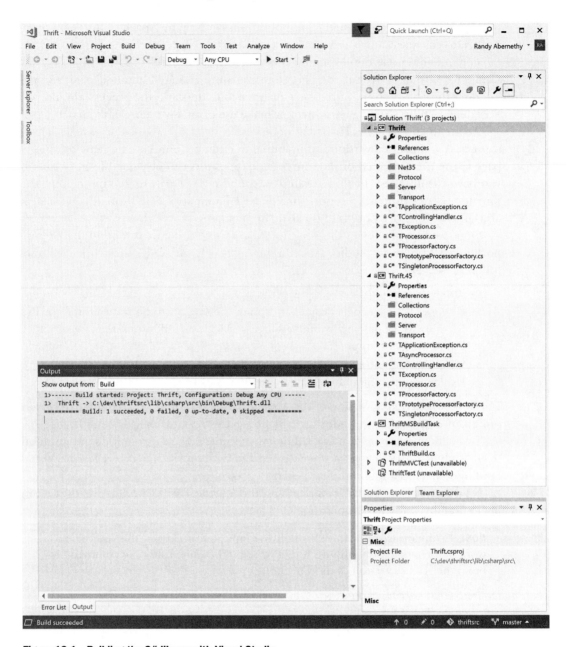

Figure 13.1   Building the C# library with Visual Studio

13.2   A simple client and server

In this section, we'll examine the build process for an Apache Thrift C# application. Before we look at a more complex code example, we'll build a simple C# RPC client and server. This Hello World example will walk you through the process of creating an RPC server and client that both use a shared library implementing the interface client/server stubs.

13.2.1   Creating a Visual Studio RPC solution

Apache Thrift clients and servers communicate through shared interfaces defined in Apache Thrift IDL. In dynamic programming languages, the code generated for these interfaces is loaded at runtime from the shared script modules generated by the IDL compiler. In purely compiled languages, the generated code is typically compiled into the client and the server. In virtual machine-based languages such as Java and C#, the interface support is often built into a shared library which is then loaded by any client or server using that interface at runtime, though many build configurations are possible and viable.

In this example we'll build the RPC client and server as separate projects and create a third project for shared interface code configured as a runtime library. To keep things organized, we'll create a Visual Studio Solution to contain all three projects.

To create the solution and our three initial projects, follow these steps:

1 Launch a new copy of Visual Studio.
2 Choose [File] > New Project.
3 On the left side of the new project dialog, select the Installed > Templates > Other Project Types item and click the Blank Solution type from the center pane.
4 In the Name text box at the bottom of the dialog, enter "hellocs" as the name for the solution and choose OK (see figure 13.2).

Figure 13.2   Creating a new C# solution

Once the solution is created we can add C# projects for the client, server, and shared interface library. We'll create Console applications for these trivial client and server apps and use a Class Library project for the shared library. Follow these steps to create the three projects:

1 To add the client project, right-click the hellocs solution in the Solution Explorer and choose Add > New Project ….

2 In the Add New Project dialog, open the Installed > Visual C# templates in the left pane, and select the Console App (.NET Framework) template in the center pane.

3 In the Name text box at the bottom of the dialog enter "helloClient" as the name for the client project and choose OK (see figure 13.3).

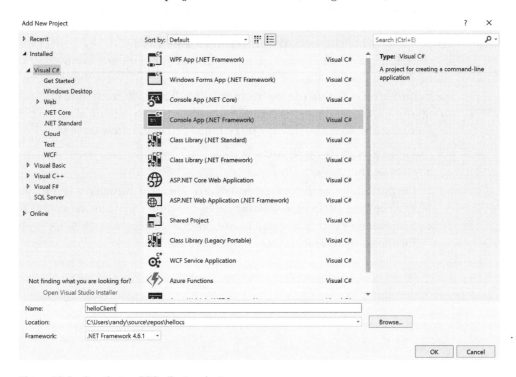

Figure 13.3   Creating an RPC client project

Repeat the previous steps to create a second Console Application project called "hello-Server". Finally complete the following steps to add the Client/Server stub shared library project:

1 To add the shared library project to house the Client/Server stub code, right-click the hellocs solution in the Solution Explorer and choose Add > New Project.

2 In the Add New Project dialog, open Installed > Visual C# in the left pane and select the Class Library (.NET Framework) template in the center pane.

3 In the Name text box at the bottom of the dialog enter "helloService" as the name for the class library and choose OK.

When complete, your solution should look something like figure 13.4. A boilerplate Program.cs file is created for each project. We'll edit the Program.cs files in the client and server projects to create our example RPC client and server shortly. First, however, we need to define an RPC service for the client and server to communicate over.

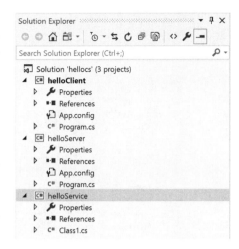

Figure 13.4 Client, server, and service interface projects

13.2.2 Creating the interface library

Now that we have our skeleton projects created, we can define a service interface for our RPC server. We'll use the same hello.thrift IDL file used throughout part 3. This trivial interface defines a single helloSvc service with one method, `getMessage()`, which takes a name string as input and returns a greeting string, as shown in the following listing.

Listing 13.1   ~thriftbook/part3/cs/hello.thrift

```
service helloSvc {
    string getMessage(1: string name)
}
```

The hello.thrift file will be used to generate all the files needed to support the service, so we'll add it to the helloService project. There's one important consideration associated with creating text files within Visual Studio. By default, Visual Studio creates text files with an encoding prefix in the file. This will look like garbage to the IDL compiler, which is expecting a plain ASCII file. We'll need to perform a save-as operation after creating our IDL file to save it with simple ASCII encoding. To add a new thrift IDL file to the helloService project, follow these steps:

1 Right-click the helloService project and choose Add > New Item.

2 From the Add New Item dialog select the Text File item and enter the name "hello.thrift" in the Name text box at the bottom of the dialog; then click Add.

3 With the hello.thrift file selected in the Solution Explorer, choose [File] > Save hello.thrift As …, then click the down arrow on the Save button and choose Save with Encoding …. Click Yes to replace the existing file; then select the US-ASCII Encoding from the Advanced Save Options dialog, and choose OK (see figure 13.5).

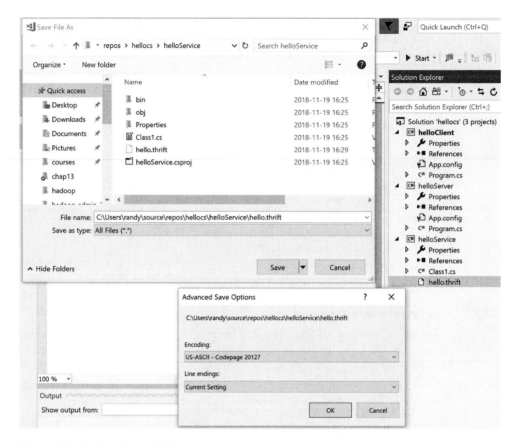

Figure 13.5   Saving files in ASCII format

Once you've created the file you can add the service definition from listing 13.1 and save your work. Your solution should now look something like figure 13.6.

The hello.thrift IDL must be compiled using the thrift.exe IDL compiler every time the IDL source is changed. Visual Studio doesn't know how to build ".thrift" files automatically. We can, however, integrate the IDL compiler into the Visual Studio build process using a pre-build event (see figure 13.7).

To add an IDL compiler pre-build event, follow these steps:

1 Right-click the helloService project in the Solution Explorer and choose Properties.
2 Click the Build Events item at the left of the dialog.
3 In the Pre-build event command line area enter the following command line:

```
thrift  -out "../../"  -gen csharp "$(ProjectDir)hello.thrift"
```

4 Choose [File] > Save All to save your work.

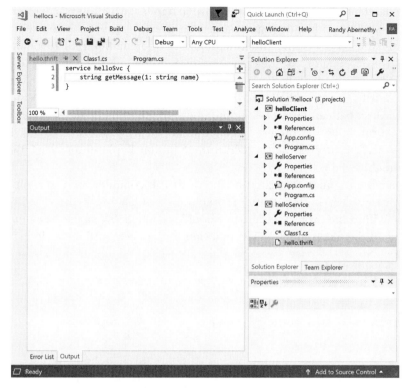

Figure 13.6 Adding the Apache Thrift IDL to the solution

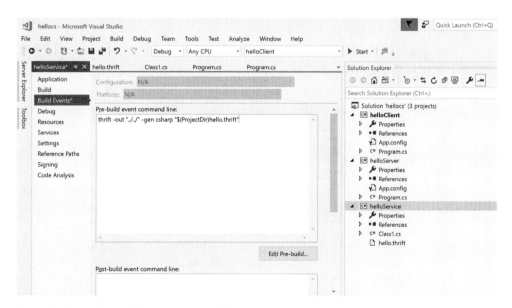

Figure 13.7 Adding an IDL compiler pre-build event

The command line you entered runs the Thrift compiler (which, as you may recall, must be on the OS search path and must be named "thrift.exe"), the –out switch tells the compiler to emit the generated files into the project directory rather than the build working directory (bin/Debug or bin/Release), the –gen switch tells the compiler to generate C# output, and the path at the end of the command line designates the IDL file to compile, hello.thrift. Note that the $(ProjectDir) variable will be replaced by Visual Studio with the project path and must be quoted in case the pathname has spaces.

Now we can build the project to generate our helloSvc stubs. To build the helloService project, right-click the project in the Solution Explorer and click Build. The project should build with no errors.

To examine the files generated by the thrift IDL compiler, we can right-click the helloService project in the Solution Explorer and choose Open Folder in File Explorer. Within the project folder you should see a helloSvc.cs file (see figure 13.8). This .cs file is the generated C# class that houses the client and server interface stubs for our helloSvc RPC service.

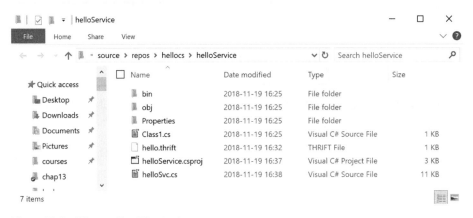

Figure 13.8   IDL compiler C# output

To build this generated helloSvc.cs file into a .NET library it needs to be included in our helloService project:

1 Right-click the helloService project in the Solution Explorer and choose Add > Existing Item.
2 Navigate to the helloSvc.cs file, select it, and click Add.

At this point we have no further use for the boilerplate Class file generated by Visual Studio. To remove it, right-click the Class1.cs file in the helloService project and choose Delete; then click the OK button in the confirmation dialog.

We now have all the library source code created; however, we're not ready to build it. Click on the helloSvc.cs file in the Solution Explorer to open it in the text editor. You'll see many IntelliSense errors, indicated by the red underlines in the source listing. These are due to a missing dependency. The generated code depends on the

Apache Thrift C# library. To resolve the dependency, we can add the library file we built at the beginning of the chapter to the project references.

To add the C# Apache Thrift library reference, right-click the References item in the helloService project in the Solution Explorer and choose Add Reference. Next use the Browse button to locate the Thrift.dll you compiled in C:\dev\thriftsrc\lib\ csharp\src\bin\Debug\Thrift.dll. Make sure a check is next to the Thrift.dll entry in the Reference Manager dialog and then click OK. After a brief pause, the Intelisense errors should clear.

To build the helloService shared library, right-click the helloService project and choose Build. This should build the helloService.dll that our client and server programs will use to communicate over the helloSvc service interface (see figure 13.9). It's worth looking through the Apache Thrift-generated C# source in helloSvc.cs if this is your first Apache Thrift C# project.

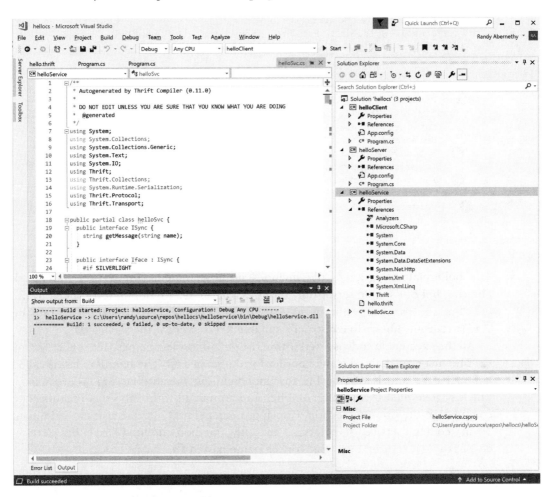

Figure 13.9   Successful helloService build

13.2.3 Creating the RPC server

Now that we have our simple helloSvc service stubs built into a shared library, we can create a server to implement the service. The Visual Studio helloServer project has a starter file called Program.cs already created. For this trivial example we'll replace the contents of this file with Apache Thrift RPC server code.

The following listing shows the simple server source.

Listing 13.2   ~thriftbook/part3/cs/helloServer.cs

```
using System;                    ❶
using Thrift.Transport;          ❷
using Thrift.Server;             ❸

namespace helloServer {                                          ❹
    public class HelloHandler : helloSvc.Iface {        ❺
        public string getMessage(string name) {             ❻
            Console.WriteLine("Received from client: " + name);
            return "Hello " + name;
        }
    }

    class Program {
        static void Main(string[] args) {
            int port = 8585;
            HelloHandler handler = new HelloHandler();              ❼
            helloSvc.Processor proc = new helloSvc.Processor(handler);   ❽
            TServerTransport trans = new TServerSocket(port, 0, true);   ❾
            TServer server = new TSimpleServer(proc, trans);     ❿
            Console.WriteLine("Server running on port " + port);
            server.Serve();                                       ⓫
        }
    }
}
```

The boilerplate Program.cs file includes using statements for several framework libraries, but our simple server only requires System ❶. We do, however, need to use the `Thrift.Transport` library to specify an endpoint transport ❷, and the `Thrift.Server` library to construct a suitable RPC server for the service ❸.

All the executable code is listed within the default project namespace, `helloServer` ❹. The first class defined is the handler for the service ❺. The handler class is called `HelloHandler` and is responsible for implementing the interface `helloSvc.Iface`, which is generated by the IDL compiler and contained within the service library we compiled in the previous section. Copying the generated interface isn't a bad way to begin coding service handlers. The only method defined for this service, `getMessage()`, returns a greeting for the name passed ❻.

The second class defined is the `Program` class itself, where the `Main()` function entry point resides. Within the `Main()` function we set up and run the RPC server. The first step to get a server running is to create an instance of the handler class for the service you wish to host ❼. Next we need to wrap the handler in the appropriate service processor to translate network traffic into calls to the handler methods ❽.

For this simple server, we set up a typical network stack for RPC operations. To host client connections over TCP we've selected the `TServerSocket` ❾ transport endpoint. The first constructor parameter configures the server socket to listen on TCP port 8585. The second parameter specifies the client timeout; 0 is the default and indicates no timeout. The third parameter is important; this Boolean enables server-side buffering when set to `true`. This should almost always be set to `true` to avoid multiple small writes to the network; the default value is `false`.

Next we configure an instance of the Apache Thrift `TSimpleServer` to host the service using the configured processor and transport ❿. Like most Apache Thrift servers, if no serialization protocol is specified, the TBinaryProtocol is used.

When everything is configured, we can call the server's `serve()` method to run the server ⓫. This causes the server to begin listening for client connections. When a client connects, the server will use the processor to handle RPC calls over the connection.

At this point, we have two unresolved dependencies in the server project. The first is a dependency on the C# Apache Thrift library, which contains the transport and server classes. You can add a reference to the thrift.dll in the helloServer project the same way you did in the helloService project.

The second dependency is on the helloService project. The server relies on the helloSvc Processor and the `helloSvc.Iface` interface. Visual Studio makes it easy to add a reference to another project in the solution. To add a reference to the helloService project, right-click the references item in the helloServer project in the Solution Explorer, and then choose Add Reference. Click the Solution item on the left side of the Reference Manager dialog, check the helloService project from the list, and choose OK.

To build the server, right-click the helloServer project in the Solution Explorer and choose Build. The output pane at the bottom of the window should report the path where the helloServer.exe is generated (see figure 13.10).

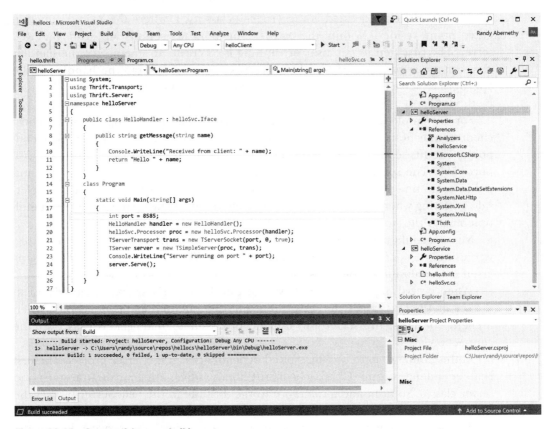

Figure 13.10   Successful server build

13.2.4   Creating the RPC client

The last step in this simple RPC example is creating a client to test the server. Having walked through most of the key build concepts in the prior two sections, putting a client together is fairly straightforward. The following listing shows the simple RPC client that you can copy into the helloClient project Program.cs file.

Listing 13.3   ~thriftbook/part3/cs/helloClient.cs

```
using System;            ❶
using Thrift.Protocol;
using Thrift.Transport;

namespace helloClient
{
    class Program
    {
        static void Main(string[] args)
```

```
        {
                TTransport trans = new TSocket("localhost", 8585);        ❷
                trans = new TBufferedTransport(trans as TStreamTransport);   ❸
     ❹         trans.Open();
                TBinaryProtocol proto = new TBinaryProtocol(trans);        ❺
     ❻         helloSvc.Client client = new helloSvc.Client(proto);
                string result = client.getMessage("Ginger");              ❼
                Console.WriteLine("Received from server: " + result);
        }
    }
}
```

Like the server, the client only requires the System .NET library, but it does depend on the Thrift `Protocol` and `Transport` libraries ❶. The client must use an endpoint transport compatible with the server's transport, so we configured a `TSocket` using port 8585 in this example ❷. The `TBufferedTransport` buffers the many small writes made by the Apache Thrift protocol layer, only transmitting data when an entire message is prepared.

In the C# language, `TSocket` is derived from `TStreamTransport`, which is in turn derived from `TTransport`. We've saved the `TSocket` with a generic `TTransport` reference to reuse the trans reference variable. However, because the `TBuffered-Transport` requires a `TStreamTransport` to wrap, we must use the "as" operator to reinterpret the trans reference to the `TSocket` as a `TStreamTransport` ❸. After reassigning the buffer-wrapped socket to the trans reference we can open the connection to the server with the `open()` method ❹. We'll take a closer look at C# Apache Thrift transports in the next section.

To complete the client I/O stack, we need to add a serialization protocol that matches the protocol used on the target server. We create a `TBinaryProtocol` here to layer on top of the transport stack ❺. We'll take a closer look at Apache Thrift C# Protocols in the next section as well.

The final step in wiring up our I/O stack is to layer the helloSvc client on top of the protocol ❻. With the client object properly configured, we can begin calling the service methods defined in the Hello Service IDL ❼.

The code is complete, but we have several unresolved dependencies. To resolve these, follow the same procedure used with the server project, adding a reference to the helloService project and the Thrift shared library. When the references are in place, right-click the helloClient project and choose Build to create the helloClient.exe.

13.2.5 *Testing the RPC application*

At this point we've generated a helloService.dll shared library for the RPC service, a helloServer.exe RPC server program, and a helloClient.exe client. To test the solution, we need to run the server and then the client.

An easy way to do this is to launch the server outside of the debugger. To do this, right-click on the helloServer project in the Solution Explorer pane and choose Set as Startup Project. Now choose [Debug] > Start Without Debugging. This will run the server in an independent console window. If your firewall warns you, be sure to allow the server to communicate over its listening port.

To test the server, run the client by right-clicking on the helloClient project and choosing Debug > Start New Instance. Your client should call the server and exit with success (0), and the server should display something similar to the output in figure 13.11.

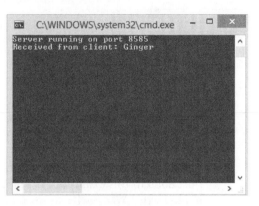

Figure 13.11   Testing helloServer.exe

13.3   C# transports, protocols, and servers

The Apache Thrift framework defines transports and server types, as well as three protocols. Not every language implementation supports all the possible Apache Thrift protocols and transports. All the C# transport and server features are realized through the .NET framework's robust set of networking and concurrency primitives.

13.3.1   C# transports

Apache Thrift transports move bytes from one place to another. The C# transport library is organized into classes, with the `TTransport` class providing the base interface for all transport implementations (essentially the methods: `open`, `close`, `read`, `write`, and `flush`). The transport base classes are

- *TTransport*—Defines the abstract Apache Thrift transport interface
- *TServerTransport*—Defines the abstract Apache Thrift server transport interface
- *TStreamTransport*—Implements `TTransport` using the C# Stream type

RPC servers require not only endpoint transports for reading and writing, but also special server-side listening transports with the ability to accept new inbound connections from clients. The `TServerTransport` defines the interface shared by all server transports, essentially the methods: `listen`, `close`, and `accept` (see figure 13.12). The C#-supported server transports include

- `TServerSocket`—Implements `TServerTransport` using the C# `TcpListener`
- `TTLSServerSocket`—Like `TServerSocket` with TLS
- `TNamedPipeServerTransport`—Implements `TServerTransport` using the C# `NamedPipeServerStream`

When two processes communicate directly over a connection, both must use the same endpoint transport. Endpoint transports hand off bytes from Apache Thrift to an

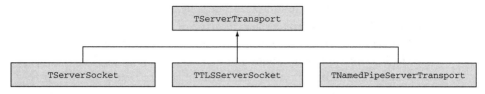

Figure 13.12 C# server transport hierarchy

external interface, typically the operating system's I/O subsystem (see figure 3.13). The most popular endpoint transport is TSocket, which allows Apache Thrift to communicate over TCP. The C# library provides a TSocket transport for raw TCP, as well as a TTLSSocket transport for TLS-encrypted TCP, and a THttpClient transport for HTTP communications over TCP.

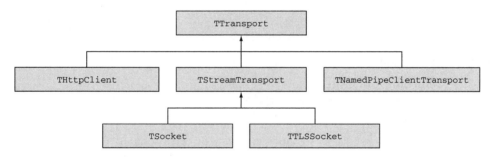

Figure 13.13 C# endpoint transport hierarchy

C# also supplies a few less common transports. The Windows platform supports an alternative to TCP, called named pipes. Named pipes use names to identify endpoints rather than port numbers. The TNamedPipeClientTransport provides client-side named pipe connectivity, and the TNamedPipeServerTransport provides the server listener.

The Windows .NET Framework has always worked well with named pipes; however, the Mono Framework for UNIX-like systems doesn't support named pipes in all Apache Thrift incarnations. You should give named pipes a test run before committing to their use if you plan to run C# in non-Windows environments.

C# also offers a memory transport, TMemoryBuffer, that collects data written into a block of memory. Memory buffers are convenient in messaging scenarios, for example, allowing you to send RPC messages over a preexisting messaging platform such as MSMQ, NATS, or Apache Kafka. The C#-supported endpoint transports include

- TSocket—Implements TStreamTransport over TCP using C#'s TcpClient
- TTLSSocket—Like TSocket with SSL/TLS
- TNamedPipeClientTransport—Implements TTransport over NamedPipes using C#'s NamedPipeClientStream
- THttpClient—Implements TTransport over HTTP using C#'s HttpWebRequest
- TMemoryBuffer—Implements TTransport using C#'s MemoryStream

Like other Apache Thrift languages, C# supplies a buffering layer and a framing layer. These layered transports can be stacked on top of existing transports to add functionality to the I/O stack. Buffering is almost always desirable, to avoid transmitting small fragments of data in lieu of complete messages. Framing is required by some server applications and provides implicit buffering (see figure 13.14). The C# layered transports are

- `TBufferedTransport`—Provides a buffering layer
- `TFramedTransport`—Provides buffering and message framing

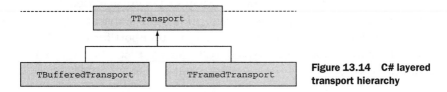

Figure 13.14   C# layered transport hierarchy

For more information on Apache Thrift transports, see chapter 3.

13.3.2 *C# protocols*

Protocols provide the means to serialize and deserialize IDL types. Three principal protocols are supported across the Apache Thrift framework and each is supported in the C# library:

- `TBinaryProtocol`—Represents data directly in binary form
- `TCompactProtocol`—Represents data directly in binary form, compressing integer types
- `TJSONProtocol`—Represents data using JavaScript Object Notation

Like connected endpoint transports, the reader and the writer in Apache Thrift must use the same serialization protocol. For more information on Apache Thrift protocols, see chapter 5.

13.3.3 *C# servers*

As a full-featured RPC framework, Apache Thrift provides not only the communications infrastructure necessary for RPC but also pre-coded servers to host RPC service implementations. C# offers three server implementations to choose from:

- `TSimpleServer`—Simple, single-threaded, single-client server
- `TThreadedServer`—Multithreaded server creating a new thread for each connection
- `TThreadPoolServer`—Multithreaded server assigning threads from a pool to process connections

The `TSimpleServer`, used in our first C# example, is fast and efficient if you plan to connect only one client at a time. This can be useful in backend applications, though the `TSimpleServer` will not process a new connection until the current client disconnects.

The TThreadedServer creates a new thread for each client connection. This allows the server to scale out, executing on all available CPUs when multiple clients make concurrent requests. The TThreadedServer maintains a maximum thread limit that can be set using the maxThreads constructor parameter; the default is 100. When the server reaches the thread limit, new connections will queue until an existing connection closes.

The final server is the TThreadPoolServer. This server uses the .NET framework ThreadPool construct to create and manage a pool of worker threads used to process client connections. The .NET ThreadPool allows threads to be returned to the pool when a connection closes, making it slightly more efficient than the TThreadedServer in certain use cases. The TThreadPoolServer min and max thread counts can be set in the TThreadPoolServer constructor; default values are 10 and 100, respectively.

The servers have only two interesting methods, serve() and stop(), which run and stop the server respectively. For more information on Apache Thrift servers, see chapter 9.

13.4 Long polling with named pipes

Now that we have a working Apache Thrift development environment and a simple RPC example under our belts, let's look at one more example demonstrating several of the more unique features of the C# Apache Thrift library.

Imagine we develop the technology for the Pacific Northwest Fish market and that we have many clients who'd like to connect to one of our servers to receive the latest trades taking place in the fish market. If our clients already interact with our servers with various languages using Apache Thrift, long polling might be an effective way to feed trade reports to connected clients.

RPC systems provide a call/response I/O model. This works well for function-call-style interaction between clients and servers. Clients make requests and servers respond with results. This is the same model provided by the HTTP protocol for the World Wide Web. On occasion this model may not fit the needs of a particular data exchange. One common case is when a server would like to supply data asynchronously to a client, as is the case in our trade reporting example. Streaming systems such as WebSocket and messaging platforms work well in this scenario.

However, if an RPC solution such as Apache Thrift is in place and performing the lion's share of the network communications effectively, it may make sense to consider long polling for moderately active asynchronous data transmission from server to client. Long polling is an RPC technique where a client makes a call to a server with the expectation that the server will not respond immediately. Rather, the server postpones responding to the client until relevant data is available to stream back to the client. As soon as the client receives a response from the server, it repeats the call to wait for the next block of asynchronous data.

The drawback of long polling is that it introduces the unnecessary overhead of repeated client calls to the server. The benefit is that it avoids introducing new communications platforms in scenarios where RPC solutions are entrenched and can perform the task effectively.

13.4.1   A long polling interface

In this section, we'll use Apache Thrift and C# to build a long polling RPC example. Our use case will be a trade report stream for the Pacific Northwest Fish Company. Clients will long poll the RPC server, which will respond asynchronously when new fish price information is available.

The following listing shows the IDL we'll use.

Listing 13.4   ~thriftbook/part3/cs/tradeStream.thrift

```
/** Apache Thrift IDL definition for the TradeStream service interface */

namespace * PNWF          ❶

enum Market {
    Unknown       = 0
    Portland      = 1
    Seattle       = 2
    SanFrancisco  = 3
    Vancouver     = 4
    Anchorage     = 5
}

typedef double USD

struct TimeStamp {
    1: i16   year
    2: i16   month
    3: i16   day
    4: i16   hour
    5: i16   minute
    6: i16   second
    7: optional i32 micros
}

union FishSizeUnit {
    1: i32   pounds
    2: i32   kilograms
    3: i16   standard_crates
    4: double  metric_tons
}

struct Trade {
    1: string        fish
    2: USD           price
    3: FishSizeUnit  amount
    4: TimeStamp     date_time
    5: Market        market = Market.Unknown
    6: i64           id
```

```
}
/**
 * Thrown when the server encounters an internal error during
 * a long polling operation.
 */
exception NetworkError {              ❷
    1: i32          error_code
    2: string       error_message
    3: set<Market>  markets_with_error
}

service TradeStream {
    /**
     * Return the next trade report
     *
     * @param fish_filter - fish to return trades for, "" for all
     * @return - the next fish trade occurring
     * @throws NetworkError - raised when the feed is delayed
     */
    list<Trade> GetNextTrade(1: string fish_filter = "")        ❸
        throws (1: NetworkError ne)
}
```

The main types listed in this interface definition file are identical to those used in the IDL section of chapter 6 ❶. For more information on Apache Thrift IDL, see chapter 6.

The two new features of this interface are the `NetworkError` exception type and the `TradeStream` service. The `NetworkError` exception type is thrown to the client when the server encounters backend errors such as pricing delays or network partitioning. The `NetworkError` type includes a message string, error code, and the set of markets affected by the error ❷.

The `TradeStream` service includes a single method, `GetNextTrade()` ❸. This method accepts an optional filter, which can specify the fish type to report on; the default is to report all fish prices. The return type is a list of fish `Trades`. The server will collect trades over a short window before returning the trade list to the client to avoid sending many small packets. The server will always return at least one trade in the list, or, per the exception specification, the server may throw a `NetworkError`.

13.4.2 *Installing Apache Thrift support through NuGet*

To create our long polling RPC example, we'll build another solution with three projects—a client, a server, and a shared interface library. However, in this iteration we'll use the Windows platform NuGet package manager to install the Apache Thrift C# library, rather than using the hand-built library.

The NuGet package manager for the Microsoft development platform makes it easy to install project dependencies such as Apache Thrift. Developers building .NET solutions use NuGet in much the same way that JavaScript developers use npm and systems administrators use Yum, apt-get, and Zypper. The NuGet client tools provide the ability to search for available packages and then add them into a project. The NuGet Gallery (http://www.nuget.org/) is the central package repository used by NuGet.

Before we can use NuGet to install Apache Thrift we'll need to follow the steps in section 13.2.1 to create a new solution. Name the new solution `TradeStream` and add C# .NET Framework Console Application projects for `tradeClient` and `tradeServer`, as well as a C# .NET Framework Class Library project for the `tradeService` project. We'll edit the project files later; for now generate default projects.

When you have all of the projects created, open the Package Manager console by choosing [Tools] > NuGet Package Manager > Package Manager Console. This will open the Package Manager Console in the lower pane of the Visual Studio display. The toolbar at the top of the pane lets you select the Package source and project to manage. Make sure the Package source is set to nuget.org and that the Default project is set to `tradeService` (see figure 13.15).

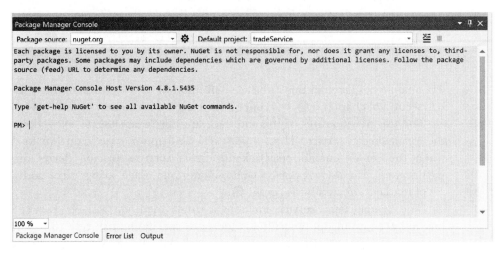

Figure 13.15 The NuGet Package Manager Console

To search for Apache Thrift-related packages, you can enter the `Find-Package thrift` command at the package manager prompt, as shown in the following code:

```
PM> Find-Package thrift

Id          Versions  Description
--          --------  -----------
Thrift      {0.9.1.3} Version based on this branch:
e51-thrift  {0.11.0.1}C# bindings for the Apache Thrift RPC system
ApacheThrift {0.9.3}   Apache Thrift .NET Library
thrift-lib  {1.0.0}    Nuget package for Thrift lib C# - built locally
apache-thrift-netcore  {0.9.3.2} For .NetCore-naive port, caution...
thrift-csharp {0.10.0} https://github.com/apache/thrift/releases/tag/0.10
...
```

Development packages will only display if the Prerelease switch is used. As you can see from the above code example, a number of Apache Thrift-related NuGet packages exist. The package with the ID "thrift-csharp" provides v0.10.0 support, matching the IDL compiler version used in this walk-through, so we'll select this one (named pipe support was added to C# in v0.9.2). To install the .NET library for use in the tradeService project, make sure the tradeService project is selected in the Package Manager Default project combo box, and then use the Install-Package command as follows:

```
PM> Install-Package thrift-csharp
```

The package installer places installed libraries under the solution "package" directory and adds a reference to the library in the selected project. You can see the location of the Apache Thrift library by right-clicking the Thrift item (in the References section of the tradeService project in the Solution Explorer) and choosing properties. NuGet offers many additional features that we leave to your exploration. For documentation, look at nuget.org or type "get-help NuGet" at the Package Manager prompt.

To complete the tradeService library project, we need to add the IDL source and build it. Follow the steps in 13.2.2 to set up the library project with the IDL from listing 13.4. Make sure to delete the unneeded Class1.cs boilerplate file and save the tradeStream.thrift file as ASCII. Add a pre-build event command line like the following to run the IDL compiler on the tradeStream.thrift file each time the project is built:

```
thrift -out "../.." -gen csharp "$(ProjectDir)tradeStream.thrift"
```

The tradeStream IDL declares several types and places everything within the PNWF namespace. When built, all of the generated .cs files will be output to the tradeService/ PNWF folder. To add the service and type .cs files to the shared library project, right-click the tradeService project and choose Add > Existing Item. In the Add Existing Item dialog navigate to the PNWF directory and select all the generated .cs files. Rather than adding the files outright, click the down arrow on the dialog Add button and choose "add as link." This will leave the files in the PNWF folder, allowing them to be updated correctly when the IDL compiler runs. If you add them without choosing "add as link," the files will be copied to the project root and then included. This will cause the build to use the stale files in the project root the next time the Apache Thrift IDL compiler emits updated files to PNWF.

When you have the tradeService library configured, build it to generate the shared tradeService.dll. Your solution should now look something like figure 13.16.

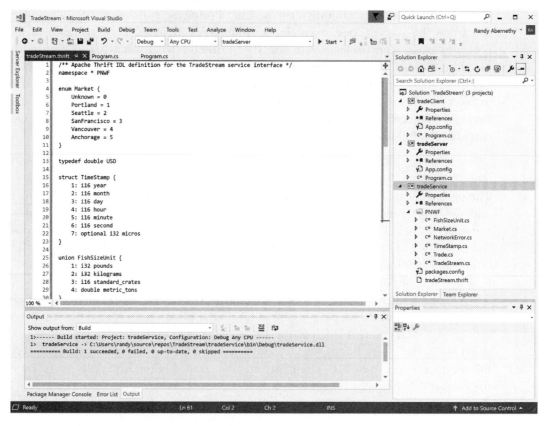

Figure 13.16   The `tradeService` project

13.4.3   *Creating a named pipe server*

Now that the service interface and type classes are generated, we can put together a server to host the `TradeStream` service. For this example, we'll build a named pipes-based server that returns fake fish trade prices to all attached clients. This will demonstrate how named pipes operate in a C# RPC setting, which, as we'll see, isn't much different than TCP sockets from a coding standpoint.

We'll also use the TCompactProtocol in this example. While its usage is identical to TBinaryProtocol, the compact protocol can materially reduce the number of bytes transmitted over the network for a small additional CPU cost.

The final new features demonstrated here will be the use of a multithreaded server and server events. We'll use the TThreadedServer, which creates one thread per client. We can easily change the code to use the TSimpleServer or the TThreadPoolServer for comparison purposes, because all three inherit the TServer interface. We examine server concurrency further in the pages ahead.

The following listing shows the source for the server.

Listing 13.5   ~thriftbook/part3/cs/tradeServer.cs

```
using System;
using System.Collections.Generic;
using System.Collections.Concurrent;
using System.Threading;
using Thrift.Transport;
using Thrift.Protocol;
using Thrift.Server;

namespace tradeServer
{
  /// <summary>
  /// Simulate trade events
  ///
  /// This class requries each client connection to be hosted by a seperate
  /// thread. A thread local event is used as a key to return a unique
  /// trade queue for each connection.
  /// </summary>
  public static class TradeEventGenerator
  {
    //Thread Local Attribute
    public static ThreadLocal<EventWaitHandle> tradeEvent =
        new ThreadLocal<EventWaitHandle>(() =>
    {
      return new EventWaitHandle(false, EventResetMode.AutoReset);
    });

    //Attributes
    private static int nextTradeId = 0;
    private static ConcurrentDictionary<EventWaitHandle,
                                      ConcurrentQueue<PNWF.Trade>> clients =
        new ConcurrentDictionary<EventWaitHandle,
                              ConcurrentQueue<PNWF.Trade>>();
    //Methods
    public static void WaitForTrades()
    {
      TradeEventGenerator.tradeEvent.Value.WaitOne();
    }
    public static ConcurrentQueue<PNWF.Trade> GetTrades()
    {
      return clients[TradeEventGenerator.tradeEvent.Value];
    }
    public static void Subscribe(ConcurrentQueue<PNWF.Trade> trades)
    {
      clients[TradeEventGenerator.tradeEvent.Value] = trades;
    }
    public static void Unsubscribe()
    {
      ConcurrentQueue<PNWF.Trade> trades;
      clients.TryRemove(TradeEventGenerator.tradeEvent.Value, out trades);
    }
```

```
//Background trade generator thread entry point
public static void ThreadProc()
{
  int[] delay = { 7000, 3000, 4000, 5000 };
  int delayIndex = 0;
  while (true)
  {
    Thread.Sleep(delay[++delayIndex % delay.Length]);
    List<PNWF.Trade> trades = GetMockTrades();
    foreach (KeyValuePair<EventWaitHandle,
                          ConcurrentQueue<PNWF.Trade>> pair in clients)
    {
      foreach (PNWF.Trade trade in trades)
      {
        pair.Value.Enqueue(trade);
      }
      pair.Key.Set();
    }
  }
}

//Internal operations
private static List<PNWF.Trade> GetMockTrades()
{
  List<PNWF.Trade> trades = new List<PNWF.Trade>();

  PNWF.Trade trade = new PNWF.Trade();
  trade.Id = ++nextTradeId;
  trade.Fish = "Halibut";
  trade.Price = 45.75;
  trade.Amount = new PNWF.FishSizeUnit();
  trade.Amount.Kilograms = 50;
  trade.Market = PNWF.Market.SanFrancisco;
  trade.Date_time = new PNWF.TimeStamp();
  DateTime now = DateTime.Now;
  trade.Date_time.Year = (short)now.Year;
  trade.Date_time.Month = (short)now.Month;
  trade.Date_time.Day = (short)now.Day;
  trade.Date_time.Hour = (short)now.Hour;
  trade.Date_time.Minute = (short)now.Minute;
  trade.Date_time.Second = (short)now.Second;
  trade.Date_time.Micros = now.Millisecond * 1000;
  trades.Add(trade);
  if (nextTradeId % 3 == 0)
  {
    PNWF.Trade trade2 = new PNWF.Trade();
    trade2.Id = ++nextTradeId;
    trade2.Fish = "Salmon";
    trade2.Price = 65.42;
    trade2.Amount = new PNWF.FishSizeUnit();
    trade2.Amount.Pounds = 31;
    trade2.Market = PNWF.Market.Anchorage;
    trade2.Date_time = trade.Date_time;
    trades.Add(trade2);
```

```
      }
      return trades;
    }
}


/// <summary>
/// Long polling Trade Stream RPC Service implementation
/// </summary>
public class TradeStreamHandler : PNWF.TradeStream.Iface
{
    //Methods
    public List<PNWF.Trade> GetNextTrade(string fish_filter)
    {
        //Wait for trades
        TradeEventGenerator.WaitForTrades();

        //Recover thread specific trade queue
        ConcurrentQueue<PNWF.Trade> trades = TradeEventGenerator.GetTrades();

        //Move the trades into the return list an return it to the client
        List<PNWF.Trade> returnTrades = new List<PNWF.Trade>();
        PNWF.Trade trade;
        while (trades.TryDequeue(out trade))
        {
            if (fish_filter.Length == 0 ||
                  fish_filter.CompareTo(trade.Fish) == 0)
              returnTrades.Add(trade);
        }
        return returnTrades;
    }
}


/// <summary>
/// Server Event Handler used to subscribe and unsubscribe each client
/// connection to the trade stream
/// </summary>
public class TradeServerEventHandler : TServerEventHandler
{
    public void preServe()
    {
        Console.WriteLine("Server ready to receive connections");
    }
    public Object createContext(Thrift.Protocol.TProtocol input,
                                Thrift.Protocol.TProtocol output)
    {
        Console.WriteLine("Client connected");
        TradeEventGenerator.Subscribe(new ConcurrentQueue<PNWF.Trade>());
        return null;
    }
    public void deleteContext(Object serverContext,
                              Thrift.Protocol.TProtocol input,
                              Thrift.Protocol.TProtocol output)
    {
        Console.WriteLine("Client disconnected");
        TradeEventGenerator.Unsubscribe();
```

```
            }
        public void processContext(Object serverContext,
                                    Thrift.Transport.TTransport transport)
        {
            Console.WriteLine("Waiting for next client trade request");
        }
    };

    class Program
    {
        static void Main(string[] args)
        {
            //Start the background mock trade generator thread
            (new Thread(TradeEventGenerator.ThreadProc)).Start();

            //Create the Service Handler and Processor
            TradeStreamHandler handler = new TradeStreamHandler();
            PNWF.TradeStream.Processor proc =
                new PNWF.TradeStream.Processor(handler);

            //Setup the I/O stack factories
            TServerTransport trans =
                new TNamedPipeServerTransport("TradeStream");
            TTransportFactory transFac = new TTransportFactory();
            TProtocolFactory protoFac = new TCompactProtocol.Factory();

            //Setup the server and register the event handler
            TServer server =
                new TThreadedServer(proc, trans, transFac, protoFac);
            server.setEventHandler(new TradeServerEventHandler());
            server.Serve();
        }
    }
}
```

This server listing is organized into four classes:

- `TradeEventGenerator`
- `TradeStreamHandler`
- `TradeServerEventHandler`
- `Program`

The `TradeEventGenerator` is responsible for simulating fish market trades and communicating them to subscribers. The `TradeStreamHandler` is responsible for accepting `GetNextTrade()` requests from clients. The `TradeServerEventHandler` uses server events to subscribe and unsubscribe client connections to the `TradeEventGenerator` trade stream. The `Main()` function in the `Program` class sets up the server and runs it. Let's look at each class in turn.

The `TradeEventGenerator` is an internal mock trade server that runs on its own background thread. The `TradeEventGenerator` is a singleton static class that accepts subscriptions from connection threads and signals them when new trades are ready for reading. Here's an abbreviated listing.

Listing 13.6 TradeEventGenerator

```
public static class TradeEventGenerator
  {
    //Thread Local Attribute
     #1
    public static ThreadLocal<EventWaitHandle> tradeEvent =
        new ThreadLocal<EventWaitHandle>(() =>
    {
      return new EventWaitHandle(false, EventResetMode.AutoReset);
    });                                                                      ❶

    //Attributes
    private static int nextTradeId = 0;                            ❷
    private static ConcurrentDictionary<EventWaitHandle,
                                ConcurrentQueue<PNWF.Trade>> clients =
        new ConcurrentDictionary<EventWaitHandle,
                            ConcurrentQueue<PNWF.Trade>>();
    //Methods
    public static void WaitForTrades()           ❹
    {
      TradeEventGenerator.tradeEvent.Value.WaitOne();
    }
    public static ConcurrentQueue<PNWF.Trade> GetTrades()    ❺
    {
      return clients[TradeEventGenerator.tradeEvent.Value];
    }
    public static void Subscribe(ConcurrentQueue<PNWF.Trade> trades)    ❻
    {
      clients[TradeEventGenerator.tradeEvent.Value] = trades;
    }
    public static void Unsubscribe()           ❼
    {
      ConcurrentQueue<PNWF.Trade> trades;
      clients.TryRemove(TradeEventGenerator.tradeEvent.Value, out trades);
    }

    //Background trade generator thread entry point
    public static void ThreadProc()
    {
      int[] delay = { 7000, 3000, 4000, 5000 };
      int delayIndex = 0;
      while (true)
      {
        Thread.Sleep(delay[++delayIndex % delay.Length]);
        List<PNWF.Trade> trades = GetMockTrades();
        foreach (KeyValuePair<EventWaitHandle,
                           ConcurrentQueue<PNWF.Trade>> pair in clients)
        {
          foreach (PNWF.Trade trade in trades)
          {
```

❸ (at `private static ConcurrentDictionary`)
❽ (at `public static void ThreadProc()`)

```
                pair.Value.Enqueue(trade);
            }
            pair.Key.Set();
        }
    }
}

//Internal operations
private static List<PNWF.Trade> GetMockTrades()          ❾
{
    List<PNWF.Trade> trades = new List<PNWF.Trade>();

    PNWF.Trade trade = new PNWF.Trade();
    trade.Id = ++nextTradeId;
    …
    return trades;
}
}
```

This class has three attributes: a per-thread event, a trade ID counter, and a dictionary of subscribed client queues. The nextTradeId is a simple integer used to generate ever-increasing trade IDs ❷. The other two attributes deserve more discussion.

The tradeEvent attribute is of ThreadLocal<EventWaitHandle> type ❶. The runtime will generate a unique EventWaitHandle for each thread spawned within the program. Because all three of the previously described Apache Thrift C# servers create a dedicated processing thread for each connection, we can use this per thread event as a key, identifying the various client connections.

It's important to note that this isn't a causal relationship. It's easy to create a server that doesn't use a separate thread for each connection. In such a situation, thread local variables wouldn't provide a means for identifying a specific connection, and a different connection key approach would be required.

The ThreadLocal tradeEvent is initialized by a special function called a value factory. In this case we create an auto reset EventWaitHandle. Each connection thread will wait on its thread-specific tradeEvent, and the TradeEventGenerator will set the event when new trades are present. After releasing the waiting thread, the event will automatically reset.

The final attribute is "clients" ❸. The client attribute is a data structure containing a set of queues used to send PNWF.Trade messages to the connected clients. Each new client connection subscribes to trade events, supplying a ConcurrentQueue, which the TradeEventGenerator will write trade messages to. The .NET ConcurrentQueue is a queue that can be written to by one thread and read from by another without locks. This makes it a good fit as a communications channel between the background TradeEventGenerator thread and the client connection thread.

The "clients" data structure is a ConcurrentDictionary using the per-thread tradeEvent as the key and the connection thread's ConcurrentQueue as the value. When the connection thread calls the subscribe() method ❻, the thread's tradeEvent is used as the key with which to store the connection's ConcurrentQueue. Because the subscribe operation updates the dictionary on the connection thread and many connections may attempt to make such an update concurrently, the dictionary must support concurrent access. The .NET ConcurrentDictionary performs this task, ensuring atomic updates with fine-grained locking.

When clients disconnect, their connection thread calls unsubscribe() to remove the trade queue from the TradeEventGenerator dictionary ❼. Client connection threads call WaitForTrades() ❹ and GetTrades() ❺ to wait for new trades and to recover queued trades, respectively.

The TradeEventGenerator background thread spends its entire life running the ThreadProc() function ❽. This function sits in an endless loop, waiting a few seconds between each iteration. Every time the thread wakes, it generates one or two pseudo-random fish trades and places them in all the subscribed client queues.

The GetMockTrades() function generates the sample fish trades ❾. This function is worth reviewing, as it demonstrates the type mappings from Apache Thrift IDL to C#. Note that all the IDL types are defined within the PNWF namespace as requested in the IDL. The code demonstrates the use of lists, structs, unions, and enumerations, among other IDL types.

The next class is the TradeStream service handler class. The TradeStream service only has one method, GetNextTrade(), which we implement in the handler class. Here's the listing.

Listing 13.7 TradeStreamHandler

```
public class TradeStreamHandler : PNWF.TradeStream.Iface      ❶
{
  public List<PNWF.Trade> GetNextTrade(string fish_filter)     ❷
  {
❸   TradeEventGenerator.WaitForTrades();
    ConcurrentQueue<PNWF.Trade> trades = TradeEventGenerator.GetTrades();
    List<PNWF.Trade> returnTrades = new List<PNWF.Trade>();
    PNWF.Trade trade;
    while (trades.TryDequeue(out trade))
    {
      if (fish_filter.Length == 0 ||
          fish_filter.CompareTo(trade.Fish) == 0)      ❹
        returnTrades.Add(trade);
    }
    return returnTrades;
  }
}
```

The TradeStreamHandler implements the PNWF.TradeStream.Iface interface generated by the IDL compiler from our TradeStream service definition ❶. The GetNext-Trade() long polling method accepts a string containing a filter which can be used to restrict the fish trades returned to a single fish type ❷.

Internally, the GetNextTrade() method begins by waiting for the trade event to signal. When the TradeEventGenerator thread queues new trades, it sets the client thread trade event, causing that thread to return from the WaitForTrades() call ❸. Due to the long polling nature of this interface, the remote client may end up waiting seconds (or even minutes in a real-world implementation) before the server responds with the requested data.

When the wait ends, the GetNextTrade() method moves all of the returned trades that meet the user's fish filter requirement (e.g. "Halibut," "Salmon") into a list that's returned to the calling client ❹.

The next class is the TradeServerEventHandler. Here's the listing.

Listing 13.8   TradeServerEventHandler

```
public class TradeServerEventHandler : TServerEventHandler
{
  public void preServe()
  {
    Console.WriteLine("Server ready to receive connections");
  }
  public Object createContext(Thrift.Protocol.TProtocol input,
                              Thrift.Protocol.TProtocol output)    ❶
  {
    Console.WriteLine("Client connected");
    TradeEventGenerator.Subscribe(new ConcurrentQueue<PNWF.Trade>());
    return null;
  }
  public void deleteContext(Object serverContext,
                            Thrift.Protocol.TProtocol input,
                            Thrift.Protocol.TProtocol output)    ❷
  {
    Console.WriteLine("Client disconnected");
    TradeEventGenerator.Unsubscribe();
  }
  public void processContext(Object serverContext,
                             Thrift.Transport.TTransport transport)
  {
    Console.WriteLine("Waiting for next client trade request");
  }
};
```

Apache Thrift C# servers support the TServerEventHandler pattern. This is described in detail in chapter 10, "Servers." The TServerEventHandler interface is implemented by user code and called by pre-built Apache Thrift servers when clients connect (createContext), disconnect (deleteContext), and before clients make a service method call (processContext). Also, a preServe event is invoked after the server is initialized but before any client connections are accepted.

In our case, the client connect and disconnect events are important. We need to subscribe to trade events when a client connects and we need to unsubscribe when a client disconnects. These event methods are called on the client's connection thread, allowing us to subscribe() ❶ and unsubscribe() ❷ at the proper time, on the proper thread.

The final class is Program, containing the Main() program entry point. Here's the listing.

Listing 13.9 Program

```
class Program
    {
        static void Main(string[] args)
        {
            (new Thread(TradeEventGenerator.ThreadProc)).Start();     ❶

            TradeStreamHandler handler = new TradeStreamHandler();
            PNWF.TradeStream.Processor proc =
                new PNWF.TradeStream.Processor(handler);
            TServerTransport trans =
                new TNamedPipeServerTransport("TradeStream");          ❷
            TTransportFactory transFac = new TTransportFactory();
            TProtocolFactory protoFac = new TCompactProtocol.Factory();

            TServer server =
                new TThreadedServer(proc, trans, transFac, protoFac);
            server.setEventHandler(new TradeServerEventHandler());      ❸
            server.Serve();
        }
    }
}
```

The Main() function begins by starting the TradeEventGenerator background thread ❶. This causes the static TradeEventGenerator to begin producing fish trades.

The next block of code prepares the server I/O stack ❷. We create an instance of the TradeStreamHandler and wrap it in a TradeStream service processor. We then create a TNamedPipeServerTransport to listen for client connections. Server transports are like factories in that they produce a new endpoint transport for each client connection. When using multithreaded servers, we generally must also supply layered transport and protocol factories to produce each of the upper layers of the stack dynamically as new connections arrive. In this example, we pass the server a generic TTransportFactory, which is a dummy class that adds nothing to the stack, and a TCompactProtocol factory, which generates a new compact protocol object for each connection.

All of these components are passed to the TThreadedServer constructor to build the multithreaded server, which is then executed using the Serve() method ❸. Before launching the server, we create an instance of the TradeServerEventHandler and register it with the server using the setEventHandler() method. This will cause the server to emit events to the supplied TServerEventHandler implementation, subscribing and unsubscribing client connections to fish trades as they come and go.

13.4.4 *Building the long polling server*

To complete the server project, we need to add references to the tradeService project and to Apache Thrift. We can add a reference to the tradeService project by
right-clicking the References item in the tradeServer project as before. To add a
Thrift.dll reference to the server project we can run the PackageManager install command again:

```
PM> Install-Package thrift-csharp
```

This creates a reference to the already installed Thrift.dll, which will be shared across
all dependent projects in the solution automatically. At this point we can build and
test run the server.

   Now that we have the server ready and running, we can build a named pipe test client.

13.4.5 *Building a named pipe client*

To test the namedpipe server, we'll create a simple client that connects to the server
and then long polls for trade events. The client will display the first 100 trade report
blocks and then exit. Here's the listing.

Listing 13.10   ~thriftbook/part3/cs/tradeClient.cs

```
using System;
using System.Collections.Generic;
using Thrift.Protocol;
using Thrift.Transport;

namespace tradeClient
{
    class Program
    {
        static void Main(string[] args)
        {
            TTransport trans =
                new TNamedPipeClientTransport("TradeStream");     ❶
            trans.Open();
❷          TProtocol proto = new TCompactProtocol(trans);
            PNWF.TradeStream.Client client =                       ❸
                new PNWF.TradeStream.Client(proto);
❹          for (int i = 0; i < 100; i++){
                List<PNWF.Trade> trades = client.GetNextTrade("");
                foreach (PNWF.Trade trade in trades) {
                    Console.Out.WriteLine(trade.Date_time.Hour.ToString("D2")+
                    ":" + trade.Date_time.Minute.ToString("D2") + ":" +
                    trade.Date_time.Second.ToString("D2") + " " + trade.Fish +
                    "-" + trade.Market.ToString() + " " + trade.Price);
                }
            }
        }
    }
}
```

The first line of our `Main()` function creates an endpoint transport to connect to the server, and the second line opens the connection ❶. Unlike TCP sockets, which connect with a host using port numbers, named pipes use pipe names. The server is listening on the pipe name `TradeStream`, so this is the name our client must connect to. The host name to connect to defaults to ".", synonymous with the localhost. To specify an explicit host name, you can use the `TNamedPipeClientTransport(server, pipe)` constructor, passing the target hostname in as the first parameter.

Named pipes are a native networking feature on Windows systems and can provide excellent performance. Windows also has a fast TCP/IP stack though, so only practical testing can give you pragmatic performance comparisons. The Windows implementation of named pipes also offers sophisticated security and authentication features. For more information on named pipes, refer to Microsoft's documentation.

To interoperate with the server we must use the same protocol as specified on the server side. To achieve this, in the client code we wrap the transport in a `TCompact-Protocol` object ❷. The protocol object is then wrapped in a `TradeStream` client object (generated by our IDL) to complete the I/O stack ❸.

The remainder of the client program simply loops 100 times ❹, making long poll requests for fish trade reports. The `GetNextTrade()` calls may linger for several seconds before returning. Long poll scenarios like this often require the client to use a background thread for the polling operation or an async callback. The Apache Thrift C# library does support client async operations; however, only over the `THttpClient` transport presently. The intrepid can roll their own async handlers.

Before we can test our system, the `tradeClient` project needs references to the `tradeService` project and the Thrift.dll. You can follow the same steps used with the server to add the references. Once the references are in place we can build the `tradeClient`.

To test the solution, right-click the `tradeServer` project in the Solution Explorer and choose Set as Startup Project. Now press F5 or choose [Debug] > Start Debugging to run the server. Next locate the tradeClient.exe executable and run several copies of the client. The client can be found in the solution TradeStream\tradeClient\bin\Debug directory. You should see output something like figure 13.17.

Figure 13.17 Three concurrent clients connected to the named pipe `tradeServer`

Summary

This chapter covered

- How to configure Apache Thrift for use with .NET on Windows
- How to create Apache Thrift applications with Visual Studio
- How to build C# RPC clients and servers with Apache Thrift
- The various endpoint transports available in C#
- The layered transports available in C#
- The C# supported protocols
- How to use C# concurrency features with multithreaded Apache Thrift servers
- How to use long polling to supply asynchronous data feeds to clients

Building Node.js
clients and servers

14

This chapter covers

- Building Node.js RPC clients and servers with Apache Thrift
- Building HTTP[S] clients with Node.js
- Using Q with RPC clients
- Multiplexing multiple services over a single connection

In the following pages, we focus on the Node.js implementation of Apache Thrift, examining basic Node.js client and server operations and working our way through most of the Node.js-specific Apache Thrift features. Complementary to this chapter is chapter 15, "Apache Thrift and the JavaScript," which explores browser-based JavaScript clients and using Node.js for building Apache Thrift web servers.

14.1 A simple client and server

Each chapter in part 3 of this book begins by creating the same simple "Hello World" service. In this section, we'll recreate the hello client and server using Node.js: each is, of course, interoperable with the "hello" clients and servers created in other languages.

HTTP is a valuable and well-understood transport, integrating with security features such as SSL/TLS as well as a range of header protocols offering authentication, network optimizations, and other benefits. On the downside, HTTP adds material overhead not always necessary in an RPC scenario. In this chapter, we'll use native TCP for optimum performance, allowing chapter 15 to cover the features and benefits of Apache Thrift over HTTP.

14.1.1 Generating client/server stubs

Before we can test our first Node.js client and server, we need to define the "hello" service and generate support code for it. We'll also need to install NodeJS and the Apache Thrift Node.js library. We'll use the standard `hello` service defined in hello.thrift from listing 11.1. The following Ubuntu 16.04 session installs NodeJS 11 with NPM and the NodeJS Apache Thrift libraries, and then compiles the hello.thrift IDL (see chapter 3 for Apache Thrift compiler installation instructions and refer to https://github .com/nodesource/distributions for modern nodejs installation instructions):

```
$ curl -sL https://deb.nodesource.com/setup_11.x | sudo -E bash -
$ sudo apt-get install -y nodejs
...
$ mkdir hello; cd hello
$ npm install thrift
...
$ cat hello.thrift
service helloSvc {
    string getMessage(1: string name)
}
$ thrift -gen js:node hello.thrift
user@ubuntu:~/hello$ ls -l
total 16
drwxrwxr-x 2 user user 4096 Nov 20 11:19 gen-nodejs
-rw-rw-r-- 1 user user   59 Nov 20 11:19 hello.thrift
drwxrwxr-x 7 user user 4096 Nov 20 11:18 node_modules
-rw-rw-r-- 1 user user 1265 Nov 20 11:18 package-lock.json
user@ubuntu:~/hello$ ls -l gen-nodejs/
total 12
-rw-rw-r-- 1 user user 6833 Nov 20 11:19 helloSvc.js          ❶
-rw-rw-r-- 1 user user  254 Nov 20 11:19 hello_types.js       ❷
user@ubuntu:~/hello$
```

When generating Nodejs code, the IDL compiler generates a `helloSvc.js` module housing all the stub code needed by `helloSvc` clients and servers ❶. The `hello_types.js` module is where the IDL compiler will place user-defined types from the hello.thrift source ❷. Our simple IDL doesn't define any types, so the hello_types.js file contains only boilerplate code.

14.1.2 Creating a Node.js server

The next listing demonstrates a simple TCP-based Node.js Apache Thrift server for the `helloSvc` service. This server is compatible with the Apache Thrift `TSocket` endpoint transport supported by all other Apache Thrift languages.

Listing 14.1   ~thriftbook/part3/nodejs/helloServer.js

```
var thrift = require('thrift');                        ❶
var helloSvc = require('./gen-nodejs/helloSvc.js');      ❷

var helloHandler = {                          ❸
  getMessage: function (name, result) {
    console.log("Received: " + name);
    result(null, "Hello " + name);
  }
};

var serverOpt = {                             ❹
  transport: thrift.TBufferedTransport,
  protocol: thrift.TBinaryProtocol,
}
var port = 8585;

thrift.createServer(helloSvc, helloHandler, serverOpt)   ❺
❻ .on('error', function(error) { console.log(error); })
   .listen(port);                                         ❼
console.log("Thrift Server running on port: " + port);
```

The listing begins with dependencies for the NodeJS Apache Thrift Library ❶ and the IDL compiler-generated module for the `helloSvc` RPC service ❷.

To implement the service, we create a simple handler class that contains a function implementing each method in the service ❸. All Apache Thrift method implementations in Node.js receive an additional final parameter, the `result()` function. To set the result of the method call, we call the `result()` function with two parameters, an exception object and a normal return value. One of these two parameters should be `null`. In the example above, we set the exception to `null` and set the desired return string as the return value. If both values are set, only the exception is used.

Before we can create a server, we need to specify the protocol and transport layers we'd like to use. The standard Node.js server uses TCP as the transport endpoint. Node.js requires a layered transport to provide buffering; either a `TFramedTransport` or a `TBufferedTransport` can be selected (see chapter 3 for full transport details). None of the Node.js servers require framing, so unless you're interoperating with other Apache Thrift components that require framing, you can use either. If no transport is specified, the server will automatically apply a `TBufferedTransport`.

The Apache Thrift Node.js implementation supports the `TBinaryProtocol`, `TCompactProtocol`, and `TJSONProtocol` serialization protocols. Here, the buffered transport and the binary protocol are selected ❹. If no protocol is specified, the server will use the `TBinaryProtocol` (for more on protocols see chapter 5).

The Node.js Apache Thrift library exposes a `createServer()` method to create a standard `TSocket`-compatible server ❺. The server requires a service module, `helloSvc`, a user-defined handler for the service, `helloHandler`, and an optional server options object, which can be used to define the transport layer and protocol to use.

The server object returned by the createServer() method is a specialization of the Node.js event emitter. This allows the server object to generate events much like built-in Node.js object types. Most applications will want to listen for the "error" event that's generated when the server encounters problems ❻. You can add event listeners to an object using the Node.js on() method, or the addListener() synonym. If you don't process error events on the server, malfunctioning clients may generate untrapped errors that will crash the server. The "error" handler is passed a Node.js error object describing the problem encountered.

Once the server is configured, it can be enabled with a call to the listen() method ❼. The listen method accepts a port parameter with the TCP port to listen on. Once running, the server will accept new client connections and service client requests until shutdown. The server can be terminated using the server close() method or by simply sending the server the TERM signal ("$ kill PID" or CTRL+C in most environments).

14.1.3 Creating a Node.js client

Now that we have a TCP-based server prepared, we need to create a simple Node.js client to test it. The sample code in the following listing creates a hello world client that calls the RPC server's one and only getMessage() method, displaying the call's result.

Listing 14.2   ~thriftbook/part3/nodejs/helloClient.js

```
var thrift = require('thrift');
var helloSvc = require('./gen-nodejs/helloSvc.js');           ❶

var connection = thrift.createConnection('localhost', 8585, {    ❷
   transport: thrift.TBufferedTransport,
   protocol: thrift.TBinaryProtocol
}).on('error', function(error) {            ❸
   console.log(error);
}).on("connect", function() {          ❹
   var client = thrift.createClient(helloSvc, connection);       ❺
   client.getMessage("Thurston Howell", function(error, result) {
       console.log("Msg from server: " + ((result) ? result : error));
       connection.end();
   });
});
```
❻ (before `client.getMessage`)
❼ (before `connection.end();`)

Like the server, this client program begins by requiring the Apache Thrift library and the service module for the hello service ❶. The next step in fabricating our client is to create a TSocket-style connection with the server.

In this area, Node.js works a bit differently than other languages. Rather than creating the RPC stack layer by layer and then calling open() on the TSocket transport, the createConnection() method is used to build a connection object, similar to a TSocket. This method requires a target host and port to connect to and a ConnectOptions object ❷. The ConnectOptions options object allows you to set the desired transport and protocol along with several other options:

- `protocol`—The protocol to use (defaults to `TBinaryProtocol`)
- `transport`—The layered transport to use (defaults to `TBufferedTransport`)
- `max_attempts`—Specifies the number of times to retry a failed connection (defaults to `0`)
- `retry_max_delay`—Maximum number of milliseconds to wait before retrying a failed connection (disabled by default)
- `connect_timeout`—The total number of milliseconds to retry a failed connection before permanent failure (disabled by default)
- `timeout`—The total number of milliseconds of inactivity before the timeout event is emitted (disabled by default)

The `ConnectOptions` object can be omitted completely if the default transport and protocol are suitable.

Like the `Server` object type, `Connection` objects inherit from the Node.js `EventEmitter` class and emit several events:

- `close`—Fired when the connection is closed
- `connect`—Fired when the connection completes
- `error`—Fired when there's an error with the connection
- `timeout`—Fired when an operation fails to complete in ConnectionOptions ::timeout milliseconds (never fired if the timeout isn't set)

Only the error event passes a parameter to its callback, that being the error in question.

The connection object attempts to connect to the specified server upon creation. Like the Node.js server object, the connection object emits the "error" event when network and other low-level problems are encountered ❸.

The connection object emits the "connect" event when the connection with the server completes. It isn't reliable to make RPC calls prior to the connection completing, so in the previous example we wait for the "connect" event before interacting with the server ❹.

When the server connection completes, we create a client for the `helloSvc` service ❺. The Apache Thrift `createClient()` method constructs a new client object using the passed-in service module and connection. The client object can then be used to invoke the methods exposed by the service. In the example here we call the one and only `getMessage()` method with the name of an important socialite ❻.

In Node.js, calls that cannot be executed instantly are implemented as asynchronous operations with few exceptions. For this reason, Node.js RPC clients generated by the Apache Thrift IDL compiler contain only asynchronous methods. Therefore, to acquire the result of the `getMessage()` call, we must provide a callback function that will be passed an error and a result object (one of which is always `null`) providing the status of the completed call. This example logs the server's response and closes the connection when the `getMessage()` call completes ❼.

The following session runs the hello server (note that certain versions of Linux use "nodejs" as the name of the node binary; substitute as needed):

```
$ ls -l
total 36
drwxr-xr-x 2 randy randy 4096 Apr 20 13:21 gen-nodejs
-rw-r--r-- 1 randy randy  519 Apr 20 13:39 helloClient.js
-rw-r--r-- 1 randy randy  525 Apr 20 15:20 helloServer.js
-rw-r--r-- 1 randy randy   61 Apr 20 13:18 hello.thrift
drwxr-xr-x 4 randy randy 4096 Apr 20 12:44 node_modules
$ node helloServer
Thrift Server running on port: 8585
Received: Thurston Howell
```

. . . and the client side:

```
$ node helloClient
Msg from server: Hello Thurston Howell
```

The hello world example described in this section demonstrates the simplest of clients and servers; many additional features are available to explore in the Apache Thrift Node.js library. In the next section, we'll look at an alternative way to code clients in Node.js.

Asynchronous error processing

The traditional approach to error management in object-oriented systems involves throwing and catching call stack–based exceptions. Apache Thrift is largely object oriented in its abstract architecture, making exceptions a basic component of the framework. In environments dominated by asynchronous code execution, such as Node.js, a call stack–based approach to error management is problematic. The code that started the asynchronous operation is typically no longer on the call stack when the asynchronous handler routine encounters an error. For this reason, asynchronous error management in Node.js is typically event-based.

RPC errors generated by the Apache Thrift framework or the server's application level handler are passed to the RPC callback when the RPC operation completes. In addition to RPC errors, all the Node.js client-side connection objects and server-side server objects may fire an "error" event when encountering network and other low-level problems. It's a good idea to provide an "error" event handler for connection and server objects, in addition to testing the error result in RPC callbacks to provide complete asynchronous error coverage.

14.2 Q

A common task in event-driven applications is that of checking the result of an asynchronous operation. This is typically handled in JavaScript with callback functions, as illustrated in the hello world RPC example. Another approach is to use a promise object as a proxy for the future result of the operation. The popular Q library has been integrated into the Node.js Apache Thrift implementation to provide promise-style access to asynchronous RPC call results. All Apache Thrift Node.js RPC methods accept an optional callback function parameter, and, in addition, return a promise that can be used to discover the result of the RPC call.

A promise can be in one of three states:

- *Pending*—The asynchronous operation hasn't yet completed.
- *Fulfilled*—The asynchronous operation has succeeded (the result is available).
- *Rejected*—The asynchronous operation failed (an error is available).

The latter two states are terminal, flagging the end of the operation. A promise that's fulfilled or rejected is said to be resolved. The Q library promise object can be tested to determine its state, and also supports callbacks that fire during state changes. Because promises are objects, they can be passed to functions, stored in arrays, and otherwise manipulated in ways that often enable elegant solutions to challenges associated with various asynchronous call management scenarios.

To get a better idea of how promises work with Apache Thrift, let's look at a version of the hello world client updated to use promises. The code that follows uses the same interface and server as the prior hello world example, but uses the Q library to perform client-side RPC operations.

Listing 14.3   ~thriftbook/part3/nodejs/helloQClient.js

```
var thrift = require('thrift');
var helloSvc = require('./gen-nodejs/helloSvc.js');
var Q = require('q');                                              ❶

var connection = thrift.createConnection('localhost', 8585, {
    transport: thrift.TBufferedTransport,
    protocol: thrift.TBinaryProtocol
}).on('error', function(error) {
    console.log(error);
}).on("connect", function() {
    var client = thrift.createClient(helloSvc, connection);
❷   var promise = client.getMessage("Thurston Howell");
    console.log("Promise fulfilled?: " + promise.isFulfilled());   ❸
    console.log("Promise rejected?: " + promise.isRejected());
    console.log("Promise pending?: " + promise.isPending());
    promise.then(function(result) {
        console.log("Msg from server: " + result);
        console.log("Promise state: " + promise.inspect().state);
    }, function(error) {                                           ❹
        console.log("Error from server: " + error);
        console.log("Promise state: " + promise.inspect().state);
    });

    var promises = [];                                             ❺
    for (var i = 0; i < 5; i++) {
        promises.push(client.getMessage(""+i));
    }
    Q.all(promises).then(function(result) {                        ❻
        console.log("Result after all promises complete: " + result);
    }).fail(function(error) {                                      ❼
        console.log("Fail after all promises complete: " + error);
```

```
    }).finally(function(){
        console.log("Finally is always called, whether sucess or failure");
        connection.end();
    });
});
```

8

This client program begins with the standard require statements and adds a require for the Q library ❶. This is only needed if you use the static library methods exposed by the Q namespace (which we do here). Q is installed as a dependency of Apache Thrift.

The call setup in this client is the same as that of the prior client; however, in this example, rather than using a callback when the RPC method is called, we use a promise to manage the asynchronous result ❷. The follow-on block of code demonstrates the various state test functions that can be used to discover the state of the promise ❸.

These tests are followed by a call to the `then()` method ❹. The `then()` method provides the ability to set a callback for success (Fulfilled) and failure (Rejected). The callbacks provided here report the result to the console and display the state of the promise (implicit in the invocation of the callback, but provided for demonstration purposes).

Another powerful feature of promises is that they can be managed in blocks. The client code demonstrates this by creating an array of promises associated with several asynchronous server calls ❺. Using the `Q.all()` method we can collect the array of promises into a single promise that we can then act on as usual ❻.

Promises provide excellent support for call chains. The example here uses `then()` to schedule a callback, which will receive the aggregate result of the promise array when all subordinate promises are resolved ❻. The promise `fail()` method provides an alternate way to schedule a callback invoked when a promise is rejected (identical to supplying a second parameter to `then()`) ❼. The promise `finally()` method is called when the promise is resolved to either the Fulfilled or Rejected state ❽. This is a good place to do generic cleanup appropriate in the face of exceptions or successful operation.

The Q library provides several other useful features, and the ways in which the features demonstrated here can be combined are numerous. For more information on Q and how to avoid the callback pyramid of doom, refer to the online documentation (http://documentup.com/kriskowal/q/).

Now that we've covered the client-side basics, let's turn our attention to the Apache Thrift NodeJS server feature set and examine several larger examples.

14.3   *Node.js servers*

There are three Node.js servers to choose from in the Apache Thrift library; each is constructed with a specific `create` function:

- `createServer(processor, handler, options)`
- `createMultiplexServer(processor, options)`
- `createWebServer(options)`

The simplest server type is created with the createServer() function. This server is perfect for backend work and is well suited to RPC exchanges with other Apache Thrift-supported languages. As we saw in the previous hello world example, the createServer() function takes a processor, handler, and ServerOptions object as input and creates an RPC server supporting a single service.

The second server is the MultiplexServer, created with the createMultiplex-Server() function. The MultiplexServer allows multiple services to be hosted on a single port. An Apache Thrift server handling RPC requests for multiple services requires additional metadata to identify which service a client would like to call when an RPC request is received. Apache Thrift supplies a standard cross-language facility known as Service Multiplexing that prepends the service name to RPC requests, making it possible for a server to host multiple services over one connection. When a service endpoint implements multiplexing, only clients configured with multiplexing support can make calls to that endpoint. The Node.js Multiplex Server implements the Apache Thrift multiplex standard, supporting multiplex clients written in any Apache Thrift language.

Multiplexing is particularly handy in scenarios where you'd like to add additional services to an application without going through the overhead of provisioning new ports and configuring firewalls, load balancers, and the like.

The createWebServer() function creates an Apache Thrift HTTP[S] server. The Web Server uses URI routes to identify the service endpoints to invoke. This makes it particularly convenient for use with browser clients, and allows multiple services to be hosted by assigning each a unique route (for example, /hello, /orderEntry, /quote, and so on). While you can use multiplexing with the WebServer, it's perhaps more common to use routes to distinguish services in a web-based environment. For more information on the Apache Thrift Node.js WebServer, see chapter 15.

The next section walks through a simple multiplexing server and client example.

14.4 *Multiplexed services*

In this section we'll build a multiplexed server hosting two services, the helloSvc we've already worked with and a new byeSvc service. The server created here only hosts two services, but there is no built-in limit to the number of services a single server can host with multiplexing.

We'll need to add a second service to our IDL file to demonstrate service multiplexing. Here's the listing for an updated interface with both the helloSvc service and a new byeSvc service defined.

Listing 14.4   ~thriftbook/part3/nodejs/mux.thrift

```
service helloSvc {
    string getMessage(1: string name)
}
```

```
service byeSvc {
   i32 bye()
}
```

Both services are trivial, allowing us to focus on the multiplexing mechanics. We'll look at using Node.js with more complex services in the last section of this chapter. Here's a sample session compiling the mux.thrift IDL:

```
$ thrift -gen js:node mux.thrift
$ ls -l gen-nodejs/
total 20
-rw-r--r-- 1 randy randy 5332 Apr 22 06:09 byeSvc.js
-rw-r--r-- 1 randy randy 6217 Apr 22 06:09 helloSvc.js
-rw-r--r-- 1 randy randy 239 Apr 22 06:09 mux_types.js
```

Note that the IDL compiler generates a separate stub file for each service defined. The code in the following listing implements the two services in a single multiplexing server.

Listing 14.5   ~thriftbook/part3/nodejs/muxServer.js

```
var thrift = require('thrift');
var helloSvc = require('./gen-nodejs/helloSvc.js');           ❶
var byeSvc = require('./gen-nodejs/byeSvc.js');

var helloHandler = {                                   ❷
  getMessage: function (name, result) {
    console.log("Received: " + name);
    result(null, "Hello " + name);
  }
};

var byeHandler = {              ❸
  counter: 0,
  bye: function (result) {
    console.log("Bye called: " + (++this.counter));
    result(null, this.counter);
  }
};

var processor = new thrift.MultiplexedProcessor();
processor.registerProcessor("helloSvc",
                      new helloSvc.Processor(helloHandler));   ❹
processor.registerProcessor("byeSvc",
                      new byeSvc.Processor(byeHandler));

var serverOptions = {
  protocol: thrift.TBinaryProtocol,
  transport: thrift.TBufferedTransport
}
var port = 8585;

thrift.createMultiplexServer(processor, serverOptions)         ❺
```

```
  .on('error', function(error) { console.log(error); })
  .listen(port);
console.log("Thrift Mux Server running on port: " + port);
```

Because we're working with two services now, we must require both service modules
❶. The `helloHandler` for the `helloSvc` is identical to the previous example ❷. The
new `byeHandler` increments a call counter each time a client calls the `bye()` method
and returns the count ❸.

The next block of code enables service multiplexing ❹. The IDL compiler-
generated processor converts network traffic into calls to the service handler. The
`MultiplexedProcessor` is a frontend for a collection of normal service processors,
providing the logic needed to strip the service prefix and call the correct service
processor for a given request.

To enable a service for multiplexing, the service processor is registered with the
`MultiplexedProcessor` using the `registerProcessor()` method. The `register-
Processor()` method takes a string as its first parameter and the service processor to
register as its second parameter. The string is the lookup key for the service and must
be the same as the string used to identify the service on the client side. Convention is
to use the exact name and case of the service as the multiplex key.

Once the `MultiplexedProcessor` is initialized, a `MultiplexServer` can be created
with the `createMultiplexServer()` function ❺. The `createMultiplexServer()`
function takes a `MultiplexedProcessor` as its first argument and a `ServerOptions`
object as its second parameter. Unlike the `createServer()` function, the `create-
MultiplexedProcessor()` function doesn't require a handler, because the `Multi-
plexedProcessor` has references to each of the service processors, and each must be
created with its own embedded handler.

Now that we have a multiplexed server put together, we can create a multiplexed
client to test it with.

Listing 14.6 ~thriftbook/part3/nodejs/muxClient.js

```
var thrift = require('thrift');
var helloSvc = require('./gen-nodejs/helloSvc.js');          ❶
var byeSvc = require('./gen-nodejs/byeSvc.js');

var connection = thrift.createConnection('localhost', 8585, {
    transport: thrift.TBufferedTransport,
    protocol: thrift.TBinaryProtocol
}).on('error', function(error) {
    console.log(error);
}).on("connect", function() {
❷    var mp = new thrift.Multiplexer();
    var helloClient = mp.createClient("helloSvc", helloSvc, connection);    ❸
    var byeClient = mp.createClient("byeSvc", byeSvc, connection);

    helloClient.getMessage("Thurston Howell", function(error, result) {     ❹
        console.log("Hello msg from server: " + result);
```

```
    });
    byeClient.bye(function(error, result) {            ❹
        console.log("Bye msg from server: " + result);
        connection.end();
    });
});
```

The client side of the multiplexing equation is also fairly straightforward. Each of the service modules to be used must be required to give access to the client-side stubs ❶. The client need not require services it isn't interested in using, however. For example, a server may support 20 services over a multiplexed connection, but a given client interested in only two of these need only require those two.

To communicate with a multiplexed server, a client must use a multiplexed protocol wrapper. In this example we create a new multiplexer that allows us to generate multiplex server-compatible clients ❷. The multiplexer `createClient()` method accepts a service key string, a service module, and a connection ❸. The service key must match the key used to identify the service on the server side. Defining these keys as IDL constants in the service definition IDL file is a good practice for production settings.

The clients generated by `createClient()` are used to make RPC calls to the multiplexed server over the shared connection ❹. Apache Thrift Node.js clients generate a sequence ID for each RPC request, allowing the client to map the RPC response back to the correct client.

From the user's perspective, multiplexed clients work exactly like normal clients, supporting promises, callbacks, and so on. Due to the modified wire mechanics, multiplexed clients are not compatible with non-multiplexed servers, and vice versa.

14.5 *Apache Thrift IDL and Node.js*

Designing interfaces is a critical aspect of distributed application development. A well-designed interface is easy to understand, easy to use, and hard to misuse. Interfaces are contracts and must therefore be fully described, yet only contain what's necessary.

A useful first step in designing any system or interface is that of identifying the entities involved. These entities turn into tables, aggregates, or column families in data stores; classes in object-oriented systems; and types in systems like Apache Thrift. They are the lingua franca of the interface. Only things that have a defined type can be passed back and forth through Apache Thrift. While Apache Thrift IDL provides all the traditional built-in types (integers, floats, strings, and so on), such base types are too fine-grained to create expressive interfaces in most cases. Fortunately, types that are more abstract, more relevant to the application at hand, can be easily created.

Apache Thrift IDL provides an expressive but concise set of tools for designing types. The IDL compiler supports not only collections, such as `list`, `set`, and `map`, but also composed types such as `struct` and `union`, in addition to convenience types such as `typedef` and `enum`.

In this section we'll look at the range of Apache Thrift IDL features available to interface designers and how these interfaces are used in Node.js. The interface we'll build defines a trade reporting feature for the Pacific Northwest Fish company. This facet of the fish market system will allow wholesalers to inspect the most recent sale prices of various types of fish in various markets in the Pacific Northwest.

The IDL for this service is more realistic than our previous trivial examples, making it a bit longer, so we'll break it into two sections. This first section describes the types that will be defined within the interface, as shown in the following listing.

Listing 14.7 ~thriftbook/part3/nodejs/trade.thrift

```
/** Apache Thrift IDL definition for the TradeHistory service interface */
namespace * PNWF

enum Market {                    ❶
    Unknown       = 0,
    Portland      = 1,
    Seattle       = 2,
    SanFrancisco  = 3,
    Vancouver     = 4,
    Anchorage     = 5,
}

typedef double USD               ❷

struct TimeStamp {               ❸
    1: i16   year,
    2: i16   month,
    3: i16   day,
    4: i16   hour,
    5: i16   minute,
    6: i16   second,
    7: optional i32 micros,
}

union FishSizeUnit {             ❹
    1: i32   pounds,
    2: i32   kilograms,
    3: i16   standard_crates,
    4: double  metric_tons,
}

struct Trade {                                           ❺
    /**The symbol for the fish traded*/
    1: string        fish,
    /**Price per size unit in USD*/
    2: USD           price,
    /**Amount traded*/
    3: FishSizeUnit amount,
    /**Date/time trade occured*/
    4: TimeStamp     date_time,
    /**Market where trade occured*/
```

```
       5: Market          market=Market.Unknown,
       /**The trade's unique identifier*/
       6: i64             id
}
```

As we examine this IDL, keep in mind that chapter 6 provides a complete Apache Thrift IDL reference, so our treatment here will be more specific to the Node.js implementation.

The IDL source begins with a namespace definition. Real-world Apache Thrift interfaces are almost always contained within a namespace. Using namespaces to contain identifiers for a subsystem is a best practice in most languages, greatly reducing global name collisions.

The first type definition is an enumeration for the markets ❶. An enumeration may be a good choice here because it allows developers to work with meaningful names rather than meaningless numbers, potentially reducing coding errors. The enumeration also ensures that each market is given a unique numeric value, which a raw integer wouldn't do. Enumerations are treated internally as integers by implementing languages, making them fast to transmit and efficient for compression, lookups, comparisons, and other operations. Enumerations contain interface master data, the fish markets in this example, making them unique among the Apache Thrift IDL constructs. All other features describe types, methods, and aggregates thereof. Adding enumeration values is acceptable, but existing values shouldn't be changed, due to the potential impact on older systems and relations that may depend on them. Enums are a fast way to mirror master data from a database without caching overhead; however, if the data is mutable or the dataset is often extended, database hosted values passed in a normal base type may be preferable.

The next definition is a simple typedef for US dollars ❷. This gives us the flexibility of a double but the benefits of a user-defined type. The user-defined type USD is self-documenting and tells us that this is a specific currency quantity and not semantically interchangeable with other non-USD doubles.

Our next type is the `TimeStamp` struct ❸. Structs are used to represent most of the complex entities within an interface in Apache Thrift. The `TimeStamp` type is composed of 16-bit integers and an optional 32-bit integer for the microseconds portion. In most Apache Thrift implementations, if this optional field isn't set, it will not be transmitted, reducing transmission overhead. Also, a receiver must test for the presence of the micros field before using it, making optionals less expensive in certain ways and more expensive in others.

The next type is the `FishSizeUnit` union ❹. This is a mutually exclusive set of values, each of which has a field name and a distinct type. Unions are the right choice when you identify a thing in your interface that can have different types at different times, yet always has only one value. The entity is consistent but the type is variable. In this case, only one amount of fish exists; however, the amount could be whole numbers of crates or fractional metric tons. The union gives us a way to allow a trade to use any amount type that's appropriate and also allows us to add new amount types in the future.

The final struct is the trade itself **❺**. As you can see, it's largely a composition of the other, more primitive types we've already defined. The market field of the trade has been assigned a default value of unknown. Default values are a useful feature in Apache Thrift IDL, ensuring there will always be a value present for the market field, even if the counterpart doesn't serialize one.

Many people think about interface design as the process of creating function signatures. However, accurately articulating the entities used in the interface is often the more important task. If you have the "things" right, the tasks that manipulate them often easily fall into place.

Our second block of IDL defines the Trade History service and its exceptions, as shown in the following listing.

Listing 14.8   ~thriftbook/part3/nodejs/trade.thrift

```
exception BadFish {                     ❶
    /**The problem fish*/
    1: string          fish,
    /**The service specific error code*/
    2: i16             error_code,
}

exception BadFishes {                           ❷
    /**The problem fish:error pairs*/
    1: map<string, i16>  fish_errors,
}

service TradeHistory {          ❸
    /**
     * Return most recent trade report for fish type
     *
     * @param fish - the symbol for the fish traded
     * @return - the most recent trade report for the fish
     * @throws BadFish - if fish has no trade history or is invalid
     */
    Trade GetLastSale(1: string fish)       ❹
        throws (1: BadFish bf),

    /**
     * Return most recent trade report for multiple fish types
     *
     * @param fishes the symbols for the fishes to return trades for
     * @param fail_fast if set true the first invalid fish symbol is thrown
     *                  as a BadFish exception, if set false all of the bad
     *                  fish symbols are thrown using the BadFishes
     *                  exception.
     * @return list of trades coooresponding to the fish supplied, the list
     *         returned need not be in the same order as the input list
     * @throws BadFish first fish discovered to be invalid or without a
     *                  trade history (only occurs if skip_bad_fish=false)
```

```
                 */
         list<Trade> GetLastSaleList(1: set<string> fishes       ❺
                                     2: bool fail_fast=false)
               throws (1: BadFish bf, 2: BadFishes bfs)
       }
```

Let's begin by examining the `TradeHistory` service ❸. The service contains two methods, `GetLastSale()` ❹ and `GetLastSaleList()` ❺. The first method, `GetLastSale()`, returns a single trade or one of the exceptions from the exception specification. Apache Thrift servers aren't allowed to throw exceptions back to clients unless they are explicitly identified in the IDL. The `GetLastSale()` method receives a fish string from the user that defines the type of fish to retrieve a trade report for. If the method is successful a trade will be returned; if the method fails it will throw a `BadFish` exception, exceptions being essentially specialized structs in the Apache Thrift IDL ❶.

The second method allows the user to retrieve trades for a variety of fish types. The fishes parameter is a collection of fish type strings. The "set" collection type makes it clear to the user that a given fish type may only be supplied once due to the nature of sets. Sets are represented as arrays in JavaScript, so, as in other dynamic programming languages, discipline is required to ensure duplicates aren't added. The second parameter is a flag indicating how the method should respond to errors. If `fail_fast` is `true`, a `BadFish` is thrown for the first fish with a problem. If `fail_fast` is `false` (the default value) and an error occurs, processing continues until all the fishes supplied are examined and a `BadFishes` exception is thrown listing all of the erroneous fish types, each with its own error code.

The `BadFishes` exception ❷ contains an Apache Thrift "map" collection that's an associative container, mapping our fish types (the string key) to their respective error codes (the i16 value). IDL maps are implemented as object hashes in JavaScript.

If successful the `GetLastSaleList()` method returns a "list" of Trades to the caller. The list is the last of the three Apache Thrift IDL collection types (set, map, and list). Lists, like sets, are implemented as JavaScript arrays.

With the IDL saved, we can build stubs for Node.js with the IDL compiler:

```
$ thrift -gen js:node trade.thrift
$ ls -l
drwxr-xr-x 2 randy randy 4096 Feb  7 00:05 gen-nodejs
-rw-r--r-- 1 randy randy 2607 Feb  7 00:47 trade.thrift
$ ls -l gen-nodejs/
-rw-r--r-- 1 randy randy 13113 Feb  7 02:41 TradeHistory.js
-rw-r--r-- 1 randy randy 13841 Feb  7 02:41 trade_types.js
```

Our next step will be building a server to implement the Trade History service.

14.5.1 *Creating full-featured IDL handlers*

Our server will be implemented as a mock, generating random trade data in response to client requests. The server listing below contains the same structural components as that of the hello world server:

- *A service handler*—For the `TradeHistory` service
- *An I/O stack definition*—`TSocket`, `TBufferedTransport`, and `TBinaryProtocol`
- *A server*—Created with `createServer()`

Here's the code.

Listing 14.9 ~thriftbook/part3/nodejs/tradeServer.js

```
var thrift = require('thrift');
var tradeTypes = require('./gen-nodejs/trade_types');            ❶
var tradeHistory = require('./gen-nodejs/TradeHistory');
var tradeUtils = require('./tradeUtils');

//TradeHistory Handler
❷ var tradeHistoryHandler = {
  GetLastSale: function(fish, result) {                          ❸
    if (!fish) {
      result(new tradeTypes.BadFish({fish: "", error_code: 5}), null);
    } else {
      var trade = getMockTrade(fish);
      tradeUtils.logTrade(trade);
      result(null, trade);
    }

  },

  GetLastSaleList: function(fishes, fail_fast, result) {         ❹
    if (!fishes) {
      result(new tradeTypes.BadFish({fish: "", error_code: 5}), null);
    } else if (!fail_fast && tradeUtils.getTimeStamp().second > 45) {
      var bf = {};
      for (var fish in fishes) { bf[fishes[fish]] = 7; };
      result(new tradeTypes.BadFishes({fish_errors: bf}), null);
    } else {
      var trades = [];
      for (var fish in fishes) {
        var trade = getMockTrade(fishes[fish]);
        tradeUtils.logTrade(trade);
        trades.push(trade);
      }
      result(null, trades);
    }
  }
};

//Setup and run the server
var port = 8585;
thrift.createServer(tradeHistory,                                ❺
```

```
                   tradeHistoryHandler,
                   { protocol: thrift.TBinaryProtocol,
                     transport: thrift.TBufferedTransport })
       .on("error", function(e){ console.log(e); })
       .listen(port);
console.log("Thrift Server running on port: " + port);
```

Let's walk through this listing in sections. At the top of the listing we require the Thrift module, as well as the generated service and types modules ❶. We've also imported another hand-coded file called tradeUtils.js. This is a Node.js module with several helper functions (for example, a mock Trade generator, a Trade logger, and so on) that will be used by the server and the client (see listing 14.11).

The next block of code defines the implementation of the TradeHistory service ❷. The GetLastSale() method returns a mock trade or throws a BadFish exception if the requested fish type isn't a valid string ❸. The GetLastSaleList() method correspondingly returns a list of Trades and every once in a while throws a BadFishes exception for testing purposes ❹. The combination of methods and exceptions in this service demonstrates use of all three Apache Thrift collections (map, list, set).

The final block of code creates and runs the server ❺. Now that the server is complete, we can look at an RPC test client.

14.5.2 *Creating a full-featured Node.js client*

To test the server, we'll build a simple Node.js client that repetitively requests trade reports from the server using both of the TradeHistory service methods, as shown in the following listing.

Listing 14.10   ~thriftbook/part3/nodejs/tradeClient.js

```
var thrift = require('thrift');
var tradeTypes = require('./gen-nodejs/trade_types');        ❶
var tradeHistory = require('./gen-nodejs/TradeHistory');
var tradeUtils = require('./tradeUtils');

var intId1 = null;        ❷
var intId2 = null;

//Connect to the server and setup a TradeHistory client
var connection = thrift.createConnection('localhost', 8585, {        ❸
  transport: thrift.TBufferedTransport,
  protocol: thrift.TBinaryProtocol
}).on('error', function(err) {        ❹
  console.log(err);
  clearInterval(intId1);
  clearInterval(intId2);
});
var client = thrift.createClient(tradeHistory, connection);        ❺

//Request trade info every 4 seconds and display result
❻ intId1 = setInterval((function() {
```

```
      var counter = 0;
      return function() {
        var fish = ["Halibut", "Salmon", "Ono", "Tuna"][++counter%4];
        client.GetLastSale(fish, function(error, success) {
          if (success) {
            tradeUtils.logTrade(success);
          }
        });
      };
    })(), 4000);

    //Request trade list info every 15 seconds and display result
➐  intId2 = setInterval(function() {
      client.GetLastSaleList(["Halibut", "Salmon", "Ono", "Tuna"],
                             false, function(error, success) {
        if (success) {
          for (var fish in success) {
            tradeUtils.logTrade(success[fish]);
          }
        } else {
          console.log(error);
        }
      });
    }, 15000);
```

This client program includes the same dependencies as the server at the top of the file without the generated types file ➊. The client code will receive objects defined in the IDL, but because JavaScript is duck typed, we don't need to declare these types unless we plan to create instances of them with the new operator.

The next bit of code declares two interval timer IDs ➋. These IDs identify the two timer-driven test methods that will drive the simulation. The createConnection() method connects a TCP socket to the server ➌. In this example we supply an error event callback that stops both interval timers if the connection fails ➍.

Once connected we can wrap the connection in the generated client defined for the service, tradeHistory, using the createClient method ➎. The last two blocks of code make RPC calls to the server using the client object.

The first block calls the GetLastSale() method every 4 seconds with a revolving set of fish types ➏. If the function succeeds, the callback logs the response. The second block of code calls the GetLastSaleList() method ➐. The server randomly fails on this call, so the code here displays the successfully returned trades as well as any BadFishes exceptions that may be returned.

This following code shows the client output while connected to a tradeServer running in another shell:

```
$ node tradeClient.js
[03:49:52] 1.Salmon, Portland 195 lbs @ 11.07
[03:49:56] 2.Ono, SanFrancisco 215 lbs @ 11.11
...
[03:50:40] 25.Salmon, Portland 195 lbs @ 10.95
```

```
[03:50:44] 26.Ono, SanFrancisco 215 lbs @ 10.99
{ name: 'BadFishes',
  fish_errors: { Halibut: 7, Salmon: 7, Ono: 7, Tuna: 7 } }
[03:50:48] 27.Tuna, Portland 235 lbs @ 11.03
[03:50:52] 28.Halibut, SanFrancisco 255 lbs @ 11.07
```

For completeness, the utility function listing used by both the client and server above is provided in the following listing.

Listing 14.11   ~thriftbook/part3/nodejs/tradeUtils.js

```
var tradeTypes = require('./gen-nodejs/trade_types');

exports.getMockTrade = (function() {
  next_trade_id = 1;
  return function(fish) {
    return new tradeTypes.Trade({
      fish: fish,
      date_time: getTimeStamp(),
      price: ((1055 + getTimeStamp().second) / 100).toFixed(2),
      amount: new tradeTypes.FishSizeUnit({
                      pounds: 175 + (next_trade_id%12 * 20)}),
      market: (next_trade_id % 2 == 0) ?
                 tradeTypes.Market['SanFrancisco'] :
                 tradeTypes.Market['Portland'],
      id: next_trade_id++
    });
  };
})();

var getTimeStamp = exports.getTimeStamp = function() {
  var date = new Date();
  return new tradeTypes.TimeStamp({
    year: date.getFullYear(),
    month: date.getMonth(),
    day: date.getDate(),
    hour: date.getHours(),
    minute: date.getMinutes(),
    second: date.getSeconds()
  });
}

var getAmountString = exports.getAmountString = function(trade) {
  var as = "";
  if (trade.amount.pounds) {
    as = " " + trade.amount.pounds + " lbs";
  } else if (trade.amount.kilograms) {
    as = " " + trade.amount.kilograms + " kg";
  } else if (trade.amount.standard_crates) {
    as = " " + trade.amount.standard_crates + " cr";
  } else if (trade.amount.metric_tons) {
    as = " " + trade.amount.metric_tons + " tons";
  }
  return as;
```

```
}

var getDateTimeString = exports.getDateTimeString = function(trade) {
  return (trade.date_time.hour<10 ? "[0" : "[") + trade.date_time.hour +
    (trade.date_time.minute<10 ? ":0" : ":") + trade.date_time.minute +
    (trade.date_time.second<10 ? ":0" : ":") + trade.date_time.second + "]";
}

var logTrade = exports.logTrade = function(trade) {
  console.log(getDateTimeString(trade) + " " + trade.id + "." +
    trade.fish + ", " + Object.keys(tradeTypes.Market)[trade.market] +
    getAmountString(trade) + " @ " + (+trade.price).toFixed(2));
}
```

Summary

Node.js has become a popular and performant platform for many organizations building distributed applications, particularly those needing to leverage the skills of their existing JavaScript developers. Apache Thrift makes it possible for Node.js applications to support high-performance Web clients while interacting with a range of backend services written in almost any language.

Most of the Apache Thrift features exposed to users, particularly those used in this chapter, are documented in the source with Javadoc. Building the source in thrift/lib/nodejs will create HTML documentation from the source comments; you can always read them directly too.

This chapter covered

- Building Node.js TSocket-compatible servers
- Multiplexing multiple services over a single connection
- Using the Q library for asynchronous operations
- Proper asynchronous error management in Apache Thrift Node.js
- How to code full-featured Apache Thrift interfaces in Node.js

15
Apache
Thrift and JavaScript

This chapter covers

- Getting up and running with Apache Thrift and browser-side JavaScript
- Building browser-based Apache Thrift RPC clients
- Building Node.js-based Apache Thrift servers for web clients
- Adding security features to web-based RPC

Though browsers generally use REST APIs to communicate with backend servers, consuming Apache Thrift RPC interfaces in browsers may also make sense in certain settings. For example, in cases where you have existing Apache Thrift services, it may be easier to consume them directly in the browser rather than creating REST wrapper/gateway services or other intermediate overhead. Apache Thrift can also operate over HTTP/2, HTTP 1.1/1.0, and, for those looking for extreme performance, WebSocket.

Apache Thrift offers two JavaScript libraries, one for Node.js and one for browser use. This chapter introduces the RPC features provided by the browser-based Apache

Thrift JavaScript libraries. We'll set up a frontend JavaScript development environment and build browser-based clients with Apache Thrift. The Apache Thrift browser libraries only support client-side RPC operations, so we'll use Node.js and the Apache Thrift Node.js libraries on the server side. This chapter assumes that you're familiar with JavaScript and the basics of web programming.

Browser and Node.js development environments share a wide array of tooling and support libraries, creating useful synergies. Though Apache Thrift has separate libraries for browser and Node.js development, both libraries are written in JavaScript and the two systems are similar, making it easy to switch between them. Many use Node.js libraries in the browser directly with tools like Webpack, Rollup, Parcel, or what have you. In this chapter, however, we're going to keep the tooling extremely simple so that we can focus on Apache Thrift. We'll explore XHR and WebSocket transports, web security features such as TLS, Cross Origin Resource Sharing (CORS), and Content Security Policy (CSP), among other useful tools.

Our first step will be to configure a frontend Apache Thrift JavaScript development environment and then test a simple browser-based Hello World RPC application.

15.1 *Apache Thrift JavaScript quick start*

We need to have a few things installed to begin working with Apache Thrift and JavaScript. The following high-level outline describes the steps involved in getting an Apache Thrift JavaScript client and server running on a clean system (Windows, OSX, or Linux). In the next section, we'll walk through each step in detail and code an example client and server, but here's the overview:

1 Install Node.js over the web (or use a package manager):
   http://nodejs.org
2 Download the Apache Thrift compiler (or use a package manager or build from source):
   http://thrift.apache.org/download
3 Open a new shell after Node.js is fully installed and create a working directory:
   $ mkdir hello_world; cd hello_world
4 Use npm to install Apache Thrift for Node.js in the working directory (N.B. Be sure the Thrift library and the compiler are the same version):
   $ npm install thrift
5 Install Bower globally using npm (more on the move from Bower to NPM later):
   $ sudo npm install -g bower
6 Use Bower to install Apache Thrift for browsers in the working directory:
   $ bower install thrift
7 Create an Apache Thrift IDL file for your service interface:
   $ vim hello.thrift...
8 Compile the IDL for JavaScript with support for browsers and Node.js:
   $ thrift -gen js -gen js:node hello.thrift

9   Create and run a Node.js server to implement the desired Apache Thrift service:
     $ node hello.js

10   Create an Apache Thrift client web page, load it in a browser, then make RPC calls!

     http://localhost:9090/hello.html

Now that we have the big picture, let's look at each step in detail.

15.2   A simple client and server

In this section, we'll build a simple Hello World Apache Thrift RPC application with a JavaScript browser client and a Node.js server. By tradition and design, the hello world application will be as simple as possible, allowing us to get the installation, configuration, dependencies, and build process sorted out before worrying about coding matters. The Node.js server will implement the standard `helloSvc` service with its one `getMessage()` method. This function will accept a name string as a parameter and return a greeting string. Our client web page will accept a user name through an input box and display the RPC server message output in response to a button click (see figure 15.1). Let's begin by setting up the development environment.

Figure 15.1   Hello World
JavaScript client

15.2.1 Installing Apache Thrift for JavaScript

While we don't strictly need to install Node.js to use Apache Thrift and JavaScript in a browser, many of the commonly used tools for browser development are written in Node.js, and it's the platform we'll use here to create servers to test our browser apps against.

The easiest and most flexible way to install Node.js is to run the installer from the Node.js website at http://nodejs.org (see figure 15.2). Modern versions of Node.js (0.10+) will also install npm, the Node Package Manager. If you're installing an old version of Node.js you may need to install npm separately (as of this writing, Node.js versions prior to 4.x are end of life). You can test your Node.js/NPM installation by executing the node and npm commands with the `--version` switch:

```
$ node --version
v10.14.2
$ npm --version
6.4.1
```

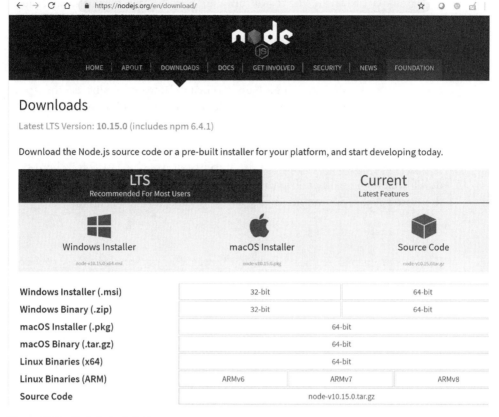

Figure 15.2   Node.js installation

The Apache Thrift Interface Definition Language (IDL) compiler is used to generate client and server stubs for RPC services. A Windows executable IDL compiler (thrift .exe) can be downloaded directly from the Apache Thrift website (http://thrift.apache .org/download). On UNIX-like systems, Apache Thrift may be available through a package manager (for example, $ sudo apt-get install thrift-compiler). In a pinch, you can always build the compiler from source (see build instructions in chapter 3).

Once Node.js, npm, and the IDL compiler are installed, you can use npm to install the current Apache Thrift libraries for Node.js. Support libraries for Node.js projects should be installed in the project's directory. To install the current Apache Thrift libraries for Node.js, create a working directory for the Hello World project and issue the npm install thrift command from within the working directory:

```
$ npm install thrift
```

A directory called node_modules is generated by npm to contain locally installed libraries. The Apache Thrift Node.js library depends on other libraries, such as node-int64 and q, all of which will be automatically installed by npm.

The Apache Thrift client-side browser libraries are currently separate from the Node.js libraries. In the future, these code bases may merge, leaving only the Node.js libraries. In the meantime, you can use the Bower package manager to install the client-side libraries (although Bower is also likely to disappear in the long run). To use Bower, you need to install it with npm. Because Bower is a utility that you can use across many projects, you should install it globally. To install Bower globally, use the npm install –g command (root permissions are typically required for global installation):

```
$ sudo npm install -g bower
```

Once Bower is installed, you can use it to install Apache Thrift for client-side browser development. The official Apache Thrift Bower package is named "thrift"; you can use the Bower install command in your working directory to install it:

```
$ bower install thrift
```

The Bower install command creates a bower_components directory that contains the Apache Thrift browser library ("./bower_components/thrift/lib/js/src/thrift.js"). Because the Apache Thrift browser library is completely contained in a single file, it's easy to copy it if you aren't interested in using Bower (you can grab it directly from the apache/thrift GitHub repo if you like).

Note that in the examples here we use Apache Thrift v0.11.0 everywhere. There may be subtle incompatibilities between the libraries and compilers of different versions of Apache Thrift, and it's almost always a bad idea to use code generated by one version and a different version of the libraries in a single program. However, using one version of Apache Thrift in a client with another version of Apache Thrift in a server is usually fine. For example, using a 0.9.3 client (compiled with 0.9.3 and using 0.9.3 libraries) with a 0.10.0 server (compiled with 0.10.0 and using 0.10.0 libraries) should work fine.

Now that we have all the Apache Thrift JavaScript support files installed, we can use Apache Thrift IDL to design an RPC interface.

15.2.2 *The Hello World IDL*

IDL is used in Apache Thrift to define a contract specifying the ways in which clients and servers may communicate. In Apache Thrift, IDL services define a set of functions that servers implement and clients call. For this Hello World walkthrough, we'll use the same helloSvc IDL used throughout part 3 of this book, as shown in the following listing.

Listing 15.1   ~thriftbook/part3/js/hello.thrift

```
service helloSvc {
    string getMessage(1: string name)
}
```

In JavaScript, IDL-generated client-side stubs come packaged in an object named "Client", and server-side stubs come in the form of a function called "Processor". The following code shows a sample session generating the necessary helloSvc JavaScript stubs for our client and server:

```
$ thrift -gen js -gen js:node hello.thrift
$ ls -l
drwxr-xr-x 3 randy randy 4096 Feb  2 12:57 bower_components
drwxr-xr-x 2 randy randy 4096 Feb  2 12:57 gen-js            ❶
drwxr-xr-x 2 randy randy 4096 Feb  2 12:57 gen-nodejs
drwxr-xr-x 3 randy randy 4096 Feb  2 12:54 node_modules

$ ls -l gen-js
-rw-r--r-- 1 randy randy 4279 Feb  5 23:05 helloSvc.js       ❷
-rw-r--r-- 1 randy randy  127 Feb  5 23:05 hello_types.js    ❸

$ ls -l gen-nodejs
-rw-r--r-- 1 randy randy 5258 Feb  5 23:05 helloSvc.js       ❷
-rw-r--r-- 1 randy randy  199 Feb  5 23:05 hello_types.js    ❸
```

The IDL compiler emits two "gen-..." directories in response to the thrift command above ❶. The –gen js switch produces the browser-side JavaScript support files and places them in gen-js. The –gen js:node switch produces the Node.js support files and places them in gen-nodejs.

Two files are generated by the IDL compiler for each environment. The first file, helloSvc.js, is named after the service and contains the client/server stubs for the service ❷. The second file, hello_types.js, contains the definitions of any user-defined types we may have created in the IDL file ❸. In this case, the types file will be empty, because we haven't created any user-defined types.

With the build tools installed and the RPC interface compiled, we're now ready to code the client and server.

15.2.3 *The Hello World Node.js server*

Implementing the helloSvc in Node.js will require several lines of boiler plate code to define a server and a few lines of code to implement the getMessage() RPC function. The Apache Thrift Node.js libraries offer a variety of Node.js servers, each useful in specific settings. The web server supports RPC services over the web and serves static files. We'll use this server to host the RPC service and to supply client-side HTML/JavaScript files to the browser.

The following listing shows the source for the Hello World Node.js server.

> **Listing 15.2 ~thriftbook/part3/js/hello.js**

```
var thrift = require('thrift');                        ❶
var helloSvc = require('./gen-nodejs/helloSvc');       ❷

//ServiceHandler: Implement the hello service
var helloHandler = {                                   ❸
```

```
    counter: 0,
    getMessage: function(name, result) {
      this.counter++;
      var msg = "" + this.counter + ") Hello " + name + "!";
      console.log(msg);
      result(null, msg);
    }
}

//ServiceOptions: The I/O stack for the service
var helloSvcOpt = {
    handler: helloHandler,
    processor: helloSvc,
    protocol: thrift.TJSONProtocol,
    transport: thrift.TBufferedTransport
};

//ServerOptions: Define server features
var serverOpt = {
    files: ".",
    services: {
        "/hello": helloSvcOpt
    }
}

//Create and start the web server
var port = 9090;
thrift.createWebServer(serverOpt).listen(port);
console.log("Http/Thrift Server running on port: " + port);
```

(4) appears beside the ServiceOptions block; (5) appears beside the ServerOptions block; (6) appears beside the web server creation block.

At the top of the listing, the Node.js require statement is used to import the server's two dependencies, the first of which is the Apache Thrift Node.js library module ❶. The Thrift module provides access to all the Apache Thrift server, transport, and protocol resources needed to build a server. The second dependency is `helloSvc` ❷; this module houses the IDL compiler-generated "processor" for the service. Apache Thrift servers can host multiple services, but in this example we configure only the hello service.

> **NOTE** In Node.js speak, modules and JavaScript files are generally in one-to-one correspondence. For example, the `require('./gen-nodejs/helloSvc')` statement loads the `helloSvc` module, which is the file helloSvc.js. Modules may also reference a folder within the node_modules folder. When searching folders, Node.js will look for a package.json file containing a "main" attribute. If this is found, Node.js will load the module using the "main" path. If a package .json file isn't found, Node.js will try to load a file called index.js. In the context of require('thrift'), Node.js reads the node_modules/thrift/package.json file and is redirected by "main" to the file node_modules/thrift/lib/nodejs/lib/ thrift/index.js. The Thrift index.js exports all the public features of the Apache Thrift implementation for Node.js.

Apache Thrift clients and servers communicate through an I/O stack involving one or more transports, a protocol, and, on the server side, a processor and handler. The processor is generated by the IDL compiler. Processors decode low-level RPC messages and then call the appropriate function in the handler.

In JavaScript, we create handler objects to implement our services, providing methods for each function in the service. Our `helloHandler` has a counter variable and an implementation for the `getMessage()` method ❸. Service methods receive the parameters defined in the service plus a `result()` callback function as arguments.

The `result()` callback function is called by the handler to set the service method's response to the client. The `result()` callback takes an optional error object as the first parameter and an optional return value as the second parameter. If an error is supplied, it will be returned to the client as an Apache Thrift exception. The second parameter passed to result is ignored if an error is set. Our trivial example has no error cases, so we invoke `result()` with `null` and the desired greeting string as a return value.

In Node.js the I/O stack for a service is specified through some combination of server create parameters and options. The `webServer` uses a `ServiceOptions` object to configure the I/O stack for each service route ❹. The `ServiceOptions` object has four properties:

- *handler*—The user-defined implementation for the service
- *processor*—The IDL compiler-generated service processor
- *protocol*—The serialization protocol
- *transport*—The layered transport

In this example we've set the handler to `helloHandler` and the processor to the generated module for our service, `helloSvc`. The serialization protocol has been set to `TJSONProtocol`. Protocols serialize the messages sent between clients and servers in a language-agnostic format. The `TJSONProtocol` uses the JavaScript Object Notation (JSON) format. Node.js also supports `TBinaryProtocol` and `TCompactProtocol`, both of which tend to be faster and more compact than JSON but less web friendly. If no protocol is defined, the server will use the `TBinaryProtocol` by default (the Apache Thrift default).

> **NOTE** At the time of this writing, the Apache Thrift JavaScript browser-side library supported only Binary and JSON protocols.

The transport field defines the transport layer to place above the network interface. The `TBufferedTransport` will buffer small protocol writes so that network transmissions are only made when a complete RPC message is ready to send. Node.js also supports the `TFramedTransport` layer that can be used in place of `TBufferedTransport`. If no transport layer is defined, the server will use the `TBufferedTransport`. For more information on Apache Thrift I/O stacks, refer to chapter 2.

After setting the options for the `helloSvc`, we need to set the options for the actual web server. In this case, the server options will define the service or services to host and the static file path to serve files from. Node.js server options are passed in a `ServerOptions` object. Most `ServerOptions` are optional (surprising, I know), though a combination of them must be provided to create a useful server. This code has configured the server to serve files from the current directory (".") and route requests for the "/hello" route to the hello service defined in the `helloSvcOpt` object ❺. For a complete list of Node.js `ServerOptions`, refer to chapter 16.

The last block of code in the server listing creates the server with the options defined and then calls the `listen()` method, which runs the server on port 9090 ❻.

Now that we have a service implemented, let's look at a simple browser-based client.

15.2.4   *The Hello World web client*

For the Hello World client, we'll create a single-page web frontend with HTML and JavaScript. To keep things simple, we'll embed JavaScript code directly in the HTML file. This isn't advisable in production, where script and HTML templates are conventionally housed in separate files.

This page prompts the user for their name and then, on a button click, calls the `helloSvc::getMessage()` function to retrieve a greeting to display to the user, as shown in the following listing.

Listing 15.3   ~thriftbook/part3/js/hello.html

```
<!DOCTYPE html>
<html lang="en">
  <head>
    <meta charset="utf-8">
    <title>Hello Thrift</title>
  </head>
  <body>
    Name: <input type="text" id="name_in">                              ❶
    <input type="button" id="get_msg" value="Get Message" >
    <div id="output"></div>

    <script src=" bower_components/thrift/lib/js/src/thrift.js ">
    </script>                                                           ❷
    <script src="gen-js/helloSvc.js"></script>
    <script>
      (function() {
        <!-- Setup Apache Thrift Client I/O Stack -->
        var transport = new Thrift.TXHRTransport("/hello");             ❸
        var protocol  = new Thrift.TJSONProtocol(transport);
        var client    = new helloSvcClient(protocol);

        <!-- Wire Apache Thrift RPC call to DOM Click Event -->
        var nameElement   = document.getElementById("name_in");         ❹
        var outputElement = document.getElementById("output");
        document.getElementById("get_msg")
          .addEventListener("click", function(){
            outputElement.innerHTML =                                   ❺
              client.getMessage(nameElement.value);
          });
```

```
    })();
    </script>
  </body>
</html>
```

This file is comprised of two parts, the HTML template for the user interface and the JavaScript program logic. The HTML template defines an input box for the user's name, a button to invoke the server `getMessage()` method, and an output div to display the result ❶.

The JavaScript code begins with script tags which load the standard Apache Thrift browser-side JavaScript library ("thrift.js") and the IDL compiler-generated client stub for `helloSvc` ("helloSvc.js") ❷. The next script tag provides our client application logic housed within an immediate function.

The first few lines of code in the main script block define the client's I/O stack ❸. Apache Thrift clients must define an I/O stack compatible with the I/O stack implemented by the server. In this example, we use the `TXHRTransport` and `TJSONProtocol` to communicate with the server. Browser-based endpoint transports may be initialized with a partial or full URI that will be used to reach the desired service, "/hello" in this case. If no URI is provided, the origin root will be used. The `TXHRTransport` uses XHR to make RPC calls over HTTP; this is the most common and widely supported transport offered by browsers.

The web server will support any HTTP request and has no problem interoperating with the browser's `TXHRTransport`. Apache Thrift browser transport operations are intrinsically buffered, so we don't need to declare a buffering layer. Of critical importance is the fact that both the client and server use the same serialization protocol. In this example, the client and server are using JSON as the common protocol.

The client object is generated by the IDL compiler and sits at the top of the stack, providing access to the `helloSvc` methods. Calling the `getMessage()` function with this I/O stack will result in the browser using the XHR POST method to send the RPC request in JSON format to the server at http://localhost:9090/hello (see figure 15.3).

The final block of code provides the UI logic. The first two lines of code get references to the input and output elements in the DOM ❹. The last few lines of code add a click handler to the HTML input button that calls the `getMessage()` function ❺. The result of the `getMessage()` call is placed in the output div.

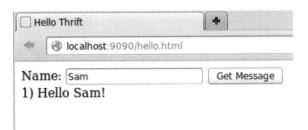

Figure 15.3 Hello World client

15.2.5 *Running the Hello World example*

To test the Hello World example, start the Node.js server in the working directory and then open the hello.html page in a browser. Once the page is open, entering a name and clicking the "Get Message" button executes the getMessage() call against the server. Here's a sample run with a browser session requesting a message for the user name "Sam" (see also figure 15.3):

```
$ ls -l
drwxr-xr-x    1 Randy    Administ        0 Mar  7 00:06 bower_components
drwxr-xr-x    4 Randy    Administ        0 Mar  7 00:13 gen-js
drwxr-xr-x    4 Randy    Administ        0 Mar  7 00:13 gen-nodejs
-rw-r--r--    1 Randy    Administ     1156 Mar  7 01:32 hello.html
-rw-r--r--    1 Randy    Administ       64 Mar  7 00:10 hello.thrift
-rw-r--r--    1 Randy    Administ     1197 Mar  7 01:12 hello.js
drwxr-xr-x    3 Randy    Administ        0 Mar  7 00:08 node_modules
$ node hello.js
Http/Thrift Server running on port: 9090
1) Hello Sam!
```

If you run the browser on the same machine that runs the server, you can open the hello.html page with the URL http://localhost:9090/hello.html.

While this example is trivial, it demonstrates how easy it is to integrate a browser-based JavaScript client with any Apache Thrift-based server supporting HTTP and JSON. We could have built the backend in C++ or Java as easily.

The RPC call in this example is synchronous, blocking the caller until the result can be returned. In other words, the getMessage() function call made in our client page does not return until the server responds or the connection times out. This makes coding easier to reason about in some settings, but it is not the JavaScript-way and can lead to usability problems in scenarios where the server might not respond promptly. In the next section we'll look at improving this situation by switching to async client callbacks.

15.2.6 *Node.js HTTP clients*

While most backend Apache Thrift services operate over raw TCP, browser-based apps use HTTP almost exclusively. HTTP adds a protocol layer on top of low-level TCP communications, enabling a range of HTTP headers and security features to be employed. HTTP clients can be built not only in the browser but also directly in Node.js. The following listing shows the source for a simple Node.js helloSvc HTTP client.

Listing 15.4 ~thriftbook/part3/js/httpClient.js

```
var thrift = require('thrift');
var helloSvc = require('./gen-nodejs/helloSvc.js');

var options = {                                    ❶
    transport: thrift.TBufferedTransport,
    protocol: thrift.TJSONProtocol,
❷  path: "/hello",
```

```
      headers: {"Connection": "close"},   ❸
  ❹  https: false
};

❺ var connection = thrift.createHttpConnection("localhost", 9090, options);
  var client = thrift.createHttpClient(helloSvc, connection);            ❻

  connection.on('error', function(error) {
     console.log(error);
  })

  client.getMessage("Thurston Howell", function(error, result) {    ❼
     console.log("Msg from server: " + result);
  });
```

At the outset, the client requires the standard Thrift library and the IDL-generated helloSvc client. Next, we set up the connection options ❶, including the server-defined protocol and transport layer, as well as a path to the service ❷. Any headers required on the call side are specified as key value pairs in the headers object hash ❸. The example here sets the "Connection: close" header, requesting the connection be closed immediately upon completing a request (efficient if you'll only make one call to the server, as in this example, otherwise it's not recommended). The last object setting is the "https" property, which is set to false here to use HTTP without TLS ❹.

HTTP connections are created using the createHttpConnection() function ❺. This function accepts a host string, TCP port number, and an options object. The host string is required. If the option object is omitted the transport defaults to TBufferedTransport, the protocol defaults to TBinaryProtocol, the route defaults to "/", and normal http is used. If the port is omitted, the connection port will default to 80.

Once the connection is prepared, a client for the desired service can be created using the createHttpClient() function ❻. The createHttpClient() function takes the service module for the service to use and the connection object as parameters. The client is then used to make calls to the service methods hosted on the server as usual ❼.

HTTP-hosted services can be multiplexed in the same way that normal TCP services are multiplexed. However, the web server ability to host different services on different routes often makes multiplexing unnecessary.

Here's a sample run of our client against the above Apache Thrift hello web server:

```
$ node httpClient.js
Msg from server: 6) Hello Thurston Howell!
$
```

15.3 *Asynchronous browser client calls*

In JavaScript one rarely has a good reason to wait, block, or sleep. The event-driven nature of JavaScript applications makes nonblocking asynchronous I/O the norm. Apache Thrift JavaScript clients support asynchronous I/O through callback functions. When used, the callback function is provided as an additional parameter at the end of an RPC call's argument list. When a callback function is provided, RPC functions return immediately after sending their request to the server. This allows the client code to do other work or return control to the browser, rather than freezing the user interface until the response is processed. When the result of an async call arrives, the callback will be invoked and passed the response. The following listing shows what the asynchronous version of the Hello World browser client looks like.

Listing 15.5   ~thriftbook/part3/js/helloAsync.html

```
<script>
  (function() {
    var transport = new Thrift.TXHRTransport("/hello");
    var protocol  = new Thrift.TJSONProtocol(transport);
    var client    = new helloSvcClient(protocol);

    var nameElement   = document.getElementById("name_in");
    var outputElement = document.getElementById("output");
    document.getElementById("get_msg")
      .addEventListener("click", function(){
        client.getMessage(nameElement.value, function(result) {     ❶
          outputElement.innerHTML = result;
        });
      });
  })();
</script>
```

The only change is the addition of a callback function to the end of the getMessage() argument list ❶. The getMessage() call returns as soon as the parameters are sent out through XHR, completing the execution of our script block. Later, when the response arrives over the network, the Apache Thrift library invokes the callback function with the function return value passed in as the "result" parameter, and the callback saves the result in the output div as before.

The subtle but important difference between this and the prior example is that the synchronous example locks up the browser until the RPC call completes. This can be invisible on a fast machine making RPC calls locally. However, users might be materially impacted by such lock ups when operating over the internet against a busy server.

15.4   *RPC error handling*

When Apache Thrift servers cannot complete their processing normally, they throw errors. Three general classes of errors exist that a server can run into:

- *Application layer errors*—When Apache Thrift processes the request but the handler on the server runs into a problem, a security violation for example, an error can be returned to the client in the form of an IDL-defined exception.
- *RPC layer errors*—When Apache Thrift cannot process an RPC request (for example, the service or function doesn't exist), an Apache Thrift framework exception will be generated and returned to the client.
- *Low-level errors*—In certain cases, low-level errors on the server can terminate server-side processing without responding to the client.

Application errors are failure cases identified and planned for in the application. Such errors are represented as user-defined exceptions in the application's IDL; they're part of the interface. IDL exceptions are raised on the server but passed back to the client for handling. RPC functions that throw exceptions must list all the exceptions they may generate in the IDL exception specification for the function. This ensures that the client can prepare for all possible application errors. Listing 15.6 provides an example IDL with an application-defined exception called badMsg.

RPC errors, the second error type, are often the result of misconfiguration. For example, if a client is configured to connect to the wrong server, none of the RPC calls it makes will succeed. When servers receive requests for unknown functions, they return an RPC error. Apache Thrift passes the (misleadingly named) TApplicationException type back to the client when encountering errors at the RPC framework level.

Low-level errors are generally the result of code flaws. Some are trapped by the server and returned in the form of RPC errors, but many terminate processing on the server. In rare cases, such errors can kill or hang the server.

In synchronous RPC, exceptions returned by the server are raised on the client in the normal fashion, requiring the client to use try/catch blocks to trap the errors. This isn't feasible in asynchronous callback scenarios. In synchronous RPC, the caller can trap exceptions as the stack unwinds. In asynchronous callback scenarios, your code isn't the caller but the callee. For this reason, when exceptions arise in async settings, the exception is passed to the callback function in place of the call result. It's important, therefore, to test the callback parameter to detect exceptions. In the context of RPC, all function calls can fail.

To get a better understanding of Apache Thrift error processing, we'll build an upgraded version of the Hello World program with support for exceptions. Imagine you're tasked with improving the HelloSvc interface by returning an error to the client when the name provided for the greeting message is zero length. The following listing shows the IDL used to add this feature to the interface definition.

> **Listing 15.6   ~thriftbook/part3/js/helloExc.thrift**

```
exception badMsg {          ❶
    1: i16      errorCode
    2: string msg
}

service helloError {
    string getMessage(1: string name)
        throws (1: badMsg bm)          ❷
}
```

This IDL is similar to the previous Hello World IDL with the addition of a user-defined exception type called badMsg ❶. Exceptions are defined like structures. If the getMessage() function in the helloError service is allowed to throw the badMsg exception, we must specify this fact in the throws clause following the function declaration ❷.

When we compile this IDL with the Apache Thrift compiler (`$ thrift -gen js -gen js:node helloExc.thrift`), it will create a helloError.js file for the service stubs and a separate helloExc_types.js file where the `badMsg` type will be defined.

Now that we've updated the interface to allow the `badMsg` to be thrown back to the client, let's revisit the server and add code to raise the exception when empty strings are supplied for name, as shown in the following listing.

Listing 15.7   ~thriftbook/part3/js/helloExc.js

```
var thrift = require('thrift');
var badMsg = require('./gen-nodejs/helloExc_types').badMsg;          ❶
var helloError = require('./gen-nodejs/helloError');

var helloHandler = {
  getMessage: function(name, result) {
    if (typeof name !== "string" || name.length < 1) {
      var e = new badMsg();
      e.errorCode = 13;                                               ❷
      e.msg = "No name";
      result(e, null);
    } else {
      result(null, "Hello " + name + "!");
    }
  }
}

var helloErrorOpt = {
    transport: thrift.TBufferedTransport,
    protocol: thrift.TJSONProtocol,
    processor: helloError,
    handler: helloHandler
};

var serverOpt = {
    files: ".",
    services: { "/hello": helloErrorOpt }
}

var server = thrift.createWebServer(serverOpt);
var port = 9099;
server.listen(port);
console.log("Http/Thrift Server running on port: " + port);
console.log("Serving files from: " + __dirname);
```

Adding exception support to the Node.js server requires two bits of code. First, we need to require the compiler-generated types file which contains the `badMsg` exception type ❶. Next, we need to add code to throw the exception when an error condition arises ❷.

As mentioned earlier, the `result()` function passed to RPC service methods takes two parameters: the first is an optional exception object and the second is an optional return value. The error processing logic here creates a new `badMsg` exception and passes it as the first parameter to `result()` when an unacceptable name string is supplied, causing Apache Thrift to return the exception to the client.

Now we are ready to add exception support to our client, as shown in the following listing.

Listing 15.8 ~thriftbook/part3/js/helloExc.html

```
<!DOCTYPE html>
<html lang="en">
  <head>
    <meta charset="utf-8">
    <title>Hello Thrift</title>
  </head>
  <body>
    Name: <input type="text" id="name_in">
    <input type="button" id="get_msg" value="Get Message" >
    <div id="output"></div>
    <script src="bower_components/thrift/lib/js/src/thrift.js"></script>
    <script src="gen-js/helloExc_types.js"></script>
    <script src="gen-js/helloError.js"></script>
    <script>
      (function() {
        var transport = new Thrift.TXHRTransport("/hello");
        var protocol  = new Thrift.TJSONProtocol(transport);
        var client    = new helloErrorClient(protocol);
        var nameElement = document.getElementById("name_in");
        var outputElement = document.getElementById("output");
        document.getElementById("get_msg")
          .addEventListener("click", function(){
            client.getMessage(nameElement.value, function(result) {
              if (result instanceof Error) {                        ❶
                outputElement.innerHTML =
                  result instanceof badMsg ? result.msg : "unknown error";
              } else {
                outputElement.innerHTML = result;
              }
            });
          });
      })();
    </script>
  </body>
</html>
```

In this example we use a callback function to receive the RPC result, error or otherwise.

All Apache Thrift exceptions inherit from the Apache Thrift `TException` type. In JavaScript `TException` inherits from the "Error" built-in type, allowing us to trap any Apache Thrift error or JavaScript error by using a test for `Error` ❶.

As exemplified in the above code, we can also test for the explicit exception types we've defined in IDL. In this example, if the Error is an instance of the badMsg type, we display the exception's msg field as output.

At this point we have enough information to start building useful JavaScript programs with Apache Thrift. That said, several other valuable features are worth discussing before we close the Apache Thrift web chapter.

15.5   *Browser RPC and jQuery*

In addition to generating code for plain browser-based JavaScript and Node.js, the Apache Thrift IDL compiler can also generate code for use with jQuery. The jQuery library is a multi-browser DOM manipulation and utility library used in many of the world's websites. jQuery provides wrappers that offer a consistent interface to the DOM and other host-oriented features, regardless of the underlying browser and version.

One of the more popular jQuery features is its XHR wrapper class, jQuery.ajax. When invoked with the –gen js:jquery switch, the Apache Thrift IDL compiler emits client wrappers that execute asynchronously and return jQuery.ajax objects. This allows those familiar with the jQuery.ajax API to write Apache Thrift client-side code as if working with any other jQuery AJAX-style interface.

To demonstrate Apache Thrift jQuery support, let's modify the previous HTML/JavaScript client to use the Apache Thrift jQuery interface. Because jQuery is a client-side library, we don't need to modify the IDL or Node.js server.

The following listing shows the jQuery version of the exception-enabled Hello World program.

Listing 15.9   ~thriftbook/part3/js/helloJq.html

```
<!DOCTYPE html>
<html lang="en">
  <head>
    <meta charset="utf-8">
    <title>Hello Thrift</title>
  </head>
  <body>
    Name: <input type="text" id="name_in">
    <input type="button" id="get_msg" value="Get Message" >
    <div id="output"></div>
    <script src="http://code.jquery.com/jquery-1.12.4.js"></script>        ❶
    <script src="bower_components/thrift/lib/js/src/thrift.js"></script>
    <script src="gen-js/helloExc_types.js"></script>
    <script src="gen-js/helloError.js"></script>
    <script>
      (function() {
        var transport = new Thrift.TXHRTransport("/hello");
        var protocol  = new Thrift.TJSONProtocol(transport);
        var client = new helloErrorClient(protocol);
        var $name = $("#name_in");                                          ❷
        var $out = $("#output");
        $("#get_msg")
          .click(function(){                                                ❸
❹         client.getMessage($name.val(), function(){})
              .success(function(result) { $out.html(result); })            ❺
              .error(function(xhr, status, e) { $out.html(e.msg || e); })
              .complete(function() { $out.append("<br>Complete"); });
```

```
            });
        })();
    </script>
  </body>
</html>
```

We need to recompile our IDL stubs with jQuery support to use this jQuery-based client. The -gen js:jquery switch outputs jQuery-compatible stubs:

```
$ thrift -gen js:jquery helloExc.thrift
```

The first modification our jQuery-based Hello World program requires is the inclusion of the jQuery library ❶. Due to jQuery's popularity, it can be pulled into the client environment from several Content Delivery Networks (CDNs). The CDN used here is code.jquery.com; however, you can also find jQuery on the Google APIs CDN (developers.google.com/speed/libraries/devguide#jquery), among others. Alternatively, you can download jQuery and place it on your own web server. Some frameworks, for example Angular, have integrated JQuery replicas you can use instead of the actual jQuery library.

By default, jQuery creates a "$" alias that can be used as a shortcut to the main jQuery library function. It's used in this example to look up DOM elements ❷. The string passed to the $ function is known as a selection because it selects the DOM element to provide a wrapper around. By convention, the jQuery objects returned by the selector are given names beginning or ending with "$", such as $name and $out. JQuery objects provide many convenience methods. In this example we use the click() method to assign a click event listener to the get_msg element ❸.

The next item of interest is the RPC call to the getMessage() function ❹. Because we've compiled with the js:jquery switch, this method returns a jQuery.ajax object.

The last parameter of getMessage(), the callback function, has been left empty. In a real application, we'd either use or omit this callback; it's shown here for reference. When provided, this callback function will execute when the RPC request completes successfully. Contrary to the non-jQuery callback, this callback will *not* be called if an error is thrown. To handle errors, you need to use the jQuery.ajax error() handler.

jQuery is credited with popularizing the chaining style of function calling in JavaScript, where each function returns the original object, allowing dot operators to add additional method calls (for example, obj.f1().f2().f3().f4();). In the example, three jQuery.ajax method calls are chained to the result of the getMessage() call ❺:

- success()
- error()
- complete()

Each of these functions registers a callback to be invoked. The success() function sets a callback that will only be called if the getMessage() function completes without error. This callback is interchangeable with the callback function supplied as an argument to getMessage(). The getMessage() callback argument is called first if both are supplied. Developers typically use one or the other of these callbacks to handle successful RPC completion.

The `error()` method registers a callback function to be invoked only if an error is thrown during the RPC operation. The error callback receives the jQuery.ajax object, a status message, and the exception object.

The final callback registration function, `complete()`, sets a callback to be invoked when the RPC operation completes, regardless of whether it succeeds or fails. The complete callback is called last when other callbacks are also set (see figures 15.4 and 15.5).

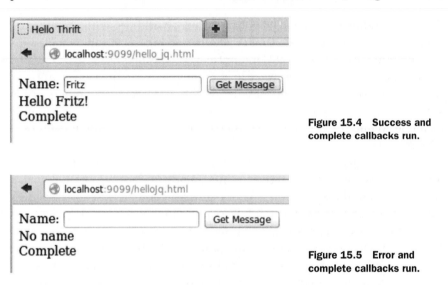

Figure 15.4   Success and complete callbacks run.

Figure 15.5   Error and complete callbacks run.

The jQuery.ajax interface is defined by jQuery rather than Apache Thrift, and many developers find these features useful beyond what's discussed here. For more jQuery information, look at the jQuery documentation (http://api.jquery.com/jquery .ajax/). The Apache Thrift jQuery stubs are XHR-based and only work with the `TXHR-Transport` transport. If you plan to use WebSocket, you'll need to use the normal Apache Thrift stubs.

15.6   Apache Thrift and web security

Security is almost always a concern when building browser-based applications. In this section, we'll examine four technologies that play an important role in securing browser-based Apache Thrift clients:

- *CORS*—Cross Origin Resource Sharing
- *CSP*—Content Security Policy
- *X-Frame options*—Clickjacking prevention
- *TLS*—Transport Layer Security

15.6.1 *Cross Origin Resource Sharing (CORS)*

By default, XHR requests from one origin to another origin (for example, abc.com -> other.com) aren't allowed by browsers, for security reasons. This is known as the "same origin policy." CORS was created to work around the limitations of the same origin policy, making it possible to selectively enable certain cross-site requests.

In the context of the same origin policy, the definition of origin includes the communications scheme (HTTP, FTP, and so on), the hostname, and the port number. Therefore, a page loaded from http://localhost:9090 cannot make an Apache Thrift RPC call over XHR to a service running on http://localhost:9091 without violating the same origin policy. Browsers also typically deny access to the local file system (for example, file://C:\Temp\my.html).

As frontend code bases grow and applications become more and more distributed, the inability to access multiple servers from a browser can become a material architecture challenge. One solution is to turn the origin server into a proxy for all the other services the client might need. This approach can be a good fit in some situations, but can conflict with integration and scaling needs and creates extra work and complexity on the server side, as each new external service required by the frontend must be passed through the proxy on the server side.

CORS provides an alternative by making it possible for foreign sites to authorize access from trusted origins. For example, if you load a web application, index.html, from the origin http://abc.com, using CORS you could make XHR calls to http://other.com if the other.com server allowed callers from abc.com.

Here's how it works: when a modern browser is asked to make an XHR request to a target other than the page's origin, the browser automatically sends a header like this to the foreign target:

```
Origin: http://localhost:9090
```

If the XHR target is willing to allow calls from pages of that origin, it would respond with the header

```
Access-Control-Allow-Origin: http://localhost:9090
```

To enable CORS on the Node.js server side, we can add the `cors` attribute to the ServerOptions object. The `cors` attribute can be `null` or undefined to deny all CORS requests, or it can be set to an object which defines the origins to allow. Origins not explicitly enabled in the `cors` object are disabled by default.

To enable an origin, add a property to the `cors` object with the origin name and a value of `true`. You can add as many origins as you like. You can also enable all origins by setting a property named "*" to `true`. To disable an origin, you set its value to `false`. This is useful because explicitly disabled origins override the all origins "*" property. Thus, to enable all origins except http://localhost:9097, you could create a Server Options object like this:

```
var server_opt = {
    ...
    cors: {
        "*":                        true,
        "http://localhost:9097": false
    }
};
```

The following listing shows our Node.js hello server reworked to support HTTP CORS requests from localhost port 9098.

```
Listing 15.10   ~thriftbook/part3/js/cors.js
```

```
var thrift = require('thrift');
var helloSvc = require('./gen-nodejs/helloSvc');

//ServiceHandler: Implement the hello service
var helloHandler = {
  getMessage: function(name, result) {
    var msg = "Hello " + name + "!";
    console.log(msg);
    result(null, msg);
  }
}

//ServiceOptions: The I/O stack for the service
var helloSvcOpt = {
    handler: helloHandler,
    processor: helloSvc,
    protocol: thrift.TJSONProtocol,
    transport: thrift.TBufferedTransport
};

//ServerOptions: Define server features
var serverOpt = {
    filePath: ".",
    services: {"/hello": helloSvcOpt},
    cors: {"http://localhost:9098": true}       ❶
}

//Create and start the web server
var port = process.argv[2];                     ❷
thrift.createWebServer(serverOpt).listen(port);
console.log("Http/Thrift Server running on port: " + port);
console.log("Serving files from: " + __dirname);
```

In this example, we've added the `cors` property to the `ServerOptions` object, enabling RPC requests from browser files with an origin of "http://localhost:9098" ❶.

To test this CORS configuration we need to load our files from a port 9098 server and make RPC calls to a server on some other port. The server source in the previous code has been modified to accept the service port on the command line to make this easy ❷.

We also need to create a version of the hello.html client from listing 15.3, which we'll call cors.html, that targets the non-origin server for its RPC calls. Apache Thrift browser transports can be initialized with a simple route, such as "/hello". This is how we've configured our transports so far. When only a route is provided, the route is added to the origin to create a URL, such as "http://localhost:9098/hello". In our case, we'd like to make RPC requests against "http://localhost:9099/hello," regardless of the origin server, so we must list the URL explicitly:

```
var transport = new Thrift.TXHRTransport("http://localhost:9099/hello");
```

Here's a transcript from our two server sessions with a browser loading hello.html from the port 9098 server and placing RPC calls against a 9099 server:

Console 1

```
$ node cors.js 9098
Http/Thrift Server running on port: 9098
Serving files from: /home/randy/thriftbook/part3/js
```

Console 2

```
$ node cors.js 9099
Http/Thrift Server running on port: 9099
Serving files from: /home/randy/thriftbook/part3/js
Hello fred!
```

In the previous example, a browser loads the hello.html file from a server at origin 9098, but executes an XHR getMessage() call against the server on port 9099. Because we've configured the server to allow this, the call is successful. To see what happened, let's look at the developer tools in the network pane in the client browser. The example screen in figure 15.6 is Firefox, though Chrome and other browsers have equally capable tools.

The browser location box (at the top of the window) shows that the origin for the hello.html file was http://localhost:9098. Look at the Request headers sent with the XHR POST method for our getMessage() call. The browser automatically supplied the Origin header for our cross-origin request and set it to http://localhost:9098, the origin of the calling code. Having the browser set this header in the XHR request keeps client code from forging or omitting the origin.

The 9098 origin is permitted by the 9099 server due to the cors config we supplied in the cors.js source. Thus the 9099 server responds with the appropriate CORS access headers and a result (rather than a CORS error). The Access-Control-Allow-Origin header value of http://localhost:9098 in the Response headers pane identifies the CORS source permitted by the call.

In certain situations, browsers may send an OPTIONS request to the non-origin server to determine CORS support prior to making the actual POST call (known as a preflight check). Refer to your favorite online web programming guide for more information on CORS headers and preflight checks.

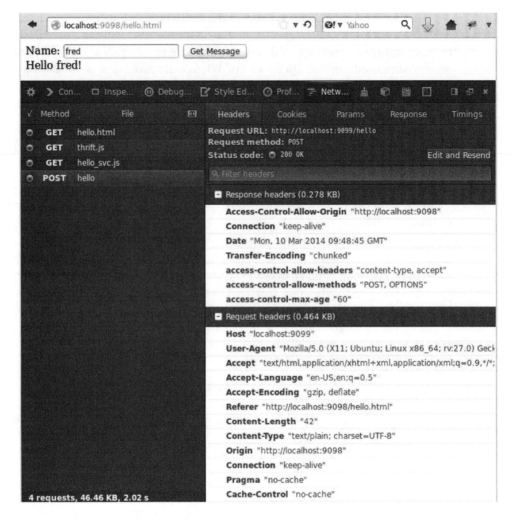

Figure 15.6   Browser network activity and CORS headers

This example demonstrates a successful cross-site Apache Thrift RPC using CORS and represents the second of three possible CORS scenarios:

- Same origin access
- Successful cross-site access using CORS
- Failed cross-site access

Our first few examples in this chapter exhibited item #1 above, same origin access. Our last example exhibited item #2 above, successful CORS access. We'll look at item #3 shortly. You can retry the same origin scenario with the new servers by pointing your browser to http://localhost:9099/hello.html. This will succeed because the XHR request will be made against the "same origin," the HTML file, and the Apache Thrift service are on the same host and port. The browser will not emit the origin header in this situation, causing the server to assume that the client is calling from the same origin.

To produce a failure, item #3, you can change the html transport target to port 9098 and retry the request, loading the cors.html page from 9099. This will fail because the origin is now 9099 and the server code is configured to only allow foreign requests from 9098. Inspecting the network interactions and headers in each of these three cases from your browser's debugger is instructive.

At this point, you might be saying to yourself, "Okay, so it's nice to stop calls to my site from browser origins I don't trust, but how do I keep my browser from making calls to sites *it* shouldn't trust?" The answer is CSP.

15.6.2 *Content Security Policy (CSP)*

CSP is a web-based security mechanism designed to augment prior web security standards and help further prevent cross-site scripting (XSS) and other attacks. CSP is a W3C project and has been in use by the broader community since 2010. CSP is supported by all modern browsers and many web frameworks.

When using CSP, the origin server provides a Content-Security-Policy header which declares types of resources (JavaScript, CSS, HTML, and so on) and the foreign hosts allowed to provide them. Here are three CSP examples:

- Content-Security-Policy: default-src 'self'
- Content-Security-Policy: default-src 'self'; connect-src 'self' https://localhost :9099
- Content-Security-Policy: default-src 'self'; img-src *; media-src *.example.com; connect-src 'self' https://localhost:9099

Each of the previous examples includes a set of types and origins separated by semicolons. The first example allows files of all types (default-src) to be loaded only from the origin ('self'). The default-src type should always be included to specify a policy for resource types not otherwise defined.

The second policy allows connections (XHR, WebSocket, and EventSource) only to the origin and localhost port 9099 using https. Attempting to connect to any foreign host other than https://localhost:9099 will generate an error in a CSP-enabled browser.

The third example shows the use of * as a wildcard. In this example, images may be loaded from any origin and media can be loaded from any example.com subdomain.

Note that when a protocol scheme (for example, https) isn't specified, the same scheme as the one used to access the protected document (for example, hello.html) is assumed. If a port number isn't specified, the browser will use the default port number for the specified scheme (80 for http, 443 for https, and so on).

WHITELIST A list of origins trusted to supply a particular type of content.

The set of origins and types defined by the CSP headers is called a whitelist. When both CORS and CSP are enabled, the origin can choose which foreign servers an application may access (CSP), and foreign servers may choose which origins they can be accessed by (CORS), providing content control at the source and destination.

CSP is particularly important when it comes to script operations. At present, the same origin policy doesn't apply to JavaScript code, allowing browsers to load Java-Script from any third-party site irrespective of CORS configuration (consider our jQuery example that loaded jQuery from a CDN in listing 15.9). CSP brings script loading under tight control. When either or both of the default-src or script-src CSP directives are in use, several standard browser features involving code execution are disabled, including

- `<script></script>` blocks with nested code
- DOM event attributes such as `onclick=""`
- Anchor tags with an `href` value that starts with `javascript:`
- Dynamic code evaluation via `eval()`
- Dynamic code evaluation through `setTimeout` or `setInterval` string arguments

In this way, the browser can ensure that all JavaScript code is retrieved from separate JavaScript files and served from an allowed origin. The combination of a concise whitelist for script loading and the inability to run code any other way makes CSP a significant improvement in browser security.

If you want to adopt CSP in your Apache Thrift JavaScript applications you need only make a few simple modifications. First, you'll have to move all your browser-based JavaScript code into separate script files. Second, you need to configure the server you use to emit the appropriate CSP headers based on your desired whitelist.

To specify custom HTTP headers using the Apache Thrift Node.js web server, you can add a headers object to the Server Options. The following listing updates our previous CORS server with a CSP header.

Listing 15.11   ~thriftbook/part3/js/csp.js

```
var thrift = require('thrift');
var helloSvc = require('./gen-nodejs/helloSvc');

//ServiceHandler: Implement the hello service
var helloHandler = {
  getMessage: function(name, result) {
    var msg = "Hello " + name + "!";
    console.log(msg);
    result(null, msg);
  }
}

//ServiceOptions: The I/O stack for the service
var helloSvcOpt = {
    handler: helloHandler,
    processor: helloSvc,
    protocol: thrift.TJSONProtocol,
    transport: thrift.TBufferedTransport
```

```
};

//ServerOptions: Define server features
var serverOpt = {
    files: ".",
    services: {"/hello": helloSvcOpt},
    cors: {"http://localhost:9098": true},
    headers: {"Content-Security-Policy":
               "default-src 'self'; connect-src http://localhost:9099"}    ❶
}

//Create and start the web server
var port = process.argv[2];
thrift.createWebServer(serverOpt).listen(port);
console.log("Http/Thrift Server running on port: " + port);
console.log("Serving files from: " + __dirname);
```

To enable CSP, we've added the "headers" property to the ServerOptions object ❶. The headers property allows us to send arbitrary headers along with any response generated by the web server. The Content-Security-Policy header set here specifies two policy elements. The first is that all content of any type not otherwise specified must come from this server (default-src 'self'). The second specifies that connections must use HTTP and target host localhost and port 9099 (connect-src http://localhost:9099). If we test the previous hello.html examples using the CSP-enabled server, the web page will fail, because our JavaScript code is embedded in the html file. This isn't allowed with CSP policies using the default-src directive. To make our hello.html file CSP-compatible, we'll need to move all the JavaScript into separate .js files. Listings 15.12 and 15.13 show a CSP-ready helloCsp.html and the new helloCsp.js, which now houses all the client code.

Listing 15.12   ~thriftbook/part3/js/helloCsp.html

```
<!DOCTYPE html>
<html lang="en">
  <head>
    <meta charset="utf-8">
    <title>Hello Thrift</title>
  </head>
  <body>
    Name:
    <input type="text" id="name_in">
    <input type="button" id="get_msg" value="Get Message" >
    <div id="output"></div>

    <script src="bower_components/thrift/lib/js/src/thrift.js"></script>
    <script src="gen-js/helloSvc.js"></script>
    <script src="helloCsp.js"></script>
  </body>
</html>
```

```
(function() {
  var transport = new Thrift.TXHRTransport("http://localhost:9099/hello");
  var protocol  = new Thrift.TJSONProtocol(transport);
  var client    = new helloSvcClient(protocol);

  var nameElement = document.getElementById("name_in");
  var outputElement = document.getElementById("output");
  document.getElementById("get_msg")
      .addEventListener("click", function(){
          client.getMessage(nameElement.value, function(result) {
            outputElement.innerHTML = result;
          });
      });
})();
```

Now if we launch two CSP servers, one on port 9098 to serve files and another on port 9099 to provide access to the hello service, we'll have a working environment that meets our CORS and CSP security policies. If we load helloCsp.html from 9098, the origin will be 9098 and CSP will allow us to load all our required JavaScript files from 9098 ('self'). Also, when we make an XHR connection to the hello service on 9099, the origin will be reported as 9098, meeting the CORS policy on the server and the CSP connect-src policy on the browser as well.

We can run two server instances the way we did in the CORS example:

Console 1

```
$ node csp.js 9098
Http/Thrift Server running on port: 9098
Serving files from: /home/randy/thriftbook/part3/js
```

Console 2

```
$ node csp.js 9099
Http/Thrift Server running on port: 9099
Serving files from: /home/randy/thriftbook/part3/js
Hello fred!
```

Figure 15.7 shows the content-security-policy response header transmitted to the browser when loading the hello.html source from the web server. This policy allows the three script files required by hello.html to be loaded from the origin and allows the Apache Thrift RPC call to connect to the 9099 server.

CSP violations are reported in different ways depending on the browser. Certain violations are ignored silently, which can make debugging a bit of a challenge. Regardless, the added security provided by CSP makes it a critical aspect of many sensitive web applications.

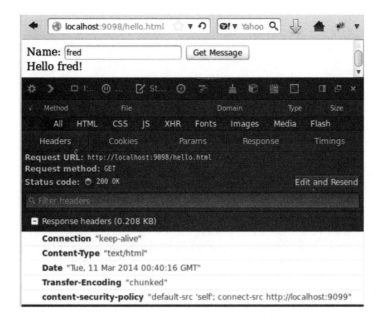

**Figure 15.7
CSP header**

15.6.3 *X-Frame-Options*

Clickjacking, also known as UI redressing, involves tricking a user into clicking on something in a browser which looks innocuous but causes unexpected malicious action. This typically involves creating a transparent IFRAME on top of normal content, then having the IFRAME hijack clicks and/or keystrokes. This exploit can be used to capture bank logins, cause unintended ecommerce purchases, or enable the user's camera and microphone, among other unpleasantness.

In 2009, Microsoft created the X-Frame-Options header to help combat clickjacking, and the header is now codified by IETF RFC 7034 and supported by most modern browsers. The X-Frame-Options header is sent by the origin host and can have one of three values:

- *DENY*—Prevents framing
- *SAMEORIGIN*—Prevents framing from external sites
- *ALLOW-FROM list*—Prevents framing from any sites other than the origins specified

To enable X-Frame-Options in our Apache Thrift web server, we can add the appropriate X-Frame-Options header to the server's header configuration object. For example, to require all frames to come from the origin, we'd specify the following header:

```
X-Frame-Options SAMEORIGIN
```

Here's our CSP `ServerOptions` example with the same origin X-Frame-Options header added:

```
var server_opt = {
    staticFilePath: ".",
    services: {
      "/hello": hello_svc_opt
    },
    headers: {
      "Content-Security-Policy": "default-src 'self';
                                  connect-src http://localhost:9099",
      "X-Frame-Options": "SAMEORIGIN",
    }
}
```

Like CSP, this is a passive feature on the server side. The server sends the headers to the browser, but all the policy enforcement takes place in the browser. It's important to ensure that a supporting browser is on the receiving end of such headers.

15.6.4 *Transport security*

In a web-based setting, communicating sensitive information in the clear is an extreme security risk. Traffic encryption is a common requirement associated with applications communicating over public networks. The Secure Socket Layer (SSL) and Transport Layer Security (TLS) protocols have been the backbone of internet encryption since the dawn of commerce on the web.

SSL, now officially deprecated, has been succeeded by TLS. Even recent versions of TLS such as TLS 1.2 have known vulnerabilities when combined with certain cipher suites. It's always a good idea to use the newest version of TLS that you can (TLS 1.3 was released in 2018), along with a cipher suite matched to the TLS version. While a full discussion of web security is beyond the scope of this book, we'll look briefly at the key aspects of TLS and Public-key Infrastructure (PKI) that empower secure Apache Thrift RPC connections.

In a PKI setting, a company, site, or server generates a key set with a public and a private key. The public key can encrypt traffic which only the private key can decrypt and vice versa. The server also generates a certificate containing the public key, which is made available to anyone (figure 15.8).

Anyone can encrypt with the public key and send secure communications to the server, though the server has no built-in way to identify the user, because everyone has access to the public key.

Conversely, the server can encrypt traffic with the private key and anyone can read it; however, the reader can be sure the traffic was sent from the private key holder. Therefore, if the certificate housing the public key can be verified as being owned by a particular company, the server can be authenticated.

To support certificate authentication, trusted Certificate Authorities (CA) sign certificates with their own private key. The signing process encrypts a hash of the

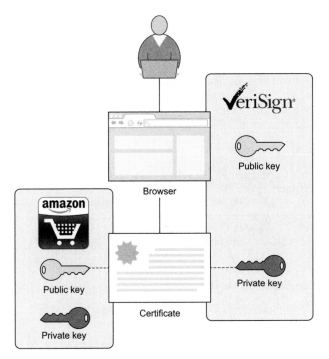

Public key

Browser

Private key

Certificate

Public key

Private key

Figure 15.8 Person trusts browser, browser trusts CA, CA trusts company.

certificate making it impossible to change the certificate without detection. All browsers have the public keys of the major certificate authorities built into them, making it difficult for attackers to fake a certificate (see figure 15.8).

With this infrastructure in place a client can connect to a website, request the site's certificate, and verify the signature with the browser's built-in CA public keys. If the site has presented a valid certificate, the client will then challenge the site with a message encrypted with the public key. If the server can decrypt this message, the client can be sure that the server is under the control of the certificate owner. Both parties then established a shared private key to use for transport encryption (public [asymmetric] key encryption is slow by comparison to private [symmetric] key encryption and only used to establish the shared private key for the session).

To use Apache Thrift RPC over TLS, you'll need to use PKI. On the client side the process is simple by design. Any browser can establish a secure channel by using the HTTPS protocol designation instead of HTTP.

On the server side, you'll need a public/private key set and a certificate to use. We'll use the open source OpenSSL toolkit to generate keys and certificates in the following example. Our keys and certificate must be stored in a format readable by the target server. The Privacy Enhanced Mail (PEM) format is understood by most Apache Thrift TLS libraries and is one of the most common file formats for such artifacts.

We'll need to generate a PEM file for the private key and another for the public key certificate. Here's an example session using `openssl` to generate a private key (key.pem) and a certificate (cert.pem):

```
# openssl req -newkey rsa:2048 -new -nodes -x509 -days 3650 -keyout key.pem
➥ -out cert.pem
Generating a 2048 bit RSA private key
...................+++
..........+++
writing new private key to 'key.pem'
-----
You are about to be asked to enter information that will be incorporated
into your certificate request.
What you are about to enter is what is called a Distinguished Name or a DN.
There are quite a few fields but you can leave some blank.
For some fields there will be a default value,
If you enter '.', the field will be left blank.
-----
Country Name (2 letter code) [XX]:US
State or Province Name (full name) []:CA
Locality Name (eg, city) [Default City]:San Francisco
Organization Name (eg, company) [Default Company Ltd]:Example Co
Organizational Unit Name (eg, section) []:Example Group
Common Name (eg, your name or your server's hostname) []:example.com
Email Address []:info@example.com
 [root@NodeA sec]# ls -l
-rw-r--r--. 1 root root 1411 Feb  8 08:42 cert.pem
-rw-r--r--. 1 root root 1704 Feb  8 08:42 key.pem
```

The `openssl req` command requests a new key set and a self-signed x509 certificate expiring in 10 years. In a production setting you'd create a Certificate Signing Request (CSR) and send it to an appropriate CA, which would return to you a signed certificate.

We can enable TLS support in our Node.js web server by supplying the private key and certificate file data through the `tls` attribute of the ServerOptions object. Here's a version of the hello server supporting TLS with the above-generated key and certificate.

Listing 15.14 ~thriftbook/part3/js/helloTls.js

```
var fs = require("fs");                    ❶
var thrift = require('thrift');
var helloSvc = require('./gen-nodejs/helloSvc');

var helloHandler = {
  getMessage: function(name, result) {
    var msg = "Hello " + name + "!";
    console.log(msg);
    result(null, msg);
  }
}

var helloSvcOpt = {
    transport: thrift.TBufferedTransport,
```

```
    protocol: thrift.TJSONProtocol,
    processor: helloSvc,
    handler: helloHandler
};

var serverOpt = {
    files: ".",
    tls: {
      key: fs.readFileSync("key.pem"),                    ❷
      cert: fs.readFileSync("cert.pem")
    },
    services: {
        "/hello": helloSvcOpt
    }
}

var port = 9099;
thrift.createWebServer(serverOpt).listen(port);
console.log("Https/Thrift Server running on port: " + port);
```

Because the private key and certificate are stored in files, we need the Node.js fs library to read the key/cert content from disk ❶. In the ServerOptions object we add the "tls" attribute with key and cert values set appropriately ❷. The tls object houses standard Node.js HTTPS TLS options. For this simple example we need only set the server private key and certificate. The Node.js fs.readFileSync() method returns the contents of the key and cert files.

It should be obvious at this point that these files, particularly the private key, are important to protect. Allowing someone to acquire a copy of your site's private key allows them to impersonate your site, attack your secure sessions, and perform many other unsavory feats.

Because your certificate is self-signed, most browsers will present a warning because the browser cannot verify the signing CA, which was you (your certificate was self-signed).

For testing purposes, you can either override the browser security warning with a browser command line switch (which is dangerous if you forget you have done so), or you can add an exception for the self-signed certificate (for example, clicking "I understand the risks" in the example Firefox dialog shown in figure 15.9).

You can run the server and test it with the simple hello.html client from listing 15.3 using the "https://localhost:9099/hello.html" URL. If you open the developer tools pane in your browser and examine the exchanges between the browser and the server you'll see that they're all encrypted (see figure 15.10). Note that this includes the Apache Thrift RPC call to getMessage().

The Node.js web server uses a clear channel by default; however, the presence of the tls property in the ServerOptions switches the server into TLS mode. If you try to connect to the server using HTTP while it's running in secure mode, the client connection will hang and eventually fail.

Figure 15.9   Self-signed certificate warning

Figure 15.10   Secure Apache Thrift RPC over TLS

Node.js is a remarkable platform for building scalable applications when deployed properly. To improve performance further, many production systems terminate TLS at a perimeter load balancer, eliminating the encryption/decryption overhead from internal systems. That said, cloud architects also use encryption everywhere to facilitate perimeterless cloud deployment. With Apache Thrift, you can work with or without TLS.

Up to this point we've used XHR as our exclusive Apache Thrift RPC transport. The final section of this chapter looks at an alternative to XHR, WebSocket.

15.7   *Using the WebSocket transport*

The world of web development has a fairly short list of communications options. The only original option for browser-based code to invoke server functionality was to load a page and all its dependencies over HTTP in one shot. In 1999 the Web became infinitely more programmable with the advent of XHR, offering the ability to make ad hoc requests for resources without a complete reload. It took another 11 years for the next major I/O feature, WebSocket, to arrive.

The WebSocket protocol first appeared in 2010 in the Chrome and Safari browsers. By 2011, all major browsers supported some form of WebSocket communications. The WebSocket protocol uses HTTP and HTTPS to establish a transport layer, but the similarities end there.

The WebSocket protocol was designed to integrate with existing web infrastructure, while being lightweight, fast, and capable of handling streaming applications effectively. All WebSocket sessions begin with an HTTP[S] session. Once the HTTP[S] connection is established and any necessary security matters are sorted out, the WebSocket client issues an "upgrade" request. If the server supports WebSocket, it will upgrade the connection to WebSocket, turning the link into a low-overhead, frame-based, two-way communication channel.

A WebSocket connection is much like a raw TCP connection with a little bit of data framing overhead. If HTTPS was used to establish the connection, the resulting WebSocket upgrade continues to use the secure transport channel. Unlike XHR, a WebSocket connection has no intrinsic request response idiom. The client can send a message to the server whenever it likes and vice versa. This makes WebSocket particularly effective in streaming or messaging scenarios.

Apache Thrift RPC can use WebSocket as a transport. No code changes are required to the standard Apache Thrift Node.js web server to support WebSocket. If the web server receives an upgrade request, it switches from HTTP to WebSocket and continues to serve RPC requests. Once upgraded to WebSocket you cannot downgrade back to HTTP.

Client-side code requires only a few modifications to use the Apache Thrift WebSocket transport. The first change is to set an appropriate transport URL. WebSocket URLs have the form "ws://" or "wss://"; the first produces a normal WebSocket connection and the second produces a secure WebSocket connection. For example, a client wishing to connect to example.com over a secure WebSocket connection would use the URL: wss://example.com.

The following listing shows a modified version of the Hello World client configured to use WebSocket for Apache Thrift RPC.

Listing 15.15   ~thriftbook/part3/js/hellows.html

```
<!DOCTYPE html>
<html lang="en">
  <head>
    <meta charset="utf-8">
    <title>Hello Thrift</title>
  </head>
  <body>
    Name: <input type="text" id="name_in">
    <input type="button" id="get_msg" value="Get Message" >
    <div id="output"></div>
    <script src="bower_components/thrift/lib/js/src/thrift.js"></script>
    <script src="gen-js/helloSvc.js"></script>
    <script>
```

```
    (function() {
❶     var loc = window.location;
      var wsUrl = ((loc.protocol === "https:") ? "wss://" : "ws://") +
                   loc.hostname + ":" + loc.port + loc.pathname;          ❷
❸   var transport = new Thrift.TWebSocketTransport(wsUrl);
    var protocol  = new Thrift.TJSONProtocol(transport);
    var client    = new helloSvcClient(protocol);
    var nameElement = document.getElementById("name_in");
    var outputElement = document.getElementById("output");
❹   transport.open();
    document.getElementById("get_msg")
      .addEventListener("click", function(){
        client.getMessage(nameElement.value, function(result) {
          outputElement.innerHTML = result;
        });
      });
    })();
  </script>
 </body>
</html>
```

While similar to the basic hello client, you'll see a few WebSocket-related changes. The first is the addition of code to capture the current window location ❶. This allows us to inspect the origin URL and determine whether to use WS:// or WSS:// with the Apache Thrift transport.

The next bit of code creates the WebSocket URL ❷. In this case, we connect back to the origin server, but any host and port could be used.

Our previous examples used the TXHRTransport in browser clients. To communicate over WebSocket we need to change to the TWebSocketTransport and construct it with the desired server URL ❸.

A final step that must be completed prior to using the WebSocket-based I/O stack involves opening the transport connection ❹. This is implicit with TXHRTransport, where calling open() is a safe noop. In the WebSocket case, the call to open is required and requests the upgrade.

Any of the hello web servers built in this chapter will work with the WebSocket client in listing 15.15. Figure 15.11 demonstrates the WebSocket client running against the TLS server we created in the previous section. Notice that the WebSocket upgrade appears as a second GET request to the origin document, hellows.html. The Request headers pane shows the Upgrade header, and the Response headers pane shows the server accepting the Upgrade with the Sec-WebSocket-Accept header. After the upgrade, the HTTP request output can no longer display the streaming WebSocket traffic.

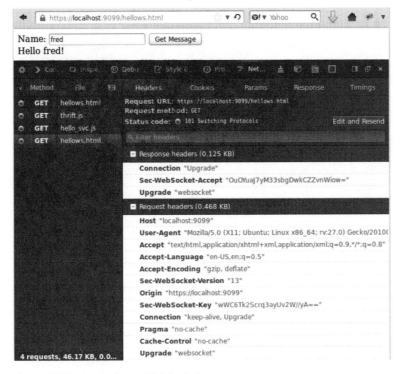

Figure 15.11 Upgrading to WebSocket

Summary

In this chapter, we looked at Apache Thrift RPC over the web. Important topics from this chapter include

- How to set up a frontend JavaScript development environment
- How to build Apache Thrift clients with JavaScript in the browser
- How to build Apache Thrift web servers with Node.js
- How to make asynchronous client calls
- How to manage RPC errors
- How to use jQuery with Apache Thrift in the browser
- How to secure RPC over the web with
  - *CORS*—Cross Origin Resource Sharing
  - *CSP*—Content Security Policy
  - *X-Frame-Options*
  - *TLS*
- How to use WebSocket for high-performance, browser-based RPC

Scripting Apache Thrift

16

This chapter covers

- Building Ruby clients and servers
- Building PHP clients
- Building Perl clients and servers
- Building Python clients and servers

Apache Thrift offers support for a wide range of dynamic programming languages. In this chapter, we'll see how to set up and build Apache Thrift clients and servers in all of the popular LAMP stack scripting languages: PHP, Perl, Python, and Ruby.

While the microservice movement and cloud native systems have largely subsumed LAMP, the LAMP languages have found a permanent home in web tech, automated test, data science, and machine learning environments, just to name a few. Scripting languages can also be used to quickly prototype services and clients using Apache Thrift. These script-based services can later be replaced by more robust solutions without violating the interface contract depended on by other parts of the system. What's more, interpreted languages that may not have been fast enough to offer complete solutions in the past can often participate in distributed solutions by offloading performance-intensive elements to other, more performant Apache Thrift-based services.

In this chapter, we'll cover Apache Thrift language library installation, Thrift compilation, and script language-specific features for each target language. If you need more details regarding the operation of Apache Thrift as an RPC platform in general, take a look at part 2 of this book, where you'll find in-depth coverage of transports, protocols, servers, and the Apache Thrift IDL.

We use a simple RPC service throughout part 3 of this book to demonstrate basic client and server operation. All of the scripting language sections that follow demonstrate a client and a server using the helloSvc, as shown in the following listing.

Listing 16.1   ~thriftbook/part3/script/hello.thrift

```
service helloSvc {
    string getMessage(1: string name)
}
```

While trivial, this service passes data from the client to the server (a name), and returns data from the server back to the client (a greeting string with name in it). The hope is that the service's simplicity will make it easy to isolate and debug language setup and configuration problems and yet prove round-trip RPC operation when you get it working. Any helloSvc client from part 3 of this book should communicate with any helloSvc server from this or any other chapter, regardless of source language.

To generate language-specific support code for an Apache Thrift IDL service, we need a copy of the Apache Thrift compiler. The Apache Thrift compiler is a C++ program that can be downloaded in binary executable form for Windows machines from the Apache Thrift website (thrift.apache.org). The Apache Thrift compiler can be installed on other operating systems using the system's native package manager or by building the compiler from source code (see chapter 3 for more details on building the Apache Thrift compiler).

Apache Thrift is tested against the most current version of supported programming languages with few exceptions, meaning that older versions of languages may have compatibility issues not trapped by the Apache CI servers. That said, Apache Thrift contributors are encouraged to make rational decisions when it comes to using cutting-edge language features within the Apache Thrift code base. Where possible, Apache Thrift code is implemented to support the widest range of language versions.

Each language in our lineup has unique traits; for example, approaches to package management, available server types, binary extensions, and other features, which we'll examine in turn. Let's begin with Ruby.

16.1 Apache Thrift and Ruby

In this section, we'll install Apache Thrift support for Ruby and build a simple Ruby RPC client and server. Ruby is a flexible programming language used for systems administration scripting, web programming, and general purpose coding. Many important devops tools are written in Ruby, such as Puppet, Chef, and Vagrant. Ruby is behind one of the most popular web frameworks, Rails, and Ruby is also a key language in many test frameworks, including RSpec. Ruby provides the best features of Perl's string processing and adds objects, functional programming features, reflection, and automatic memory management. When combined with Apache Thrift, Ruby becomes an effective RPC service platform and a versatile language for RPC service mocking and testing.

To build Apache Thrift clients and servers in Ruby, you'll need to install the Apache Thrift IDL compiler and the Apache Thrift Ruby library package. In Ruby, reusable library modules are packaged in the Gem format and can be installed using the RubyGems "gem" package manager. More than 9,000 Ruby gems are hosted on RubyGems.org, the central repository for publicly available Ruby packages. A search for "Thrift" on the RubyGems.org site produces a list of more than 30 gems, including the official Apache Thrift Ruby library, which is named "Thrift".

If you have a working Ruby installation, it's fairly easy to install support for Apache Thrift. Here's an example:

```
$ sudo gem install thrift
Building native extensions. This could take a while...
Successfully installed thrift-0.11.0.0
Parsing documentation for thrift-0.11.0.0
Installing ri documentation for thrift-0.11.0.0
Done installing documentation for thrift after 2 seconds
1 gem installed
$
```

This example installs the latest version of the Apache Thrift Gem, which contains the library code needed to execute Ruby-based Apache Thrift clients and servers. The Apache Thrift Ruby library includes an optional C language native extension designed to improve serialization performance. This is automatically built (if possible) by the Gem installer. The Ruby Development packages are typically required to build native extensions. To install full Ruby support on an Ubuntu 16.04 system you could use a command something like the following:

```
$ sudo apt-get install ruby ruby-dev
```

Once we have the Thrift Gem installed, our next step is to generate client and server stubs for the helloSvc service:

```
~/thriftbook/part3/script/ruby$ thrift --gen rb ../hello.thrift      ❶
~/thriftbook/part3/script/ruby$ ls -l gen-rb                              ❷
-rw-r--r-- 1 randy randy  161 Oct 26 17:37 hello_constants.rb
-rw-r--r-- 1 randy randy 1647 Oct 26 17:37 hello_svc.rb
-rw-r--r-- 1 randy randy  139 Oct 26 17:37 hello_types.rb
~/thriftbook/part3/script/ruby$ head gen-rb/hello_svc.rb      ❸
#
# Autogenerated by Thrift Compiler (0.11.0)
#
# DO NOT EDIT UNLESS YOU ARE SURE THAT YOU KNOW WHAT YOU ARE DOING
#
```

```
require 'thrift'
require 'hello_types'

module HelloSvc        ❹
```

The `thrift` command ❶ generates Ruby code to support all the Apache Thrift interface components described in hello.thrift. The generated code will be emitted in a subdirectory called "gen-rb", as displayed in the listing above ❷. The top few lines of the `hello_svc.rb` are displayed with the head command ❸. As you can see from the comments, this file should be treated as read only: to change it you should change the IDL source and recompile it with the Thrift compiler. The output also shows that Ruby packages each service within a module, module `HelloSvc` in this case ❹. For more information on the Apache Thrift IDL compiler or the Apache Thrift IDL, see chapter 6.

The IDL compiler generates three files to support our IDL definitions: *_constants .rb files contain all of the constants defined in the IDL (none in our case), *_types.rb files contain all of the user-defined types from the IDL (again, none in our case), and *.svc.rb files define the service client and server stubs required to support the services defined in the IDL.

In Ruby, the svc file contains a module for each IDL service, "HelloSvc" in our case. A service module contains a "Client" class used by service clients and a "Processor" class used by servers to process service requests. Each service method will also have a class definition for the arguments passed to the server and the result returned from the server. These classes are for use by the client and the processor and aren't typically accessed directly by user code.

16.1.1 A Ruby server

Now that we have the Thrift libraries installed and our service client/processor code is generated, we can code up a quick RPC server. The following listing shows an example.

Listing 16.2   ~thriftbook/part3/script/ruby/hello_server.rb

```
#!/usr/bin/env ruby

❶ require 'thrift'
   $:.push('gen-rb')          ❷
   require 'hello_svc'

   class HelloHandler          ❸
     def getMessage(name)
       return 'Hello ' + name
     end
   end

❹ port = 9095
   handler = HelloHandler.new()
   proc = HelloSvc::Processor.new(handler)      ❺
❻ trans_ep = Thrift::ServerSocket.new(port)
   trans_buf_fac = Thrift::BufferedTransportFactory.new()      ❼
```

```
⑧ proto_fac = Thrift::BinaryProtocolFactory.new()
   server = Thrift::SimpleServer.new(proc,trans_ep,trans_buf_fac,proto_fac)   ⑨

   puts "Starting server on port #{port}..."
⑩ server.serve()
```

The server source begins with a require statement to include Apache Thrift library support ❶, then adds the gen-rb directory to the library path ❷, before requiring the IDL-compiler generated hello_svc.rb file. This provides access to both the core Thrift library and the code needed to implement helloSvc.

Thrift takes care of all the service plumbing, leaving only the implementation of the service methods to us. The `HelloHandler` class provides a method for each method defined in the Apache Thrift IDL helloSvc ❸.

After defining the service methods in the handler, we can create a server to host the service. In this example, the server is configured to run on port 9095 ❹. The IDL compiler-generated processor for the helloSvc is initialized with a new instance of the handler class ❺. The server will use the processor to pass network calls to the handler methods and return the responses.

This example server uses a common Apache Thrift protocol stack:

- `TSocket`
- `TBufferedTransport`
- `TBinaryProtocol`

The `TSocket` layer provides TCP communications with the client, and on the server side we use the `ServerSocket` factory class ❻. The server transport will listen for new connections and create a new socket for each connecting client. The `BufferedTransportFactory` allows the server to create transport buffers for each connection, collecting response data together until a complete RPC response is ready to transmit back to the client ❼. The `BinaryProtocolFactory` allows the server to create a new binary protocol serializer for each connecting client ❽.

With the I/O stack created, we're ready to construct the server that will orchestrate all of these components. In this example, we use the `SimpleServer` ❾. The `SimpleServer` will only accept one client connection at a time, queuing connection requests until the current client disconnects. After constructing the server with an initialized processor, transport stack, and protocol, we can run it by calling the `serve()` method ❿.

Running the Ruby server should look something like this:

```
$ ruby hello_server.rb
Starting server on port 9095...
```

16.1.2   A Ruby client

Next let's look at a basic Ruby client we can use to test our server.

Listing 16.3   ~thriftbook/part3/script/ruby/hello_client.rb

```ruby
#!/usr/bin/env ruby

require 'thrift'
$:.push('gen-rb')                    ❶
require 'hello_svc'

❷ begin
    trans_ep = Thrift::Socket.new('localhost', 9095)
    trans_buf = Thrift::BufferedTransport.new(trans_ep)    ❸
    proto = Thrift::BinaryProtocol.new(trans_buf)
  ❹ client = HelloSvc::Client.new(proto)

    trans_ep.open()                          ❺
  ❻ res = client.getMessage('world')
    puts 'Message from server: ' + res
    trans_ep.close()                         ❼
❽ rescue Thrift::Exception => tx
    print 'Thrift::Exception: ', tx.message, "\n"
  end
```

The client has the same dependencies as the server ❶, requiring the Thrift library and the generated hello_svc code. The I/O stack is also identical, including the Socket endpoint transport and a transport buffer layer, as well as the binary serialization protocol ❸.

The main client code listing is wrapped in a `begin` rescue block ❷. The `rescue` clause will trap any Thrift exceptions and display them to the console ❽.

On the client side, to connect with the server we use the transport `open()` method ❺. With the connection open, we can use the helloSvc client instance ❹ to make calls to the server using the service interface ❻. When the client's session is complete, the connection can be closed with the transport `close()` method ❼.

16.1.3   Ruby features

Ruby is a popular language with a mature Apache Thrift implementation. The Apache Thrift Ruby libraries support most of the top-shelf Apache Thrift features.

When using Apache Thrift IDL, the type mappings from Ruby to Apache Thrift are fairly intuitive, as shown in table 16.1.

Table 16.1   Apache Thrift-to-Ruby type mapping

Apache Thrift type	Ruby type
bool	True or False
byte, i8, i16, i32, i64	Integer (for example, 8, 0, -394)
double	Float (for example, 3.1415, -42.42)
binary	String (for example, "\xE5\xA5\xBD")

Table 16.1 Apache Thrift-to-Ruby type mapping *(continued)*

Apache Thrift type	Ruby type
string	String (for example, 'hi Mom')
list	Array (for example, [1,2,3,4,5])
map	Hash (for example, {'red' => 'FF0000', 'blue' => '0000FF' })
set	Set (for example, Set.new([1,2,3,4,5]))
struct	Object (for example, myType.new({'name'=>'Bob, 'age'=>24}))
union	Object (for example, myUnion.new({'color'=>'red'}))

Ruby also supports IDL namespaces. In Ruby, an IDL namespace generates a module. For example, placing the statement "namespace rb FishCo" at the top of an IDL file would place all the generated code in the Ruby module "FishCo." Ruby will also create modules for wildcard namespaces, for example `namespace * FishCo`.

Ruby supports most of the common Apache Thrift endpoint transports:

- *TCP sockets*—`Thrift::Socket`
- *HTTP*—`Thrift::HTTPClientTransport`
- *UNIX domain sockets*—`Thrift::UNIXSocket`
- *Memory buffers*—`Thrift::MemoryBufferTransport`
- *Arbitrary streams*—`Thrift::IOStreamTransport`

Ruby I/O stacks should include either the buffered transport (`Thrift::Buffered-Transport`) or the framed transport (`Thrift::FramedTransport`) for performance, avoiding transmitting partial messages. Certain servers (typically nonblocking servers) require a frame header, in which case the framed transport must be used.

Ruby also supplies all three common serialization protocols:

- *Binary*—`Thrift::BinaryProtocol`, `Thrift::BinaryProtocolAccelerated`
- *Compact*—`Thrift::CompactProtocol`
- *JSON*—`Thrift::JsonProtocol`

A native implementation of the binary protocol can be accessed through `Binary-ProtocolAccelerated` and `BinaryProtocolAcceleratedFactory` classes. The native extension is a compiled C language drop-in replacement for the Ruby-based `Binary-Protocol`. In the client program in listing 16.3, we could replace the `BinaryProtocol` type with the `BinaryProtocolAccelerated` type to use the faster native extension. On the server, you'd replace the `BinaryProtocolFactory` with the `BinaryProtocol-AcceleratedFactory`. The speed improvement varies by platform and application.

The native extension may improve RPC performance; however, it may not build successfully on all target systems. Whether you choose the Ruby or the C implementation of `BinaryProtocol`, the bits on the wire are the same, and the client or server on the other end of the connection won't be impacted by your choice.

Ruby also supplies a useful set of prebuilt servers you can quickly deploy:

- *Single-threaded server*—`Thrift::SimpleServer`
- *Multithreaded server*—`Thrift::ThreadedServer`
- *Thread pool server*—`Thrift::ThreadPoolServer`
- *Nonblocking server*—`Thrift::NonblockingServer`
- *HTTP server*—`Thrift::ThinHTTPServer, Thrift::MongrelHTTPServer`

The single-threaded simple server handles one client at a time. The multithreaded server creates a new thread for each client, allowing multiple clients to connect in parallel. The standard Ruby interpreter runs one user thread at a time. I/O and system operations can take place in parallel, but the Ruby code associated with a server cannot. Scale in cloud-native systems is generally achieved horizontally by running multiple copies of a given server; you can also scale Ruby servers vertically by running them with an application server like Passenger.

The thread pool server creates a pool of threads (configurable through the last parameter of the server's initialize method; 20 by default) and assigns each thread to a connecting client. When all threads are in use, connections queue until a thread is freed by a closing connection.

The nonblocking server is the most complex of the servers. It uses a pool of worker threads to process inbound user requests from an arbitrary number of clients. The thread pool can be set in the server's initialize method and defaults to 20.

The Ruby library offers two HTTP server implementations. The first is based on the Thin Ruby gem. Thin is a Ruby web server that combines the Mongrel parser, the `EventMachine` network I/O library, and the Rack webserver interface. The second implementation is based completely on Mongrel, a popular Ruby web server.

For more details regarding servers and threading models, see chapter 10 in part 2.

16.2 *Apache Thrift and PHP*

PHP was invented in 1994 and originally stood for Personal Home Page, currently restyled as the recursive backronym: PHP Hypertext Preprocessor. Though it took 20 years, PHP acquired its first language specification in 2014. PHP is a simple server-side scripting language, often embedded in HTML and interpreted by web server native extensions or CGI programs. Several web metrics platforms estimate that nearly 40% of all web servers support PHP.

Because most PHP code runs in an interpreter behind a web server, it's not commonly used as an Apache Thrift server platform. In fact, the Apache Thrift IDL compiler only generates client-side code by default; you must request server stubs using the "–gen php:server" switch (see chapter 6 for more IDL compiler information). While you can create Apache Thrift servers using PHP, they generally run within a web server, such as Apache HTTPD, and therefore the transport in use must be HTTP-based.

Because web servers form the first tier of many layered applications, calling high performance backend Apache Thrift services from within PHP can be a useful capability. In this section, we'll look at building an Apache Thrift PHP client for the helloSvc in listing 16.1. We can test the examples against the Ruby server from listing 16.2 (or a helloSvc server written in any other language).

At the time of this writing, PHP7 is the current PHP version, yet many Apache Thrift users still rely on PHP5 (PHP6 was abandoned). PHP7 can be twice as fast as PHP5 in many situations and yet is almost completely backward-compatible.

PHP can be installed fairly easily on almost any modern server, including 64-bit Windows (http://php.net/). Most Linux systems will install a suitable PHP for Apache Thrift (v5.3+) through native packages. For example, on Ubuntu 16.04

```
$ sudo apt-get install php
$ php --version
PHP 7.0.15-0ubuntu0.16.04.4 (cli) ( NTS )
Copyright (c) 1997-2017 The PHP Group
Zend Engine v3.0.0, Copyright (c) 1998-2017 Zend Technologies
    with Zend OPcache v7.0.15-0ubuntu0.16.04.4, Copyright (c)
    1999-2017, by Zend Technologies
$
```

While you can run PHP programs directly in the PHP interpreter, PHP is not the most convenient language for command-line scripting. More likely you'll use PHP in combination with a web server. It's not uncommon to find servers preconfigured with everything needed to run a PHP website. You can also install a complete LAMP stack using packages from XAMPP or Zend. For our example, we'll install PHP, Apache HTTPD, and the Apache HTTPD PHP module.

On an Ubuntu 16.04 system, the following command installs all the web server and PHP bits needed:

```
$ sudo apt-get install apache2 php
➥ libapache2-mod-php
```

16.2.1 *A PHP program*

Our simple Apache Thrift PHP example requires a web UI, which will run in a browser, a PHP program, which will run in a web server module, and an Apache Thrift server, which will run stand-alone.

We'll create a PHP program to produce the browser UI and interact with the backend Apache Thrift server, as illustrated in figure 16.1. We'll use the Ruby server from section 16.1 as the backend server for testing.

To simplify debugging, we'll tackle the construction of this example in two steps. As a first step, we'll get a simple PHP program up and

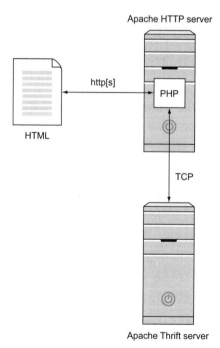

Figure 16.1   PHP and Apache Thrift

running on the web server. This will verify the configuration of the web server and round trip browser operation. As a second step, we'll add in an Apache Thrift server and call it from the PHP program.

Our PHP program will emit a simple web form requesting the user's name. We can embed PHP code in the form, allowing it to post back to itself, whereupon the PHP code can process the form data and re-render the HTML accordingly. The following listing shows the code.

Listing 16.4   ~thriftbook/part3/script/php/hello_test.php

```php
<?php
❶ $uname = "Anonymous";
  if ($_SERVER['REQUEST_METHOD'] === 'POST' &&
      array_key_exists('hello_form', $_POST) &&
      $_POST['hello_form'] == "Submit") {        ❷
❸    $uname = $_POST['user_name'];
  }
?>

<!DOCTYPE html>
<html lang="en">
  <head>
    <meta charset="utf-8">
    <title>Hello Thrift</title>
  </head>
  <body>
    <form name="hello_form" method="post" action="hello_test.php">
      Name:
      <input type="text" name="user_name">
      <input type="submit" name="hello_form" value="Submit">
    </form>
    <br>
    <div><?php echo "Hello $uname"; ?></div>        ❹
  </body>
</html>
```

The main PHP code block in this application initializes the user name to "Anonymous" ❶ and then tests to see if it was called as the result of a hello_form POST operation ❷. If so, we overwrite the $uname variable with the posted user name string ❸. When the browser initially requests the PHP page, it will do so with a GET request, causing "Anonymous" to be displayed as the value of $uname in the div at the bottom of the HTML page ❹.

Having created the hello_test.php program from listing 16.4, we now need to deploy it to a web server. In this example, we'll copy the program to the web server's default HTML directory:

```
$ sudo cp hello_test.php /var/www/html/hello_test.php
```

Once deployed, you can browse to http://localhost/hello_test.php to view the page.
The HTML displays a simple form allowing
the user to enter their name and submit
the form (see figure 16.2). Entering your
name and clicking "Submit" posts the text
in the input box back to the PHP program,
which saves the user name as $uname, out-
putting a new page with the user's name
displayed in the div after the text "Hello".

Figure 16.2   hello_test.php

16.2.2 *A PHP Apache Thrift client*

With the test program running smoothly, we can move on to step two, calling an
Apache Thrift service from PHP. To make calls to Apache Thrift services from PHP,
we'll need the Apache Thrift PHP libraries and PHP client stub code for the helloSvc
service.

You can use Composer to install the Apache Thrift PHP library. Composer is a PHP
system designed to install libraries and their dependencies automatically. Composer
dependencies are configured in a composer.json file in the project directory. Package
lookups are supported by Packagist, the main Composer repository. The official
Apache Thrift PHP libraries can be found at the following Packagist link: https://
packagist.org/packages/apache/thrift.

Our simple Apache Thrift client will depend on only the Apache Thrift library.
Referring to the Packagist link in the previous paragraph, you can require Apache
Thrift 0.10.0 by creating a composer.json file as shown in the following listing.

> **Listing 16.5   ~thriftbook/part3/script/php/composer.json**

```
{
    "require": {
        "apache/thrift": "0.10.0"
    }
}
```

Composer can be installed by passing the Composer installer to the PHP interpreter.
For example

```
$ curl -sS https://getcomposer.org/installer | php

#!/usr/bin/env php
All settings correct for using Composer
Downloading...

Composer successfully installed to:
     /home/randy/thriftbook/part3/script/php/composer.phar
Use it: php composer.phar
```

The Composer installer creates a composer.phar (PHP archive) file that you can run to install all the dependencies defined in your composer.json:

```
$ ls -al
drwxrwxr-x 3 randy randy    4096 Feb  5 14:58 ./
drwxrwxr-x 4 randy randy    4096 Feb  4 23:37 ../
-rw-rw-r-- 1 randy randy      60 Feb  5 14:56 composer.json
-rwxr-xr-x 1 randy randy 1053395 Feb  5 14:58 composer.phar*
-rw-rw-r-- 1 randy randy     978 Feb  5 14:54 hello_client.php
-rw-rw-r-- 1 randy randy     517 Feb  5 13:50 hello_test.php
$ php composer.phar install
Loading composer repositories with package information
Updating dependencies (including require-dev)
Package operations: 1 install, 0 updates, 0 removals
  - Installing apache/thrift (0.10.0): Cloning b2a4d4ae21 from cache
Writing lock file
Generating autoload files
```

The final preparatory step involves generating the PHP client stub code to support the helloSvc. The Thrift compiler generates PHP code in response to the `--gen php` switch. Execute the following command to build client code for the helloSvc:

```
~/thriftbook/part3/script/php$ thrift -gen php ../hello.thrift
~/thriftbook/part3/script/php$ ls -l
-rw-rw-r-- 1 randy randy      60 Feb  5 14:56 composer.json
-rw-rw-r-- 1 randy randy    1747 Feb  5 15:13 composer.lock
-rwxr-xr-x 1 randy randy 1053395 Feb  5 14:58 composer.phar
drwxrwxr-x 2 randy randy    4096 Feb  5 14:50 gen-php
-rw-rw-r-- 1 randy randy     517 Feb  5 13:50 hello_test.php
drwxrwxr-x 4 randy randy    4096 Feb  5 15:13 vendor
```

With the Apache Thrift library installed and the helloSvc code generated, we're ready to add an RPC request to the hello_test.php program, as shown in the following listing. The new program will take the name string posted by the browser and pass it to helloSvc::getMessage(), displaying the result in the HTML output div as before.

Listing 16.6   ~thriftbook/part3/script/php/hello_client.php

```php
<?php
❶  require 'vendor/autoload.php';
    require 'gen-php/Hello/helloSvc.php';          ❷

❸  $msg = 'No server response';

    if ($_SERVER['REQUEST_METHOD'] === 'POST' &&
        array_key_exists('hello_form', $_POST) &&
        $_POST['hello_form'] == "Submit") {          ❹
❺    try {
        $trasn_ep = new Thrift\Transport\TSocket('localhost', 9095);    ❻
❼      $trans_buf = new Thrift\Transport\TBufferedTransport($trasn_ep);
        $proto = new Thrift\Protocol\TBinaryProtocol($trans_buf);    ❽
❾      $client = new Hello\helloSvcClient($proto);
```

```
⑩  $trasn_ep->open();
    $msg = $client->getMessage($_POST['user_name']);   ⑪
⑫  $trasn_ep->close();
  } catch (Thrift\Exception\TException $tx) {           ⑬
    error_log( 'TException: '.$tx->getMessage()."\n" );
  }
 }
?>

<!DOCTYPE html>
<html lang="en">
  <head>
    <meta charset="utf-8">
    <title>Hello Thrift</title>
  </head>
  <body>
    <form name="hello_form" method="post" action="hello_client.php">
      Name:
      <input type="text" name="user_name">
      <input type="submit" name="hello_form" value="Submit">
    </form>
    <br>
    <div><?php echo "$msg"; ?></div>
  </body>
</html>
```

Listing 16.6 begins by requiring the Apache Thrift library ❶. Because we used Composer and defined a dependency on Apache Thrift in the composer.json, we need only require the autoload.php file under the vendor directory. Now when we use "new" to create classes like TSocket, defined in the Apache Thrift library, autoload.php will automatically load them. The next line of code requires the generated PHP code supporting the helloSvc service ❷.

After declaring dependencies, we initialize the $msg variable, which we output in the div at the bottom of the HTML page. As before, if the client is getting the page for the first time, we return the HTML with the default message ❹. However, if the client is submitting the hello_form with the POST verb, we take the user's input and use it to call the backend Apache Thrift service.

Because network communications are prone to failure, it's a good idea to protect client-side RPC code within a try block ❺. The first few lines of code in the try block set up the I/O stack we'll use for the remote procedure call. First, we create a TSocket endpoint to connect to the server on port 9095 ❻, the port the Ruby server from section 16.1 runs on.

We wrap the endpoint socket in a buffer using the TBufferedTransport ❼. The input and output buffer sizes default to 512 bytes. You can increase this by passing additional arguments to the buffered transport constructor. The buffer should typically be made large enough to hold the largest message you might send to the server. For example

```
$tb = new Thrift\Transport\TBufferedTransport($trasn_ep, 1024, 1024);
```

The next line wraps the transport buffer in the binary protocol ❽, which is then passed to the constructor for the service client ❾. With the I/O stack constructed, we can open the socket connection ❿, call the service ⓫, and close the connection ⓬. In the example code, the exception `catch` block only traps Apache Thrift exceptions ⓭, displaying them in the web server's error log.

PHP errors typically manifest on the server side within the context of the web server. You can debug PHP programs using a variety of methods, but a basic approach includes examining the web server's error log. On an Ubuntu 16.04 system, this file is located at /var/log/apache2/error.log. If you're having difficulties getting things running, it's not a bad idea to tail the error log and keep an eye on it while testing (for example, $ `tail -f /var/log/apache2/error.log`).

To give our PHP program a test run, we need to use a URI that the web server can map to the project directory, or copy the project directory to a location the web server is already configured to serve. In this example, we'll copy the project directory to /var/www/html (refer to your web server docs for the appropriate file path on your system):

```
~/thriftbook/part3/script/php$ sudo cp -r . /var/www/html/
~/thriftbook/part3/script/php$ ls -l /var/www/html/
-rw-r--r-- 1 root root      61 Apr 29 13:06 composer.json
-rw-r--r-- 1 root root    1700 Apr 29 13:06 composer.lock
-rwxr-xr-x 1 root root 1836198 Apr 29 13:06 composer.phar
drwxr-xr-x 2 root root    4096 Apr 29 13:06 gen-php
-rw-r--r-- 1 root root    1111 Apr 29 13:06 hello_client.php
-rw-r--r-- 1 root root     515 Apr 29 13:06 hello_test.php
-rw-r--r-- 1 root root   11321 Apr 29 12:38 index.html
-rw-r--r-- 1 root root     608 Apr 29 13:06 README.md
drwxr-xr-x 4 root root    4096 Apr 29 13:06 vendor
~/thriftbook/part3/script/php$
```

To test the program, we need to run the Ruby helloSvc server from listing 16.3. It's important to note that the client I/O stack must be configured to be compatible with the server I/O stack. In this case, we used Sockets and the BinaryProtocol on both the client and the server.

If everything is in order, you can browse to the hello_client.php program, enter a name, click Submit, and see the message returned from the Apache Thrift server displayed in the new web page emitted by the PHP program (see figure 16.3).

Figure 16.3   PHP RPC round trip

16.2.3 PHP features

PHP is one of the original Apache Thrift languages, and it offers good support for most of the key Apache Thrift technologies. PHP clients can communicate with services using several transports:

- *TCP sockets*—Thrift\Transport\TSocket
- *HTTP*—Thrift\Transport\THttpClient, Thrift\Transport\TCurlClient
- *Memory buffers*—Thrift\Transport\TMemoryBuffer
- *PHP streams*—Thrift\Transport\TPhpStream

The TSocket transport is the most universally supported Apache Thrift transport; however, PHP provides support for HTTP, serializing to memory and to PHP streams as well. Two HTTP transports exist, the first of which uses fopen to connect to the URI, and the second uses libcurl. PHP also supports buffering and framing transport layers.

PHP supports all three common serialization protocols:

- *Binary*—Thrift\Protocol\TBinaryProtocol, Thrift\Protocol\TBinaryProtocolAccelerated
- *Compact*—Thrift\Protocol\TCompactProtocol
- *JSON*—Thrift\Protocol\TJSONProtocol

PHP also supports multiplexing, allowing a server to support multiple services over a single transport.

PHP supplies two servers:

- *Single-threaded server*—Thrift\Server\TSimpleServer
- *Multiprocessing server*—Thrift\Server\TForkingServer

The simple server is a single-threaded, single-client-at-a-time server. The forking server forks a new instance of itself to support each new client connection, allowing multiple clients to connect concurrently. The performance of the PHP servers is presently not up to par when compared with most other Apache Thrift languages.

16.3   *Apache Thrift and Perl*

Perl is a scripting language originally developed for report processing in 1987. Perl5 is the primary Perl dialect in common use today. Perl6 has been in development since 2000 and is a separate language, not completely compatible with Perl5. The current Apache Thrift library is designed to work with Perl5 versions 5.6+.

Over the years, Perl has become a Swiss Army knife language of sorts, but it excels at text processing. This has made Perl a strong player in the hypertext and markup/down world of the web. Perl's long history with *nix has led most *nix distributions to include Perl in even the most basic system configurations. If you're working on a system where you need to install Perl, you can find a wide range of options through package managers and installers from perl.org (https://www.perl.org/get.html).

One of the most remarkable things about the Perl ecosystem is the Comprehensive Perl Archive Network (CPAN). CPAN was launched in 1993 and is arguably the inspiration for all language library/package managers that followed. Today CPAN indexes more than 140,000 Perl modules (http://www.cpan.org/). At the time of this writing, CPAN doesn't host an official Thrift module and those present are fairly old.

CPAN files are commonly used in conjunction with the `cpanm` module manager to automate the installation of module dependencies. Fortunately, `cpanm` can install modules directly from GitHub, which is the path we'll take to install Apache Thrift Perl support. To begin, we need to make sure that `cpanm` is installed on the local system. On most systems with Perl present you can install `cpanm` as follows:

```
$ curl -L https://cpanmin.us | perl - --sudo App::cpanminus
...
--> Working on App::cpanminus
Fetching http://www.cpan.org/authors/id/M/MI/MIYAGAWA/
    App-cpanminus-1.7043.tar.gz ... OK
Configuring App-cpanminus-1.7043 ... OK
Building and testing App-cpanminus-1.7043 ... [sudo] password for user:
OK
Successfully installed App-cpanminus-1.7043
1 distribution installed
```

We can now use `cpanm` to install Apache Thrift Perl support. The Apache Thrift GitHub repository contains the Perl library within a subdirectory inside the main source tree. If you use `cpanm` to install the Apache Thrift repository from this repository, you'll get the entire Apache Thrift tree (all 20+ languages), and `cpanm` won't know where to find the module Makefile.PL. Until a better solution is in place, you can install the current and prior releases of the Apache Thrift Perl library from a GitHub repository managed by the author. The URL is http://github.com/RandyAbernethy/ThriftPerl, and the repository is a mirror of the https://github.com/apache/thrift/tree/master/lib/perl, updated to Thrift 0.12.0.

To install Apache Thrift 0.11.0 from the Perl subtree, use the following `cpanm` command:

```
$ sudo cpanm git://github.com/RandyAbernethy/ThriftPerl.git@0.11.0
```

This will install version 0.11.0 in the system's standard Perl library path. If you leave the `sudo` out, `cpanm` will place the library in your home directory under a directory called perl5. You can use the "–local-lib" switch to specify an alternative installation path.

With Perl and the Apache Thrift Perl library installed, we're ready to build a Perl RPC client.

16.4 *Apache Thrift Perl clients*

In typical Apache Thrift fashion, building RPC clients in Perl is fairly easy. The first step is to generate client stub code for the service you wish to call. We'll build a simple Perl client for the helloSvc. To generate client code for the helloSvc, use the following Thrift IDL compiler command:

```
~/thriftbook/part3/script/perl$ thrift --gen perl ../hello.thrift
~/thriftbook/part3/script/perl$ ls -l
drwxrwxr-x 2 user user 4096 Apr 29 13:41 gen-perl
```

```
-rw-rw-r-- 1 user user   449 Apr 28 17:08 HelloClient.pl
-rw-rw-r-- 1 user user   537 Apr 28 17:08 HelloServer.pl
   ~/thriftbook/part3/script/perl$ ls -l gen-perl/
-rw-rw-r-- 1 randy randy  197 Feb  6 12:42 Constants.pm
-rw-rw-r-- 1 randy randy 6305 Feb  6 12:42 helloSvc.pm
-rw-rw-r-- 1 randy randy  177 Feb  6 12:42 Types.pm
```

The IDL compiler creates a gen-perl directory for the generated Perl source. The
service interface is saved in a file with the same name as the service, gen-perl/
helloSvc.pm. All IDL constants are saved in the Constants.pm file, and all IDL user-
defined types are stored in the Types.pm file.

Having generated the stub code for the service, we can create a simple Perl client
program to call our helloSvc server, as shown in the following listing.

Listing 16.7   ~thriftbook/part3/script/perl/HelloClient.pl

```perl
#!/usr/bin/env perl

use lib './gen-perl';        ❶

use Thrift::Socket;
use Thrift::BufferedTransport;       ❷
use Thrift::BinaryProtocol;
use helloSvc;

   my $trans_ep  = Thrift::Socket->new("localhost", 9095);    ❸
❹ my $trans_buf = Thrift::BufferedTransport->new($trans_ep);
   my $proto     = Thrift::BinaryProtocol->new($trans_buf);   ❺
❻ my $client    = helloSvcClient->new($proto);

$trans_ep->open;
my $msg = $client->getMessage("World!");     ❼
$trans_ep->close;

print $msg."\n"      ❽
```

The script begins with a "use" statement, to tell Perl to search for dependencies in the
gen-perl directory, where our generated service code is located ❶. The next block of
use statements tells Perl we'll use the listed modules ❷.

The first actionable code in our script creates a socket endpoint to connect to a
server on localhost port 9095 ❸. The endpoint is wrapped in a buffer ❹, which is, in
turn, wrapped in the binary protocol ❺. The binary protocol is passed to the service
client constructor to complete the I/O stack ❻.

The final bits of code open the connection to the server, make a `getMessage()`
RPC call, and then close the socket ❼. The message is then displayed to the console to
complete the program ❽.

Twelve lines of code to call an RPC server isn't bad. You may note that this code
doesn't make any provision for trapping exceptions. While there are modules you can
add to Perl programs with convenient exception handling mechanisms, many Perl

scripts are simple and short executable code bits wherein an attendant person or process can cope with errors should they arise.

To run this program, we can start a compatible server. The Ruby server from listing 16.2 is used here. Next, pass our script to the Perl interpreter:

```
$ perl HelloClient.pl
Hello World!
```

Perl is both simple and powerful, making it a great language for quick projects that require access to Apache Thrift services. It's also easy to build RPC servers in Perl, which we look at next.

16.5 *Apache Thrift Perl servers*

While Perl RPC servers aren't going to be a good fit for your heavily loaded production environment, they can be a great way to build test mocks, to whip together networked IT tools, and any number of other household tasks. The code that follows demonstrates a simple Perl RPC server supporting our helloSvc service.

Listing 16.8 ~thriftbook/part3/script/perl/HelloServer.pl

```
#!/usr/bin/env perl

use lib './gen-perl';

use utf8;          ❶
use strict;        ❷
use warnings;      ❸

use Thrift::ServerSocket;
use Thrift::Server;
use helloSvc;

package HelloSvcHandler {          ❹
    sub new {                       ❺
        my ($class, %opts) = @_;
        bless {}, $class;
    }

    sub getMessage {          ❻
        my $self = shift;
        my $input = shift;

        return "Hello ".$input;
    }
}

my $trans  = Thrift::ServerSocket->new(9095);          ❼
my $proc   = helloSvcProcessor->new(HelloSvcHandler->new);          ❽
my $server = Thrift::ForkingServer->new($proc, $trans);          ❾

$server->serve;          ❿
```

While similar to the HelloClient, we've added a few additional features to the Perl server to increase its robustness. The first new statement is "use utf8" **❶**. This is a Perl pragma that tells the parser to allow UTF-8 characters in the program text in the current lexical scope. UTF-8 is the definitive string format used by the Apache Thrift Binary, Compact, and JSON protocols. Clients can add this pragma if they need to represent non-ASCII characters in strings. Servers should always use this pragma to ensure compatibility with any client that may connect.

The Perl "use strict" pragma appears next **❷**. This causes Perl to disallow problematic legacy features and unsafe statements; again, not a bad idea on clients, but even more important on servers requiring the stability to service multiple clients. The "use warnings" pragma is similar and causes Perl to display all warnings regarding likely code flaws **❸**, complementing the `use strict` pragma.

The next block of interesting code is the service handler **❹**. The server must supply an implementation of the service it hosts. In Perl, this is typically accomplished by creating a package that can act like a class in other languages. The new subroutine **❺** initializes instances and associates them with the `HelloSvcHandler` class, using the `bless` statement. The `getMessage()` subroutine **❻** provides the actual implementation for the one-and-only service function, returning the `$input` string passed in with "Hello" prepended.

On the server side, we need to listen at the port our clients will connect to using a server version of the transport. In this case, we've created a `ServerSocket` to listen on port 9095 **❼**. Next we create a processor to dispatch network requests to the handler **❽**. The processor is generated by the IDL compiler and placed in the helloSvc.pm source file.

The last step is to create and run the server. The `ForkingServer` from the `Thrift::Server` package is used here **❾**. The server is constructed with the protocol and endpoint transport defined in the two prior lines. Perl servers can also accept a third and fourth argument, a layered transport factory, and a protocol factory, respectively. If not specified, Perl uses a buffering layer and the binary protocol.

The last statement calls the server's `serve` method **❿**, which runs the server. To test the server, you can run it with the Perl interpreter in one shell and then run the previously coded Perl client in another shell. For example

```
> server$ perl HelloServer.pl
(wait for all client requests then CTRL+C to cancel)
> ^C
> server$


================================================================


< client$ perl HelloClient.pl
< Hello World!
< client$ perl HelloClient.pl
< Hello World!
```

16.5.1 Apache Thrift Perl features

Now that we've seen the practical side of Apache Thrift and Perl, we can look at the transports, protocols, and servers supported by Perl.

Perl supports a basic set of transports:

- *TCP sockets*—`Thrift::Socket`
- *UNIX sockets*—`Thrift::UnixSocket`
- *HTTP*—`Thrift::HttpClient`
- *Memory buffers*—`Thrift::MemoryBuffer`

The Apache Thrift Perl library can interact with Socket and HTTP servers and the utility memory endpoint transport. Perl also supports buffering and framing transport layers on top of these endpoints, as well as SSL.

The Apache Thrift Perl library only provides direct support for the binary serialization protocol:

- *Binary*—`Thrift::BinaryProtocol`

Perl supports modules created and compiled in the C language. These modules are often significantly faster that interpreted Perl script. One such example is the `Thrift::XS` library by Andy Grundman. This library can be found on CPAN (https://metacpan.org/pod/Thrift::XS) and not only includes a drop-in replacement for the binary protocol and `MemoryBuffer` transport, but also a complete `CompactProtocol` implementation.

Perl supports multiplexing and offers two server implementations:

- *Single-threaded server*—`Thrift::SimpleServer`
- *Multiprocessing server*—`Thrift::ForkingServer`

The single-threaded simple server serves one client connection at a time. The forking server forks a new process for each inbound client.

With Perl under our belts, we'll close this chapter with a short look at Python.

16.6 Apache Thrift and Python

In this section, we look at installing Python and working across Python versions 2 and 3. The key features of Apache Thrift Python are covered in chapters 1 through 10 of this book, Python being one of our three demonstration languages in part 2.

Python has two active major versions, Python 2 and 3. Version 2 is fading away and is officially end of life in 2020, so you may find it more convenient to code new Apache Thrift applications in version 3.

Apache Thrift supports both major versions of Python. Several key incompatibilities impact Apache Thrift across Python 2 and 3, especially changes in support for strings and binary data. Fortunately, the Python six library provides a cross-platform interface to the problem features.

Apache Thrift libraries for Python are available through the standard Python package manager, Pip. Pip may not be installed on your system, but it's easy to add. For example, on Ubuntu 16.04 you can install Pip for Python 2.x and Python 3.x:

```
$ sudo apt-get install python-pip
...
$ pip --version
pip 8.1.1 from /usr/lib/python2.7/dist-packages (python 2.7)

$ sudo apt-get install python3-pip
...
$ pip3 --version
pip 8.1.1 from /usr/lib/python3/dist-packages (python 3.5)
```

If your Pip version complains that it's out-of-date when you use it, you can use Pip to upgrade Pip:

```
$ pip install --upgrade pip
```

With Pip installed, we can easily install the Apache Thrift Python support library:

```
$ pip install thrift
Collecting thrift
Collecting six>=1.7.2 (from thrift)
  Using cached six-1.10.0-py2.py3-none-any.whl
Installing collected packages: six, thrift
Successfully installed six-1.10.0 thrift-0.10.0
```

The previous command installs Thrift for Python 2, because we used the Python 2 version of Pip. To run our Hello World Python example (also demonstrated in chapter 1) under Python 2, we can gen stubs and run the server directly:

```
~/thriftbook/part3/script/python$ thrift -gen py ../hello.thrift

~/thriftbook/part3/script/python$ python hello_server.py
[Server] Started
[Server] Handling client request: world
```

To test the server with a client, we can run the client under Python 2 in another shell:

```
~/thriftbook/part3/script/python$ python hello_client.py
[Client] received: Hello world
```

However, we can also run the client under Python 3 by installing Thrift with Pip 3:

```
~/thriftbook/part3/script/python$ pip3 install thrift
Collecting thrift
  Using cached thrift-0.10.0.zip
Collecting six>=1.7.2 (from thrift)
  Using cached six-1.10.0-py2.py3-none-any.whl
Building wheels for collected packages: thrift
  Running setup.py bdist_wheel for thrift ... done
  Stored in directory:
    /home/user/.cache/pip/wheels/e7/f1/d3/b472914d95caa1781fb29b1257
  b85808324b0bfd1838961752
Successfully built thrift
Installing collected packages: six, thrift
```

```
Successfully installed six-1.10.0 thrift

~/thriftbook/part3/script/python$ python3 hello_client.py
[Client] received: Hello world
```

In the previous session, we installed the Python 3 Thrift library and ran the same client program used above with Python 2 under Python 3. Writing cross-version-compatible Python RPC code is fairly easy: as you can see from the example, Apache Thrift often takes care of all the details.

If you'd like more Python examples, browse through part 2 of this book. Python examples for transports, protocols, IDL, types, services, exceptions, and servers can be found in chapters 4–10, respectively.

Summary

This chapter has covered

- Installing Apache Thrift for Ruby
- Creating Ruby RPC clients
- Creating Ruby RPC servers
- Installing Apache Thrift for PHP
- Creating RPC clients in PHP
- Installing Apache Thrift for Perl
- Creating RPC clients in Perl
- Installing Apache Thrift for Python 2 and 3

Thrift in the enterprise

In the pages leading up to this final chapter, we've had a chance to see how Apache Thrift is organized architecturally as well as how several high-profile languages integrate with the Apache Thrift framework. Here we step back from the mechanics a bit to examine ways Apache Thrift can solve challenges facing large-scale distributed applications. Apache Thrift is billed as a cross-language framework for high-performance RPC applications, the key phrases being "cross-language" and "high performance." Let's start by looking at the value of cross-language support.

17.1 *Polyglot systems*

Apache Thrift is well suited to building distributed applications in a single language; however, one of the marquee features of Apache Thrift is its ability to weave together services coded in a variety of languages.

The strong cross-language support in Apache Thrift is particularly valuable when building distributed systems, which tend toward polyglot composition for a range of reasons:

- *Design*—Systems may be designed to use different languages, where each language is best suited to its part of the system.
- *Evolution*—Companies may transition to new languages more suitable to the system over time, requiring support for old and new.
- *Greenfield*—New parts of a system may be created with new languages.
- *Acquisition*—Acquirers may need to integrate technologies from acquirees divergent from their own.
- *Test*—Test automation languages are often selected independently from application development languages.
- *Performance*—Maturing systems may need to evolve parts under strain to new languages for performance reasons.

Apache Thrift can help architects and developers future-proof service and messaging interfaces, making language changes and additions to various parts of a system nearly painless.

The last bullet in the list of scenarios causing firms to consider new programing languages is performance. You might ask, "If I need to adopt a new language for performance reasons in a part of my application, will Apache Thrift be fast enough?" We'll answer that question in the next section.

17.2 *Service tooling and considerations*

Distributed applications vary widely when it comes to load profiles, communications patterns, and message payload types and sizes. Even within the fairly modern and narrow world of microservices, performance isn't a one-size-fits-all proposition. That said, we'll use the next few pages to develop basic intuition around Apache Thrift networked service performance.

17.2.1 *Services*

A service is a self-contained collection of invokable operations. The SOA and microservices approaches to system development decompose systems into encapsulated, individually testable services. Such services frequently consume other services, making inter-service communications performance an important consideration in microservice architectures.

Distributed systems can be decomposed into services in varying ways. Service interfaces can be defined with objects, functions, and/or resources. Systems organized around objects are supported by technologies such as COM and CORBA; however, the stateful nature of such services presents scaling challenges and has caused them to fall out of favor. RPC-style services, perhaps the oldest service scheme, organize services around related sets of functions. Such systems are suitable for the implementation of discrete operations and resonate with traditional software approaches and modern functionally oriented systems. Resource-oriented services organize sets of related resources into services, typically using HTTP, JSON, and elements of the RESTful approach.

Given that RPC and RESTful services are the only practical choices for most developers, let's compare and contrast the two to surface the strengths and weaknesses of each.

17.2.2 Interface comparisons

RPC-style services have traditionally had interfaces defined in a formal interface definition language. IDLs define only the features of a service necessary to form a contract with the calling client. IDLs therefore define all the mechanical aspects of an interface. Well-crafted interfaces also include the semantic information clients will require in the form of concise type and parameter names, as well as integrated docstrings.

RPC INTERFACES

Though RPC services are embodied by sets of operations, those operations often accept and return complex data types or entities. For example, an interface designed to return stock trade reports might use a `TradeReport` type used with a `TradeHistory` service interface. The following listing illustrates such a service in Apache Thrift IDL.

Listing 17.1 Simple Apache Thrift interface in IDL

```
struct TradeReport {
    1: string  symbol,
    2: double  price,
    3: i32     size,
    4: i32     seq_num
}

exception BadSymbol {
    1: string symbol
    2: string error_msg
    3: i16    error_code
}

service TradeHistory {
    list<TradeReport> get_trades_by_symbol(
        1: string symbol  //Security ticker
        2: i32 limit=10)  //Trade count to return from newest to oldest
        throws (1: BadSymbol err) //Thrown when symbol is not found
}
```

The Apache Thrift interface definition language has several subtle but important strengths. First, and perhaps foremost, it's remarkably compact and simple. It's also expressive, allowing rich types and services to be described easily with support for lists, sets, and maps, and a full complement of interface evolution features. For more information on Apache Thrift IDL, see chapter 6.

The interface defined in listing 17.1 exposes an RPC service called `TradeHistory` with a single self-describing method called `get_trades_by_symbol()`, which returns a `TradeReport` list. The `TradeReport` type is defined independently of the service, allowing multiple methods and services to reuse the type without defining it repeatedly. The `TradeReport` type can also be independently serialized and transmitted over messaging systems like NATS and Kafka with cross-language support (more on this shortly).

Large-scale systems may require many much longer IDL files to fully describe their interfaces. Such a collection of interface definitions would, however, represent a mere fraction of the code necessary to implement the interfaces. The ability to summarize service functionality at a high level of abstraction is one of the key features of IDL.

Benefits frequently attributed to IDL-based systems include:

- *Documentation*—Interface definition languages are designed to simplify service descriptions by eliminating implementation details, making IDL a perfect base for interface documentation.
- *Abstraction*—The absence of implementation affords engineers and architects the ability to scrutinize the pure interface and consider the interactions in the abstract, simplifying efforts to identify and reduce server roundtrips, making it easier to identify and remove nonessential data and methods, and so on.
- *Domain-centric*—As a simple abstract language, IDL sources in whole or in part can be used to confer with users and domain experts about the veracity of a design.
- *Cross-language/platform support*—IDLs aren't implementation languages; they necessarily describe interfaces in a platform/language-agnostic way.
- *Specification*—IDL and associated standards can directly define an ABI.
- *Code generation*—A robust IDL enables tooling to generate client and server stubs, simplifying and improving the reliability of client and server construction.
- *Rigor*—IDL can add type safety and other forms of rigor in critical interfaces, even when implementation languages (such as scripting languages) provide no such support.

While less interesting in smaller projects, features such as those listed above pay dividends when architecting larger systems.

REST INTERFACES

To provide contrast, let's look at a RESTful interface definition with the same functionality as our IDL service listed previously. Restful service interfaces can be described using various technologies, such as the OpenAPI Specification (OAS), RAML, API Blueprint, WADL, and others. While some would argue that no unifying standard exists,

the OAS specification, which carries on where Swagger 2.0 left off, appears to be well
positioned to unite the industry. The following listing provides an OAS definition for a
RESTful service interface functionally equivalent to the Apache Thrift RPC service
found in listing 17.1.

Listing 17.2   Simple REST interface in OAS

```
openapi: 3.0.0
paths:
  /symbols/{symbol}/trades:
    get:
      operationId: get-trades-by-symbol
      parameters:
        - name: symbol
          in: path
          description: Security ticker
          required: true
          schema:
            type: string
        - name: limit
          in: query
          description: Trade count to return from newest to oldest
          required: false
          schema:
            type: integer
            format: int32
            default: 10
      responses:
        '200':
          content:
            application/json:
              schema:
                $ref: "#/components/schemas/Trades"
        '404':
          description: Given symbol not found.
components:
  schemas:
    TradeReport:
      required:
        - symbol
        - size
        - price
      properties:
        symbol:
          type: string
        size:
          type: integer
          format: int32
        seqnum:
          type: integer
          format: int32
        price:
          type: number
```

```
        format: double
Trades:
  type: array
  items:
    $ref: "#/components/schemas/TradeReport"
```

It's a bit more verbose than the Apache Thrift equivalent, yet clearly identifies the `TradeReport` type and the IRI (International Resource Identifier) used to retrieve trades by symbol. Rather than calling the `get_trades_by_symbol()` RPC function with a stock ticker and optional limit, a user of the RESTful version of the interface would invoke the HTTP `GET` method on an IRI something like this:

```
GET /symbols/AMZN/trades?limit=1
```

RPC VERSUS REST

The preceding Apache Thrift and OAS examples highlight several of the more important differences between RPC services and ROA(Resource Oriented Architecture) services. RPC services are decomposed into functions/operations, and ROA services are decomposed into resources/entities. In the RPC service, the symbol is a function parameter, but in the ROA service, the symbol is a resource and is represented by an IRI.

While it's possible to model RPC functions directly with IRIs (for example, `GET /get_last_sale?symbol=GOOG`), to do so misses the point of REST. One might ask what it means to `PUT /get_last_sale?symbol=CSCO`? HTTP methods have distinct semantics defining safety, idempotence, and support, or lack thereof, for the upload of a document body, along with HTTP header implications and more, though these are occasionally countermanded by (often inexperienced) interface designers.

Because REST is an architectural style with no associated standard, the range of implementations and approaches varies widely. A given REST IRI may be invoked with any one of several HTTP methods (`POST`, `OPTIONS`, `GET`, `HEAD`, . . .); may receive and return a document body in various formats; may accept path parameters, query parameters, and matrix parameters; and may define interactions with any number of HTTP headers. RESTful services are, in essence, highly customizable interfaces integrated into the HTTP protocol.

In contrast, RPC services often run directly over TCP, the protocol below HTTP. When RPC systems such as Apache Thrift and SOAP use HTTP, they tunnel within HTTP `POST` methods, making no practical use of HTTP features like methods, headers, and status codes. GRPC is an RPC system open-sourced by Google in 2015 that requires HTTP/2 and makes much deeper use of the underlying protocol, though it still uses the POST verb exclusively.

HTTP integration brings many advantages to ROA systems. First and foremost, HTTP is the protocol of the web, and the web is the largest distributed system ever created by mankind. Consequently, properly designed RESTful services integrate naturally with most pieces of internet-facing networking software and hardware. For example, a `GET` request for a given IRI may be safely returned from cache in many cases. Every browser, proxy server, and reverse proxy server in the world understands this. It's hard to imagine a client/server interaction faster than one that returns the response from an in-process cache.

The advantages of HTTP integration over the web, and the ease of adoption associated with its widespread use and tool-less nature, make RESTful services a great choice for internet-facing APIs.

If that is the case, then why do we need Apache Thrift? The short answer might be: APIs consumed by clients over the internet and APIs consumed by microservices in platform backends have distinct and separate requirements and priorities.

Frontend systems run in browsers and mobile apps; backend systems more often than not run on clusters of cloud instances. Frontend systems run on one (often mobile) device; backend systems are composed of many services working together. Frontend systems communicate through browsers, proxies, reverse proxies, gateways, and other standardized web tech systems, while backend systems typically don't. Frontend systems are physically resource-constrained, while backend systems in the cloud have effectively unlimited resources.

Building backend service APIs in the same way as frontend service APIs offers technology and knowledge leverage (not to be underestimated), but their target operating environments and composition are profoundly different.

The concise abstraction provided by IDL (Apache Thrift or others) can be a critical success factor when building large-scale backends in greenfield systems. In brownfield environments (faced by most enterprises), decomposing monolithic systems into function-based microservices greatly simplifies system migration and modernization. It is easy to take a few functions or methods from a monolith and repackage them as a microservice. On the other hand, taking a few functions or methods from a monolith and converting them into a service with a resource-based interface is more work and less likely to be a drop-in replacement for existing clients of the functionality.

Other benefits aside, in microservice-oriented backend systems, Apache Thrift offers one particularly killer feature: performance. If you need responsiveness and/or support for extreme request rates in backend systems, or the ability to run services in resource-restricted embedded systems, Apache Thrift may be the perfect tool. Performance can also be particularly important in microservice-based architecture, due to the dramatic increase in network RPC traffic created over that of traditional monolithic applications. We'll examine relative interface performance in the next section.

A PRACTICAL SERVICE COMPARISON

Let's build a simple REST-style service and a corresponding Apache Thrift RPC service to better understand the strengths and weaknesses of each approach. Every programming language worth its salt provides at least one, likely several, frameworks for implementing REST-style services. We'll build our services in Java and use Jersey, the reference implementation of JAX-RS, the Java REST API standard. The following listing provides the REST service source code.

```java
import javax.ws.rs.GET;
import javax.ws.rs.Path;
import javax.ws.rs.Produces;
import javax.ws.rs.QueryParam;
import javax.ws.rs.core.MediaType;

@Path("tradehistory")                          ❶
public class RestServer {
    public static class TradeReport {    ❷
        public String  symbol;
        public double  price;
        public int     size;
        public int     seq_num;

        public TradeReport(){}
        public TradeReport(String symbol, double price,
                           int size, int seq_num) {
            this.symbol = symbol;
            this.price = price;
            this.size = size;
            this.seq_num = seq_num;
        }
    }

    @GET
    @Path("/get_last_sale")                    ❸
❹  @Produces(MediaType.APPLICATION_JSON)
    public TradeReport get_last_sale(@QueryParam("symbol") String symbol) {
        return new TradeReport(symbol, 25.50, 100, 1);
    }
}
```

The service in listing 17.3 is designed to provide a direct comparison with our upcoming Apache Thrift example, so it isn't particularly resource-oriented. It does, however, demonstrate the JAX-RS approach to REST services and exhibit the performance characteristics of the platform effectively. JAX-RS uses annotations to identify mappings between code and interface elements; other popular Java frameworks such as Spring use a similar approach. For example, the `@Path` annotation causes the `RestServer` class to handle all IRIs with the `tradehistory` path ❶. Similarly, the `get_last_sale()` method will handle all of the GET requests to the subresource tradehistory/get_last_sale IRI ❸. The `get_last_sale()` method returns a `TradeReport` ❷ instance. The `@Produces` annotation ❹ causes the returned object to be converted into a JSON string and placed in the response body.

Embedding the interface into the server code represents a significant difference in approach to that of IDL-style systems. Rather than generating code from IDL, the Jersey framework generates IDL from the code. The Jersey-generated IDL is known as WADL, Web Application Description Language, and is a distant relative of the SOAP WSDL interface definition language. However, unlike WSDL, WADL isn't a W3C standard and

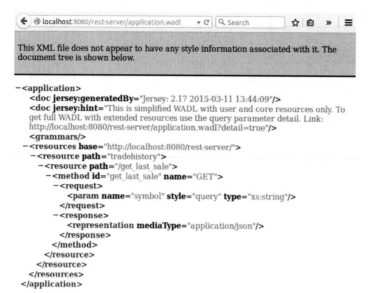

Figure 17.1
TradeHistory in WADL

not all REST adherents use it. The WADL generated from a JAX-RS server is available through the application.wadl IRI, exemplified in figure 17.1. You may note that there is no mention of the TradeReport type. In this case, the WADL simply identifies that a TradeReport is returned by the get_last_sale() method as a JSON response.

As it stands, the WADL in figure 17.1 isn't complete enough to generate full client or server stubs. For this and other reasons, specifications such as OAS have been developed as WADL alternatives, making it easier to use an "IDL first" or "round trip" approach to interface development.

The JAX-RS REST service in listing 17.3 can be built using the Apache Maven project included with the book's source code. The Maven project includes support for running the service within an Apache Tomcat 7 application server, one of the most common hosts for RESTful web services. Here's a sample run of the REST server:

```
thrift@ubuntu:~/ThriftBook/part3/ws/rest/rest-servlet$ mvn clean package
...
thrift@ubuntu:~/ThriftBook/part3/ws/rest/rest-servlet$ mvn tomcat7:run
...
```

The first command, mvn clean package, removes intermediate files and targets, then builds the servlet into a war file (target/rest-server-1.0-SNAPSHOT.war). The second command runs a Tomcat 7 server to host the servlet.

One of the great features of REST services is the ease with which you can invoke them using a plain vanilla browser. Figure 17.2 shows a browser invoking our new service.

A JAX-RS-based client is also provided in the book's sources to test the server. This client uses the GET verb to invoke the tradehistory/get_last_sale URI, with the symbol

**Figure 17.2
Calling a REST
service from a
browser**

set to AAPL. This client GETs the tradehistory/get_last_sale IRI one million times in a tight loop. Here's a sample timed run of the client:

```
thrift@ubuntu:~/ThriftBook/part3/ws/rest/rest-client$ time mvn exec:java
...
real    5m3.331s
user    1m15.539s
sys     0m54.374s
```

The client code is located in the part3/ws/rest/rest-client directory of the book's source and also includes a Maven project file. In the previous session we clean and build the client jar, then run it under the Linux time command. The run takes a little more than five minutes to complete on the test system, producing one server round trip per 303 microseconds. As you can see from the timing data, most of the elapsed time on the client is spent waiting for the server to respond. Out of the elapsed five minutes, the client consumed 75 seconds of CPU in user mode and 54 seconds of CPU in kernel mode.

If we needed things to run faster, we could consider Apache Thrift as an alternative to REST. In the following listing we'll create an Apache Thrift example as close to the REST technology platform as possible. As in the REST example, we'll begin by creating an Apache Thrift RPC server using a Java servlet running under Tomcat 7 with the JSON serialization protocol. The only practical difference between our new Apache Thrift service and the prior REST service is that the REST service is IRI-based and uses Jersey to parse and serialize, and the Apache Thrift service is RPC-based and uses generated Apache Thrift code to parse and serialize. The code for the simple Apache Thrift service appears in the following listing.

Listing 17.4   ~/ThriftBook/part3/ws/thrift/thrift-servlet/src/main/java/ThriftServer.java

```java
import org.apache.thrift.protocol.TJSONProtocol;
import org.apache.thrift.server.TServlet;

public class ThriftServer extends TServlet {
    public static class TradeHistoryHandler implements TradeHistory.Iface {
        @Override
        public TradeReport get_last_sale(String symbol) {
            return new TradeReport(symbol, 25.50, 100, 1);
        }
    }

    public ThriftServer() {
        super(new TradeHistory.Processor(new TradeHistoryHandler()),
            new TJSONProtocol.Factory());
    }
}
```

The Apache Thrift service implements the interface defined in the IDL from the book sources found at part3/ws/thrift-servlet/src/main/thrift/trade_report.thrift. This interface is functionally equivalent to the WADL for our REST service. As illustrated in listing 17.4, using the Java servlet API makes implementing an Apache Thrift server a trivial affair, but how does it perform?

Here's a session building and running the Apache Thrift servlet server:

```
thrift@ubuntu:~/ThriftBook/part3/ws/thrift-servlet$ mvn clean package
...
thrift@ubuntu:~/ThriftBook/part3/ws/thrift-servlet$ mvn tomcat7:run
...
```

With the server up and running, we can perform a throughput test by running the book's sample RPC test client in another shell. The thrift-servlet project has an exec:java goal to run the client, which makes the exact same 1,000,000 get_last_sale() calls used to test in the REST service. Here is the output from the client session:

```
thrift@ubuntu:~/ThriftBook/part3/ws/thrift-servlet$ time mvn exec:java
...
real    3m3.130s
user    0m21.790s
sys     1m22.852s
```

With the same system and conditions, the Apache Thrift server completes the run in 3/5ths the time of the Rest service. The Apache Thrift test transfers more bytes than the REST example, because the REST GET operation only has a payload on the response side, while the Apache Thrift client POSTs its request to the server in the request body. The key differentiator is serialization efficiency. Even though both example programs use HTTP and JSON, the REST example uses a general-purpose framework (Jersey) and JSON serializer (Moxy), while the Apache Thrift program uses a compiled, purpose-built JSON serializer created for the TradeReport type by the Apache Thrift IDL compiler.

While this is a significant performance improvement, we can do better. If we need more performance, we can leave the Tomcat server and the HTTP protocol behind and implement the exact same service with one of the Apache Thrift servers and the TSocket TCP transport. The following listing provides the source for such a server.

Listing 17.5   ~/ThriftBook/part3/ws/thrift/thrift-json/ThriftServer.java

```
import java.io.IOException;
import org.apache.thrift.transport.TServerSocket;
import org.apache.thrift.transport.TTransportException;
import org.apache.thrift.protocol.TJSONProtocol;
import org.apache.thrift.server.TThreadPoolServer;

public class ThriftServer {
    public static class TradeHistoryHandler implements TradeHistory.Iface {
```

```
        @Override
        public TradeReport get_last_sale(String symbol) {
            return new TradeReport(symbol, 25.50, 100, 1);
        }
    }

    public static void main(String[] args)
            throws TTransportException, IOException {
        TradeHistory.Processor proc =
            new TradeHistory.Processor(new TradeHistoryHandler());
        TServerSocket trans_svr =
            new TServerSocket(9090);
        TThreadPoolServer server =
            new TThreadPoolServer(new TThreadPoolServer.Args(trans_svr)
                .protocolFactory(new TJSONProtocol.Factory())
                .processor(proc));
        System.out.println("[Server] listening of port 9090");
        server.serve();
    }
}
```

Not only does this server eliminate the Tomcat overhead, it also eliminates the reliance on HTTP (methods, headers, and the like). Here's a sample run of a TCP-based Apache Thrift server (still using the JSON protocol):

```
thrift@ubuntu:~/ThriftBook/part3/ws/thrift-json$ ant runServer
Buildfile: /home/thrift/ThriftBook/part3/ws/thrift-json/build.xml

runServer:
     [java] [Server] listening of port 9090
```

Now we can run the TCP client, which uses the same 1,000,000 calls to get_last_sale():

```
thrift@ubuntu:~/ThriftBook/part3/ws/thrift-json$ time ant runClient
Buildfile: /home/thrift/ThriftBook/part3/ws/thrift-json/build.xml

runClient:

BUILD SUCCESSFUL
Total time: 29 seconds

real    0m30.055s
user    0m10.641s
sys     0m7.038s
```

In this test, the TCP-based server is an order of magnitude faster than the HTTP REST server. Also, by eliminating the HTTP overhead, this example reduces request and response size by a factor of two.

For even more performance, we can switch from the slow-to-parse JSON protocol to the Apache Thrift binary or compact protocol. Here's an example run of the service from listing 17.5 using the TBinaryProtocol instead of TJSONProtocol. The server first

```
thrift@ubuntu:~/ThriftBook/part3/ws/thrift$ ant runServer
Buildfile: /home/thrift/ThriftBook/part3/ws/thrift/build.xml

runServer:
     [java] [Server] listening of port 9090
```

Now the client's 1,000,000 call timing output

```
thrift@ubuntu:~/ThriftBook/part3/ws/thrift$ time ant runClient
Buildfile: /home/thrift/ThriftBook/part3/ws/thrift/build.xml

runClient:

BUILD SUCCESSFUL
Total time: 15 seconds

real     0m15.370s
user     0m4.196s
sys      0m3.896s
```

The TBinaryProtocol version of the client/server solution is 20 times faster than the REST solution. The number of bytes exchanged in this case is comparable to the preceding JSON example due to the trivial nature of the interface, but the elimination of JSON parsing does improve performance by a factor of almost two. Another important service consideration in many environments is memory consumption. The Tomcat 7 Jersey-based REST servlet initially reserves about 500K of private memory in the previous tests, while the final Apache Thrift server example reserves about 75K of private memory. You can use tools such as WireShark, nethogs, iptraf, top, htop, ps, and pmap to examine the footprint and performance features of these and other services you may wish to bench test.

Figure 17.3 shows the relative performance of the various examples shown earlier in this chapter and adds a comparable SOAP example. The SOAP web service is the slowest of the bunch largely because it incurs all the overhead of the REST service plus the additional size and processing burden of XML encoding in both directions. The SOAP server and client can be found in the book's source in the part3/ws/soap folder.

PERFORMANCE CAVEATS

While the preceding examples are useful for developing basic performance intuition, they should be taken with a grain of salt and are no substitute for practical testing of real interfaces using your languages and your production loads. Many important factors have been overlooked in this simple comparison. That said, even the limited nature of this comparison demonstrates why companies such as Google (with Protocol Buffers and gRPC), Facebook, and Twitter (both users of Apache Thrift) have adopted non-REST solutions for high-performance backend services.

It's also important to consider the impact of HTTP/2. HTTP/2 is a backward-compatible next generation standard for HTTP with significant performance enhancements introduced in 2015. Many REST APIs will receive a material bump in

Service performance comparison

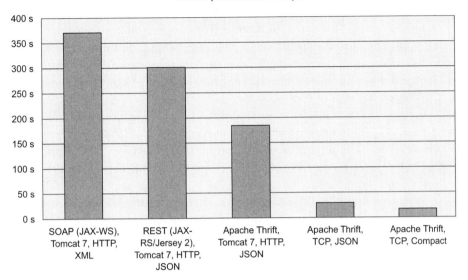

Figure 17.3 Seconds required to complete 1 million API calls with various technologies

performance as HTTP/2 becomes more and more ubiquitous. Google recently contributed an RPC system to the CNCF, which operates over HTTP/2, called gRPC. In tests run by the author, the same `get_last_sale()` service implemented above in gRPC is much faster than the comparable REST service, but approximately four times slower than the corresponding `TBinaryProtocol`-based Apache Thrift equivalent.

17.3 Messaging

Networked services based on request/response models are only half of the distributed system communications story. Most enterprise-scale distributed applications also make heavy use of messaging systems. Messaging systems provide a robust and flexible way to decouple services and allow them to communicate asynchronously. Many messaging systems use message brokers to host queues or manage pub/sub facilities that allow applications to send messages without knowing who's listening or when messages will be received, a premise at the heart of loosely coupled systems.

Most mature cloud-based PaaS offerings include messaging solutions. For example, Amazon AWS offers the SQS (Simple Queue Service) and Kinesis Streams, while Google Cloud Platform offers Cloud Pubsub, and Microsoft Azure offers Service Bus Queues and Topics. In-house platform teams can deploy one of the many open source or commercial messaging solutions such as CNCF NATS, Apache Kafka, Apache RocketMQ, or Pivotal's RabbitMQ.

A typical messaging use case involves passing predefined data types between messaging participants. However, even when both parties use the same programming language, data types typically need to be serialized into a common communications format. Serialization takes into account the operations necessary to encode collections and to address platform byte ordering, among other factors.

One of the best features of Apache Thrift is its ability to provide cross-language communications solutions in both RPC and messaging settings. IDL types such as the TradeReport struct from listing 17.1 are self-serializing in Apache Thrift. Any Apache Thrift IDL type can be easily serialized into a message body and then received and deserialized by another system.

Imagine that you need to build a production trade logging system in Java and want to create a quick mock TradeReport message generator in Python to test it with. To complete this task, you can create a Python trade message generator to emit TradeReport messages and use a message broker to queue the messages for the Java application to read.

To get a better understanding of how Apache Thrift works with messaging systems, we'll build an example using RabbitMQ as the message broker. RabbitMQ is a popular messaging platform and can be quickly run in a Docker container, installed from the rabbitmq.com web site, or installed through the package manager on most Linux systems. Here's an example install on Ubuntu 16.04:

```
thrift@ubuntu:~/ThriftBook/part3/mq$ sudo apt-get install rabbitmq-server
...
```

Before we can begin coding to the RabbitMQ system in Python, we'll need to install one of the Python RabbitMQ communications libraries. The following example code uses the Python Pip package manager to install the pika RabbitMQ support library:

```
thrift@ubuntu:~/ThriftBook/part3/mq$ sudo pip install pika
...
```

We can generate Python serialization code for our TradeReport messages using Apache Thrift. We'll use the Apache Thrift IDL from the trade_report.thrift IDL in Listing 17.1:

```
$ thrift --gen py --gen java trade_report.thrift
```

Now we can build a Python messaging program to mock a normal market data feed in a few lines of code, as shown in the following listing.

Listing 17.6   ~/ ThriftBook/part3/mq/Quotegen.py

```
#!/usr/bin/env python
import sys
import pika
import time

sys.path.append("gen-py")
from thrift.transport import TTransport
```

```
from thrift.protocol import TCompactProtocol
from trade_report import ttypes

connection = pika.BlockingConnection(
        pika.ConnectionParameters(host='localhost'))
channel = connection.channel()
channel.queue_declare(queue='trade_reports')            ❶

trans = TTransport.TMemoryBuffer()              ❷
proto = TCompactProtocol.TCompactProtocol(trans)        ❸
tr = ttypes.TradeReport()                 ❹
trans.open()

for seq_num in range(1,20):
    time.sleep(seq_num%4)

    tr.symbol = ["CSCO", "MSFT", "IBM", "VMW", "INTC"][seq_num%5]
    tr.price = 25.50
    tr.size = 500                                                        ❺
    tr.seq_num = seq_num

    trans.cstringio_buf.seek(0)                 ❻
    trans.cstringio_buf.truncate();            ❼
    tr.write(proto)                 ❽
    channel.basic_publish(exchange='',                                   ❾
                          routing_key='trade_reports',
                          body=trans.cstringio_buf.getvalue())
    print("Sent trade for " + tr.symbol)

connection.close()
```

The Python program in listing 17.6 demonstrates basic use of Apache Thrift in a messaging environment. RabbitMQ offers a host of features; our example simply creates a queue called `trade_reports` ❶ and then sends messages to it.

The Apache Thrift I/O stack is constructed here in much the same way as we'd create an I/O stack for RPC. The differences are that we use a `TMemoryBuffer` as our endpoint ❷, and, because we won't make RPC calls, we have no need for a service client. The serialization protocol we use in this example is the `TCompactProtocol` ❸. An instance of the `TradeReport` type will be used to serialize our messages ❹. The Trade-Report type is emitted inside the trade_report package `ttypes` module when generating Python code with the IDL compiler.

The program emits 20 mock trades in a loop before exiting. Each loop iteration initializes the `TradeReport` with made-up data ❺. Because we're reusing the Python `TMemoryBuffer` for each message, we need to reset ❻ and clear ❼ the buffer on each iteration.

Serializing the `TradeReport` into the `TMemoryBuffer` is as easy as calling the Trade-Report `write()` method on the I/O stack ❽. We use the RabbitMQ `channel.basic_publish()` method to send the serialized message to the trade_reports queue ❾.

We can execute our trade generator directly if the file is given execute permissions:

```
thrift@ubuntu:~/ThriftBook/part3/mq$ ./QuoteGen.py
Sent trade for MSFT
Sent trade for IBM
Sent trade for VMW
...
```

Because we're using the RabbitMQ message broker as middleware, the receiver need not be running at the time we send the messages. This contrasts with RPC, where the client and the server must both be running for communications to take place. The rabbitmqctl program allows us to see queues with pending messages:

```
thrift@ubuntu:~/ThriftBook/part3/mq$ sudo rabbitmqctl list_queues
Listing queues ...
trade_reports    14
...done.
```

To complete the cross-language messaging demonstration, we can code up the Java service that will consume the TradeReport messages, as shown in the following listing.

Listing 17.7   ~/ThriftBook/part3/mq/trade_reader/src/main/java/TradeReader.java

```java
import com.rabbitmq.client.ConnectionFactory;
import com.rabbitmq.client.Connection;
import com.rabbitmq.client.Channel;
import com.rabbitmq.client.QueueingConsumer;

import org.apache.thrift.TException;
import org.apache.thrift.transport.TTransportException;
import org.apache.thrift.transport.TMemoryBuffer;
import org.apache.thrift.protocol.TCompactProtocol;

public class TradeReader {
    private final static String QUEUE_NAME = "trade_reports";

    public static void main(String[] argv)
        throws java.io.IOException,
                java.lang.InterruptedException,
                java.util.concurrent.TimeoutException,
                TException,
                TTransportException {

        ConnectionFactory factory = new ConnectionFactory();
        factory.setHost("localhost");
        Connection connection = factory.newConnection();
        Channel channel = connection.createChannel();
        channel.queueDeclare(QUEUE_NAME, false, false, false, null);
        QueueingConsumer consumer = new QueueingConsumer(channel);
        channel.basicConsume(QUEUE_NAME, true, consumer);

        System.out.println("Waiting for trade reports...");
```

```
        while (true) {
            QueueingConsumer.Delivery delivery = consumer.nextDelivery();    ❶
  ❷        byte[] data = delivery.getBody();
            TMemoryBuffer trans = new TMemoryBuffer(data.length);            ❸
            trans.write(data, 0, data.length);
  ❹        TCompactProtocol proto = new TCompactProtocol(trans);
            TradeReport tr = new TradeReport();                             ❺
            tr.read(proto);
            System.out.println("[" + tr.seq_num + "] " + tr.symbol +
                                " @ " + tr.price + " x " + tr.size);
        }
    }
}
```

The trade reader code in listing 17.7 is similar to the Python writer, connecting to the local RabbitMQ server and then creating a channel attached to the trade_reports queue that the Python program wrote to. The Java program read loop reads and displays each new trade message arriving.

The consumer.nextDelivery() method blocks the loop until a new message is available ❶. When a message is available, we can read the serialized body with the delivery.getBody() method ❷. To deserialize the bytes read we need to load them into a TMemoryBuffer ❸. With the data in a transport buffer, we can create a TCompactProtocol ❹ to deserialize the bytes into a new TradeReport. The TradeReport.read() method ❺ reconstitutes the TradeReport object from the message payload.

The code supplied with the book includes a Maven project that will build the Apache Thrift stubs and pull in the RabbitMQ Java library from Maven Central. We can use the exec:java goal to run the program:

```
thrift@ubuntu:~/ThriftBook/part3/mq/trade_reader$ mvn exec:java
[INFO] Scanning for projects...
[INFO] ------------------------------------------------------------------
[INFO] Building Trade Reader
[INFO]     task-segment: [exec:java]
[INFO] ------------------------------------------------------------------
[INFO] Preparing exec:java
[INFO] No goals needed for project - skipping
[INFO] [exec:java {execution: default-cli}]
Waiting for trade reports...
[1] MSFT @ 25.5 x 500
[2] IBM @ 25.5 x 500
[3] VMW @ 25.5 x 500
...
```

In essence, the types we pass describe our application-specific messaging interface: TradeReport. Because Apache Thrift IDL allows us to describe services as well as types, we can easily define unified interfaces that move key application domain entities, like our TradeReport, through messaging systems and RPC interfaces.

If your distributed system boils down to RPC services and messaging systems, the lion's share of your interface definition tasks can be managed by Apache Thrift. Having a single solution within which you can describe all the principle interfaces of a distributed system is a high-value proposition to many software architects.

17.4 *Best practices*

At this point we've taken a detailed look at the form and function of Apache Thrift, identifying the roles Apache Thrift can play in the design and implementation of enterprise-scale distributed applications. We've also discussed the distinct features and roles played by RESTful services, Apache Thrift services, and messaging systems in distributed systems; and how all three often come together to create a powerful combined solution.

This final section closes the book with a set of suggestions for building interfaces which are efficient, reliable, easy to evolve, and easy to maintain.

17.4.1 *IDL*

- Keep interfaces simple.

  Apache Thrift interfaces (services and UDTs) can evolve avoiding the need for Big Design Up Front (BDUF).

- Use only letters and numbers in IDL file names: begin with a letter, and end with .thrift.

  Apache Thrift IDL filenames are used as identifiers in the output of many language generators. Spaces and other non-alphanumeric characters may generate code which will not compile in certain languages. You can convince the IDL compiler to compile source files without a .thrift extension, but this can cause problems with other tools and IDL include statements. The underbar character, "_", can be treated as a letter for file naming and works with all current Apache Thrift code generators.

- Always define a * namespace.

  Interface names are often widely visible; namespacing them avoids global namespace pollution by placing IDL elements within a package/namespace or similar name partition in various target languages. Avoid language-specific namespaces; if a namespace is a good idea in one language, it's probably a good idea in others, and using one consistent name is less confusing and hazardous than discrete language namespaces.

- Prefer coded documentation to commented documentation.

  Choose self-documenting types (use bool for true/false values rather than byte or i32) and self-documenting identifiers (name the field "requires_authorization" not "flag").

- Document interface semantics not made clear by the code in comments.

  Semantics are as important to an interface definition as mechanics.

- Use base types for map keys.

    Many languages don't support complex keys.

- Don't depend on ordering in sets and maps.
- Initialize bools with "true" and "false" literals only, never numbers.
- Always give fields explicit positive IDs.
- Initialize enum constants with positive integers; then always use the enum constant identifier elsewhere in IDL (never the integer value).
- Prefer string and binary to list<byte>.

    Collections are serialized per element; string and binary types are serialized in one operation. Therefore a 200-byte collection will cause a protocol to make about 202 (type, size, el1, el2, and so on) transport writes; a 200-byte string/binary will require two transport writes (size, string).

17.4.2 *Interface evolution*

- Use structs to support attribute evolution.

    If you need the flexibility to add or remove fields to a thing over time, use a struct.

- Use unions to support type evolution.

    If you need the flexibility to change a thing's type over time or to represent it with different types call-by-call, use a union.

- Use collections to support cardinality evolution.

    A collection can hold 0 things, 1 thing, or many things.

- Never change interface literals.

    Changing ordinals, default values, or constants can create distributed systems where clients and servers hold different views of the value of such an element.

- Consider returning a struct from service methods to allow return evolution.

    Integral return types cannot change type or cardinality (if you return an i32 you must always return one i32). Collections cannot change type (if you return a list<i32>, you can only return i32s). Structs can contain any number of fields of any type, can use all levels of requiredness, and support the addition and removal of fields, allowing the application to evolve more flexibly.

17.4.3 *Service design*

- Carefully consider and document the exceptions that will be part of the interface.

    Anything passed between system components is part of an interface, and Apache Thrift exceptions are passed from servers to clients. Exception specification is an important but often overlooked interface design responsibility.

- Always list every exception a service method may throw in the method exception list.

- Consider extending interfaces (interface inheritance) when adding methods to reuse code, and simplify support for old servers implementing the base interface.

- Avoid deep interface hierarchies and the complexity associated with them.

- Prefer default requiredness parameters and supply them with default values to maximize support for interface evolution.

- Only use `required` with parameters which are immutably bound to the interface.

  Never mark any field as required unless it's mechanically attached to the interface and cannot possibly change or be removed. Required fields cannot evolve in type and cannot be deleted or added. That said, `required` makes these requirements clear in the rare case where such constraints exist. Because required fields are bound to the interface, if you need to change them you must change the entire interface. The benefits of required fields are that they have the lowest overhead of any field type and are the only field type where it's safe to change the default value across revisions of the interface (this is because required values are always serialized, even if the writer is using the default value, ensuring the reader sees the same default value as the writer).

- Comment out deleted parameters rather than removing them (documenting their prior existence), and never reuse their ordinals.

17.4.4 Type design

- Prefer default requiredness for struct fields.

  Make all fields default (normal) requiredness to support interface evolution unless the field isn't always necessary, in which case it can be made optional.

- Provide default values for default requiredness fields where possible.

  Give normal fields a default value to enable support for versions of the interface that do not have that field (whether older or newer).

- Use list<> for ordered collections.

  `set` and `map` values aren't required to be ordered.

- Don't rely on Apache Thrift to enforce set uniqueness.

  Certain implementations don't have or don't use a `set` construct to implement IDL sets, making it possible for IDL-generated sets to contain duplicates.

- Use optional for optimization not evolution.

  Fields that are semantically optional within a problem domain can be defined using default requiredness, where a default value indicates an unset field, or using optional requiredness. Both have their benefits.

  Optional fields do not add interface evolution features beyond those provided with default (normal) requiredness. Optional fields do, however, add overhead and complexity. Both Default and Optional fields can be added/removed without breaking backward compatibility. Neither Default nor Optional fields support type, ordinal, or default value changes without breaking backward compatibility.

The advantage of optional fields is that they can be unset and therefore elided in serialization streams. The disadvantage is that they must be tested for and flagged as set when assigned to.

- Avoid assigning default values to optional fields.

Understand that optional fields given default values are no longer semantically optional (unset-able). If a default value is assigned to an optional field, both the reader and the writer will initialize the field with the default value. If the reader doesn't find the optional field in the stream, it will use the default value, making it impossible for the optional value to not be present when deserialized.

- Only use `required` with fields that are immutably bound to the interface.

See service notes.

- Comment out deleted fields and never reuse their ordinals.

This best practice also applies to enum members.

17.4.5 Coding practices

- When extending Apache Thrift, code to idiomatic Apache Thrift interfaces, not specific implementations (for example, code to `TProtocol` not `TBinaryProtocol`, `TTransport` not `TSocket`).

- Always ensure the transport stack includes a buffer.

Protocols make many small writes to the underlying transport. If the underlying transport is an unbuffered network connection, each write may generate a network packet that will need to be reassembled on the server. Adding a transport buffer (`TBufferedTransport` or `TFramedTransport`) ensures that a single packet is sent to the server for each request. Note that framed transports are self-buffering and that the Java `TSocket` is also self-buffering.

- Use a `TFramedTransport` layer to avoid OOM attacks and to enhance server optionality.

Determining the size of an unframed message requires de-serializing it. Most Apache Thrift servers attempt to read inbound messages into memory. Adversaries and poorly formed client messages can cause servers to allocate huge amounts of memory, potentially crashing the server or worse. Framing adds a 4-byte message size prefix to the beginning of every message (RPC calls and responses). The Apache Thrift `TFramedTransport` framing layer uses a maximum message size (configurable on construction) to reject oversized messages.

Also, nonblocking servers require message framing. By using framing with all I/O stacks you leave open the option to change the server side of a connection to or from a nonblocking server without disrupting the client code.

Summary

Here are the most important points to take away from this chapter:

- Apache Thrift is often used as a high-performance backend platform for REST-based frontend systems.
- Apache Thrift offers a crisp but expressive IDL that can be used to define RPC-style service interfaces as well as messaging system message structures.
- Organizations migrating from monoliths to microservices may find function-based RPC technologies more direct, faster, and easier to work with than resource-oriented REST-based solutions.
- IDLs provide a vernacular with which developers, domain experts, and architects can maximize abstraction and simplify the design process of large-scale, service-based systems.
- Apache Thrift provides significant performance benefits and is more memory compact than many comparable service interface technologies.
- Adopting Apache Thrift best practices can improve the long-term viability and maintainability of Apache Thrift-based interfaces and systems.

index

MORE TITLES FROM MANNING

C++ Concurrency in Action, Second Edition
by Anthony Williams

> ISBN: 9781617294693
> 592 pages
> $69.99
> February 2019

Kubernetes in Action
by Marko Lukša

> ISBN: 9781617293726
> 624 pages
> $59.99
> December 2017

Netty in Action
by Norman Maurer and Marvin Allen Wolfthal

> ISBN: 9781617291470
> 296 pages
> $54.99
> December 2015

For ordering information go to www.manning.com